# The Discoveries of Manuscripts from Late Antiquity

## Their Impact on Patristic Studies and the Contemporary World

### Conference Proceedings
### 2nd International Conference on Patristic Studies

edited by

Patricia CINER
Alyson NUNEZ

BREPOLS

© 2021, Brepols Publishers n.v., Turnhout, Belgium.

All rights reserved.
No part of this publication may be reproduced,
stored in a retrieval system, or transmitted,
in any form or by any means, electronic, mechanical,
photocopying, recording, or otherwise
without the prior permission of the publisher.

D/2021/0095/19
DOI 10.1484/M.STR-EB.5.121558
ISBN 978-2-503-59149-0
E-ISBN 978-2-503-59150-6
E-ISSN 2566-073X
Printed in the EU on acid-free paper.

# TABLE OF CONTENTS

Patricia CINER
*Introduction: The Discovery of Manuscripts from Late Antiquity: An Open Debate in Patristic Studies and in Contemporary Times*     9

CHAPTER 1
THE DISCOVERY OF THE MANUSCRIPTS OF QUMRAN
AND THE APOCRYPHAL LITERATURE:
THEIR IMPACT ON PATRISTIC STUDIES

Magdalena DÍAZ-ARAUJO
*Brief Introduction to the Topic*     17

Alberto D'ANNA
*Manuscripts of Christian Apocrypha: The Texts and their Use*     21

Adolfo D. ROITMAN
*The Mystery of Melchizedek in Early Christianity in Light of the Dead Sea Scrolls*     37

Juan Carlos ALBY
*Health and Disease in Qumran Texts and Jewish Aprocryphal Literature*     67

CHAPTER 2
THE DISCOVERY OF ORIGEN'S MANUSCRIPTS AND THOSE
OF THE ALEXANDRIAN TRADITION: THEIR IMPACT
ON PATRISTIC STUDIES

Anders-Christian JACOBSEN
*Brief Introduction to the Topic*     87

TABLE OF CONTENTS

Lorenzo PERRONE
*Origen's* Renaissance *in the Twentieth Century and the Recovery of his Literary Heritage: New Finds and Philological Advancement*     91

Rubén PERETÓ RIVAS
*Self-knowledge and Dispersion in the Alexandrian Tradition*     111

CHAPTER 3
THE DISCOVERY OF THE NAG HAMMADI GNOSTIC LIBRARY: ITS IMPACT ON PATRISTIC STUDIES

Mariano TROIANO
*Brief Introduction to the Topic*     133

Francisco GARCÍA BAZÁN
Corpus Gnosticum. *Noticias y fuentes sobre los Gnósticos incluida la Biblioteca de Nag Hammadi y otros hallazgos anteriores menos conocidos*     137

David BRAKKE
*What Difference Does the* Gospel of Judas *Make?*     163

Mariano TROIANO
*Magic and Theology. Barbaric Utterances in the* Pistis Sophia *and their Different Levels of Interpretation*     181

CHAPTER 4
THE DISCOVERY OF COPTIC AND SYRIAC MANUSCRIPTS: THEIR IMPACT ON PATRISTIC STUDIES

Patricia CINER
*Brief Introduction to the Topic*     201

Alberto CAMPLANI
*The Discovery of Coptic Manuscripts and the Development of Patristic Studies: Methodological and Epistemological Issues and the Challenge of Some New Research Projects*     205

Luise Marion FRENKEL
*Recovering Late-Antique Christian Identities: The Ongoing Discovery and Rediscovery of Syriac Manuscripts, their Diversity, and Limitations*     243

## Chapter 5
### THE DISCOVERY OF COLLECTIONS OF LETTERS FROM THE PATRISTIC ERA: ITS IMPACT ON WESTERN HISTORY

Patricia CINER
*Brief Introduction to the Topic* 279

Oscar VELÁSQUEZ
*The Vision of God and Augustine's* De uidendo Deo liber unus
(= ep. *147*) 283

Bronwen NEIL
*Pope Leo I's Letters on "The Manichean Perversity"* 301

## Chapter 6
### MANUSCRIPTS FROM LATE ANTIQUITY AND FROM THE PATRISTIC PERIOD: THEIR DISCOVERY, CONSERVATION AND DIGITAL PUBLICATION

Patricia CINER
*Brief Introduction to the Topic* 321

Ira RABIN
*Writing Materials of the Dead Sea Scrolls* 325

Cesare PASINI
*La "vocación patrística" de la Biblioteca Vaticana* 333

Angelo DI BERARDINO
*The Impact of Recent Archaeological, Historical and Literary Discoveries for the Study of Patristics* 357

## Chapter 7
### THE DISCOVERY OF MANUSCRIPTS FROM LATE ANTIQUITY AND ITS IMPACT ON THE CONTEMPORARY WORLD

Patricia CINER
*Brief Introduction to the Topic* 387

Theodore DE BRUYN
*Papyri, Parchments, and Ostraca and the Study of Ancient Christianity Today* 391

Marco RIZZI
*The Impact of the Rediscovery of Manuscripts on Theology and Religious Culture after the Second World War* 411

PATRICIA CINER
*Universidad Católica de Cuyo, Argentina*

# INTRODUCTION
## THE DISCOVERY OF MANUSCRIPTS FROM LATE ANTIQUITY: AN OPEN DEBATE IN PATRISTIC STUDIES AND IN CONTEMPORARY TIMES

Time has an obvious lineal component where past, present, and future seem to play out inevitably one after the other. However, time also has an enigmatic and reversible component by which the past can transform the present and future. This mysterious aspect of time seems to have been revealed in the discoveries of the Manuscripts of Late Antiquity, manuscripts discovered during the twentieth and twenty-first centuries. Apparently as if by chance, complete libraries of manuscripts as well as individual documents of great importance for our understanding of historical authors and situations have come to light after having been buried for millennia. Just some examples are the incredible discoveries of the Nag Hammadi Gnostic library, the Dead Sea Scrolls, Origen of Alexandria's homilies, and Augustine's sermons, among others.

These manuscripts are not passive documents. They pose numerous questions to specialists from a diverse array of fields, demanding new evaluations of a past that was thought to be already understood and judged. Some of the questions to emerge include:

- What meaning and implications does the discovery of the Dead Sea Scrolls have for an understanding of the Judaism of Late Antiquity and for the beginning of Christianity?

- Can these newly discovered manuscripts contribute new information about the social and cultural context within which Jesus lived and died?

- Can the Gnostic and Apocryphal gospels provide us with a more complete vision of Christianity?

- Does the discovery of the Coptic and Syriac manuscripts modify our current perspective of the West?
- Is it possible that the discovery of Origen's homilies will change the judgement that the history of theology has passed on this controversial author?
- What new information about Early Christianity's practices does the discovery of Saint Augustine's sermons provide?

Scholars attempted to answer all of these questions during the 2nd International Conference on Patristic Studies, organized by the Catholic University of Cuyo in San Juan, Argentina, 28–31 March 2017. During this academic event, we sought to respond to these and other questions with the greatest academic rigor possible, intending for our responses to contribute to enriching our understanding of both the specific realm of Patristic Studies and the general realm of the contemporary world. The articles contained in this book are the presentations which were given by renowned national and international specialists who, without a doubt, gave great prestige to this event.

## *Fruitful Efforts: A Brief History of Patristic Studies at the Catholic University of Cuyo*

San Juan is a small and picturesque province in western Argentina. The imposing surrounding mountains make the city popular with tourists and impact its economic activities, which include mining and viticulture. However, a rich tradition and production in Patristic Studies is also part of the city's cultural heritage, as more than twenty years ago the Catholic University of Cuyo formed a center of in-depth study of the first centuries of our era.

The history of Patristic Studies in the province begins thanks to the work of a tireless pioneer in the field: Dr María Isabel Larruari. While she was serving as Rector of the Catholic University of Cuyo in 2009, a graduate certificate course in Patristic Studies was implemented, with its central topic being "Church Fathers in Dialogue with Contemporary Times". This course was given by notable international and national specialists. In 2010, the Institute of Patristic Studies was officially inaugurated. The creation of this Institute allowed scholars to present the results of their research being carried out in San Juan and also sought to facilitate dialogue with important academic centers around the world. The methodology used was characterized by: a) the use of specific research categories that recognized the plurality and richness of theological and philosophical positions which had coexisted during the approximate six centuries of the Patristic era and b) the need to connect Patristic Studies with the contemporary world, thereby demonstrating the importance of this fascinating era of Western history.

The use of this methodology was considered essential due to the fact that Patristic Studies currently addresses the diverse problems that arose during this period of Western history from a two-part perspective. On the one hand, Christian schools of thought and thinkers are studied as they relate to the diverse schools of the time and in this sense making reference to the historical category of Late Antiquity as a framework for understanding the diverse theories and doctrines of Patristic authors is preferable.[1] On the other hand, these topics are addressed from a specifically Patristic point of view. This does not mean that Christian authors lose their identity, it simply implies framing them within the context in which the authors themselves carried out their analyses. As such, we must not forget, for example, that both the Church Fathers and the Gnostics were men of their time and were well aware of the cultural, political and philosophical-theological positions of the era. It is also necessary to highlight the fact that the specificity of Christianity was at the same time multiple, as the existence of a variety of schools of thought in Early Christianity is indisputable for contemporary research. In this sense, the reflection made by G. Luttikhuizen in his book *The Diversity of Earliest Christianity* synthesizes the methodology that inspired this task through the years:

> The discovery during the last century of Jewish and Christian sources, sources until then unknown, most especially

---

[1] P. Hadot, *Exercices spirituels et philosophie antique* (París: Études augustiniennes, 1981), P. Brown, *The World of Late Antiquity: From Marcus Aurelius to Muhammad*, Londres (London: Thames and Hudson, 1971).

the Qumran Cave Scrolls and the Nag Hammadi library, led to a profound revision of the traditional concept of Second Temple Judaism, of Early Christianity, and of the religious world of Late Antiquity in general. In terms of Christianity, these sources offer us a completely new vision of Early Christianity and of the great diversity that characterized its first centuries of existence.[2]

We must also add that for various reasons this historical period cannot be considered a closed-off era that requires no further research. This is so firstly because the consequences of several theological positions are still seen today in the contemporary world. And secondly, the discovery of manuscripts which had been lost for centuries has changed our vision of this time. Taking into account this information allows us to affirm that only when we understand this period of humanity will we be able to truly understand our present and open new paths for the future.

As a way of consolidating this research work, two international conferences were organized by the Catholic University of Cuyo in San Juan. These conferences represented milestones for Patristic Studies and its impact in the contemporary world. In 2012, the 1st International Conference on Patristic Studies was organized around the theme "The Identity of Jesus: Unity and Diversity in the Patristic Era" with the participation of scholars from fifteen countries. In March 2017, the 2nd International Conference on Patristic Studies was organized around the theme "The Discovery of Manuscripts from Late Antiquity: Its Impact on Patristic Studies and the Contemporary World" and its most notable presentations gave rise to this volume you are reading today. As can be imagined, the work carried out by the Catholic University of Cuyo for more than twenty years has brought fruits of international recognition as an important center for the study of Patristics.

---

[2] G. P. Luttikhuizen, *The Diversity of Earliest Christianity* (London: Parthenon, 2012).

INTRODUCTION

## *Structure of this Volume*

This volume has been organized into seven chapters, each of which is structured around a different topic. Each one starts with a brief introduction of the topic and presents the specialists responsible for its development. Some chapters prioritize the geographical locations where manuscripts were found, while others center on specific authors and their recent manuscripts discovered. The chapters are as follows:

1. The Discovery of the Nag Hammadi Gnostic Library: Its Impact on Patristic Studies
2. The Discovery of Origen's Manuscripts and those of the Alexandrian Tradition: Their Impact on Patristic Studies
3. The Discovery of the Qumran Manuscripts and Apocryphal Literature: Their Impact on Patristic Studies
4. The Discovery of Coptic and Syriac Manuscripts: Their Impact on Patristic Studies
5. The Discovery of Augustine's Manuscripts and Letters from the Patristic Era
6. The Discoveries of Manuscripts of Late Antiquity and the Patristic Era: Their Preservation, Diffusion and Digital Publication
7. The Discovery of Manuscripts from Late Antiquity and Its Impact on the Contemporary World

## *Acknowledgements*

This volume is the result of generosity from numerous institutions and individuals. In this regard, I close this introduction by mentioning those who have offered financial support, time, and energy to collaborate with this wonderful project.

Firstly, I must thank Brepols, undoubtedly one of the oldest and most prestigious publishing houses in the world. Brepols trusted that a small university far from the principal academic centers of the world could produce a quality publication. I am truly grateful to Dr Tim Denecker for this opportunity.

I would again like to mention the engine of Patristic Studies in San Juan, our dear Dr María Isabel Larrauri, who had the clarity of vision to see that San Juan could be a national and international center of knowledge. I also highlight the aid and constant encouragement given by the Rector of the Catholic University of Cuyo, Dr Claudio Larrea; the University Directors; the Vice-Rector of Education, Father José Juan García; the former Dean of the School of Philosophy and Humanities, Prof. Jorge Bernat Gigantino; the former Rector of the Seminary, Father Jorge Harica; and the Secretary of Publications, Susana Lahoz. Despite the difficulties that arose, they always had a kind word of encouragement and enthusiasm. I must also mention our dear bishops, Monsignor Alfonso Delgado and Monsignor Jorge Lozano, who, with their wisdom and prudence, placed their trust in us. As regards the Government of San Juan, which also provided financial support for this conference, I would like to give special thanks to the Under Secretary of Scientific and Technological Activity, Dr Pablo Diez, who always supported us generously and enthusiastically.

Of course, this conference would not have been possible without the invaluable contributions of prestigious national and international scholars who accepted our proposal for the conference and later for the publication of this volume, providing us with their knowledge and wisdom. Each and every one deserves special thanks. They honored us with their presence and ensured that a topic as passionate and controversial as is "The Discovery of Manuscripts from Late Antiquity and Its Impact on Patristic Studies and the Contemporary World" could be addressed with the highest degree of academic rigor possible. Finally, I would like to thank our incredible team, with whom I have worked for many years. I feel truly honored to be able to work with such extraordinary human beings. They include: Father Pedro Fernández (Director of the Institute of Patristic Studies), Dr José Antonio Carrascosa Fuentes, Prof. Susana Villalonga, Father Leonardo Pons, Prof. Alyson Nuñez (co-editor of this volume) and Fabricio Echegaray. Without them, this adventure would have been impossible.

# CHAPTER 1
# THE DISCOVERY OF THE MANUSCRIPTS OF QUMRAN AND THE APOCRYPHAL LITERATURE: THEIR IMPACT ON PATRISTIC STUDIES

MAGDALENA DÍAZ ARAUJO
*Universidad Nacional de Cuyo, Argentina*

# BRIEF INTRODUCTION TO THE TOPIC

First, I would like to express my gratitude to Dr Patricia Ciner, as well as to all the organizers of this conference, for the honor of coordinating this conversation between eminent specialists: Dr Adolfo Roitman (Lizbeth and George Krupp Curator of the Dead Sea Scrolls and Head of the Shrine of the Book at the Israel Museum, Jerusalem), Dr Alberto D'Anna (Università degli Studi Roma Tre), and Dr Juan Carlos Alby (Universidad Católica de Santa Fe and Universidad Nacional del Litoral).

The subject of this Section, "The discoveries of manuscripts of Qumran and apocryphal literature: their impact on Patristic Studies," addresses a wide spectrum of research, revitalized 70 years ago. In 2017 we celebrated the 70th anniversary of the discovery of the Dead Sea manuscripts, and this panel presented an exceptional *hommage*. The discovery of over 900 manuscripts in eleven, or possibly twelve,[1] caves near Khirbet Qumran came to transform not only our knowledge of Second Temple Judaism, but also all studies of Early Christianity and Late Antiquity. To mention just a few fundamental issues that have created controversy in the *status quaestionis*, I would refer to the extensive discussions regarding the characteristics (in terms of celibacy, poverty, purification, etc.) of communities associated with such manuscripts, their exegetical and liturgical practices, the figure of the Teacher of Righteousness, among other topics. On the other hand, these questions continue to be renewed as the research on the scrolls advances, which has even been shaken by the recent

---

[1] On this recent discovery, see http://new.huji.ac.il/en/article/33424.

appearance of numerous additional forged fragments. These fragments have been at the center of relevant works since 2002, querying their authenticity and provenance, expressed by Eibert Tigchelaar, Årstein Justnes, Torleif Elgvin, Esther Eshel, Hanan Eshel, James H. Charlesworth, Kipp Davis, Ira Rabin, Ines Feldman, Myriam Krutzsch, Michael Langlois, and Hasia Rimon, among other scholars.[2]

Likewise, this debate increases with the constant discoveries and revisions of apocryphal literature, both Jewish and Christian. As examples, I can mention the discovery of a Coptic version of *2 Enoch* in 2009,[3] and the strenuous editing work carried out by the teams working under the direction of Tobias Nicklas,[4] or in different associations, such as the *North American Society for the Study of Christian Apocryphal Literature*,[5] the South American *Grupo Oracula* Seminars,[6] the *Association pour l'Étude de la Littérature Apocryphe Chrétienne*,[7] which publishes the *Series Apocryphorum, Corpus Christianorum*. Precisely, Dr Alberto D'Anna addresses here three main issues: the concept and traits of "apocryphal", the progress made regarding the knowledge of Christian apocryphal texts thanks to the discovery of new witness manuscripts, and the status and use of those texts.

These important discoveries revealed the enormous richness and complexity of ideas and beliefs circulating in the early days

---

[2] For a comprehensive bibliographical list, see the useful work accomplished by Årstein Justnes and Ludvik A. Kjeldsberg: https://lyingpen.com/2017/09/09/post-2002-dead-sea-scrolls-like-fragments-online-a-really-exhausting-guide-for-the-perplexed/.

[3] A. A. Orlov, G. Boccaccini & J. M. Zurawski (eds), *New Perspectives on 2 Enoch: No Longer Slavonic Only* (Leiden-Boston: Brill, 2012). I stress as well the relevance for this domain, of the various meetings organized by the *Enoch Seminar*, see http://enochseminar.org/.

[4] I cannot introduce here the extensive work of this scholar; see for instance: T. Nicklas, *The Oxford Handbook of Early Christian Apocrypha* (Oxford: Oxford University Press, 2015). I would like to stress as well the remarkable research, projects, and publications housed by the Centre for Advanced Studies "Beyond Canon" Heterotopias of Religious Authority in Ancient Christianity, see https://www.uni-regensburg.de/research/beyond-canon/home/index.html.

[5] For this innovative work, see http://www.nasscal.com/e-clavis-christian-apocrypha/; and http://www.nasscal.com/manuscripta-apocryphorum/.

[6] Published in the journal *Oracula*; see https://www.metodista.br/revistas/revistas-ims/index.php/oracula/index.

[7] On this behalf, see http://wp.unil.ch/aelac/aelac/.

of Christianity. Within this perspective, Patristic Studies benefits from a greater understanding of the controversies and traditions that the first Fathers convey. A remarkable example of these contributions is observed in the study of Christology, as Dr Adolfo Roitman elucidates, through the examination of the messianic figure of Melchizedek. Certainly, as Roitman states "the discovery of this manuscript could be key to revealing the "mystery" that has enveloped the surprising exegetical development of Melchizedek in Early Christianity". Additionally, the correlations between sickness, theodicy and purification of Early Christianity are enriched by Dr Juan Carlos Alby's analysis of the Jewish texts of the Second Temple, where, according to Alby, "legal and liturgical aspects overlap with sanitary ones."

However, dealing with these complex dialogues between different communities is nothing less than arduous. In fact, the multiplication of publications on these textual *corpora* implies an increasing level of difficulty and can be seen in the compartmentalization into isolated disciplines. For that reason, I commend gatherings such as this which encourage multiple perspectives, perspectives that are actually themselves implied in the texts.

ALBERTO D'ANNA
*Università Roma Tre, Italy*

# MANUSCRIPTS OF CHRISTIAN APOCRYPHA: THE TEXTS AND THEIR USE

I structure this paper into three parts: I will begin with a preliminary reflection on the concept of "apocryphal" and the features of the tradition of Christian apocryphal texts; I will then provide some examples of discoveries of manuscripts that have improved our knowledge of Christian apocrypha; finally, I will consider how these discoveries shed light on the status of apocryphal writings and on their use.

## 1. *Christian Apocrypha*

Talking about the manuscripts of Christian apocrypha requires some preliminary remarks. First of all, it is necessary to remember what we mean by the expression "Christian apocrypha": we refer to anonymous or pseudepigraphic literary works which – because of their content, or the author to whom they are attributed, or both – present themselves as bearers of a portion of that "memory of the Christian origins" which is a paradigmatic and intrinsically normative reference for believers in Jesus, from many points of view – doctrinal in the first place, but also disciplinary, liturgical, cultural, devotional – works which, however, have not become part – at least, not in a uniform manner in space and stable in time – of that normative collection which is the Christian canon of Scripture.[1]

---

[1] For a wide and deep reflection on the meanings of the term "apocryphal", with rich examples, see at least: R. Gounelle, "Christian apocryphal literature: An overview", in *The Apocryphal Acts of Apostles in Latin Christianity*, ed. by

It is a modern and scientific meaning of the expression, which has some late-antique precedents, but which above all distances itself from the two ideologically connoted meanings that the term "apocryphal" assumed in the first centuries of Christian history: in a positive sense (especially used by the Gnostics, but not only),[2] relative to a secret knowledge reserved for a few elected; and in a negative sense (prevalent in the great Church), relative to heretical falsifications.[3]

In its modern use, without either positive or negative ideological connotations, the term "apocryphal", when applied to Christian literary works, ends up constituting a category closely related to another category, that of "canonical", or "testamentary". It is, therefore, a category only applicable *a posteriori*, in relation to the constitution of the canon of Christian Scriptures. Of the works included in it, the category of "apocryphal" only says that they do not achieve the authoritative status of "Sacred Scripture". Paradoxically, while Wilhelm Schneemelcher sets the fourth century – that is, the time of the definitive consolidation of the canon of the Christian Bible – as the final chronological limit for the use of the term "apocryphal", after which we should only speak of hagiographical works,[4] according to the meaning just exposed that same chronological limit rather marks the beginning of the composition of works *ab origine* apocryphal. Of those composed before, we must instead affirm that "they have become apocryphal".

---

E. Rose, Proceedings of ISCAL, 1 (Turnhout: Brepols, 2014), pp. 7–30; T. Burke, "Entering the Mainstream: Twenty-five Years of Research on the Christian Apocrypha?", in *Rediscovering the Apocryphal Continent: New Perspectives on Early Christian and Late Antique Apocryphal Texts and Traditions*, ed. by P. Piovanelli and T. Burke, Wissenschaftliche Untersuchungen zum Neuen Testament, 349 (Tübingen: Mohr Siebeck, 2015), pp. 19–47; P. Piovanelli, *Apocryphités. Études sur les textes et les traditions scripturaire du judaïsme et du christianisme anciens*, Judaïsme ancien et origines du christianisme, 7 (Turnhout: Brepols, 2016).

[2] See, e.g., *Col* 2:3.

[3] Attestations of use of the category of "apocryphal" in E. Preuschen, *Analecta. Kürzere Texte zur Geschichte der alten Kirche und des Kanons*, II: *Zur Kanonsgeschichte* (Tübingen: Mohr Siebeck, 1910[2]).

[4] See E. Junod, "'Apocryphes du Nouveau Testament': une appellation erronée et une collection artificielle. Discussion de la nouvelle définition proposée par W. Schneemelcher", *Apocrypha*, 3 (1992), pp. 17–46.

This first premise was necessary to explain that to speak of "manuscripts of Christian apocrypha" means to take into consideration, with a necessarily synthetic expression, an ancient situation observed from a modern point of view. In reality, for many of the works we are dealing with, it would be more correct to say: "manuscripts of works that have become apocryphal"; and although it may be true on the one hand that even the oldest works found in a medieval manuscript would be already perceived as completely apocryphal by the copyist as much as by us today,[5] on the other hand the same cannot be said with the same confidence about the oldest books, produced when the limits of the canon of Christian Scripture were still rather uncertain and mobile, presenting at times considerable regional differences.

A second point, in many ways clearly related to what has just been said, must now be introduced. It is necessary to consider the tradition of the apocrypha and its characteristics. In this respect too, the formation of the canon of Christian Scripture is a decisive factor. Before the fixation of the canon, we see that the works which *de facto* belong or claim to belong (whether the claim is implicit or external to the text itself) to that mythical memory of Christian origins, are all subject to the normal process of textual reproduction of antiquity, including also more or less extensive forms of reworking and reuse of pre-existing works. Among the literature that has become canonical, the most famous cases in this respect are perhaps the rewriting of *Mark* (or of a "proto-*Mark*"), by both *Matthew* and *Luke*, the double ending of the *Fourth Gospel*, and the patchwork of Paul's *Second Letter to the Corinthians*. The process of reproduction also originated more or less large variants, which led to the progressive differentiation of the texts of a work and to the development of the famous textual types, widely studied by New Testament philology. This same science teaches us that the fixation of the canon has determined the end of the period of greatest textual mobility of the works included in it, and the stabilization of the texts, now

---

[5] *Epistola tertia ad Corinthios quae autentica non est* is, for example, the title that can be read in a manuscript of the thirteenth century (Laon, Bibliothèque municipale, cod. 45).

reproduced with the accuracy and respectful deference due to the books of Sacred Scripture.

A different and, in some ways, opposite destiny was met by those works which were progressively marginalized and then completely excluded from the Christian canon, that is to say "became apocryphal", as well as those works which were composed after the substantial closure of the canon. Not only, in fact, did they continue to be reproduced "normally", that is, without that special care due to the sacred text, and therefore undergoing the usual multiple phenomena of textual innovation; but the voluntary and conscious reworking of these works was even encouraged by their exclusion from the canon and by the contextual spread, in the great Church, of the negative meaning of the category "apocryphal", as comprising "compositions later than works containing the authentic memory of the origins, produced by heretics, finalized to the propagation of their doctrines among the faithful of the Church".[6] On the one hand, in fact, works marked by the stigma of inauthenticity have been forgotten, if not destroyed voluntarily. On the other hand, devotion and liturgy above all, but also theology and controversy, enriched by now by a great deal of data about Jesus, his Mother, and the apostles transmitted through texts that had become apocryphal, still required the preservation, if not of those works, at least of many traditions handed down through them. Moreover, even outside the great Church, among the religious movements that most used these works (Manichaeans, Priscillianists), we see phenomena of textual reworking, with the aim of adapting the text to the doctrines of those movements. We may accordingly recognize two types of widespread phenomena.

– Dismemberment. This is the phenomenon exemplarily represented by the fate of the acts of the individual apostles: typically, the story of the martyrdom of the apostle is separated from the rest of the work. Martyrdom, inserted in hagiographic collections or in liturgical texts, enjoys wide reproduction and

---

[6] Athanasius' 39th *Festal Letter* (for Easter 367) is an excellent example of this meaning of "apocryphal". See: Atanasio di Alessandria, *Lettere festali*. Anonimo, *Indice delle Lettere festali*, ed. by A. Camplani, Letture cristiane del primo millennio, 34 (Milano: Paoline, 2003), pp. 498–518, part. 512.

diffusion, as well as translation in languages different from the original. The story that preceded is easily lost and is seldom preserved in its integrity; what remains survives thanks to a very few and often maltreated witnesses, sometimes exclusively through ancient translations.

- Rewriting. In reality, this phenomenon can be of two types, depending on the size of the intervention. We have, in fact, the production of new versions of the same work, or actual compositions of new works, which substantially re-elaborate a previous work. In the first case, new contexts of fruition of a work and new functions attributed to it lead to the writing of successive versions, with the textual changes suitable for its re-functionalisation. In the second case, a work, or part of it, is rewritten and transformed into a new work, rescuing from the source exclusively what was intended to be preserved from the inevitable loss, which would result from its official condemnation. Rewriting may also involve the change of literary genre (often contents of ancient apocryphal texts are transmitted in the form of homilies) and / or the attribution of the work to a fictitious author, different from that to which the source was attributed (if it was not anonymous). The examples are countless: the most famous is the rewriting of the so-called *Protoevangelium of James*, but there are also many of the acts of apostles, or of their martyrdoms (a perfect example being the process whereby the *Martyrdom of Peter* – separated from the *Acts* of the apostle himself –, passes through the *Pseudo-Linus*, the *Pseudo-Hegesippus*, the *Pseudo-Marcellus*, and arrives at the *Pseudo-Abdias*), of works on Jesus (such as the so-called *Gospel of Nicodemus*), or on the Virgin (the *dormitiones*). The tendency is to have more manuscripts of the derivative works and less of their sources, if they survive at all, as they are basically replacements of one work for another.

The most evident consequence of these phenomena, typical of the tradition of texts that have become apocryphal or were born as such, is the fact, only apparently contradictory but understandable in the light of what has just been said, of the extreme scarcity, even total loss, of witnesses of some works or parts of them (that is, those that have been dropped or reused as sources of later rewrites), for the conservation of which the ancient translations into languages of peripheral areas of the Christian world are often fundamental; and, on the other hand, the much better attestation, which sometimes amounts to overabundance, of the manuscript tradition of other works, or parts of works, namely those that have managed to pass the scrutiny of the ecclesiastical authorities or that have even been promoted by them and that, for this reason, I like to call, with what is only an apparent oxymoron, "institutional apocrypha".

The effects on the methodology for the critical edition of works characterized by this type of manuscript tradition are also evident. The extreme textual mobility of certain apocrypha leads us to reflect on how to conceive of their critical edition. For a work of which, for example, there are various redactions, even in different languages, one must ask oneself if it is more philological, that is more in keeping with historical reality, to try to trace back a text presumed to be close to the archetype, but of which nothing assures that it is not a sort of abstract reconstruction of a textual form that in reality has perhaps never existed as such, or rather renounce this ambition and provide the edition of single textual forms that contain several innovations with respect to the archetype, but which can be published with a good degree of reliability and have circulated in historical contexts that can be reconstructed with good approximation.[7] Another problem that is sometimes posed to the critical editor of apocryphal texts is represented by the superabundant traditions: the complete collation of all the witnesses of an apocryphon may well prove to be an insurmountable impediment and it becomes necessary therefore to identify specific *loci critici* on which to base the comparison.

## 2. *Discoveries of Manuscripts of Apocrypha*

Having said this, it is certainly easier to understand how progress in the knowledge of the tradition of the Christian apocrypha has

---

[7] In-depth methodological considerations of these kinds of ecdotic problems are set forth in: R. Gounelle, "L'édition de la recension grecque ancienne des *Actes de Pilate*. Perspectives méthodologiques", *Apocrypha*, 21 (2010), pp. 31–47.

been proportional to the fortune and the textual history of the individual works. Of some of them we still know too little, having to rely exclusively on a few surviving fragments, while of others an already solid tradition has been further enriched by the advance of knowledge of manuscripts.

If we take as a starting point the three large collections of critical editions of Christian apocrypha published between the mid-nineteenth century and the beginning of the twentieth – the *Evangelia Apocrypha* by Tischendorf (1853; 1876²), the *Apocalypses Apocryphae* again by Tischendorf (1866), and the *Acta Apostolorum Apocrypha* by Lipsius and Bonnet (1891–1903) – we certainly record some subsequent discoveries of important manuscripts – in some cases of otherwise unknown works – but above all the questioning of many of the editors' choices. Without any claim to completeness, I mention some of these discoveries and new editions.

The tradition about Jesus has certainly been enriched by new texts, many of them fragmentary, such as the *Gospel of Peter*,[8] or the *Berlin-Strasbourg Apocryphon* (the so-called *Gospel of the Saviour*[9]), but in some instances complete texts, such as the *Gospel of Thomas*,[10] in the Coptic version discovered in Nag Hammadi, or the *Gospel of Judas*,[11] also in the Coptic version, otherwise unknown (except for the Irenaeus' mention). In 1912 Guerrier published the critical edition of the Ethiopian text of the so-called *Epistle of the Apostles*, in actual fact a dialogue with the Risen Christ, the Greek text of which remains, to this day, unknown.[12] And if the discovery of Papyrus Bodmer V (which we will come back to) has not substantially changed our knowledge of the text

---

[8] See M. Geerard, *Clavis Apocryphorum Novi Testamenti* (from here forward: CANT) (Turnhout: Brepols, 1992), n. 13.

[9] CANT, n. 6 and A. Suciu, *The Berlin-Strasbourg Apocryphon. A Coptic Apostolic Memoir*, Wissenschaftliche Untersuchungen zum Neuen Testament, 370 (Tübingen: Mohr Siebeck, 2017).

[10] CANT, n. 19.

[11] CANT, n. 39 and P. Nagel, *Codex apocryphus gnosticus Novi Testamenti*, I: *Evangelien und Apostelgeschichten aus den Schriften von Nag Hammadi und verwandten Kodizes. Koptisch und deutsch*, Wissenschaftliche Untersuchungen zum Neuen Testament, 326 (Tübingen: Mohr Siebeck, 2014), pp. 261–309.

[12] CANT, n. 22. Even before the Ethiopian text, a Latin fragment was known in a palimpsest from Bobbio; in 1919 Schmidt published a defective Coptic text.

of the *Protevangelium of James*,[13] the choices of the editors of the *Gospel of the Pseudo-Matthew*[14] and the *Liber de nativitate Mariae*[15] (Gijsel and Beyers), for the Series Apocryphorum of Corpus Christianorum, have been very different from those of Tischendorf, favouring, among the versions of the texts (four for *Pseudo-Matthew*, two for the *Liber*), those now recognized as being the oldest and the starting point of the later revisions.

Among the apocryphal acts of the apostles, a much better understanding of the *Acts of Paul*,[16] exemplary both for the phenomenon of dismemberment and for that of rewriting, can now be obtained thanks above all to the publication of the Coptic Papyrus of Heidelberg (1904) and of the Greek Papyrus of Hamburg (1936), by Schmidt. These two ancient books, from the sixth and fourth centuries, although damaged and incomplete, allow us to have a better idea of the original narrative structure of the *Acts*. Thus, we are now able to reconstruct the context from which the section on Paul and Thecla – in many respects, the first Christian novel – was very early extracted, a section known already to Lipsius through eleven Greek manuscripts (as well as through ancient translations), and nowadays through around fifty witnesses: it is a typical case of dismemberment of an apocryphon. The *Martyrdom* was also extracted from these same *Acts*; few witnesses remain of it, however, because it was supplanted by later revisions, which are otherwise well attested, such as, for example, the *Passion of the Pseudo-Linus*,[17] known today thanks to more than a hundred manuscripts.

But great progress has been made in the knowledge also of other apocryphal acts. For example, the initial part of the *Acts of Andrew*[18] (the first thirty-two chapters) was discovered thanks to the publication of two Greek manuscripts, from Sinai and Athens, in 1982, by Détorakis. A manuscript of Athos, discovered in 1974 by Bovon and Bouvier, has allowed a substantial improve-

---

[13] CANT, n. 50.
[14] CANT, n. 51.
[15] CANT, n. 52.
[16] CANT, n. 211.
[17] CANT, n. 212.
[18] CANT, n. 225.i.

ment in our knowledge of the *Acts of Philip*,[19] the text of which, however, is reconstructed on only three Greek witnesses, except for the martyrdom, which is transmitted by about fifty manuscripts.

As far as epistolary literature is concerned, the case of the so-called *Third Letter to the Corinthians*[20] is in many ways exemplary, both for the evolution of the status of the work and for the discoveries related to its text. *3 Corinthians*, actually a pseudepigraph correspondence between Paul and the Corinthians composed in Greek, was included in the *corpus paulinum* by the *Vetus Syra* and remained, in the Armenian Bible, in a fully canonical position until the seventh century. It had an initial diffusion as a Pauline text also in the West, with two translations in Latin. Decisive for its exclusion from the *corpus paulinum* was its transmission not only as an independent text, but also as part of the *Acts of Paul*. The early refusal of the authenticity of the latter, already attested by Tertullian, also involved the correspondence, the memory of which was lost in the West. Only from the end of the nineteenth century were they progressively discovered: between 1891 and 1953, five Latin witnesses of the independent text; in 1904, the Coptic papyrus of Heidelberg with correspondence within the *Acts of Paul*; and, finally, in 1959, the Papyrus Bodmer X, to date the only Greek witness of the *3 Corinthians*, transmitted in the independent form. Even today the debate concerning its original editorial form is still open: whether it was composed independently, before the *Acts of Paul*, and then inserted in them (as is thought to have happened to the traditions on Thecla), or whether it was instead composed by the author of the *Acts* himself and then extracted from them (like the *Acts of Paul and Thecla*). What is certain is that *3 Corinthians* has also circulated independently and that it represents one of the clearest examples of the fact that the apocryphal status of a text (at least in the sense that we have given to the term) is an extrinsic and relative feature.

Progress due to the discovery of new manuscripts also involves the apocalypses. The Latin tradition of the *Apocalypse of Paul*

---

[19] CANT, n. 250.
[20] CANT, n. 211.iv.

(*Visio Pauli*),[21] to be distinguished from the Gnostic work by the same title discovered at Nag Hammadi, is now known in much better detail thanks to Silverstein's research, published between 1935 and 1997, which led to the discovery of more than fifty witnesses of various versions of the *Visio Pauli*. A redaction of the Latin *Vision of Ezra*,[22] preceding the other three already known, was discovered in a Vatican manuscript in 1984 by Bogaert.

## 3. *Manuscripts and the Status of Works that we Call Apocryphal*

After this cursory overview of the discoveries that followed the great editions of Tischendorf and Lipsius-Bonnet, I would like to conclude, referring to the initial premises, with a reflection on the status of these works, considered in the light of progress in the knowledge of manuscripts. I will mention two cases which I have dealt with directly during my research, cases that well exemplify, in my opinion, the contribution of the study of manuscripts to the knowledge of the phenomenon "apocryphal".

The first case is actually well known and has been studied by eminent specialists: it is the codex of the Bodmer collection (LDAB 2565) that I have already mentioned twice, because it is the oldest witness of the *Protevangelium of James* (*Nativity of Mary*) and the oldest, and the only Greek witness of *3 Corinthians*.

It is a papyrus multiple-text composite codex (sometimes called in the literature "Bodmer Miscellaneous Codex" or, with reference to the three New Testament texts contained in it, P[72]), coming from Upper Egypt, probably from the region of Panopolis, assembled in around the middle of the fourth century, purchased by Martin Bodmer in 1956[23] and published by Michel Testuz in four volumes, between 1958 and 1960. It belonged to a library on the consistency of which opinions are still very discordant

---

[21] CANT, n. 325.

[22] CANT, n. 341.

[23] See J. M. Robinson, *The Story of the Bodmer Papyri. From the First Monastery's Library in Upper Egypt to Geneva and Dublin* (Cambridge: Clarke & Co., 2013), pp. 35–47; B. Nongbri, *God's Library. The Archaeology of the Earliest Christian Manuscripts* (New Haven-London: Yale U.P., 2018), pp. 157–215.

(a recent inventory proposal counts forty units).[24] Also, with regard to the environment of production and use of the books available in this library, there is no agreement among scholars; the most convincing proposal, in my opinion, is that of a culturally elevated environment of lay scribes-readers, united by a network of personal relations and shared doctrinal interests, a prodrome not yet institutionalized of the later lay brotherhoods, present in Christian Egypt in the fifth–seventh centuries.[25]

Codicological and paleographic analyses tell us that the book resulted from the assembly of three pre-existing units,[26] the first and the third of which are slightly older (late third–early fourth century) than the second (mid fourth century). These three units appear thematically coherent within themselves,[27] and although some scholars are more reluctant than others on this point,[28] the same may be said with regard to the assemblage of the three parts.[29] The codex, therefore, was organized, not mechanically assembled.

---

[24] See J.-L. Fournet, "Anatomie d'une bibliothèque de l'Antiquité tardive: l'inventaire, le faciès et la provenance de la 'Bibliothèque Bodmer'", *Adamantius*, 21 (2015), pp. 8–40.

[25] See K. Haines-Eitzen, *Guardians of Letters. Literacy, Power, and the Transmitters of Early Christian Literature* (New York: Oxford University Press, 2000), pp. 96–104; A. Camplani, "Per un profilo storico-religioso degli ambienti di produzione e fruizione dei Papiri Bodmer: contaminazione dei linguaggi e dialettica delle idee nel contesto del dibattito su dualismo e origenismo", *Adamantius*, 21 (2015), pp. 98–135.

[26] See P. Orsini, "I Papiri Bodmer: scritture e libri", *Adamantius*, 21 (2015), pp. 60–78; B. Nongbri, "Recent Progress in Understanding the Construction of the Bodmer 'Miscellaneous' or 'Composite' Codex", *Adamantius*, 21 (2015), pp. 171–72. The first nucleus includes the *Nativity of Mary* (the so-called *Protevangelium of James*) (= *P.Bodm.* V), the *Correspondence between Paul and the Corinthians (Third letter to the Corinthians)* (*P.Bodm.* X), the *Ode of Solomon* XI (*P.Bodm.* XI), the *Letter of Judas* (*P.Bodm.* VII), the Melito of Sardis' *Homily on the Passover* (*P.Bodm.* XIII), a fragment of a liturgical hymn (*P.Bodm.* XII). The second includes the *Apology of Fileas* (*P.Bodm.* XX) and *Psalms* 33 and 34 (*P.Bodm.* IX). The third (since 1969 separated from the rest and preserved in the Vatican Library) includes the *First* and *Second Letters of Peter* (*P.Bodm.* VIII), copied from the same hand as *P.Bodm.* X, XI, VII.

[27] See Camplani, "Per un profilo storico-religioso", pp. 113–22.

[28] See T. Nicklas and T. Wasserman, "Theologische Linien im *Codex Bodmer Miscellani*?", in *New Testament Manuscripts. Their Text and Their World*, ed. by T. J. Kraus and T. Nicklas, Texts and Editions for New Testament Study, 2 (Leiden-Boston: Brill, 2006), pp. 161–88.

[29] See D. G. Horrel, "The Themes of 1 Peter: Insights from the Earliest Manuscripts (the Crosby-Schøyen Codex ms 193 and the Bodmer Miscellaneous Codex

In the perspective of this reflection, it is interesting that this book attests to the coexistence, side by side, of both canonized works and others that have become apocryphal. This is true for both the first nucleus and the final assembly. Of the latter, it is important to highlight both the period, hardly prior to the middle of the fourth century, and the fact that the two *Letters of Peter* appear to have been separated from another pre-existing book, to be then joined to this.[30]

This coexistence, in the Bodmer Composite Codex, of canonized works and works that have become apocryphal is described by Eldon Jay Epp as the presence of "unexpected books" in a "New Testament manuscript".[31] Using such categories for a book like this means forcing the evidence it represents into ideological categories that are absolutely inadequate for a real historical perspective (and it must be said that Epp uses them with a declared awareness of such inadequacy). If we want, on the other hand, to get rid of *a posteriori* classifications, we must recognize that the Bodmer codex is the proof of the double fluidity, which Epp himself points out and which has already been mentioned here: on the one hand the fluidity, or rather the absence among some Egyptian Christians, between the third and fourth centuries, of a scriptural canon of such normative impact as to separate some works from others, leading them to constitute "special" collections; and on the other hand the fluidity of the text themselves of these works.

We do not know, in fact, what was the status attributed to *Protevangelium, 3 Corinthians, Ode of Solomon, Judas, 1* and *2*

---

containing P[72])", *New Testament Studies*, 55 (2009), pp. 502–22 [republished in Id., *Becoming Christian. Essays on 1 Peter and the Making of Christian Identity*, Library of New Testament Studies, 394 (London-New York: Bloomsbury T & T Clark, 2013), pp. 45–72]; Haines-Eitzen, *Guardians of Letters*, pp. 102–04; Camplani, "Per un profilo storico-religioso", p. 122.

[30] See B. Nongbri, "The Construction of P.Bodmer VIII and the Bodmer 'Composite' or 'Miscellaneous' Codex", *Novum Testamentum*, 58 (2016), pp. 394–410.

[31] E. J. Epp, "Issues in the Interrelation of New Testament Textual Criticism and Canon", in *The Canon Debate: On the Origins and Formation of the Bible*, ed. by L. M. McDonald and J. A. Sanders (Peabody, MA: Baker Academic, 2002), pp. 485–515 [republished in Id., *Perspectives on New Testament Textual Criticism. Collected Essays, 1962–2004*, Novum Testamentum, Supplements, 116 (Leiden-Boston: Brill, 2005), pp. 595–639].

*Peter* by those who collected them; it is clear, however, that the compiler (or the compilers) of the manuscript had no reason to distinguish and separate them, and brought them together, according to a conscious editorial project, in a single book, which did not induce any extrinsic qualitative evaluation among the works contained in it. Talking about apocryphal and canonical texts, in a case like this, makes no sense at all, from a historical perspective. Moreover, if we "enter" into the texts, we discover that the Bodmer codex, although the oldest witness known to date, nevertheless does not transmit the best text of either the *Protevangelium* or *Judas*, but a text already subjected to some important innovations.[32] The book, therefore, also attests to this other type of fluidity: two works destined to reach different status in the history of Christianity and to enjoy entirely different textual traditions, were in that context still united also by the same quality of reproduction.

The second case I would like to deal with concerns a work and a manuscript that are much less well-known than those I have just mentioned. The work is the *Passio Petri et Pauli*, called "of Pseudo-Marcellus",[33] composed, according to Lipsius, in the middle of the fifth century. It provides an excellent example of the process of rewriting a previous work, as well as of composition *ex novo*. It is based, in fact, on the general bipartite scheme of the *Acts of Peter*, as we know them from the Vercelli manuscript:[34] conflict between the apostle and Simon the magician, followed by the martyrdom of the apostle. It also draws on the *Acts of Peter* for specific elements (such as the flight of Simon, the *Quo vadis, Domine?*, the inverted crucifixion of Peter), but profoundly reworks the story and introduces several new elements, notably the presence of Paul at Peter's side in the conflict against Simon and in the condemnation suffered, and the setting of the conflict in the presence of Nero, who almost acts as judge. The tradition of this work represents a typical case of superabundant tradition: if Lipsius had catalogued seventy-seven manuscripts, nowadays

---

[32] See Epp, "Issues", pp. 492–93 [605]; A. Frey, "Protévangile de Jacques", in *Écrits apocryphes chrétiens*, vol. I, ed. by P. Geoltrain and F. Bovon, Bibliothèque de la Pléiade, 442, (Paris: Gallimard, 1997), pp. 67–104.

[33] CANT, n. 193.

[34] CANT, n. 190.iii.

more than two hundred are known. Already this issue, compared to the only Vercelli manuscript of the *Acts of Peter*, should make us reflect on the phenomenon of rewriting: that is, the fact that, if elements considered unacceptable for various reasons are purged (in this specific case, all the doctrinal reflections and the very fact that Peter was martyred independently and in the absence of Paul are lost from the ancient *Acts of Peter*), certain traditions could continue to live openly in the ecclesiastical sphere and also enjoy excellent health, giving rise to texts that we may call apocryphal, in the scientific sense of the term, just as those that they replaced, but which in fact were certainly not considered to be apocryphal in the negative sense of heretical forgeries. The manuscript tradition, however, tells us even more: the oldest witness known to date, which Lipsius was not aware of and was published only in 1944, is an important liturgical book, the *Lectionary of Luxeuil*, written just before 700, intended for the cathedral of Langres, where it was used for a long time, still in the ninth century.[35] This precious lectionary, witness of the Gallican liturgy, also contains the *Passio Petri et Pauli*, from which the first reading of the Mass of June 29 was taken: on the margin of the text, in fact, a hand wrote *lege ad mesa*[*m*] e [*fi*]*nit* next to the points where the first reading in the Mass of the feast of Peter and Paul was to begin and end.[36] This manuscript, in short, not only shows ecclesiastical tolerance towards works that we today call apocryphal and that we recognize consist essentially of legendary stories; it also attests to the full approval of such works by the episcopal authority and to the fact that they were *de facto* placed on the same level, in the liturgy, with texts that have become canonical; *a fortiori*, the definition of them as "institutional apocrypha" seems the most appropriate to me.

---

[35] See P. Salmon, *Le Lectionnaire de Luxeuil (Paris, ms. lat. 9427). Édition et étude comparative. Contribution à l'histoire de la Vulgate et de la Liturgie en France au temps des Mérovingiens*, Collectanea biblica latina, 7, (Roma-Città del Vaticano: Abbaye Saint-Jérôme-Libreria Vaticana, 1944); Id., *Le Lectionnaire de Luxeuil (Paris, ms. lat. 9427). II: Étude paléographique et liturgique suivie d'un choix de planches*, Collectanea biblica latina, 9, (Roma-Città del Vaticano: Abbaye Saint-Jérôme-Libreria Vaticana, 1953.

[36] See Salmon, *Le Lectionnaire de Luxeuil* [I], pp. xxxi–xxxvi; 182–83.

## *Abstract*

The paper addresses two main themes: the progress in the knowledge of Christian apocryphal works, thanks to the discovery of new late antique or medieval manuscripts, and the reflection on the status of those works and their use, starting from the data of their material transmission.

ADOLFO D. ROITMAN
*The Israel Museum, Jerusalem*

# THE MYSTERY OF MELCHIZEDEK IN EARLY CHRISTIANITY IN LIGHT OF THE DEAD SEA SCROLLS[1]

## *Introduction*

The figure of Melchizedek is expressly mentioned only two times in the Hebrew Bible: Gn 14, 18–20 and Ps 110, 4. In both passages, this figure is enigmatic and ambiguous, without his literary, historical and theological significance having been clarified by contemporary scholars.[2]

Therefore, it is not surprising that this mysterious and challenging character has called the attention of Jewish exegetes of

---

[1] This is an abbreviated version of a presentation given at the 2nd International Conference on Patristic Studies held at the Catholic University of Cuyo (San Juan, Argentina) in March 2017. The complete Spanish version was published in *Bandue: a Journal of the Spanish Society of Religious Sciences* (2018), pp. 199–232.

[2] For different interpretations of these two biblical passages by modern critics, see A. D. Roitman, "La identidad mesiánico-sacerdotal de Jesús. La exégesis de Génesis 14, 18–20 en la Epístola a los Hebreos a la luz del judaísmo antiguo," in *Actas del Primer Congreso Internacional de Estudios Patrísticos: "La identidad de Jesús: unidad y diversidad en la época de la Patrística"* (A. Hernández; S. Villalonga; P. Ciner and P. Fernández [eds]; San Juan: Universidad Católica de Cuyo, 2014), pp. 86–90, 130–31; F. L. Horton, *The Melchizedek Tradition. A Critical Examination of the Sources to the Fifth Century A.D. and in the Epistle to the Hebrews* (Cambridge et al.: Cambridge University Press, 1976), pp. 12–53; M. Delcor, "Melchizedek from Genesis to the Qumran Texts and the Epistle to the Hebrews," *JSJ* 2 (1971), pp. 115–23; A. Steudel, "Melchizedek", in *Encyclopedia of the Dead Sea Scrolls* [*EDSS*] (L. H. Schiffman and J. C. VanderKam [eds]; New York: Oxford University Press, 2000), vol. 1, p. 535; E. F. Mason, *'You are a Priest Forever.' Second Temple Jewish Messianism and the Priestly Christology of the Epistle to the Hebrews* (STDJ 74; Leiden-Boston: Brill, 2008), pp. 138–46; idem, "Melchizedek Traditions in Second Temple Judaism," in *New Perspectives on 2 Enoch: No longer Slavonic Only* (A. Orlov, G. Boccaccini, J. Zurawski [eds]; Leiden: Brill, 2012), pp. 343–45.

Antiquity, both in the Second Temple[3] and Rabbinic eras,[4] who interpreted the figure of Melchizedek principally as a human and historic being,[5] identifying him in rabbinical sources with Shem, Noah's son.[6] This figure was the center of controversies in pious

[3] Specifically: *Genesis Apocryphon* col. XXII, 12–17; *Pseudo-Eupolemus* (apud Eusebius, *Praeparatio Evangelica* 9.17.6); Philo of Alexandria (*On Abraham* § 235; *On Mating with the Preliminary Studies* § 99; *Allegorical Interpretation* III §§ 79–82); Flavius Josephus (*Antiquities* 1.179–81; *War* 6.438); *11QMelchizedek* (11Q13); *2 Enoch*. Melchizedek is also mentioned in Hellenistic synagogue prayers (*Apostolic Constitutions*, books 7–8), which, despite being Christian liturgical material in their current state, could have had Greek-Jewish elements from the first centuries of our era as origin. For its part, the current version of the book *Jubilees* in classical Ethiopian (*Ge'ez*) (13, 22–29) regarding Abraham's military feats recounted in Gn 14 has come to us with empty spaces between verses 25–28, with precisely the corresponding reference to Abraham's encounter with Melchizedek missing. Nevertheless, in this same space appears the insertion of a text dealing with tithing regulations (vv. 25b–27). The presence of this discussion in this literary context could suggest that these are the remains of a lost original.

[4] Specifically: Targum (*Tg. Ps.-J., Frg. Tg.*, and *Tg. Neof.* to Gn 14, 18); Talmud (*b.Ned.* 32b; *b.Sukk.* 52b); and Midrash (*'Abot R. Nat.* A 34; *Gen. Rab* 43, 1; 43, 7; 56, 14; *Lev. Rab.* 25, 6; *Num Rab.* 4, 8; *Cant. Rab.* 2.13.4; *Pesiq.* 51a; *Pirqe de-Rabbi Eliezer* 8, 2; 27, 3; *Midrash Tehilim* 76, 3.

[5] With the possible exception of some testimonies, for example: Philonean exegesis in the *Allegorical Interpretation III* § 80, which understands Melchizedek to be "straight reason" (ὁ ὀρθὸς λόγος) (the Greek text follows the version from F. H. Colson and G. H. Whitaker [trans.], *Philo*, [LCL], vol. I, London-New York, 1929), implying that for this Jewish philosopher the king-priest of Salem must have had supernatural-divine meaning. Another case is that present in the Talmud (*b.Sukk.* 52b) and in the Midrash (*Cant. Rab.* 2.13.4; *'Abot R. Nat.* A 34; y *Pesiq.* 51a), where Melchizedek takes on an eschatological role. Finally, *2 Enoch* and *11QMelchizedek* (11Q13) are the most extreme cases in this respect, presenting the figure of Melchizedek in supernatural terms. For Medieval Jewish developments on Melchizedek as a heavenly priest and eschatological judge, see M. Poorthuis, "Enoch and Melchizedek in Judaism and Christianity: A Study in Intermediaries," in *Saints and Role Models in Judaism and Christianity*, M. Poorthuis y J. Schwartz [eds] (Brill: Leiden-Boston, 2004), p. 119.

[6] On the figure of Melchizedek in Jewish literature from the Second Temple Era and in rabbinical sources, see Roitman, "La identidad mesiánico-sacerdotal de Jesús," pp. 93–108; Mason, '*You are a Priest Forever,*' pp. 138–90; idem, "Melchizedek Traditions," pp. 346–60; Horton, *The Melchizedek Tradition*, pp. 54–86, 114–30; Steudel, "Melchizedek," pp. 536–37; B. A. Pearson, "Melchizedek in Early Judaism, Christianity, and Gnosticism," in *Biblical Figures Outside the Bible* (M. E. Stone and Th. A. Bergren; Harrisburg, Pennsylvania: Trinity Press International, 1998), pp. 180–86; Delcor, "Melchizedek from Genesis," pp. 124–25, 127–32; M. McNamara, "Melchizedek: Gen 14, 17–20 in the Targums, in Rabbinic and Early Christian Literature," *Biblica* 81 (2000), pp. 1–31; R. Hayward, "Shem, Melchizedek, and Concern with Christianity in the Pentateuchal Targumim," in *Targumic and Cognate Studies: Essays in Honour of Martin McNamara* (K. J. Cathcart and M. Maher [eds]; JSOT Sup. 230

circles (*hasidim*) and with the Pharisees in their disputes with the Hasmoneans, Enoch-Noachic groups and Christians.[7]

Moving on to the exegesis of the figure of Melchizedek in Christian tradition, the first known testimony is that which is found in *Epistle to the Hebrews* (chap. 5–7), and more specifically in 7, 1–10, when upon interpreting the encounter between the former king-priest of Salem and the patriarch Abraham in Gn 14, 18–20,[8] the former was characterized by the author of *Hebrews* in the following terms: v. 3a (1) "without father" (ἀπάτωρ); (2) "without mother" (ἀμήτωρ); (3) "without genealogy" (ἀγενεαλόγητος); v. 3b: (4) "having neither beginning nor end of life" (μήτε ἀρχὴν ἡμερῶν μήτε ζωῆς τέλος ἔχων); v. 3c: (5) "but resembling the Son of God" (ἀφωμοιωμένος δὲ τῷ Υἱῷ τοῦ Θεοῦ); y v. 3d: (6) "he remains a priest forever" (μένει ἱερεὺς εἰς τὸ διηνεκές).[9]

---

Sheffield: Sheffield Academic Press LTD, 1996), pp. 67–80; C. T. R. Hayward, "Melchizedek as Priest of the Jerusalem Temple in Talmud, Midrash, and Targum," in *Targums and the Transmission of Scripture into Judaism and Christianity*, (*idem* [ed.] Leiden-Boston: Brill, 2010), pp. 377–99.

[7] On the controversial use of Melchizedek in ancient Judaism, see J. J. Petuchowski, "The Controversial Figure of Melchizedek," *HUCA* 28 (1957), pp. 127–36; R. Longenecker, "The Melchizedek Argument of Hebrews: A Study in the Development and Circumstantial Expression of New Testament Thought," in *Unity and Diversity in the New Testament Theology: Essays in Honor of George E. Ladd* (R. A. Guelich [ed.]; Grand Rapids, Michigan 1978), pp. 164–67; A. A. Orlov, "Melchizedek," in *The Eerdmans Dictionary of Early Judaism* [*EDEJ*] (J. J. Collins y D. C. Harlow [eds]; Grand Rapids, Michigan/Cambridge, U.K.: William B. Eerdmans Publishing Company, 2010), pp. 931–32; *idem*, "Melchizedek Legend of 2 (Slavonic) Enoch," *JSJ* XXXI/1 (2000), pp. 27–31; *idem*, "The Heir of Righteousness and the King of Righteousness: The Priestly Noachic Polemics in 2 Enoch and the Epistle to the Hebrews," *JThS*, NS, 58/1 (2007), pp. 50–55; Poorthuis, "Enoch and Melchizedek," pp. 112–15; M. Simon, "Melchisédech dans la polémique entre juifs et chrétiens et dans la légende," *RHPR* XVII (1937), pp. 58–93; A. Aschim, "Melchizedek and Levi," in *The Dead Sea Scrolls. Fifty Years After Their Discovery*. Proceedings of the Jerusalem Congress, July 20–25, 1997 (L. H. Schiffman, E. Tov and J. C. VanderKam [eds]; Jerusalem: Israel Exploration Society, in cooperation with The Shrine of the Book, Israel Museum, 2000), pp. 773–88.

[8] On the exegesis of Gn 14, 18–20 in *Hebrews* 7, see Roitman, "La identidad mesiánico-sacerdotal de Jesús," pp. 112–22; H. Attridge, *The Epistle to the Hebrews: A Commentary on the Epistle to the Hebrews* (Hermeneia Series, vol. 72; Philadelphia: Fortress Press, 1989), pp. 186–97; P. Ellingworth, "'Like the Son of God': Form and Content in Hebrews 7, 1–10," *Biblica* 64/2 (1983), pp. 255–62.

[9] If not indicated differently, biblical citations (Hebrew, Christian Bible and Apocrypha) follow the translation of the New Revised Standard Version w/Apoc-

This text key to *Hebrews* 7's reasoning for the immutability and perfection of the celestial and eternal High Priesthood of Jesus, which characterizes its prototype Melchizedek as an eternal being, has become a true *crux interpretum* in the history of scholarly research, leading academics to adopt a variety of strategies for its interpretation.[10] But whichever the original idea that the author of *Hebrews* had about Melchizedek's nature,[11] from this point forward this figure became an important *topos* in Patristic literature, playing an important role in the controversy between Orthodox Christianity and diverse Christian heresies and Judaism, as well as being a popular theme in Byzantine iconography.[12]

More specifically, a careful reading of the exegetical traditions regarding Melchizedek present in Early Christian literature allows for the identification of two different approaches to this character. On the one hand, from the second century onward, Orthodox Christianity (Justin Martyr, Tertullian, Jerome and Epiphanius of Salamis, among others) consciously developed a Christological interpretation of Melchizedek as a "priest of the Most High and

---

rypha (online: https://www.biblestudytools.com/apocrypha/nrsa/). The Greek text comes from the *Nuevo Testamento Trilingüe*, J. María Bover, J. O'Callaghan and C. M. Martini [eds] (Madrid: Editorial Católica, 1977).

[10] For some examples, see Roitman, "La identidad mesiánico-sacerdotal de Jesús," pp. 116–18; Horton, *The Melchizedek Tradition*, pp. 160–64; Mason, '*You are a Priest Forever,*' pp. 28–33; *idem*, "SBL 2007 Presentation: Hebrews 7: 3, Melchizedek, and the Nature of Jesus's Priesthood" (online: https://hebrews.unibas.ch/documents/2007Mason.pdf); Attridge, *The Epistle to the Hebrews*, pp. 189–92; D. W. Rooke, "Jesus as Royal Priest: Reflections on the Interpretation of the Melchizedek Tradition in Heb 7," *Biblica* 81 (2000), p. 84; G. Granarød, "Melchizedek in Hebrews 7," *Biblica* 90/2 (2009), p. 202; J. W. Thompson, "The Conceptual Background and Purpose of the Midrash in Hebrews VII," *NT* XIX/3 (1977), pp. 211–15.

[11] For more on this point, see below section "The Mystery of Melchizedek in Early Christianity."

[12] G. Bardy, "Melchisédech dans la tradition patristique," *RB* XXXV (1926), pp. 496–509; XXXVI (1927), 25–45; Horton, *The Melchizedek Tradition*, pp. 87–114; Simon, "Melchisédech dans la polémique entre juifs et chrétiens;" P. Piovanelli, "'Much to say and hard to explain'. Melchizedek in Early Christian Literature, Theology, and Controversy," in *New Perspectives on 2 Enoch, op. cit.* [*supra*, n. 1], pp. 411–29; E. Revel-Neher, "The Offerings of the King-Priest: Judeo-Christian Polemics and the Early Byzantine Iconography of Melchizedek," in *Continuity and Renewal. Jews and Judaism in Byzantine-Christian Palestine* (L. I. Levine [ed.]; Jerusalem, 2004), pp. 270–98.

priest of the uncircumcised",[13] emphasizing his human condition, in clear continuation with the long Jewish exegetical tradition in this sense since the Greco-Roman era. This theological focus had its origin in the need to mitigate the supernatural-divine nature of Melchizedek promoted by heretical circles (more later) in order to avoid compromising the ontological superiority of Christ.[14]

On the other hand, perhaps stemming from a radical exegesis of *Hebrews* 7, 3,[15] the king-priest of Salem was considered in heterodox speculation by some Christian sects (called the heresy of the "Melchizedekeans" by Epiphanius of Salamis in his book *Panarion* LV)[16] as a celestial "great power" (μεγάλην τινὰ δύναμιν)

---

[13] See Justin Martyr, *Dialogue with Trypho* § 33. On Justin's use of Melchizedek, see J. L. Marshall, "Melchizedek in Hebrews, Philo, and Justin Martyr," *SE* 7 (1982), pp. 339–42.

[14] See Poorthuis, "Enoch and Melchizedek," pp. 115–19; Pearson, "Melchizedek in Early Judaism," pp. 186–88; C. Gianotto, "Melchizedek," in *Encyclopedia of Ancient Christianity* (A. Di Berardino [ed. gral.]; Downers Grove, Illinois: IVP Academic, 2014), vol. 2, p. 756; Horton, *The Melchizedek Tradition*, pp. 87–89. Another strategy was to present "biographical" developments on the origin and life of the king-priest of Salem (which Pioivanelli called: an "orthodox" narrative reaction), as is the case of the popular "History of Melchizedek" (a work written in Greek at the end of the fourth century or at the beginning of the fifth, translated into all the languages of the Christian Orient, including: Syriac, Coptic, Arabic, Ethiopian, Armenian, Georgian, Slavic and Romanian). For more detail on this work and its text, see P. Piovanelli, "The Story of Mekchizedek with the Melchizedek Legend from the *Chronicon Paschale*," in *Old Testament Pseudepigrapha. More Noncanonical Scriptures* (R. Bauckham, J. R. Davila, A. Panayotov [eds]; Grand Rapids, Michigan/Cambridge, U.K: William B. Eerdmans Publishing Company, 2013), vol. 1, pp. 64–81; idem, "'Much to say'...," pp. 424–27; S. E. Robinson, "The Apocryphal Story of Melchizedek," *JSJ* 18/1 (1987), pp. 26–39; M. Skowronek, "On Medieval Storytelling. The Story of Melchizedek in Certain Slavonic Texts (Palaea Historica and the Apocryphal Cycle of Abraham)," *Studia Ceranea* 4 (2014), pp. 171–91. Another example in this sense is *The Cave of Treasures* (31, 13–17), written in Syriac in the fourth century.

[15] According to Horton, "we have found no system which does not make use of Hebrews, especially Heb. vii.3 and the understanding of Ps. cx.4 to be found in Hebrews (cf. Heb. v.6, 10; vi.20; vii.11, 15, 17, 21)" (*The Melchizedek Tradition*, p. 111). Nevertheless, Attridge rejects Horton's categorical statement: "[t]he earliest witness to this movement, Hippolytus, does not give any indication of the use of Hebrews or Ps 110 in the development of the theory about Melchizedek..." (*The Epistle to the Hebrews*, p. 194). For the text of (Pseudo)-Hippolytus, see *infra* n. 17.

[16] According to some academics, this sect never existed, rather it was a mere invention on the part of Epiphanius. See Bardy, "Melchisédech," p. 505; Horton, *The Melchizedek Tradition*, p. 98; Pearson, "Melchizedek in Early Judaism," p. 189.

superior to Christ (the Theodotus the banker's group, active in Rome at the end of the second century),[17] acting as a celestial intercessor in favor of the angels (according to the testimony of Pseudo-Tertullian, *Adv. Haer.* 8),[18] and coming to be identified with the "Holy Spirit" (Hierax the Egyptian, beginning of the fourth century [Epiphanius, *Pan.* LXVII, 3, 2–4])[19] or with the "Son of God" (Epiphanius, *Pan.* 5.7.3),[20] the "Logos" or "God" (θεός) himself before the incarnation (see Mark the Hermit's testimony, a hermit who lived in the desert of Judea in the fifth century, in his treatise *On Melchizedek* [PG 65, 1117–1140, esp. 1120]).[21]

---

[17] (Pseudo)-Hippolytus's testimony in his *Refutation of All Heresies* goes: "Different questions having arisen among them, a certain one, himself called Theodotus, a banker by trade, attempted to say that a certain Melchizedek is the great power, and this one is greater than Christ, in whose likeness, they say, the Christ happens to be. And they, like the aforementioned Theodotians, say that Jesus is a man and just like them that the Christ came down unto him" (VII, 36 [cited by Horton, *The Melchizedek Tradition*, p. 90]).

[18] "Nam illum Melchisedech praecipua ex gratia caelestem esse virtutem, [...] Melchisedech facere pro caelestibus angelis atque virtutibus" (cited by Attridge, *The Epistle to the Hebrews*, p. 194 n. 109).

[19] For Epiphanius's testimony on Hierax, see: http://ldysinger.stjohnsem.edu/@texts/ 0395_epiphanius/01_panarion-sel.htm. According to Pearson ("Melchizedek in Early Judaism," p. 191), this doctrine is again found in a Latin work of the fourth century, traditionally attributed to Saint Augustine (*Quaestiones Veteris et Novi Testamenti* CXXVII, question 109).

[20] According to Pearson ("Melchizedek in Early Judaism," p. 191), this notion of Melchizedek seems to have been preeminent in certain monastic communities of Egypt (cf. *Apophthegmata Patrum* [PG 65, 160]).

[21] For details on the Christian heresies regarding Melchizedek, see Bardy, "Melchisédech," passim; Pearson, "Melchizedek in Early Judaism," pp. 188–92; Gianotto, "Melchizedek," p. 756; Horton, *The Melchizedek Tradition*, pp. 90–114; Piovanelli, "'Much to say'...," pp. 420–23. Nevertheless, Jerome tells of "heterodox" disputes regarding the nature of Melchizedek within Christian orthodoxy itself when he states the following: "And first, I met the first homily of Origen on Melchizedek; and in this explanation of Genesis, the author drawn by the very extent of his discussion, comes to the point of declaring that this pontiff was an angel. To establish his assumption, he uses the same arguments roughly as your writer to establish his own. From there I went to Didymus his disciple, and I saw a man who threw himself right in the opinion of his master. I then went to consult Hippolytus, Irenaeus, Eusebius of Caesarea, and that of Emesa, Apollinaris, and our Eustathius, who the first of the bishops of Antioch sounded his brilliant trumpet the combat against Arius; and I found that all by different arguments and paths, led to the same conclusion, to declare that Melchizedek was a Chananean, king of this city which first was called Salem, then Jebus,

In this same spirit, Melchizedek was interpreted in some works of Gnostic literature to be a soteriological figure, with a celestial-angelical-priestly-warrior character, when in some cases *Hebrews* 7, 3 served as a base text (the fragment *Bala'izah*; NHC IX, 1: *Melchizedek*), while in others it didn't (*2 Jeu* and *Pistis Sophia* [books 4; 1–3]).[22]

How can we explain this radical transformation in the way Melchizedek is understood, who went from being a human king-priest in an ancient Israelite biblical tradition, Jewish tradition (in its majority) and Christian (orthodox) tradition, to becoming a heavenly-angelical being in some circles of heterodox ancient Christianity (and subsequently, in medieval Jewish circles)? Was this last exegetical development a Christian creation *ex novo* or would it have had pre-Christian roots? When was the point of inflection in the history of the interpretation of this mysterious figure? What was the social and religious framework that would have made this exegetical development possible?

In order to continue and complement my previous work presented at the First International Conference on Patristic Studies in 2012, in which I studied in detail the interpretations of Melchizedek found in Jewish literature in the Second Temple era as a king-priest of Salem (Gen 14),[23] the purpose of this work is to explore a unique text from the era, found among the Dead Sea Scrolls, which presents Melchizedek as a heavenly-angelical being, that is: *11QMelchizedek* (11Q13). The hypothesis I wish to demonstrate is that in this sectarian exegetical tradition resides the key to understanding the mutation suffered by the pre-Christian Melchizedek at the end of the Greco-Roman era, which itself would have served as a background or even as inspiration for the

---

and finally Jerusalem." (*Epistle* 73, 2 [cited from: https://sites.google.com/site/aquinasstudybible/home/jerome-letter-73-to-evangelus).

[22] For details and texts, see Pearson, "Melchizedek in Early Judaism," pp. 192–98; *idem*, "The Figure of Melchizedek in Gnostic Literature," in *idem*, *Gnosticism, Judaism and Egyptian Christianity* (Minneapolis: Fortress Press, 1990), pp. 108–23; *idem*, "Melchizedek," in *ABD*, vol. 4, p. 688; Horton, *The Melchizedek Tradition*, pp. 131–47, J. M. Robinson (dir.), *The Nag Hammadi Library in English* (Leiden: E. J. Brill, 1977), pp. 399–403; A. Piñero, J. Montserrat Torrents and F. García Bazán (eds), *Textos gnósticos. Biblioteca de Nag Hammadi III: Apocalipsis y otros escritos* (Madrid: Editorial Trotta, ³2016), pp. 187–96.

[23] See *supra*, n. 2.

later development of this figure in Early Christianity (Epistle to the Hebrews, heterodox sects, and Gnosticism).

## 11QMelchizedek *(11Q13)*

### a. Editing, Physical Description, and Dating

The Dead Sea scroll *11QMelchizedek* (11Q13) was found among the manuscripts of cave number eleven near Qumran in the year 1956 and was published in *editio princeps* by A. S. van der Woude in the year 1965 under the auspices of the Royal Netherlands Academy of Arts and Sciences.[24] Due to its physical state of deterioration, reading this document has been quite difficult, requiring numerous corrections and restorations since then in subsequent publications.[25]

The present document written on animal hide consists of numerous fragments (between ten and fifteen pieces), though there is no complete agreement among researchers on the best way to count and configure them. The general consensus is that portions of three consecutive columns have been able to be reconstructed, with column II being the most well-preserved despite its various blank spaces and numerous fragments. Nevertheless, twenty-five lines of this column have been recovered (it probably originally contained twenty-seven lines) but none of them is complete (only the words at the beginning of the column have been preserved), forcing specialists to develop various proposals for the restoration of the original text. The character, size, and position of these columns in the original document are unknown, but due to the content of the document, we do believe

---

[24] A. S. van der Woude, "Melchisedek als himmlische Erlösergestalt in den neugefundenen eschatologischen Midraschim aus Qumran Höhle XI," Oudtestamentlische Studiën 14 (1965), pp. 354–73.

[25] F. García Martínez, E. J. C. Tigchelaar and A. S. van der Woude (eds), *Qumran Cave 11. II 11Q2–18, 11Q20–31* (Oxford: Clarendon Press, 1998), pp. 221–41; J. J. M. Roberts, "Melchizedek (11Q13 = 11QMelch)," in *The Dead Sea Scrolls: Hebrew, Aramaic, and Greek Texts with English Translations*, vol. 6b: *Pesharim, Other Commentaries, and Related Documents* (J. H. Charlesworth et al. [eds]; Tübingen: Mohr Siebeck-Louisville: Westminster John Knox Press, 2002), pp. 264–73; E. Qimron, *The Dead Sea Scrolls. The Hebrew Writings* (Jerusalem: Yad Ben-Zvi Press, 2013), vol. 2, pp. 278–80 (in Hebrew).

that the preserved columns would have been located at the end of the original.

The document is written in Hebrew, and using its written form, paleographical dating has been evaluated diversely, with variations from the first half or the first century BCE (Milik), to the second half of the first century BCE (Kobelski, García Martínez et al.), and even to the first half or middle of the first century CE (van der Woude, Horton, Bertalotto).[26] Using formal criteria, which include certain formulas for citation and interpretation (Steudel), dependence on the book of Daniel (García Martínez), or the supposed controversy surrounding the document against the Maccabees appropriating the title of "priest of the most high God" in Gn 14, 18 (Puech),[27] it has been concluded that the original work was composed in the middle or at the end of the second century BCE.[28]

### b. Content and Literary Genre

As was previously stated, only a good part of column II has been able to be satisfactorily reconstructed enough to enable an evaluation of the content of the document. According to this reconstruction, the document presents an eschatological description of "the last days" (אחרית הימים) (line 4),[29] beginning with the tenth and last jubilee (lines 6–7).

---

[26] For details, see García Martínez-Tigchelaar-van der Woude, *Qumran Cave 11*, pp. 221, 223; Mason, *'You are a Priest Forever,'* pp. 168–70; idem, "Melchizedek Scroll (11Q13)," in *EDEJ*, p. 932; P. J. Kobelski, *Melchizedek and Melkireša'* (The Catholic Biblical Quarterly Monograph Series 10; Washington: The Catholic Biblical Association of America, 1981), p. 3; Horton, *The Melchizedek Tradition*, p. 82; P. Bertalotto, "Qumran, Messianism, Melchizedek, and the Son of Man," in *The Dead Sea Scrolls in Context. Integrating the Dead Sea Scrolls in the Study of Ancient Texts, Languages, and Cultures*. Vol. I, Supplements to *Vetus Testamentum* 140/1; A. Lange, E. Tov, and M. Weigold [eds], in association with B. H. Reynolds III (Leiden-Boston: Brill, 2011), p. 331.

[27] On this topic, see Roitman, "La identidad mesiánico-sacerdotal de Jesús," pp. 126–28.

[28] Steudel, "Melchizedek," p. 536; F. García Martínez, "Textos de Qumrán," in *Literatura judía intertestamentaria* (G. Aranda Pérez, F. García Martínez and M. Pérez Fernández [eds]; Estella [Navarra]: Editorial Verbo Divino, 1996), p. 85.

[29] If not otherwise indicated, the Hebrew text follows the edition of García Martínez-Tigchelaar-van der Woude, *Qumran Cave 11*. The English transla-

The document presents an eschatological interpretation of midrashic character of different passages from the Scriptures, in some cases cited *verbatim* and in others only alluded by some phrases, following the style of the typical thematic *pesharim* (as is the case of 4Q*Florilegium* [4Q174], 4QCatena[a] [4Q177], o 4QCatena[b] [4Q182]) of the sectarian literature of the Dead Sea Community.[30]

In its first part (lines 2–14), the *pesher* is based on Lev 25 (on the jubilee year), on Dt 15 (on debt remission in the sabbatical year) and on Ps 7 and 82 (on divine judgement), centering on the figure of "Melchizedek." In the second part (lines 15–22), the *pesher* cites and explains Is 52 (proclaiming freedom of captives), where it makes reference to the "messenger."[31]

The central theme around which all of these texts are based is the salvation of the "sons of light" from the domain of Belial and from the spirits of his lot, in total agreement with the apocalyptic character of the Dead Sea Community,[32] in which a character named "Melchizedek" would play a crucial role.

---

tion follows G. Vermes, *The Dead Sea Scrolls in English* (London *et alli*: Penguin Books, revised and extended fourth edition, 1995).

[30] For details on the literary genre of the *Pesharim* in Qumran, see Sh. Berrin Tzoref, "Pesharim," in *EDEJ*, pp. 1050–55, esp. p. 1051. According to Steudel ("Melchizedek," p. 536), *Melchizedek*.

[31] Regarding the identification of the "messenger" with the eschatological prophet expected in 1QS and 4Q175, see García Martínez, "Las tradiciones sobre Melquisedec en los manuscritos de Qumrán," *Biblica* 81 (2000), p. 79. For an alternative interpretation, identifying the figure of "Melchizedek" and that of the "eschatological prophet" as making reference to the "Anointed One" (not necessarily heavenly) of the end of times, see A. Cavicchia, "'Malky-sedeq', 'unto', profeta-araldo, sacerdote e re nel giubileo escatológico" (11QMelch II,2–14), *Biblica* 91/4 [2010], pp. 518–33). On the identification of "Melchizedek" with the "messenger," see Bertalotto, "Qumran Messianism," p. 337. On the co-references in *11QMelchizedek* assuming that "Melchizedek," the "messenger," and the "anointed one" are all references to the same figure, see L. Guglielmo, "11Q13, Malchî Ṣedek, Co-Reference and Restoration of 2 18," *Henoc* 33 (2011), pp. 61–72. For some information on this last proposal, see D. Bock, "Is That All There Is? A Response to Lara Guglielmo's 11Q13, Malchî Ṣedek, Co-Reference, and Restoration of 2 18," *ibid.*, pp. 73–76.

[32] On the apocalyptic character of the Dead Sea Community, A. D. Roitman, *Sectarios de Qumrán. Vida cotidiana de los esenios* (Barcelona: Ediciones Martínez Roca, 2000), pp. 85–92. According to García Martínez ("Las tradiciones sobre Melquisedec," p. 71 n. 8), both the terminology and the content of this document demonstrate that it must have been the product of the Dead Sea Community.

## c. Name and Character of Melchizedek

According to what has been stated previously, "Melchizedek" is the central figure in much of column II of the document.[33] His name is written in the document with two words מלכי צדק (*mlky ṣdq*) (lines 5 [two times], 8, 9, 13, [25]), identical to the practice in use in the biblical masoretic מַלְכִּי-צֶדֶק (*mlky ṣdq*) (Gn 14, 18; Ps 100, 4) and targumic traditions (*Tg. Onq.* מלכי צדק [*mlky ṣdq*]; *Tg. Ps.-J.* מלכא צדיקא [*mlkʾ ṣdqʾ*]; *Tg. Neof.* מלכא צדק [*mlkʾ ṣdq*]; *Frg. Tg* מלכי צדק [*mlky ṣdq*]).[34]

With the exception of the presence of this name in *Genesis Apocryphon* (a work of non-sectarian character which would have formed part of the Jewish literature common in the Second Temple period), *11QMelchizedek* is the only document found among the Qumran manuscripts in which the name "Melchizedek" appears expressly and completely,[35] to the point of even being "atypical" in Qumranic literature (Horton).[36] According to Dimant, the choice of this name could be due to the predilection on the part

---

[33] Because of the fragmented state of the current document, we are unable to know if the centrality of Melchizedek in column II was an essential characteristic of the original lost work or rather a secondary characteristic.

[34] Unlike this compound form of the name, in LXX (Μελχισεδεκ) and in *Pseudo-Eupolemus* (Μελχισεδεκ) the form of the name is joined. It seems to be that this unified form is the oldest, while the compound form seen in the biblical masoretic and targumic traditions and in *11QMelchizedek* reflects the etymology that explains the name as "just king" (βασιλεὺς δίκαιος) (Josephus, *Antiquities* 1.180; Philo, *Allegorical Interpretation III* § 79) or "king of justice" (βασιλεὺς δικαιοσύνης) (Hb 7, 2), which was popularized at the end of the Second Temple period. On this topic, see Kobelski, *Melchizedek and Melkireša*, pp. 55–56.

[35] According to the reconstruction proposed by C. Newsom (*DJD* XI, p. 205), the name Melchizedek was present in one of the manuscripts of the work entitled *Songs of the Sabbath Sacrifice*: צדק כוהן בעד[ת אל] [מלכי] ("[Melchi]zedek, priest in the assemb[ly of God]" (4Q401 11 3). Davila maintains that this figure was also referred to in 4Q401 22 3 and 11Q17 3 II 7. Likewise, it has been suggested that the name also could have appeared in a series of manuscripts from Qumran (4Q ʿAmramᵇ, 4Q280 and 4Q286), which coincidentally has not been discovered in any of the preserved texts, but rather, due to the content of these documents in which his angelic opponent Melkirešaʿ is present, would be expected. On the value of these reconstructions, D. Dimant states: "...the figure of Melchizedek is solitary even in the Qumran literature. The reconstructions of his name in the Songs of the Sabbath Sacrifice and in the Visions of Amram are speculative and should not be exploited to develop further theories" ("Melchizedek at Qumran and in Judaism: A Response," in *New Perspectives on 2 Enoch* [supra, n. 2], p. 366).

[36] Cf. Horton, *The Melchizedek Tradition*, p. 79.

of the Qumran sectarians for choosing compound words with the word "justice" (צדק [ṣdq]), which in the sectarian nomenclature designates the essence of the power of the Light.[37]

But who was this "Melchizedek" mentioned in column II of the document? Due to issues intrinsic to the document itself, both its fragmented state and its jumbled and somewhat confusing content, the issue of the identity of this figure has been dealt with intensely by scholars. Despite the exegetical alternatives proposed, arguing that with the name "Melchizedek" the author wishes to make reference to a divine hypostasis (Milik), a Davidic messiah (Rainbow), a divine human being (Fletcher Louis), the angel Michael (Cockerill, Kobelski), the leader of the Qumran Community (Knohl), the eschatological anointed one (Cavicchia), or to Yahweh himself (Manzi),[38] the majority of researchers (Mason and García Martínez, among others) believe that this name is tied to or exegetically derived from the biblical character of the same name in Gn 14, 8 and Ps 110, 4, despite there not being any express reference or even simple allusion to those biblical texts in our document.[39]

---

[37] Dimant, "Melchizedek at Qumran," p. 365.

[38] For bibliographical references, see P. Rainbow, "Melchisedek as a Messiah at Qumran," *BBR* 7 (1997), pp. 179–94; G. L. Cockerill, "Melchizedek or 'King of Righteousness'," *EvQ* 63 (1991), pp. 305–12; Kobelski, *Melchizedek and Melkireša*, pp. 71–74; Cavicchia, "Malky-sedeq," pp. 518–33; I. Knohl, "Melchizedek: A Model for the Union of Kingship and Priesthood in the Hebrew Bible, *11QMelchizedek*, and the Epistle to the Hebrews," in *Text, Thought, and Practice in Qumran and Early Christianity*. Proceedings of the Ninth International Symposium of the Orion Center for the Study of the Dead Sea Scrolls and Associated Literature, Jointly Sponsored by the Hebrew University Center for the Study of Christianity, 11–13 January, 2004 (R. A. Clements y D. R. Schwartz [eds], STDJ 84; Leiden-Boston: Brill, 2009), pp. 255–66, esp. 259–64. For an attempt at reconciling some of these proposals, see R. Van de Water, "Michael or Yhwh? Toward Identifying Melchizedek in 11Q13," *JSP* 16/1 (2006), pp. 75–86. For a review of these proposals and their criticisms, see A. Aschim, "Melchizedek and Jesus: 11QMelchizedek and the Epistle to the Hebrews," in *The Jewish Roots of Christological Monotheism. Papers from the St Andrews Conference on the Historical Origins of the Worship of Jesus* (C. C. Newman, J. R. Davila, and G. S. Lewis [eds]; Brill: Leiden-Boston-Köln, 1999), pp. 133–35; Mason, '*You are a Priest Forever*,' pp. 185–90; *idem*, "The Identification of *MLKY ṢDQ* in 11QMelchizedek: A Survey of Recent Scholarship," *QR* 17 (2009), pp. 61–61.

[39] On the exegetical dependence of Gn 14, 18 and Ps 110, 4 and the figure of Melchizedek in *11QMelchizedekc*, see *infra*, section e.

However, even if scholars were correct in deriving the figure of "Melchizedek" in our document from his biblical antecedent, our figure in *11QMelchizedek* seems to be of a totally different nature than that of the king-priest of Salem with clear human-earthly traits in Gn 18, 14. More specifically, "Melchizedek" in our document seems to allude to a heavenly-angelical being, notwithstanding the fact that nowhere is he expressly called "angel" (מלאך).[40]

This conclusion regarding the heavenly and sublime nature of "Melchizedek" in our document[41] is in agreement with the probable manner of referring to Melchizedek in other Qumran texts. In this sense, one case would be the testimony present in *Songs of the Sabbath Sacrifice* (a work first known as *Liturgia Angelical*), in which, according to the reconstruction carried out by C. Newsom (*DJD* XI, p. 205), the name Melchizedek would have likely been present in one of the manuscripts of the work: [מלכי] צדק כוהן בעד[ת אל ("[Melchi]zedek, priest in the assemb[ly of God]" (4Q401 11 3). Considering the fact that this work

---

[40] This identification was preliminarily presented at the beginning of research carried out by M. de Jonge and A. S. van der Woude, "11QMelchizedek and the New Testament," *NTS* 12 (1965–1966), pp. 301–26. For opinions of contemporary scholars, see Mason, *'You are a Priest Forever,'* pp. 182–83; Kobelski, *Melchizedek and Melkireša*, pp. 59–62; Dimant, "Melchizedek at Qumran," p. 365; J. R. Davila, "Melchizedek: King, Priest, and God," in *The Seductiveness of Jewish Myth. Challenge or Response?* (S. D. Breslauer [ed.]; Albany: State University of New York Press, 1997), p. 222; Ch. A. Gieschen, "Enoch and Melchizedek: The Concern for Supra-Human Priestly Mediators in 2 Enoch," in *New Perspectives on 2 Enoch* [*supra*, n. 1], p. 378; F. Du Toit Laubscher, "God's Angel of Truth and Melchizedek," *JSJ* 3/1 (1972), pp. 46–51. For critiques of this identification, see as an example Rainbow, "Melchizedek as a Messiah," pp. 182-87. For a somewhat ambivalent and less categorical position, see H. Attridge, "Melchizedek in Some Early Christians Texts and 2 Enoch," in *New Perspectives on 2 Enoch* [*supra*, n. 1], p. 390.

[41] García Martínez summarizes the issue stating: "If Melchizedek in 11QMelch is neither God nor a divine hypostasis, he certainly is a heavenly and sublime character. The text attributes to him power over the celestial armies; he is the leader of all the angels (the אלים) and of all the sons of God. Moreover, it is he who directs the battle against Belial and the spirits of his lot and who carries out divine revenge against them. Melchizedek is described with the same characteristics with which the *Community Rule* and the *Damascus Document* describe the 'Prince of Light,' and as a double for the archangel Michael, just as is described in the *War Scroll*" ("Las tradiciones sobre Melquisedec," pp. 73–4). On the functions of Melchizedek, see the next section.

of probable Qumranic origin includes thirteen hymns sung by different angels in the heavenly temple,[42] one for each Saturday or *Shabbat*, it would be evident then in this literary context that "Melchizedek" in this work, be it only in this specific case or also in the other suggested cases (4Q401 22 3; 11Q17 3 II 7), would have also had an angelic character, performing as priest in the heavenly temple.[43]

These last considerations on the possible celestial, sublime, and angelical nature of Melchizedek in this document naturally lead us to explore the functions that this character would have carried out in "the last days", hoping to find a correlation between his nature and his functions.

### d. The Functions of Melchizedek

The beginning and the end of column II have as a central theme the topic of freedom. From biblical texts dealing with freeing and debt remission (Lv 25, Dt 15), the author of our text presents Melchizedek as a liberator of "captives" (referring to the men of the Community themselves) in "the last days" when the expected salvation would occur in the tenth jubilee (lines 4–7).

According to these texts then, Melchizedek would have had the role of liberator at the end of times, rescuing "captives" (השבויים) (line 4),[44] probably also referred to as "the inheritance

---

[42] For details, García Martínez, "Textos de Qumrán," pp. 205–10; C. Newsom, "Songs of the Sabbath Sacrifice," in *EDEJ*, pp. 1246–48.

[43] According to Newsom (*DJD* XI, p. 205), 4Q401 11 3 would be the only opportunity in *Songs of the Sabbath Sacrifice* in which an angel would be called by his name. Likewise, she affirms that this same text in which the word "priest" (כוהן) is used to characterize the function of Melchizedek in the "assembly of God" (עדת אל) is also unusual in this work. If she is indeed correct in her affirmations, then all of this information would lead us to conclude that Melchizedek would have been considered by the author of *Songs*, and by the Community accustomed to singing these songs on Saturdays, as a figure high up in the heavenly court. Nevertheless, we must recognize that the value of this argument for validating Melchizedek's angelical condition is quite problematic, as the same reconstruction adopted by Newsom was carried out with *11QMelchizedekc*, undermining the strength of the argument. For a critique in this sense, see Rainbow, "Melchizedek as a Messiah," p. 183 n. 12. Cf. also *supra*, n. 35.

[44] A clear allusion to Is 61, 1. Line 6 also makes an allusion to this biblical passage. Other allusions and phrases of Is 61, 1–2 occur in other parts of column II, that is: 9, 13, 14, 18 and 20. The massive recurrence of Is 61, 1–2 in

of Melchizedek" (נחלת מלכי צדק) (line 5), of his sinful condition ("[the wrong-doings] of all of his iniquities") (משא [כול עוונותיהמה) (line 6). More specifically, this text establishes that this soteriological action would take place at the end of the tenth jubilee, that is, the "Day of Atonement" (lines 7–8).

The statement that salvation would occur on the eschatological "Day of Atonement", together with the usage of the verb "atone" in its infinitive form (לכפר),[45] allows us to conclude that Melchizedek in this passage was imagined as a High Priest who, like his human counterpart in the Israelite ritual (Lv, 16), would carry out during the *Yom hakippurim* (Day of Atonement) at the end of time the expiation rites to condone the iniquities of the "captives" subject to the control of Belial.[46]

Despite the fact that this function does not appear expressly established in the text, Melchizedek's priestly function would be more than reasonable in this literary context in light of biblical tradition (Gn 14, 18; Ps 110, 4), of the probable reconstruction in *Songs of the Sabbath Sacrifice* – "[Melchi]zedek, priest in the assemb[ly of God]" (4Q401 11 3) –, and of other circumstantial considerations of his condition as a "High Priest" in early Jewish tradition (Philo [*On Abraham* §235; *Frg. Tg.*; *Tg. Neof.*; *Apostolic Constitutions* [8.12.13]), among other arguments.[47]

---

this text confirms the importance that it had for the literary structure and message of *11QMelchizedek*, functioning as a sort of *stichwörter* ("key word"). Apparently, the author saw in Is 61, 1–2 the key for eschatological times. For more details, see M. P. Miller, "The function of Is 61 1–2 in 11Q Melchizedek," *JBL* 88/4 (1969), pp. 467–69. On Jesus in his role as eschatological liberator, carrying out the function that other Jewish traditions assign to Michael or Melchizedek, see G. Brooke, "Melchizedek (11QMelch)," in *The Anchor Bible* Dictionary [*ABD*] (D. N: Freedman ed.; New York *et al.*: Doubleday, 1992), vol. 4, p. 687; D. R. Schwartz, "On Quirinus, John the Baptist, the Benedictus, Melchizedek, Qumran and Ephesus," *RQ* 13 (1988), pp. 635–46, especially 639–43.

[45] This infinitive form of the verb does not allow us to establish with certainty that the subject of the action is Melchizedek. Nevertheless, the majority of interpreters understand the text flatly in this way. See García Martínez, "Las tradiciones sobre Melquisedec," p. 74; Mason, *'You are a Priest Forever,'* p. 184.

[46] The members of the Dead Sea Community believed that they were living in an era controlled by Belial (1QS I,18.23–24; II,19; CD XII,23; XV5,7; 1QM XIV,9–10).

[47] For a positive evaluation of Melchizedek as a priest in this text, see Kobelski, *Melchizedek and Melkireša*, pp. 64–71; Aschim, "Melchizedek and Jesus," pp. 139–40; Davila, "Melchizedek," p. 223.

In addition to his function as liberator and priest, Melchizedek would have also served as an eschatological judge at the end of time, who, in his role of *'Elohim* as a member of God's celestial court (אל), would judge Belial and his followers for their rebelliousness (lines 8–12). But Melchizedek would not only serve as heavenly judge at the end of time, at the same time he would also be the one to carry out the punishment, performing revenge in the name of God against angelical opponents with the help of "the gods of justice" (lines 13–15). Using language belonging to Qumranic dualism, Melchizedek as an eschatological warrior would destroy Belial's forces and the spirits of his lot in the last days, and with this victory would inaugurate the era of salvation ("the day of [peace/salvation]" (יום ה[שלום]) (lines 15–25), described with the words of Is 52, 7 and 61, 2–3.[48]

This presentation of Melchizedek as the leader of the heavenly armies who conquers Belial's armies reminds us with his characteristics of the "Prince of Light" (1QS III, 20; CD-A V, 18; 1QM XIII, 10) and, specifically, of the archangel Michael (1QM XVII, 6–7), so much so that some scholars have concluded that the author of the text consciously presented Melchizedek with attributes and characteristics traditionally associated with Michael.[49]

To sum up then, we use Mason's words when he successfully articulates the totality of Melchizedek's functions: "In summary, 11QMelchizedek presents Melchizedek as a heavenly, eschatological figure in the service of God. He will deliver the righteous on God's behalf and will execute judgement on Belial and his lot. Also, Melchizedek will make atonement for those of his own lot."[50]

---

[48] We suppose that column III of the text, of which very few words were preserved, would have described in detail the punishment and destruction of Belial, as the words "will consume Belial with fire" (יתממ[ו] בליעל באש) (line 7) seem to indicate. On this popular topic in apocalyptic literature, cf. *1 Hen* 10, 6.13–14.

[49] On this topic, see Kobelski, *Melchizedek and Melkireša*, pp. 71–74. On Melchizedek assuming the former role of Michael the archangel as leader of the divine forces in the eschatological war, see J. R. Davila, "Melchizedek, Michael, and War in Heaven," *SBL 1996 Seminar Papers* (Atlanta, Georgia, 1996), pp. 270–71. For a rejection of this identification, see M. Bodinger, "L'énigme de Melkisédeq," *RHR* 211/3 (1994), p. 325.

[50] Mason, *'You are a Priest Forever,'* p. 185. For a brief presentation of Melchizedek in the Dead Sea Scrolls, with particular emphasis on *11QMelchizedek*,

In light of this set of functions on the part of this heavenly-angelical being,[51] García Martínez goes further in his understanding of this enigmatic character, concluding that Melchizedek would have been considered by the Dead Sea Community to be a "heavenly messiah".[52] If this was the case, the figure of Melchizedek in *11QMelchizedek* as a messianic-heavenly character would remind us of the figure of the "son of God"/"son of the Most High" in 4Q246[53] and of the "Son of man" as a preexisting and transcendent "Messiah" of heavenly origin, witnessed in Jewish apocryphal literature (*The Book of Parables of Enoch* [48, 10; 52, 4]; *IV Esdras* [7, 28; 12, 32]) and in the New Testament (Mt 25, 31–46).[54]

e. The Transformation of Melchizedek

If we are correct that Melchizedek, in *11QMelchizedek* and with some likelihood in other texts of the Dead Sea manuscripts (*Songs of the Sabbath Sacrifice*, 4Q ʿAmramᵇ, 4Q280 y 4Q286), was conceived of as a being of heavenly-angelical nature, we must ask ourselves: How did the enigmatic king-priest of Salem, presented as an active human being in pre-Israelite times (Gn, 14) and thought of as such by the majority of Jewish authors at the

---

see E. R. Mason, "Hebrews 7: 3 and the Relationship between Melchizedek and Jesus," *BR* 50 (2005), pp. 50–61.

[51] According to Cavicchia ("Malky-sedeq," p. 532), however, Melchizedek's functions in *11QMelchizedek* do not necessarily suppose a heavenly being, rather they could have also belonged to a human "anointed" one, a God's deputy on earth.

[52] García Martínez, "Las tradiciones sobre Melquisedec," p. 76.

[53] See García Martínez, "Textos de Qumrán," pp. 82–83. On the differences between Melchizedek in *11QMelchizedek* and the protagonist in 4Q246, see the reflections of Bertalotto, "Qumran Messianism," pp. 331–35.

[54] García Martínez, "Las tradiciones sobre Melquisedec," p. 76. Cf. also D. Flusser, "Melchizedek and the Son of Man," in *idem, Jewish Sources in Ancient Christianity. Studies and Essays* (Tel Aviv: Sfriat Poalim, second printing, 1979), pp. 275–82 (in Hebrew) (= "Melchizedek and the Son of Man," *Christian News from Israel*, April 1966, pp. 23–29). On the parallels and differences that exist between Melchizedek in *11QMelchizedek* and the "Son of Man" in the *The Book of Parables of Enoch*, see Bartalotto, "Qumran Messianism," pp. 336–39. See also the thoughts of J. Harold Ellens ("The Dead Sea Scrolls and the Son of Man: An Assessment of 11Q13," *Henoc* 33/1 [2011], pp. 77–87, esp. pp. 83–87) on the common traits present between Melchizedek in our text and the "Son of Man" in different Second Temple traditions (Daniel, *Enoch*, and the Gospels), considering Melchizedek a virtual "Son of Man".

end of the Second Temple period (Genesis Apocryphon, Pseudo-Eupolemus, Philo of Alexandria, and Flavius Josephus), radically transformed in sectarian Qumranite circles[55] to become a "heavenly messiah" that would perform judicial, priestly, and military functions at the end of time?

Two different strategies can be identified in the scientific literature to answer this question. The first is characterized by an understanding of the sudden appearance of the heavenly-angelical Melchizedek as the resurgence of an ancient myth, forgotten intentionally by circles that promoted monotheistic faith in ancient Israel.[56] According to the reconstruction proposed by Davila, Melchizedek would have originally been a king made divine after death and transformed into a divinity after death in the pre-Israelite period, in accordance with the funerary cults of western Semitic religion and, upon being accepted by the Davidian dynasty, would have become part of the Temple cult along with the Melchizedek priesthood.[57] But due to the fact that pre-exilic Israelite literature was transmitted and manipulated by Deuteronomist circles opposed to funerary cults (cf. Dt 18, 9–12; 1 S 28), it is not surprising that this cult of Melchizedek was eliminated from the canon of the Hebrew Bible. His conclusion is that "[t]hus, Melchizedek was allowed to remain in the Hebrew Bible as a human priest and king and the patron of a Davidic priesthood. Nevertheless, Melchizedek the god survived in the apocalyptic, esoteric, and gnostic transformations of the royal cult, in which he became an angelic redeemer figure."[58]

Because of the hypothetical nature of this reconstruction, it is difficult to accept it as a satisfactory explanation of the "mystery" of Melchizedek. The second strategy developed by researchers

---

[55] Until now we have not found another testimony regarding Melchizedek similar to that presented in *11QMelchizedek* in the Jewish literature of the Second Temple period. As such, with our present state of knowledge, we must treat this exegetical development as an original result of Qumranite religious thought.

[56] See Davila, "Melchizedek," p. 224.

[57] For details of his argument, see *ibid.*, pp. 225–29.

[58] *Ibid.*, p. 230. Another hypothesis in this same spirit is that proposed by M. Bodinger ("L'enigme de Melkisédeq," pp. 309, 332), according to which the sun god Sedeq would be behind the figure of Melchizedek in our document.

seems to be more promising and certain, as it seeks the origins of Melchizedek's transformation not in supposed "lost myths" of antiquity, but rather in the way in which Jews in antiquity would have read the biblical traditions on this character in Gn 14 and Ps 110.[59] In other words, the genetic key would be found in *exegesis* of the Scriptures, despite not having any citation or direct allusion to these texts in *11QMelchizedek*.[60]

One proposal along these lines was made by Kobelski when he argued that some elements in the account of Genesis, such as the reference to Melchizedek as the "king of Salem" (מלך שלם) and "priest of the Most High God" (כהן לאל עליון) or his untimely appearance in the narration, could have suggested to the author of *11QMelchizedek* that Abraham had met an angel when these elements in Genesis were read in light of popular concepts and ideas about angels that the Jews of the time maintained.[61] Likewise, the similarities between Psalms 110 and *11QMelchizedek* are so notable and basic that Kobelski concludes that such a fact could not be a coincidence.[62]

This same interpretative line has also been adopted by A. Aschim. According to his suggestion, Gn 14 and Ps 110 could have served as inspiration for the elaboration of this angelical, priestly, warrior and eschatological judge character. In accordance with his argumentation, for example, like the "You" in Psalms 110, 4, Melchizedek occupies in the Qumran text a position

---

[59] In the words of Kobelski: "The background for the development of the figure of Melchizedek in 11QMelch is the author's understanding of the description of Melchizedek in Genesis 14 and Psalms 110" (*Melchizedek and Melkireša*, p. 51).

[60] It is a fact that in the fragments we have there is no indication at all of the use of these two texts. This information has led Fitzmyer to conclude that "[t]he fragmentary state of the text, however, prevents from saying whether this midrash has any connection with either Gn 14: 18–20 or Ps 110, the two places in the OT where Melchizedek is explicitly mentioned. What is preserved is a midrashic development which is independent of the classic OT *loci*" ("Further Light on Melchizedek from Cave 11," in *idem*, *Essays on the Semitic Background of the New Testament* [London: Geoffrey Chapman, 1971] p. 254). Nevertheless, Aschim rejects this conclusion, arguing somewhat rightly that "[t]he argument fails to do justice to the fragmentary character of 11QMelch, however. The fact that no such reference is *preserved* does not necessarily mean that no such reference ever *existed*" ("Melchizedek and Jesus," p. 136) (Italics are the author's).

[61] See details in Kobelski, *Melchizedek and Melkireša*, p. 52.

[62] *Ibid.*, p. 54.

near God in the heavens (Ps 110, 1; 11Q13 II 9–14), "governing" from "Zion" (Ps 110, 2; 11Q13 II 23–25), and taking part in the eschatological battle (Ps 110, 1.2.5–6; 11Q13 II 13–14) and in judicial activity (Ps 110, 6; 11Q13 II 9–13.23).[63] Likewise, elsewhere Aschim affirms that the elaboration of Melchizedek in *11QMelchizedek* could have had as origin a peculiar reading of Gn 14, which would have interpreted the figure of Melchizedek king-priest in the Pentateuch as Abraham's heavenly assistant and, as such, he would have played a fundamental role in the rescue of Lot.[64]

Despite the fact that this last interpretative strategy is rather convenient for understanding the mechanism that would have made Melchizedek's transformation possible, it provides no answer to the question of the circumstances, the ideological frameworks, and the reasons that would have led the Qumranite group, in whose interior this interpretation prospered, to develop this new notion of the biblical Melchizedek.[65]

According to our proposal, the key to this surprising exegetical development lies in the general phenomenon of the re-mythologization of the cosmos and of history present in Early Judaism,[66] within the framework of which figures like Moses, Enoch, and Elijah, once "human beings" in biblical tradition,[67] transformed

---

[63] Aschim, "Melchizedek and Jesus," p. 136. Also Gieschen ("Enoch and Melchizedek," pp. 377–78) and Mason ("SBL 2007 Presentation", p. 15) consider that *11QMelchizedek* would have been inspired by Ps 110 because of its thoughts on Melchizedek.

[64] For a more detailed analysis, see A. Aschim, "Melchizedek the Liberator. An Early Interpretation of Genesis 14?," *SBL 1996 Seminar Papers* (Georgia, 1996), pp. 243–57.

[65] According to M. Astour ("Melchizedek [person]," in *ABD*, vol. 4, p. 684), however, this transformation or sublimation of Melchizedek into a supernatural figure would already have been outlined or insinuated originally in Ps 110, which, according to his hypothesis, was composed in the Greek era.

[66] See M. E. Stone, "Three Transformations in Judaism: Scripture, History, and Redemption," *Numen* XXXII/2 (1985), p. 227.

[67] Despite being presented in biblical tradition as real beings, Enoch and Elijah are the only figures in the Hebrew Bible who are said not to have died naturally, implying that these figures would have continued existing in limbo or in a supranatural reality. In the case of Enoch, it is said that he "he was no more, because God took him" (Gn 5, 24). As regards the prophet Elijah, it is said that he was walking with his disciple Elijah when "a chariot of fire and horses of fire separated the two of them, and Elijah ascended in a whirlwind into heaven"

at the end of the Second Temple period into quasi-divine or glorified beings associated with eschatological times and esoteric knowledge (specifically Enoch).[68] Together with angels like Michael, Gabriel, or Uriel,[69] or with divine attributes personified such as Wisdom, the "Logos", or the *Mêmrâ*, these quasi-divine figures acted as mediator beings between God and men.[70] So much so these entities or divine heroes were perceived as being near the angelical world, that Moses was "equal on glory to the holy ones" and elected "out of all humankind" (LXX Si 45, 2.4), and Enoch came to be identified with the archangel Michael and the angel Metatron (*2 Enoch* 22, 5–10; *3 Enoch* 4, 2–3).[71]

This phenomenon of the religion of Israel in Greco-Roman Judaism, in which the ancient ontological separation between heaven and earth assumed in the Hebrew Bible had lost ground to ontic continuity,[72] to the point of conceiving as possible the divinization of distinguished characters (*theios aner*) (as in the case of Moses), the ascension of the elect to heaven (particularly Enoch), and the transformation of heroes into angels

---

(2 K 2, 11). Moses is said to have died and been buried (by God?), and his death is also shrouded in mystery, as the Hebrew Bible tells us that "but no one knows this burial place to this day" (Dt 34, 6). These three idiosyncratic traditions about the mysterious disappearances of these characters in the Hebrew Bible could suggest that biblical tradition already associated these ancient men with the supernatural and esoteric world, and in the specific case of Elijah, that he was linked with eschatological expectation (cf. Ml 3, 23–24).

[68] On Moses, Elijah, and Enoch in Second Temple Judaism, see S. Carbullanca Núñez, "Elías, Profeta," in *Gran Diccionario Enciclopédico de la Biblia* [*GDEB*], A. Ropero Berzosa [ed. gral.] (Barcelona: Editorial Clie, 2013), pp. 723–25; A. A. Orlov, "Enoch," in *EDEJ*, pp. 579–81; D. K. Falk, "Moses," in *EDEJ*, pp. 967–70.

[69] On renewed interest in angels in the Second Temple era, see A. T. Wright, "Angels," in *EDEJ*, pp. 328–31.

[70] Mediator figures are understood as beings or entities that act as vehicles of revelation, of redeeming action, or the governing of God. For details, see L. W. Hurtado, "Mediator Figures," in *EDEJ*, pp. 926–29.

[71] Cf. E. Isaac, "Enoch and the Archangel Michael," in *The Bible and the Dead Sea Scrolls*. Vol. Two: The Dead Sea Scrolls and the Qumran Community. The Second Princeton Symposium on Judaism and Christian Origins (J. H. Charlesworth [ed.]; Waco, Texas: Baylor University Press, 2006), pp. 363–75, esp. 367-71. On the transformations of Enoch in *2 Enoch* and in *3 Enoch*, see the observations of Gieschen, "Enoch and Melchizedek," pp. 379–82.

[72] On ontological separation as a fundamental characteristic of biblical theology, see the enlightening article by B. Uffenheimer, "Biblical Theology and Monotheistic Myth," *Immanuel* 14 (1982), pp. 7–24.

("angelification"),[73] could have been the religious framework that facilitated the transformation of biblical Melchizedek[74] from a real, human king-priest in his origin (at least in Gn 14) to an angelical "heavenly messiah" in *11QMelchizedek*.[75]

[73] On the "divinization" of Moses in Hellenistic Jewish literature, see D. L. Tiede, "Aretalogy," in *ABD*, vol. 1, pp. 372-73; W. L. Liefeld, "The Hellenistic 'Divine Man' and the Figure of Jesus in the Gospels," *JETS* 16/4 (1973), pp. 195-97, esp. pp. 199-201. On the ascension of Enoch into heaven, see M. Himmelfarb, "The *Book of the Watchers* and Tours of Heaven," in *Jewish Spirituality. From the Bible Through the Middle Ages* (A. Green [ed.]; New York: Crossroad, 1988), pp. 145-65; S. Pfann, "Abducted by God? The Process of Heavenly Ascent in Jewish Tradition, From Enoch to Paul, From Paul to Akiva," *Henoc* 33/1 (2011), pp. 113-28. On the phenomenon of angelification in Second Temple Judaism, see J. H. Charlesworth, "The Portrayal of the Righteous as an Angel," in *Ideal Figures in Ancient Judaism* (J. J. Collins and G. W. E. Nickelsburg [eds]; Ann Arbor, MI: Scholar Press, 1980), pp. 135-51; M. Smith, "Two Ascended to Heaven – Jesus and the Author of 4Q491," in *Jesus and the Dead Sea Scrolls* (J. H. Charlesworth [ed.]; New York et al.: Doubleday, 1992), pp. 290-301; A. F. Segal, "The Risen Christ and the Angelic Mediator Figures in Light of Qumran," *ibid.*, pp. 302-28, esp. pp. 304-13. On useful taxonomy for classifying the nature of soteriological figures for the eschatological era ("human", "revived", "angelomorphic", and "celestial") in Qumran literature, see F. García Martínez, "Figuras salvadoras al final de los tiempos en los manuscritos de Qumrán," in *Mediadores y mediación con lo divino en el mediterráneo antiguo* (María Luisa Sánchez León [ed.]; Palma de Mallorca: Universitat de les Illes Balears, 2015, pp. 917-33). In this regard, we must mention the important thoughts by A. Piñero (*Guía para entender a Pablo de Tarso* [Madrid: Trotta, 2015], pp. 407-23) on the Pauline perception of Jesus as Messiah as both human and divine at the same time, in light of Jewish theology of the Second Temple regarding the double nature of God's agents.

[74] On the hypothesis that Melchizedek had undergone a new transformation in Medieval times, becoming the "youth" of the "Palace Literature" (*Hekhalot*) in late Jewish mysticism, see J. R. Davila, "Melchizedek, the 'Youth,' and Jesus," in *The Dead Sea Scrolls As Background to Postbiblical Judaism and Early Christianity*. Papers from an International Conference at St Andrews in 2001 (STDJ XLVI; *idem* [ed.]; Leiden-Boston: Brill, 2003), pp. 262-66.

[75] This same religious framework could also be the origin of the legend of the miraculous birth of suprahuman priest Melchizedek and his condition as an eschatological mediator-savior in 2 *Enoch* (a Jewish work probably written in Greek in Egypt [Alexandria?] in the first century CE before the destruction of the Temple of Jerusalem). As Pearson affirms ("Melchizedek in Early Judaism," p. 184), there might even be structural parallelism in this work between the figures of Melchizedek and Enoch. On the different strategies used by researchers to understand the origin, function, significance, and evolution of this fascinating literary tradition, see Delcor, "Melchizedek from Genesis to the Qumran Texts," pp. 127-30; A. Orlov, "Melchizedek Legend of 2 (Slavonic) Enoch," *JSJ* 31 (2000), pp. 23-38; *idem*, "The Heir of Righteousness and the King of Righteousness: The Priestly Noachic Polemics in 2 Enoch and the Epistle to the Hebrews," *JThS*, NS 58/1 (2007), pp. 45-65; Ch. Böttrich, "The Melchizedek Story

This exegetical development regarding the figure of Melchizedek achieved such weight due to the particular interest that the Dead Sea Community took in topics related to angels, eschatology and messianism.[76] More specifically even, this new ontological perception of Melchizedek was possible because the anthropological conception itself of this community neutralized or shortened the distance between the divine and the human, making possible communion between the righteous and the angels, in total agreement with apocalyptic-Enochic tradition.[77]

Finally, one question prevails: What was the immediate trigger that motivated the men of Qumran to take a specific interest in the figure of Melchizedek? Scarce references to this character in the Dead Sea Scrolls makes it practically impossible to provide a definitive response. Nonetheless, the hypothesis suggested above that the original version of *11QMelchizedekc* was composed in the middle or at the end of the second century BCE would fit chronologically with the fact that certain circles of the time had shown a marked interest in the figure of Melchizedek.

As is evident in some compositions from the third and second centuries BCE,[78] as is the case of *Jubilees* and the Aramaic Levi Document [ALD], both with a strong presence among the Qumran manuscripts, the figure of Melchizedek would have served as inspiration for certain alienated circles of the cult of Jerusalem and its priesthood to exalt the figure of Levi.[79] And if we add to this the fact that the figure of Melchizedek as an ideal

---

of '2 (Slavonic) Enoch': A Reaction to A. Orlov," *JSJ* 32/4 (2001), pp. 445–70; Attridge, "Melchizedek in Some Early Christian Texts," pp. 394–406; Gieschen, "Enoch and Melchizedek," pp. 382–85.

[76] On angels in the Dead Sea Scrolls, see M. Mach, "Angels," in *EDSS*, vol. 1, pp. 24–27. On messianism and eschatology in Qumran thought and religion, see J. J. Collins, "Eschatology," in *EDSS*, vol. 1, pp. 256–61; C. A. Evans, "Messiahs," *ibid.*, pp. 537–42; J. VanderKam y P. Flint, *The Meaning of the Dead Sea Scrolls* (New York: Harper San Francisco, 2002), pp. 264–73.

[77] Mach, *op. cit.*, pp. 26–27; D. Dimant, "Sons of Heaven : the doctrine about angels in the book of Jubilees and in the writings of the Qumran community." in *idem, Connected Vessels: The Dead Sea Scrolls and the Literature of the Second Temple Period* (Jerusalem: Bialik Institute, 2010), pp. 153–54 (in Hebrew).

[78] Without forgetting, of course, the interest in Melchizedek present in other contemporary works, as is the case of *Genesis Apocryphon* and *Pseudo-Eupolemus*.

[79] For details, see Roitman, "La identidad mesiánico-sacerdotal de Jesús." pp. 124–26.

prototype of the king-priest had been adopted by the new dynasty of Hasmonean governors and high priests to justify their political and religious ambitions (1 M 14, 41; Josephus, *Ant.* 6.163; *Testament of Moses* 6, 1; *bRosh Hashaná* 18b),[80] then it would not be absurd to suppose that this renewed love for the king-priest Melchizedek throughout the second century BCE, in marked contrast with the marginalization of this character in ancient biblical tradition, would have served as a stimulus for the Qumranites to reflect on the heavenly-angelical nature of Melchizedek.

## *The Mystery of Melchizedek in Early Christianity: A Proposal for its Resolution*

Having reached this point in our research, we believe that we are now able to answer the questions posed at the beginning of this work. Firstly, the discovery of the *11QMelchizedek* manuscript among the Dead Sea Scrolls would definitively prove that the conception of a supernatural (heavenly-angelical) Melchizedek, attested to in some circles of Early Christianity (principally heterodox circles), was not a Christian creation *ex novo* but rather an innovation of Judaism from the Greco-Roman era.

More precisely, this exegetical development regarding the figure of Melchizedek as a "heavenly messiah" would have been the fruit of religious intuitions promoted by the Dead Sea Community at the end of the second century or beginning of the first century BCE, in light of renewed interest in the figure of Melchizedek on the part of different Jewish groups of the time (priests alienated from Jerusalem or Hasmonean governors). This spiritual conception would have been possible due to the Qumranite's particular interest in issues referring to "the last days" (eschatology and messianism) and to the structural changes to Second Temple Judaism in questions related to world view (*weltanschauung*), which

---

[80] More specifically, this strategy was promoted in the times of John Hyrcanus I (134–104 BCE) as an integral part of his political propaganda of presenting this dynasty as being elected by God (1 M 5, 62), and John Hyrcanus I as having "three crowns": royalty, priesthood and prophecy (Josephus, *Ant.* 13, 282.99; *bSotah* 33a). On this matter, see Roitman, *op. cit.*, pp. 126–28; Longenecker, "The Melchizedek Argument," pp. 162–64.

understood as possible the transformation of humans (heroes and righteous people) from Israel's mythical past into glorified or angelical beings.

If we are correct in the answers proposed, the discovery of this manuscript could be the key to revealing the "mystery" that has enveloped the surprising exegetical development of Melchizedek in Early Christianity. More specifically, *Melchizedek* or some similar tradition which is yet unknown, established by pious Jewish circles at the end of the Greco-Roman era, could have served as the backdrop, or even as direct or indirect inspiration, for speculations of an eternal, heavenly, angelical, warrior, and savior Melchizedek in the *Epistle to the Hebrews*, in the literature of the Church Fathers (the heresy of the "Melchizedekeans"), and in Gnostic texts.[81]

For example, let us take a closer look at the case of *Hebrews*. The statement reiterated in chapter seven of this work about the eternal nature of Melchizedek,[82] which constitutes one of the author's fundamental theological arguments for affirming the eternity and immutability of the High Priesthood of Jesus "like Melchizedek",[83] does not seem to have been a conclusion derived from the use of "hermeneutic tools",[84] but rather had its origin in extra-biblical traditions of the heavenly-angelical nature of Melchizedek and, more specifically, in the exegesis of this figure in *11QMelchizedek*.

---

[81] Although our work has centered on *11QMelchizedek* specifically to explore the possible echoes and influences of this pre-Christian Jewish exegetical tradition regarding Melchizedek in Early Christianity, research on this topic would not be complete without carrying out a similar study of the case of 2 *Enoch*. Similar research, however, goes beyond the objectives of our present work.

[82] That is: "he remains a priest *forever*" (μένει ἱερεὺς εἰς τὸ διηνεκές) (3d); "it is testified that *he lives*" (ἐκεῖ δὲ μαρτυρούμενος ὅτι ζῇ) (8b); "but through the power of an *indestructible life*" (ἀλλὰ κατὰ δύναμιν ζωῆς ἀκαταλύτου) (16b).

[83] "The implication that Melchizedek 'remains' a priest continually permits a measure of understanding of Christ as the abiding, eternal priest. The 'eternal' nature of Melchizedek priesthood is its distinguishing feature. It is the one element above all others that interests the writer as he prepares to present Christ as the high priest 'like Melchizedek'" (W. L. Lane, *Hebrews 1–8* [WAC 47A; Dallas, Texas 1991], p. 167).

[84] As was affirmed by G. Granerød, "Melchizedek in Hebrews 7," *Biblica* 90/2 (2009), p. 202.

Although some authors have shown reservations and even clear rejection of such a possibility,[85] the great majority of academics have adopted a position in favor of such an hypothesis, varying in their manner of evaluating the data. While some scholars have demonstrated a certain sense of caution due to the fact that the parallels between *Hebrews* and *11QMelchizedek* are not exact or exhaustive, and have preferred to speak generally of "certain influences," of "some affinities," or of "indirect influences,"[86] others have adopted a more assertive position, affirming that *11QMelchizedek* allows us to understand the way in which the author of *Hebrews* argues in favor of the superiority of Christ as a High Priest with respect to Levite priesthood, significantly highlighting their Christology.[87] Finally, there are researchers who have adopted an unwavering position in favor of a more direct and specific dependency between *Hebrews* and the traditions of Melchizedek in Qumran,[88] speaking of "shared views" (Mason)[89] and "striking similarities" (Aschim),[90] to the point of categorically stating, as in the case of Longenecker, that "I suggest in particular that in 11QMelch we have an important key for the understanding of the treatment of Melchizedek in the letter".[91] This supposed relationship of dependence between both compositions even led Bodinger to suggest that the author

---

[85] As is the case of Horton, *The Melchizedek Tradition*, p. 164. See also Dimant, "Melchizedek at Qumran," p. 367; P. Ellingworth, "Like the Son of God," p. 258.

[86] See Attridge, *The Epistle to the Hebrews*, p. 194). Cf. also Poorthius, "Enoch and Melchizedek," p. 112.

[87] As Fitzmyer states, "Further Light on Melchizedek," p. 253.

[88] This statement must be evaluated in light of possible contacts existing between the Dead Sea Scrolls and *Hebrews*. On the nature of these contacts, see F. C. Fensham, "Hebrews and Qumran," *Neotestamentica* 5 (1971), pp. 9–21; Y. Yadin, "The Dead Sea Scrolls and the Epistle to the Hebrews," *Aspects of the Dead Sea Scrolls* (Scripta Hieroslymitana IV) (Ch. Rabin and Y. Yadin [eds]; Jerusalem: The Hebrew University, 1965, 2° ed.), pp. 36–55.

[89] See Mason, *'You are a Priest Forever,'* p. 203). See also *idem*, "Hebrews 7:3," pp. 59–62; "SBL 2007 Presentation," pp. 19–23. In this same vein, see Knohl, "Melchizedek," p. 266.

[90] Aschim, "Melchizedek and Jesus," pp. 135–47.

[91] Longenecker, "The Melchizedek Argument," p. 172. For details of the argumentation, see *ibid.*, pp. 172–79.

of *Hebrews* "connaissait la tradition qumranienne, peut-être même la source primitive de la tradition sur Melkisédeq".[92]

Numerous scholars affirm that *11QMelchizedek* would also be the key understanding the exegetical-theological development of the former biblical king-priest of Salem in Christian heterodox circles (the "Melchizedekeans" of Epiphanius of Salamis), when he went from being a real and historical human being to being a heavenly-angelical being. According to suggestions put forward by many, speculations on Melchizedek as a heavenly "great power" (μεγάλην τινὰ δύναμιν) superior to Christ ([Pseudo]-Hippolytus VII, 36), an angel (Origen according to Jerome, *Epistle* 73, 2), or a heavenly intercessor in favor of the angels (Pseudo-Tertullian, *Adv. Haer.* 8) in marginalized Christian circles would not have been the fruit of original and independent thoughts on Hebrews 7, 3,[93] but rather elaborations based on traditions inherited from the Judaism of the Greco-Roman era, of the type present in *11QMelchizedek*. As Kobelski suggests: "It is significant, however, that some Christian sects would have interpreted Melchizedek in Hebrews as an angelic leader who plays an intermediary role between God and humanity. It is probable that a tradition such as the one expressed in 11QMelch stands behind their interpretation of Melchizedek in Hebrews."[94]

The same interpretative approach is followed by scholars who understand the soteriological, heavenly-angelical, priestly, and warrior nature of Melchizedek present in some Gnostic texts in light of his presentation in *11QMelchizedek*. One example in this sense is when the tradition of Melchizedek as an eschatological avenger in the Qumranite text (*11QMelchizedek*, II 13) is confronted with his presentation as a high priest and warrior in NHC IX,1: 26, 2–9. The similarities between these two presentations are remarkable, to the point of having led academics to consider a possible genetic dependence between both traditions.[95]

---

[92] Bodinger, "L'enigme de Melkisédeq," p. 329.
[93] See *supra*, n. 15.
[94] Kolbelski, *Melchizedek and Melkireša'*, p. 60 n. 36. For other favorable opinions in this sense, see Attridge, *The Epistle to the Hebrews*, p. 194; Piovanelli, "Much to say...," p. 421.
[95] Piovanelli, "Much to say...," p. 419. See also Pearson, "The Figure of Melchizedek," p. 112.

A similar conclusion was reached upon analyzing the presentation of Melchizedek in another Gnostic work, *Pistis Sophia*, in which he appears as a heavenly savior transferring particles of light (souls saved) to the Treasure of Light. This soteriological action by Melchizedek reminds one of his redeeming action in *11QMelchizedek*, in which he is presented as the redeemer of the "sons of light"/the "lot of Melchizedek" from the control of Belial (II, 4–8, 25). These similarities led Pearson to state categorically that "Pistis Sophia's treatment of Melchizedek can easily be seen as a Gnostic reinterpretation of that found in 11QMelch".[96]

If all of this is true then, the discovery of *11QMelchizedek* would have allowed us to resolve the "mystery" of Melchizedek through the recovery of the "missing link", reconstructing the processes that would have affected Melchizedek's transformation at the end of Greco-Roman Judaism, converting the former king-priest of Salem in the Hebrew Bible (Gn 14), with his real and historical human nature, into an angelical-heavenly, priestly, savior, warrior being in certain circles of Early Christianity (centuries I–IV).

Finally, as this specific study on the traditions of Melchizedek has allowed us to see, underground communication links between the Judaism of the Greco-Roman era and some Christian heterodox groups (the "Melchizedekeans" and Gnostics) did exist in the first centuries of our era, permitting the spread of ideas, beliefs, and literature from dissident apocalyptic groups from Second Temple Judaism, as is the case of the Qumranites. In this sense, this work is a modest contribution to a promising field of research that has recently awakened the interest of specialists, that is: the way in which the Jewish traditions of the Second Temple period were transmitted and reinterpreted in Christian circles at the end of the ancient era.[97]

---

[96] Pearson, "The Figure of Melchizedek," pp. 122–23. See also Aschim, "Melchizedek the Liberator," p. 258. On the phenomenon of the generalized use of Jewish sources in Gnostic literature, B. A. Pearson, "Jewish Sources in Gnostic Literature," in *Jewish Writings of the Second Temple Period. Apocrypha, Pseudepigrapha, Qumran Sectarian Writings, Philo, Josephus* (M. E. Stone [eds]; Van Gorcum, Assen/Fortress Press, Philadelphia, 1984), pp. 443–81.

[97] On this topic, see M. Kister, H. Newman, M. Segal, and R. Clements (eds), *Tradition, Transmission, and Transformation from Second Temple Literature*

*Abstract*

The figure of Melchizedek, which appears expressly mentioned in the Scriptures only twice in the Hebrew Bible (Gen 14, 18-20, Ps 110, 4), and once in the New Testament (Heb 7), became an important topic in patristic literature, as well as in the polemic of Christianity against various heresies and Judaism, becoming a popular theme in Byzantine iconography. The Epistle to the Hebrews was a turning point in the way of perceiving this character in antiquity, when the former king-priest of Salem of earthly character in ancient Jewish sources (Gen 14, Genesis Apocryphon, Pseudo-Eupolemus, Philo of Alexandria, and Flavius Josephus), was characterized in the New Testament as an eternal being (7, 3). From that moment on, the figure of Melchizedek played a significant role in the heterodox speculations of some Christian sects (for example, the heresy of the "Melchizedekites"), considering it a heavenly "great power" superior to Christ (Theodotus the banker), an "angel" (Origins), or even identifying it with the "Holy Spirit" (Hieracas the Egyptian). Likewise, Melchizedek was interpreted as a soteriological figure in Gnostic literature, having a celestial-angelic, priestly and warrior character. How can one explain this radical transformation in the way of apprehending the figure of Melchizedek? The hypothesis of this work is that the sectarian-qumranite exegetical tradition present in 11QMelquisedec (11Q13) would be the key to understanding the mutation suffered by the pre-Christian Melchizedek at the end of the Greco-Roman period, which would have served as background, or even as inspiration, for the later development of this figure in ancient Christianity.

*through Judaism and Christianity in Late Antiquity*. Proceedings of the Thirteenth International Symposium of the Orion Center for the Study of the Dead Sea Scrolls and Associated Literature, Jointly Sponsored by the Hebrew University Center for the Study of Christianity, 22–24 February, 2011 (STJD 113; Brill, 2015).

JUAN CARLOS ALBY
*Universidad Católica de Santa Fé, Argentina*

# HEALTH AND DISEASE IN QUMRAN TEXTS AND JEWISH APROCRYPHAL LITERATURE

## Introduction

Upon examining Jewish tradition, it is not easy to prove that there existed a specific medical class in Israel during Old Testament times, as was the case, for example, of the surgeons in Babylon who were considered artisans, or of the "house of life" in Egypt, which can be interpreted to have been a medical school and which appears in famous shrines. The absence of a medical class in Israel can be explained for different reasons, of which we highlight the following:

a) On the one hand, the rejection of dissection practices in order to prevent contamination through the handling of dead bodies: "Whoever touches the dead body of anyone will be unclean for seven days."[1] This prescription extends to anyone out in the open who touches someone who has been killed with a sword or anyone who touches a human bone or a grave.[2]

Through these cultural prescriptions, Israel expresses a radical demystification as well as a desanctification of death, as Yahweh is "God of the living" and not of the dead. Those who are excluded from life and communion with God are outside his cult (Ps 88, 11–13).[3]

---

[1] Num 19, 11.
[2] Cf. Num 19, 16.
[3] Cf. Von Rad, G. *Teología del Antiguo Testamento*, vol. I, Salamanca, Sígueme, 1986, p. 349.

b) On the other hand, the analogical consequences deduced from the study of animals and applied to man do not seem very convincing, in light of the privileged position he holds in the order of creation:

> Now the Lord God had formed out of the ground all the beasts of the field and all the birds of the air. He brought them to the man to see what he would name them; and whatever the man called each living creature, that was its name. So the man gave names to all the livestock, the birds of the air and all the beasts of the field. But among them no suitable helper was found.[4]

Keeping in mind that "to name" in this context means "to take possession of," man's relevant place rising in dignity and strength over other living species becomes clear from this account. For this reason, it is uncertain how conclusions taken from the study of animals are valid for our understanding of the human organism. Despite this absence of institutionalized medicine in Israel, there were doctors for external wounds[5] though priests intervened in all serious diseases. The concept of disease was linked to its value as being sacred, to such an extent that mistrusting divine intervention for its cure by requesting medical advice was considered an act of reckless lack of faith.[6] Only Yahweh could cure: "I am the Lord who heals you (*rōpā*)."[7] Only once the patient had put his trust in the Lord did medicines begin to be considered. Leprosy, which was called "death's firstborn,"[8] was considered to be the most serious bodily impurity in existence and, as such, priests were to pay special attention to curing it.[9]

This tradition, which will be projected with continuities and modifications into the apocalyptic realm of the Judaism of Late Antiquity, can be found in apocryphal literature from the time,

---

[4] Gn 2, 19–20.

[5] Cf. Ex 21, 19.

[6] Cf. 2 Chr 16, 12.

[7] Ex 15, 26. This expression appears in a controversial context, on the occasion of the transformation of the bitter waters (*Marah*) (Ex 15, 22–27). Here, the people are told that by obeying God's commands, they will be kept safe from the diseases suffered in Egypt. Cf. also 2 Re 5, 7.

[8] Jb 18, 13.

[9] Cf. Lv 13.

such as in some Qumran documents. We will first consider some of those texts found in the Qumran Caves. Secondly, we will analyze aspects related to disease and cures found in documents from the profuse apocryphal literature, illustrative of the eschatological atmosphere of that time, within the framework of its current classifications.

## 1. *Health and Disease in Qumran Documents*

The Qumran community which emerged in the second century BC from the Essene movement accounts for a textual plurality that includes writings with a markedly eschatological tendency, both those produced by the community itself and those taken from the Judaism of Late Antiquity.

Firstly, two works belonging to the Qumran library, the *Apocrypha of Genesis* (1Q20) and the *Prayer of Nabonidus* (4Q292/4QPrNab), deserve particular consideration as they are the two cases in which exorcism is mentioned as a remedy for disease, considered to be an effect of demonic possession. Nevertheless, the Hellenistic medical tradition, based on the use of curative herbs, was also taken into account, as Josephus from the first century of the Common Era demonstrates in his praise of the Essenes:

> They have studied the ancient writings extensively, taking away that which is beneficial for their bodies and souls and as such, they tend to reach the virtue of many herbs, plants, roots and stones. They know each one's strength and power and analyze this information with great diligence.[10]

Behind this knowledge is the illustrious figure of Solomon who, according to the Jewish historian, had achieved a high level of expertise on these topics, including the art of expelling demons:

> The sagacity and wisdom that God conferred upon Solomon were so great that they exceeded that of the elderly; they were not inferior to the Egyptians, of whom it was said were the most intelligent in the world, but whose sagacity was clearly

---

[10] Flavius Josephus, *Guerras de los judíos* II, VII, 6, in *Las guerras de los judíos. Tomo I*, Tarrasa (Barcelona), CLIE, 1983, p. 219.

inferior to that of the king [...] He wrote five thousand books of odes and songs, three thousand of parables and the like; he wrote a parable about each type of tree, from the hyssop to the cedar; he also wrote about animals and all living beings on the Earth, in the sea or in the air because he did not ignore any of their characteristics nor did he ever cease to research them; he described them as a philosopher would, revealing impressive knowledge of their diverse properties. God also conferred upon him the ability to expel demons, a science which was both useful and curing. He composed spells to relieve pain and left mankind ways of using exorcisms by which demons were cast away so as never to return. This method of healing continues to be widely used to the present day.[11]

Later, Josephus mentions a man called Eleazar who practiced exorcisms in the presence of Vespasian, his sons and his captains.

> Healing occurred as follows: he brought a ring stamped with the root of one of the classes mentioned by Solomon up to the nasal passages of the possessed, made him to breathe it in and extracted the demon by the nose. The man would fall to the floor immediately while he exorcised the devil from ever entering the body again, repeatedly mentioning Solomon's name and reciting the spell he had composed. When Eleazar wanted to convince and demonstrate to the spectators that he held this power, he put a glass or recipient full of water at a certain distance and order the devil, upon leaving the man's body, to knock it over as a way of making the abandonment public. Having done this, Solomon's abilities and wisdom were clearly put on display.[12]

In the same century that Josephus was writing, Philo of Alexandria also highlights the medical abilities of a sect known as the *Therapeutae* whom he mentions in addition to the Essenes, as the treatise *On the Contemplative Life* or *On the Beggars* opens chapter one as the continuation of a previous book, according to which is read "having already taken up the topic of the Essenes." It is highly probable that the book in question has been largely lost, a book known as the *Apology for the Jews* or *Hypothetica*, registered

---

[11] Flavius Josephus, *Antigüedades de los judíos* VIII, II, 5, in *Antigüedades de los judíos. Tomo II*, Tarrasa (Barcelona), CLIE, 1988, p. 73s.

[12] Flavius Josephus, *op. cit.*, p. 74.

in fragments by Eusebius of Cesarea in his *Praeparatio Evangelica* VIII, 6, 1–9, VIII, 7, 1–20 and VIII, 11, 1–18.[13] The differences between Essenes and Therapeutae relate mainly to goods and work, to permiting women to enter the sect as is the case with the Therapeutae and to the leniency or severity of dietary customs.[14] Chapter two reads:

> The choice that these philosophers make can clearly be seen in their names: they are called Therapeutae or Therapeutides, be it because they profess an art of healing superior to that of the cities – these cure only the physical body, whereas the former also cure souls, those souls afflicted with awful and serious diseases caused by pleasures and lust, sadness and fear, ambition, insanity and injustice and by the infinite heap of other passions and vices – be it because they were educated by nature and by sacred laws to serve the Existent One, who is superior to good, purer than one and more native than the monad.[15]

Highlighted here is the issue of therapy of the soul in addition to therapy of the body, as well as a listing of causes that afflict it, these characterize the superiority of their medicine in relation to other communities. Eusebius of Cesarea, who was familiar with this book, talks about the meaning of this *therapeía* whose roots refer to the therapy of body and soul at the service of God:

> Firstly, in the book he titled *On the Contemplative Life* or *Beggars*, Philo makes it clear that he will not add anything against the truth or of his own making to what he will express. He says that they were called *Therapeutae* and the women that were with them *Therapeutisses* and he adds the reasons for such names: either because as doctors they freed the souls of those who approached them from sufferings caused by evil, healing them and caring for them, or because of the cleansing and purity of their service to the divinity.[16]

---

[13] Cf. Martín, José Pablo (Introduction, translation and notes), *Filón de Alejandría. Obras completas*, Volumen V, Madrid, Trotta, 2009, p. 148, n. 10. On the historical existence of this sect and the state of the matter, see the complete "Introduction" that the author provides to *On the Contemplative Life*, pp. 147–56.

[14] Cf. Martín, J. P., *op. cit.*, p. 154.

[15] Philo of Alexandria, *De vita contemplativa* 2, in Martín, J. P., *ibidem*, p. 157.

[16] Eusebius of Cesarea, *Historia eclesiástica* II, 17, 3, in Velasco-Delgado, Argimiro (Spanish version, introduction and notes), *Eusebio de Cesarea. Historia Eclesiástica I*, bilingual text, Madrid, BAC, 1997 (2ª. ed.), p. 91.

From these readings, we gather that both the Essenes – from which the Qumran community broke off – and the therapeutae of Alexandria, despite their differences, coincided in their need for mental as well as physical healing. In the case of the Essenes, the recourse to Hellenistic medical teachings based on the Hippocratic pharmacopeia of medicinal herbs and to exorcism is sufficiently documented. In a passage from *Every Good Man is Free*, Philo would have us understand that, perhaps in some cases, medical help for the suffering was sought outside the community when he refers to payment of medical fees from a common fund:

> The sick are not left without care because they cannot contribute, rather, they are given the expected resources for the treatment of their illness, resources that the common fund makes available to them, so that they are at complete liberty to use the sufficiently healthy fund for their expenses.[17]

In the Qumran documents that refer the healing of illnesses to the expelling of evil spirits for the forgiveness of sins, we see firsthand the *Genesis Apocryphon*. The typological classification offered by Florentino García Martínez in his translation of the Qumran texts locates this writing in group V, which corresponds to parabiblical literature. It includes works which both expand upon the base biblical text and recount it differently, merging it with different traditions to such a point that the biblical origin of the account seems to become lost within the composition. This is not the case of the *Genesis Apocryphon*, in which the original biblical text is easily discernable.[18] The passage from this treatise which interests us here is based on Gen 12, 10–19, a story which is repeated with Abimelech instead of the Pharaoh in Gen 20, 1–18. Fearing that he will lose his life because of the desire that Sarah's beauty awoke in the Pharaoh Zoan, Abraham concocted an astute plan to make him believe that Sarah was his sister instead of his wife. The Pharaoh believed him, but that same night, in response to Abraham's pleas, God sent an evil spirit to afflict him and his household.

---

[17] Philo of Alexandria, *Todo hombre bueno es libre* 87, in Triviño, José María, *Obras completas de Filón de Alejandría*, Tomo V, Buenos Aires, Acervo Cultural, 1976, p. 82.

[18] Cf. García Martínez, Florentino (edición y traducción), *Textos de Qumrán*, Madrid, Trotta, 2009 (6ª. ed.), p. 269.

Additionally, Zoan could not come near to Sarah nor have sexual relations with her during the two years she was under his control. After these two years, plagues against him and the members of his household intensified. The Pharaoh requested the assistance of all the magicians and healers in Egypt, but none succeeded in finding the cure as the spirit attacked them and caused them to flee. One of his ministers, warned by Abraham's nephew Lot that the patriarch couldn't intercede for the sovereign while Sarah was with him, told the king that all of the plagues were due to the fact that he held Sarah, Abraham's wife. The Pharaoh reproached Abraham for his trickery and told him:

> I have there your wife, take her away! Go. Leave the cities of Egypt. But first, pray for me and for my household so that this evil spirit will be expelled. I prayed for [...] and laid my hands upon his head. The plague was removed from him; [the evil spirit] was expelled [from him] and lived.[19]

The control exerted over the evil spirit is expressed through the use of the term געד [*g'r*], a verbal root which appears only in the *qal* form in the Old Testament and conveys the idea of "reprimanding," but also "reprimanding with voices" or "shouts" as an activity belonging to the exorcist. The strictly theological use of the term connects especially to reprehension in battle and appears in different references to the battle waged by the Lord against chaos (Ps 104, 7; Jb 26, 11; Ne 1, 4; Ps 68, 31; 106, 9; 18, 16).[20] For his part, H. Kee maintains that it really means "dominating a hostile force."[21] We believe that the root גבר [*gbr*] is more in line with that meaning, "superiority," "vigor," "strength," than that which appears in the Qumran text.[22] In this document, "a spirit of festering evils" is spoken of, though in the original biblical account it is said that in the case of Abimelech and his family, the punishment consisted of infertility because God "had closed all the wounds

---

[19] *Génesis Apócrifo* (1Q20), Col. XX, 27–29, in García Martínez, F., *op. cit.*, p. 284.

[20] Cf. Jenni, E., Westermann, C., *Diccionario teológico manual del Antiguo Testamento* I, Madrid, Cristiandad, 1978, p. 609.

[21] Cf. Kee, Howard K., *Medicina, milagro y magia en tiempos del Nuevo Testamento*, Córdoba, El Almendro, 1992, p. 45.

[22] Cf. Jenni, E., Westermann, C., *op. cit.*, p. 569.

of Abimelech's house." In any case, we see here one of the many cases in which illness or demonic persecution is a consequence of evil works. In this respect, rabbinic tradition is conclusive, as can be noted in certain saying attributed to R. Hiyya bar Abba (Tannaíta, *c.* 200 AD):

> An ill man does not recover from his illness until all his sins have been forgiven, as it is written: "He forgives all your sins and heals all your diseases" (Ps 103, 3).
>
> Healing the diseased is a miracle far greater than pulling Ananias, Misael and Azarias from the fire; these three are affected by a human fire which anyone can put out, but the fire blazing inside the diseased comes from the heavens, who shall put it out?[23]

In the account found in the *Genesis Apocryphon*, no mention is made of medicinal herbs or magical formulas, instead only the simple removal of pain for the forgiveness of sins through the laying on of hands.

In this same line of parabiblical literature, the second treatise to consider is that known as the *Prayer of Nabonidus*. The king of Babylon had been struck down by a malicious disease that left him marginalized from the community of man, similar to that described in Dan 4 as a loss of sanity regarding what happened to King Nebuchadnezzar. After praying to God Almighty, Nabonidus's sin was forgiven by an exorcist:

> Word of prayer pronounced by Nabonidus, king of the coun[try of Babylon], [great] king, [when he began to suffer] from a malicious inflammation, by decree of G[od Almi]ghty, in Teiman. [I, Nabonidus], suffered [from a malicious inflammation] for seven years and was cast far away [from man until I prayed to God Almighty] and my sin was forgiven by an exorcist.[24]

---

[23] *Talmud de Babilonia* (*TB*), *Nedarim* 41 a, in Perez Fernandez, Miguel, *Tradiciones mesiánicas en el Targum Palestinense. Estudios exegéticos*, Valencia-Jerusalén, Institución San Jerónimo, 1981, p. 70.

[24] *4Q Oración de Nabonida* (4Q242[4QPrNab]), Frag. 1, 1–4, in García Martínez, F., *ibidem*, p. 333.

The term גזרין (*gzryn*), as it appears in Dan 5, 11, is better translated as "exorcist," as F. García Martínez translates, than as "seer."[25]

With respect to biblical vocabulary regarding cures, the Qumran continues with the theological use of the Hebrew Bible. In Yahwist monotheism, healing action had been monopolized by Yahweh. From here comes the well-known saying: "Yahweh wounds but he also binds up" (Deut 28, 27.35; 32, 39; Os 6, 1; Ps 60, 4; Job 5, 18). Only by way of subsequent theological reflections upon its own history will Israel understand health as being tied to justice and disease as a type of future punishment for apostasy and infidelity. Hence, the necessary apposition regarding "the sun of justice" in Malachi's text to understand healing: "But for you who fear my name, the sun of justice will arise with healing (*-mrp'*) in its wings."[26] But the medicinal language directed toward God's action remained inalterable within the new salvation context and, in this way, appeared in the *Hôdayôt* of Qumran Cave 1. The term *-mrp'* appears in two of these hymns. In the first, if he who is speaking in first person is the Master of Justice, medicine is attributed to himself:

> I am a trap for transgressors, medicine for all those who distance themselves from sin, prudence for the simple, firmness for the shy of heart.[27]

If this text can be interpreted in the light of Isa 53, 5: "by his wounds we are healed (*-mrp*)," then the Master of Justice is portrayed as medicine for his followers. Nevertheless, there are those who do not share this interpretation.[28]

The second passage in which *-mrp* appears refers to personal healing, but not to medicine for others:

> Your admonition has become for me joy and delight, my plague eternal healing and perpetual [happiness], my adver-

---

[25] Ricardo Cerni translates in this way in *Antiguo Testamento interlineal hebreo-español* IV: *Libros proféticos*, Barcelona, CLIE, 2002, Dn 5, 11, p. 676.

[26] Mal 3, 20.

[27] *1QHôdayôt*ᵃ (1QHᵃ), Col. X (= II), 8–9, in García Martínez, F., *idem*, p. 366.

[28] For example, H. Michaud, who prefers to associate the term *-mrp'* with the language of the wise according to Prov 12, 18: "the tongue of the wise brings healing (*-mrp'*)", rather than with the Master of Justice, in "A propos d'un passage des hymnes (1Q Hôdayôt) II, 7–14", *Revue de Qumrân* 1 (1958), 413–16. Cf. Perez Fernandez, M., *op. cit.*, p. 71, n. 116.

sary's mockery a crown of glory, and my weakness eternal strength.[29]

> The Spirit of the Sovereign Lord is on me, because the Lord has anointed me to proclaim good news to the poor, to bind up the brokenhearted, to proclaim freedom for the captives and release for the prisoners.

Additionally, it is interesting to compare the Hebrew text of Isa 61, 1 referring to the Messenger with the LXX, as the former does not mention any physical healing nor does the verb *rf'* appear:

In the LXX, on the other hand, the expression "to bind up the brokenhearted" is translated as "to heal" and physical healing is added to the text: "and to restore vision to the blind." In Qumran theology, the Messenger is identified as the Messiah, as can be seen in 11QMelch:

> And the herald of good news is [the annoint]ed one of the spirit of whom Da[niel] spoke [... and the herald of] good news that announces salva[tion is he of whom it is written that [he will send "to console the afflicted, to watch over the afflicted of Zion"].[30]

If this Messenger is called Melchizedek, this is probably due to the etymology of this name, King of Justice or Just King. But no healing action is attributed to him. We must wait until the New Testament for the figure of the Messenger to become one with the Messiah healer, when Jesus takes over this title introducing himself not only as he who proclaims the Good News to the poor, but also as he who heals the lepers, makes the lame walk, the deaf hear, and the blind see (Luk 7, 22).

## 2. *Health and Disease in the Apocryphal Literature of the Judaism of Late Antiquity*

These documents are considered to be apocryphal as they are not part of the official canon established in Yabne at the end of the first century AD. The political circumstances that accentuated

---

[29] 1QH³, Col. XVII (= 9), 25, in García Martínez, F., *idem*, p. 384.
[30] *11QMelquisedec* (11Q13[11QMelch]), Col. II, 18–19, in García Martínez, F., *idem*, p. 187.

Judaism's crisis triggered the reaction of theologians who became obligated to explain God's plan with a historical perspective. Thus, a great part of the literature from this period, such as the *Book of Jubilees, Daniel* chapters 7–12, part of *1Enoch* and the *Testament of Moses*, among others, are pierced by certain historical determinism. The anguish and calamity of the present do not escape God's sight, and He will soon be forced to intervene decisively in history to punish the heathen and reward the just. In this context, mentions of disease, demonic possession and its subsequent liberation appear, as do references to health and purification rites in which legal and liturgical aspects overlap with sanitary ones.

The book of Tobias was probably written during the first twenty five years of the second century BC. Here is mentioned the case of Tobias's blindness caused by the feces of sparrows falling onto his eyes, and the physicians' failed attempt to cure him.[31] After four years, he was cured with the same remedy that had been used to expel the demon Asmodeus, namely the bile, heart and liver of one fish.[32] It is understandable, then, that the angel who guides Tobias in his journey to his family's house, reclaims his betrothed and expels the demon that had caused the deaths of his seven previous wives on their wedding nights, be called Raphael which means: "God heals."[33] This angel appears once more in the Cycle of Enoch, whose first book makes reference to fallen angels who lived together with women and who corrupted the human race by teaching man science, spells and magical formulas. These angels gave birth to three races, the giants, who themselves gave birth to the *Nefilim* and these to the *Eliud*. They multiplied and

---

[31] Cf. Tb 2, 9–10: "The same night also I returned from the bathing, and slept by the wall of my courtyard, with my face uncovered because of the heat. And I knew not that there were sparrows in the wall, and mine eyes being open, the sparrows muted warm dung into mine eyes, and a whiteness came in mine eyes. I went to the physicians for a cure, but the more remedies they applied, the less I saw because of the whiteness until I remained completely blind."

[32] Cf. Tb 6, 7–9: "And he said unto him: 'Brother Azarias, what remedy is there in the heart, liver and bile of a fish?' He responded: 'If you burn the heart or liver of a fish before a man or woman tortured by a demon or by a bad spirit, smoke banishes all evil and makes it disappear forever. Spreading bile upon the eyes of a man attacked by whiteness and blowing on these stains cures him.'"

[33] Cf. Tb 8, 1–3; 11, 8–14.

revealed mysteries that were to remain hidden to man. Consequently, Noah is warned of the destruction of the human race and Raphael is instructed to tie down the evil angels for eternal punishment.

This interest in the nature of the world of the angels just as in the calendar, whose invention is attributed to this mysterious biblical character, are perhaps some of the reasons that explain the fact that this apocryphon of the Old Testament has received more attention than all others. This attention has only increased since the discoveries of Qumran.[34]

The corruption of the human race is attributed to the prohibited teachings that these races passed on to man, such as knowledge of herbs and plants to be used for diverse means, astrology, metallurgy and even knowledge of cosmetic for female beauty, as well as knowledge of weapons of warfare and magical spells. We read, for example:

> And they took women; each one chose his own and they began to live together and unite themselves to them, teaching them spells and incantations and training them to collect roots and plants. They became pregnant and gave birth to enormous giants three thousand cubits tall each [...]. Azazel taught the men to make swords, knifes, shields, breastplates, metals and their techniques, bracelets and decorations; how to put alcohol over their eyes and beautify their eyebrows, how to distinguish which stones are precious, all the colors and metallurgy. There was great impiety and much fornication, they erred and corrupted their customs:[35]

---

[34] The material recovered consists of seven copies of three of the five sections of the Ethiopian Enoch (*1 Enoch*) and four copies of the *Astronomical Book* (*1 En.* 72–82) (4QEnastr[abcd]), eight copies of the *Book of the Giants* (1QEnGiants, 6QEnGiants, 4QEn[c] [= 4QEnGiants[a]], 4QEnGiants[abcde?]) and at least two copies of the *Book of Noah* (1QNoé, 4QNoé[4QMessAram]); cf. Vegas Montaner, Luis, "Los textos de Qumrán y la literatura apócrifa judía", in Trebolle Barrera, Julio (coordinador), *Paganos, judíos y cristianos en los textos de Qumrán*, Madrid, Trotta, 1999, cap. 8, pp. 181–211 (here, p. 187s.).

[35] *1 En. (Et)* 7, 1–2; 8, 1–2. The Ethiopian text can be compared with the Greek version of the same passages: "These and all the rest, in the year 1170, took wives for themselves and began to go into them and were promiscuous with them until the moment of the cataclysm. They bore them three races. The first, large giants. These bore the *Nefilim*, and these the *Eliud*. They increased in number, remaining the same size, and they themselves learned, and taught their wives, spells and incantations. Azazel, the tenth ruler, was the first to teach them to make

> And the Lord said to Raphael: "Chain up Azazel by his hands and feet and throw him to the darkness; strike open the desert in Dudael and throw him there. Throw rough, sharp stones upon him and cover him in darkness [...] and on judgement day he will be sent to the fire.[36]

In his diachronic classification of apocryphal literature, G. W. E. Nickelsburg includes *1 En.* 72–82 or the *Astronomical Book* and *1 En.* 1–36 or the *Book of the Watchers* in group II which corresponds to the Palestine of Alexander the Great.[37] This becomes very important for our topic, as the *Book of Ecclesiasticus* or the *Book of the All-Virtuous Wisdom of Joshua ben Sira*, which contains the well-known passage on the value of physicians in the Judaism of the Alexandrian period, is in the same group:

> Honor the physician for the need thou hast of him, for the most High hath created him. For all healing is from God, and all gifts are from the king. The skill of the physician shall lift up his head, and in the sight of great men he shall be praised. The most High hath created medicines out of the earth, and a wise man will not abhor them... the most High hath given knowledge to men, that he may be honored in his wonders. By these he shall cure and shall allay their pains, and of these the apothecary shall make sweet confections.[38]

Later, the Sirach makes clear that healing comes from God, and that falling into the hands of a physician could be the consequence of straying from the Maker:

> My son, in thy sickness neglect not thyself, but pray to the Lord, and he shall heal thee. Turn away from sin and order thy hands aright, and cleanse thy heart from all offense. Offer incense, a memorial of fine flour and a generous offer-

---

swords, shields and all types of instruments for warfare; also about metals of the earth and gold – how to work with them and make adornments for the women – and silver. He also taught them how to make up the eyes, to beautify themselves, about precious stones and dyes; they sinned and made the saints err." *1 En.* (Gr$^5$) 7, 1–2; 8, 1–2, in Diez Macho, Alejandro, *Apócrifos del Antiguo Testamento IV*, Madrid, Cristiandad, 1982, pp. 43–45.

[36] *1 En.* 10, 4–6, p. 47.

[37] Cf. Nickelsburg, G. W. E., *Jewish Literature between the Bible and the Mishnah*, Philadelphia, Fortress Press, 1986, pp. 43–44.

[38] Eccl 38, 1–7.

ing as you can. Then give place to the physician, for the Lord created him; for there is a time when thou must fall into his hands. And they also beseech the Lord, that He would prosper what they give for ease and remedy. He that sinneth in the sight of his Maker, shall fall into the hands of the physician.[39]

For his part, Vega Montaner classifies the treatises of the Cycle of Enoch in group 6 typologically, treatises corresponding to parabiblical writings of an apocalyptic character.[40] One variation of this criteria is that which we find in the classification for Qumran literature proposed by F. García Martínez. This author locates the Enoch material recovered at Qumran in group V which corresponds to parabiblical literature, together with the writings already analyzed from the *Genesis Apocryphon* and the *Prayer of Nabonidus*.[41] That is to say that both in the historical diachronic criteria and in the literary typology, we find a definite correspondence to analyze the notions of health and disease and learn of the value that the physician had in that period.

Another text of Jewish apocalypse written in the middle of the second century BC, the *Book of Jubilees*, shares with the *Ecclesiasticus* the notion that medicinal herbs form part of the order of creation and that they were revealed to the chosen people of God. At the same time, just as in *1 Enoch*, this book makes reference to the fallen angels and, especially, to their leader Mastema, who incited the Egyptians to harass Moses and the sons of Israel:

> And one of us He commanded that we should teach Noah all their medicines; for He knew that they would not walk in uprightness, nor strive in righteousness [...]. And we explained to Noah all the medicines of their diseases, together with their seductions, how he might heal them with herbs of the earth. And Noah wrote down all things in a book as we instructed him concerning every kind of medicine. Thus the evil spirits were precluded from the sons of Noah. And

---

[39] Eccl 38, 9–15.
[40] Cf. Vega Montaner, L., "Los textos de Qumrán y la literatura apócrifa judía", in Trebollé Barrera, J. (coord.), *Paganos, judíos y cristianos en los textos de Qumrán*, Madrid, Trotta, 1999, cap. 8, p. 186.
[41] Cf. García Martínez, F., *idem*, p. 269.

he gave all that he had written to Shem, his eldest son; for he loved him exceedingly above all his sons.[42]

And the prince Mastema stood up against thee [Moses] and sought to cast thee into the hands of Pharaoh, and he helped the Egyptian sorcerers, and they stood up and wrought before thee the evils indeed we permitted them to work, but the remedies we did not allow to be wrought by their hands.[43]

The *Book of Jubilees* shares Nickelsburg"s group III "reform-repression-rebellion" (175–164 BC) with Dan 7–12, the *Testament of Moses* and *1 Enoch* 83–90 (*Book of Dreams*), the aforementioned group 6 of Trebolle and group V parabiblical literature according to García Martínez's typological variant. The importance that Qumran gave to the *Book of Jubilees* is demonstrated by the twelves copied found at that location. In each case, the spirit of the time is sufficiently attested to. Israel lives in sin and error; the existence of malicious angelic powers marks the growth of corruption. The following stand out: the desecration of the temple, the bad conduct and ignorance of the priests, the use of an erroneous calendar, the rupture of the Alliance, the transgression of the Law and the incorrect interpretation of the Torah. All of these evils give rise to social injustices committed by priests and rulers and, with these, the loss of health which is worsened by demonic possession. All of this will be overcome by divine intervention in the history of Israel and the repentance and purification that will need to be adjusted to both legal and sanitary prescriptions.

## Final Considerations

When studying the concepts of health, illness and medicine in the Jewish tradition of Late Antiquity in general, and of the Essenes in particular, we must distinguish between and examine three separate aspects. On the one hand, the literary genre of "apocalypses" and works that belong to this genre. On the other hand, "apocalypticism" as a social movement from which the Essene movement and the Qumran community are born. And finally, "apocalyptic"

---

[42] *Book of Jubilees (Jub.)* 10, 10–14, in Diez Macho, A., *op. cit.* II, p. 108.
[43] *Jub.* 48, 9–10, p. 184.

eschatology understood as the ideological and symbolic horizon that finds its expression in the apocalypses and that determines the hermeneutics with which these texts interpret the books of the Old Testament authorized for religious teaching. This set of ideas and representations crystalized into the Essene movement and later found its institutional expression in the Qumran community, which split from the Essene majority school of thought.[44] As such, these literary works present the bipolar character of the Judaism of the time, specifically, that of halakhic revelation and interpretation, both in line with the double mission given to the Master of Justice according to the *Damascus Document*:

> And God considered their deeds, for they sought Him with a perfect heart, and He raised for them a Master of Justice in order to direct them in the way of His heart. [...] And He made known to later generations what He had wrought in a former generation, the generation off treacherous men.[45]

It is precisely this apocalyptic character or revelation which allows both the Master of Justice and the Qumran community to access the biblical texts that contain legal prescriptions and modify them according to new interpretation. The following passage of the hymn seems to infer this:

> But you have set me as a flag for those chosen in justice, as a wise disseminator of marvelous secrets.[46]

The healing of illnesses is understood in this context. According to the passages of the Dead Sea manuscripts and the Jewish apocalyptica analyzed, there is no negative valuation of physicians as was found in Late Antiquity Judaism, where the sole exception found was the praise of Egyptian embalming physicians to whom Joseph entrusted the body of his father Jacob.[47] In the prophet

---

[44] Cf. Trebolle Barrera, J., *La Biblia judía y la Biblia cristiana. Introducción a la historia de la Biblia*, Madrid, Trotta, 2013 (4ª ed.), p. 248s.

[45] *Damascus Document*ª (CD-A), Col. I, 10–12, in García Martínez, F., *idem*, p. 80.

[46] 1QHª, Col. X (= II), 13, 2–4, in García Martínez, F., *idem*, p. 366.

[47] Cf. Gen 50, 1–3.

Jeremiah, however, we find ironic expressions regarding the inefficiency and even absence of physicians:

> Is there no balm in Gilead? Is there no physician there? Why then is there no healing for the wound of my people?[48]

> Go up to Gilead, capital of Egypt, and get balm; but you multiply remedies in vain. There is no healing for you.[49]

In Sirach times, the situation changes abruptly as physicians are to be taken into account seeing as though God has given them the science to relieve suffering, in addition to making remedies accessible through their mediation. The influence that Greek medicine has on the valuing of physicians in Israel is an indicator of the Hellenization experienced by these peoples on all fronts. During this time, nevertheless, the ancient idea of association between illness and the demonic and God acting through the exorcist to bring about healing is maintained, as we have seen in the *Genesis Apocryphon* and the *Prayer of Nabonidus*. However, the reworking of scripture involving material from the period in question allows us to consider the physician's actions as necessary and positive for human health, while human pain and suffering are the product of demonic operation, according to that presented by *1 Enoch* and the *Book of Jubilees*. Therefore, the concepts of health and illness, while prolonging the ancient teaching, find new and positive expressions in the Qumran community and in apocryphal literature, to the point of influencing the esteem with which physicians are held the Roman world.

## *Abstract*

The Qumran community which emerged in the second century BC accounts for a plurality of texts which includes writings with a marked eschatological tendency. These texts are both their own production and those from late Judaism. These latter writings are considered apocryphal because they are not part of the official canon established in Jabneh at the end of the first century AD. The political circumstances that accentuated the crisis of Judaism motivated the reaction from

---

[48] Jer 8, 22.
[49] Jer 46, 11.

theologians, who were forced to explain the plan of God in a historical perspective. Hence, much of the literature of the time such as the *Book of Jubilees, Daniel* in its chapters 7-12, part of *1 Enoch* and the *Testament of Moses*, among others, are crossed by certain historical determinism. The anguish and calamities of the present do not escape the foresight of God, who very soon was to intervene decisively in history to punish the wicked and reward the righteous. In this context there are references about disease, demonic possession and its consequent liberation, about health and purification rites where legal and liturgical aspects overlap with health aspects. Besides these texts, certain works belonging to the Qumran library such as the *Genesis Apocryphon* (1Q20) and the *Prayer of Nabonidus* (4Q292 / 4QPrNab) deserve consideration. In order to specify the medical, religious, and liturgical practices regarding the health-disease relationship in the different periods of the Jewish apocalyptic literature and in their respective literary contexts, this set of writings are analyzed within their current classification frameworks. They are: the historical and diachronic criterion provided by Nickelsburg, the typological method for apocryphal literature used by Trebolle Barrera, and the typological of Qumran by García Martínez.

CHAPTER 2

# THE DISCOVERY OF ORIGEN'S MANUSCRIPTS AND THOSE OF THE ALEXANDRIAN TRADITION: THEIR IMPACT ON PATRISTIC STUDIES

ANDERS-CHRISTIAN JACOBSEN
*Aarhus Universitet, Denmark*

# BRIEF INTRODUCTION TO THE TOPIC

For this audience I hardly need to define what we understand by "Alexandrian tradition". In the broadest sense the label "the Alexandrian tradition" designates the wide and long traditions of literature, philology, philosophy and religious movements, which during the Antique and Late Antique period had their home in Alexandria in Egypt.[1] All the philosophical schools of that time were present in Alexandria creating specific versions and schools of the different philosophies. Many religious movements were at home there as well. In addition to what from a Christian perspective are often labeled as "Greek" or "pagan" religions, Judaism and Christianity in different versions were also present in Alexandria. Philo of Alexandria (*c.* 20 BCE – 40 CE) is probably the most important and well-known representative of the Jewish traditions. Being an Origen-scholar myself, I would say that the main figure in the Christian Alexandrian tradition is Origen of Alexandria (185–253/54), but Origen stood on the shoulders of or in opposition to his predecessors, for example Clement from Alexandria (around 150–215) and more of the so-called Gnostic Christian groups.

Prof. Lorenzo Perrone's lecture will deal with manuscripts containing Origen's writings and is entitled "Origen"s Renaissance in the Twentieth Century and the Recovery of His Literary

---

[1] Concerning the intellectual environment in Alexandria, see T. Georges – F. Albrecht – R. Feldmeier, eds, *Alexandria* (Moh Siebeck, Tübingen 2013); Alfons Fürst, *Christentum als Intellektuellen Religion. Die Anfänge des Christentums in Alexandria* (Verlag Katholisches Bibelwerk, Stuttgart 2007).

Heritage: New Finds and Philological Advancement'. Prof. Perrone represents the best of contemporary philological work on manuscripts containing Origen's work.

As regards manuscripts and philology, we should not forget that the Christian theologians from Alexandria stood in a proud philological tradition, reaching far back in the history of Alexandrian literary and philological scholarship. It is in this philological tradition that we find the first examples of systematic philological and text critical works trying to establish a coherent Homeric literary tradition. This is of utmost importance for understanding Origen's philological and text critical work represented in his *Hexapla*.

Origen – the main figure in the Christian Alexandrian tradition – was followed by a number of important theologians and groups, who took the legacy of Origen in different directions. A number of theologians could be mentioned, for example Didymus the Blind (313–98) and Evagrius Ponticus (345–99), who both contributed to establishing a learned monastic tradition building on Origen's theology.

Prof. Rubén Peretó Rivas' article "Revisiting Evagrius Ponticus' Orthodoxy in the *Kephalaia Gnostica*" represents another important perspective on the Alexandrian theological tradition, namely whether Origen and his heirs ended up outside or inside the boundaries of the upcoming Christian orthodoxy.

Our knowledge of these important Alexandrian traditions and the authors mentioned above depends completely on the manuscript tradition. The philological and theological study of this huge corpus of manuscripts is therefore of utmost importance. The premodern and modern philological work on manuscripts containing texts from the Alexandrian tradition goes far back in time to the humanist movement represented by Erasmus (*c.* 1466–1536). Since then, there has been continuous production of critical editions of texts from the Alexandrian tradition. Important examples include P. D. Huet (1630–1721), *Origeniana* (1668);[2] the ten volumes of Origen's texts in J. P. Migne *Patrologia Graeca*

---

[2] E. Rapetti, "Pierre-Daniel Huet's *Origeniana*. Origenian Scholarship in Early Modern France", in A. Fürst (ed.), *Origenes in Frankreich. Die Origeniana Pierre-Daniel Huets*, Adamantiana 10 (Aschendorff Verlag, Münster 2017), pp. 35–73.

(vol. 10–17) published around 1860; the ten volumes of Origen's texts in *Griechische Christliche Schriftsteller* (GCS) published in Leipzig and Berlin by the Royal Prussian Academy during the first decades of the twentieth century, and the very many Origen volumes published in the French series *Sources Chrétiennes* during the last half of the twentieth century.[3] In addition to the Origen editions published in these important series, a number of editions of individual works of Origen have been published over the years. One of the latest and most important editions is Lorenzo Perrone's edition of the recently discovered *Homilies on the Psalms*.[4]

The philological work on texts from the Alexandrian tradition has fortunately from time to time been inspired by the findings of hitherto unknown manuscripts which include already known texts as well as unknown texts. In 1941, important papyri were discovered in Tura in Egypt. These papyri contained portions of Origen's and Didymus the Blind's texts.[5] In 2012, a collection of homilies on the Psalms was discovered by Marina Molin Pradel in the State Library in Munich. This manuscript is now published by Lorenzo Perrone in cooperation with other Italian colleagues.

The philological work on manuscripts from the Alexandrian tradition is thus still ongoing and the specialists in this chapter contribute in important ways to establishing new critical editions and to interpreting the content of these traditions.

---

[3] Concerning this history of editions of Origen's works see Christoph Markschies, "The Reception and Transformation of Origen's works in modern editions. Some comparative views on editions in Britain, France, Italy, and Germany", in A.-C. Jacobsen (ed.), *Origeniana Undecima. Origen and Origenism in the History of Western Thought* (Peeters, Leuven 2016), pp. 165–89.

[4] "Origenes, Die neuen Psalmenhomilien. Eine kritische Edition des Codex Monacensis Graecus 314", ed. by L. Perrone, *Origenes XIII, Die griechischen christlichen Schriftsteller der ersten Jahrhunderte* N.F. 19 (De Gruyter, Berlin 2015).

[5] See further about the Tura papyri, L. Doutreleau, "Que savons-nous aujourd'hui des papyrus de Toura", *Recherches des Sciences Religieuses* 43 (1955), pp. 161–93, including plates; H. C. Puesch, "Les nouveaux écrits d'Origine et de Didyme découverts à Toura", *Revue d'Histoire et de philosophie religieuses* 31 (1951), pp. 293–329.

LORENZO PERRONE
*Università di Bologna, Italy*

# ORIGEN'S *RENAISSANCE* IN THE TWENTIETH CENTURY AND THE RECOVERY OF HIS LITERARY HERITAGE: NEW FINDS AND PHILOLOGICAL ADVANCEMENT

*The Century of Origen's Renaissance: Novel Access to his Writings*

It is true that since the beginnings of the modern age, starting with the first editions of the *Opera Omnia* by Jacques Merlin (1512) and Erasmus of Rotterdam (1536), Origen and his writings were never out of sight of academics.[1] Yet perhaps no other century has devoted so much attention to the Alexandrian as the past one. It is not exaggeration to speak of the twentieth century as a "renaissance" of Origen, unparalleled by previous studies and his longstanding reception in so many different periods of history.[2] Even before a new interest for the Church Fathers arose in France between the two World Wars with the so-called *ressourcement*, a movement of a "return to the sources" inspired by the influential Roman Catholic theologians Henri de Lubac and

---

[1] G. Lettieri, "Origenismo (in Occidente, secc. VII–XVIII)", in *Origene. Dizionario: la cultura, il pensiero, le opere*, ed. by A. Monaci Castagno (Rome: Città Nuova, 2000), pp. 309–21; A. Fürst, "Klassiker und Ketzer: Origenes im Spiegel der Überlieferung seiner Werke", in Id., *Von Origenes und Hieronymus zu Augustinus. Studien zur antiken Theologiegeschichte* (Berlin-New York: De Gruyter, 2011), pp. 209–36. The abbreviations of Origen's writings are given according to: *Origenes Werke*, 13. Bd.: *Die neuen Psalmenhomilien. Eine kritische Edition des* Codex Monacensis Graecus 314, ed. by L. Perrone with M. Molin Pradel, E. Prinzivalli, and A. Cacciari, GCS. NF 19 (Berlin: De Gruyter, 2015), pp. 64–69.

[2] M. Alexandre, "La redécouverte d'Origène au XXe siècle", in *Les Pères de l'Église dans le monde d'aujourd'hui*, ed. by C. Badilita and Ch. Kannengiesser (Paris-Bucuresti: Beauchesne-Curtea Veche Publishing, 2006), pp. 51–93.

Jean Daniélou,[3] in Germany, Adolf von Harnack, together with other prominent Protestant scholars, launched the "Griechische Christliche Schriftsteller der ersten drei Jahrhunderte" (GCS) at the Berlin Academy of Sciences, a series devoted to new critical editions of the Greek authors of early Christianity until Eusebius of Caesarea. In this program, the Alexandrian occupied an important place from the start, as shown by the publication in 1899 of the first two volumes of the "Origenes-Werke", including the *Exhortation to Martyrdom*, the *Against Celsus* and the *Treatise on Prayer*.[4] In spite of the criticisms that especially the *Against Celsus* raised of its editor Paul Koetschau, these volumes marked the commencement of a successful recovery of Origen's literary heritage.[5] It would subsequently inspire further enterprises of a similar nature, be they of greater or lesser extent, above all the "Sources Chrétiennes", which is now the largest and best known series of Patristic texts worldwide.[6]

The fact that the GCS project opened the edition of Origen with the three works just mentioned is in a sense revealing. Among the extant writings of the Alexandrian, the *Exhortation to Martyrdom*, the *Treatise on Prayer (Orat)*, and the *Against Celsus*

---

[3] M. Fédou, "Le Cardinal Henri de Lubac: Méditation sur les Pères", in *Les Pères de l'Église aux sources de l'Europe*, ed. by D. Gonnet and M. Stavrou (Paris: Les Éditions du Cerf, 2014), pp. 37–56; M. Alexandre, "Le Père Daniélou: la construction d'une 'cohérence intérieure'. Mystère de l'histoire et incarnations du christianisme", in *Les Pères de l'Église aux sources de l'Europe*, ed. by D. Gonnet and M. Stavrou, pp. 57–102.

[4] Ch. Markschies, *Origenes und sein Erbe. Gesammelte Studien* (Berlin-New York: Walter de Gruyter, 2007), pp. 239–49 ("Origenes in Berlin. Schicksalswege eines Editionsunternehmens"), 251–66 ("Die Origenes-Editionen der Berliner Akademie. Geschichte und Gegenwart. Anhang: Liste der Origenes-Editionen in den GCS").

[5] Ch. Markschies, "The Reception and Transformation of Origen's Works in Modern Editions: Some Comparative Views on Editions in Britain, France, Italy, and Germany", in *Origeniana Undecima. Origen and Origenism in the History of Western Thought*, Papers of the 11th International Origen Congress, ed. by A.-C. Jacobsen (Leuven: Peeters, 2016), pp. 165–89.

[6] J.-N. Guinot, "Éditer et traduire les écrits des Pères dans 'Sources Chrétiennes': regard sur soixante-dix ans d'activité éditoriale", in *Patristic Studies in the Twenty-First Century*. Proceedings of an international conference to mark the 50th anniversary of the International Association of Patristic Studies, ed. by B. Bitton-Ashkelony, Th. de Bruyn, and C. Harrison (Turnhout: Brepols, 2015), pp. 221–46. At present the collection comprises more than 40 volumes with Origen's works.

(*CC*) are the only ones that have been integrally, or at least almost completely, preserved in their original language. The text of *Orat* presents only some *lacunae* in the initial section of the unique manuscript transmitting the treatise,[7] while the indirect tradition of the *CC* in the *Philocalia*, an anthology going back to the fourth century,[8] displays in addition to its selection of passages from the apology just a short piece not attested to in the direct tradition.[9] These three happy cases of preservation should make us aware of the largely unhappy history of the manuscript tradition of Origen's works in Greek and, although to a far lesser extent, also in Latin. This is a chapter that has not yet been fully written in the studies on the Alexandrian, apart from the preparatory works for the editions or the introductions accompanying the publication of the single works, also because we simply know too little about the whole story.[10]

We assume that the transmission of Origen's writings must essentially go back to the library and the *scriptorium* of Caesarea and that it depended upon the care that its librarians, first and foremost Pamphilus and Eusebius, assured for their finding and preservation. After all, we possess relatively good information about the first Christian library that allows us to reconstruct its stock, insofar as Eusebius exploited it in his works, especially in the *Ecclesiastical History*, often providing lists with the titles of books and excerpts from them.[11] But something had already gotten lost

---

[7] See especially *Orat* I; II,1.4; III,1.4: *Origenes Werke*, 2. Bd.: *Buch V–VIII Gegen Celsus, Die Schrift vom Gebet*, hg. v. Paul Koetschau, GCS 3 (Lipsia: Hinrichs, 1899), pp. 298–99, 302, 304, 306).

[8] É. Junod, "Questions au sujet de l'anthologie origénienne transmise sous le nom de 'Philocalie'", in *Lire en extraits. Lecture et production des textes de l'Antiquité à la fin du Moyen Âge*, ed. by S. Morlet (Paris: Presses de l'Université Paris-Sorbonne, 2015), pp. 149–66.

[9] *Phil* 15, 19: *Origène. Philocalie, 1–20: Sur les Écritures* et *La Lettre à Africanus sur l'histoire de Suzanne*, Intr. trad. et notes par M. Harl et N. De Lange, SCh 302 (Paris: Les Éditions du Cerf, 1983), pp. 437–38.

[10] See, for instance, W. A. Baehrens, *Überlieferung und Textgeschichte der lateinisch erhaltenen Origeneshomilien zum Alten Testament* (Lipsia: Hinrichs, 1916).

[11] A. Carriker, *The Library of Eusebius of Caesarea* (Leiden-Boston: Brill, 2003); A. Grafton and M. Williams, *Christianity and the Transformation of the Book. Origen, Eusebius, and the Library of Caesarea* (Cambridge/Ma.-London: The Belknap Press of Harvard University Press, 2006); Lorenzo Perrone, "Eine 'verschollene Bibliothek'? Das Schicksal frühchristlicher Schriften (2.-3. Jh.) –

at the beginning, as we see from the catalogue of Origen's writings. Eusebius appended it to the *Life of Pamphilus*, his teacher, who first tried to bring together the books of the Alexandrian as much he could. However, the list survives only in the Latin translation by Jerome in his *Ep.* 33 to Paula – an invaluable document, even if it is not complete. Jerome apparently got weary of transcribing the long series of titles and omitted two important writings, precisely the *CC* and *Orat*.[12] What is worse, some pieces no longer existed when Eusebius drew up the list of Pamphilus' collection, as we hear from Jerome with regard to Origen's commentaries on the psalms, for instance. Moreover, some that the Alexandrian himself occasionally mentions do not figure among the items recorded by Jerome.[13]

If we face these problems from the start, this means that Origen truly wrote too much to avoid the risk that parts of his huge literary production would get lost and dispersed.[14] As a consequence, the writings of the Alexandrian, because of their often exceptional dimensions, were submitted to a process of selection and short-cutting of which we observe several traces, primarily but not exclusively in the exegetical *catenae*. But such a process had already taken place earlier with the *Commentary on Matthew*, thus giving way to distinct compendious recensions.[15] The damage inflicted to the majority of the great exegetical commentaries was therefore not primarily the effect of the condemna-

---

am Beispiel des Irenäus von Lyon", *Zeitschrift für Kirchengeschichte*, 116 (2005), pp. 1–29; Id., "Eusèbe de Césarée face à l'essor de la littérature chrétienne au IIe siècle: Propos pour un commentaire du IVe livre de l'Histoire Ecclésiastique", *Zeitschrift für Antikes Christentum*, 11 (2007), pp. 311–33.

[12] P. Nautin, *Origène. Sa vie et son œuvre* (Paris: Beauchesne, 1977), pp. 227–41.

[13] Jerome, *Ep.* 34, 1. See M.-J. Rondeau, *Les commentaires patristiques du Psautier (IIIe-V[e] siècles)*. I: *Les travaux des Pères grecs et latins sur le Psautier. Recherches et bilan* (Rome: Pontificium Institutum Orientale, 1982), p. 51.

[14] L. Bossina, "Réduire Origène. Extraits, résumés, réélaborations d'un auteur qui a trop écrit", in *Lire en extraits. Lecture et production des textes de l'Antiquité à la fin du Moyen Âge*, ed. by Sébastien Morlet (Paris: Presses de l'Université Paris-Sorbonne, 2015), pp. 199–216. Fürst, "Klassiker und Ketzer: Origenes im Spiegel der Überlieferung seiner Werke",, p. 211 stresses instead the repercussions of the condemnation on the textual transmission in general.

[15] L. Bossina, "Le diverse redazioni del *Commento a Matteo* di Origene. Storia in due atti", in *Il Commento a Matteo di Origene. Atti del X Convegno di Studi del Gruppo Italiano di Ricerca su Origene e la Tradizione Alessandrina*, ed. by T. Piscitelli (Brescia: Morcelliana, 2011), pp. 27–97.

tion of Origen as a heretic in 553, though this obviously did not favour the circulation of his books. Surely, the dogmatic censure had a very negative impact on the textual transmission of the *Perì archôn*, usually regarded as the theological "masterpiece" of the Alexandrian and the most debated among his works. In fact, the text has reached us only in a controversial Latin translation by Rufinus, whereas thanks to the *Philocalia* we have in Greek only two large portions from the 3rd and the 4th books, on the doctrine of free will and biblical hermeneutics, respectively. Yet the *Commentary on John* and the *Commentary on Matthew*, whose imposing remains still impress us, must have suffered their heavy losses mainly because of their discouraging size in the eyes of copyists and later readers. This situation led Rufinus to abridge the *Commentary on Romans* and the *Commentary on the Canticle of Canticles* in his translation.

In the end, we owe the survival of the Greek Origen to unique manuscripts, the only exception being the *Commentary on Matthew*.[16] Our codices were supposedly all connected with Constantinople as the main centre of learning in Byzantine Christianity and became available to western scholars in the wake of Humanism and the Renaissance. However, not in every case was it a swift process, as is shown by the *editio princeps* of *Orat* that had to wait until 1686 to see the light, due to the wanderings of its manuscript throughout Europe from the early sixteenth century onwards.[17]

The same can be said of Origen's homilies. We cannot thank our two Latin translators, Rufinus and Jerome, enough for having saved for us a considerable amount of the gigantic homiletic corpus of the Alexandrian, even if the quality of their versions regularly demands to be checked. Until the seventeenth century, when the *Homilies on Jeremiah* were first edited (once again on the basis of a unique codex), no group of Origen's sermons was available in the original language, despite their popularity and their vast

---

[16] Fürst, "Klassiker und Ketzer: Origenes im Spiegel der Überlieferung seiner Werke", p. 219.

[17] L. Perrone, "Zur Edition vom 'Perì Euchês' des Origenes: Rückblick und Ausblick", in *Von Homer bis Landino. Beiträge zur Antike und Spätantike sowie zu deren Rezeptions- und Wirkungsgeschichte. Festgabe für Antonie Wlosok zum 80. Geburtstag*, ed. by B. R. Suchla (Berlin: Pro BUSINESS, 2011), pp. 269–318.

dissemination throughout the Middle Ages.[18] Even if the Latin tradition goes back to a period earlier than the Greek one at our disposal, as shown in particular by the textual transmission of the *Homilies on Genesis* or the *Perì archôn* (liable to be reconstructed so far back as the sixth and seventh centuries),[19] it is still a derivative one and the possible finding of the original texts in Greek cannot but invariably represent the dream of every scholar. Now, such a dream has come true twice in the span of less than a century, first in 1941 with the discovery of the Tura papyri and then in 2012 with that of the Munich codex.

## New Finds I:
## Tura (1941) – The Unexpected Origen "in Debate"

The accidental finding in August 1941 of a conspicuous stock of papyrus codices in Tura (near Cairo), with several texts from Origen and Didymus the Blind, was a "sensation" that had to wait until the end of the 2nd World War and even longer to be fully appreciated. The first report of these findings in an article actually appeared only five years later.[20] Yet it was the most important discovery of the last century with regard to the ecclesiastical literature of Alexandrian Christianity and preceded by just a few years the spectacular unearthing of the Nag Hammadi library. The joining of the two names Origen and Didymus, who with Evagrius

---

[18] Fürst, "Klassiker und Ketzer: Origenes im Spiegel der Überlieferung seiner Werke", p. 228.

[19] See the latest presentations in the editions respectively by Peter Habermehl and Samuel Fernández: *Origenes Werke*, 6. Bd.: *Homilien zum Hexateuch in Rufins Übersetzung*, Teil 1: *Die Homilien zu Genesis* (Homiliae in Genesim), ed. by P. Habermehl, GCS.NF 17 (Berlin: De Gruyter, 2012), pp. xii–xiii; *Orígenes. Sobre los principios*. Introducción, texto crítico, traducción y notas de S. Fernández (Madrid: Ciudad Nueva, 2015), pp. 52–63).

[20] O. Guéraud, "Note préliminaire sur les papyrus d'Origène découverts à Toura", *Revue d'Histoire des Religions*, 131 (1946), pp. 85–108; H.-Ch. Puech, "Les nouveaux écrits d'Origène et de Didyme découverts à Toura", *Revue d'Histoire et de Philosophie Religieuses*, 31 (1951), pp. 293–329; L. Doutreleau, "Que savons-nous aujourd'hui des papyrus de Toura?", *Recherches de Science Religieuse*, 43 (1955), pp. 161–93. See also B. Witte, *Die Schrift des Origenes "Über das Passa"*. Textausgabe und Kommentar (Altenberge: Oros Verlag, 1993), p. 13; and A. Cacciari, "From Tura to Munich. Seventy Years of Origenian Discoveries", in *Origeniana Undecima. Origen and Origenism in the History of Western Thought*, ed. by Jacobsen, pp. 191–200.

Ponticus were condemned at the Second Council of Constantinople (553), has led some to think that the papyri were put in the gallery of a stone quarry used during the times of the Pharaohs in the aftermath of their condemnation. For others, on the contrary, they were hidden there before the Arab invasion of Egypt in the first half of the seventh century. The dating of the papyri has oscillated between the first half of the sixth and the beginnings of the seventh century, though at present the first alternative seems to have gained more consensus. In light of a note written by the copyist at the end of the extracts from the *Commentary on Romans*, a connection with the unorthodox stigmatization of Origen cannot be excluded: "I attest that I always admire you as learned, but I never read you as an orthodox" (Μαρτύρομαι ὡς ἀεί σε θαυμάζω ὡς ἐλλόγιμον, οὐδέποτε δὲ ἀναγινώσκω ὡς ὀρθόδοξον).[21]

However, the assortment of texts selected from the works of the Alexandrian, presumably originating in the nearby Chalcedonian monastery of St Arsenius,[22] seems rather to emphasize his role as a "teacher of the Church", at least from the most unexpected and surprising one: the debates recorded in the so-called *Disputation with Heraclides*. Together with this previously unknown text of Origen, the codices include excerpts from the first two books of the *CC* as well as from the fifth and sixth books of the *Commentary on Romans* (on Rom. 3, 5–5, 7), which unexpectedly came to enrich the indirect tradition of these two works previously represented by the *Philocalia* or by fragments in the *catenae*. Furthermore, we find excerpts from the famous *Homily on the Witch of Endor* (on 1 Sam. 28), the only one preserved in Greek apart from the *Homilies on Jeremiah* and known in direct tradition once again through a unique manuscript. Finally, there is another text which was completely unknown before, a treatise *On Easter* (*Pas*) in two parts. In this way, the Tura papyri of Origen, in spite of the presumably casual nature of the stock,

---

[21] CRmG 4: *Le Commentaire d'Origène sur Rom. III. 5-V. 7, d'après les extraits du Papyrus n° 88748 du Musée du Caire et les Fragments de la Philocalie et du Vaticanus Gr. 762. Essai de reconstitution du texte et de la pensée des Tomes V et VI du Commentaire sur l'Épître aux Romains*, ed. by J. Scherer (Le Caire: Institut Français d'Archéologie Orientale, 1957), pp. 49 and 232 app. crit.

[22] Cacciari, "From Tura to Munich. Seventy Years of Origenian Discoveries", p. 193.

mirror several aspects of his literary activity by renewing the image of the Alexandrian as apologist (*CC*), as exegete (*CRm* and *Pas*), as preacher (*HReG*), and as a renowned theologian (*Dial*).

As hinted at before, the Tura papyri give evidence of the process of selection and short-cutting that the writings of Origen underwent in Antiquity. Nevertheless, their witness is not at all devoid of interest. On the contrary, these excerpts can be very useful when we compare them with the entire text, as is the case with *CC* and *HReG*, or with the Latin translation of *CRm* by Rufinus. As for the great apology, the Tura papyrus supports the textual choices made by Paul Koetschau in his edition of the *CC*. He mainly relied on the thirteenth century Vatican codex (**A**), from which all the other witnesses depend, against the fragmentary tradition preserved in the manuscripts of the *Philocalia*.[23] The new testimony, whose text is older than these and much closer to **A** (since it goes back to the same archetype), contributed to appeasing, if not to definitively concluding, a longlasting quarrel among classical philologists over Koetschau's editorial preferences. The papyrus helps not only to occasionally ameliorate the text of the main testimony, but also supports the corrections and additions made by a second copyist on **A**, on account of a better model at his disposal.[24] A new edition of the *CC* by Marcel Borret happily profited from the papyrus, but did not preclude another, more recently, by the efforts of Miroslav Marcovich, whose results however seem to demand some caution and further improvement.[25]

The expectations raised by the extracts from the *Commentary on Romans* were even greater, on account of the unique value

---

[23] See Koetschau's introduction to *CC*: *Origenes Werke*, 1. Bd.: *Die Schrift vom Martyrium. Buch I–IV Gegen Celsus*; 2. Bd.: *Buch V–VIII Gegen Celsus, Die Schrift vom Gebet*, ed. by Paul Koetschau, GCS 2–3 (Lipsia: Hinrichs, 1899), p. lxxi.

[24] After J. Scherer, *Extraits des Livres I et II du* Contre Celse *d'Origène*, d'après le Papyrus n° 88747 du Musée du Caire (Le Caire: Institut Français d'Archéologie Orientale, 1956), see now *Origène. Contre Celse*. Tome I (Livres I et II), ed. by M. Borret, SCh 132 (Paris: Les Éditions du Cerf, 1967), pp. 34–46.

[25] See *Origen. Contra Celsum*. Libri VIII, ed. by M. Marcovich (Leiden-Boston-Köln: Brill, 2001) and the critical remarks by J. Arnold, "Textkritisches zu Origenes' 'Contra Celsum'", *VigiliaeChristianae*, 64 (2010), pp. 54–73. The same author has meanwhile published an important book on Celsus' *True Discourse*: J. Arnold, *Der* Wahre Logos *des Kelsos. Eine Strukturanalyse*, JAC.E 39 (Münster: Aschendorff, 2016).

of such a large section from a work that is otherwise only accessible in Greek through minor fragments in the *Philocalia* or, though less reliably, through the *catenae*. Yet, on the one hand, Rufinus' translation derives from a reduction of the original commentary and, on the other hand, the excerpts themselves experienced a selection and abridgment.[26] This situation explains the lively debate that arose after Scherer's edition was published between those who contested the value of Rufinus' text (as did the editor himself) and those who defended it,[27] while evoking once more the impression of a textual transmission that was "compromised" quite early.

In contrast to that picture, the papyri of Tura enlarged the corpus of Origen's writings with two new works, the *Treatise on Easter* and *The Disputation with Heraclides*, both substantially enriching our portrait of the Alexandrian, especially thanks to the remarkable evidence of the latter. The *Treatise on Easter* has received less attention in scholarship, as the text, due to its lamentable state of preservation, was made available only in 1979,[28] almost thirty years after the discovery. The textual reconstruction was partially facilitated by the quotations from the first part of the treatise contained in the *Octateuch Catena* of Procopius of Gaza.[29] It is certainly an interesting document of Origen's exegesis and teaching activity in the ethnically and religiously mixed milieu of Caesarea, though its presumable background and finality still leaves many questions open. While the first part of the treatise, commenting upon Ex. 12, supports the Jewish etymology of "Easter" as "passage" (διάβασις) and rejects the connection with "passion" or "suffering" (πάσχω) generally assumed by Christian interpreters, the second deals with the distinction between the ancient Passover of the Jews and the sacrifice of Christ. Still, the

---

[26] Bossina, "Réduire Origène. Extraits, résumés, réélaborations d'un auteur qui a trop écrit", p. 210.

[27] See respectively *Le Commentaire d'Origène sur Rom. III. 5-V. 7*, p. 85, and H. Chadwick, "Rufinus and the Tura Papyrus of Origen's 'Commentary on Romans'", *Journal of Theological Studies*, 10 (1959), pp. 10–42.

[28] See *Origène. Sur la Pâque*. Traité inédit publié d'après un papyrus de Toura par O. Guéraud et P. Nautin (Paris: Beauchesne, 1979).

[29] For the echoes before and after the *editio princeps*, see Witte, *Die Schrift des Origenes "Über das Passa"*, pp. 9–10.

differences of content and style in the second part raise an issue of authenticity or secondary refashioning that is not yet completely out of place, in spite of the remarkable research done in recent years by Bernd Witte and Harald Buchinger.[30] Actually, it seems to be one of those cases in Origen where we face the problem of the composition of his writings through dictation and, at the same time, realize the idea of a chronological evolution in his thought.[31] If the second part does go back to the later period of his literary activity, i.e. after the *CC* and the *Commentary on Matthew*, then the newly discovered *Homilies on the Psalms*, to be dated likewise after these works, might perhaps supply a helpful term of comparison.

Finally, the *Disputation with Heraclides on the Father, the Son and the Soul*, for many the most unforeseen and the most rewarding of the finds of Tura, was also the first of the codices to be published. The title provides matter for discussion, since the Greek word διάλεκτος (usually meaning "language" in Origen) is often rendered as "dialogue" or "conversation", beginning already with the *editio princeps* by Jean Scherer in 1949.[32] It is a term that recalls the διαλέξεις of Origen, of which we hear both from Eusebius in the *Ecclesiastical History* and from the Alexandrian himself.[33] In different circumstances of his life he was involved in public "debates", both inside and outside the Church (for instance, with heretics like Candidus or with Jews in Caesarea). Yet, contrary to what was at the disposal of the bishop of Caesarea, who explicitly attests to the existence of a collection of διαλέξεις, before the Tura discovery there was no direct record of this activity. Due to his celebrity, Origen on occasion was invested with official respon-

---

[30] See respectively Witte, *Die Schrift des Origenes "Über das Passa"*, and H. Buchinger, *Pascha bei Origenes*, I–II (Innsbruck-Wien: Tyrolia Verlag, 2005).

[31] *Origene. Sulla Pasqua. Il papiro di Tura*, Introd., trad. e note di G. Sgherri (Milano: Edizioni Paoline, 1989), pp. 33–42; Id., "Pasqua", in *Origene. Dizionario: la cultura, il pensiero, le opere*, ed. Monaci Castagno, p. 342. Also Buchinger, *Pascha bei Origenes*, p. 319 supports the idea of a temporal distance between the two parts.

[32] See *Entretien d'Origène avec Héraclide et les évêques ses collègues sur le Père, le Fils et l'âme*, ed. by J. Scherer (Le Caire: Institut Français d'Archéologie Orientale, 1949) and also *Entretien d'Origène avec Héraclide*, Introduction, texte, traduction et notes de Jean Scherer, SCh 67 (Paris: Les Éditions du Cerf, 1960).

[33] For instance, in *CC* I,45.

sibility, as shown by his participation in a synod convened in Arabia to discuss the unorthodox tenets of Beryllus, the bishop of Bostra.[34]

The papyrus thus constitutes an extraordinary source for our picture of the Alexandrian, inasmuch as it presents Origen in debate and registers the ups and downs of the conversations and discussions that he engaged in with his partners who, like Heraclides, all seem to have been bishops. Perhaps it was because of such live-transcript that the *Disputation* survived, despite the fact that the doctrinal debates which occupy Origen reflect, so to say, a still archaic state of theology. Surely, this is not entirely the case at least for the "trinitarian" section of the *Disputation*, in which the Alexandrian by means of his maieutic questions gradually leads Heraclides to abandon his monarchian views and to recognize the distinction of the Son from the Father as a "second God". At any rate, Origen, resting on the liturgical practice of the Church, restates the doctrine of the Father as the adressee of prayer, in accordance with the ideas expressed in *Orat*. Furthermore, the other topics dealt with in the subsequent disputes openly mirror "backward problems" such as the controversial identification of the soul with the blood, on account of several biblical passages, or even the mortal condition of the soul at the moment of death. For other aspects, for instance the motif of the two men, the "outer" and the "inner" according to 2 Cor 4, 16, and the related doctrine of the spiritual senses, the *Disputation* fully betrays a more typical Origenian imprint.

Perhaps the multiplicity of the themes raised in the debates points to a conflated text that, upon closer literary analysis, demands to be more carefully distinguished as far as the profile of its single units is concerned. As was interestingly suggested recently by Marco Rizzi, we ought perhaps to recognize that the disputation with Heraclides is endowed with a different status – that is as an ἀνάκρισις, an authoritative and definitive "inquiry" –, when compared to the subsequent debates in which Origen answered the "questions" (προβλήματα) of his listeners more free-

---

[34] Eusebius, *HE* VI,33,3.

ly.[35] Even if we should reckon with an assemblage of records taken on different occasions, the *Disputation* opens up a unique window into the passionate personality of the Alexandrian as a teacher concerned with asserting his exegetical and theological program against the resistance manifested by a different approach to Christian beliefs, by far less spiritualizing than his own.

### New Finds II: Munich (2012) – A Preacher and Commentator of the Psalms in his Later Years

For more than seventy years there was no discovery of Origen texts comparable to Tura. Only some modest remains of papyri became now and again the object of studies,[36] such as the *Papyri Bononienses* with two exegetical pieces on the Gospels of Luke and Matthew attributed to the Alexandrian[37] or the *Papyrus Egerton* 2 (Inv. 3), containing a text that has not been identified with certainty but might belong to a lost book of the *Commentary on John*.[38] Hence the discovery in April 2012 of the Munich Codex with 29 *Homilies on the Psalms* was a most welcome surprise.[39] This time it did not happen by accident but as a result of that most thankless and beneficial exercise of philology, editing a catalogue of manuscripts. Marina Molin Pradel, while preparing a more precise description of the anonymous *Codex Monacensis Graecus* 314 than the one made two hundred years ago (1806) by Ignaz Hardt in his catalogue of the Greek codices of the Bayerische Staatsbibliothek, was at first able to identify Origen as the author

---

[35] M. Rizzi, "La seconda parte del 'Dialogo con Eraclide': l'anima è il sangue?", *Adamantius*, 21 (2015), pp. 269–83.

[36] K. McNamee, "Origen in the Papyri", *Classical Folia*, 27 (1973), pp. 28–53.

[37] R. Otranto, "Origene, Omelia XXXV sul Vangelo di Luca: P. Bon. 1+P. Haun. Inv. 319", in *E sì d'amici pieno. Omaggio di studiosi italiani a Guido Bastianini per il suo settantesimo compleanno*, ed. by A. Casanova, G. Messeri, and R. Pintaudi: 1 – Papirologia – Egittologia (Florence: Edizioni Gonnelli, 2016), pp. 17–24; Cacciari, "From Tura to Munich. Seventy Years of Origenian Discoveries", pp. 195–96. The one (on Lk. 12, 59) stems from the first section of *HLc* XXXV, while the other (on Mt. 24, 3–5) might go back to *CMt*.

[38] Cacciari, "From Tura to Munich. Seventy Years of Origenian Discoveries", pp. 196–98.

[39] The list includes the following homilies: *H15Ps* I–II; *H36Ps* I–IV; *H67Ps* I–II; *H73Ps* I–III; *H74Ps*; *H75Ps*; *H76Ps* I–IV; *H77Ps* I–IX; *H80Ps* I–II; *H81Ps*.

of four homilies on Psalm 36 thanks to the corresponding pieces in Rufinus' translation (= *H36PsL* I–IV).[40] She then extended the attribution to other homilies whose fragments are transmitted by the *catenae*.[41] Finally, I was happy to confirm her indications myself by recognizing the whole collection of sermons as a work of Origen.[42]

Since I have presented this exceptional discovery on so many occasions, here I will deal with it briefly mainly in order to show what contribution the new texts make to a better understanding of the Alexandrian. First of all, one should consider the substantial enrichment of the ensemble of sermons in Greek. In fact, the 29 homilies constitute the largest series in the original language and, by adding to them the five further homilies on Pss. 36–38 translated by Rufinus (*H36PsL* V; *H37PsL* I–II; *H38PsL* I–II), we reach more than a fourth of the *Homilies on the Psalms*, as recorded in Jerome's list (that is, 34 of 120 pieces).[43] Setting aside the chance to analyze the language and style of the preacher and to inspect them comparatively, in light of the *Homilies on Jeremiah* – to my eyes a very promising field for future research[44] –, such a remarkable group of sermons allows us to revisit one of the most important and fascinating chapters in Origen's interpretation of the Scriptures, the exegesis of the Psalter, a biblical book that not only accompanied the Alexandrian throughout his writings, as attested to by the abundance of quotations, but also led him to

---

[40] Cf. *H36–38PsL*.

[41] The *catenae* attest generally short excerpts as follows: *H36Ps* I–IV; *H67Ps* I–II; *H74Ps*; *H75Ps*; *H76Ps* I; *H76Ps* IV; *H77Ps* I–IX; *H80Ps* I–II; *H81Ps*.

[42] M. Molin Pradel, "Novità origeniane dalla Staatsbibliothek di Monaco di Baviera: il Cod. graec. 314", *Adamantius*, 18 (2012), pp. 16–40; L. Perrone, "Rediscovering Origen Today: First Impressions of the New Collection of Homilies on the Psalms in the Codex Monacensis Graecus 314", in *Studia Patristica*. Vol. LVI, Papers presented at the Seventeenth International Conference on Patristic Studies held in Oxford 2011, ed. by M. Vinzent, Volume 4: *Rediscovering Origen* (Leuven-Paris-Walpole/MA: Peeters, 2013), pp. 103–22. On the first echoes of the discovery see now M.-O. Boulnois, "Chronique d'une découverte et de ses retombées scientifiques: les nouvelles Homélies sur les Psaumes d'Origène", *Revue des Études Tardo-Antiques*, 5 (2015–2016), pp. 351–62.

[43] See the list in Nautin, *Origène. Sa vie et son œuvre*, pp. 249–50: 258.

[44] As preliminarily proved by C. Barilli, "La lingua delle nuove omelie sui Salmi: osservazioni introduttive", *Adamantius*, 20 (2014), pp. 226–37.

several literary enterprises of different scope and finality throughout the course of his life.

Origen explained the Psalms first of all in the form of commentaries (*tomoi*), initially in Alexandria and later on in Caesarea. Secondly, he commented on them both in his homilies and also by means of *scholia*, perhaps conceived as autonomous work or as a preparation for future commentaries.[45] Apart from the evidence provided by Jerome's catalogue with its impressive amount as far as the number of the *tomoi* and of the sermons, the exact contours of Origen's activity on the Psalms are still debated.[46] Our fragmentary knowledge of his comments on the Psalter was essentially restricted to the modest remains in the *Philocalia* or the *catenae*,[47] whereas at present we dispose of detailed explanations commenting on the texts of several Psalms verse by verse. Instead of relying mostly upon scraps of exegesis as before, often – as we already know – through reduction and adaptation, we can now follow Origen's interpretation in its entirety. As a further motive of interest, for me indeed the most important, the new homilies introduce us to the exegete at work, whereby the Alexandrian, even when preaching, does not spare himself or his audience at all. As a matter of fact, he exploits the different techniques he was acquainted with as a former grammarian, from repeated recourse to textual criticism and grammatical analysis to the use of rhetorical devices and the discussion of "problems".[48]

---

[45] F. X. Risch, "Zur lateinischen Rezeption der 'Scholia in Psalmos' von Origenes", in *Origeniana Undecima. Origen and Origenism in the History of Western Thought*, ed. by Jacobsen, pp. 279–80.

[46] See especially Nautin, *Origène. Sa vie et son œuvre*, pp. 261–92; Rondeau, *Les commentaires patristiques du Psautier (III*ᵉ*-V*ᵉ *siècles)*. I: *Les travaux des Pères grecs et latins sur le Psautier*, pp. 44–51; R. E. Heine, *Origen: Scholarship in the Service of the Church* (New York: Oxford UP, 2010), pp. 115–20; Id., "Restringing Origen's Broken Harp. Some Suggestions Concerning the Prologue to the Caesarean Commentary on the Psalms", in *The Harp of the Prophecy. Early Christian Interpretation of the Psalms*, ed. by B. E. Daley and P. R. Kolbet (Notre Dame/Indiana: Notre Dame UP, 2015), pp. 47–74; G. Dorival, *Les chaînes exégétiques grecques sur les Psaumes. Contribution à l'étude d'une forme littéraire*, Tome 5 (Leuven: Peeters, 2018), pp. 370–78.

[47] Only in a few cases we possess significant evidence as particularly with *CPs* 4 (= *Phil* 26) and *FrPs* 118.

[48] A. Cacciari, "Nuova luce sull'officina origeniana. I LXX e 'gli altri'", *Adamantius*, 20 (2014), pp. 217–25; L. Perrone, "The Find of the Munich Codex: A Collection of 29 Homilies on the Psalms", in *Origeniana Undecima. Origen*

Going beyond the literary and technical aspects of scriptural exegesis, the homilies help us to refine our picture of the Alexandrian, first and foremost, as a man of the Bible and "a teacher of the Church". Certainly, his polemical targets are once more the Gnostics and the Marcionites, as we knew before from elsewhere,[49] but Origen seems to be especially concerned with the Marcionites because of their doctrine of the world and its creator.[50] Perhaps as a reaction to them, more than in his other writings here he appears to be sensitive to the beauty of the world created by God. Even if he feels obliged to criticize the Judaizing tendencies in his community of Caesarea with regard to ritual observances,[51] he does not conceal his satisfaction for what he confidently regards as the victory of orthodoxy over heresy. He indeed observes that the present situation of the Church has changed significantly when compared to what happened in his youth. At that time unorthodox teachers drew to their "schools" (διδασκαλεῖα) many who were yearning for a more mature knowledge of Christianity than the simple beliefs shared by most of the faithful.[52] These remarks carry with them the imprint of an autobiographical "confession" from a man who has already reached old age. He unquestionably identifies himself with one of those teachers who between the second and third centuries assured in his eyes the success of the "Great Church".

The Munich homilies offer further clues for tracing a chronological framework and assigning it to the last period in the literary activity of the Alexandrian. On the one hand, he avows to have changed his mind on a characteristic point of his teaching, the doctrine of the "angels of the nations" (based on Dt. 32, 8–9)

---

*and Origenism in the History of Western Thought*, ed. by Jacobsen, pp. 201–33. For example, see the treatment of the imperative mood in *H67Ps* I,2 (p. 175,1–18) or the advocacy of the method of *quaestiones et responsiones* for the study of the Bible in *H77Ps* I,6 (pp. 362,17–363,13). A remarkable display of rhetorics can be found in *H76Ps* II,1 (pp. 313,1–315,15).

[49] A. Le Boulluec, "La polémique contre les hérésies dans les 'Homélies sur les Psaumes' d'Origène (Codex Monacensis Graecus 314)", *Adamantius*, 20 (2014), pp. 256–74. Among the many passages, see *H77Ps* I,1 (pp. 352,14–353,22).

[50] See in particular *H76Ps* I, III–IV.

[51] A. Fürst, "Judentum, Judenchristentum und Antijudaismus in den neu entdeckten Psalmenhomilien des Origenes", *Adamantius*, 20 (2014), pp. 275–86. He mentions the Ebionites in *H76Ps* II,1 (pp. 313,16–17; 314,2).

[52] *H77Ps* II,4 (pp. 371,15–372,6).

and the establishment of the "elect people". According to his new opinion, it should no longer be dated to the time of the tower of Babel and the confusion of tongues but rather in relation to Israel's exodus from Egypt.[53] Such a correction is really surprising, inasmuch as the Alexandrian regularly exposes the former view until the *CC*, the last of his great works together with the *Commentary on Matthew* (both written around 248–49).[54] On the other hand, Origen once reminds his audience of his *Commentary on Hoseah*.[55] According to Eusebius, this was among his writings composed at the end, so that we may regard the *Homilies on the Psalm* (or at least the nine sermons on Ps. 77) as the ultimate witness of Origen's activity as preacher and writer.

Finally, the new sermons, in addition to completely overthrowing the chronology once suggested by Nautin (for whom the *Homilies on the Psalms* were the first to be preached by Origen),[56] enable us for the first time to develop a synoptic examination of the Latin translation by Rufinus and of the original text, or at least of four homilies. Since for a great part of Origen's *corpus*, first and foremost the homilies, we depend on translated texts, it is easy to understand how this unique opportunity proves to be delicate and important.[57] Now the synopsis tends to confirm Rufinus' substantial fidelity to the Greek text, although he occasionally feels free to intervene in order to adapt it to his Roman audience and facilitate its understanding. A more precise elucidation of the criteria followed by the translator will be of great help so as to adequately evaluate the other Latin texts available in Rufinus' versions without their Greek original.

---

[53] *H77Ps* VIII,1 (pp. 449,1–451,2).

[54] P. W. Martens, "'On the Confusion of Tongues' and Origen's Allegory of the Dispersion of Nations", *The Studia Philonica Annual*, 24 (2012), pp. 107–27.

[55] See *H77Ps* IX,6 (475,15–17) and Eusebius, *HE* VI,36,2 (p. 590,18–22 Schwartz).

[56] A. Monaci Castagno, "Contesto liturgico e cronologia della predicazione origeniana alla luce delle nuove Omelie sui Salmi", *Adamantius*, 20 (2014), pp. 238–54; L. Perrone, "The Dating of the New Homilies on the Psalms in the Munich Codex: The Ultimate Origen?", *Proche-Orient Chrétien*, 67 (2017), pp. 243–51.

[57] E. Prinzivalli, "A Fresh Look at Rufinus as a Translator", in *Origeniana Undecima. Origen and Origenism in the History of Western Thought*, ed. by Jacobsen, pp. 247–75.

## The Progress of Philology: A Field Waiting for Further Research

I conclude with a brief note on a phenomenon definitely less striking than the exceptional discoveries of texts mentioned so far, but very promising and fruitful in several aspects – the hard philology work quietly going on in the broad field of Origen studies aimed at further recovery of his texts. Unfortunately, there have been some obstacles for the project of a new edition of the *Hexapla*,[58] although the steady progress of research into the Septuagint will undoubtedly create more favourable conditions for this meritorious undertaking, much needed nowadays, almost a century and a half after Field's momentous publication.[59] To fully appreciate the quality and extent of the work done by the Alexandrian on the Bible we should also be able to go through his immense editorial enterprise.[60] Although we must deal with fragmentary evidence of the *Hexapla*, it is nevertheless possible to cast new light on it and to catch some glimpses of Origen at work.[61] In any case, the partial exploitation of the Syro-hexaplaric materials leads one to hopefully expect a significant advancement of our knowledge in the future.[62]

A more precise and encouraging picture emerges from another scenario of Origen's studies. The arduous investigation conducted on the exegetical *catenae* has never ceased, even if perhaps the interest for this genre of philological application seems to be less

---

[58] *Origen's Hexapla and Fragments.* Papers Presented at the Rich Seminar on the Hexapla, Oxford Centre for Hebrew and Jewish Studies, 25th-3rd August 1994, ed. by A. Salvesen (Tübingen: Mohr Siebeck, 1998).

[59] *Origenis Hexaplorum quae supersunt*, ed. Frederick Field, I–II (Oxford: Clarendon Press, 1875).

[60] Grafton and Williams, *Christianity and the Transformation of the Book. Origen, Eusebius, and the Library of Caesarea*, pp. 86–132.

[61] O. Munnich, "Un dossier d'Origène: Les notes marginales de la Syro-Hexaplaire de Daniel", in *Lire en extraits. Lecture et production des textes de l'Antiquité à la fin du Moyen Âge*, ed. by Morlet, pp. 167–98; F. Schironi, "P. Grenf. 1.5, Origen and the Scriptorium of Caesarea", *Bulletin of the American Society of Papyrologists*, 52 (2015), pp. 181–223.

[62] See, for instance, T. M. Law, *"Origenes Orientalis": The Preservation of Origen's Hexapla in the Syrohexapla of 3 Kingdoms* (Göttingen: Vandenhoeck & Ruprecht, 2011).

prominent than in the past.[63] However, in the last years we have seen the publication of important traces of Origen's exegesis, such as the edition of the Greek fragments on the *Canticle* by Maria Antonietta Barbàra,[64] as well as the preliminary work done by Karin Metzler for the excerpts on *Genesis* in the framework of her edition of the *Commentary on Genesis* by Procopius of Gaza.[65]

By far, the most rewarding investigation in the field of the *catenae* might prove to be that addressing the excerpts on the Psalter under the auspices of the Berlin Academy, also thanks to the discovery of the *Homilies on the Psalms*.[66] Beyond the few cases in which the indirect tradition can improve the text of the Munich manuscript,[67] the new sermons offer a precious term of comparison. Not only has Origen's *usus scribendi* now become a more suitable tool for inner criticism, but also his typical constellations of scriptural passages may provide a reliable criterion for assessing the authenticity of the excerpts in the name of the Alexandrian or that should eventually be assigned to him. The evidence of the *catenae* also enables us to retrace a path in the transmission of Origen's writings, as shown for instance by the fact that in the eleventh century Nicetas of Heraclea had access to a manuscript of the *Homilies on the Psalms* that was not anonymous and was

---

[63] Notwithstanding that, see now Dorival, *Les chaînes exégétiques grecques sur les Psaumes*, with the completion of his longstanding work (five volumes!) on the *catenae* of the Psalter.

[64] *Origene. Commentario al Cantico dei Cantici. Testi in lingua greca*, a cura di M. A. Barbàra, Biblioteca Patristica 42 (Bologna: Edizioni Dehoniane Bologna, 2005).

[65] *Prokop von Gaza. Eclogarum in libros historicos Veteris Testamenti epitome. Teil 1: Der Genesiskommentar*, hg. von K. Metzler, GCS.NF 22 (Berlin: De Gruyter, 2015) and K. Metzler, "Auf Spurensuche. Rekonstruktion von Origenes-Fragmenten aus der so genannten Oktateuchkatene des Prokop von Gaza", in *Quaerite faciem eius semper. Studien zu den geistesgeschichtlichen Beziehungen zwischen Antike und Christentum. Dankesgabe für Albrecht Dihle zum 85. Geburtstag aus dem Heidelberger "Kirchenväterkolloquium"*, ed. by A. Jördens, H. A. Gärtner, H. Görgemanns, and A. M. Ritter (Hamburg: Verlag Dr Kovač, 2008), pp. 214–28.

[66] See the newly edited introductory texts to the Psalter: *Die Prologtexte zu den Psalmen von Origenes und Eusebius*, hg. von C. Bandt, F. X. Risch u. B. Villani, TU 183 (Berlin: De Gruyter, 2019).

[67] C. Bandt, "The Reception of Origen's Homilies on Psalms in the Catenae", in *Origeniana Undecima. Origen and Origenism in the History of Western Thought*, ed. by Jacobsen, pp. 235–46.

preserved in the Patriarchal Library of Constantinople.[68] It is not yet clear what precisely is the relationship between the *Homilies* and the *Scholia*,[69] but the concise explanation provided by the latter, as soon as we shall have better access to them than in the edition of René Cadiou,[70] will probably show Origen's exegesis of the Psalter, so to say, *in nuce*, by drawing for us the profile of what was known to Jerome as the *Enchiridion*.[71]

Nicetas of Heraclea, in a sort of postface to his vast *catena* on the Psalms, wrote that he did not make much use of Origen and "rejected the most of him" (τὰ πολλὰ ἀπεδοκιμάσαμεν) because he was by far "more accurate than necessary" (περιεργότερος τοῦ δέοντος).[72] Ironically, Nicetas had recourse to the Alexandrian more than he was disposed to admit – further proof that Origen's literary and exegetical heritage is something more or less unavoidable and that now and again it resurfaces – to the joy of more open and interested readers who will never get enough of him.[73]

*Abstract*

The paper first discusses the transmission of Origen's writings and their modern editions, pointing to the preoblems raised by both processes. Secondly, it analyzes the discoveries of new texts of Origen from the papyrus found at Toura, near Cairo, in 1941 until the find of the Munich Codex Graecus 314 with the "Homilies on the Psalms". Finally, it briefly deals with the perspectives for future research, by stressing the necessity of advancing the studies of philological nature and opening in this way the path to new critical editions.

---

[68] *Ibid.*, p. 242.

[69] *Ibid.*, p. 244.

[70] R. Cadiou, *Commentaires inédits des Psaumes. Étude sur les textes d'Origène contenus dans le manuscrit* Vindobonensis 8 (Paris: Les Belles Lettres, 1936).

[71] Risch, "Zur lateinischen Rezeption der 'Scholia in Psalmos' von Origenes", in *Origeniana Undecima. Origen and Origenism in the History of Western Thought*, ed. by Jacobsen, p. 279.

[72] Bandt, "The Reception of Origen's Homilies on Psalms in the Catenae", in *Origeniana Undecima. Origen and Origenism in the History of Western Thought*, ed. by Jacobsen, p. 237.

[73] See also C. Stewart, "Psalms and prayer in Syriac monasticism: clues from Psalter prefaces and their Greek sources", in *Prayer and Worship in Eastern Christianities, 5th to 11th Centuries*, ed. by B. Bitton-Ashkelony and D. Krueger (New York: Routledge, 2016), pp. 44–62 for the promising hints with regard to the Syriac *catenae* on Psalms.

RUBÉN PERETÓ RIVAS
*Universidad Nacional de Cuyo – CONICET, Argentina*

# SELF-KNOWLEDGE AND DISPERSION IN THE ALEXANDRIAN TRADITION

One of the characteristics of the School of Alexandria and of its theological tradition was its *internationalism*. In fact, the most prestigious intellectuals from various regions of the Empire met there in the first centuries of the Christian era. Clement was from Athens and Evagrius came from the Pontus in Asia Minor, for example. This diversity was not reduced to the nationalities of the Alexandrian authors but reflected over the following centuries and spread even to such remote places as the Middle East or the Galia.

One of the spaces where the Alexandrian influence could be found is in Nestorian theology, which developed in Persia from the fifth century. Nestorius himself was of Alexandrian origin and though the School of Nisibis closely followed the Antiochean exegetic tradition, the presence of Alexandrian authors was also felt. This was the case of Joseph Hazzāyā, considered to be the father of Syriac mysticism. In the first part of this work, I propose to show conceptual elements that appear in this author and acknowledge a clear belonging to Alexandrian theological tradition. I will do so from a perspective that incorporates elements both from psychology and theology. The aim is to show the preference given in his texts to the necessity of self-knowledge and, consequently, to the dangers found in dispersion. In the second section, I will focus on the same concepts as are approached by Evagrius Ponticus, Hazzāyā's undisputed inspirer.

## Stages of Self-knowledge in Hazzāyā

It would seem that the knowledge of oneself is not only difficult to reach, but that it is a higher knowledge demanding a process that not everyone is able to follow. On many occasions, it is assimilated to the *full conscience*, or *mindfulness*, of oneself, or rather to the conscience not only of one's personal reality, but also of the outer world and of God. These three successive grips of conscience, three types of knowledge, are *standardized* in a process that recognizes three stages that have received different names throughout history.

One of the first authors to grant a name to these stages and characterize them was Evagrius Ponticus. He called them *practical*, *physical* and *theological*, and dedicated a book to each one. The first book consists of self-knowledge through government of the passions and culminates in *apátheia*; the second, of the knowledge of the physical world, finally reaching the contemplation of the second natures; and the third of the knowledge of the spiritual world, reaching the contemplation of the first natures. This is an ascending process in that the object of knowledge is higher each time, while at the same time it is a process of inner deepening, which instead of leading man to an egotistical, and probably even pathological, solipsism, *heals* him inasmuch as it reveals his own intimate truth and that of everything surrounding him.

In fact, this whole process is framed within a theological and ascetic plane. This is not some sort of *natural philosophy* or a *natural healing of the soul*. For Evagrius or Hazzāyā, the supernatural element is an essential component of the process. In other words, this self-knowledge is possible because what is reached is the knowledge of God. Or rather, it is God who, through his grace, makes it possible for man to go through the three stages of perfection or spiritual life.

Joseph Hazzāyā was one of Evagrius Ponticus' most distinguished disciples within Syriac limits. He is important because what we know of his work gives witness to the repercussion of Evagrian doctrine on the three stages of monastic life enjoyed by Syriac Christianity in the Middle East, which flourished most importantly during the Sassanid Empire and declined at length after the Muslim invasions.

What we know about Joseph Hazzāyā's life is only a few facts from the *Book of Chastity*.[1] He was born between 710 and 713, and at the age of seven was sold as a slave to a Christian in the region of Qardou. He was baptized and entered a monastery in the province of Erbil, the current capital of Kurdistan. He was a hermit all his life and the head of several monasteries in Eastern Christianity. He died toward the end of the eighth century.[2]

According to his contemporaries, his work was voluminous. In this paper, I will work with the *Letter on the Three Degrees of the Spiritual Life*, a text attributed for many years to Filoxeno of Mabbug until the works of Paul Harb and François Graffin restored them to its true author.[3] The influence of Evagrius Ponticus in Joseph Hazzāyā is evident. Throughout his voluminous work, Evagrius described with precision and sharpness the process by which the evil thoughts or *logismoi*, while distracting the monk's attention, obstruct the knowledge of God and thrust him into the fearful world of ignorance.[4]

The *Letter on the Three Degrees of the Spiritual Life* is actually a *treatise* about monastic life. It is divided into three parts dedicated to each of the stages of the spiritual life, although the space dedicated to each one is very unequal, especially the third stage which is very brief, possibly because at this stage experiences are ineffable and difficult to express with words. These three stages, the *somatic*, *psychic* and *pneumatic*, reflect the tripartite division of man (body, soul and spirit) according to Pauline tradition (I Tes. 5, 23).

---

[1] Cf. J.-B. Chabot, "Le livre de la chasteté, composé par Jésusdnah, évêque de Baçra", *Mélanges d'archéologie et d'histoire de l'École française de Rome* XVI (1896), 225–91.

[2] Cf. R. Beulay, *La Lumière sans forme: Introduction à l'étude de la mystique chrétienne syro-orientale* (Chevetogne: Editions de Chevetogne, 1987), 215.

[3] For the discussion on the authorship, see the *Introduction* of the critical edition: Joseph Hazzāyā, *Lettre sur les trois étapes de la vie monastique*, ed. by P. Harb & F. Graffin, Patrologia Orientalis t. 45, fasc. 2, nº 202 (Turnhout, Brepols, 1992), 266–69. Cf. the Spanish edition: Yauseph Hazzaya, *Las tres etapas de la vida espiritual. Seguida de Apuntes sobre la oración*, ed. by F. J. López Sáez (Salamanca: Sígueme, 2017).

[4] Cf. R. Peretó Rivas, "Conocimiento e ignorancia en Evagrio Póntico", *Cauriensia* 9 (2014), 75–93.

The first step that Hazzāyā mentions, and with which he initiates either monastic life or the process of conversion or self-knowledge, is that of *leaving the world*. It means distancing himself from everything that *distracts*, or rather, diverts from the object of perfection what he who has entered monastic life has planned.

When dealing with this first decision, Joseph Hazzāyā insistently repeats the term *motion or movement* (ܙܘܥܐ) which has a series of relevant connotations. In the first place, and most immediate of all, it deals with a process that is initiated by a voluntary act. This is a first sign that the beginning of the process is available to everyone because everyone is able to carry out a voluntary act that initiates the *movement* of his conversion. It is a decision or a preference – a positive act of the will – by which one chooses to "leave the world", equivalent to "returning to himself". *Leaving the world* is not *suffered* but *practiced*; there is no passion but rather an action begun by the same subject. And every human subject is capable of making this choice.

The movement that Joseph Hazzāyā speaks about may be approached from another point of view that places it among the constellation of Christian authors of the Alexandrian tradition. It is the same term (ܙܘܥܐ) that Evagrius uses to explain the fall of the *noes* or intelligences from the original Unity. Within the cosmology of these writers, two creations by God are accepted. In the first one the spiritual world was created – the intelligences – which remained united to God in permanent contemplation and, at a given moment, and due to a *movement*, drew away or fell from this unity, turning into angels, souls, or demons. This is where the second creation takes place, as an act of mercy from God, in which He creates the material world, and in it the body so that human souls may not continue to fall and have the possibility of returning to their original state. Evagrius mentions this *movement* engenderer of every evil in several chapters of his *Kephalaia gnostika*. For example, "the first movement of rational creatures is the separation of the intellect from the unity that is in it".[5] In every case he uses the same Syriac term (ܙܘܥܐ) that Hazzāyā uses.

---

[5] Evagrius of Pontus, *Kephalaia gnostica* III, 22, ed. by I. Ramelli (Atlanta: SBL Press, 1985), 107.

Origen also makes use of the word *movement* to explain the fall. Rufinus' translation of his *Peri archon* says "Recedendi autem causa in eo erit, si non recte et probabiliter dirigatur motus animorum. Voluntarios enim et liberos motus a se conditis mentibus creator indulsit".[6] The cause of the fall or "distancing" was a disoriented movement of the intelligences which instead of remaining continuously turned to the Creator, leant toward other ends, away from Unity. And, in this case, the coincidence does not happen only in the term used – *motus* according to the Latin text, probably translated from the Greek κίνησις or physical movement –, but also with the insistence that Origen gives to freedom. The intelligences were created free by God and they decided freely to draw away from Him. Voluntarily and due to negligence, according to Evagrius, or to satiety according to Origen, the rational beings preferred to stop tending toward God and to draw away from his sight.

It is a kind of specular reflex. Joseph Hazzāyā's text reflects, as in a mirror, that of Evagrius and Origen. In the same way as the *movement* was the occasion of the distancing of the intelligences from the contemplation of God and the beginning of their misfortune, Hazzāyā grants *movement* a contrary value and, in this case, is the occasion of redemption or, better still, of remaking freely that which had been freely badly made, that is, distancing from God.

I must also point out another aspect. Origen speaks of the cause of *distancing* (*recedo*) and refers to the distancing from God, or from original Unity, but this distancing of the intelligences from what most intimately constitutes them – to live in continuous and constant contemplation of the divine beauty – was also a distancing from themselves, or rather an estranging or alienating from themselves, since the aim of their creation was, precisely, the contemplation of the Divine Being. Therefore, the *leaving the world* of which Joseph Hazzāyā speaks *copies* the Origenist tale: the intelligences distanced themselves from the Unity and fell; in

---

[6] "But the cause of the withdrawal will lie in this, that the movements of their minds are not rightly and worthily directed. For the Creator granted to the minds created by him the power of free and voluntary movement, ...". Origen, *On First Principles* II, 9, 2, ed. by J. Cavadini (Notre Dame: Ave Maria Press, 2013), 162.

order to return they *must leave* or distance themselves from the world. In both cases it is the same concept.

In this case we can also adopt the image of the mirror: if the whole cosmic drama began with a *recedere* or distancing, the solution should start contrarily, that is to say by a *redere* or return, and the first step of this return is the return to oneself, to know oneself, to be conscience of one's own reality as a being alienated from the aim of his original existence and to freely wend his way back. If at the beginning it was an *exitus*, for Joseph Hazzāyā, leaving the world is a *reditus*.

But what are the conditions of possibility for this task? Is it possible for man to start on his way back? This is not an idle question since, in the history of Christianity, many opinions have arisen that consider the gravity of the stain originated by the distancing, or by that original fall, to be so deep as to render man unfit for even the least good work with which to commence his redemption. The human soul is completely vitiated and its salvation is only possible by an act of divine will. By himself, man can do nothing good or meritorious.

Joseph Hazzāyā does not argue the question in such a definite way, but both elements, freedom and grace, are present. He writes: "The first movements toward leaving the world are the natural seeds of good that were sown by God in us in the nature of the first creation. Because they germinate continuously in us until they find a will slightly leaning toward good, and then the occasion arises for the Angel of Providence to approach the soul".[7] There exist in man "seeds of good" that are natural. Or, it may be said that human nature was not wholly destroyed after the fall or original distancing; *seeds* or possibilities of regeneration were hidden in it. They belong to their own proper nature because they were placed by God at the very moment of creation. However, in the same way as every seed needs water and light to germinate, or conditions that will allow it to grow, the same happens to man. He might at most dispose himself toward good and this will be the occasion and possibility of help from God.

---

[7] Joseph Hazzāyā, *Lettre sur les trois étapes de la vie monastique* 6, 293.

## *Dispersion in Evagrius Ponticus*

Evagrius Ponticus speaks in several of his works about the *logismoi* or evil thoughts behind which demons hide, charged with troubling man so as to prevent him from reaching *apatheia*, in this way and as a last instance, salvation. He also mentions a lower demon that he calls δαίμων πλάνος or *vagabond demon*, which has the particular mission of distracting the monk and disposing him to the attacks of more dangerous and injurious demons.[8]

Beyond curiosity about demonology, which may appear picturesque or fanciful, what these authors are dealing with is the actual fact of *wandering*, be it physical or mental, and which ends by generating a series of reflections that impact the structure of the ascetic system and its psychology as well. In fact, Evagrius grants great relevance to the mindfulness of the present and the act of avoiding the dispersion produced by disorderly thoughts. This will be the initial and basic condition for any significant progression in the spiritual life and of psychic health as a consequence.

"Ἔστι δαίμων πλάνος λεγόμενος", "There is a demon called the Vagabond", says Evagrius. And it is a demon characterized by being a wanderer, roaming here and there, unable to remain stable in one place and occupied in permanent dispersion. Some years later, John Cassian writes in his *Conferences* that there exist some demons "qui Planos vulgus appellat" and which are characterized by being liars and comedians. They are found on the roads but they are not interested in tormenting the travellers they deceive, they only laugh at them and mock them and try to simply wear them out instead of harming them.[9]

However, in Evagrius, the characterization is different. In some ways it is more complex through two descriptions: one, brief and enigmatic, and the other lengthier and more detailed.

---

[8] Cf. Evagrius Ponticus, *On Thoughts* 9, in R. Sinkewicz, *Evagrius of Pontus. The Greek Ascetics Corpus* (Oxford: Oxford University Press, 2003), 159.

[9] Jean Cassian, *Conférences* VII, 32, ed. by E. Pichery, SC 42 (Paris: Cerf, 2008), 271–73.

## First Characterization

Evagrius writes that this demon "presents himself to the brothers especially about the time of dawn (ἠώς)".[10] This characteristic has to do with the time of day when the demon appears. Why dawn? This is the moment when the monk is waking up to start his *synaxis* or daily prayer; when he is not yet fully awake but has come out of deep sleep or dreaming. He finds himself in the state of drowsiness that usually precedes waking up. Guillaumont comments on this passage that Evagrius is referring to dreams that usually accompany paradox sleeping.[11]

In contemporary medicine, this phase of sleep is called REM (*Rapid Eye Movement*) and is one of two phases of sleep. During the night, a person has four or five periods of REM sleep, at first very brief but with longer periods towards the end of the night, constituting about 25% of the whole sleep period. It is common to wake up lightly at the end of each phase and it is this REM sleep which often precedes full awakening. What is most interesting in our case is that it is exactly at this phase when the most intense dreams occur, when the dreamed experiences are most vivid and real.

Science explain chemical phenomena that appear during REM sleep which are linked to neurotransmitters: a high percentage of acetylcholine and a very low presence of monoamines such as norephedrine, serotonin and histamine. But, beyond the phenomenal, there is no consensus as to the mechanism or functions of this phase of sleep. Hypotheses are multiplie and scientists are very cautious in their statements since there is no evidence yet to allow for definite conclusions.

Evagrius Ponticus suggests a hypothesis: REM sleep is produced by a *wandering demon*. It is he who provokes the monk's imagination and memory so that they may be peopled, or infected, by vivid images that may annoy him sufficiently during a state of vigil to prevent the prayer and concentration necessary for carrying out his duties. This demon is not only an errant and wan-

---

[10] Evagrius Ponticus, *On Thoughts* 9, 159.
[11] Cf. Evagre le Pontique, *Sur les pensées* 9, ed. by P. Géhin, C. Guillaumont and A. Guillaumont, SC 438 (Paris: Cerf, 1998), 181, n. 2.

derer but also an *early riser*, because it is in the early morning, just when the monk begins to awaken, that he launches his attack. But why does he do it? What is the motive of his onslaughts?

## Second Characterization

The provocation of annoyances during sleep is not the principal aim of the wandering demon. It is simply a strategy. It would seem that this is what Evagrius wanted to show when he opened this chapter with that oneiric reference. This demon's most important characteristic is the capacity to provoke in the monk's mind (*nous*) an incessant process of wandering: "...he leads the mind around from city to city, from village to village, and from house to house".[12] This is not about the monk actually leaving the desert and going to the city, but only of *wandering* within his mind. The monk's imagination wanders in distractions that are not necessarily sinful in themselves, although they finally do resort to sin, as we will see later.

This wandering process is gradual. It begins at first with casual and brief encounters, but later his conversations with those he meets in his daily life become slowly more prolonged and thus, slowly the monk begins distancing himself little by little from the knowledge of God and from virtue and forgets even his profession. These are the consequences provoked by the wandering demon's attacks. According to Evagrian thought, this is the gravest thing that may happen to a monk. On the one hand, the *science of God* is the ultimate aim toward which every man is ordained. The practical, gnostic and theological stages are straightened in order to reach divine knowledge. This is the way to inner transformation and realization of the ultimate end. Wandering causes a distancing from that aim toward which the monk's life is primarily directed, as well as that of every man's.

The second consequence is as grave as the first. It consists of *forgetfulness* (λήθη) of what one is: "he forgets even his own profession", as Evagrius writes referring to the *office* of being a monk. We have already seen on other occasions the cause of alienation from

---

[12] Evagrius Ponticus, *On Thoughts* 9, 159.

reality over which Evagrius so frequently insists.[13] To forget what one really is leads inexorably to a life lost in a world of fantasy, away from reality. And it is in that type of world, a *metareal* one, in which the demons will have greater power over the monk. This is also one of the effects provoked by the demon of *acedia*, seemingly related to the vagabond demon. In fact, Joseph Hazzāyā does indeed identify them, as we will see later.

We can therefore reach a first conclusion that the wandering demon is the *demon of alienation* or, in other words, that the wandering mind leads inexorably to a distancing from God and, worse still, to the forgetfulness of one's own reality and estrangement from oneself. This dissociation has consequences not only in the spiritual life but also affects man's psychical life, as we are faced with a breakdown that may become pathological.

Evagrius proposes attentiveness or attention to what is happening as a defense mechanism: "The anchorite must therefore *observe* this demon".[14] The author uses *teréo* (τηρέω), a word with military connotations, and with it has highlighted the function of *watching the enemy's movements*. That is to say that the monk must go over what movements and images the wandering demon proposes – "where he starts from and where he ends up" – which have finally caused the dispersion and evil thoughts. Because as the author expresses clearly, the demon does not follow this route at random but rather with a calculated plan, so that the monk will end up prey to the demon of fornication, of anger, or of sadness. These three may seriously ruin the splendor of his state.

For Evagrius then, the vagabond demon is a minor demon charged with obtaining victims for other greater demons. His work is to people or infect the monk's mind, for example through particularly vivid dreams that occur minutes before waking, so that through wandering or association of images, he may become the victim of attacks from other more dangerous demons – those of fornication, anger, and sadness that *ruin* (λῡμαίνομαι) the state of splendor of the *nous*.

---

[13] Cf. R. Peretó Rivas, "La acedia y Evagrio Póntico. Entre ángeles y demonios", in *Cappadocian Writers. The Second Half of the Fourth Century*, ed. by M. Vinzent, Studia Patristica 67 (Leuven: Peeters, 2013), 239–45.

[14] Evagrius Ponticus, *On Thoughts* 9, 159.

## Dispersion in Joseph Hazzāyā

In his *Letter on the Three Degrees of the Spiritual Life*, Hazzāyā speaks about the battles a monk will have to wage against the demons and introduces the wandering demon. Although assigning it a secondary role, he admits a repeated presence of this demon throughout the process of struggling against temptations. He states:

> The first combat the brother will wage in his cell will be against the demons of acedia and boredom, and when he has been vanquished by these two, they will deliver him into the hands of the other three demons that will lower him to the depths of the Sheol of ignorance. This is, in the first place, the *wandering demon* that makes the monk's thoughts wander from room to room, from monastery to monastery and from mountain to mountain.[15]

This first description quickly brings to mind the description Evagrius Ponticus makes of the demon of acedia in his *Praktikos*: "Then he compels the monk to look constantly towards the windows, to jump out of his cell, to watch the sun to see how far it is from the ninth hour, to look this way and that lest one of the brothers... He leads him on to a desire for other places..."[16] This association is introduced by the same Hazzāyā who writes, following the text just quoted: "This is the demon of whom blessed Evagrius says that he wanders around the soul from the third to the tenth hour, and that if the days of this combat were not abridged, no flesh could survive".[17]

This demon owns an auxiliary character or *facilitator* with respect to others since "when the wandering demon forces the monk's intellect to wander over all the places mentioned, he then delivers him to the demon of gluttony"[18] and then to the demon of fornication. Joseph Hazzāyā writes:

> To begin with, [the demon of fornication] in the middle of sleep approaches [the monk] and forms repugnant ghosts

---

[15] Joseph Hazzāyā, *Lettre sur les trois étapes de la vie monastique* 88, 363.
[16] Evagrius Ponticus, *The Monk: A Treatise on the Practical Life* 12, in R. Sinkewicz, *Evagrius of Pontus*, 99.
[17] Joseph Hazzāyā, *Lettre sur les trois étapes de la vie monastique* 88, 363.
[18] Joseph Hazzāyā, *Lettre sur les trois étapes de la vie monastique* 88, 363.

in front of him [...], to the extreme of soiling his body with the fluids that flow from it, caused by the great amount of humours in the body and caused by the weight of abundant food, and to the extreme of breaking the balance of the intellect because of the terrifying visions. Once [the monk] is awake [the demon] presents him with all the visions and repugnant ghosts that he had shown him in dreams [and the brother] remains all day long occupied with the idolatrous images that [the demon] represents in front of him.[19]

Several features in this description liken the wandering demon to what Evagrius writes about his intervention at the moment of dreaming, its intensity at the moment of waking and the annoyances it provokes throughout the entire day by the "idolatrous images" that remain in his memory.

Once the demon of lust has accomplished his task, the demon of anger takes his turn, which will make him "boil with fury, like fire, against his brothers at the monastery".[20] And when this has occurred, the wandering demon approaches again and drives the monk back over all the places shown to him before so that the monk may be filled with vainglory imagining how he will be praised in those places. He will then be delivered into the hands of the demons of anxiety and sadness and finally to the demon of despair.[21]

This brief account of demonology by Joseph Hazzāyā is characterized as being more descriptive and narrative than Evagrius Ponticus', while at the same time more superficial since it lacks the psychological angle found in the other. It characterizes the wandering demon as a figure whose role consists of dispersing the monk by driving his mind over different places so that he may be attacked by other more powerful demons. It is fundamentally the same idea that circulates in the Evagrian text.

## *Therapeutics*

In the same way as they differ about characterization, both authors also differ about the "remedies" they offer. While Hazzāyā dedi-

---

[19] Joseph Hazzāyā, *Lettre sur les trois étapes de la vie monastique* 89, 363.
[20] Joseph Hazzāyā, *Lettre sur les trois étapes de la vie monastique* 89, 365.
[21] Joseph Hazzāyā, *Lettre sur les trois étapes de la vie monastique* 90–91, 365.

cates himself exclusively to exposing the method of combating the demon of acedia, surely because it is followed by all the rest, Evagrius proposes special "therapies" against the wandering demon.

Contrary to what happens in other cases when the *greater* demons must be forcibly ejected even wrathfully as soon as they appear in the conscience, in the case of the wandering demon, he advises another strategy: to observe and not to frighten him; even more, to give him leeway for "another day or two, to bring his game to completion".[22] He warns that one must be careful in this process because this demon wants to go unnoticed and hides so as not to be discovered. This is, briefly, to adopt the hunter's attitude, observing his prey's movements in order to know what strategy will allow for chase with greater ease.

This will succeed, that is to say, the demon will be unmasked with "a word". The process of following the demon's strategy culminates when, once it is uncovered, the monk exposes it or brings it to light with a *word*. This is an element known in the Evagrian system: the power of the word to heal or, in this case, to uncover and thus rid oneself of a demon. The *Logos* acts like a ray of light that illumines the demon that lies hidden, thus neutralizing his strategy. Basically, it is the intelligibility of the situation that allows for escaping from it. It is only by thinking or reflecting or, better still, by knowing and considering it, that it is possible to identify the dark points to be illuminated.[23] This is a constant in the spirituality taught by Evagrius Ponticus, man will be able to reach his salvation, or return to the Unity from which he fell, by acting *kata physin*, that is to say, according to his spiritual nature. He is *nous* and only the action proper to the *nous* – intelligibility – will make his healing possible.

The wandering demon cannot bear the shame of being uncovered. This is why it is easy to know if the monk has said the right word because, in this case, the demon will escape and liberate the monk from his roaming.[24] It is therefore necessary to find the right word, the word that will effectively send the wandering

---

[22] Evagrius Ponticus, *On Thoughts* 9, 159.

[23] Cf. S. Vázquez, "El lógos como *phármakon*. Una introducción al estudio de la capacidad curativa de la palabra en Evagrio Póntico", *Rivista di Storia e Letteratura Religiosa* 53 (2017), 3-31.

[24] Cf. Evagrius Ponticus, *On Thoughts* 9, 159.

demon into flight. Even if Evagrius insists considerably on this aspect of the word, he gives no hint as to which word it should be or how it can be discovered. It does not seem to mean appealing to Biblical phrases, as in the case he presents in his *Antirrhétikos*, destined to reply to the eight *logismoi*.[25] It is rather a personal process of discovering the adequate *Logos*. With his memory, each monk must go over the process by which he was made a victim of the wandering demon, in order to find the adequate word, the one most appropriate to the situation.

Evagrius indicates the way to carry out this process of rememorizing: "Sit down and recall for yourself the things that happened to you".[26] Καθέζομαι is the verb he uses, which refers to the bodily posture that the monk adopted for most of the time spent in his cell: sitting on the floor, with his legs folded and his head leaning over or between his knees. In the *Life of Saint Pacome*, several instances of this manner of remaining in his cell are mentioned. For example, "Theodore remained sitting... with his head resting on his knees..." or "Theodore remained sitting... with his face leaning over his knees...".[27]

The same Greek word, καθέζομαι, is used in John's gospel when he describes that after the death of Lazarus, while Martha went out to meet Jesus, Mary "remained at home": Μαριὰμ δὲ ἐν τῷ οἴκῳ ἐκαθέζετο (Jn. 11, 20). It means, therefore, to remain sitting, but not as an expression of repose or light heartedness, rather of being in the right place, concentrated and turned toward oneself, trying to discover in one's own inner world the realities affecting one. In this case, it is the monk carrying out his monastic office.

Joseph Hazzāyā also proposed remedies, but remedies designed to vanquish the demon of acedia. Let us remember that, according to this author, this is the first temptation that assaults the monk, from which all the others are unleashed. "When this one is vanquished [the demon of acedia], so are easily all the others" he assures.[28] The strategy he plans consists of vanquishing this

---

[25] Cf. Evagrio Póntico, *Talking Back. Antirrhêtikos. A Monastic Handbook for Combating Demons*, ed. by D. Brakke (Collegeville: Liturgical Press, 2009).

[26] Cf. Evagrius Ponticus, *On Thoughts* 9, 159.

[27] *La Vie de saint Pachôme selon la tradition copte*, ed. by A. Veilleux, Spiritualité Orientale 38 (Bégrolles-en-Mauges: Bellefontaine, 1984), 139 and 169.

[28] Joseph Hazzāyā, *Lettre sur les trois étapes de la vie monastique* 95, 369.

principal temptation first. And the methods of doing so are two: psalmody and to remain in the cell without yielding to the temptation of abandoning it.

Psalmody consists of the repetition of a brief sacred text, going beyond a mere rational comprehension. The words of Psalm 41 (v. 6) are significant: "Quare tristis est anima mea, et quare conturbas me? Spera in Deo..." This constant repetition of versicles implies, in the monastic context, inner penetration and the need to repeat in order to reach longlasting presence in the heart. A ritual element also intervenes which ensures novelty and renewal, since it is not a boring and monotonous repetition but, rather, salutary, as Evagrius affirms, stressing the physical and bodily dimension of this exercise.[29]

As for the cell and the need to remain in it, we must understand the significance of that space in the monastic environment. The cell is not only the monk's place, it is more of a space with value as an environment of spiritual training and reflection necessary for the mental and physical discipline demanded by solitary life in the desert. The *Apophthegmata Patrum* relate the case of a monk who went to Abba Moses in search of advice, to which the old man replied simply that his cell would teach him all things. He should, therefore, remain in it no matter how strong the temptation to leave it could be.[30] This advice is repeated throughout the writings of the Egyptian Fathers of the Desert and also in the Syriac monasteries, as we see through Hazzāyā. The cell becomes the door to heaven through which one enters the kingdom of God.[31]

Apart from the contributions currently being made regarding the structure of monastic cells by archaeologists and recent exca-

---

[29] Cf. Evagrius Ponticus, *The Monk:...* 27, 102. See also L. Dysinger, "The Significance of Psalmody in the Mystical Theology of Evagrius of Pontus", in *Biblica et Apocrypha, Ascetica, Liturgica*, ed. by E. A. Livingstone, *Studia Patristica XXX* (Leuven: Peeters, 1997), 176–82; L. Dysinger, *Psalmody and Prayer in the Writings of Evagrius Ponticus* (Oxford: Oxford University Press, 2005).

[30] Cf. *Les apophtegmes des pères* 2, 19; ed. by J.-C. Guy, SC 387, (Paris: Cerf, 2013), 134.

[31] For this issue see D. L. Brooks Hedstrom, "The Geography of the Monastic Cell in Early Egyptian Monastic Literature", *Church History* 78/4 (2009), 756–91.

vations in Egyptian monasteries,[32] what is even more relevant for us is the testimony found in literary sources. And there the idea appears that the cell is where the monk combats the demons that push him to distraction and depression. These sources suggest that the physical aspect of the space had a spiritual meaning for the monks, since it is there that they exercised in order to perfect their hearts and minds.

Henri Lefebvre elaborates a distinction between *place* and *space* which is useful to keep in mind in this work. He considers space as a given "interval" in a determined place that is not empty. This *space* contains "things". It is the individuals that interact among themselves in a determined place that transform it into a *space*.[33] In this sense, the *monastic cell* would not be a *place* but a *space*. It is much more than a physical structure because ascetic practices are developed within its confines that endow it with a certain *performativity*. In this sense, the geography of monasticism is *transformative* since every individual creates a space that, in turn, transforms he who inhabits it.[34] It is the monk who *makes* the cell since he removes it from its undefined nature to transform it into space, but it is also the cell which makes the monk since it *transforms* him.

The words and rites developed by the monk in his cell have a performative character, which is to say, they *make* or *transform*. Over the last years, semiotic specialists have dedicated themselves to studying the performative capacity that words and rites possessed in Late Antiquity and the Middle Ages.[35] From this perspective, prayers and ritual gestures carried out by the monk in his cell led to an interiorization of it within his heart and mind. It was a process that, if it was faithful and persevering, led him to free himself in some way from the physical conditions of the cell and

---

[32] See the researching carried out by Samuel Rubenson and scholars of the University of Lund. See also the paper presented by M. G. Genghini: "'Go, sit in your cell and your cell will teach you everything'. How the Physical Enviroment Shaped the Spirituality of Early Egyptian Monasticism", at the 17th International Conference on Patristic Studies, Oxford, 10–14 de agosto de 2015.

[33] Cf. H. Lefebvre, *The Production of space*, trad. D. Nicholson-Smith (Oxford: Blackwell, 1991), 2.

[34] Cf. B. Hedstrom, "The Geography...", 762.

[35] See, for exemple, I. Rossier-Catach, *La parole efficace. Signe, rituel, sacré* (Paris: Seuil, 2004), and N. Bériou, J.-P. Boudet & I. Rosier-Catach, *Le pouvoir des mots au Moyen Âge* (Turnhout: Brepols, 2014).

to begin to inhabit the true cell hidden inside his heart. Thus, the physical cell was an image of the inner cell inhabited by God. This ambivalence of the cell, with an external aspect and an internal one, implied that the mandate given by Abba Moses to the young monk "Go and sit in your cell" implied deep consequences that go beyond the mere physical and bodily fact.[36]

Thus, the cell possessed a definite purpose for the monk and his positioning within it transformed him. However, the monk had to transcend the physical conditions of that impact and recognize that the cell was only the representation of a sacred space that nourished his inner self. This space could be made internal and turn into the inner cell. And, as Carruthers points out, the monk inhabiting both cells – the external and internal – could devote himself to μνήμη τοῦ Θεοῦ (*mnéme tou Theou*), the memory of God that exorcises the demon of acedia and heals.[37] This explains the insistence of Joseph Hazzāyā of remaining in his cell, as it is really about remaining in his own self; not abandoning and dispersing himself in a world leading to alienation but liberating himself from the dangerous demons of anger, fornication, and despair.

## *Conclusions*

An appropriate question that could trigger conclusions of this work might be the following: Up to what point can the *vagabond demon* of which Evagrius Ponticus and Joseph Hazzāyā speak be placed in the category of *demonology*? Or rather, would it be possible to place him in another category? And this question is apt because, in this case, the *antirrhesis* or reply which it proposes in order to drive away this evil spirit, consists simply of behaving *according to nature* or *according to reason*, or more exactly *according to the nous*, remaining in the inner cell of one's own heart.

Evagrius proposes no exorcisms, nor does he appeal to magic to frighten away his demons. He has recourse to the *Logos*, to the

---

[36] On the performative rites, see C. Bell, *Ritual: Perspectives and Dimensions* (Oxford: Oxford University Press, 2009), and G. Brown, "Theorizing ritual as performance: explorations of ritual indeterminacy", *Journal of Ritual Studies* 17/1 (2003), 3–18.

[37] Cf. M. Carruthers, *The Craft of Thought. Meditation, Rhetoric, and the Making of Images. 400–1200* (Cambridge: Cambridge University Press, 1998), 2.

*word*, which is the most complete and characteristic fruit of activity according to man's nature. It is not necessary to resort to external means or any sort of artifice. It is sufficient *to remain sitting* in the cell, turned toward oneself, analyzing the memory of self-experience to discover the enemy's ruses. If man is a fallen *nous*, his possibility of return or salvation consists of the development of his *noetic* activity, that is to say, *kata physin*, in accordance with his most proper nature.

If what provokes the mind's distraction and the monk's consequent dispersion is a wandering demon that presents distracting *thoughts*, Evagrius proposes eradicating them with another thought or word. This is a kind of special *homeopathy: similia similibus curantur*. From this point of view, the Evagrian recourse is maintained, at least at first, within the natural environment. There are no supernatural references. It is an activity that can be carried out exclusively through one's own and proper natural activity: the exercise of the *nous*.

This is the reason why we began the conclusion by asking ourselves about the demoniacal category of this evil spirit. In this case, it is very clear that without denying the character of concrete reality that Evagrius and Hazzāyā attribute to the demons, these also represent psychological recourses. This means that different psychological circumstances that may cause annoyances in life are presented by Evagrius as demons. This recourse opens a wide field of discussion as it would appear that thought is built up like an action by a thinking agent external to the person who thinks. This is the externalization of a process that contemporary psychology assumes is of the subject or of the subject's self. Evagrius, on the contrary, externalizes it, which therefore leads us to ask ourselves about the conception of the *self* or of the monastic self.

At this point I would like to broach a subject that goes beyond the limits of this work but that I would like to leave open to discussion. Richard Sennett stated in 1977 in his book *The Fall of Public Man* that the concept of individuality crystallized at the beginning of modern times. It did not exist previously.[38] Sennett confuses *individuality* with *individualism*, which may perhaps be

---

[38] Cf. R. Sennett, *The Fall of Public Man* (New York: W. W. Norton & Company, 1992).

the fruit of modernism. The individuality of the monk is not an individualism that rejects authority and accentuates self-assertion. On the contrary, the monk lives in a state of constant analysis of himself which leads him to compose his individuality. It is true that in the majority of cases, this meticulous and permanent examination has as its aim the detection of sin in order to eradicate it, which drives him to a sort of *suspicion* of his own inner self. Guy Stroumsa speaks of two synchronic movements: at the same time as the self widens and unifies through the idea of a man created in God's image, it breaks down in another way. The division is not now between soul and body but inside the same subject.[39] The Egyptian monks' demonology is probably the expression of Stroumsa's theory.

In fact, by resorting to a demon that they call *wandering* and carefully characterizing him, both authors are indicating what may be the central point for safeguarding the monk's psychological balance when spending his days in solitude: to live the mindfulness of himself in the present moment and avoid dispersion.

## *Abstract*

The aim of this paper is to analyse a particular aspect of Alexandrian and Syriac demonology based on the so-called δαίμων πλάνος (daimon planos) or wandering demons, which Evagrius Ponticus presents in his treatise *On Thoughts*. This demon's particular mission is to distract the monk from his own purpose and to dispose him to the attack of more dangerous and harmful demons. This figure was inaugurated by Evagrius and taken up again some centuries later by Syrian authors who developed and applied it in various ways in their spiritual works. In addition to the Evagrian text, I will focus on the work of one of his most renowned commentator: Joseph Hazzaya in the *Letter on the Three Stages of Monastic Life*. In this text it can be observed that the treatment of the very fact of wandering, whether physical or mental, causes in Hazzaya a series of reflections that impact on the structuring of their ascetic or spiritual systems, and on the reservations with

---

[39] Cf. G. Stroumsa, "'Caro salutis cardo': Shaping the Person in Early Christian Thought", *History of Religions* 30/1 (1990): 25–50; G. Stroumsa: *The End of Sacrifice: Religious Transformations in Late Antiquity* (Chicago: The University of Chicago Press, 2009). I thank I. Graiver (Tel Aviv University) for suggest to me these bibliographical references.

which they warn the monks about the importance of stability – which ultimately ends up in the *hesykhía* –, and the dangers of abandoning the cell. Therefore, in addition to the conclusions directly related to spiritual theology, this analysis also allows us to enter into considerations of a psychological nature, specifically, the importance and necessity of living the present with full awareness, avoiding the dispersion that is the product of disordered thinking.

# CHAPTER 3
# THE DISCOVERY OF THE NAG HAMMADI GNOSTIC LIBRARY: ITS IMPACT ON PATRISTIC STUDIES

MARIANO TROIANO
*Universidad Nacional de Cuyo, Argentina*

# BRIEF INTRODUCTION TO THE TOPIC

The finding of the Nag Hammadi texts in Upper Egypt in 1945, together with the Manuscripts of Qumran, constitutes one of the greatest discoveries of ancient texts of the Contemporary Age.[1] They have fundamentally changed the modern studies on the History of Judaism, the Origins of Christianity and Late Antique philosophy. In fact, the Nag Hammadi texts reveal a movement full of nuances and contradictions, eager to incorporate the most varied traditions that converged in the political unity proposed by the Roman Empire. The thirteen codices, with their more than fifty treatises, many of which were previously unknown to researchers, greatly increase the number of direct sources included in the three codices that had been studied up to this point (the Bruce Codex, the Askew Codex and the Codex of Berlin) and the testimonies transmitted by some heresiologists.

Since its discovery, the collection of Nag Hammadi has been surrounded by controversy and its history includes situations common to Hollywood productions. The narrative of such incredible adventure, described by James Robinson in 1979 in his *The Discovery of the Nag Hammadi Codices*,[2] and more extensively in two

---

[1] A. Piñero, "Prologo", in *Textos gnósticos. Biblioteca de Nag Hammadi I: Tratados filosóficos y cosmológicos*, ed. por Antonio Piñero et al., (Madrid: Trotta, 2001), pp. 9–10.

[2] J. Robinson, "The discovery of the Nag Hammadi codices", *Biblical Archaeology* vol. 42, (1979), pp. 206–24.

volumes in 2014,[3] has recently been challenged with articles written by Mark Goodacre and Nicola Denzey Lewis.[4]

Finally, these controversies also involve recent discoveries ranging from the widely publicized and polemical "Gospel of Judas" in 2006 to the controversial "affair" of the so-called "Gospel of Jesus' Wife" in 2012, in which the scientific prestige of Harvard University was called into question and which included discussion that involved renowned specialists. Although mainly concerning scholars, we cannot avoid the questions posed by Hugo Lundhaug and Lance Jenott in *The Monastic Origins of the Nag Hammadi Codices* (2015),[5] which raise doubts about the origin of the texts and delay their redaction.

And to the above we could add the numerous novels and films that have momentarily attracted the interest of the "masses" about these ancient codices.

One question arises then: Why does Gnosticism regularly manage to shake academic parsimony with new controversies? What secrets do its pages enclose that attract scholars from different fields of historical, psychological, philosophical and religious studies? We will propose a general, but no less genuine, answer concerning these Gnostic texts (as Einar Thomassen,[6] we have decided to use this category in the absence of a new one, which shall be at least as descriptive). These ancient authors suggest rational, philosophical and exegetically based answers to some of the essential questions that concern not only Second Temple and Rabbinic Judaism, the Fathers of the Church and the philosophers who inherit from the Platonic tradition, but also the apparently modern and hyper-connected women and men of our time.

The following chapter relies on the presence of two of the greatest specialists in the field. Professor Francisco García Bazán

---

[3] J. Robinson, *The Nag Hammadi Story (2 vols.). From the Discovery to the Publication*, (Leiden: Brill, 2014).

[4] M. Goodacre, "How reliable is the story of the Nag Hammadi discovery?", *Journal for the Study of the New Testament* 35/4 (2013), pp. 303–22 and N. Denzey Lewis & J. Blount, "Rethinking the origins of the Nag Hammadi Codices", *JBL* 133 n. 2 (2014), pp. 399–419.

[5] H. Lundhaug & Lance Jenott, *The Monastic Origins of the Nag Hammadi Codices*, (Tübingen: Mohr Siebeck, 2015).

[6] E. Thomassen, *The Coherence of "Gnosticism"*, (Berlin, Boston: De Gruyter, 2020).

will present his research that supports the coherence of "gnostic" thinking. He proposes "the task of ordering, enumerating and confronting this set of texts with other writings classified in their own Codices, which are also possessed in Coptic and other ancient languages and which are chronologically later" with the aim of establishing a *Corpus Gnosticum*. For his part, Professor David Brakke will introduce us to the world of the *Gospel of Judas*, leading us to "an understanding of the varieties of Christianity in the second and third centuries and of the questions that divided them". Finally, I hope that my intervention will demonstrate, through the joint analysis of *Pistis Sophia* and several Valentinian Nag Hammadi texts, the breadth of philosophical knowledge and the depth of the exegetical analysis that the Gnostic authors put into play in the creation of their "barbaric utterances".

FRANCISCO GARCÍA BAZÁN
*Conicet-Ancba-Fundtard, Argentina*

## *CORPUS GNOSTICUM.* NOTICIAS Y FUENTES SOBRE LOS GNÓSTICOS INCLUIDA LA BIBLIOTECA DE NAG HAMMADI Y OTROS HALLAZGOS ANTERIORES MENOS CONOCIDOS

Las primeras noticias que leemos en griego sobre los "gnósticos" son indirectas y remontan a Pablo de Tarso y las Epístolas Pastorales (desde mediados del siglo I d. C. a comienzos del siglo II). Las informaciones se amplían extraordinariamente, sin embargo, cuando aflora en el último cuarto del siglo II la impugnante corriente cristiana heresiológica (Ireneo de Lyón, Hegesipo, Hipólito de Roma, y la recapitulación histórica de estas noticias ofrecida posteriormente por Eusebio de Cesarea). No obstante todos los autores de este círculo y los escritos que han producido reconocen de hecho la preexistencia de los personajes que condenan a los que llaman "herejes" y de las escrituras que rechazan a las que similarmente denominan "escritos heréticos". Del material abordado extenso y variado, se ha conservado una apreciable cantidad de fuentes e incluso un conjunto de coherente aire de familia de más de cincuenta manuscritos catalogados en trece códices, la llamada Biblioteca de NagHammadi descubierta casualmente en 1945 y de azaroso trámite de edición hasta 1977. Tomando por base y punto de partida esta masa de fuentes conservadas en diversos dialectos del copto y traducidas en su totalidad al español en la última década del siglo XX,[1] se considera que es necesario emprender con urgencia la tarea de ordenación, enumeración y confrontación de este conjunto de textos con los otros escritos asimismo clasificados en sus propios códices, que se poseen también en copto y otras lenguas antiguas y que cronológicamente son

---

[1] Cfr. A. Piñero, F. García Bazán, J. Montserrat Torrents, *Textos gnósticos. Biblioteca de NagHammadi*, I–II-III, Ed. Trotta, Madrid, 1997, 1999, 2000.

posteriores (por ejemplo los libros contenidos en el *Papiro gnóstico de Berlín 8502*, *El libro del gran discurso iniciático* y la *Pistis Sophía*), hasta concluir el siglo V.

## *Gnosis arcaica*

Sobre el fondo histórico de la "diversidad una", o sea, teniendo en cuenta la pluralidad de orientaciones diversas que se registran entre los seguidores inmediatos de Jesús en Israel por el impacto de la experiencia histórica con el Cristo – la vida colectiva del cristianismo más arcaico –, se insinúan tres formas contemporáneas de grupos cristianos con distintas orientaciones religiosas: el grupo de los judeocristianos, el de los gnósticos y el de los protocatólicos. A estos últimos hay que agregar a Pablo de Tarso con cuya asimilación y escritos se fortalece la estructura del bloque protocatólico.

La *Epístola a los Gálatas* de Pablo, el fariseo convertido en el camino hacia Damasco en el año 32, redactada unos veinte años después, abre la posibilidad de investigar y confirmar esta diversidad triple mencionada de una comunidad plural y flexible de creyentes cristianos al escribir:

> Luego de allí [desde Damasco en torno al año 35], a tres años subí a Jerusalén [alrededor del año 38] para conocer a Cefas y permanecí quince días en su compañía. Y no vi a ningún otro apóstol, y sí a Santiago, el hermano del Señor.[2]
>
> Luego al cabo de catorce años (año 52), subí nuevamente a Jerusalén...Y reconociendo la gracia que me había sido concedida [la aparición del Cristo Resucitado en el camino hacia Damasco], Santiago, Cefas y Juan [un pariente y un representante de las dos parejas más antiguas de discípulos: Pedro (de la dupla de Pedro y Andrés) y Juan (del dúo integrado por Santiago de Zebedeo – ya fallecido por ajusticiamiento – y su hermano Juan], que eran considerados como columnas, nos tendieron la mano en señal de comunión a mí y a Bernabé [...] nosotros nos iríamos a los gentiles y ellos a los circuncisos.[3]

---

[2] Gál 1, 16–19.
[3] Gál 2, 1 y 9. Sobre la cronología cfr. O. Cullman, *Le Nouveau Testament*, P.U.F., París, 1966, pp. 55–57 y con mayor amplitud, S. Vidal, *Las Cartas originales de Pablo*, Trotta, Madrid, 1996, 71–117, esp. pp. 71–73.

El pasaje recordado es el relato que da sustento a la historia sagrada de la tradición católica nacida en el Asía Menor con centros en Antioquía de Siria y en Esmirna y con cabezas visibles en Evodio, Ignacio, Papías y Policarpo. El relato incluye dos elementos que crecerán con organización propia: **A**) un aspecto es la admisión de Santiago, el hermano del Señor, el líder de la comunidad judeocristiana, integrando la crónica más antigua del cristianismo, un grupo que continuará residiendo en Jerusalén. Ciudad que posteriormente con Elio Adriano en el año 132 será denominada *Aelia Capitolina* y **B**), el otro aspecto a registrar seguidamente es la confirmación histórica de la existencia de la gnosis, a la que Pablo se refiere explícitamente en el año 55 y a la que no sólo no parece adherir, sino también condenar, según las palabras de la *Primera Epístola a los Corintios*: "Os recuerdo, hermanos, la Buena Nueva que os prediqué, que habéis recibido y en la que permanecéis firmes y por la que seréis también salvos, si la guardáis tal como os la prediqué. Si no, habréis creído en vano. Porque os transmití, en primer lugar, lo que a mi vez recibí". Una enseñanza, por lo tanto, en la convicción paulina, tradicional; recibida y que se debe transmitir fielmente. Esto primero, es una posición formalmente legítima, pero lo que escribe a continuación referido al contenido del mensaje, ofrece mayor problema en cuanto a su justificación y, por eso, parte de los judeocristianos, seguidores de Santiago y de buena memoria respecto del "*homo inimicus*" – es decir, Saulo – que ha estado entre los perseguidores de la predicación de Jesús, no lo pueden admitir. Dicho de otro modo y según la interpretación judeocristiana: el contenido de las visiones extraordinarias de Pablo en el camino hacia Damasco no son confiables, pues ¿cómo es posible reconocer la identidad de una voz o figura personal que no se ha conocido con anterioridad?[4] Las tradiciones evangélicas más arcaicas no son anuladas por esta polémica de los judeocristianos contra Pablo que trataba de legitimar su función de Apóstol. Aunque estas dudas, por otra parte, podrían explicar la exuberancia de pruebas personales que Pablo aduce, insertándose en la tradición de las apariciones del Nazareno de la primera hora, válidas para

---

[4] Ver dentro de la tradición judeocristiana, *Les Reconnaissances du pseudo Clément. Roman chrétien des premiers siècles*, trad., intr. et notes par A. Schneider & L. Cirillo, Brepols, Turnhout, 1999, 70.1–8 (pp. 138–39).

las tres corrientes cristianas y que los gnósticos sabiamente llamen a Pablo "el Apóstol de la Resurrección" en sentido profundo, ya que como todo gnóstico es un resucitado antes de la muerte física, pues lo es por experiencia íntima de conocimiento. Dice Pablo, en consecuencia:

> Porque os trasmití, en primer lugar, lo que a mi vez recibí: que Cristo murió por nuestros pecados, según las Escrituras; que fue sepultado y que resucitó al tercer día, según las Escrituras; que se apareció a Cefas y luego a los Doce; después se apareció a más de quinientos hermanos a la vez, de los cuales todavía la mayor parte viven y otros murieron. Luego se apareció a Santiago, más tarde a todos los apóstoles. Y en último término se me apareció también a mí, como a un abortivo. Pues yo soy el último de los apóstoles, indigno del nombre de apóstol, por haber perseguido a la Iglesia de Dios... Ahora bien, si se predica que Cristo ha resucitado de entre los muertos ¿cómo andan diciendo algunos de entre vosotros que no hay resurrección de muertos. Si no hay resurrección de muertos, tampoco Cristo resucitó. Y si no resucitó Cristo, vana es nuestra predicación, vana también vuestra fe (1Cor 15, 1-9; 12-14).

Ahora bien, con estas palabras últimas el Pablo exotérico se ubicaba en una atmósfera de censuras anticipadas que años después se refuerzan paulatinamente en las Epístolas Pastorales. De este modo escribe la *I Epístola a Timoteo*: "Evita las palabrerías profanas y las objeciones del conocimiento de falso nombre (*tês seudónymou gnosis*), algunos que lo profesaban se han apartado de la fe" (6, 20). Este presunto error condenado, lo ratifica asimismo la *2Timoteo* refiriéndose a Himeneo y Fileto al afirmar que: "La resurrección ya ha tenido lugar". Y es que la cuestión de la resurrección de los muertos incluye dos acepciones controvertidas en la época en relación con el cuerpo terrestre o sin él y cuándo tiene lugar, y los gnósticos son claros al respecto habiendo optado por la primera interpretación, como lo dice el *Tratado sobre la resurrección* de la biblioteca de NagHammadi. Porque la resurrección es: "La revelación de lo que es y la transformación de las cosas y una transición hacia la novedad. Pues la incorruptibilidad desciende sobre la corrupción y la luz se vierte sobre la oscuridad, absorbiéndola".[5]

---

[5] TrRes 48.33-49.3. A. Piñero, J. Montserrat Torrents, F. García Bazán (eds), *Textos gnósticos. Biblioteca de Nag Hammadi III*, Trotta, Madrid, 2000,

Por eso el gnóstico es el que posee la gnosis y:

> De esta manera el que posee el conocimiento es de lo alto. Si es llamado escucha, responde y se vuelve hacia quien lo llama para ascender hacia él. Y sabe cómo se llama. Poseyendo el conocimiento hace la voluntad de quien le ha llamado, quiere complacerle y recibe el reposo. Su nombre propio aparece. Quien llegue a poseer el conocimiento de este modo sabe de dónde viene y adónde va. Sabe cómo una persona que habiendo estado embriagada ha salido de su embriaguez, ha vuelto a sí misma y ha corregido lo que les es propio.[6]

La gnosis es, como se dice vulgarmente, "un conocimiento que salva".

## *Verdadera gnosis*

Teniendo en cuenta al movimiento de la gnosis arcaica y tratando de desplazar su originalidad de conocimiento liberador o salvífico, han surgido dos tipos de críticas posteriores y condenatorias: la de la línea católica alejandrina, más compleja, y la de la tradición heresiológica episcopal antioqueno-romana, más simple. El enfoque alejandrino verificable en Clemente de Alejandría (150–220) incluye en alianza íntima a judeocristianos y católicos. Evita a la gnosis originaria condenándola, pero elabora al mismo tiempo respecto de la naturaleza de la experiencia religiosa cristiana distinguiéndolas, la fe y la gnosis. Considera la fe, en interpretación diversa a *Epístola a los hebreos* 11, 1, como un conocimiento imperfecto y la gnosis como el conocimiento profundo que cultivan y trasmiten los maestros. La gnosis verdadera, además, enfrenta a la gnosis arcaica, frente a su autenticidad, considerándola como falsa gnosis. Dicho con otras palabras. En términos históricos reconoce

---

p. 209). Ver al respecto, Outi Lehtipuu, *Debates over the Resurrection of the Dead*, Oxford University Press, 2015 y el resumen del prefacio en *Vigiliae Christianae* LXIX/5 (2015), p. 576. Sobre el pasaje de la Epístola extensamente explicado cfr. *First Corinthians. A New Translation with Introduction and Commentary* by Joseph A. Fitzmyer, S. J., The Anchor Yale Bible, Yale University Press, 2008, 539–52 y 557–63.

[6] Cfr. *Textos gnósticos. Biblioteca de Nag Hammadi* II, 22, 2-20 (p. 150) y ver con mayor amplitud, F. García Bazán, "Sobre el gnosticismo y los gnósticos. A cuarenta años del Congreso de Mesina", en *Gerión* 26/2 (2008), pp. 111–34, esp. 118–19.

el hecho de la gnosis arcaica como preexistente, pero asimismo como errónea y perversa que hay que reemplazarla por la verdadera gnosis y de esta caracterización participan tanto creyentes católicos como judeocristianos, sin discriminarlos. Por eso dicen las *Hypotyposeis* de Clemente: "Porque después de la Ascensión del Salvador Pedro, Santiago y Juan, aunque habían sido los predilectos del Salvador, no se adjudicaron este honor, sino que eligieron obispo de Jerusalén a Santiago el Justo" (VII, 10) y un poco más adelante: "El Señor, después de la resurrección, hizo entrega del conocimiento (*gnôsis*) a Santiago el Justo, a Juan y a Pedro, y éstos se lo trasmitieron a los demás apóstoles, y los demás apóstoles a los setenta, uno de los cuales era también Bernabé...".[7]

## Gnosis herética

Pero la gnosis como falso conocimiento, el contenido de la tradición católica de la heresiología que inicia Justino con el respaldo del episcopado romano (obispo Higinio 135–42) y que asume con oportunidad e intransigencia el obispo Ireneo de Lión, llega también a establecer un pacto con la heresiología jerosolimitana por el acuerdo de Hegesipo y culmina con Hipólito, Tertuliano, Epifanio y antes de éste Orígenes, aunque el erudito alejandrino sin apartarse de sus inquietudes especulativas.[8] Es la biblioteca

---

[7] VII, 13, ver M. Merino Rodríguez, *Clemente de Alejandría* (Fuentes Patrísticas 24), Ciudad Nueva, Madrid, 2010, p. 327, lo que ratifican las *Stromata*, cfr. J. Daniélou, "La tradition selon Clément d'Alexandrie", en J. Daniélou y otros, *Conferenze Patristiche II. Aspetti della Tradizione*, InstitutumPatristicum "Augustinianum", Roma, 1972, 5–18, esp. 7–10. Ver con mayor extensión: P.Th. Camelot, *Foi et Gnose. Introduction à l'étude de la connaissance mystique chez Clément d'Alexandrie*, Vrin, París, 1945; A. Méhat, *Étude sur les "Stromates" de Clément d'Alexandrie*, Éditions du Seuil, París, 1966; idem, "'Vraie' et 'Fausse' Gnose d'après Clement d'Alexandrie", en B. Layton (ed.), *The Rediscovery of Gnosticism I. The School of Valentinus*, Brill, Leiden, 1980, 426–33; Salvatore R. Lilla, *Clement of Alexandria. A Study in Christian Platonism and Gnosticism*, Oxford University Press, 1971; Alain Le Boulluec, *La notion d'hérésie dans la literature grecque II$^e$-III$^e$ siècles*, Études Augustiniennes, París 1985, II, 263–438; idem, *Alexandrie antique et chrétienne. Clément et Origène*, Institut d'Études Augustinienne, (édition établie par Carmelo Giuseppe Conticello), París, 2006, pp. 213–19, 255–74; Andrew C. Itter, *Esoteric Teaching in the Stromateis of Clement of Alexandria*, Brill, Leiden, 2009 y el extenso comentario de esta obra por S. Lilla en *Augustinianum* L/II (2010), 577–91.

[8] Cfr. F. García Bazán, *El papado y la historia de la Iglesia*, El Hilo de Ariadna, Buenos Aires 2014, pp. 49–52.

de NagHammadi al haber descubierto documentos directos de la corriente gnóstica auténtica, la que exige la elaboración de un nuevo enfoque y marco de investigación, históricamente válido y confirmatorio de la diversidad una del cristianismo de los primeros tiempos de la Iglesia.[9]

Al contrario, la condena de la gnosis que hemos llamado "gnosis arcaica", la propia e inconfundible de los gnósticos, también es explícita. El nacimiento y la formación progresiva de la heresiología desde el último tercio del siglo II explica este nuevo fenómeno cristiano, nacido en Jerusalén a mediados del siglo II, fortalecido en Roma y alimentado en Lión desde el año 175 con el apoyo del flamante obispo Ireneo de Lión. El nuevo enfoque niega rotundamente la diversidad una de la Iglesia primitiva tratando de seducir con su empuje a la Iglesia de Occidente basándose en la organización de la Iglesia romana que ya había descubierto el resorte de su efectividad (la afirmación, sostenimiento y difusión del cuidado o caridad para con los pobres – *agape*). Se pueden descubrir así históricamente dos conceptos de "herejía" que finalmente se simplifican y unifican. El primer concepto es el de los judeocristianos de Jerusalén, lo escribe Hegesipo en sus *Memorias* y lo registra Eusebio de Cesarea a continuación en su *Historia Eclesiástica*.

La comunidad de la Iglesia de Jerusalén tiene su carácter propio siendo la más próxima a Jesús, pues su base son los parientes directos del Galileo manteniéndose con una sucesión igualmente parental: su hermano primogénito Santiago, seguido por su primo hermano Simón hijo de Cleofás, y así va a seguir su posteridad. Pero cuando a la muerte de Santiago lo siguió legítimamente Simeón bar Clopás, hubo un rechazo frontal por parte de Tibutis, sacerdote probablemente del grupo de los convertidos, algunos quizás esenios, según cuentan los *Hechos de los apóstoles*.[10] Tibutis rechazó la elección del pariente directo e insistió en que la sucesión legítima le correspondía a él por su ministerio de sacerdote. Eusebio aclara que este fue el origen de las herejías, o sea, un cisma de carácter práctico justificado en un juicio sobre la sucesión legítima

---

[9] Cfr. F. García Bazán, *La Biblioteca gnóstica de NagHammadi y los orígenes cristianos*, El Hilo de Ariadna, Buenos Aires, 2013, capítulos IV y V.

[10] Hechos 6,7 y ver las explicaciones de. A. Fitzmyer, *Los Hechos de los Apóstoles* (Vol. 1), Sígueme, Salamanca, 2003, p. 479, n. 7.

y no en la interpretación de la enseñanza. Ireneo, sin embargo, y con él, antes y después, la sucesión de los heresiólogos principales: Justino, Tertuliano, Hipólito y Epifanio firmes en la línea de las epístolas católicas, como hemos visto, consideran que la "herejía" es una elección doctrinal de falso contenido.[11]

En resumen, se han afirmado tres tesis: 1º La gnosis arcaica surgida en los orígenes cristianos entre discípulos emparentados con Jesús: Santiago y Tomás. Pedro y Juan, apóstoles, así lo han reconocido; 2º Pablo de una generación posterior de discípulos, desde el comienzo es rechazado por la corriente judeocristiana, ha aceptado algunos elementos de la gnosis, y muchos del protocatolicismo. 3º El protocatolicismo ha rechazado a la gnosis auténtica y posteriormente a los judeocristianos. Gnósticos y cristianos alejandrinos han sido limitados por el protocatolicismo que elabora con sus sedimentos, la teología protocatólica, libre de elementos arcaicos dudosos.[12]

---

[11] Cfr. Ireneo, *Adversus haereses*, así como antes Justino, aunque sosteniendo asimismo el sentido gentil general del vocablo "escuela". Cfr. F. García Bazán, "Haíresis/secta en los primeros tiempos cristianos", en *Revista bíblica* (1977) I, pp. 29-35. La versión de los juaninos tiene asimismo sus características protocatólicas propias Ver 1 Jn 2, 18-29, que señala lamentándolo la ruptura de la comunidad de Juan primitiva. Cfr. R. E. Brown, "Cuando se escribieron las cartas", en *La comunidad del discípulo amado. Estudio de la eclesiología juánica*, Sígueme, Salamanca, 1983, pp. 89-136 y F. García Bazán, poniendo el acento en: "Salieron de entre nosotros; pero no eran de los nuestros. Si hubiesen sido de los nuestros, habrían permanecido con nosotros..." (1 Jn 2, 19), *Jesús el Nazareno y los primeros cristianos. Un enfoque desde la historia y la fenomenología de las religiones*, Lumen, Buenos Aires, 2006, cap. IX.

[12] La interpretación alejandrina ha sido la más influyente en la caracterización contemporánea del esoterismo judío y la Cábala (G. Scholem, *Les grands courants de la mystique juive*, Payot, París, 1960), aspectos del esoterismo islámico (M. Cruz Hernández, "Los precedentes gnósticos del 'Irfan'", *Anales del Seminario de Historia de la Filosofía* 17 (2000), 15-36) y del esoterismo cristiano (R. Guénon, *Aperçus sur l'ésotérisme chrétien*, Villain et Belhomme-ÉditionsTraditionnelles, París, 1969 y con sus lagunas, Jérôme Rousse-Lacordaire, *Ésotérisme et christianisme. Histoire et enjeux théologiques d'une expatriation*, Cerf, París, 2009). Cfr. Además, J. Daniélou, "Les traditions secrets des Apôtres", *Eranos-Jahrbuch* 31 (1962), 199-215; ídem, "La tradition selon Clément d'Alexandrie", en *Conferenza Patristiche II. Aspetti della tradizione*, Institutum Patristicum "Augustinianum", Roma, 1972, 5-18; A. Orbe, S. J., "Ideas sobre la tradición en la lucha antignóstica, ibídem, pp. 19-33; F. García Bazán, *Aspectos inusuales de lo sagrado*, Trotta, Madrid, 2000, pp. 103ss; ídem, *La gnosis eterna. Antología de textos gnósticos griegos, latinos y coptos I*, Trotta-Edicions de la Universitat de Barcelona, 2003; ídem, "Sobre el gnosticismo y los gnósticos. A cuarenta años del Congreso de Messina", en *Gerión* 26/2 (2008), 111-34;

## Escritos gnósticos directos

Un proyecto que aspire a proporcionar un cuadro lo más exhaustivo posible de documentos gnósticos directos, debería dividir los textos accesibles al investigador en tres estratos diversos:

1° Documentos gnósticos en griego y latín proporcionados por los heresiólogos y datables por su uso entre estos autores. En este cuadro podemos inventariar: *La Gran Revelación* de Simón el Mago,[13] los *fragmentos* de Basílides transmitidos por Hegemonio como *Actas de Arquelao y Mani* 67, 4-12; Clemente de Alejandría, *Stromata* IV, 81, 1 a 83, 1 y IV, 86, 1, y Orígenes, *Comentario a la Epístola a los Romanos* VI, 1: sobre su hijo y discípulo Isidoro y otros discípulos Clemente, *Stromata* II. VI y III.[14] Sobre Epífanes el hijo de Carpócrates, poseemos también un singular fragmento de su libro *Sobre la justicia*, conservado por Clemente de Alejandría.[15] En los *Hechos de Tomás*, en referencia al hermano y gemelo de Cristo, apóstol de Siria y la India, se presenta al integrante del grupo de los "doce" como discípulo, receptor y mediador de las revelaciones secretas de Jesús. La doctrina gnóstica se expresa en este caso por una composición poética, *El Himno de la Perla*.[16] En el círculo de los valentinianos, son varias las fuentes compiladas: nueve fragmentos directos de Valentín (seis por Clemente,

---

ídem, *La Biblioteca gnóstica de Nag Hammadi y los orígenes cristianos*, El Hilo de Ariadna, Buenos Aires, 2013; ídem, *El papado y la historia de la Iglesia*, El Hilo de Ariadna, Buenos Aires, 2014.

[13] Hipólito, *Elenchos* VI, 9–18 – F. García Bazán, *La gnosis eterna Antología de textos gnósticos griegos latinos y coptos I*, Trotta-Edicions de la Universitat de Barcelona, Madrid, 2003, pp. 49–56, y previamente las justificaciones de que "el conocimiento más genuino de la doctrina gnóstica simoniana lo aportan los únicos fragmentos directos de la llamada *Gran Revelación*, que Hipólito de Roma adquirió con otros libros gnósticos y que glosa externamente al irla copiando. Después de esta exposición parafrástica coloca su interpretación heresiológica y condenatoria al resumir lo que Justino de Roma e Ireneo de Lyon habían expresado – ibídem pp. 48–49. La *Revelación de la Gran Potencia* también se registra por su uso entre los gnósticos naasenos, p. 109. Ver asimismo el *Pensamiento de nuestro Gran Poder* NHC VI,4 (*Textos gnósticos de Nag Hammadi* III, 115–28). En este documento hay también una referencia a Judas en 41. 15–22.

[14] Cfr. *La gnosis eterna I*, pp. 139–44 y el comentario sobre el escrito el *Libro de Baruc* del gnóstico Justino, en F. García Bazán, *Gnosis la esencia del dualismo gnóstico*, Castañeda, 1978, pp. 120–24 y 291–97.

[15] *Stromata* III, 5,2–9,3: *La gnosis eterna I*, 149–51.

[16] Cfr. García Bazán, o. c., pp. 152–58.

dos por Hipólito y uno por Antimo).[17] Pero Epifanio de Salamina ha registrado en su *Panarion* una *Carta dogmática valentiniana* y una *Carta a Flora de Ptolomeo*.[18] A su vez el alejandrino Orígenes en su *Comentario al Evangelio de Juan* ha citado literalmente y examinado, cuarenta y ocho fragmentos del valentiniano Heracleón, y Clemente de Alejandría en las *Eclogae* y *Stromateis* otros dos fragmentos. Este material se amplía por el patriarca Focio en la *Epístola 134* con otro fragmento.[19] Igualmente el Alejandrino registra en polémica con otro maestro valentiniano unos *Extractos*

---

[17] Ver F. García Bazán, *La gnosis eterna I*, 160-63. Entre los años 177-80 el escritor medioplatónico Celso escribe su acerba diatriba contra los cristianos conocida como la *Doctrina verdadera (Alethéslógos)*. El amigo, mecenas y discípulo de Orígenes, Ambrosio, se la hace conocer a éste y le pide una réplica. Esta tarea la realiza el escritor alejandrino en el 238. Celso no separa a los gnósticos de los cristianos comunes y demuestra tener un conocimiento directo de la corriente de los gnósticos que trata, según son reflejados por Orígenes en el *Contra Celso V*, 61-65 y VI, 21-40. Mientras que en la primera parte afirma que estos cristianos creen en un Dios diferente al de los judíos y opuesto a él, de quien ha venido el Hijo, y que hay cristianos psíquicos y pneumáticos, otros aceptan a Jesús, pero quieren vivir según la Ley judía (judeocristianos). Ostentan estos creyentes asimismo una diversidad de subcorrientes que centran su identidad en una figura femenina: simonianos, marcelinianos, harpocratianos – discípulos de Salomé –, discípulos de Mariamme y otros de Marta, y también marcionitas, y dirigidos por un demon practican tenebrosas ceremonias como las tíasas de Egipto, amigos de la discordia y de un odio implacable, radicalmente separados y arrogantes, nada comprenden de las doctrinas que quisieran conocer. En la segunda parte habla Celso del esquema de los ofitas, que Orígenes ha tratado de rastrear, el platónico, según el escritor alejandrino, confunde con una ceremonia de iniciación mitraica, pero que se trata de un diseño cosmológico de diez esferas, las siete cósmicas – por las que asciende el alma – y las tres más altas de la ogdóada con las dos suprauránicas, seguido de un formulario ritual sobre los ritos de ascenso del alma y el espíritu. Se han podido seleccionar al menos ocho puntos principales de la descripción en relación con la noticia de los ofitas de Ireneo. Los paralelos con las figuras de animales de los arcontes se repiten en el *Apócrifo de Juan* y la *Pístis Sophía*, las analogías con los "misterios de la Luz" de la última obra citada y del *Libro del gran discurso iniciático* con sus formas rituales, sus sellos y sus marcas, están asimismo presentes, advirtiéndose también la denominación de "gnósticos" atribuida a estos creyentes y su difusión bajo formas diversas por Roma y Egipto, aunque conservando palabras y fórmulas de pasaje en lengua aramea. Todo esto insinúa que se trata de un grupo arcaico de gnósticos originariamente de la Siria aramaica, entre los que la ejecución reglada de los misterios iniciáticos son claramente indisociables de las doctrinas que asumen sus miembros, siempre en vínculo con estos rituales (ver F. García Bazán, *La Biblioteca gnóstica de Naga Hammadi*, pp. 62-63).

[18] Cfr. García Bazán, *La gnosis eterna I*, pp. 163-65 y 185-91, respectivamente.

[19] Cfr. García Bazán, *La gnosis eterna I*, 210-29.

*de las obras de Teodoto y de la escuela llamada oriental en el tiempo de Valentín.*[20]

2° En ampliación de estas noticias directas catalogadas, pero constituyendo una biblioteca independiente se pueden consultar los 53 manuscritos en papiro que contienen los 13 códices de la Biblioteca de NagHammadi, conocidos desde 1945 y editados y estudiados consecutivamente desde la década de 1950. Son traducciones del griego a diversos dialectos del copto, al sahídico, al bohaírico y al akhmímico y subakhmímico de la zona de Akhmían. Los códices están encuadernados en cuero de cabra y varios de ellos tienen apuntaladas las cubiertas con material en desuso, fragmentos de escritos, facturas de compra e inventarios de materiales en depósito, estos comprobantes están fechados lo que ha permitido inferir la data de la encuadernación de los códices y así conjeturar el lugar geográfico de origen. Las hojas de estos cuadernos escritos en copto han debido ser más antiguas que la manufacturación de su armado y encuadernación y asimismo siendo versiones del griego al copto los originales han debido ser anteriores, por eso hay un término de finalización del proceso de encuadernación, pero no una fecha para el origen, debiéndose investigar para cada escrito la posibilidad de su cronología particular. Los escritos probablemente más antiguos son: el *Evangelio de Tomás*, el *Evangelio de los Egipcios*, el *Libro secreto de Juan* – del que contamos con cuatro originales, tres en esta biblioteca y uno en el *Códice de Berlín 8502* –, el *Evangelio de la Verdad*. Los desafíos de fijación y catalogación de los códices son casi insuperables, y porque describir la tarea insumiría un largo rato,[21] a modo de ilustración

---

[20] Cfr. F. García Bazán, *La gnosis eterna I*, pp. 229–47. Sobre el nivel filosófico de estas composiciones cfr. Chr. Markshies, "Valentiniangnosticism: Toward the Anatomy of a School", en J. D. Turner & A. Mcguire, *The Nag Hammady Library after Fifty Years. Proceedings of the 1995 Society of Biblical Literature Commemoractión*, Brill, Leiden, M1997, 401–38. En este apartado no se debe omitir el apoyo de las obras de Tertuliano: *De praescriptione haereticorum* (E. Alcover, *Estudios Eclesiásticos* 75 (2000), 235–301), *Adversus valentinianos* (ed. y trad. A. Marastoni), Gregoriana Editrice, Padua 1971; *AdversusPraxean* (edición, trad. y comentarios de G. Scarpat, Loescher Ed., Torino, 1959.

[21] Cfr. F. García Bazán, "Las primeras bibliotecas cristianas: *Aelia Capitolina*, Cesarea de Palestina, NagHammadi y Roma", en *Anales de la Academia Nacional de Ciencias de Buenos Aires*, tomo XLIX – Año 2015, Buenos Aires, 2017, pp. 51–72. (especialmente pp. 62–70). Asimismo cfr. *La Biblioteca gnóstica de NagHammadi y los orígenes cristianos*, pp. 117–37 y las nuevas conjeturas de H. Lundh-

nos detendremos sólo en un ejemplo, en el Códice de Nag Hammadi I. Éste se compone de cinco escritos y el que cierra el códice es un tratado carente de título, el más extenso de toda la Biblioteca y dividido en tres partes, el *Tratado tripartito*. Teniendo en cuenta de que este tratado de 77 folios es de naturaleza valentiniana y altamente reflexivo y que en su redacción resaltan rasgos estrechos de contraste con el pensamiento de Plotino según se expresa en las Enéadas que forman la "gran tetralogía" del curso lectivo romano de 265–66, es posible justificar la hipótesis de que se trata de un extenso escrito abiertamente antiplotiniano y que los cuatro escritos que le preceden: *Oración del Apóstol Pablo, Carta esotérica de Santiago, Evangelio de la Verdad y Tratado sobre la Resurrección (Epístola a Regino)*, formaban con él un conjunto ordenado más extenso, como un bloque unitario de cinco escritos. Clave de la hipótesis es el examen de elementos materiales del códice en relación con la caligrafía y la composición, puesto que si el *Tratado sobre la resurrección* (NHC I,4) ocupa siete páginas sin numeración y es de la mano de un copista diferente al de los restantes escritos del códice,[22] es igualmente cierto que ha copiado este trabajo sobre unas hojas dejadas a propósito en blanco – por eso carecen de foliación – entre el *Evangelio de la Verdad*[23] y el *Tratado tripartito*.[24] Pero hay un dato más. Posiblemente el autor de este escrito y asimismo del *Tratado tripartito* tenía presente que en esta enseñanza doctrinal sobre el concepto de resurrección (*anástasis*), había además puntualizaciones que tenían por blanco ideas de Plotino sobre la resurrección que tocaban tangencialmente a la doctrina cristiana gnóstica.

En efecto en En III, 6 (26), 6 al final que está al comienzo de las lecciones sobre los "problemas del alma" correspondientes al año lectivo 264/65 e inmediatamente anterior a la "Gran tetralogía"

---

aug/L Jenott, *The Monastic Origins of the Nag Hammadi Codices*, MohrSiebeck, Tübingen, 2015 y H. Marx-Wolf, *Spiritual Taxonomies and Ritual Authority. Platonits, Priests, and Gnostics in the Thrd Century* CE, University of Pennsylvania Press, Philadelphia, 2016, cap. III (pp. 73–99 y 158–64).

[22] Aunque sí es de la misma mano del amanuense que ha copiado la primera parte del NHC XI (*La interpretación del conocimiento y La exposición valentiniana* con sus suplementos sobre la unción, el bautismo y la eucaristía).

[23] Que concluye en la página 43 y cuya mitad inferior y reverso utiliza.

[24] Que comienza en el anverso de la página 51.

y que se encuentra integrado en la atmósfera propedéutica de ésta, el filósofo llegaba a sostener: "Pero la verdadera vigilia es una real resurrección (*anástasis*) separada del cuerpo y no con él. En efecto, el cambio con el cuerpo es como la ida de un cuerpo a otro, del mismo modo como se pasa de un lecho al otro; pero la resurrección por entero verdadera es fuera de los cuerpos, cuya naturaleza siendo la opuesta al alma, es esencialmente algo diferente", o sea, dicho llanamente, la "elevación" del alma implica el logro de su aspecto particular en la universalidad del alma del mundo, en este estado se encuentra en auténtica vigilia, hasta que un nuevo ciclo la pueda sumergir en el devenir del universo. La *Epístola sobre la Resurrección* es tajante al respecto en cuanto a lo que piensa el valentinismo:

> El Salvador ha absorbido la muerte – tú no debes ser considerado ignorante –, en efecto él ha abandonado el mundo perecedero, se ha cambiado en un Eón imperecedero y se ha erguido por sí mismo, una vez que absorbió lo visible por lo invisible y nos facilitó el camino de nuestra inmortalidad. Entonces, como el Apóstol lo ha dicho, hemos sufrido con Él, y hemos resucitado con Él y hemos subido al Cielo con Él. Pero si somos manifestados en este mundo revistiéndole somos sus rayos y somos rodeados por Él hasta nuestra declinación, que es nuestra muerte en esta vida (*bíos*); somos atraídos al cielo por Él como los rayos por el sol, sin ser obstaculizados por nada. Tal es la resurrección espiritual, que absorbe a la psíquica tanto como a la carnal. Si hay alguno, empero, que no cree no es posible persuadirle; ya que se trata de la esfera de la fe, hijo mío, y no de la persuasión. El que está muerto resucitará y (si) hay alguno entre los filósofos de este mundo que cree, él, sin embargo, resucitará. El filósofo de este mundo, en cambio, no acepta creer que él sea alguien que retorna sobre sí y (nosotros) por nuestra fe, ya que hemos conocido al Hijo del Hombre y hemos creído que ha resucitado de entre los muertos y es de Él del que decimos que "llegó a ser la destrucción de la muerte", a tal punto es grande Aquél en quien se cree. Los que creen son inmortales. El pensamiento de los que son salvados no perecerá. El intelecto de los que le han conocido no perecerá (45, 13–46, 23).

Además, una hoja sobrante de las mencionadas sin numeración se utilizó por el primero de los escribas cuando todavía no se había encuadernado el códice con su forma definitiva, para copiar la *Oración de Pablo*, que debía preceder a todos los demás escritos y que encaja perfectamente con el conjunto, cuando el organizador del códice se aseguró de que era posible copiar su *Tratado sobre la resurrección*, que dedicó a Regino, dando solidez doctrinal plena al libro. De esta manera el códice se completaba con el más reciente mensaje valentiniano gnósticamente tradicional en tanto que su doctrina hundía sus raíces en la enseñanza mítica del relato de los gnósticos arcaicos barbelognósticos-setianos, asimilaba de esta manera la sofisticación filosófica cristiana naciente que en contacto íntimo con la técnica del platonismo pitagorizante había alcanzado la perfección teosófica del valentinismo capaz de representar la concepción plena de la realidad profunda ante las imperfecciones del pensamiento griego y judío, siempre siervos de la manifestación cósmica inestable. Por eso como se ha ido observando, en primer lugar la *Oración del Apóstol Pablo*, modelo de plegaria cristiana, debía abrir el códice con el patrocinio del Apóstol de la Resurrección, cuya inesperada experiencia de gnosis transformante – sobre un "aborto" – le permitía hacerse entender por pneumáticos y psíquicos, en camino hacia una perfección superior. La *Carta esotérica de Santiago*, integraba la autoridad primera del "hermano del Señor", la corriente esotérica judeocristiana o jacobita, por encima de la inclinación a la experiencia del secreto último de Dídimo Judas Tomás (*Evangelio de Tomás*) y del protocatolicismo petrino (*Carta de Pedro a Felipe, el Hecho de Pedro*). Coherentemente estas revelaciones esotéricas se perfeccionan durante el tiempo fuerte que media entre la Resurrección y Ascensión del Salvador. Por otra parte, el *Evangelio de la Verdad* – la buena noticia que proviniendo gratuitamente de la Verdad trae "alegría" a quienes la reciben – nace de la experiencia personal profunda del mismo Valentín y el sentido inequívoco de la Resurrección como la gnosis en sí misma que cambia lo mudable en incommovible y permite que la ambivalencia del mismo Pablo aparezca en su propia luz la confirma como una misiva imprescindible entre hermanos – Regino, una cabeza visible – de cofradías emparentadas que buscan el mutuo fortalecimiento, la *Carta a Regino sobre la Resurrección*. Confirmada de esta manera la cadena tradicional de la vieja escuela teosófica cristiana de raigambre judía en sus hitos espirituales fundamentales, y teniendo como fondo para la contrarréplica el curso cerrado de un filósofo con discípulos reconocidos, se torna posible didácticamente escribir un tratado completo de filosofía cristiana en el que sistema intelectual, actividad ritual y ética y política comunitarias se desarrollan en unidad con el fin aspirado de la liberación. Y al enfrentar polémicamente las pretensiones culturales exclusivistas de un pensador griego, Plotino, se revela el libro como una pieza elocuente de apologética o credencial de identidad del credo esotérico cristiano. No parece que ningún tratado filosófico de pensamiento cristiano autónomo y en todas sus partes, ni en Roma ni en Alejandría, se haya adelantado a éste de un maestro valentiniano – insistimos en Aquilino, ver *Vita Plotini de Porfirio* – escrito en el año 267 exponiendo la teosofía gnóstica completa al responder al alegato antignóstico de Plotino del curso lectivo 265–66. El hueco en blanco de siete páginas era el espacio necesitado por Aquilino para insertar en él la copia de su propio escrito, el *Tratado sobre la resurrección*, para concluir un proyecto valentiniano de sólida respuesta pneumática contra el filósofo antignóstico Plotino.[25]

3° Los originales gnósticos de los siglos II a IV en prolongación de continuidad y de cronología relativa. Tenemos a nuestra disposición cuatro códices investigados consecutivamente desde fines del siglo XIX hasta las primeras dos décadas del siglo XXI: A. El Papiro gnóstico de Berlín 8502. B. El Códice de Askew y la Pistis Sophía. C. El Códice de Bruce. yD. El Códice Tchacos.

A. El *Papiro berolinensis* es un códice pequeño con hojas de papiro con un total de 141 páginas. Varios de los folios se han perdido. Fue adquirido en 1896 en El Cairo por el Museo de Berlín. Proviene de la región de Ahkmín y las cuatro obras que contiene están traducidas del griego al copto sahídico. Son el *Evangelio de María*, el *Libro secreto de Juan*, la *Sabiduría de Jesucristo* y el *Hecho de Pedro*. Este códice como los de la Biblioteca de NagHammadi ha sido compuesto con un fin de unidad en relación con la enseñanza gnóstica. El escrito que lo encabeza introduce, al que lo lea o comente, en el mensaje del pneuma cautivo en el dominio del dios creador; el segundo, ofrece la gran enseñanza doctrinal sobre los

---

[25] Cfr. asimismo F. García Bazán, *La gnosis eterna. Antología de textos gnósticos griegos, latinos y coptos III. Gnósticos libertinos y testimonios hermético gnósticos, alquímicos y neoplatónicos*, Trotta, Madrid 2017, 85–108.

antecedentes metafísicos, las particularidades internas de la plenitud espiritual, la quiebra de esa misma plenitud y el retorno salvífico a través del proceso temporal; la *Sabiduría de Jesús* hace hincapié sobre el aspecto soteriológico de los anteriores escritos.[26] Este códice que coloca en su centro la figura de María Magdalena, representante de la tradición jacobita, une por ella a Santiago y Pedro en la línea de la *Carta esotérica de Santiago* (NHC I,2), el *1Apocalipsis de Santiago* (NHC V,3) y *Los dos libros de Ieu*.[27]

B. El *Codex Askewianus* que contiene la conocida obra *Pístis Sophía* recibe esta denominación de su comprador, Antonino Askew, un médico y coleccionista de manuscritos londinense que probablemente adquirió el original en 1750 de un librero en Londres. Muerto Askew en 1772, el códice fue comprado por el British Museum en 1785. El filólogo C. G. Woide fue el primer especialista que estudió el manuscrito por indicación del mismo Askew y el que asimismo le dio el pertinente título de *Pístis Sophía*, aunque la transcripción de los caracteres coptos que realizó nunca se publicó.[28] La edición crítica del texto de la *Pístis Sophía* que se mantiene como referente es la de C. Schmidt, quien la publicó en 1905.[29] Efectivamente obedeciendo al título de la obra el escrito

---

[26] Del mismo modo que en NHC III,2 lo lleva a cabo con *Eugnosto, el Bienaventurado*, al que allí precede el *Apócrifo de Juan* en su versión extensa – los paralelos en la mentalidad de la conformación codicológica son constantes.

[27] Finalmente, la acción ejemplar o *Hecho de Pedro*, refiere la curación milagrosa de su bella hija – y posteriormente el contramilagro de que es sujeto la misma joven – y ratifica mediante el simbolismo de la prodigiosa actividad petrina el sentido de la verdadera salvación que superando al milagro físico, señala a la regeneración espiritual de la pareja matrimonial, sola capaz de liberar al pneuma del gobierno inferior y demiúrgico.

[28] Un nuevo intento para publicar el manuscrito se hizo en 1848 por parte de M. G. Schwartze, que fue enviado con este fin a Inglaterra por la Real Academia de Ciencias de Berlín. Su trabajo fue publicado póstumamente por J. H. Petermann incluyendo una edición del texto copto y su traducción latina. La posterior traducción anónima que figura en el *Dictionnaire des apocryphes* de J.-P. Migne (París, 1856, 1, cols 1.191–1.286) y la inglesa de George R. S. Mead, secretario de H. P. Blavatsky, aparecida en 1896, se originan en esta versión latina, por más que un año antes de esta última E. Amélineu había publicado la primera traducción directa a una lengua moderna, al francés.

[29] Por encargo de la Comisión de Padres de la Iglesia de la Academia de Ciencias de Berlín, el original de esta edición cuando todavía estaba inédita fue traducida al alemán y apareció en el mismo año con anotaciones con los escritos del *Codex Brucianus*. El mismo autor publicó en 1925 la edición crítica con una segunda versión mejorada de la primera traducción, la misma que editó en nuevas impre-

es un diálogo entre Jesús resucitado y María Magdalena, María, la madre de Jesús, y otros discípulos y discípulas (Juan, Tomás, Andrés, Felipe, Mateo, Pedro, Simón el Cananeo, Salomé y Marta).[30] La relación de este escrito tanto con largos extractos de escri-

siones W. Till en 1954 y 1959 y, más tarde, con la nueva colaboración de H. M. Schenke, en 1981. En el año 1978 Violet MacDermot retomó la edición crítica de 1925 de C. Schmidt y la publicó con una traducción inglesa en la Editorial Brill de Leiden dentro de la colección de los Nag Hammadi Studies. El manuscrito de que se dispone es una traducción del griego al sahídico. Paleográficamente el original en copto data de la segunda mitad del siglo IV y el testigo griego que fue la base de la traducción, se debió de redactar un siglo antes, entre la mitad y el final del siglo III. El códice de pergamino consta de cuatro partes: las primeras dos partes abarcan las páginas 1–126 y 127–255, respectivamente. En esta última aparecen dos títulos: al comienzo "El libro II de la Fe (*Pístis*) Sabiduría (*Sophía*)". Y al final, "Una parte de los rollos del Salvador". La parte III va de las páginas 256–352, su título es igualmente, "Una parte de los rollos del Salvador", y la parte IV que comprende las páginas 353–85, aparece sin título. Se trataría, entonces, de "Los (cuatro) rollos o libros del Salvador sobre la Fe Sabiduría".

[30] En su transcurso el Salvador les amplía la enseñanza reservada para ellos, anunciada, pero no desarrollada. Los libros I, II y parte del III deben haber sido los primitivos de la compilación y hay que distinguirlos de la parte final del III y el IV. El tema central del escrito gira sobre la enseñanza e interpretación que el Resucitado da sobre la actividad de la Fe Sabiduría, o sea, de la Sabiduría en su función de adhesión al designio del Padre de la Luz, colaborando así en la obra salvífica como intermediadora entre lo psíquico y lo pneumático, lo que se agrega es la posterior descripción de los ritos que celebra el Salvador. La primera parte trata sobre la actividad de Sabiduría caída, debajo del Eón décimo tercero, su causa por desconcentración de la espontaneidad de la acción ritual al ver la Luz de arriba y desearla ("suspensión de la ejecución del misterio del décimo tercer Eón", I,43, 10–25, García Bazán, p. 56; "Y cesé en los misterios y descendí al Caos", II, 180, 19–18, p. 128) y su arrepentimiento en forma paralela a como se conoce didácticamente esta parte del relato gnóstico por medio de la enseñanza valentiniana, con la doble sutileza del agregado del origen de la caída debido a una debilitación de la actividad mistérica en el Pleroma y la advertencia, al mismo tiempo, de que en el plano de la fe ya los *Salmos de David y Salomón* y cinco de las *Odas de Salomón* anticipaban prefigurativamente la profundidad de esta comprensión gnóstica, tanto en relación con el origen de la deficiencia como con sus consecuencias de cautiverio para las almas particulares. La segunda parte de la obra avanza otro grado en la doctrina, puesto que describe la liberación de Sofía como el comienzo ejemplar de la liberación de los espíritus. La tercera parte retoma el sentido de la primera descripción en torno a *Pístis Sophía*, pero ahora aplicado a los pneumáticos, en esclavitud a causa de la falta primordial de Sabiduría, pero rescatados a partir de su conversión. Un sentido que se va precisando por medio del diálogo cuyo significado está encerrado en varias *palabras* transmitidas del Señor. La segunda sección de la parte III y la parte IV, por su parte, introducen progresivamente en lo más cumplido del Pleroma, el reino de los Eones, mediante las referencias al sentido oculto de las formulaciones de los nombres secretos y de los ritos inefables, completándose así el mensaje esotérico del Salvador concretado en su obra liberadora de redención: descenso, ascenso y donación del conocimiento completo de

tos bíblicos provenientes de la traducción griega de los Setenta como con los dos *Libros de Ieu* (= *el Libro del gran discurso iniciático*), libro II, 246, 20; libro III, 349ss. y libro IV, debe tenerse en cuenta como una doble respuesta gnóstica, tanto a cristianos católicos de Egipto como a las actividades de cultos de misterio aborígenes en el mismo medio, conjunto de actos que se rescatan como profundamente cristiano-gnósticos.

Lo últimamente acotado se muestra como fundamental en el aparentemente abigarrado escrito gnóstico, el que debe datarse entre mediados y fines del siglo III, siendo obviamente posterior a los *Libros de Ieu* de comienzos del mismo siglo y procediendo ambos de un medio cristiano gnóstico egipcio grecoparlante de acuerdo con lo que se ha señalado sobre sus fuertes características culturales. Su versión al copto, además, debe haber formado parte de la gran empresa de traducción de originales gnósticos emprendida durante los siglos III y IV por grupos próximos de la zona de Alejandría. Es digno de señalar, además, que la *Pistis Sophia* comience indicando que la enseñanza impartida por el Salvador resucitado haya abarcado los once años posteriores a la resurrección, es decir, los tiempos cronológicamente más oscuros y filón de polémicas dentro de la historia cristiana primitiva, pero asimismo los años inmediatamente anteriores a la conversión de Pablo de Tarso (año 36) y subsiguientes, cuando se traslada a Damasco, Arabia, nuevamente a Damasco y tres años después se presenta ante Pedro, predicando con autonomía. En esta obra, en efecto, a partir de un eje central, una fotofanía, una manifestación intensa de luz que envuelve e invade al Salvador – en contrarréplica al portento luminoso experimentado por Saulo –, se manifiesta a los discípulos una comprensión de la realidad salvífica ordenada y brillante por oposición al Caos y las tinieblas, que antes poseían como información externa, pero no en su significado interior. De la totalidad de la revelación, no obstante, participa el cuerpo estable de los discípulos y discípulas, pero entre los que se distinguen niveles de entendimiento – utilizándose una terminología filosófica precisa colindante con la del neoplatonismo –, el de quienes

---

lo verdaderamente real, momentos que se hacen efectivos por el cumplimiento de los ritos intramundanos de iniciación inseparables de los misterios de la Luz e imprescindibles para el logro de la liberación.

comprenden más a fondo (María Magdalena, Juan) – recibiendo los elogios de beneplácito de Jesús cuando aportan explicaciones – y el grupo de los que entienden menos, igualmente predestinados a la gloria. Jesús, por tanto, no ha dividido ni segregado a ningún miembro del conjunto, al contrario, los ha orientado armónicamente para que no se separen valorizando a cada uno en su nivel – de este modo apacigua los conatos de controversia entre Pedro y María Magdalena, rispideces que se tornan agudas en otros documentos gnósticos, como el *Evangelio de María*, el *Evangelio de Tomás*, o bien, el más recientemente conocido, el *Evangelio de Judas*. Desde luego, el plano gnóstico-esotérico o de espiritualidad pura es el que guía al exotérico, aunque la entrega de "las llaves del reino" abraza ambas posibilidades cristianas. El libro IV, próximo por varios aspectos estudiados de su contenido al *Libro del gran discurso iniciático* del *Códice de Bruce*, que se presenta como la clave para la interpretación de los "grandes misterios" que él mismo encierra, completa y pone el broche de oro a la gran suma teórico-práctica de la doctrina gnóstica que es la *Pistis Sophia*. Redactado el escrito, según razonable hipótesis, en torno a la mitad del siglo III en un medio de cristianos egipcios, como se ha dicho, la Fe (ascendida a) Sabiduría no es sólo una revelación de la enseñanza gnóstica – que por el enfoque filosófico aplicado a María Magdalena en el libro III puede haber influido en el estrato femenino de la Escuela neoplatónica de Alejandría si se recuerda la figura de Hipatía –, sino que al mismo tiempo aspira a facilitar al lector la versión gnóstica de la historia más antigua del cristianismo primitivo – anterior incluso a la del eslabón representado por la noticia sobre Tibutis proporcionada por Eusebio de Cesarea, el más antiguo heresiarca en relación con la tradición judeocristiana –, haciendo pie en la fotofanía extraordinaria del Jesús resucitado, en la que la interpretación del misterio del bautismo de perdón ocupa un lugar exegético axial, un hecho del Resucitado que se relata experimentado por todos los discípulos en la carne, lo que la difundida y más tardía teofanía luminosa invocada por Pablo en el camino de Damasco no podía garantizar.[31]

---

[31] Cfr. F. García Bazán, *La gnosis eterna. Antología de textos gnósticos griegos, latinos y coptos II. Pístis Sophía/Fe Sabiduría*, Trotta, Madrid, 2007, pp. 11-29.

C. El denominado *Codex Brucianus* es un manuscrito en copto constituido originalmente por 78 hojas de papiro, escritas por ambos lados (156 páginas), de las que faltan siete.[32] Este manuscrito encierra dos escritos, el denominado por la *Fe Sabiduría* (*Pístis Sophía*) como "los dos libros de Ieu", al que corresponde el título único de: "El libro del gran discurso iniciático" y un escrito más breve carente de título. La primera copia del manuscrito copto la realizó C. G. Woide y una vez que falleció esta copia fue adquirida por la Clarendon Press de Oxford.[33] La forma final que adquirió el códice es la dada por C. Schmidt en 1892.

Los escritos que contiene el códice son los dos libros del *Libro del gran discurso iniciático* (94 páginas incluidas las 6 de tres hojas faltantes) y el *Tratado sin título* (62 páginas incluidas las 8 de los cuatro folios perdidos). Las ocho hojas de fragmentos acompañan al primer manuscrito. Las tres escrituras están traducidas del griego al sahídico, pertenecen a escribas diferentes y asimismo difiere el contenido de los manuscritos. El primero, es anterior a la *Fe Sabiduría*, puesto que ésta lo cita, y pese a su aparente exotismo, asume una interpretación gnóstica de los misterios helenísticos, con abundantes referencias a la magia ritual y a la función de Jesús como gran mistagogo, ritos en los que ocupan un importante lugar

---

[32] Este códice formaba parte de un lote mayor de escrituras en árabe, etiópico y copto que fue adquirido por el viajero escocés James Bruce en torno al 1773 en Medinet Habu en el Alto Egipto.

[33] En 1848 la Biblioteca Bodleiana compró tanto el códice como la transcripción de Woide. Sobre el texto original trabajaron posteriormente M. G. Schwartze y E. Amélineau, lo que permitió establecer correcciones en la copia de C. G. Woide. La copia inconclusa de M. G. Schwartze había llegado finalmente a las manos de A. Herman y fue éste junto con A. von Harnack los que habilitaron a C. Schmidt para que con el apoyo económico de la Academia de Ciencias de Berlín trabajara conjuntamente con el manuscrito original cotejándolo con las copias de Woide y Schwartze. C. Schmidt descubrió que en el códice había dos manuscritos y algunos fragmentos. Puso los folios en orden sucesivo e hizo una nueva transcripción y publicó su edición crítica con una traducción alemana y un comentario en 1892. En 1905 publicó una traducción revisada, agregando a la anterior edición, la traducción y comentario de la *Pistis Sophía*. Posteriormente aparecieron nuevas ediciones de esta obra bajo la responsabilidad de W. Till. Por otra parte F. Lamplugh realizó una traducción al inglés del *Tratado sin título* basada en la versión francesa de E. Amélineau, mientras que C. A. Baynes realizó la misma tarea en 1933, pero basándose sobre el texto original, la transcripción de C. Schmidt y las copias de Woide y Schwartze. A diferencia de Schmidt colocaba las cinco últimas hojas al comienzo.

tanto los varones como las mujeres.³⁴ Ellas adquieren una preeminencia que no se ofrecen en otros testimonios directos: "Jesús dijo a su discípulos que estaban reunidos con él, los doce discípulos y las discípulas (*mathetría*). Rodeadme, mis doce discípulos y discípulas, para que os hable de los grandes misterios del Tesoro de la Luz, éstos que nadie conoce, (que) están en el Dios invisible".³⁵

El Tratado *sin título*, en cambio, es doctrinal e himníco, pone el acento en el momento de la regeneración del Unigénito o culminación del ascenso del pneuma y de sus experiencias de carácter ultrapleromático, en el seno del Padre.³⁶

---

[34] El escrito en consecuencia contiene numerosos criptogramas, diagramas y nombres místicos y divinos, que ratifican tanto las figuras, el orden y disposiciones de paso de los actos rituales, como los estados concomitantes del ascenso iniciático y espiritual. En este sentido el libro conserva valiosos testimonios sobre las prácticas esotéricas que ahora pueden comprenderse mejor gracias al material paralelo que nos han deparado los escritos asimismo en copto de Nag-Hammadi.

[35] 54,7–12, también 124 [75], al final, sobre los doce discípulos. Completa asimismo los nombres de "las siete mujeres" (expresión también mencionada en SabJC al comienzo). Frente al ejemplar lacunoso del *I Apocalipsis de Santiago* del NHC V,3,40,25: Salomé, María, Marta, Arsinoe aludidas en ambas versiones, el *Santiago* del Códice Tchacos 29, 1–10 amplía la lista con Safira, Susana y Juana. Un posible paralelo, pero con las féminas como aliadas del amoralismo libertino lo encontramos posteriormente en Epifanio en el capítulo 26 del *Panarion* sobre los gnósticos disipados. Cfr. F. García Bazán, *La gnosis eterna III*, pp. 18–29.

[36] Las preferencias de las consideraciones a menudo con el carácter de bendiciones y alabanzas, se centran en el Hijo u Hombre perfecto vuelto interiormente a la profundidad del vientre paterno, tripotente y en silencio. El Uno Solo supera el retorno oculto, pero desde aquí se torna al principio, perfilándose asimismo reiteradamente la ordenación descendente e incluso la situación de ocultamiento o encierro en la maldad y la materia. Las vinculaciones del texto con el vocabulario y temática de la llamada gnosis barbelógnóstica, pero según la tradición primordial setiana enriquecida comunitariamente por los nombres de varios visionarios y profetas transmisores del mensaje, son dignas de advertir y en este sentido se revela asimismo el contenido de los himnos inefables, la "acción de gracias" que entonan los iniciados. Estas himnodias completan aspectos de lo que se dice y describe sobre la doctrina y el rito en el escrito anterior, dando unidad al códice. Se reconoce, por lo tanto, igualmente el aire familiar común con apocalipsis de trámite paralelo como los que encerraban las experiencias o revelaciones sublimes del Unigénito alcanzadas por el "divino Set" y en su línea, por Marsanes, Fosilampo y Nicoteo, citado este último por Porfirio en su *Vida de Plotino* XVI, pero al mismo tiempo se facilita una terminología precisa, aclaratoria y ampliada acerca de la utilizada por Plotino en algunos tramos eneádicos de su polémica antignóstica. Por lo tanto este escrito tiene que ser, como el *Tratado tripartito*, posterior a la apología plotiniana y ponerse en relación doctrinal con este último tratado, como también lo está el *Marsanes*. En este sentido admitimos que el orden correcto de las hojas del escrito es el establecido por C. Schmidt y ratificado por W. Till y V. Macdermot. Difieren en la interpretación M. Tardieu – J.-D. Dubois. El manuscrito del

D. La publicación del *Códice Tchacos* en junio de 2007 conteniendo los facsímiles de *El evangelio de Judas* (33, 1-58, 28) y enriquecida la edición con nuevas conjeturas sobre el texto copto transcrito y las interpretaciones incluidas en las versiones inglesa (M. Meyer, F. Gaudard) y francesa (R. Kasser), ha exigido la actualización tanto del texto como del comentario a la primera traducción al castellano que realizáramos y fuera publicada por Editorial Trotta en mayo de 2006.

Este códice se descubrió en 1978 en el Egipto Medio, en Mughagha, a 60 km al norte de Al-Mynia, en una caja de caliza, en una tumba, en el interior de una cueva, posiblemente de propiedad de un asceta. Ver nuestra edición, traducción y comentario de *El evangelio de Judas* (2006) de Trotta, en cuyo Estudio Preliminar ofrecimos las observaciones de naturaleza histórico-críticas pertinentes, las traducciones de fuentes griegas y latinas de los heresiólogos más autorizados al respecto (Ireneo de Lión, Pseudo Tertuliano y Epifanio de Salamina) y los testimonios de escritos canónicos, patrísticos y apócrifos en relación con las leyendas cristianas sobre Judas Iscariote. Ver posteriormente la nueva versión y comentario en *Textos gnósticos. Biblioteca de NagHammadi III. Apocalipsis y otros escritos*, 2ª. ed., Trotta, Madrid, 2009, 347-56. Desde fines del siglo II y después que el episcopado monárquico romano se consolidara, la doctrina de Ireneo de Lión del Evangelio escrito bajo cuatro formas se impuso asimismo en la Iglesia alejandrina. El género literario evangélico de carácter narrativo se ha considerado por largos siglos el normal y exclusivo. Hay comprobaciones de que no es así y que aunque la tradición del "Evangelio tetramorfo" es muy antigua y registra a sus espaldas ciertas concordancias de "Recuerdos de los Evangelios" (Justino Mártir) y de armonías evangélicas cuádruples (*diatessáron*), hubo también escritos de naturaleza evangélica tan arcaicos o más que los citados, constituidos por series de palabras del Señor sin explicaciones biográficas (el *Escrito Q* que subyace a los Evangelios de Mateo y de Lucas o el *Evangelio de Tomás*), y otros de factura dialogada comu-

---

*Tratado sin título* parece proceder del siglo IV, en tanto que los folios de los libros de Ieu son algo posteriores, la compaginación de los escritos, por lo tanto, es obra de un creyente gnóstico posterior. Ver ahora asimismo, *Les "Deux Livres de Iéou" (MS Bruce 96, 1-3)*, textes établs, traduits et présentés par E. Crégheur, Les Presses de l'Université Laval/Éditions Peeters, Québec, Louvain, Paris, Bristol, 2019.

nes a corrientes diversas judeocristianas o gnósticas (*Evangelio de los hebreos, Evangelio de los egipcios, Carta esotérica de Santiago, Diálogo del Salvador*). *El evangelio de Judas* (*peuaggelionnïoudas*) es una traducción del griego al copto sahídico en papiro del siglo III, pertenece al último tipo señalado y posee una identidad de contenido inconfundiblemente gnóstica.

No es el primer evangelio gnóstico directo de que se dispone, pues, por la Biblioteca de Nag Hammadi conocemos otros ejemplos, como el *Evangelio de Felipe*, el *Evangelio de la Verdad* y el *Evangelio de Tomás* del que se poseían fragmentos en griego provenientes del vaciadero de Oxirrinco, también en Egipto. Con larga anterioridad, en 1896, sabemos que el *Papiro gnóstico de Berlín 8502* ofreció un *Evangelio de María*. Y existieron algunos otros similares de los que los heresiólogos nos han dejado los títulos, aunque escasas noticias del contenido. El mundialmente publicitado *Evangelio de Judas* ahora está exhumado, pero antes sólo era aludido y hecho circular entre gnósticos "cainitas", que gozaron de pésima reputación entre los heresiólogos. La lectura directa de *El evangelio de Judas* que forma parte del Códice de Tchacos, sin embargo, permite confirmar actualmente lo escrito por los heresiólogos y obtener asimismo mayor información. El *Códice Tchacos* se abre con la *Carta de Pedro a Felipe* (pp. 1, 1–9, 12) de la familia valentiniana (cfr. NHC VIII,2) y es seguida por un escrito titulado *Santiago* (pp. 10, 1–30, 26) que precede a *El evangelio de Judas*. Este documento es digno de tenerse en cuenta, porque es el mismo que se posee en NHC V,3, como hemos visto en una nota anterior. Si bien el escrito retiene rasgos valentinianos similares a noticias aportadas por san Ireneo (cfr. Adv. Haer. I 21, 4–5) el contenido de su redacción mantiene un estilo propio que lo pone en contacto con materiales de *Eugnosto, el Bienaventurado* y la *Sabiduría de Jesucristo*. El escrito parece relativamente tardío e interpreta en clave gnóstica al judeocristianismo. Este discurso salvífico puede haber sido escrito en Egipto hacia fines del siglo III en un medio interesado en mostrar la superioridad del espiritualismo gnóstico. El texto se conserva en sahídico en un papiro de mala calidad. Pero el recientemente aparecido *Santiago* en el *Códice Tchacos* es más completo en algunos aspectos y es de sumo interés para la reconstrucción del esoterismo judeocristiano que este documento parece tener interés en reivindicar. Este segundo original es más extenso que el anteriormente conocido, contiene elementos que no era posible leer en la versión anterior – v.gr. la función de "segundo maestro" y de medio de las enseñanzas secretas por parte de Santiago, transmitidas a Addai y conservadas por sus descendientes y las "siete mujeres", la superación de la fe por la gnosis, la piedad profunda del personaje, la oración atribuida al dios justo y el rechazo del sacerdocio de este mundo y las alusiones al sufrimiento de Santiago – con equivalencias y paralelos en *El evangelio de Judas* – e informaciones sobre el juicio y ejecución de Santiago. Permite asimismo esta versión completar lagunas del primer manuscrito o ampliar parcialmente noticias, bien sea por ofrecer folios de papiro mejor conservados o por contener informes más explicativos. Inversamente el manuscrito de la biblioteca de Nag Hammadi también presta auxilio para que se puedan completar líneas faltantes de éste últimamente encontrado en páginas 13, 14 y 29. Para finalizar, el códice se cierra por unos fragmentos de un documento denominado *Allógenes* (pp. 59, 2–66, 24), un título aplicado al Salvador, como de otra raza. Es posible observar que este códice se insinúa en su comienzo como valentiniano, crece como del judeocristianismo esotérico y se completa con el estrato hebreocristiano más antiguo, el evangelio setiano, en el que se incluye al gnóstico Judas Iscariote. Su unidad conserva la integridad del mensaje gnóstico con sus diversos recursos expresivos.[37] Debido a que *El evangelio de Judas*, será motivo de una exposición particular en esta sección por parte del profesor David Brakke, podemos concluir nuestro análisis.

## *Resumen*

Las noticias más antiguas en griego sobre los "gnósticos" remontan a Pablo de Tarso y las Epístolas Pastorales. Las informaciones se amplían cuando aflora en el último cuarto del siglo II la corriente cristiana heresiológica (Ireneo de Lyón, Hegesipo, Hipólito de Roma

---

[37] Ver la nueva versión y comentario en *Textos gnósticos. Biblioteca de Nag Hammadi III. Apocalipsis y otros escritos*, señalado más arriba, y mayor información en F. García Bazán, *La Biblioteca gnóstica de Nag Hammadi y los orígenes cristianos*, pp. 137–49 y asimismo el anticipo de D. Brakke, *Los Gnósticos. Mito, ritual y diversidad en el cristianismo primitivo*, Sígueme, Salamanca, 2013, 15–18 y *passim*.

y Eusebio de Cesarea). Los autores de este círculo y los escritos que han producido reconocen de hecho la preexistencia de los personajes que condenan a los que llaman "herejes" y de las escrituras que rechazan que denominan "escritos heréticos". Del material abordado se ha conservado una cantidad de fuentes de más de cincuenta manuscritos catalogados en trece códices, la llamada Biblioteca de Nag Hammadi. Tomando por base y punto de partida esta masa de fuentes conservadas en diversos dialectos del copto y traducidas en su totalidad al español en la última década del siglo XX, se considera que es necesario emprender con urgencia la tarea de ordenación, enumeración y confrontación de este conjunto de textos con otros escritos que se poseen también en copto y otras lenguas antiguas y que son posteriores, hasta concluir el siglo V.

DAVID BRAKKE

*Ohio State University, USA*

# WHAT DIFFERENCE DOES THE *GOSPEL OF JUDAS* MAKE?

Although the manuscript that contains the *Gospel of Judas*, known as Codex Tchacos, was most likely discovered in the 1970s, an edition and translation did not become available to the wider scholarly community until 2006.[1] The original editors, translators, and publishers promoted it as revolutionary. The gospel's allegedly positive presentation of Judas Iscariot, its attacks on the other disciples as evil and ignorant, and its Gnostic view that the God of Genesis is not the ultimate God and Father of Jesus Christ but a lower ruler – these views sharply contradicted wider Christian tradition. As one prominent scholar put it, the *Gospel of Judas* represents "Christianity turned on its head".[2] Early publicity focused especially on the idea of a "good" Judas, for the primary point of comparison was the gospels of the New Testament (and their highly negative views of Judas) rather than the range of early Christian sources from the second century, when the new gospel probably originated. More recently, however, most scholars have agreed that the character of Judas in the gospel is either negative, ambiguous, or tragic – not virtuous and exemplary – and so we can now turn away from comparisons with the canonical gospels and consider more carefully how, if at all, the discovery of the

---

[1] On the discovery of the manuscript and its circuitous journey to publication, see H. Krosney, *The Lost Gospel* (Washington: National Geographic Society, 2006).

[2] B. D. Ehrman, "Christianity Turned on Its Head: The Alternative Vision of the *Gospel of Judas*", in *The Gospel of Judas*, ed. by R. Kasser, M. Meyer, & G. Wurst (Washington: National Geographic Society, 2006), pp. 77–120.

*Gospel of Judas* changes our picture of second- and third-century Christianity.

This paper does not discuss every contested point in the interpretation of *Judas*, nor does it provide a survey of the state of scholarship. Rather, it seeks to assess the impact of the discovery from the wider perspective of Patristic Studies. With only a decade of scholarship behind us, it is more accurate to speak of the gospel's potential impact rather than its actual impact. On the one hand, the gospel appears to provide new evidence for debates about clerical authority, ritual, and possibly martyrdom among rival Christian groups of the second century. On the other hand, it may have greater potential to change how we understand the development of what we call "Sethianism" or "Gnosticism" and its relationship to other Christian groups.

We can appreciate the significance of *Judas* better with some consideration of the impact that the earlier discovery of the Nag Hammadi manuscripts has had on Patristic Studies. By some measures that impact has been small. For example, if one reads the programs for recent Oxford Patristics Conferences or for meetings of the North American Patristics Society (NAPS), one will find very few papers devoted to sources from Nag Hammadi. At the 2014 meeting of NAPS, my paper on *Judas* was one of only two papers on "Gnosticism". Many more such papers appear at meetings devoted to the New Testament or Coptology, such as the Society of Biblical Literature and the quadrennial International Congress of Coptic Studies. Although *Vigiliae Christianae* has always published a healthy number of articles on Gnosticism and Nag Hammadi writings, thanks in part to the leadership of the late Gilles Quispel, the same cannot be said of the *Journal of Early Christian Studies*, even though I edited it for ten years. Yet no one can deny that the Nag Hammadi codices have significantly enhanced our understanding of so-called heretical forms of Christianity during the pre-Constantinian era, including the Valentinians.

One reason for the marginalization of Nag Hammadi codices within Patristics is that most of the original editors, translators, and interpreters of the texts were New Testament scholars by training. They understood the new tractates in terms of New Testament genres and concepts, and they often dated the texts as early as possible, to bring them into "the New Testament era". They analyzed them by asking the traditional questions of *neutestamentliche Wissenschaft*: Can we identify the text's sources and layers of redaction? Does the text give us access to oral traditions of Jesus' sayings or to lost sources for the New Testament writings? These are not the questions and concerns of Patristics. Most likely the survival of the texts in Coptic rather than in Greek, Latin, or even Syriac has provided another obstacle to greater use of the Nag Hammadi writings by Patristics scholars.

The New Testament approach to Nag Hammadi has gradually eroded over the last decade. Some historians have gone in the exact opposite direction. Represented best by the so-called Oslo School, these scholars now treat the Nag Hammadi codices as sources primarily for Egyptian Christianity, especially monasticism, around the turn of the fifth century.[3] Works that scholarly consensus has dated to the second or third centuries, like the *Gospel According to Philip*, they place in the fourth or early fifth, possibly even composed in Coptic rather than Greek.[4] Meanwhile, the *Gospel According to Thomas* once seemed, of all the Nag Hammadi works, the one most likely to come from the first century and so to be as useful to the study of the historical Jesus as the canonical gospels. Now it seems to be settling into the early second century – or even later.[5] With these changing perspectives we may find the Nag Hammadi codices increasing their impact in the study of Patristics.

Meanwhile, more studies are appearing that integrate Nag Hammadi works into the study of pre-Constantinian Christianity without segregating them into the category of Gnosticism.

---

[3] For example, H. Lundhaug & L. Jenott, *The Monastic Origins of the Nag Hammadi Codices* (Tübingen: Mohr Siebeck, 2015); L. Jenott, "Recovering Adam's Lost Glory: Nag Hammadi Codex II in its Egyptian Monastic Environment", in *Jewish and Christian Cosmogony in Late Antiquity*, ed. by L. Jenott & S. Kattan Gribetz (Tübingen: Mohr Siebeck, 2013), pp. 222–43.

[4] H. Lundhaug, "Begotten, Not Made, to Arise in This Flesh: The Post-Nicene Soteriology of the *Gospel of Philip*", in *Beyond the Gnostic Gospels: Studies Building on the Work of Elaine Pagels*, ed. by Eduard Iricinschi *et al.* (Tübingen: Mohr Siebeck, 2013), pp. 235–71.

[5] N. Denzey Lewis, "A New Gnosticism: Why Simon Gathercole and Mark Goodacre on the *Gospel of Thomas* Change the Field", *Journal for the Study of the New Testament*, 36 (2014), pp. 240–50.

For example, Denise Buell studies *The Tripartite Tractate* and *The Gospel According to Philip* with the *Shepherd of Hermas* and Justin Martyr's *Dialogue with Trypho* in her book on early Christian ethnic reasoning.[6] In one book, Benjamin Dunning explores the theme of alienation and sojourning in the *Apocryphon of James*, *Hermas*, and the *Epistle to Diognetus*, and in another he examines sexual difference and the legacy of Paul in *On the Origin of the World*, Clement of Alexandria, Irenaeus, and Tertullian.[7] These studies demonstrate that the works in the Nag Hammadi manuscripts can enrich our knowledge of early Christian diversity and shed new light on the traditional texts and church fathers of Patristic scholarship, especially if we do not consider the Nag Hammadi sources as a monolithic category.

No one can deny, however, that the codices have had a profound impact on the study of Gnosticism, even if that impact has not resulted in a clear scholarly consensus. For the most part, scholars agree that the works are strikingly diverse and seldom correspond to the sects and teachings that appear in the heresiological reports – with two important exceptions. First, several writings appear to have come from Valentinian Christians, most prominently *The Tripartite Tractate, The Gospel of Truth, The Gospel According to Philip*, and *The Treatise on Resurrection*.[8] These texts have provided significant evidence for the teachings, rituals, and even social organization of Valentinian groups, and they have revealed how Valentinian authors may have disagreed about such significant topics as Christology and free will and determinism. Second, nearly all scholars have accepted Han-Martin Schenke's hypothesis that several Nag Hammadi writings come from a single Gnostic tradition, which he and others usually call "Sethian"; these include *The Secret Book According to John, The Revelation*

---

[6] D. K. Buell, *Why This New Race: Ethnic Reasoning in Early Christianity* (New York: Columbia University Press, 2005).

[7] B. H. Dunning, *Aliens and Sojourners: Self as Other in Early Christianity* (Philadelphia: University of Pennsylvania Press, 2009); *Specters of Paul: Sexual Difference in Early Christian Thought* (Philadelphia: University of Pennsylvania Press, 2011).

[8] E. Thomassen, "Notes pour la delimitation d'un corpus valentinien à Nag Hammadi", in *Les textes de Nag Hammadi et le problème de leur classification*, ed. by L. Painchaud & A. Pasquier (Quebec: Presses de l'Université Laval; Leuven: Peeters, 1995), pp. 243–59.

*of Adam, Zōstrianos,* and others.[9] The inexact but unmistakable correspondence of a major part of *The Secret Book According to John* with Irenaeus's account of the myth of "Gnostics" confirms that this tradition existed in the middle of the second century.[10] The Sethian hypothesis is surely the most important advance in the study of Gnosticism after Nag Hammadi, even if historians do not agree about the origin, social character, and exact boundaries of Sethianism.

On the other hand, far from clarifying what Gnosticism was, the Nag Hammadi discovery has renewed and invigorated the debate over how, if at all, to define this phenomenon. Scholars have taken every possible position. On the extremes, Michael Williams argues for the complete abandonment of the category, and Birger Pearson claims that there was an actual Gnostic religion, which included the Sethians, the Valentinians, the Manichaeans, the Mandaeans, and many other sub-groups.[11] Others, such as Christoph Markschies, argue for a heuristic use of a typological category called "Gnosticism", and April DeConick calls Gnosticism a transgressive form of spirituality separate from and yet entangled with specific religions like Judaism and Christianity.[12] A small group, which includes Mark Edwards, Alastair Logan, Bentley Layton, and me, argue for the restriction of the term "Gnostic" in a sectarian sense to a specific group of early Christians, roughly equivalent to Schenke's Sethians.[13] An important

---

[9] H.-M. Schenke, "Das sethianische System nach Nag-Hammadi-Handschriften", in *Studia Coptica*, ed. by Peter Nagel (Berlin: Akademie, 1974), pp. 165–73; Schenke, "The Phenomenon and Significance of Gnostic Sethianism", in *The Rediscovery of Gnosticism: Proceedings of the International Conference on Gnosticism at Yale*, ed. by B. Layton (Leiden: Brill, 1981), II, pp. 588–616.

[10] Irenaeus, *Against Heresies* 1.29.

[11] M. A. Williams, *Rethinking 'Gnosticism': An Argument for Dismantling a Dubious Category* (Princeton: Princeton University Press, 1996); B. A. Pearson, "Gnosticism as a Religion", in *Was There a Gnostic Religion?*, ed. by A. Marjanen (Helsinki: Finnish Exegetical Society; Göttingen: Vandenhoeck & Ruprecht, 2005), pp. 81–101.

[12] C. Markschies, *Die Gnosis* (Munich: C.H. Beck, 2001); A. D. DeConick, *The Gnostic New Age: How a Countercultural Spirituality Revolutionized Religion from Antiquity to Today* (New York: Columbia University Press, 2016).

[13] M. J. Edwards, "Gnostics and Valentinians in the Church Fathers", *Journal of Theological Studies*, n.s. 40 (1989), pp. 26–47; M. J. Edwards, "Neglected Texts in the Study of Gnosticism", *Journal of Theological Studies*, n.s. 41 (1990), pp. 26–50; A. H. B. Logan, *Gnostic Truth and Christian Heresy: A Study in the History*

study by Tuomas Rasimus builds upon and complicates that hypothesis.[14] There is no reason to expect or indeed to hope for a resolution to this discussion, which raises important methodological questions in the historical study of religion: How do we identify and define religious groups? What do we mean by such terms as "religion", "sect", "tradition", or "spirituality"? How, if at all, can we move from text to social reality? These are crucial and intellectually exciting questions. We Patristics scholars should be glad that we have a topic that encourages us to wrestle with them, almost certainly without end.

In 2006 the *Gospel of Judas* appeared on the scene.[15] To be sure, it is not the only significant tractate that Codex Tchacos contains. The manuscript provides texts of two works already known from Nag Hammadi: *The Letter of Peter to Philip* (Nag Hammadi Codex VIII, 2) and *The (First) Apocalypse of James* (Nag Hammadi Codex V, 3). The Tchacos text of the latter appears to be superior to that of Nag Hammadi.[16] The work that the editors entitled *Book of Allogenes* does not correspond to the Nag Hammadi work of similar name (Nag Hammadi Codex XI, 3) and thus represents a new, albeit highly fragmentary source. Nonetheless, as valuable as these works are, their significance pales in comparison to the

---

*of Gnosticism* (Edinburgh: T & T Clark, 1996); Logan, *The Gnostics: Identifying an Early Christian Cult* (London: T & T Clark, 2006); B. Layton, "Prolegomena to the Study of Ancient Gnosticism", in *The Social World of the First Christians: Essays in Honor of Wayne A. Meeks*, ed. by L. M. White & O. L. Yarbrough (Minneapolis: Fortress, 1995), pp. 334–50; D. Brakke, *The Gnostics: Myth, Ritual, and Diversity in Early Christianity* (Cambridge, Mass.: Harvard University Press, 2010).

[14] T. Rasimus, *Paradise Reconsidered in Gnostic Mythmaking: Rethinking Sethianism in Light of the Ophite Evdience* (Leiden: Brill, 2009).

[15] The original critical edition is found in R. Kasser *et al.*, *The Gospel of Judas Together with the Letter of Peter to Philip, James, and a Book of Allogenes from Codex Tchacos: Critical Edition* (Washington: National Geographic, 2007), but for editions that include the fragments that appeared subsequently, see L. Jenott, *The 'Gospel of Judas': Coptic Text, Translation, and Historical Interpretation of the 'Betrayer's Gospel'* (Tübingen: Mohr Siebeck, 2011), and F. Bermejo Rubio, *El Evangelio de Judas: Texto bilingüe y comentario* (Salamanca: Ediciones Sígueme, 2012).

[16] W.-P. Funk, "The Significance of the Tchacos Codex for Understanding the *First Apocalypse of James*", in *The Codex Judas Papers: Proceedings of the International Congress on the Tchacos Codex held at Rice University, Houston Texas, March 13–16, 2008*, ed. by A. DeConick (Leiden: Brill, 2009), pp. 509–33.

potential impact the *Gospel of Judas* may have on our understanding of second-century Christianity.

But is the *Gospel of Judas* actually from the second century? The date of the work depends primarily on whether Irenaeus refers to the original Greek of the work that we have in Coptic when he mentions a *Gospel of Judas* in his *Against the Heresies* of around 180. His report reads in full:

> And furthermore – they say – Judas the betrayer was thoroughly acquainted with these things; and he alone was acquainted with the truth as no others were, and (so) accomplished the mystery of the betrayal. By him all things, both earthly and heavenly, were thrown into dissolution. And they bring forth a fabricated work to this effect, which they entitle *The Gospel of Judas*.[17]

Irenaeus reports three things about the contents of the *Gospel*. First, Judas knew "these things": it is not clear which of the many things Irenaeus has just described Judas knew. Some of the mythological motifs and stories Irenaeus has narrated in the preceding sections are found in our *Gospel of Judas*, but many more are not, including the things that Irenaeus attributes to the "others" (i.e., other Gnostics) just before he mentions *Judas*. It may be relevant on this point that our *Judas* is a relatively short work. Second, Irenaeus says that "Judas alone was acquainted with the truth as no others were, and accomplished the mystery of betrayal". Our *Gospel of Judas* emphasizes Judas's knowledge of Jesus's true identity and the ignorance of the other disciples; Jesus reveals the nature of God and the origin of this cosmos to Judas alone; and the gospel concludes with Judas's agreement to hand Jesus over to Jewish leaders. Third, Irenaeus says that by Judas's act "all things, both earthly and heavenly, were thrown into dissolution". In our gospel, Jesus tells Judas that Judas will sacrifice the human being that the savior inhabits; Jesus then announces that "[... the thrones] of the aeon have been [defeated, and] the kings have become weak, and the races of the angels have groaned, and the evils

---

[17] Irenaeus, *Against Heresies* 1.31.1, translated in B. Layton, *The Gnostic Scriptures* (Garden City, N.Y.: Doubleday, 1987), p. 181.

that [...] the ruler is destroyed".[18] This sounds very much like what Irenaeus describes – the dissolution of the present world order, both earthly and heavenly.

Brief as it is, every point in Irenaeus's description of the *Gospel of Judas* that circulated before 180 matches our newly discovered work; he does not say anything about the work that rules out our gospel. Thus, Gregor Wurst, one of the original editors, concluded that the newly discovered text is most likely a Coptic translation of a Greek work that Irenaeus mentions.[19] Most subsequent scholars have agreed, but there is no clear consensus as to whether Irenaeus had read the gospel or had merely heard about it. Immediately after his reference to the *Gospel of Judas*, Irenaeus goes on to say, "And, moreover, I have also collected their writings in which they exhort to dissolve the works of the Womb; they call the creator of heaven and earth Womb".[20] Taking this statement to be adversative to the preceding one about *Judas*, Wurst concludes that Irenaeus likely knew the gospel "only from hearsay".[21] Johannes van Oort argues that the references to "dissolution" suggest instead that *Judas* was one of the works that Irenaeus collected and thus had likely read.[22]

Some scholars question the identification of Irenaeus's *Gospel of Judas* with the one from Codex Tchacos, however. Simon Gathercole, for example, cautions that the correspondences between Irenaeus's account and our gospel are slight and that we have examples from early Christianity of different works with the same name.[23] John Turner and Gesine Schenke Robinson argue that Irenaeus must have known an earlier version of the

---

[18] *Gospel of Judas* 57: 4–10.

[19] G. Wurst, "Irenaeus of Lyon and the Gospel of Judas", in Kasser *et al.*, *The Gospel of Judas*, pp. 121–35. Wurst's identification of the Gnostics in question as "the Cainites" (p. 128), however, must be rejected; it is not Irenaeus's term, but one that later heresiologists added.

[20] Irenaeus, *Against Heresies* 1.31.2 (my translation).

[21] Wurst, "Irenaeus of Lyon," pp. 127–28.

[22] J. van Oort, "Irenaeus on the *Gospel of Judas*: An Analysis of the Evidence in Context", in *Codex Judas Papers*, ed. by DeConick, pp. 43–56.

[23] S. Gathercole, *The Gospel of Judas: Rewriting Early Christianity* (Oxford: Oxford University Press, 2007), pp. 119–23.

*Gospel of Judas* or even a different text altogether.[24] In part, they make this claim based on what Irenaeus does *not* say about the gospel; that is, both assert that if Irenaeus had known the text that we have, he would have summarized and/or criticized certain features about which he is silent. These include the gospel's highly negative portrayal of the disciples other than Judas and the specifically Sethian aspects of the gospel's mythology. Like nearly all other scholars, Turner and Schenke Robinson believe that our *Judas* should be included among Sethian writings. But they claim that the gospel's simpler version of the Sethian myth and its Christian character suggest that it originated late in the history of Sethianism, no earlier than the second quarter of the third century. I find the argument based on what Irenaeus does not say unconvincing. It is difficult to know what Irenaeus would have considered worthy of mention in his brief report, and, as we have seen, it remains possible that he had not read the gospel himself, but reported what he had heard about it from someone else. Moreover, the placement of the gospel late in Sethian history depends on an already hypothetical reconstruction of that history and thus includes a significant element of circularity.[25] It remains simplest and most probable that the Coptic text we have is a translation of the *Gospel of Judas* that circulated in Greek in the middle of the second century.[26]

If so, then it appears to provide evidence for a passionate debate over the authority of the clergy and the validity of the Eucharist in this early period. Lance Jenott has made one of the most thorough

---

[24] G. Schenke Robinson, "The *Gospel of Judas*: Its Protagonist, its Composition, and its Community", in *Codex Judas Papers*, ed. by DeConick, pp. 75–94; J. D. Turner, "The Sethian Myth in the *Gospel of Judas*: Soteriology or Demonology?" in *Codex Judas Papers*, ed. by DeConick, pp. 95–133; Turner, "Dating the *Gospel of Judas*", in *Judasevangelium und Codex Tchacos: Studien zur religionsgeschichtlichen Verotrung einer gnostischen Schriftensammlung*, ed. by E. E. Popkes & G. Wurst (Tübingen: Mohr Siebeck, 2012), pp. 321–32.

[25] On this question see D. Brakke, "The *Gospel of Judas* and the End of Sethian Gnosticism", in *Envisioning God in the Humanities: Essays on Christianity, Judaism, and Ancient Religion in Honor of Melissa Harl Sellew*, ed. by C. J. P. Friesen (Salem, Or.: Polebridge, 2018), pp. 133–52.

[26] Cf. Jenott, *Gospel of Judas*, pp. 5–6; Bermejo Rubio, *Evangelio de Judas*, pp. 31–33.

arguments for this interpretation.[27] The gospel opens with the disciples gathered and "making eucharist (ⲣ-ⲉⲩⲭⲁⲣⲓⲥⲧⲓ) over the bread", but Jesus mocks their ritual as offered to the wrong god.[28] Later the disciples have a vision of priests who offer multiple sacrifices on an altar, treat each other with respect, and yet commit terrible sins. Jesus identifies the disciples as the priests who invoke his name and the people that they lead as the animals they sacrifice.[29] The author seems to be criticizing an ordained clergy that made claims to apostolic succession, presented itself as a priestly class, and presided over the Eucharist as over a sacrifice – what we might call the priestly-sacrificial model of religious authority. The existence of this model may come as something of a surprise for the middle of the second century: Was there already a dominant church structure with a priestly clergy, one so strong as to provoke condemnation as intense as that found in the *Gospel of Judas*? To be sure, already in *1 Clement*, from the last decade of the first century, we find some of the ingredients of this model: the author compares the Christian clergy to the biblical priests and the church's rituals to "offerings" and "sacrifices" (θυσίαι); he claims that bishops and deacons received their authority in succession from the original apostles.[30] About two decades later Ignatius of Antioch grounded the bishop's authority in part in his exclusive right to preside at the Eucharist, which he described as taking place at an "altar" (θυσιαστήριον), and he compared the bishops and presbyters to God and the apostles.[31] But much second-century "proto-orthodox" literature between Ignatius and Irenaeus lacks these ideas or at least lacks them as a package, and one usually thinks of Origen of Alexandria and Cyprian of Carthage in

---

[27] Jenott, *Gospel of Judas*, pp. 37–69; cf. L. Painchaud, "Polemical Aspects of the *Gospel of Judas*", in *The Gospel of Judas in Context: Proceedings of the First International Conference on the Gospel of Judas*, ed. by M. Scopello (Leiden: Brill, 2008), pp. 171–86.

[28] *Gospel of Judas* 33: 22–34: 11.

[29] *Gospel of Judas* 38: 1–40: 26.

[30] *1 Clement* 40: 1–5; 41: 2; 42: 4–5; 44: 1–3. See C. A. Bobertz, "The Development of Episcopal Order", in *Eusebius, Christianity, and Judaism*, ed. by H. W. Attrdige & G. Hata (Detroit: Wayne State University Press, 1992), pp. 183–211, esp. 184–89.

[31] Cf. Ignatius, *Magnesians* 6: 1; *Philippians* 4, 7: 2; *Ephesians* 5: 2; *Smyrnaeans* 8: 1.

the third century as the true witnesses to the spread and development of the priestly, apostolic identity of the clergy and the corresponding sacrificial understanding of the Eucharist. And yet here we seem to have in *Judas* an attack on all of this, and at a level of vehemence that suggests that the priestly-sacrificial model had achieved a high level of authority.

For some scholars, this feature of the text alone might suggest that it belongs to the third century rather than the second, that is, that it belongs to the world of Origen and Cyprian more than to that of Justin Martyr and Valentinus. Instead, however, I see the *Gospel of Judas* as providing new evidence for the development of proto-orthodox understandings of clerical authority and the Eucharist during the second century, the importance of which we should not exaggerate. The situation that the author describes pertains primarily to his own local context, whatever that may have been, and should not necessarily be projected onto the wider screen of "second-century Christianity". The claims to apostolicity and priesthood to which the author responds he may have found primarily in texts like *1 Clement*, although the passionate nature of his response suggests that he was engaged in a lively debate with other Christians. One may also ask whether the gospel opposes the Eucharist *per se* or only emerging clerical claims to authority over it and its connection to their "angry" God of the Old Testament.[32] In any event, future scholarship on the rise and authority of the clergy and on the Eucharist in the second century will need to take *Judas* into account.

The interpretation of the gospel's sacrificial imagery as Eucharistic and of its polemic as anti-clerical appears in some of the earliest studies of the gospel,[33] but it has not gone unchallenged. Bas van Os, for example, argues that the gospel refers to baptism (perhaps along with the Eucharist) when it depicts human sacrifice: starting with Paul (Romans 6: 1–11) early Christians frequently

---

[32] Such is the position of Jenott, *Gospel of Judas*, pp. 55–56. For the argument that the gospel rejects the Eucharist entirely, see F. Williams, "The Gospel of Judas: Its Polemic, its Exegesis, and its Place in Church History", *Vigiliae Christianae*, 62 (2008), pp. 371–403.

[33] In addition to Williams, "The Gospel of Judas," A. van den Kerchove, "La maison, l'autel et les sacrifices: Quelques remarques sur la polémique dans l'*Évangile de Judas*", in *Gospel of Judas in Context*, ed. by Scopello, pp. 311–29.

called baptism a death, the human being's crucifixion with Christ. Because the crucifixion and resurrection are not the means to salvation, *Judas* "sets out an alternative version to counteract the 'apostolic' narrative and its Easter call to baptism".[34] It is indeed plausible that the author polemicizes against "proto-orthodox" baptism. Toward the end of his dialogue with Jesus, Judas asks him, "Come then, what will those who have been baptized in your name do?"[35] Jesus's answer is lost in a lacuna of four lines and is impossible to reconstruct, but it is possible that his answer would have criticized baptism in his name, for earlier Jesus severely condemns "the priests" who "are invoking my name": "In my name [they] shamefully have planted fruitless trees".[36] Presumably the (Sethian) Gnostic community that produced and read the gospel practiced the distinct form of Gnostic baptism that appears in other Gnostic works and that almost certainly did not invoke the name of Jesus.[37] The Gnostic *Revelation of Adam* claims that others have "defiled the water of life".[38] Jesus's missing answer to Judas's question about baptism in his name might have provided additional evidence for polemics between Gnostic Christians and other Christians over the correct practice of baptism.

Other historians, most notably Karen King and Elaine Pagels, have seen in *Judas* evidence for debate over the value of martyrdom.[39] When Jesus accuses the disciples of leading people astray and sacrificing them like animals on an altar, the author may be condemning martyrdom as misguided sacrifice to the lower created god. After all, Ignatius of Antioch had presented his impend-

---

[34] B. van Os, "Stop Sacrificing! The Metaphor of Sacrifice in the *Gospel of Judas*", in *Codex Judas Papers*, ed. by DeConick, pp. 366–86 (386).

[35] *Gospel of Judas* 55: 23–25.

[36] *Gospel of Judas* 39: 7–17.

[37] J.-M. Sevrin, *Le dossier baptismal Séthien: Études sur la sacramentaire gnostique* (Québec: Les presses de l'Université Laval, 1986); J. D. Turner, "Ritual in Gnosticism", in *Gnosticism and Later Platonism: Themes, Figures, and Texts* (Atlanta: Society of Biblical Literature, 2000), pp. 83–139 (87–97); E. Pagels, "Baptism and the *Gospel of Judas*: A Preliminary Inquiry", in *Codex Judas Papers*, ed. by DeConick, pp. 353–66.

[38] *Apocalypse of Adam* 84: 17–18.

[39] E. Pagels & K. L. King, *Reading Judas: The Gospel of Judas and the Shaping of Christianity* (New York: Viking, 2007); cf. E. Iricinshi, L. Jenott, & P. Townsend, "The Betrayer's Gospel", *The New York Review of Books*, 53 (2006), pp. 32–37.

ing martyrdom as a "sacrifice" (θυσία) and "a libation to God" poured out on an "altar" (θυσιαστήριον); he described his body as bread reminiscent of that of the Eucharist, "ground by the teeth of the wild beasts".[40] In this case, the author of *Judas* condemns the sacrifice of one's body, for salvation belongs to the true spiritual self, which must return to its heavenly origin. Here, however, we face the problem that little evidence for a debate over martyrdom or indeed for martyrdom itself as a central issue survives from the middle of the second century. Recent scholarship has played down the frequency of martyrdom and has argued for dating the *Martyrdom of Polycarp*, a traditional source for martyrdom in the middle of the second century, to the third century instead of the 160s.[41] The gospel's use of the Greek term *eucharist* supports the case that the sacrificial imagery of the disciples' vision refers to that ritual; we lack the same kind of support for a reference to martyrdom, and thus debate over this hypothesis is likely to continue.[42] In any case, the martyrological and Eucharistic interpretations are not mutually exclusive, and together they expand evidence for conflicts over ideas about the clergy, ritual, and martyrdom in the period between Ignatius and Irenaeus.

I believe that the *Gospel of Judas* has greater potential to make a difference in how we understand the Gnostics, specifically those we have called the Sethians, during the second century. If we accept that it is the gospel to which Irenaeus refers, then it becomes the earliest securely dated Gnostic work that we have, and it suggests that the Gnostics were fully engaged with the wider Christian movement from the start. In addition, Irenaeus shows knowledge of the myth that appears in the *Secret Book According to John*. Although we cannot be certain that Irenaeus knew any of the versions of the *Secret Book* that survive in four Coptic manuscripts, we can hypothesize that some version of this work also circulated at the same time as the *Gospel of Judas* originated.

---

[40] Ignatius, *Romans* 2: 2; 4: 1–2.

[41] C. R. Moss, "On the Dating of Polycarp: Rethinking the Place of the *Martyrdom of Polycarp* in the History of Christianity", *Early Christianity*, 1 (2010), pp. 539–74; Moss, *The Myth of Persecution: How Early Christians Invented a Story of Martyrdom* (San Francisco: HarperOne, 2013).

[42] C. R. Moss, *Ancient Christian Martyrdom: Diverse Practices, Theologies, and Traditions* (New Haven: Yale Univ. Press, 2012), p. 161.

Together these two works form the most secure basis for reconstructing (so-called Sethian) "Gnosticism" at the middle of the second century.[43]

The *Secret Book According to John* and the *Gospel of Judas* share several significant figures, confirming their relationship to the same group of Gnostics. First, they both feature a revelation dialogue between Jesus (or Christ) and a disciple, which provides information about God, the origin of the cosmos, the structure and population of the heavens, and the origin and early history of humanity. In each case, the divine revealer departs at the conclusion of the dialogue.[44] Second, both gospels situate themselves in relation to the Fourth Gospel. The *Secret Book* makes John, the purported author of the Gospel, its main character, and Johannine elements appear in both the frame story and the revelation dialogue.[45] *Judas* shows knowledge of Matthew and Luke,[46] and its dramatic opening scene of Judas's "confession" is clearly modeled on the "confession" of Peter in the Synoptic Gospels (Matthew 16: 13–20 and parallels). Still, the gospel's concluding scenario, showing Judas just outside the location of the Last Supper, seems to presuppose the departure of Judas from the guest room in John 13: 30.[47] Third, they share a set of theological or mythical motifs that they arrange into a similar story. An unknowable ultimate source, the Invisible Spirit, emanates two other divine hypostases, the Barbēlō (or a "luminous cloud") and the Self-Originate aeon, the latter of which has four attendants.[48] From these emanate multiple other divine aeons, among which are heavenly proto-

---

[43] For a more detailed argument, see Brakke, "The *Gospel of Judas*".

[44] *Gospel of Judas* 58: 5–26.

[45] J.-D. Dubois, "La tradition johannique dans l'*Apocryphe de Jean*", *Adamantius*, 18 (2012), pp. 108–17.

[46] S. Gathercole, "Matthean or Lukan Priority? The Use of the NT Gospels in the *Gospel of Judas*", in *Judasevangelium und Codex Tchacos*, ed. by Popkes and Wurst, pp. 291–302.

[47] S. Emmel, "The Presuppositions and the Purpose of the *Gospel of Judas*", in *Gospel of Judas in Context*, ed. by Scopello, pp. 33–39.

[48] Judas's statement to Jesus early in the gospel – "I know who you are and where you have come from. You have come from the aeon of the Barbēlō, the immortal (aeon). But as for the one who sent you, I am not worthy to proclaim his name" (35:17–21) – refers explicitly to the Barbēlō and obliquely to the Invisible Spirit. In his later cosmological revelation, Jesus refers explicitly to the Invisible Spirit and obliquely to the Barbēlō ("a luminous cloud") (47: 14–21).

types of Adam and the posterity of his son Seth. The universe in which we live, in contrast, is created and ruled by a hostile power, named Ialdabaōth and/or Saklas, who is identified as the god of Genesis. At the top of the hierarchy within this cosmos preside twelve rulers, doubtless corresponding to the twelve signs of the Zodiac, for both works closely identify the power structure of this universe with the heavenly bodies. Five names of rulers occur in both works in the same order – only five because that is as many as the *Gospel of Judas* names.[49]

Fourth, both works identify the saved people as a *genea*, a "race" – for example, "the immovable race" in the *Secret Book* and "the strong and holy race" in the *Gospel of Judas*.[50] Both works place in the spiritual realm an archetypal progeny of Seth: "the seed of Seth" in the *Secret Book* and "the incorruptible race of Seth" in the *Gospel of Judas*.[51] Neither, however, explicitly identifies human beings in the material realm as the descendants of Seth. The name "Seth" appears only three times in the entire *Secret Book*, and the *Gospel of Judas* speaks of a final exaltation of (perhaps a portion of) "the great race of Adam".[52] Given the prominence of Adam in both works and the lesser role of Seth, the name "Sethian" does not seem the most apt choice for these materials.[53] Finally, both works refer to "the perfect (τέλειος) human being", with whom the saved are associated, early in the narratives. In the *Secret Book* the Savior tells John to share what he is about to reveal with persons from "the immovable race of the perfect human being".[54] In his first dialogue with the disciples, Jesus challenges them to "bring forward the perfect human being".[55] Together the *Secret Book* and the *Gospel of Judas* provide a set of teachings and mythological ele-

---

[49] *Gospel of Judas* 52: 3–14; *Apocryphon of John* BG 40: 5–9 par.
[50] *Apocryphon of John* BG 73: 9–10 par.; *Gospel of Judas* 36: 25–26.
[51] *Apocryphon of John* BG 36: 3–4 par.; *Gospel of Judas* 49: 5–6.
[52] *Secret Book*; in addition to the previous citation, BG 35: 21; 63: 14 par. *Gos. Jud.* 57: 11–12.
[53] Schenke himself remarked on the artificial nature of the name "Sethian": his text group could, he wrote, just as easily be called the "X-group" ("Phenomenon and Significance", p. 590).
[54] *Apocryphon of John* BG 22: 15–16; II 2: 24–25.
[55] *Gospel of Judas* 35: 3–4.

ments that can be the basis for a new understanding of the Gnostic school of thought.

The two works also differ in important ways. In the *Gospel*'s opening dialogue, as I have mentioned, Judas makes a confession of Jesus' identity similar to Peter's confession at Caesarea Philippi in the Synoptic Gospels: "I know who you are and where you have come from. You have come from the aeon of the Barbēlō, the immortal (aeon). But as for the one who sent you, I am not worthy to proclaim his name".[56] Despite the prominence of the Barbēlō in this important statement, the *Gospel of Judas* gives remarkably less attention to that aeon in its theology than does the *Secret Book*, leaving it unnamed as a "luminous cloud" in Jesus's later revelation.[57] The two works differ also in how the rulers of this cosmos originated. In the *Secret Book*, Ialdabaōth comes into being when the aeon Wisdom attempts to think without the consent of her male consort: Ialdabaōth is a kind of glitch in divine thought, an error. In the *Gospel of Judas*, by contrast, one of the immortals, most likely Ēlēlēth, calls Ialdabaōth and his fellow rulers into being.[58] This scenario appears also in the *Holy Book of the Great Invisible Spirit* (or *Gospel of the Egyptians*), which shares other key features with *Judas*.[59] The error and fall of the aeon Sophia, which scholars have tended to highlight as a central feature of Sethian Gnosticism, was only one of seemingly two possible Sethian explanations for how the imperfect lower divinities originated from the serene perfection of the Entirety.

The standard account of "Sethianism" places its origins among "heterodox" non-Christian Jews and minimizes its Christian character as secondary and superficial. But if we consider the new evidence that the *Gospel of Judas* presents us, then it appears that this movement originated and developed in close interactions with competing Christian claims to revelation and authority, claims in which literary depictions of the original disciples of Jesus figured prominently. Both the *Secret Book According to John* and the *Gos-*

---

[56] *Gospel of Judas* 35: 15–21.
[57] *Gospel of Judas* 47: 14–21.
[58] *Gospel of Judas* 51: 3–15.
[59] *Gospel of the Egyptians*. III 56: 22–59: 9; see Jenott, *Gospel of Judas*, pp. 94–99.

*pel of Judas* are revelations – apocalypses – akin in their literary forms to the Revelation to John in the New Testament and the *Shepherd of Hermas* outside of it. Theologically they participate in the lively debate among second-century Christians over how to relate the new revelation of Jesus to the Septuagint, the Jewish Law, and the God of Genesis – a debate that the teachings of Paul and the Gospel of John set up and that Christians ranging from Basilides to Marcion to Valentinus and Justin took up with vigor. The narrative of secondary and superficial Christianization appears much less plausible.[60]

The *Gospel of Judas* has the potential to make a very significant difference in how we understand "Sethianism", "Gnosticism", or whatever we wish to call the remarkable religious group that produced this gospel and so alarmed Irenaeus and other church fathers. Although the gospel has the potential to provide oblique evidence for second-century debates over the clergy, rituals like the baptism and the Eucharist, and martyrdom, it is here that this manuscript discovery could have its greatest impact on Patristic Studies.

## Abstract

After its publication in 2006, scholars initially studied the *Gospel of Judas* within the paradigm of New Testament studies, just as they had the Nag Hammadi Codices in earlier decades. If we consider the new gospel within its second-century context, however, its potential impact on Patristic Studies is twofold. On the one hand, the gospel appears to provide new evidence for debates about clerical authority, ritual, and possibly martyrdom among rival Christian groups of the second century. On the other hand, it may have greater potential to change how we understand the development of what we call "Sethianism" or "Gnosticism" and its relationship to other Christian groups.

---

[60] Cf. Bermejo Rubio, *Evangelio de Judas*, p. 71.

MARIANO TROIANO
*Universidad Nacional de Cuyo, Argentina*

# MAGIC AND THEOLOGY. BARBARIC UTTERANCES IN THE *PISTIS SOPHIA* AND THEIR DIFFERENT LEVELS OF INTERPRETATION

*Introduction*

This work emerges within the framework of the Cenob project ("Corpus des énoncés des noms barbares"), financed by the French National Research Agency, and as a complement to the article "Rituels et énoncés barbares dans la *Pistis Sophia*" published in 2018.[1] Cenob's objective was to establish a scientific and multilingual database that brings together the so-called "barbarian names" (ὀνόματα βάρβαρα) from the Mediterranean basin between the sixth century before and after our era. Such "barbaric utterances" appear mainly in magical documents and texts, but also in philosophical (especially Neoplatonic) and theological (especially Gnostic) writings.

According to Michel Tardieu, the term "barbarian names or utterances" refers to "the divine names or attributes and functions of the gods, or even vocal effects that occur within the framework of rituals".[2] This designation comes from the fact that the phonet-

---

[1] M. Troiano, "Rituels et énoncés barbares dans la Pistis Sophia", in *Langage des dieux, langage des démons, langage des hommes dans l'Antiquité*, éd. par Luciana Soares & Philippe Hoffmann, (Turnhout: Brepols, 2018), pp. 61–76.

[2] Tardieu explains: "L'expression 'noms barbares' (ὀνόματα βάρβαρα) sera toujours utilisée dans ce volume pour désigner des noms divins, ou bien des attributs et fonctions de divinités, ou bien encore des effets vocaux intervenant dans le cadre de rituels". M. Tardieu, "Introduction", in *Noms barbares I. Formes et contextes d'une pratique magique* dir. par M. Tardieu *et al.*, Bibliothèque de l'École des Hautes Études 162, (Turnhout: Brepols, 2013), p. 11, note 2. The expression appears for the first time used with this sense towards the middle of the first century AD by the stoic philosopher Chaeremon of Alexandria, master of Nero fr. 4, ap. Porphyr, *Letter to Anebon*, quoted by Eusebius, *PE*, V 10, 5–8 (ἄσημα ὀνόματα καὶ βάρβαρα, "indistinct and barbarous names"), and then in the following cen-

ics of these names seemed strange to a Greek or Latin reader. "It was about – explains the French scholar – especially in the exercise of the denomination of the sacred, expressing the inexpressible in words supposedly stronger and more foreign than the autochthonous form of designating the gods by means of their own common names or by the absence of any proper name".[3] These are, then, invocative or exegetical formulas, consisting of sequences of sounds or names of deities and/or demons that usually enter in a register that does not belong to the language of the document in which they are inscribed. They have usually been considered meaningless and can rarely be cut into easy units to pronounce and interpret. In certain cases the researcher can differentiate the ritual context in which the statements are presented, in other cases they are included in philosophical, theological and religious works whose ritual character is absent or subject to debate but within which are found names that have been converted or used as "barbarian names". Such broader conception of documents capable of containing these utterances contributes to a better understanding of the use of "barbaric utterances" in Antiquity, including meta-discourses on these "names".[4]

The *Pistis Sophia* is a Gnostic text[5] which possesses a rich variety of these "barbaric utterances", more than 400. The treatise forms part of the Askew Codex, one of the earliest known Gnostic texts prior to the discovery of the Nag Hammadi Collection.

---

tury used by Plutarch, *De Superstitione*, 3, 166 B 5–6 (ἄτοπα ὀνόματα καὶ ῥήματα βαρβαρικὰ, "foreign names and barbarous words"), by Lucian of Samósata, *Menippus* or *Necromancy* 9 (βαρβαρικὰ ὀνόματα) and by the *Chaldean Oracles*, fr. 150 (ὀνόματα βάρβαρα), from where it was transmited to Neoplatonism. cf. PGM VIII 20–21 (βαρβαρικὰ ὀνόματα) and Pliny the Elder, HN, 28, 20 (*externa uerba atque ineffabilia*). Synonym of "barbarian names" by ethnic and cultural determination: "Egyptian names", Αἰγύπτια ὀνόματα (*Corpus Hermeticum*, XVI 2). Tardieu, "Introduction", p. 11, note 2.

[3] Tardieu, "Introduction", p. 12.

[4] http://www.cenob.org/Project/Description (consulted on March 13th 2017).

[5] For the use of the category "Gnostic" and "Gnosticism" we follow the arguments proposed by Einar Thomassen in E. Thomassen, *The Coherence of "Gnosticism"*, (Berlin, Boston: De Gruyter, 2020), pp. 5-6 and 34-36, A. Piñero & J. Montserrat, "Introducción General", in *Textos gnósticos Biblioteca de Nag Hammadi I: Tratados filosóficos y cosmológicos*, ed. por A. Piñero *et al.*, (Madrid: Trotta, 2000²), pp. 33–37 and J.-D. Dubois, *Jésus Apocryphe*, (Jésus et Jésus-Christ 99), (Paris: Mame-Desclée, 2011), pp. 16–17.

Michel Tardieu and Jean-Daniel Dubois date the composition of the original in Greek towards 330 and its Coptic translation ten years later.[6]

The *Pistis Sophia* consists in dialogues of the risen Jesus with his disciples (men and women) and especially with Mary Magdalene. Through these dialogues, Jesus proposes the exegesis of barbaric utterances that entail a revelation of the ineffable name of the transcendent Father and introduce rites of enchantment that assure to the disciples the possession of the gnosis. Although the magic recipes mainly concern Book IV, they are distributed throughout the four parts of the treatise.[7] These parts make up an homogeneous whole[8] which reveals the activity of Wisdom as a collaborator in the process of salvation, a process which can be synthesized, following the structure of the text, as: descent, ascent and the gift of knowledge. In spite of the importance that the *nomina barbara* have in this document, they have been neglected by researchers and only the crossing of gnostic, patristic and philosophical sources has allowed us to evaluate the wealth of meaning that they contain.[9]

---

[6] M. Tardieu & J.-D. Dubois, *Introduction à la littérature gnostique I*, (Clamecy: CERF, 1986), p. 80. See in this regard the associations reported by the authors between this codex and the book called *Questions of Mary* quoted and summarized by Epiphanius in *Panarion*, XXVI 8, 1–2. The Askew Codex, whose origin is unknown and which is now preserved in London, was named after its first owner, a collector of ancient manuscripts who bought it in 1772. It is a translation from Greek into dialect Coptic Sahidic, which consists of 178 sheets, 356 pages, written in two double-sided columns. The work, divided into four distinct parts or books, could be the result of the work of two scribes. *Introduction à la littérature gnostique*, p. 66.

[7] The first book includes an exegesis of the *Psalms of David* and the *Odes of Solomon* in function of the fall and the repentance of Pistis Sophia. The second part describes the salvation of Pistis Sophia and the consequences for the individual soul. The third book is about the nature of sin and repentance, considered from the exegesis of the *logoi* of Jesus. Finally, the last book proposes, through the exegesis of *symbola magica*, a revelation of the ineffable name of the transcendent Father and introduces rites of enchantment to assure the possession of the gnosis by the disciples.

[8] *Introduction à la littérature gnostique*, pp. 74–75. Nevertheless, according to Francisco García Bazán, books I, II and part of book III would be more primitive and should be distinguished from the end of book III and book IV. F. García Bazán (trad.), *La gnosis eterna II. Pístis Sophia/Fe Sabiduría*, (Madrid: Trotta, 2007), p. 12.

[9] In fact, the *Pistis Sophia* does not present a list of barbaric utterances with specific recipes according to the objectives fixed by the operator, nor details

Thus, the aim of this study is to show not only the diversity and complexity of the *nomina barbara* detailed in this book, but also to support the idea that their study is essential for our understanding of theology, cosmogony and anthropology in Late Antiquity, where Philosophy and Religion, Patristics and Gnosticism, converge in the exegesis of new concepts. Concepts enunciated in different languages and whose interpretation requires addressing multiple levels in order to provide them with meaning.

Therefore, on the one hand, we will propose the study of the co-text (both immediate and extended) surrounding these expressions and, on the other hand, we will conduct a parallel research on philosophical sources such as Plotinus *Enneads*, on patristic sources, such as the writings of Irenaeus of Lyon or Clement of Alexandria, and on other Gnostic texts such as the Valentinian texts of the Nag Hammadi Collection. These levels will allow diverse but confluent paths, providing a new perspective to elucidate the meaning of these barbaric utterances and to expose the ideas that they convey.

## *Iaō: Verb, Son and Intellect*

In the previous article mentioned above, we analyzed the six barbaric chains [10] from Book IV of *Pistis Sophia*, which are presented

---

such as the description of the objects and the rituals to perform in order to achieve the desired result, as is the case of PGM (Papyri Graecae Magicae) or the Coptic Barbaric Utterances published by Angelicus Kropp. K. Preisendanz (ed.), *Papyri Graecae Magicae: die Griechischen Zauberpapyri, I–II*, new edition by A.Henrichs, (Stuttgart: B.G. Teubner, 1973–1974) (1$^{st}$ ed. Preisendz 1928–1931). See also H.-D. Betz (ed.), *The Greek Magical Papyri in Translation: including the Demotic Spells, vol. 1: Texts*, (Chicago-London: University of Chicago Press, 1996) (1$^{st}$ ed. 1986). For Coptic utterances see: A. Kropp, *Ausgewählte koptische Zaubertexte*, (Bruxelles: Fondation Égyptologique Reine Elizabeth, 1931). The *Nomina Barbara* present in the Codex Askew are a strong argument supporting the originality of the problem addressed by the Cenob project. In fact, the common flaw of the current indexations is to extract the barbarian name from its co-text (and usually also its context); while the analysis of the barbaric utterances present in the *Pistis Sophia* makes it clear that the examination of the co-text in which the *nomina barbara* are inserted is essential to investigate their interpretation.

[10] A "barbaric chain" is a concept established by the Cenob project that defines a compact and binder mass of characters, particularly impressive for its length, which spans one after another a sequence of these barbarian utterances

in two groups of three chains each. We established that both groups form part of two rituals practiced by Jesus and his disciples, which we called the "ascension ritual" (PS IV, 136, 353–54) and the "ritual of absolution" (PS IV, 142, 369–72).

In this paper, we would like to focus on a particular aspect of both rituals that was briefly dealt with in that article and which include three of the mentioned chains: the first two of the first ritual and the first of the second ritual.

The first (PS IV, 136, 353, 9–12)[11] and the third (PS IV, 142, 370, 11–18)[12] of these chains repeat, with variations, certain barbaric utterances that have been studied by Michel Tardieu.[13] However, we would like to draw attention to the reiteration in all the three chains, with repetitions and variations, of the name Iaō:

or names; and whose particular difficulty is to find a safe reference point for cutting them according to its meaning and thus to obtain short, easy-to-pronounce words. Sometimes these chains have divisions that allow us to establish the separation between utterances. However, despite the abundance of *nomina barbara* present in the *Pistis Sophia* (more than 400 barbaric utterances), there are only seven of these "barbaric chains".

[11] The first chain reads as follows: 'ⲀⲈⲎⲒⲞⲨⲰ· ⲒⲀⲰ· ⲀⲰⲒ̈· ⲰⲒ̈Ⲁ· ⳨ⲒⲚⲰⲐⲈⲢ· ⲐⲈⲢⲚⲰ⳨· ⲚⲰ⳨ⲒⲦⲈⲢ· ⲌⲀⲄⲞⲨⲢⲎ· ⲠⲀⲄⲞⲨⲢⲎ· ⲚⲈⲐⲘⲞⲘⲀⲰⲐ· ⲚⲈ⳨ⲒⲞⲘⲀⲰⲐ· ⲘⲀⲢⲀⲬⲀⲬⲐⲀ· ⲐⲰⲂⲀⲢⲢⲀⲂⲀⲨ· ⲐⲀⲢⲚⲀⲬⲀⲬⲀⲚ· ⲌⲞⲢⲞⲔⲞⲐⲞⲢⲀ· Ⲓ̈ⲈⲞⲨ· ⲤⲀⲂⲀⲰⲐ·'. *Pistis Sophia*, ed. by Carl Schmidt and transl. by Violet MacDermot, (Leiden: E.J. Brill, 1978), pp. 706–07.

[12] The third chain reads as follows: 'Ⲓ̈ⲀⲰ· Ⲓ̈ⲞⲨⲰ· Ⲓ̈ⲀⲰ· ⲀⲰⲒ̈· ⲰⲒ̈Ⲁ· ⳨ⲒⲚⲰⲐⲈⲢ· ⲐⲈⲢⲰ⳨ⲒⲚ· ⲰⲨⲒⲐⲈⲢ· ⲚⲈⲪⲐⲞⲘⲀⲰⲐ· ⲚⲈⲪⲒⲞⲘⲀⲰⲐ· ⲘⲀⲢⲀⲬⲀⲬⲐⲀ· ⲘⲀⲢⲘⲀⲢⲀⲬⲐⲀ· ⲒⲎⲀⲚⲀ ⲘⲈⲚⲀⲘⲀⲚ· ⲀⲘⲀⲚⲒⲀ ⲦⲞⲨ ⲞⲨⲢⲀⲚⲞⲨ· Ⲓ̈ⲤⲢⲀⲒ̈ ϨⲀⲘⲎⲚ ϨⲀⲘⲎⲚ· ⲤⲞⲨⲂⲀⲒ̈ⲂⲀⲒ̈· ⲀⲠⲠⲀⲀⲠ· ϨⲀⲘⲎⲚ · ϨⲀⲘⲎⲚ· ⲀⲈⲢⲀⲀⲢⲀⲒ̈ϨⲀ ⲠⲀϨⲞⲨ ϨⲀⲘⲎⲚ ϨⲀⲘⲎⲚ· ⲤⲀⲢⲤⲀⲢⲤⲀⲢⲦⲞⲨ ϨⲀⲘⲎⲚ ϨⲀⲘⲎⲚ· ⲔⲞⲨⲔⲒⲀⲘⲒⲚ ⲘⲒⲀⲒ̈ ϨⲀⲘⲎⲚ ϨⲀⲘⲎⲚ· Ⲓ̈ⲀⲒ̈· Ⲓ̈ⲀⲒ̈· ⲦⲞⲨⲀⲠ ϨⲀⲘⲎⲚ ϨⲀⲘⲎⲚ· ⲘⲀⲒ̈Ⲛ ⲘⲀⲢⲒ· ⲘⲀⲢⲒⲎ· ⲘⲀⲢⲈⲒ· ϨⲀⲘⲎⲚ ϨⲀⲘⲎⲚ ϨⲀⲘⲎⲚ·', *Pistis Sophia*, pp. 740–41.

[13] Michel Tardieu, "Nethmomaoth", in *Mélanges bibliques et orientaux en l'honneur de M. Delcor*, ed. by A. Caquot et al. (Alter Orient und Altes Testament 215) (Neukirchen-Vluyn: Butzon & Bercker, 1985), pp. 403–07. On the other hand, Michela Zago explains that Zagoure is one of the seven names of the visible manifestation of the creator god and also related to Iaō: "L'invocation au dieu créateur, ouverte et close circulairement par la transcription grecque du tétragramme hébreu, *Iao*, est accompagnée par une série d'autres appellations, sept au total. Les Sept noms peuvent se référer tant au dieu suprême qu'aux figures angéliques, 'les premiers anges apparus'. Ils semblent être la manifestation visible du dieu créateur, comme s'ils en constituaient des émanations ou, si l'on veut, des 'puissances'. Les sept noms sont, dans l'ordre: *Iao, Sabaoth, Arbathiao, Zagoure, Arath, Adonaíos* et *Basemm*, que je considérerais plutôt comme une figure autonome et distincte." M. Zago, "Le nom physique du Dieu", in *Noms barbares I. Formes et contextes d'une pratique magique* dir. par M. Tardieu et al., Bibliothèque de l'École des Hautes Études 162, (Turnhout: Brepols, 2013), p. 211.

1. First chain: ⲁⲉⲏⲓⲟⲩⲱ· ⲓ̈ⲁⲱ· ⲁⲱⲓ̈· ⲱⲓ̈ⲁ· (PS IV, 136, 353, 9)
2. Second chain: ⲓ̈ⲁⲱ · ⲓ̈ⲁⲱ · ⲓ̈ⲁⲱ· (PS IV, 136, 353, 22)
3. Third chain: ⲓ̈ⲁⲱ· ⲓ̈ⲟⲩⲱ· ⲓ̈ⲁⲱ· ⲁⲱⲓ̈· ⲱⲓ̈ⲁ· (PS IV, 142, 370, 11)

The first and the third chains are preceded by an invocation addressed to the Father: "Hear me, my Father, thou father of all fatherhoods, thou infinite Light (ⲥⲱⲧⲙ̅ ⲉⲣⲟⲓ̈ ⲡⲁⲉⲓⲱⲧ" · ⲡⲉⲓⲱⲧ' ⲙ̅ ⲙ̅ⲛⲧⲉⲓⲱⲧ ⲛⲓⲙ' ⲡⲁⲡⲉⲣⲁⲛⲧⲟⲛ ⲙ̅ⲡⲟⲩⲟⲉⲓⲛ·)".[14] However, only the second chain presents an interpretation of the utterance: ⲓ̈ⲁⲱ · ⲓ̈ⲁⲱ · ⲓ̈ⲁⲱ. "This is its interpretation: iota, because the Whole has emanated (ⲓ̈ⲱⲧⲁ ϫⲉ ⲁⲡⲧⲏⲣϥ̅ ⲉⲓ 'ⲉⲃⲟⲗ); alpha, because it will return to the interior (ⲁⲗⲫⲁ ϫⲉ ⲥⲉⲛⲁⲕⲧⲟⲟⲩ ⲉϩⲟⲩⲛ); omega (double or long), because the completion of all completions will happen[15] (ⲱ'ⲱ' ϫⲉ ϥⲛⲁϣⲱⲡⲉ ⲛ̅ϭⲓ ⲡϫⲱⲕ ⲛ̅ⲛ̅ϫⲱⲕ ⲧⲏⲣⲟⲩ)" (PS IV, 136, 353, 22–25).[16]

We begin with an analysis of the verbs used by this interpretation to establish links with philosophical, gnostic and heresiological texts that can clarify the meaning of such formula.[17]

The double or long omega (ⲱ'ⲱ') refers to the Coptic verb ⲱⲱ, "to conceive", "to be pregnant",[18] then the sense of producing or giving birth (ϣⲱⲡⲉ) to the last fullness (ⲡϫⲱⲕ ⲛ̅ⲛ̅ϫⲱⲕ ⲧⲏⲣⲟⲩ). The Coptic construction ⲁⲡⲧⲏⲣϥ̅ ⲉⲓ' ⲉⲃⲟⲗ translated as "the Whole has emanated" or "unfolded",[19] as well as the terms ⲥⲉⲛⲁⲕⲧⲟⲟⲩ ⲉϩⲟⲩⲛ (= will return to the interior);[20] and the Coptic verb ϫⲱⲕ, used as noun, which also has a sense of end and fullness,[21] indicate links with certain philosophical interpreta-

---

[14] *Pistis Sophia*, pp. 706–07 and 740–41. Concerning the relations between rituals, invocations and barbaric chains, see our article mentioned in n. 1.

[15] The meaning can also be read as "the end of all ends". *A Coptic Dictionary*, comp. by W. Crum, (Oxford: Clarendon Press, 1962²), p. 761a and *Lexique copte (dialecte sahidique)*, ed. by P. Cherix, (Copticherix: UniGe, 2007), p. 82a.

[16] *Pistis Sophia*, pp. 706–07.

[17] See also M. Philonenko, "L'Anguipède alectorocéphale et le dieu Iaô", *Comptes Rendus des séances de l'Académie des Inscriptions et Belles-Lettres*, 2 (1979), pp. 297–304.

[18] *A Coptic Dictionary*, p. 518a.

[19] Also in the sense of "deploying", or "manifesting itself". See *A Coptic Dictionary*, p. 71b.

[20] Verb under ⲧⲕⲧⲟ, *A Coptic Dictionary*, p. 127b.

[21] The term ⲧⲏⲣϥ̅ also has the meanings of "the whole" and "the creation". *A Coptic Dictionary*, p. 424 a-b.

tions of the three moments in the genesis of the Second Principle or Intellect in the treatises of Plotinus 10 (*Ennead* V, 1, 7) and 38 (*Ennead* VI, 7, 16), but particularly in Treatise 11 (*Ennead* V, 2, 1). In the next section, we would like to highlight some passages of the Neoplatonic philosopher.

### *Plotinus and the Gnostics*

In Treatise 10, 6, 39–49, Plotinus explains the narrow link connecting the three hypostases (One, Intellect and Soul), and also confirms that the Intellect is "the verb (λόγος)[22] and the act of the One", which must look toward the One in order to become Intellect.

This union is evident when Plotinus describes the three stages of the generation of the Intellect and describes how they are produced by the One and how the Soul is generated in the same way. Treatise 11 states:

> the One, perfect because it seeks nothing, has nothing, and needs nothing, overflows (ὑπερερρύη), as It were, and Its superabundance (ὑπερπλῆρες) makes (πεποίηκεν) something other than Itself. This, when It has come into being, turns back (ἐπεστράφη) upon the One and is filled (ἐπληρώθη), and becomes Intellect by looking (βλέπον) towards It (i.e. the One). Its halt and turning towards the One constitutes Being, Its gaze upon the One, Intellect. Since It halts and turns towards the One that it may see, It becomes at once Intellect and Being. Resembling the One thus, Intellect produces in the same way, pouring forth (προχέας) a multiple power – this is a likeness of It – just as that which was before it poured it forth. This activity springing from the substance of Intellect is Soul [...].[23]

---

[22] Émile Bréhier adds: "Le logos (verbe) en est venu à exprimer une fonction plutôt qu'un être; chaque hypostase est le logos de la précédente et ne désigne pas comme dans la théologie chrétienne une hypostase unique". Plotin, *Les Ennéades. Ennéades V*, trad. par É. Bréhier, (Paris: Les Belles Lettres, 2003⁷), p. 23, note 1.

[23] *Enn*. V, 2 (11), 1, 7–16. *Plotinus in seven volumes V. Enneads V. 1–9*, transl. by A. Armstrong, (LCL 444), (Cambridge: Harvard University Press, 1984), pp. 58–61. Also, Plotin, *Les Ennéades V*, pp. 33–34.

It is, then, the superabundance of the One that gives birth to the Intellect, and then, turning to look at It, is fulfilled[24] by the creative power of the One, thus becoming Being.[25] In the *Ennead* V, 1 (10), 7, 17-24, Plotinus shows how the manifold comes into existence after the division undertaken by the Intellect to attain the possibilities manifested in the creative power of the One:

> But Intellect sees, by means of Itself, like something divided proceeding from the undivided, that life and thought and all things come from the One [...] For this reason that One is none of the things in Intellect; but all things come from Him.[26]

The intellect divides itself to be able to fix the multiple possibilities existing in the generating power of the One and the synthesis, by which each part has taken each of the things that will come from the One, allows it, at the same time, to give exact account of the multiple unity of the One and to give birth to the Being.

On the other hand, if we briefly examine some Valentinian texts, we find similar interpretations. The *Tripartite Tractate* (NHC I, 5) is an eighty-eight-page text from the beginning of the third century, which brings together the whole of Gnostic mythology from cosmogony to eschatology and which is attributed to a Christian writer of Valentin's school. The beginning of the Treatise presents a clear similarity between the One of Plotinus and the Valentinian Father. This, says the text, is the One who is alone, unique, immutable, "without beginning" and

---

[24] *A Greek-English Lexicon*, comp. by H. Liddell & R. Scott, revised and augmented edition by H. Stuart Jones, (Oxford: Clarendon Press, 1996⁹), pp. 1419b–1420b.

[25] In the *Ennead* V, 1 (10), 4, 21-28 Plotinus clarifies the relationship between Intellect and Being: "But Intellect is all things. It has therefore everything at rest in the same place, and it only is, and it 'is' is forever and there is no place for the future for then too – or for the past – for nothing there has passed away – but all things remain stationary forever, since they are the same, as if they were satisfied with themselves for being so. But each of them is Intellect and Being, and the whole is universal Intellect and Being, Intellect making Being exist in thinking it, and Being giving Intellect thinking and existence by being thought". *Plotinus in seven volumes V*, pp. 22-25.

[26] *Plotinus in seven volumes V*, pp. 36-37.

"without end";[27] the one who "existed before anything other than himself came into being".[28] The text adds: "and since he has the ability to conceive (ⲛⲟⲉⲓ) of himself, to see (ⲁⲛⲉⲩ) <himself>, to name (ⲣⲉⲛ) <himself> and to comprehend (ⲁⲙⲁ2ⲧⲉ) himself, he alone is the one who is his own intellect (ⲛⲟⲩⲥ)".[29] He wants to give the knowledge to be known (ⲧⲣⲟⲩⲥⲟⲩⲱⲛϥ), by the superabundance (ⲙ̄ⲡ2ⲟⲩⲟ) of its sweetness (ⲛⲧⲉϥ2ⲙⲛⲧⲁϭⲉ). So that by knowing and conceiving Himself as He is, He has a Son who subsists in Him, "in an unbegotten way, he is the one (i.e. the Son) in whom He (i.e. the Father) knows Himself who begot Him having a thought, which is a thought of Him, that is, the perception (ⲁⲓⲥⲑⲏⲥⲓⲥ) of Him".[30] The Son, for his part, is called the firstborn (ⲟⲩϣⲣ̄ⲡ ⲙ̄ⲙⲓⲥⲉ), He alone exists because no one exists after Him; but He wanted to be known, because of the wealth (ⲧⲙ̄ⲛⲧⲣⲙ̄ⲙⲁⲟ) of his sweetness (ⲙ̄ⲛⲧ2ⲁϭⲉ).[31] Thus the Son, admiring himself as Father; it is also in Him (i.e. the Unity Father-Son) that He conceives Himself as Son and from both of Them comes an innumerable and illimitable and yet indivisible offspring called the Church,[32] "innumerable offspring of aeons (ⲛ̄ⲛⲓϫⲡⲟ ⲛ̄ⲛⲁⲓⲱⲛ ⲛ̄ⲛⲁⲧⲁ[ⲡⲟ]ⲩ)".[33] This unity is the Pleroma (ⲡⲓⲡⲗⲏⲣⲱⲙⲁ) that

---

[27] *TriTrac* 52, 32 et 36. "The Tripartite Tractate", transl. by H. Attridge & E. Pagels, in *The Coptic Gnostic Library. A Complete of Nag Hammadi Codices, Volume I*, ed. by J. Robinson, (Leiden-Boston – Köln: Brill, 2000), pp. 194–95. Also, "Traité Tripartite (NH I, 5)", trad. par L. Painchaud & E. Thomassen, in *Écrits Gnostiques*, dir. par J.-P. Mahé & P.-H. Poirier, (Paris: Gallimard, 2007), p. 126. And *Le Traité Tripartite* (NH I, 5), trad. par L. Painchaud & E. Thomassen, (coll. Bibliothèque Copte de Nag Hammadi 19), (Québec: Les Presses de l'Université Laval, 1989), pp. 54–55.

[28] *TriTrac* 51, 6–8. "The Tripartite Tractate", pp. 192–93. Also, *Le Traité Tripartite*, pp. 50–51.

[29] *TriTrac* 55, 3–6. "The Tripartite Tractate", pp. 198–99. Also, *Le Traité Tripartite*, pp. 60–61.

[30] *TriTrac* 56, 32–34. "The Tripartite Tractate", pp. 200–01. Also, *Le Traité Tripartite*, pp. 64–65.

[31] *TriTrac* 57, 18–29. "The Tripartite Tractate", pp. 202–03. Also, *Le Traité Tripartite*, pp. 66–67.

[32] *TriTrac* 58, 8–30. "The Tripartite Tractate", pp. 202–03. Also, *Le Traité Tripartite*, pp. 68–69.

[33] *TriTrac* 59, 7. "The Tripartite Tractate", pp. 204–05. Also, *Le Traité Tripartite*, pp. 70–71.

exists eternally in the thought of the Father,[34] formed by the aeons about which the text affirms: "Like the Verb (ⲙ̄ⲡⲗⲟⲅⲟⲥ) He (i.e. the Father) begot Them, subsisting spermatically (ⲥⲡⲉⲣⲙⲁ), and the ones whom He was to beget had not yet come into being".[35]

In order for the aeons to understand the Father, He made Them know the Son, because the Son and the Pleroma Itself are the way that allows the knowledge of the Father.[36] In fact, the Son is the Whole, the Pleroma and the name of the Father:

> Each one of the aeons is a name <that is>, each of the properties and powers of the Father, since He exists in many names, which are intermingled and harmonious with one another. It is possible to speak of Him because of the wealth of the Verb, just as the Father is a single name, because He is unity, yet He is innumerable in His properties and names.[37]

The reading of the *Tripartite Tractate* agrees with some interpretations that, through a different method, refer to the same concepts presented by Plotinian extracts, which in turn have allowed us to understand the barbaric utterances of the *Pistis Sophia*. This confluence, which on occasion reaches significant complementarity, is evident in the following passage of the Valentinian treatise:

> Now He (i.e. the Son) who arose from Him (i.e. the Father) when He stretched himself out for begetting and for knowledge (ⲟⲩⲥⲁⲩⲛⲉ) on the part of the Totalities, He (is) [...] all of the names (ⲡⲉ ⲛⲓⲣⲉⲛ ⲧⲏⲣⲟⲩ), without falsification, and He is [...] the face of the invisible, the logos of [the] unutterable (ⲡⲗⲟⲅⲟⲥ ⲙ̄[ⲡⲓⲁⲧⲟⲩ] ⲁϩⲙⲉϥ), the intellect of the inconceivable (ⲡⲛⲟⲩⲥ ⲙ̄ⲡⲓⲁⲧⲣ ⲛ̄[ⲟⲉⲓ ⲙ̄] ⲙⲁϥ), the fountain which flowed from Him.[38]

---

[34] *TriTrac* 59, 36–60, 3. "The Tripartite Tractate", pp. 206–07. Also, *Le Traité Tripartite*, pp. 70–73.

[35] *TriTrac* 60, 34–37. "The Tripartite Tractate", pp. 206–07. Also, *Le Traité Tripartite*, 74–75.

[36] *TriTrac* 65, 17–35 and 71, 20–25. "The Tripartite Tractate", pp. 214–15 and 224–25. Also, *Le Traité Tripartite*, pp. 86–87 and 100–01.

[37] *TriTrac* 73, 8–18. "The Tripartite Tractate", pp. 228–29. Also, *Le Traité Tripartite*, pp. 104–07.

[38] *TriTrac* 66, 5–18. "The Tripartite Tractate", pp. 216–17. Also, *Le Traité Tripartite*, pp. 88–89.

The Son, the first one after the Father, is the expression of the Father who wants the existence of His knowledge and His knowledge is the Son, who has risen from the Father so that He may be known. Then, the Intellect, knowing the intelligible, made possible the existence of the Pleroma.

At this point, we could continue to establish relationships between numerous Plotinian interpretations and other Valentinian texts, such as the *Gospel of Truth* (I, 3), and even deepen the meaning of the barbaric utterances that concern us with an analysis of the notion of the name, including the affirmations of Mark the Magician referred to the "Symbolic Name" (τὸ ἐπίσημον ὄνομα) and the Jewish speculations about the origins of this aspect of the Son / Savior.[39] These topics, however, would go far beyond the objective of this paper, so we will limit ourselves to analyzing a few paragraphs from the *Excerpts of Theodotus*, another disciple of Valentinus, reported by Clement of Alexandria (150–220 AD), which clarified a range of points about the nature of the Son.

In an exegesis on the beginning of the prologue to the *Gospel of John* ("In the beginning was the Verb and the Verb was with God, and the Verb was God" [Jn 1, 1]), Theodotus states, according to Clement: "'In the Beginning' they say (i.e. the Gnostics = Theodotus), is the One [...] and it is the Verb who is 'in the Beginning', that is, in the Unborn, in the Intellect (νοῦς) and the Truth",[40] and the text continues: "Thus he who came out of 'knowledge' (γνώσεως), that is, from the thought of the Father (πατρικῆς Ἐνθυμήσεως), became also 'knowledge' (Γνῶσις), that is, the Son, because it is through the Son that the Father has been known (ἐγνώσθη)".[41]

---

[39] Jean-Daniel Dubois explains: "Nous touchons ici un aspect important du contenu du 'Nom insigne', sur le nom du Sauveur. Les spéculations marcosiennes, mais aussi valentiniennes en général sur le Nom divin, s'appuient sur des spéculations juives sur l'ineffabilité du Nom de Dieu, et sur le caractère imprononçable du tétragramme, alors que la figure divine du Nom – Shem – manifeste le caractère exprimable de la divinité". J.-D. Dubois, "Le 'Nom Insigne' d'après Marc le mage", in *Noms barbares I. Formes et contextes d'une pratique magique* dir. par M. Tardieu *et al.*, Bibliothèque de l'École des Hautes Études 162, (Turnhout: Brepols, 2013), p. 259.

[40] *Clément d'Alexandrie, Extraits de Théodote*, trad. by F. Sagnard, (Sources Chrétiennes 23), (Paris: Cerf, 1970), pp. 64–65. On the differences with the doctrine of Ptolemy exposed by Irenaeus see *Extraits de Théodote*, p. 67 note 2.

[41] *Exc. Theod.* 7, 1. *Extraits de Théodote*, pp. 66–69.

Therefore, while the individual aeons are only "shadows of the Name" and cannot individually express the perfect and flawless unity of the Pleroma; the Son as an absolute name [42] is the first manifestation of the Father, which makes his knowledge possible; but it is also He who defines the unity of the Pleroma, who establishes its form, its limits, and its existence.

## Mark, the Magician

If we return to the multiple levels of interpretation revealed by the analysis of the barbaric utterances, Iaō and its multiple variations represent the genesis of the Intellect, issued as Plotinus explains. It is also the Name / Son through which the Father is known and, likewise, the origin of the manifestation of the multiple in the Pleroma. Having understood this, the vowels included in the barbarian statements and the variations of Iaō find a coherent sense through the mythology of Mark the Magician, transmitted in Book I of *Against Heresies*:

> In 14, 7, Irenaeus of Lyon states:
>
> At once the Silence would have told Mark that the Symbolic number (ἀριθμὸν ἐπίσημον) has as an auxiliary the greatness of seven numbers, to express the fruits that by his will he has conceived. [...] The first heaven resounds the *alpha*, the second the *epsilon*, the third the *eta*, the fourth (which is also the midst of the seven) utters the power of the *iota*, the fifth the *omicron*, the sixth the *upsilon*, and the seventh (which is also the fourth from the middle) the *omega*.[43]

The identification of the vowels with the pleromatic powers is explicit in the following paragraph: "All these powers together, she says (i.e. the Silence to Mark), embracing one another, sing and glorify the Pro-Patōr who emitted them with songs of praise. The echo of this glorification fell on the earth, she says, to become

---

[42] On the immensity and incomprehensibility of the Father's name see AH I, 14, 2. *Irénée de Lyon, Contre les hérésies. Livre I, tome II*, ed. et trad. par A. Rousseau & L. Doutreleau, (Sources Chrétiennes 264), (Paris: Cerf, 1979), pp. 214–15.

[43] AH I, 14, 7. *Contre les hérésies*, pp. 226–29.

the Plasterer and the Begetter of terrestrial beings (φεφόμενόν φησι πλάστην γενέσθαι καὶ γεννήτορα τῶν ἐπὶ τῆς γῆς)".[44] These pleromatic powers praise the Verb/Logos, the first manifestation of the Father: "As, then, he says (i.e. Mark), the seven Powers glorify the Verb, so also the soul of babies, weeping and moaning give glory."[45]

Consequently, the Pleroma of Divine Manifestation is contained in the seven vowels ⲁⲉⲏⲓⲟⲩⲱ. But Mark indicates, through the description of its order, the importance of three of these vowels: iota at the very center of the series and alpha and omega on the extremes, with interchangeable roles as the beginning and the end (the fourth is also the midst of the seven and the seventh is also the fourth from the middle). This is why the barbaric chains of the *Pistis Sophia* are composed of different variants of these letters: ⲁⲉⲏⲓⲟⲩⲱ ⲓⲁⲱ ⲁⲱⲓ ⲱⲓⲁ among others.

Thus, the barbaric utterance iaō, that is ⲓⲁⲱ ⲁⲱⲓ ⲱⲓⲁ, represents a whole series of interpretive levels that include speculations about the Son-Logos contained in the Pleroma, voice that manifests the Father and origin of everything created. Or in philosophical Plotinian terms, as the Intellect through which the One communicates and manifests Itself to allow the multiplicity and the emitter of the Soul of the World, demiurge of creation.

At this point, it is evident the complexity of the initiation necessary to reach a complete understanding of the different levels of knowledge that such enunciations imply.[46] But this cryptic and mythological language is indispensable for expressing the theological truths, as the *Gospel of Philip* (NH II, 3) explains:

---

[44] AH I, 14, 7. *Contre les hérésies*, pp. 228–29.
[45] AH I, 14, 8. *Contre les hérésies*, pp. 230–31.
[46] As stated by Roy Kotansky: "The words of the gold leaf, for the most part, may not be meaningless syllables at all, but words whose sense would have been known to the maker, and conceivably to the 'initiated' wearer, as well; yet, since they prove to be foreign words written in Greek (just as *voces magicae* ultimately are), the syllables themselves become secret formulas, or powerful 'mantras', whose interpretation remains unknown to the masses. To the informed 'insider' they are recognizable words of power; to the 'outsider' they remain mysterious and arcane syllables. The distinction between 'meaningful' text and 'secret' formulas becomes subtlety blurred, perhaps even intentionally so, when it comes to texts such as this. We do not, in point of fact, know whether the words of the gold leaf were understood as meaningful or merely viewed as esoteric passwords for the deceased". R. Kotansky, "A gold *lamella* for 'blessed' abalala", *Acta Classica, Univ. Scient. Debrecen*, LII, (2016), 7–20 (p. 10).

If they (i.e. the names) were in the eternal realm (aeon), they would at no time be used as names in the world. Nor were they set among wordly things. They have an end in the eternal realm. One single name is not uttered in the world, the name which the Father gave to the Son; it is the name above all things: the name of the Father. Fort the Son would not become Father unless he wore the name of the Father. Those who have this name know it, but they do not speak it. But those who do not have it do not know it.[47]

If it is not possible to use words directly, there is, however, a way of transmitting the Truth through images. Language and words can express the Truth if they use images (because they are images), applying the relationship between them and their model: "The Truth did not come into the world naked, but it came in types and images (ⲚⲦⲨⲠⲞⲤ ⲘⲚ̄ Ⲛ̄ⲈⲒⲔⲰⲚ). The world will not receive Truth in any other way".[48]

This way is valid to express the Truth that holds the philosophy of the names, since the words, well that imperfect, can keep and transmit the Truth. It is not a question of two different languages but of one and the same: "although we refer to them by the same names. There are other names, however, they are superior to every pronounced name (ⲈⲦⲞⲨⲢ̄ⲞⲚⲞⲘⲀⲌⲈ)".[49]

## Conclusion

In his article "Magic", Wouter Hanegraff presents an historical reconstruction of the conceptions of the term magic, that is to say, what the contemporaries understood when they spoke of magic.[50]

---

[47] *Gos. Phil* 54, 1–14. "The Gospel according to Philip", transl. by W. Isenberg, in *Nag Hammadi Codex II, 2–7*, ed. by B. Layton, (Leiden-New York-Kobenhavn-Köln: Brill, 1989), pp. 146–47.

[48] *Gos. Phil.* 67, 9–11. "The Gospel according to Philip", pp. 174–75. And so the origin of All/Mainfold can also be signified with a myth based on the Verb/Logos and the emission of syllables on frames or sounds and letters of the name. See AH I, 14, 1.

[49] *Gos. Phil.* 76, 617. "The Gospel according to Philip", pp. 194–95.

[50] W. Hanegraff, "Magic", in *The Cambridge Handbook of Western Mysticism and Esotericism*, ed. by G. A. Magee, (Cambridge: Cambridge University Press, 2016), pp. 393–404. See also, E. Thomassen, "Gnostic Semiotics: The Valentinian Notion of the Name", *Temenos* 29, (1993), pp. 141–56.

For Hanegraff, the initial moment is "Magic as ancient wisdom" and he explains it as follows: "Here magic was understood very positively as referring to the wisdom of the ancients that had been passed on through history to Plato and the Platonists but had later come to be confused with demonic and superstitious practices of all kinds".[51] It is, says the Dutch author, a hidden philosophy, divine knowledge that should not be confused with minor practices.

In the same sense does Origen understand it when he affirms in *Against Celsus* I, 24–25 that magic is an "ineffable divine science (θεολογίας ἀπορρήτου)", a "philosophy of names (ὀνομάτων φιλοσοφίας)",[52] which very few know[53] and it is on the basis of this science that the divine names have been transmitted. These names, says the Alexandrian in V, 45, have an effective power (δύναται) if their original language is respected.[54] Similarly, the Neoplatonic commentators of the *Chaldean Oracles* explain: "Never change foreign names".[55]

It is necessary, then, to know the name in its original language and to declare it during the ritual without permutations, as Origen states: "It is necessary to add to the theory of names what the experts transmit in the practice of incantations (τῶν ἐπῳδῶν): to pronounce the incantation in its own dialect, is to fulfill what the incantation promises; translate the same incantation into any other language, is to see it without force or effect".[56]

---

[51] The author continues: "It is on this basis, for example, that Cornelius Agrippa wrote his famous *De occulta philosophia* in an attempt to restore magic to its ancient state of honor. It also led to endless repetitions of the apologetic argument that true magic is a good and divine thing but should not be confused with the despicable dark practices of *goetia*". "Magic", p. 400.

[52] *Against Celsus* I, 24–25. Origène, *Contre Celse, tome I (livres I et II)*, trad. M. Borret, (Sources Chrétiennes 132), (Paris: Cerf, 2005 (1967)), pp. 138–43.

[53] On the wisdom of these scribes see J. Yoyotte, "La Parole et l'objet, et vice-versa", in *Noms barbares I. Formes et contextes d'une pratique magique,* dir. par M. Tardieu *et al.*, Bibliothèque de l'École des Hautes Études 162, (Turnhout: Brepols, 2013), pp. 37–49.

[54] *Against Celsus* I, 24–25 and V, 45. *Contre Celse, tome I*, pp. 138–43 and Origène, *Contre Celse, tome III (livres V et VI)*, trad. M. Borret, (Sources Chrétiennes 147), (Paris: Cerf, 1969), pp. 130–33.

[55] Fr. 150. *Oráculos Caldeos. Numenio de Apamea. Fragmentos y Testimonios*, trad. por F. García Bazán, (Biblioteca Clásica Gredos 153), (Madrid: Gredos, 1991), p. 91 and note 267.

[56] *Against Celsus* I, 25. *Contre Celse I*, pp. 142–43.

Hence the importance of the name, as Valentin explains, since it completes the form granted to the spirit by gnosis:

> What is the cause of the image? The greatness of the person who provided (παρεσχημένου)[57] the model for the painter, so that he might be honoured through his name. For the form was not regarded as equal to the original, but the name filled out (ἐπλήρωσεν = πληρόω)[58] what was lacking in the artefact. For the invisibility of God (Rom 1, 20) as well contributes to faith in the created work.[59]

Einar Thomassen explains: "In other words, the Name, though it cannot be contained in speech, can nevertheless somehow be made present in speech by an act of faith in grace".[60]

Thus, the study of the barbaric utterances present in the *Pistis Sophia* manifests the existence of a Christianity impregnated with Egyptian realities[61] that feeds, for its esoteric and ritual practices, from various sources. Various interpretive methods are possible, but our research confirms the semantic complexity transmitted by these names.

Of course, a direct relationship between the *Pistis Sophia* and Plotinian and Valentinian texts cannot be confirmed.[62] However,

---

[57] παρέχω means also "produce", "cause" and of incorporeal things "display on one's own part". *A Greek-English Lexicon*, p. 1338a-b.

[58] The verb meaning allows "make full", "complete", and even "impregnate". *A Greek-English Lexicon*, pp. 1419b–1420a.

[59] "τίς οὖν αἰτία τῆς εἰκόνος; μεγαλωσύνη τοῦ προσώπου παρεσχημένου τῷ ζωγράφῳ τὸν τύπον, ἵνα τιμηθῇ δι' ὀνόματος αὐτοῦ οὐ γὰρ αὐθεντικῶς εὑρέθη μορφή, ἀλλὰ τὸ ὄνομα ἐπλήρωσεν τὸ ὑστερῆσαν ἐν πλάσει. συνεργεῖ δὲ καὶ τὸ τοῦ θεοῦ ἀόρατον εἰς πίστιν τοῦ πεπλασμένου." (Valentín, *Fragment*, 5 – Clem. Alex. *Str.* IV 13, 89, 6–90, 1). E. Thomassen, *The Spiritual Seed. The Church of the 'Valentinians'*, (Leiden-Boston: Brill, 2006), p. 465 and *Clément d'Alexandrie, Les Stromates. Stromate IV*, trad. par A. Van den Hoek, (Sources Chrétiennes 463), (Paris: Cerf, 2001), pp. 204–05.

[60] "Gnostic Semiotics", p. 152.

[61] *Introduction à la littérature gnostique*, p. 82.

[62] Similar speculations on the first divine manifestation can also be found in the so called "sethian texts". See J. D. Turner, "From Baptismal Vision to Mystical Union with the One: The Case of the Sethian Gnostics", in *Practicing Gnosis: Ritual, Magic, Theurgy and Liturgy in Nag Hammadi, Manichaean and Other Ancient Literature. Essays in Honor of Birger A. Pearson*, ed. by A. D. DeConick et al., (Leiden-Boston: Brill, 2013), pp. 411–31 and K. Corrigan, "The Meaning of 'One' Plurality and Unity in Plotinus and Later Neoplatonism", in *Practicing Gnosis*, pp. 523–36.

we consider to have demonstrated that the study of philosophical interpretations and the Valentinian exegesis is a valid method for understanding the reasoning behind the conception of certain barbaric utterances. Indeed, its interpretation compels the researcher to analyze both the immediate co-text of each utterance or chain and the whole treatise.[63] As well as sources "a priori" consider as outside the so-called magical texts.

We can affirm that the Valentinians' mythology, Plotinus' philosophical analysis and the barbaric utterances of the *Pistis Sophia*, show, in different ways, questions linked to the same subject: knowledge of the divine structure, the passage of One to the multiple and the mechanism of creation. The barbaric utterances are, then, an indispensable complement to the *nomen ignotum* [64] that allows us to understand the unknowable without naming it.[65]

---

[63] We can even continue our analysis by discovering how our studies allow us to explain the importance of the first barbaric chain present in Book I (PS I, 10, 16–18). Indeed, the message that pleromatic beings send to Jesus in the garment of glory shows how the philosophical data presented in this paper can help to explain the interpretations presented by the *Pistis Sophia*. These pleromatic beings name Jesus as "the mystery through which the all exists", he is everything from which everything emanates and the whole that emitted all the emissions and everything that is within them. In addition, they claim that he is the "first mystery that exists in the One before it arrives". The similarity with Plotinian and Valentinian interpretations is evident, but also with the interpretation of the second barbaric chain that we have analyzed about the name Iao. See "Rituels et énoncés barbares dans la Pistis Sophia", p. 68.

[64] See about it M. Tardieu, "Introduction", p. 12 note 4.

[65] The complexity of the different interpretive levels enclosing the barbarian names is expressed by Jean-Daniel Dubois: "En donnant accès au 'Nom insigne', la gnose marcosienne récapitule les étapes primordiales du monde pléromatique, les événements survenus dans le plérôme aboutissant à la descente du Sauveur, ainsi qu'à la mission terrestre du Jésus de l'économie. Ce sont les diverses dimensions du Nom divin qu'analyse aussi Einar Thomassen dans un bel article sur la notion valentinienne du Nom où il met en valeur les contextes protologiques des emplois du Nom, les contextes sotériologiques et leurs dimensions épistémologiques; chez les valentiniens, il y a en effet un tas de noms d'anges ou d'éons à interpréter, mais il y a aussi de vrais noms et de faux noms. Cette pluralité de contextes pour les emplois valentiniens des noms nous pousse à poser la question simple suivante: est-ce que les spéculations de Marc le mage sur le Nom insigne sont partagées par les autres valentiniens? Nous pensons donner une réponse positive à cette question, et sans pouvoir traiter de tout ce qu'implique le sujet, nous voudrions pour terminer indiquer quelques directions de recherches encore à exploiter à partir d'autres textes du corpus valentinien". "Le 'Nom Insigne' d'après Marc le mage", p. 261.

## Abstract

The expressions "barbarian names or utterances" refers to invocative or exegetical formulas, consisting of sequences of sounds or names of deities and/or demons that usually enter in a register that does not belong to the language of the document in which they are inscribed. They have usually been considered meaningless and can rarely be cut into easy units to pronounce and interpret.

The aim of this study is to show not only the diversity and complexity of the *nomina barbara* detailed in the *Pistis Sophia*, but also to support the idea that their study is essential for our understanding of theology, cosmogony and anthropology in Late Antiquity. For that purpose, on the one hand, we will study the co-text (both immediate and extended) surrounding these expressions and, on the other hand, we will conduct a parallel research on philosophical sources such as Plotinus *Enneads*, on patristic sources, such as the writings of Irenaeus of Lyon or Clement of Alexandria, and on other Gnostic texts such as the Valentinian texts of the Nag Hammadi Collection. These levels will allow diverse but confluent paths, providing a new perspective to elucidate the meaning of these barbaric utterances and to expose the ideas that they convey.

# CHAPTER 4
# THE DISCOVERY OF COPTIC AND SYRIAC MANUSCRIPTS: THEIR IMPACT ON PATRISTIC STUDIES

PATRICIA CINER
*Universidad Nacional de Cuyo, Argentina*

# BRIEF INTRODUCTION TO THE TOPIC

This chapter is dedicated to two lines of research that have reached great levels of excellence in Patristic Studies during the twentieth and twenty-first centuries: Coptic Studies and Syriac Studies. Two distinguished specialists in these areas, Dr Alberto Camplani and Dr Luise Frenkel, have contributed articles to this section.

Dr Alberto Camplani is undoubtedly one of the most renowned scholars in the field of Coptology. He worked tirelessly to organize the X International Congress of Coptic Studies in Rome in 2012, which gave rise to the magnificent volume *Coptic Society, Literature and Religion from Late Antiquity to Modern Times. Proceedings of the Tenth International Congress of Coptic Studies, Rome, September 17–22, 2012 and Plenary Reports of the Ninth International Congress of Coptic Studies, Cairo, September 15–19, 2008*. On this occasion, he presents an interesting article entitled "The Discovery of Coptic Manuscripts and the Development of Patristic Studies: Methodological and Epistemological Issues and the Challenge of Some New Research Projects". Dr Camplani clearly and precisely synthesizes this line of research stating:

> The beginning of Coptic Literature as a discipline is due not only to discoveries of manuscripts in the course of the archaeological excavations (as well as in the context of illegal private trade) or their study in academic and ecclesiastical libraries, but above all to the intellectual passion and the philological attitude which during the 18th century lead scholars to recover a forgotten literary heritage, to catalogue and reconstruct dismembered manuscripts containing works of known

and unknown authors, either translated from Greek or originally created in Coptic. The great questions concerning the origins of Coptic literary activity and the relationship of Coptic culture to Greek (Christian and secular) culture have been interpreted by scholars according to different models more or less influenced by an uninterrupted sequence of discoveries and identifications. In this paper these models will be discussed as well as their relationship to manuscript discoveries; moreover, we will look at the influence of some discoveries on the development of Patristic studies.

Dr Camplani's work breaks down this line of research into various components that offer the reader an updated and detailed view of what is currently happening in this field. For example, in the section dedicated to the notion of discovery and the peculiarity of Coptic philosophy, Dr Camplani provides a clear definition of what must be understood when we speak of Coptic language and literature, a topic that is sometimes ambiguous and difficult to define. Other important sections describe the most important ongoing research projects in Coptic Studies, PATHS (Tracking Papyrus and Parchment Paths: An Archaeological Atlas of Coptic Literature) and CMCL (Corpus de Manoscritti Copti Letterari), providing detailed descriptions of their work and illustrating their potential. In synthesis, this is a generous article written by a generous specialist which provides the methodological keys for carrying out a serious study of the impact of Coptic Studies on the contemporary Patristic world.

For her part, Dr Luise Frenkel is a promising young Brazilian academic specializing in the field of Syriac Studies and its relationship with Patristics. In addition, she has a solid research base after having worked at various European research centers. Her contribution to this volume presents the challenging topic of "Recovering Late-Antique Christian Identities: The Ongoing Discovery and Rediscovery of Syriac Manuscripts, Their Diversity, and Limitations".

Following specialists that include Joseph-Marie Sauget and Sebastian Brock, Dr Frenkel's objective is to show the decisive importance of the legacy of Syriac manuscripts for a broader and more complete understanding of Patristics. She expresses this stating that "the importance of Syriac manuscripts as conveyors of Patristic literature, whether in translations, especially from the Greek, including many not extant in the original language, or in works originally written in Syriac, has been recognized by European scholars for half a millennium".

Her article reflects a clear defense of increasing our knowledge of the Syriac world and its influence in order to better understand both the Christianity of Late Antiquity and many present-day Christian communities. In this sense, and as a conclusion, Dr Frenkel maintains:

> This section has thus shown that the corpus of Syriac manuscripts has a clear Patristic bias, which is unrepresentative of the full range of the cultural traditions in which they were made and used over a wide timeframe. Focusing on narratives of the destruction of manuscripts and cultural scenarios in which they or their content was or was not meaningful, this paper has shown that active engagement with the riches of the collections and electronic depositories of Syriac manuscripts is essential for a proper understanding of the New Testament, Early Church, Latin or Greek fathers, papal primacy, asceticism, monasticism, the philosophical legacy of the Cappadocians, Ps.-Dionysius the Areopagite, and Maximus the Confessor, among other topics of Patristic Studies. The Syriac manuscripts have and will continue to yield new texts and important information on their philosophical and political implications. Their preservation and interdisciplinary research is essential for Patristics Studies.

ALBERTO CAMPLANI
*Sapienza Università di Roma, Italy*

# THE DISCOVERY OF COPTIC MANUSCRIPTS AND THE DEVELOPMENT OF PATRISTIC STUDIES
## METHODOLOGICAL AND EPISTEMOLOGICAL ISSUES AND THE CHALLENGE OF SOME NEW RESEARCH PROJECTS[1]

The aim of this contribution is to offer some methodological considerations on the influence that the modern discoveries of Coptic manuscripts have exerted and will exert on both the evolution of Patristic studies and the modeling of the Coptic textual heritage within the context of Christian literatures produced in Greek and Oriental languages.[2] Particular attention will be paid to the extensive semantic range of the word "discovery" when applied to the

---

[1] This essay has benefited from my long-standing conversations with my teacher Tito Orlandi and my colleague Paola Buzi, as well as with my more distant colleagues Anne Boud'hors and Stephen Emmel. Responsibility for the statements found in my article is obviously entirely mine. I am grateful to Emanuel Fiano for revising my English text.

[2] The following abbreviated forms will be used throughout this essay:
*ICCopt 4* = *Actes du IV<sup>e</sup> Congrès Copte, Louvain-la-Neuve, 5–10 septembre 1988*, ed. by M. Rassart Debergh & Julien Ries (Louvain: Institut Orientaliste, 1990).
*ICCoptS 5* = *Acts of the Fifth International Congress of Coptic Studies, Washington 12–15 August 1992*, ed. by T. Orlandi (Roma: CIM, 1993).
*ICCoptS 6 (1999)* = *Ägypten und Nubien in spätantiker Zeit. Akten des 6. Internationalen Koptologenkongresses Münster, 20.-26. Juli 1996*, vol. 2: *Schrifttum, Sprache und Gedankenwelt*, ed. by S. Emmel, M. Krause, S. Richter & S. Schaten, Sprachen und Kulturen des Christlichen Orients, 6 (Wiesbaden: Reichert, 1999).
*ICCoptS 7* = *Coptic Studies on the Threshold of a New Millenium: Proceedings of the Seventh International Congress of Coptic Studies, Leiden, August 27 – September 2, 2000*, ed. by M. Immerzeel, J. Van Der Vliet & C. Van Zoest, Orientalia Lovaniensia Analecta, 133 (Louvain: Peeters, 2004).
*ICCoptS 8 Bilans* = *Huitième congrès d'études coptes (Paris 2004) Bilans et perspectives 2000–2004*, ed. by A. Boud'hors & D. Vaillancourt, Cahiers de la Bibliothèque copte, 15 (Paris: de Boccard, 2006).

recovery and reconstruction of ancient artefacts: just to take into consideration the two most extreme senses of this range, suffice it to say that, on the one hand, a discovery can be the result of archaeological excavations or negotiations with still active ancient libraries or other ecclesiastical institutions (for example the White Monastery near Sohag), accompanied by the more or less detailed description of the archaeological and documentary context by the protagonists of the discovery; on the other, it can consist in the identification of texts within codices preserved in modern libraries, originally obtained through excavations (clandestine in some cases) or the antiquarian market, with no information on the circumstances of the acquisition and the place of provenance.

Coptic studies during the twentieth century became integrated in the patristic studies, a rapidly evolving field of research that was losing progressively its confessional character and becoming familiar with the methods of philology and history as practiced in secular centres of learning. In the first part of the twentieth century the Medinet al-Madi discovery of Manichaean writings and the Nag Hammadi finding of a series of codices preserving texts mainly attributable to Gnostic tendencies made the Coptic textual heritage attractive not only for historians of Christian literature and history and specialists of the ancient translations of the Bible, but also for historian of religions and Late Antiquity. Nowadays there exist very few centers of study in which a confessional perspective on Coptic texts is prevalent. In a sense, we can state that Coptic studies as a field has both benefited from the progressive secularization of the researches on Christian literature

---

*ICCoptS 8* = *Actes du huitième congrès international d'études coptes, Paris, 28 juin – 3 juillet 2004*, ed. N. Bosson – A. Boud'hors, Orientalia Lovaniensia Analecta, 163 (Leuven: Peeters, 2007).

*ICCoptS 9–10* = *Coptic Society, Literature and Religion from Late Antiquity to Modern Times: Proceedings of the Tenth International Congress of Coptic Studies, Rome, September 17th–22nd, 2012, and Plenary Reports of the Ninth International Congress of Coptic Studies, Cairo, September 15th–19th, 2008*, ed. by P. Buzi, A. Camplani, & F. Contardi, Orientalia Lovaniensia Analecta, 125 (Leuven: Peeters, 2016).

CE = *Coptic Encyclopedia*, ed. by A. S. Atiya (New York: Macmillan, 1991) now online: http://ccdl.libraries.claremont.edu/cdm/landingpage/collection/cce.

CMCL = Corpus dei Manoscritti Copti Letterari.

PATh s = *PATh s – Tracking Papyrus and Parchment Paths: An Archaeological Atlas of Coptic Literature. Literary Texts in their Geographical Context. Production, Copying, Usage, Dissemination and Storage.*

and propelled the latter through discoveries of texts outside the bounds of the orthodox tradition. When studied with correct methodologies, these texts can provide a new, richer, and more varied image of early Christianity and Gnosticism.

The first contacts European civilization had with the Coptic Church and its rich textual heritage – in both Coptic and Arabic languages – surrounded negotiations in view of the latter's unification with the Catholic Church. The first Coptic collection in Italy was formed thanks to a missionary activity, as shown by the reconstruction of the arrival of the first Coptic codices to the Vatican Library.[3] Even at later times, when antiquarian and historical interests began to emerge, it was Catholic and subsequently other Christian missions in Egypt that constituted the main channel for Coptic codices to reach Italian and European centres of study and preservation.[4]

As Tito Orlandi has put it, studies on Coptic literature and language have "a prehistory, a beginning that can be considered official, and a scientific beginning".[5]

Their prehistory dates back to the activity of the ancient scholars of Byzantine and Arabic Egypt, attested to by Byzantine lists of words in two or three languages and later by the *scalae* that were meant to Arabic speakers' study of the Coptic language. To these works Orlandi adds the activities of those seventh- through ninth-century "Coptic scholars" who collected and systematized past literary works adding to them long titles that contained several information about the texts' authors, contents and contexts of composition. This work can be considered "as a first sketch of the history of Coptic literature (and therefore of Patristics),

---

[3] D. V. Proverbio, "Per una storia del fondo dei Vaticani Copti," in *Coptic Treasures from the Vatican Library. A Selection of Coptic, Copto-Arabic and Ethiopic Manuscripts. Papers collected on the accasion of the Tenth International Congress of Coptic Studies (Rome, September 17$^{th}$-22$^{nd}$, 2012)*, ed. by P. Buzi & D. V. Proverbio. Studi e testi, 472 (Città del Vaticano: Biblioteca Apostolica Vaticana, 2012), pp. 11–19.

[4] S. Emmel, "Coptic Studies before Kircher," in *ICCopt 7*, vol. 1, 1–11; A. Hamilton, *The Copts and the West 1439-1822. The European Discovery of the Egyptian Church* (Oxford: Oxford University Press, 2006).

[5] T. Orlandi, "La documentation patristique copte. Bilan et prospectives," in *La documentation patristique. Bilan et prospective* (Laval-Paris: Les Presses de l'Université Laval et Les Presses de l'Université de Paris Sorbonne, 1995), pp. 127–47 (128).

although unfortunately it testifies more to the image those ancient scholars had of contemporary cultural heritage than to their knowledge of the real cultural development of Coptic literature".[6] It goes without saying that texts such as those found in the Nag Hammadi codices had ceased being copied within the Coptic Church long time before.

The official beginning of Coptic studies may be dated to the Council of Florence (1439–1443). A delegation sent by Patriarch John XI (1427–1452) and headed by Andrew, abbot of the monasteries of Antony and Paul (near the Red Sea), participated in the council, leaving a good number of Copto-Arabic codices as a gift. These materials constitute the oldest Coptic fonds in the Vatican Library. Various attempts were subsequently made to study the language of Biblical and liturgical manuscripts in several centres of learning and with different results. We can mention the names of Julius Caesar Scaliger (1484–1565), Jean-Baptiste Raimondi (1540–1610), Pietro della Valle (1586–1652), Tommaso Obicini (1585–1632), Nicholas Peiresc (1580–1637: formation of the fonds of Bibliothèque Royale, now Nationale, in Paris), Claude Saumaise (1588–1653), Athanasius Kircher (1602–1680), the compiler of the first Western grammar modeled on the Copto-Arabic grammars (1636), a tool that paved the way for the scientific study of Coptic.[7]

The "scientific beginning" of the discipline may be set at this time. Coptology became a limited but important field of studies within the broader field of Christian studies. It was cultivated in all the most active European cultural centres, such as Rome, Venice, Paris, Oxford, and Berlin. The focus was understandably on language, liturgy, and biblical philology, as little information in terms of historical knowledge could be drawn from the scarce corpus of literary codices available until the early nineteenth century, the time when various kind of manuscripts began to reach the European libraries.

It is at this time that Stefano Borgia and George Zoëga began to collaborate. Their joint efforts were a turning point in the study

---

[6] T. Orlandi, "La documentation patristique copte," p. 129.

[7] P. Buzi, "*Roma e la riscoperta della 'perduta e morta lingua egizia dei Cofti' tra il Concilio di Firenze e la pubblicazione di* Lingua Aegyptiaca restituta," *Rivista Storica Italiana*, 120 (2020), 158-180.

of the growing Coptic literary corpus, as has been demonstrated by Paola Buzi.[8] Coptic codices were considered no longer antiquarian objects or mere sources for biblical studies, but rather testimonies to a rich literature, both in translation from Greek and original – indeed testimonies to an entire civilization. Zoëga's Egyptological and Coptological activities have been studied in a recent Congress.[9] Tito Orlandi has contextualized Zoëga's philological attitude in the history of seventeenth century scholarship.[10] Anne Boud'hors has offered some observations on his method, with particular attention to his recovery of the literary heritage of Shenoute of Atripe in the leaves preserved in the Borgia collection.[11] The Sahidic materials were in a bad state of preservation. On the codicological level, there existed a set of several hundred of sheets of parchment in disarray, and no complete manuscript. Various scribal hands could be recognized, some of which very similar, difficult to distinguish and to date, in the absence of comparative elements. Linguistically, in the leaves of the Borgia collection there emerged a variety of Coptic (i.e. the Sahidic dialect) still very poorly attested to in his time. From a the literary perspective, these leaves transmitted works, some of which previously unknown. The most spectacular results of Zoëga's catalogue was the identification of about thirty-five manuscripts attributable to the same author, Shenoute, hitherto totally unknown (apart from Quatrèmere):

> Le principal accomplissement de Zoëga fut en effet l'identification de ce que nous appelons aujourd'hui "unités codico-

---

[8] P. Buzi, *Catalogo dei manoscritti copti Borgiani conservati presso la Biblioteca "Vittorio Emanuele II" di Napoli, con un profilo scientifico del cardinale Stefano Borgia e Georg Zoëga*, Atti dell'Accademia dei Lincei, Anno CDVI, Classe di scienze morali. Storiche e filologiche. Memorie, serie IX, Volume XXV, Fascicolo 1 (Roma: Bardi, 2009). Of course Zoëga's work was inspired by that of other philologists, such as Giovanni Luigi Mingarelli (1722–1793), on whom see P. Buzi, "Giovanni Luigi Mingarelli e il 'primo tentennare per vie nuove': gli studi copti a Bologna nella seconda metà del XVIII secolo e la nuova stagione dei caratteri tipografici copti," in *Aegyptiaca et Coptica. Studi in onore di Sergio Pernigotti*, ed. by P. Buzi, D. Picchi & M. Zecchi (Oxford: British Archaeological Reports, 2011), pp. 33–57.

[9] *The Forgotten Scholar: Georg Zoëga (1755–1809). At the Dawn of Egyptology and Coptic Studies*, ed. by K. Ascani, P. Buzi & D. Picchi (Leiden: Brill, 2015).

[10] T. Orlandi, "Gli studi copti fino a Zoëga," in *The Forgotten Scholar*, pp. 195–205.

[11] A. Boud'hors, "Chénouté et Zoëga: l'auteur majeur de la littérature copte révélé par le savant danois," in *The Forgotten Scholar*, pp. 206–15.

> logiques", c'est-à-dire, d'ensembles de feuillets appartenant à un même livre. Parfois ces feuillets étaient encore solidaires, mais dans d'autres cas ils étaient détachés. Pour arriver à ce résultat, il fallait combiner des critères paléographiques et codicologiques (écriture, pagination, signatures de cahiers) et des critères de contenu, parfois directs (titres, mention de l'auteur), parfois indirects (sujets traités et style). Comme il a été dit, trente-cinq de ces unités furent attribuées par Zoëga à Chénouté. Plus d'un siècle après Zoëga, Johannes Leipoldt poursuivit la tâche en ajoutant aux unités codicologiques de la collection Borgia des feuillets nouvellement découverts. Il put aussi proposer un degré de classement supplémentaire, à savoir le titre de l'oeuvre, attribué par lui en fonction du sujet.[12]

This was the beginning of the study of Coptic literature, a literature in fragments that deserved an enormous philological effort to be reconstructed.

During the nineteenth century and the first half of the twentieth, discoveries of manuscripts followed one another at an increasing rate, through excavations and "discoveries" made on the antiquities market. This period witnessed also the sad phenomenon of the dismemberment of codices and of the scattering of their leaves across different European libraries. At the same time, the range of kinds of manuscripts and works retrieved continued to widen. Scholars were forced to reckon with novel linguistic forms (literary "dialects"), new kinds of codices, containing apocryphal and gnostic literature (e.g. *Berolinensis gnosticus* 8509), texts in Latin, Greek and Coptic, coexisting either in the same codex or in codices deriving from the same library. The Nag Hammadi codices and the Bodmer Papyri are among the results of this intense hunt for manuscripts.

Johannes Leipoldt was responsible for the first critical attempt at creating an outline of Coptic literature. According to Leipoldt, Shenoute and Besa (the fourth-fifth centuries abbots of the monastery of Atripe) represented the summit as well as the final stage of Coptic literature. At the same time, he was persuaded that the translations of authentic Greek texts as well as all the hagiographic and homiletic falsifications so numerous in the Coptic

---

[12] *Ibid.*, p. 209.

manuscripts should be attributed to Shenoute.[13] This representation of Coptic literature has come under serious scrutiny in recent decades.

## 1. *The Notion of Discovery and the Peculiarity of Coptic Philology*

To begin this discussion, working definitions of Coptic language and literature are needed:

- Coptic literary production may be defined as the corpus of writings, of mainly religious content, produced in Egypt between the third and the eleventh centuries in the Coptic language, in its different dialects.[14]

- Coptic developed in a context in which Greek was the official language, provided with great cultural strength. The literary genres of works found in Coptic manuscripts between the fourth and the sixth centuriy are fewer than the genres represented by works preserved in contemporaneous Greek manuscripts. In Coptic there are no poetry comparable to the the Greek, no technical tractates, with the exception of some alchemical treatises, or a treatise on the letters of the alphabet),

---

[13] J. Leipoldt, "Geschichte der Koptischen Litteratur," in *Geschichte der Christliche Litteraturen des Orients*, ed. by C. Brockelmann (Leipzig: C.F. Amelang, 1907), pp. 131–82.

[14] The reader may use the following reports about the studies on Coptic literature: T. Orlandi, "The Future of Studies in Coptic Biblical and Ecclesiastical Literature," in *The Future of Coptic Studies*, ed. by R. McL. Wilson (Leiden: Brill, 1978), pp. 1–22; Id., "The Study of Coptic Literature, 1976–1988," in *ICCoptS 4*, vol. 2, pp. 211–23; Id., "The Study of Biblical and Ecclesiastical Literature, 1988–1992," in *ICCoptS 5*, pp. 129–49; Id., "Lo studio della letteratura copta (1992–1996)," in *ICoptS 6* (1999), vol. 2, 23–37; S. Emmel, "A Report on Progress in the Study of Coptic Literature, 1996–2004," in *ICCoptS 8 Bilans* (2007), vol. 1, pp. 173–204; Id., "Coptic Literature in the Byzantine and Early Islamic World," in *Egypt in the Byzantine World, 300–700*, ed. by R. S. Bagnall (Cambridge – New York: Cambridge UP, 2007), pp. 83–102; H. Behlmer, "Research on Coptic Literature (2004–2008)," in *ICCopt 9–10* (2016), vol. 1, pp. 15–48; *Ead.*, "New Research on Coptic Literature (2008–2012)," in *ICCopt 9–10* (2016), vol. 1, pp. 303–33. Of course, some of Tito Orlandi's presentations of Coptic literature should be used as a starting point for further study: e.g. T. Orlandi, "Testi patristici in lingua copta," in *Patrologia*, ed. by A. di Berardino (Torino: Marietti, 2000), vol. 5, pp. 487–566; Id., "Literature, Coptic," in *CE*, vol. 5, pp. 1450–60.

and no professional philosophy (apart from certain Gnostic compositions).
- Coptic, differently from Greek (and in part also Latin) does not have a public role in society until the sixth century. Its role in the Church grew over time, but in the tenth century the official use of Greek by the Patriarchate will be replaced not by Coptic, but by Arabic.[15]

With regard to the contents of the discoveries initiated by Zoëga, a quadripartite taxonomy emerges: 1) New witnesses useful to broaden the textual base of already known Greek patristic works, and in some cases to improve their critical reconstruction; 2) Works by Greek patristic authors lost in their original language (occasionally preserved in other oriental languages), to whose existence a Coptic codex or even a short Coptic fragment constitutes the only testimony; 3) New Coptic authors completely unknown in the traditional patristics (Shenoute, Besa); 4) Texts pseudoepigraphically attributed to great Greek patristic authors but composed in reality in Coptic. This type of literary operation was often performed to confer greater authority to the composition in particular cases in which the need was felt to emphasize the importance of a religious festival or building (to defend their antiquity, the right to restoration, or a new construction, either in front of the Arabs, or in competition with the Chalcedonians).

At a more general level some facts connected to the discovery of manuscripts should be considered:
- A discovery may take place during an archaeological excavation. In this case, it can be accompanied by more or less detailed reports, which might provide clues to the context of preservation of the codices and therefore to the nature of their production;
- It may consist in the acquisition of a manuscript on the antiquities market;

---

[15] J.-L. Fournet, *The Rise of Coptic. Egyptian versus Greek in Late Antiquity* (Princeton: Princeton UP, 2020); A. Camplani, "Il copto e la chiesa copta. La lenta e inconclusa affermazione della lingua copta nello spazio pubblico della tarda antichità," in *L'Africa, l'Oriente mediterraneo e l'Europa. Tradizioni e culture a confronto*, Africana ambrosiana 1 (Milano-Roma: Biblioteca Ambrosiana-Bulzoni, 2015), pp. 129–53.

- It may coincide with the identification of the contents of a codex preserved in a modern library or in some other kind of repository;
- At a more basic level, it may consist in the reconstruction of a codex starting from its "pieces", which in turn may be discovered in the three ways above mentioned. This is often the case in Coptic studies.

When may a manuscript discovery be qualified as "ideal"? When it can be described, recorded, filmed. These operations allow for the preservation of information about the archaeological remains and their documentary contexts. One could think of the monastery of Apollo at Deir Bala'izah,[16] or of the Monastery of Epiphanius in Thebaid,[17] where clear examples of codices complete with their documentary and archaeological context have been found.[18] Other discoveries that had an impact on Patristic studies were certainly those concerning Coptic Manichaean writings. The famous discovery of Medinet Madi has now been supplemented with that of Kellis, where not only literary codices were found, but also documentary papyri coming from some Manichaean families. These discoveries meet all the criteria of an "ideal" manuscript discovery: literary and paraliterary manuscripts are found close to documentary papyri in an archaeological context that has been described and documented.[19]

---

[16] P. E. Kahle. *Bala'izah. Coptic texts from Deir El-Bala'izah in Upper Egypt* (London: Cumberlege, 1954).

[17] H. E. Winlock and W. E. Crum, *The Monastery of Epiphanius at Thebes*, 2 vols (New York: Metropolitan Museum, 1926-1933).

[18] With regard to Bishop Pisenthius' archive and its relation to literary production, see R. Dekker, *Episcopal Networks and Authority in Late Antique Egypt. Bishops of the Theban Region at Work*, Orientalia Lovaniensia Analecta, 264 (Leuven-Paris-Bristol: Peeters, 2018), pp. 203-75.

[19] For the Medinet Madi manuscript discovery, now part of an edition projects of Manichean writings, see C. Schmidt & H. J. Polotsky (mit einem Beitrag von H. Ibscher), "Ein Mani-Fund in Ägypten. Originalschriften des Mani und seiner Schüler," *Sitzungsberichte der Preussischen Akademie der Wissenschaften, phil.-hist. Klasse*. Sonderasugabe (Berlin: Akademie der Wissenschaften–de Gruyter, 1933), 4-90; J. M. Robinson, *The Manichaean Codices of Medinet Madi* (Cambridge: James Clarke & C, 2015). For the Kellis discovery and the documentary papyri see *Coptic Documentary Texts from Kellis: P. Kellis VII (P. Kellis Copt. 57-131)*, ed. by I. Gardner, A. Alcock & W.-P. Funk, Dakhleh Oasis Project: Monograph, 16 (Oxford: Oxbow Books, 2014). The collection "Dakhleh Oasis

More examples could be quoted of recent and less recent discoveries of Coptic manuscripts in which information about the archaeological context, as well as about the historical conditions of their preservation, production, and commission is clearly reported. And all of this becomes even more exciting when lists of books emerge attesting to their circulation in a given milieu.[20]

This, however, is not the rule. Indeed the "ideal" discovery happens in a minority of cases. Thus, the problems specific to Coptic philology include:

- the mostly modern (seventeenth- through nineteenth-century) dispersion of portions of originally complete codices across several libraries has imposed as scholars' primary task the recomposition of dismembered codices. This has stimulated the study of Coptic codicology and paleography, as well as the production of tools such as databases of information and digital images;

- the difficulty in dating a number of Coptic works that are unknown in other literary traditions. These include: a) works attributed to Athanasius, Chrysostom, Cyril, or other famous patristic authorities, or simply without attribution, which correspond to well-known texts preserved in Greek or other oriental languages, translated either as early as the third / fourth century, or later, in the fifth-seventh century; b) texts falsely attributed to one of those famous patristic authorities, sometimes written later than the sixth century and directly in Coptic, with the aim of bolstering Egyptian cultural, ecclesiastical,

---

Project: Monograph" has published most of the results of this extraordinary discovery: literary texts in Coptic and Aramaic, para-literary and documentary texts. For a general presentation of the discovery see I. Gardner, "The Manichaean Mission in Egypt," in *Quand les dualistes polémiquaient. Zoroastriens et manichéens*, ed. by F. Ruani & M. Timuş, Orient & Méditerranée, 34 (Leuven : Peeters, 2020), pp. 201–229. See also the discussion about the impact of this discovery on the debate concerning the origins and significance of the Nag Hammadi codices in A. Camplani, "From Ismant Al-Kharab to Nag Hammadi. Some Observations about Ideological Diversity in Fourth Century Groups of Coptic Manuscripts," *Studi e Materiali di Storia delle Religioni*, 86 (2020), 117–140.

[20] On the importance of these lists in the papyrological documentation see now É. Mazy, "Livres chrétiens et bibliothèques en Égypte pendant l'antiquité tardive: le témoignage des papyrus et ostraca documentaires," *Journal of Coptic Studies*, 21 (2019), 9–56.

or monastic identities. The titles of works in Coptic manuscripts tend to be generic also in the case of ancient texts; they are therefore to be considered independently from the works to which they refer.[21]

However, certain advantages in studying Egyptian material are not to be forgotten, even in relation to other Eastern Christian literatures:

- Coptologists can count more often than scholars of other Eastern Christian literary traditions – though still rarely – on the possibility of locating codices geographically over a long period of time. In medieval and modern times ancient Christian codices from Eastern regions were often preserved in important libraries formed thanks to the acquisitions of other lost libraries (Ravenna is an exception). Archeological excavations in Egypt have enabled a study of the establishment and evolution of several libraries from late ancient libraries, that in some cases have been identified.
- The relationship between literary activity and the literacy of the milieus in which it is practiced can be outlined in much greater detail in Coptic than in other literatures. The discoveries illuminate therefore not only the literature itself, but also the economic, administrative and monastic context in which it developed.

Therefore, as Orlandi has put it, "The works which constitute the Coptic literature, and their relative manuscripts, are not easily classified according to a general and consistent critical and historical arrangement. The main obstacles which have determined this situation are well known, and easily appreciated, but also hard to cope with. First is to be mentioned the fragmentary condition of most documents, due to the vicissitudes of the manuscripts after the death of Coptic as a spoken language, and later on their disordered transportation outside of Egypt; secondly, to the peculiar instability which characterizes the text of the literary (patristic) works as they have been transmitted in Coptic."

---

[21] See P. Buzi, *Titoli ed autori nella tradizione copta. Studio storico e tipologico* (Pisa-Roma: Giardini, 2005).

The problems typicallly faced by Coptologists can be summarized as follows: "Too frequently, when we speak of a 'codex', we do not mean something that we really have in our hands, but a number of sheets once belonging to a complete codex, but now dispersed in several collections. And when we speak of a work, we do not mean an established text with one consistent tradition, but something that was often reshaped by scribes or clerks more or less competent, in order to accommodate the text to new exigencies; or even fragments of such a text." [22]

## 2. *Textual Contributions of Discoveries*

### 2.1 Manuscripts or Fragments Belonging to Already Known Texts: Their Philological Contribution

We will begin with the easiest type of discovery, the one which takes place when a scholar is able to recognize the fragment or the leaves he or she is studying as part of an already known text, originally written either in Coptic or in Greek. If it is a Coptic text, the philological problems are those shared by ancient literature in all languages: is this a fragment belonging to an already-identified dismembered manuscript or a new manuscript witness? As for the text, does it contain variants due to textual evolution or corruption, to its dialectological variety (which was the literary language of the original?), or a plurality of recensions? The identification of a fragment coming from an already known Greek (or Syriac) [23] writing adds to these problems new important ones: To what family of Greek manuscripts is it a witness? Is it a different translation from the one already known? Is it a trace of a textual situation not attested by the Greek documentation? The two following examples drawn from my own activity with Coptic and Greek texts found in Egypt are meant to give the reader an idea of what can happen with new identifications of Coptic transla-

---

[22] T. Orlandi, "A Terminology for the Identification of Coptic Literary Documents," *Journal of Coptic Studies*, 15 (2013), 87–94 (87–88).

[23] On the possibility of a direct translation from Syriac to Coptic, see A. Suciu, "The Sahidic Version of Jacob of Serugh's Memrā on the Ascension of Christ," *Le Muséon*, 128 (2015), 49–83.

tions of Greek writings, in particular when Coptic translations broaden our knowledge of a lost Greek tradition.

*P. Vindob.* K 10157 is a roll of papyrus written on both sides.[24] The recto has has been identified as Cyril's *Festal Letter* 1, written for Easter 413, in Coptic translation, specifically in Achmimic.[25] What is more impressive in this identification is the fact that it allows to perceive a severe corruption in the entire Greek tradition of the letter, consisting in the conflation of the first section of *Letter 1* (Easter 413) and the second section of *Letter 2* (Easter 414). Only the first part of the Coptic letter has a parallel in the Greek text published in *Patrologia graeca* and now in *Sources chrétiennes*.[26] When reading in parallel the Greek text and the Coptic version, one can easily realize that at some point the latter deviates from the former, naturally continuing up to the announcement of Easter of 413 and the list of episcopal successions in Egypt for that year, according to the typical style of the festal letters. The Greek text at that point does not present obvious errors of syntax or grammar, but a logical leap in the argumentation can be detected. Then, differently from the Coptic version, it continues until the announcement of Easter of 414. Probably a mechanical error occurred in the Greek tradition (the loss of a quaternion?), which was followed by an activity of "textual restauration" by a scribe, whose copy is at the origin of the Byzantine textual tradition. The lack of a letter announcing the Easter date corresponding to the first year of Cyril's episcopate, AD 412–13, had been noted for some time. Someone had supposed that this absence was due to the obscure circumstances surrounding the beginning of Cyril's episcopate. The Coptic text allows us to solve this prob-

---

[24] *Osterbrief und Predigt in akhmimischem Dialekt*. Mit Übersetzung und Wörterverzeichnis, herausgegeben von W. Till, Studien zur Epigraphik und Papyruskunde, 11 (Leipzig: Dieterich'sche Verlag, 1931).

[25] A. Camplani, "La prima lettera festale di Cirillo di Alessandria e la testimonianza di *P. Vindob.* K 10157," *Augustinianum*, 39 (1999), pp. 129–38. See also the notes of comment upon the episcopal list: A. Camplani & A. Martin, "Lettres festales et listes épiscopales dans l'Église d'Alexandrie et d'Égypte. À propos de la liste épiscopale accompagnant la première lettre festale de Cyrille d'Alexandrie conservé en copte," *Journal of Juristic Papyrology*, 30 (2000), 7–20.

[26] Cyrille d'Alexandrie, *Lettres Festales*, I–VI, Introduction générale par P. Évieux, Introduction critique, texte grec par W. H. Burns, Traduction et annotation par L. Arragon, M.-O. Boulnois, P. Évieux, M. Forrat, B. Meunier, Sources Chrétiennes, 372 (Paris: Cerf, 1991).

lem. This text, moreover, by revealing that the Greek text is the product of the conflation of two different letters, offers an answer to the question concerning the comparatively excessive length of the so-called "First Festal Letter" in the Greek tradition.

What is lacking in my own study is both an accurate description of the artefact and a hypothesis about the reason of the choice of a roll as a support for the text. The papyrus is described by Stephen Emmel in the following terms: "three columns (of varying dimensions) of a roll (later than 413), from which at least one column is missing at the beginning but possibly no more at the end, 280 × 780 mm but originally both taller and longer [...]; on the back, an unidentified homiletic work was written *transversa charta* (so in *rotulus* form), starting at the beginning of the roll".[27] This form is an oddity in Coptic. It is to be compared with few other examples of Coptic rolls containing festal letters, monastic letters or excerpts of canonical literature. In the case of the Vienna papyrus one reason for the choice of this particular support was the imitation of the typical format of the Greek festal letters (probably this was specifically the form in which that of 413 was circulating).

There remains an open question about the dating of the papyrus. The script of the roll appears very ancient. A fifth century dating of it seems reasonable also based on the history of the literary dialect in which the text is written (Achmimic), which, after a fourth / fifth century *acme*, experienced a decline already in the following century. However, we are unable to establish whether our papyrus is really a copy of the translation of the Greek letter in Coptic made in the spring of the year 413. Although such an early dating and immediate translation are in no way proven, they cannot be excluded either. An alternative hypothesis is suggested by a comparison with other texts preserved in this format, from which it appears that rolls and *rotuli* could be used to give

---

[27] S. Emmel, "5.2. Book forms", in P. Buzi and S. Emmel, "5. Coptic Codicology", in *Comparative Oriental Manuscript Studies. An Introduction*, ed. by A. Bausi (General Editor) (Hamburg: Tredition, 2015), pp. 137–53 (140–41). See now N. Carlig, "Les rouleaux littéraires coptes de papyrus (ca. 300-VII[e] siècle)", in *Études coptes XVI. Dix-huitième journée d'études (Bruxelles, 22-24 juin 2017)*, ed. by A. Boud'hors *et al.*, Cahiers de la Bibliothèque copte, 23 (Paris : Boccard, 2020), pp. 229–49 (pp. 239–40).

a document the appearance of a normative text. Of course, these same texts could be transcribed in other book-forms, for example a papyrus codex, to become properly literary works.

Another beautiful example is provided by Epiphanius' *Ancoratus*. Eduard Schwartz had already supposed that in the final chapters of this work a Byzantine scribe had substituted the Constantinopolitan Creed to the Nicene one, which was originally in Epiphanus' text and is in a sense presupposed by the author's comments before and after the quotation.[28] The following quotation from Bibliothèque Nationale de France, Copte 131.5 f. 36 bolsters Schwartz's hypothesis: [...] ⲁⲩⲱ ϥⲛⲏⲩ ⲉⲕⲣⲓⲛⲉ ⲛⲛⲉⲧ[ⲟ]ⲛⲍ ⲙⲛ ⲛⲉⲧⲙⲟⲟ[ⲩⲧ] ⲁⲩⲱ ⲍⲙ ⲡⲉⲡⲛ̅[ⲁ ⲉ]ⲧⲟⲩⲁⲁⲃ [29] ("and he will come to judge the living and the dead; and [I believe] in the Holy Spirit"): these expression are typical of the Nicene Creed, not of the Constaninopolitan one. The same has been demonstrated by Bernd Weischer in relation to the Ethiopic translation.[30]

This is only one of the dozens of examples which could be mentioned to demonstrate that a new identification can change the reconstruction of the tradition of a text. Coptic variants often offer a new perspective on the Greek tradition, for example on the indirect one. An example is the Coptic version of John Chrysostom's *On David and Saul III*, several of whose readings, not attested in the direct Greek tradition, occur in the indirect tradition, suggesting that they should be considered in the establish-

---

[28] E. Schwartz, "Das Nicaenum und das Constantinopolitanum auf der Synode von Chalkedon", *Zeitschrift für die neutestamentliche Wissenschaft*, 25 (1926), 38–88.

[29] Christian Bull is now editing all the Coptic fragments of Epiphanius' *Ancoratus*. About other features of the Coptic translation see also A. Camplani, "Epifanio (*Ancorato*) e Gregorio di Nazianzo in copto: identificazioni e *status quaestionis*," *Augustinianum*, 35 (1995), 327–47; D. V. Proverbio, "Introduzione alle versioni orientali dell'*Ancoratus* di Epifanio," *Miscellanea Marciana*, 12 (1997) 67–91.

[30] For the text and the new textual witnesses see *Epiphanius I. Ancoratus und Panarion Haer 1–33*. 2., erweiterte Auflage, ed. by Marc Bergermann and Christian-Friedrich Collatz. GCS. Neue Folge. Band 10/1 (Berlin-Boston: de Gruyter, 2013), pp. 533–36. On the Ethiopic texts see B. M. Weischer, "Die ursprüngliche nikänische Form des ersten Glaubenssymbols im Ankyratos des Epiphanios von Salamis," *Theologie und Philosophie*, 53 (1978), 407–14; Id., *Qerellos IV/2. Traktate des Epiphanios von Zypern und des Proklos von Kyzikos*, Äthiopistische Forschungen, 6 (Wiesbaden: Franz Steiner, 1979).

ment of the Greek text.³¹ This is also the case with another recent exceptional discovery: the identification by Sofía Torallas Tovar of a very ancient Coptic translation of Athanasius' *Letter to Dracontius* in a papyrus roll of the fourth / fifth century preserved in the Montserrat Monastery. Also this Coptic text contains a number of variants which must be taken into consideration for a new edition of the Greek letter.³²

## 2.2 Identification of Lost Works Written in Coptic or Translated from Greek

Of course, a more exciting event in Coptic studies is the identification or discovery of texts that were not previously known. I will deal later with the question, too often neglected, of the cultural significance of works that at one point were eliminated for the most various reasons from the literary corpus that was considered worthy of being handed down. Here I would like to offer a few examples. The first concerns a set of texts which were preserved for a long time and made it through all the steps of selection, while the others deal with texts progressively marginalized.

The first example is the recovery of Shenoute's works,³³ a great and multifaceted discovery to be attributed to a plurality of protagonists of the modern Coptic scholarship. I will return later to the research project about Shenoute which aims not only to deal with his works, but also to reconstruct their bibliological organization. For the moment, two aspects should be stressed about the progressive recovery of this literary corpus. On the one hand, Shenoute, the archimandrite of the monastery of Atripe or "White Monastery", one of the greatest saints of the Coptic Church, known until the seventeenth century as a holy man, was recognized by Émile Quatremère and Georg Zoëga as an important author of Coptic texts. These were to be

---

[31] F. P. Barone, "Una versione copta dell'omelia *De Dauide et Saule* III di Giovanni Crisostomo trádita da un papiro del Museo Egizio di Torino (VIII Orlandi)," *Orientalia Christiana Periodica*, 75 (2009), 463–73.

[32] S. Torallas Tovar, "Athanasius' Letter to Dracontius: A 4th Century Coptic Translation in a Papyrus Roll (P.Monts.Roca inv. 14)," *Adamantius*, 20 (2018), 22–38.

[33] See A. Crislip, "Shenoute Studies," in *ICCoptS 9–10*, 335–64.

reconstructed through a complex philological effort of recomposition of groups of leaves coming to Europe through the activity of the missionaries and the antiquities market. On the other hand, the remnants of the library of the Monastery of Shenoute were discovered by Gaston Maspero in a small room behind the eastern staircase of the church. However things went after this discovery, we have to aknowledge that it created the conditions to establish a close connection between the codices disseminated in Europe and their original storage site.[34] The library of the monastery of Atripe can now be at least described for what concerns its contents.[35] The monastery itself has become a fruitful object of archaeological research, as has been demonstrated by the recent discovery of Shenoute's tomb.

It is interesting to observe that Shenoute's works survive in codices coming mainly from the library of his own monastery. According to Stephen Emmel "from the White Monastery library there survive parts of about one hundred codices containing works of Shenoute, perhaps about 10% of the total number of codices for which there is evidence that they formed the library's holdings'.[36]

---

[34] S. Emmel, *Shenoute's Literary Corpus*, 2 vols, CSCO 599, Subsidia 111 (Leuven: Peeters, 2004), I, 13–24; Id. & C. Römer, "The Library of the White Monastery in Upper Egypt / Die Bibliothek des Weißen Klosters in Ober Ägypten," in *Spätantike Bibliotheken. Leben und Lesen in den frühen Klöstern Ägyptens*, ed. by H. Froschauer and C. E. Römer (Vienna: Phoibos Verlag, 2008), pp. 5–24; C. Louis, "Nouveaux documents concernant l' 'affaire des parchemins coptes' du Monastère Blanc", dans *ICCopt 8*, vol. I, p. 99–114; C. Louis, "The Fate of the White Monastery Library," in *Christianity and Monasticism in Upper Egypt*, vol. 1: *Akhmim and Sohag*, ed. by G. Gabra and H. N. Takla (Cairo and New York: The American University in Cairo Press, 2008), pp. 83–90; T. Orlandi & A. Suciu, "The End of the Library of the Monastery of Atripe," in *Coptic Society, Literature and Religion from Late Antiquity to Modern Times: Proceedings of the Tenth International Congress of Coptic Studies, Rome, September 17–22, 2012, and Plenary Reports of the Ninth International Congress of Coptic Studies, Cairo, September 15th–19th, 2008*, 2 vols, ed. by P. Buzi, A. Camplani, & Federico Contardi, Orientalia Lovaniensia Analecta, 247 (Leuven: Peeters, 2016), pp. 891–918.

[35] T. Orlandi, "The Library of the Monastery of Saint Shenute at Atripe," in *Perspectives on Panopolis: An Egyptian Town from Alexander the Great to the Arab Conquest. Acts from an International Symposium Held in Leiden on 16, 17 and 18 December 1998*, ed. by A. Egberts, B. P. Muhs, & J. van der Vliet (Leiden: Brill, 2002), pp. 211–31.

[36] S. Emmel, "Shenoute the Archimandrite: The Extraordinary Scope (and Difficulties) of His Writings," *Journal of the Canadian Society for Coptic Studies*, 10 (2018), 9–36 (13–14).

The reconstruction of Shenoute's literary heritage was achieved by combining on the one hand codicology and palaeography (in order to recover dismembered codicological units), and on the other hand bibliological and textual analysis (in order to capture the structure of Shenoute's literary corpus). The edition of Shenoute's literary heritage will contribute greatly to the undertaking of mining Shenoute's writings for information about ecclesiology, monastic discipline and theology.[37]

The real events that unfolded in relation to the Nag Hammadi's discovery as well as its connection with the antiquities market are still far from being clarified.[38] In any event, this finding concerns peculiar and archaic-looking codices. Unlike Shenoute's works, these writings were not subsequently transcribed and preserved, but rather quickly marginalized from the mainstream Coptic textual transmission. This process was likely due to the doctrine and religious language they employed, which at a certain point in time (possibly after the second half of the fifth century) could no longer be accepted. No discovery of Coptic manuscripts had as strong an impact on Patristic studies as the Nag Hammadi finding. Scholars saw in the codices the possibility of a direct access to a Gnostic library, constituted by texts reflecting Gnosticism's doctrine without the mediation of Christian authors as well as by other texts that, though not qualified as properly Gnostic, were at least the product of varieties of Christianity that had disappeared

---

[37] J. Timbie, "Shenoute of Atripe", in *The Wiley Blackwell Companion to Patristics*, ed K. Parry (Chichester UK, Wiley Blackwell, 2015), pp. 184–96.

[38] On this much-debated issue see M. Goodacre, "How Reliable is the Story of the Nag Hammadi Discovery?," *Journal for the Study of the New Testament*, 35 (2013), 303–22; N. J. Denzey Lewis and J. A. Blount, "Rethinking the Origins of the Nag Hammadi Codices," *Journal of Biblical Literature*, 133 (2014), 397–419. See the documentation in J. M. Robinson, *The Nag Hammadi Story*. Vol. 1: *The Discovery and Monopoly*. Vol. 2. *The Publication*, Nag Hammadi and Manichaean Studies, 86 (Leiden: Brill, 2014); *Histoire des manuscrits coptes. La Correspondance Doresse-Puech 1947–1970*, présentée par M. Tardieu, éditée par E. Cregheur, J. M. Robinson & M. Tardieu, Bibliothèque copte de Nag Hammadi, Études, 9 (Québec – Louvain – Paris: Les Presses de l'Université Laval – Peeters, 2015). To all this is to be added N. Denzey Lewis's response: "Rethinking the Rethinking of the Nag Hammadi Codices," *Bulletin for the Stuidy of Religion*, 45 (2016), 2, 39–45 (see at p. 45 the balanced estimation of what we really know: "that the codices gradually appeared on the antiquities market; that they apparently came from the Jebel al-Tarif; and that they share details such as binding styles and scribal hands.").

in the course of its evolution (among other examples, the *Gospel of Thomas*).[39]

Needless to say that, alongside texts that had a parallels in those cited by the heresiological tradition, others appeared completely new: the influence of this discovery on early Christian studies is not comparable to the much more modest one of the "Gnostic" codices that arrived in London and Berlin between the eighteenth and nineteenth centuries.[40] Nowadays, after more then seventy years since the discovery, a more nuanced evaluation can be offered about the codices and the works they contain. The initial enthusiasm and the marked tendency to move back their dating as far as possible over time have given way to a detailed study of the various religious and textual traditions that went into their composition. While this study has led to confirm the antiquity of some writings, it has also highlighted in some cases a strong tendency to rewrite texts and update their religious language. Thus a good portion of these texts is to be considered a late literary product, to be dated to the end of the third or the beginning of the fourth century. The library of Nag Hammadi itself, the result of the confluence of several subgroups of codices, should no longer be considered the product of fourth-century Gnostic groups comparable to those of the second century. It must be placed in relation, instead, to a plurality of intellectual, clerical, monastic milieus which were part of the rich Egyptian religious landscape.[41] In addition, the documents preserved in the covers pose interesting problems concerning the connection between

---

[39] For the debate about the notion of Gnosticism in relation the Nag Hammadi codices, see M. A. Williams, *Rethinking "Gnosticism". An Argument for Dismantling a Dubious Category* (Princeton NJ, Princeton UP, 1996); K. King, *What is Gnosticism?* (Cambridge: Belknap, 2003); D. Brakke, *The Gnostics: Myth, Ritual, and Diversity in Early Christianity* (Harvard: Harvard UP, 2012).

[40] On the Coptic codices known before the appearance of the Nag Hammadi library, see M. Tardieu & J.-D. Dubois, *Introduction à la littérature gnostique*. T. 1: *Collections retrouvées avant 1945* (Paris: Cerf-CNRS, 1985).

[41] A discussion about the possible contexts in which the Nag Hammadi library could be situated can be read in H. Lundhaug & L. Jenott, *The Monastic Origins of the Nag Hammadi Codices*, Studien und Texte zu Antike und Christentum, 97 (Tübingen, Mohr, 2015); for a critique of their proposal see P. Piwowarczyk & E. Wipszycka, "A Monastic Origin of the Nag Hammadi Codices," *Adamantius*, 23 (2017), 432–58.

their productions and their impact onto the lay and monastic worlds.[42]

A very instructive example, among many, of the discovery among a group of fragments preserved in a library of an early lost work, about which antiquity has provided no information, is *P. Berlin* 20915, a fourth-fifth century papyrus codex reduced to little fragments. The long effort of its editors has resulted in the reconstruction of a sequence of sheets whose textual content appears exceptional.[43] The text contained in this codex speaks, in a first part, of the creation of the human being in a sophisticated, biblically and philosophically nourished language, and then discusses the effects that divine wrath, provoked by human sins and transgressions, could have on humanity and the created world. The title contained in the lost first sheets of the codex is missing and the overall structure of the text is not completely penetrable. It is not sure that the two blocks of fragments of different content belong to the same work. Nevertheless, an argument in favor of the work's unity could come from a comparison with a homily falsely attributed to Basilius of Caesarea, contained in a rather ancient codex, dedicated to creation, God's economy in the history of salvation, and his wrath.[44] *P. Berol.* 20915 contains a great number of quotations, drawn from the Christian Scriptures, the *Epistle of Barnabas*, the *Sybilline Oracles*. The citation style has been shown to be comparable to Clement of Alexandria's. As it is

---

[42] The texts are published in *Nag Hammadi Codices: Greek and Coptic Papyri from the Cartonnage of the Covers*, ed. by J. W. B. Barns, G. M. Browne, & J. C. Shelton, Nag Hammadi Studies, 16 (Leiden: Brill, 1981); see the observations by E. Wipszycka, "The Nag Hammadi Library and the Monks: A Papyrologist's Point of View," *Journal of Juristic Papyrology*, 30 (2000), 179–91.

[43] Edition: *Das Berliner "Koptische Buch" (P. 20915): Eine wiederhergestellte frühchristlich-theologische Abhandlung*, ed. by G. Schenke Robinson, CSCO 610–11, Scriptores coptici 50–51 (Leuven: Peeters, 2004).

[44] Good observations on the text and its style of quotation can be found in H.-M. Schenke, "Der Barnabasbrief im Berliner Koptischen Buch (*P. Berlin.* 20915)," *Enchoria*, 25 (1999), 43–75; A. van der Hoek, "*Papyrus Berolinensis* 20915 in the Context of Other Early Christian Writings from Egypt," in *Origeniana Octava. Origen and the Alexandrian Tradition*, ed. by L. Perrone, Bibliotheca Ephemeridum Theologicarum Lovaniensium, 164 (Leuven: Peeters, 2004), pp. 76–92, with very useful appendices about the citation of Scripture and early Christian writings in comparison with Clement of Alexandria. For the homily attributed to Basil, see *Clavis Coptica* 0076 and E. A. Wallis Budge, *Coptic Homilies in the Dialect of Upper Egypt* (Oxford: Oxford UP, 1910), n. VIII.

obvious, the similarity of citation style does not authorize setting a date for the Greek original, which could be later. This Coptic translation is a trace of the interest of those intellectuals who used the Coptic language for very complex writings. The subsequent disappearance of this work from the Coptic literary tradition was due more to the difficulty of its contents and style than to its anthropological and theological ideas.

### 2.3 Methodological Remarks on Coptic Libraries and Evolving Portraits of Coptic Literature

What can new manuscript discoveries teach us about the transformations of the Coptic textual heritage in the course of time – in its entirety or in its regional dimensions – that is, about the selection, preservation, and accretion of the textual canon?

The textual competence, articulating the contents of Coptic literature, has a long history, which begins in late antiquity. Each historical phase, especially after the Council of Chalcedon, has its own image of the literary heritage, its own selection of the textual "competence" or "competences". This image is diverse and composite in itself at each time and, additionally, it changes over time. As far as Sahidic literary tradition is concerned, we have inherited the image transmitted by the clergy and intellectuals active in the eighth and ninth centuries, while the images created in previous periods are precluded to us, at least in part.

Manuscript discoveries allow us to overcome the limitations of a phase of textual selection by taking notice of the existence of ancient codices prior to these phases, containing texts later relegated for various reasons to the margins of the main stream of textual heritage. These findings provide us with new snapshots of the Coptic textual situation in different phases of the religious controversies, or, in a synchronic and spatial perspective, in different regions, dioceses, and monastic settlements.

The study of individual libraries, of their remains, or of the lists of book titles, offers important traces to reconstruct the textual selection and the cultural life of regions and even entire churches.

As far as the dating of Coptic manuscripts is concerned, most of them are attributable to the period from the ninth to the eleventh centuries, that is, much later than a good number of the texts they contain. Most of these manuscripts are collections put together for liturgical purposes, bringing together texts of various origins and dates. Those texts may have been rewritten through the centuries.

Therefore, it is important to study manuscripts preceding the ninth century and to interpret correctly the textual transmission after that date. We must always keep in mind different possibilities:

1) An original Coptic text or a translation from Greek is preserved in a manuscript that can be dated to a time after the phase of selection of the ninth century:

    a. we should keep in mind that this does not mean that the text is late; we should consider, if it is an ancient text, that it has passed through previous phases of selection. Shenoute's corpus in the context of the White Monastery is such a case;

    b. however we should not exclude the possibility that a text has been composed immediately before the selection phase; in this case, the textual analysis, the study of the title and other stylistic and linguistic elements will suggest a possible dating;

2) texts preserved in ancient codices (fourth to sixth century) have been marginalized for the most different reasons and then disappeared. It is precisely in these cases that the discoveries of manuscripts preceding the great phases of cultural selection allow us not only to know new texts, but also to get an idea of the cultural currents active in different historical periods, textual competences different and probably larger than those found after the selection and addition of new, later texts. The most impressive example is that of the Nag Hammadi codices.

This kind of analysis should be repeated for group of manuscripts coming from known milieus: a monastery, a church, etc. It is useful for example to compare the Turin collection, coming from This, with what was circulating in Coptic before the seventh century and what was to become the standard textual competence in the following centuries. Very acute observations have been proposed in this regard by Tito Orlandi.[45] According to him, the originality

---

[45] T. Orlandi, "The Turin Coptic Papyri", *Augustinianum*, 53 (2013), 501–30.

of the fund – a clear sign of its antiquity – is revealed by the fact that, out of a total of thirty-eight identified works, eighteen are not represented in any other identified Coptic manuscript: "this means that when the library was assembled many texts were still in use, which later became obsolete". Among them, there is the *Life of Aphu*, as has been demonstrated above, one of the most important texts of Coptic literature. The This Library would reflect the textual competence and the ideological perspectives of the seventh-eighth century, before the turn of what Orlandi qualifies as "the synaxarial systematization":

> Before the sixth century its (= Coptic literature's) character does not differ from that of the contemporary international (Greek) Christian literature. But after that time the Chalcedonian separation and the Arab conquest had the effect of giving way 1) first to a group of Coptic writers (mainly learned bishops) who wanted to replace older texts for some special liturgical feasts; 2) then to the anonymous production of cyclical texts, whose scope was to reassess the history of Egyptian Christianity, for the edification of the contemporary public, and for anti-Islamic polemic; 3) later still, at the beginning of the ninth century, with the crisis of the Coptic Church, the main work of the Coptic intellectuals was to choose the texts to be saved, especially for liturgical reasons, and having them copied in classical codices which we call *synaxaries*. In the Turin papyri (which I would call the library of Tin) most of the texts are translations from the Greek, which can be reasonably assigned to around the fifth century. None belongs to the late sixth century literary group mentioned above, and only five belong to the "cycles".[46]

Paola Buzi has corroborated Orlandi's observation in an article in which the provenance and the modern history of the collection is revisited and enriched with new details:[47]

> The layout of the codices is normally in two columns – with three exceptions – the writing is in evolution, and the titles

---

[46] *Ibid.*, 527.

[47] P. Buzi, "The Coptic Papyrus Codices Preserved in the Museo Egizio, Turin: New Historical Acquisitions, Analysis of the Codicological Features, and Strategies for a Better Understanding and Valorization of the Library from Thi(ni)s", *Adamantius*, 24 (2018), 39–57.

always stand before the works they refer to. *Subscriptiones* (or final titles) occasionally survive, but no longer represent the main titles. As for the contents, there is a meaningful presence of Greek patristic works translated into Coptic in the fifth century (the so-called "classical translations", according to Tito Orlandi's classification), some apocrypha (such as the *Acta Pilati*), old-style works that reflect the theological controversies of the end of the 4th century (for instance, the *Vita Aphou*, transmitted exclusively by a Turin codex), some original works of the 6th century (such as Damian of Alexandria, *De Nativitate*), a few pseudoepigraphal works and a selection of normative works, such as the *Gnomai Concilii Nicaeni*, and last but not least the *De iudicio* of *Shenoute*, which represents, so far, the most ancient manuscript transmitting a work of Shenoute. It is useless to stress how important is the presence of this work in the Thi(ni)s codices for the reconstruction of the dissemination of the works of the archimandrite of Atripe.

Of course, there are texts in Turin whose significance should be emphasized. The *Vita Aphu* has changed our perception of the Origenistic controversy. It is probably a text of the fifth or sixth century which reveals the ideological configuration of a great part of the monastic world about such crucial themes as the human being in God's image and the place of vision in prayer. In this text there emerges a Christian perspective distant from the traditional one of the Alexandrian milieus with their spiritualistic anthropology and allegorical exegesis. In the perspective of the *Vita Aphu* the unity of the human components, body and spirit, is stressed against dualism, and emphasis is lain on the role of the body in the glorification of God, also by the ascetics as well as on the concreteness of the vision of God during the prayer.[48]

The few remains of older manuscripts that were found at the White Monastery are all the more precious for the history of the

---

[48] See D. Bumazhnov, *Der Mensch als Gottes Bild im christlichen Ägypten. Studien zu Gen 1, 26 in zwei koptischen Quellen des 4.-5. Jahrhunderts*, Studien und Texte zu Antike und Christentum, 34 (Tübingen: Mohr Siebeck, 2006), and, especially for bibliographical discussion, A. Camplani, "Il dibattito sulla visione di Dio e sull'"uomo ad immagine' nel monachesimo egiziano: interpolazioni e riscritture nei testi copti attribuiti ad Agatonico di Tarso", in *L'anti-Babele. Sulla mistica degli antichi e dei moderni*, ed. I. Adinolfi, G. Gaeta, & A. Lavagetto (Genova: Il nuovo melangolo, 2017), pp. 149–83.

textual competence in that monastery.[49] And in any case, there are smaller groups of manuscripts coming from other monasteries which could predate the reorganization into collections.[50] The monasteries of Scete have yelded the Bohairic manuscripts (ninth to eleventh century) that reached the Vatican Library. Fifty codices of the monastery of St Michael in the Fayyūm, datable to the ninth to tenth century, are now preserved in the Pierpont Morgan Library. Monasteries of the Theban region have given us remains of forty-five codices (seventh to eighth century);[51] and manuscripts from the monasteries or churches of the region of Esna are now in the British Library.

Other libraries are less defined, such as that of Nag Hammadi or the Bodmer papyri, to which a conference has been devoted recently.[52] Also this last library demonstrates a coexistence of Greek, Latin and Coptic which was destined to decline over time, and an intellectual and religious curiosity that was to be contained and channeled. Other codices of the period from the fourth to the fifth century clearly show a great variety of ideological positions, concerning anthropology, Christology, spirituality, and eschatology: they are the sign of living debates, of a Coptic Christian culture open to different ideas and theories. The effects of the Christological controversies and of ecclesiastical divisions and conflicts, as well as of the Persian invasion and the Arabic domination, were to reduce the spaces of freedom and the wide range of ideological options that can still be observed in the earliest centuries of Coptic literature.

---

[49] T. Orlandi, "The Library of the Monastery of Saint Shenute at Atripe", in *Perspectives on Panopolis: An Egyptian Town from Alexander the Great to the Arab Conquest*, ed. A. Egberts, B. P. Muhs, & J. van der Vliet, Papyrologica Lugduno-Batava, 31 (Leiden: Brill, 2002), pp. 211–31.

[50] A. Boud'hors, "The Coptic Tradition", in *The Oxford Handbook of Late Antiquity*, ed. S. F. Johnson (Oxford: Oxford UP, 2012), pp. 224–46.

[51] A. Boud'hors, "À la recherche des manuscrits coptes de la région thébaine", in *From Gnostics to Monastics. Studies in Coptic and Early Christianity in Honor of Bentley Layton*, ed. D. Brakke, S. J. Davis, & S. Emmel, Orientalia Lovaniensia Analecta, 263 (Leuven: Peeters, 2017), pp. 175–212.

[52] G. Agosti, P. Buzi, & A. Camplani, "Bodmer Papyri. Libraries, ascetic congregations, and literary culture in Greek, Coptic, and Latin, within Late-Antique Egypt", *Adamantius*, 21 (2015), 6–172.

## 3. The Research about Coptic Literature: Questions and Initiatives

### 3.1 Methodological Awareness in Some Research Projects

If an "ideal" discovery of manuscripts is that which takes place in the course of an archaeological excavation – which in turn is recorded in accurate reports addressed to both archaeologists and philologists – and often is accompanied by the unearthing of documents, such as private letters and list of books (Kellis' and the Theban region's manuscripts and papyri, among others, could be mentioned as two prominent examples of this double level of textual documentation) illustrating not only the everyday life of the environment, but also the degree of literacy of the intellectual milieu which commissioned these manuscripts, or got them from elsewhere (even those that have been found in well documented archaeological contexts may represent a 'secondary deposition', that is, they were not found in their original location),[53] we have to admit that a great part of the known Coptic manuscripts preserved in modern libraries do not meet these criteria. Therefore, it is necessary that new research projects on Coptic manuscripts declare in advance which are the limits of the information we have about the consistency of groups of codices (also when they are dismembered), the modern history of their acquisition, their ancient history and their archaeological context, in the lucky case in which this has been recorded.

Investigators of recent projects are aware of the complexities of Coptic literary documentation. It is to be underlined that a quite well organized association has promoted the researches through congresses and form of updating. I am referring to the *International Association for Coptic Studies* (IACS), whose stat-

---

[53] See *Coptic Literature in Context (4th-13th cent.): Cultural Landscape, Literary Production, and Manuscript Archaeology*. Proceedings of the Third Conference of the ERC Project "Tracking Papyrus and Parchment Paths: An Archaeological Atlas of Coptic Literature. Literary Texts in their Geographical Context ('PAThs')", ed. by P. Buzi (PAST – Percorsi, Strumenti e Temi di Archeologia 5), Roma 2020. In particular P. Buzi discusses the topic in her essay, "The Places of Coptic Literary Manuscripts: Real and Imaginary Landscapes. Theoretical Reflections in Guise of Introduction", pp. 15–16.

ute explicitly declares that "the Association shall be a non-profit organization designed to encourage and contribute to the progress of all aspects of Coptic Studies. It shall promote international cooperation among individuals as well as among organizations and institutions. It shall advance the dissemination of information about works in progress, new discoveries and new results, organize periodic Congresses on Coptic Studies." Along the years, the International Congresses of Coptic Studies have become a place of dialogue and training for young scholars. Suffice it to mention the use to entrust to some scholars, changing over time, the task of presenting the status of the studies on the sub-fields of Coptology, such as Coptic art, Coptic archaeology, Coptic literature, Coptic Bible, Gnostic and Manichaean studies, Coptic linguistics, Coptic papyrology, Coptic epigraphy, Coptic history, Coptic monasticism.[54]

Before speaking of two initiatives specifically dedicated to creating methodologies and cognitive models meant to manage information on Coptic manuscripts in their relationship with the book production of the context, such as the CMCL and PAThs, I deem it necessary to mention a few examples of individual and collective initiatives with an impact on Patristic studies.

The project about Shenoute's literary corpus is a great international enterprise of edition of texts, born by the initiative of Bentley Layton and Stephen Emmel, that includes the discussion of methodological questions related to the history of transmission. Identifications of the contents of single sheets or fragments are inserted in a bibliological model which is not a modern artificial construction, but the result of the documented ancient practice of work classification. Stephen Emmel has recently declared about his own research on Shenoute's literary corpus (2004) that:

> a fundamental discovery during the first decade of that research was the bibliographical structure of the Shenoutean corpus as it was transmitted into the medieval period. Sparse evidence for the existence of this structure had been observed by previous scholars, and certainly I was not the first to work on the puzzle that the White Monastery library's holdings had become during the eighteenth and nineteenth centuries,

[54] http://www.cmcl.it/~iacs/.

but in fact it was only on the basis of a comprehensive codicological reconstruction of the manuscripts containing Shenoute's works that it became possible to see the underlying pattern that for the most part determined their contents. The core of Shenoute's surviving writings is a corpus of at least seventeen volumes of collected (but probably also selected) works: nine volumes of *Canons* and eight volumes of *Discourses*. The codices themselves employ the Greco-Coptic word *kanōn* to designate the nine volumes of the *Canons*, although individual works in these volumes are most often designated as *epistolē*, "letter," a term that is well attested for this purpose in Shenoute's own usage. The term that is typically associated with the contents of the eight volumes of the *Discourses* is the Greco-Coptic word *logos*, which might be translated in various ways, including "discourse" or "sermon"; but here also *epistolē* "letter" occurs not infrequently [...] In addition to the seventeen volumes of the *Canons* and *Discourses*, there is a collection of *Letters* in the usual proper sense (as distinct from the "letters" in the *Canons* and *Discourses*), addressed to various persons outside the monastery, including archbishops of Alexandria (possibly each of them from Timothy I through Timothy II) and clerics, officials of the provincial government, residents of Panopolis, local landowners, and villagers. As is often the case in the corpora of letters of Greek and Latin Patristic authors of late antiquity, the corpus of Shenoute's *Letters* includes some items of which he was not the author but the recipient (for example, several letters addressed to Shenoute by Cyril of Alexandria and by Cyril's successor Dioskoros). Unfortunately, this part of Shenoute's corpus is particularly poorly preserved'.[55]

Emmel explains the reasons for the bibliological division of Shenute's writings: *Canons* are more related to the inner life of Shenoute's federation of monasteries, the *Discourses* normally deal with questions arising in the area surrounding the monastery and also the diocese of Panopolis. Whereas Shenoute himself shaped his nine-volume set of *Canons*, the volumes of *Discourses* were composed after Shenoute's death.

---

[55] S. Emmel, "Shenoute the Archimandrite: The Extraordinary Scope (and Difficulties) of His Writings," 15–16.

The research project on the edition of Shenoute's corpus, born in 2000, will have the following tasks: 1) the updating of the reconstruction of dismembered codices, containing Shenoute's work, as offered by Stephen Emmel in 2004,[56] by adding new items and finding for them the codicological and bibliological context (to which one of the hundreds of codices known to us does the new item belong? Or is the new item part of an unknown codex? In which subset of Shenoute's corpus the work attested to by the new item is to be inserted?); 2) the diplomatic transcription of each codex; 3) the edition of Shenoute's works on the basis of the diplomatic transcriptions.[57]

The project *The Canons of Apa Joannes the Archimandrite*, coordinated by Diliana Atanassova, focuses on the works of a Coptic author, Apa John the Archimandrite, who was one of the successors of Shenoute at the direction of the White Monastery between the sixth and the seventh century. Also in the case of John's works, the word "canon" should be interpreted in the sense of exhortations directed to the monks and concerning the inner life of the monastic federation. Apa John's canons are contained in dismembered parchment manuscripts from eighth to the eleventh centuries originally preserved in the White Monastery. The research will provide a complete diplomatic edition (already online) of the reconstructed codices accompanied by an English translation.[58]

Other projects, such as *Scriptorium*, coordinated by Caroline Schroeder and Amir Zeldes, are more oriented to linguistic analysis of Coptic works than to codicology. The grammatical and syntactical tagging of a consistent corpus of different authors and the sophisticated tools of analysis are meant to improve our knowledge of both Sahidic language in general and the particular Sahidic idiom of such authors as Shenoute, Besa, John the Archimandrite, or that of the translations of the Old Testament or *Apophthegmata Patrum*[59] – an indispensable knowledge in order to make good editions of text.

---

[56] S. Emmel, *Shenoute's Literary Corpus*.

[57] S. Emmel, "Shenoute the Archimandrite: The Extraordinary Scope (and Difficulties) of His Writings," 21.

[58] http://coptot.manuscriptroom.com/web/apa-johannes/codices.

[59] http://copticscriptorium.org/.

The *Digital Edition of the Coptic Old Testament*, based in the Göttingen Academy of Sciences and Humanities, coordinated by Heike Behlmer, aims "to provide a complete documentation of the manuscript evidence, digital editions of all OT manuscripts, critical editions of all OT books, corpus-linguistic analyses and translations into English, German and Arabic."[60] The fate of the White Monastery's codices, as well as other libraries, certainly did not spare the biblical manuscripts. For that reasons, the codicological and textual reconstruction of all extant witnesses to the Coptic-Sahidic Old Testament is the main focus of this research. The diplomatic transcription will be followed by an edition and translation in modern languages. The corpus of texts will be tagged in order to give the scholars the possibility of linguistic analysis through the tools provided by *Scriptorium*.

Alin Suciu's blog, *Patristics, Apocrypha, Coptic Literature and Manuscripts*,[61] is not really part of an official research project, but can be really qualified as a useful tool for research. One of the main tasks of its author is to identify new works, connect fragments, provide the edition of short texts, give information on congresses, workshops, discoveries, didactic initiatives. Bibliographical information, links to websites, photographs, are tools that give this initiative a fresh taste and show openess to the future. Its connection with both the CMCL and PAThs, the identifications proposed by Alin Suciu are well contextualized in the codicological and literary culture.

### 3.2 The Challenge of Two Comprehensive Projects on Coptic Literature

CMCL and PAThs project are characterized by a more general approach to the whole of the Coptic literature, with the exception of the liturgical and biblical manuscripts, which, although dealt with, remain at the margins of the fundamental interest of both. Tito Orlandi's *Corpus dei manoscritti copti letterari*[62] is a project meant to connect in a systematic way the information we have

---

[60] http://coptot.manuscriptroom.com/.
[61] http://alinsuciu.com.
[62] http://www.cmcl.it.

on Coptic manuscripts and Coptic literature, in order to recover dismembered manuscripts and literary works, and to study their preservation and circulation. Two main results of this project should be emphasized:

1) The first is the database that allows the virtual reconstruction of Coptic literary codices from the leaves scattered in different libraries and shows their distinctive features and their contents, the whole being linked to a system of digitalized images. This database allows scholars to check the palaeographical and codicological description provided by one of the sections of the database with the image of a manuscript, in order to improve its description, and finally to contribute to the reconstruction of codices by singling out new leaves;

2) The second is the electronic edition of Coptic texts (whose methods are in line with the new developments of the philological theory). that allows their computer analysis, so that indices, concordances, and grammatical categorization may be produced automatically.

If we take into account the fact that these two sections of the project are tied also to a Coptic grammar with its analytical tools, a bibliography, and a history of Coptic literature, the whole appears to be a very ambitious project, which is in need of the cooperation of a plurality of scholars.

Orlandi's attempt to give Coptic literature a more formalized structure in relation to both the information on Coptic manuscripts and the edition of texts is linked to his engagement in computer science. The reflection upon the methodology of humanities computing has influenced not only the way of conceiving the edition of Coptic texts and the notion of "text", but also the creation of a model of description of Coptic literary production and the formalization of the intellectual operations involved in its analysis.

It is interesting to notice that a parallel evolution can be seen in Tito Orlandi's approach to both Humanities Computing and Coptology. Issues of encoding of the sources have imposed a reformulation of the means by which the information of a text is reproduced in an electronic text. The text is not only a sequence of signs, but also a system in which we can identify a plurality of levels.

This system can be expressed by the production of a model containing both the symbols representing the graphemes and the symbols representing the extra-graphematic features of the text itself. Therefore, it is necessary to use a number of formal structures that constitute what is called a model.[63]

The initial project was a collection of the photographs of all the fragments, so that scholars could easily browse through them and find which fragments are complementary to which others in having belonged to an original codex. This program was later expanded to include the whole field of Coptic literature: according to Tito Orlandi's reconstruction, it was soon evident that the photos must be accompanied by a systematic and analytical archive in which all relevant information on the manuscripts themselves, and also on the Coptic literature in its different manifestations, could be stored and retrieved. The activity was structured upon the following items: 1. Photographic archive; 2. Catalogue of manuscript collections; 3. History of the manuscripts; 4. Catalogue of Coptic literary texts; 5. Reconstruction of the White Monastery Library; 6. Bibliography of the Coptic Literature, then general Coptic bibliography; 7. Publication of texts with introduction and translation.

During the following years in which this work was being carried on, technology made great progresses, improving the possibility of managing images and disseminating information. Accordingly, the CMCL changed its tools, although maintaining the same purpose, with the creation of an environment, properly defined by Tito Orlandi as "Modeling the Coptic Literature." It includes: 1) The web page – *i.e.* the major vehicle of dissemination of the results obtained from research, with its possibilities of inquiry (the *grammar*, the *clavis*, the *manuscripts*, the *bibliography*, and the *texts*); 2) The data stored and manipulated in the electronic archives (a relational database, divided into data about manuscripts, data about literary works – the *clavis coptica* – and the texts themselves; 3) The software for the management of data (made up of Unix scripts).

---

[63] See T. Orlandi, "Linguistica, sistemi e modelli," in *Il ruolo del modello nella scienza e nel sapere (Roma, 27–28 ottobre 1998)*, Contributi del Centro Linceo Interdisciplinare, 100 (Roma: Accademia dei Lincei, 1999), pp. 73–90 (82–83).

The multimedial critical edition of some Coptic works offered in the CMCL website can give a good insight into this complex system. The scholar will find in it the images of the fragments, provided with a codicological and palaeographical description; their connection to form manuscripts; their diplomatic transcription with a set of symbols corresponding to both graphematic and extra-graphematic features; the edition of the text reconstructed on the basis of the manuscript witnesses; its translation, its annotation. This kind of encoding makes it possible the automatic passage from one level to another. Several tools can be created to analyze the different levels of the model.

During the International Congress of Coptic Studies of 2008 held in Cairo Tito Orlandi has proposed a new terminology for Coptic literature, able to reflect the peculiarities of the literary production and its transmission. Given the fact the scholars of Coptic literature have rarely to do with real entire manuscripts and stable literary works, as well as with real authors, his new system of identification of manuscripts and literary products is based on "units", as the following list can show: Codicological units, Bibliological units (ancient or modern, with their *scriptoria*); Textual units (with their literary genres); Author units; Narrative units.[64]

The deep between the CMCL and the ERC Advanced project *PAThs – Tracking Papyrus and Parchment Paths: An Archaeological Atlas of Coptic Literature. Literary Texts in their Geographical Context. Production, Copying, Usage, Dissemination and Storage* (= PAThs), coordinated by Paola Buzi, Sapienza Università di Roma, are motivated first of all by the fact that Paola Buzi was, as myself, a student of Tito Orlandi; second, the two scholars share a deep passion for Coptic manuscripts, their history, their circulation, their reconstruction, and for the literature they convey.[65]

---

[64] T. Orlandi, "Terminology for the Identification of Coptic Literary Documents", *Journal of Coptic Studies*, 15 (2013), 87–94.

[65] https://atlas.paths-erc.eu/, a very rich and documented site, with a database containing detailed and structured information on manuscripts, an atlas with the places of Coptic manuscript discoveries, some tools of analysis and an important "mission statement". See also the already mentioned rich collection of essays concerning questions of research connected to PAThs: *Coptic Literature in Context (4th-13th cent.)*, ed. P. Buzi.

The main focus of PAThs is the relationship between codices and geography. It "aims to provide an in-depth diachronic understanding and effective representation of the geography of Coptic literary production."[66] In a recent report, three members of the staff have provided the description of their work, which deserves a quotation:

- Conception and implementation of the relational database, on which the archaeological atlas of Coptic literature is based, and setting up of the GIS – that makes use of ancient cartography as well as of satellite images – to be used for the geographical representation.
- Complete classification of Coptic literary works (c. 1200) by a systematic attribution of a *Clavis Coptica* (CC) identification number, integrating the work already done in this field by CMCL.
- Complete classification of 114 "Coptic authors", through the attribution of stable identifiers. Moreover, a detailed form of description for each author has been elaborated. This includes a biographical profile and a classification according to the following categories: original author (no matter if Greek or Coptic); stated author (by titles, colophons, tradition, etc.); author of the master work.
- Complete classification of Coptic titles (c. 760) through the attribution of a CC identification number.
- Complete digital edition (with English translation) of the entire corpus of Coptic titles (third to eleventh centuries).
- Complete classification of Coptic colophons or scribal subscriptions by means of a stable identifier (c. 180).
- Ongoing complete digital edition (with English translation) of the entire corpus of Coptic colophons.
- Complete classification of 6135 Coptic manuscripts (or better codicological units), by means of the attribution of stable identifiers, in order to have univocal coordinates of reference

---

[66] P. Buzi, J. Bogdani, & F. Berno, "The 'PAThs' Project: An Effort to Represent the Physical Dimension of Coptic Literary Production (Third–Eleventh centuries)", *COMSt Bulletin*, 4/1 (2018), 39–58 (39).

to the entire Coptic book production. Such a classification is progressively expandable as soon as new manuscripts are discovered or identified.
- Elaboration of a protocol of detailed (digital) codicological description to be gradually applied to all collected manuscripts (at the moment between 20% and 25% of the corpus has been described in detail).
- Mark-up (in TEI XML) of a selected corpus of literary works that are consistent in terms of their area of production and intellectual milieu, to be used for a tentative identification of places and geographical areas where specific works and literary genres were conceived. This corpus is stored online at <https://github.com/paths-erc/coptic-texts>.
- Complete census of the relevant sites (c. 450 until now), known as places where single manuscripts (such as codices buried with a body, as a funerary kit) or entire "collections" (for example a monastery library) have been found or produced, or important for reconstructing the cultural and religious landscape of late antique and medieval Egypt.
- Elaboration of an accurate form of description of the classified places, including an archaeological description, precise coordinates, information on more ancient and more recent phases of occupation and usage, on the eventual function of the site as episcopal see, etc.

As the reader may understand, great emphasis is given to the information about the manuscripts and their place of provenance, because, as we have seen, this relationship is one of the areas in which Coptic literary studies are rather weak and in need of an improvement. The project aims to provide all the data on places of Coptic culture, through consultation of reports and personal surveys on those places by the members of the staff themselves. Another activity which is methodologically relevant is the attribution of identifiers to all the discrete elements which can be identified in a manuscript: titles of works, colophons, name of authors (real or pseudoepigraphical, etc.): here the influence of Tito Orlandi's proposal of a system of classification (units) is evident. The proposal of a model of manuscript description, which can be tested in the manuscript data base, is a real progress and will mark the future study of Coptic codicology.[67]

So, as we can learn from the site and other presentations, the project aims to stimulate Coptic studies to take into consideration Coptic literature as a cultural phenomenon not independent of its material context. The combination of philology, codicology, archaeology and digital humanities, according to the promoters, will allow scholars to describe the birth of a manuscript from production to diffusion and storage, and the creation of Coptic works in relation to the geographical contexts of origin of both the texts themselves and their related writing supports. The most visible product will be an interactive atlas of late antique and early medieval Egypt, searchable at different chronological, regional and thematic levels, and illustrating (1) the places where Coptic manuscripts have been found or produced, with a focus on monastic settlements, episcopal sees, tombs, and urban contexts; (2) the places where the works were conceived and created; (3) the codicological features of the manuscripts (book format, writing support, ruling system, presence of a binding, etc.) and their development in relation to a specific period and a specific region; (4) information related to the manuscript makers (places where they practiced their trade, places where they obtained their writing supports, etc.).

\* \* \*

One of the main features of the projects I have discussed above is their interconnectedness, as shown by their websites. This allows scholars to move from one project to another. For example, it is helpful to go from exploring the wealth of information on Coptic codices, their history, and their geographical provenience found on the PAThs website to perusing the structure, style, and contents of the works contained in those codices as described in

---

[67] It is to be remarked that Paola Buzi has written important contributions on Coptic manuscripts in the COMSt handbook, another research network which has reached great results: see *Comparative Oriental Manuscript Studies. An Introduction*, edited by A. Bausi (Hamburg: Tredition, 2015): "Catalogues of Coptic Manuscripts", pp. 481–83; "Coptic Palaeography", pp. 283–86; "Coptic Codicology" (with S. Emmel), pp. 137–53.

CMCL. Additionally, if *Scriptorium* offers a tagged transcription of those same works, it is possible to consult their advanced linguistic analysis. Taken collectively, these projects allow scholars to realize the need to submit Coptic manuscripts to a multi-layered analysis and to ask the right questions about their history, in order to experience the multiple implications of the notion of "manuscript discovery."

## *Abstract*

The aim of this contribution is to offer some methodological considerations on the influence that the modern discoveries of Coptic manuscripts have exerted on both the evolution of Patristic studies and the modeling of the Coptic textual heritage. Born in connection to the missionary activity of the Catholic church and later of other Christian Churches, the scholarly interest in Coptic culture and manuscripts became independent from ecclesiastical centres during the nineteenth century, when a great number of Coptic codices and fragments came to the European and American libraries. This contribution discusses the notion of "discovery", its textual relevance, its relation to the evolving portraits of Coptic textual heritage over time. The third part shows how some recent research projects on Coptic manuscripts (CMCL and PAThs in particular) organize the knowledge about the Coptic manuscripts preserved in modern libraries and those discovered within the archaeological activity.

LUISE MARION FRENKEL
*Universidade de São Paulo, Brazil*

# RECOVERING LATE-ANTIQUE CHRISTIAN IDENTITIES: THE ONGOING DISCOVERY AND REDISCOVERY OF SYRIAC MANUSCRIPTS, THEIR DIVERSITY, AND LIMITATIONS [1]

## 1. *Patristics and Syriac Literature*

The importance of Syriac manuscripts as conveyors of Patristic literature, whether in translations, especially from the Greek, including many not extant in the original language, or in works originally written in Syriac has been recognised by European scholars for half a millennium. European contact with Syriac speakers during the Middle Ages was largely sporadic. It paid little attention to Syriac manuscripts and was seldom related to scholastic endeavours.[2]

---

[1] I thank the Universidade de São Paulo for granting leaves for fellowships at the Institute for Textual Scholarship and Electronic Editing (ITSEE, Birmingham, supported by the Brazil Visiting Fellowship Scheme), St Edmund's College (Cambridge) and the Max Weber Centre for Advanced Cultural and Social Studies (MWK Erfurt, supported by resources of the Deutsche Forschungsgemeinschaft, DFG, within the framework of the research group "Religious individualisation in historical perspective"). Writing the conference paper and this chapter would not have been possible without the resources of these institutions. Some funding for participation at the conference was awarded as PROAP e-Convênios (n° 38860 SICONV – 817757/2015). The invaluable comments which J. F. Coakley, Geoffrey Greatrex, Theresia Hainthaler, Jeremiah Coogan, Walter F. Beers, Jack Tannous, Michael Penn, Elizabeth Key Fowden and others made could only occasionally be incorporated to the chapter, so that it remained as close as possible to the presentation at the conference. Finally, I thank the organisers, especially Dr Patricia Ciner for the invitation to contribute this paper.

[2] See below on twelfth-century contact with Maronites and on pre-1498 visits of Latin Christians, mostly papal envoys, to Malabar and other areas in India, see K. C. Zachariah, *The Syrian Christians of Kerala: Demographic and Socio-Economic Transition in the Twentieth Century* (New Delhi: Orient Longman, 2006), p. 55.

In the last century, several papers by leading researchers reported stories of their publication or analysed some of the most influential editions, which contributed to momentous reappraisals, for example, in conciliar studies and fifth-century Christological controversies. Such is the case with Joseph-Marie Sauget's 1976 talk in Geneva, which he then published in 1978 in the "Revue de Théologie et de Philosophie".[3] He digressed on representative examples with the authority of someone who used to work daily with Syriac manuscripts in the Vatican Library.

Sebastian Brock, perhaps the most known and influential scholar of Syriac culture nowadays, at least in Anglophone academia,[4] has often promoted Syriac manuscripts, as in the recent papers on their contribution to the translation and standardisation of biblical texts, and on hagiography.[5] His 1996 paper presents the limitations of traditional views about Early Christianity and the development of the various orthodox Churches. An enticing story about manuscripts in the Syriac legacy is narrated in an article on the abbot of Deir al-Surian.[6]

Also Françoise Briquel-Chatonnet, who researches the whole chronological and geographical range of Syriac manuscripts and has advanced our palaeographical and codicological knowledge about them, devotes several publications to their importance.[7]

---

[3] J.-M. Sauget, "Études syriaques. L'apport des traductions syriaques pour la patristique grecque", *Revue de Théologie et de Philosophie*, 110 (1978), 139–48; republished in *Littératures et manuscrits des chrétientés syriaques et arabes (recueil d'articles publ. par Louis Duval-Arnould et Frédéric Rilliet; préf. de Léonard E. Boyle)*, Studi e testi 389 (Città del Vaticano: Biblioteca apostolica vaticana, 1998).

[4] See G. A. Kiraz, "Sebastian Paul Brock: *Haddaya* of Syriac Studies", *Journal of Assyrian Academic Studies*, 18:1 (2004), 5–8.

[5] Respectively S. P. Brock, "Charting the Hellenization of a Literary Culture: The Case of Syriac", *Intellectual History of the Islamicate World*, 3:1–2 (2015), 98–124 (p. 102) and S. P. Brock, "Saints in Syriac: A Little-Tapped Resource", *Journal of Early Christian Studies*, 16:2 (2008), 181–96.

[6] S. P. Brock, "The 'Nestorian' Church: A Lamentable Misnomer", *Bulletin of the John Rylands Library*, 78:3 (1996), 23–35, S. P. Brock, "Without Mushē of Nisibis, Where Would we be? Some Reflections on the Transmission of Syriac Literature", *Journal of Eastern Christian Studies*, 56 (2004), 15–24, and references in n. 21 below.

[7] See F. Briquel-Chatonnet, "Les manuscrits syriaques", in *Sources syriaques*, ed. by R. Jabre-Mouawad, *Nos sources: arts et littérature syriaques*, 1 (Antélias-Beyrouth: Centre d'Études et de Recherches Orientales CERO, 2005), pp. 43–

Although many collections of Syriac manuscripts no longer have a dedicated specialist, the outreach work of librarians and curators continues. For example, Columba Stewart often advances the relevance of Syriac manuscripts for Patristic scholarship,[8] and regularly points to their living meaningfulness for the social identity of various groups and several Christian communities. The damage, loss, and destruction of manuscripts has also been mentioned in the media coverage of the destruction of archaeological, artistic, and manuscript patrimony in African, European, and Asian areas in which Syriac literature flourished. Scholars have taken more or less clear stances in relation to the claims and socio-political issues at stake, accounting for the losses and promoting projects and archives which can contribute to the preservation of the material and intellectual Syriac legacy.[9] Many other scholars, librarians, and writers tried to convince academic or religious groups and society at large of the importance of Syriac manuscripts for their identities and the Humanities.[10]

Since Late Antiquity and especially since the Fourth Crusade, a few Syriac manuscripts have reached Europe as part of eccle-

---

73, F. Briquel-Chatonnet & M. Debié, "Introduction", in *Manuscripta Syriaca. Des Sources de Première Main*, ed. by F. Briquel-Chatonnet & M. Debié, *Cahiers d'études syriaques*, 4 (Paris: Geuthner, 2015), pp. 1–7, P. G. Borbone, F. Briquel-Chatonnet & E. Balicka-Witakowska, "Codicology of Syriac Manuscripts", in *Comparative Oriental Manuscript Studies: An Introduction*, ed. by A. Bausi et al. (Hamburg: COMSt; Tredition, 2015), pp. 252–66, and F. Briquel-Chatonnet & M. Debié. *Le Monde syriaque: Sur les routes d'un christianisme ignoré* (Paris: Les Belles lettres, 2017), pp. 89–116.

[8] See, for example, the lecture on 6 February 2017 at Fordham University on *Out of the Flames: Preserving the Manuscript Heritage of Endangered Syriac Christianity in the Middle East*.

[9] See C. Stewart, "Yours, Mine, or Theirs? Historical Observations on the Use, Collection and Sharing of Manuscripts in Western Europe and the Christian Orient", in *Malphono w-Rabo d-Malphone. Studies in Honor of Sebastian Paul Brock*, ed. by G. A. Kiraz, Gorgias Eastern Christian Studies 3 (Piscataway: Gorgias, 2008), pp. 603–30 (pp. 627–30), C. Stewart, "HMML and Syriac Manuscripts", in *Manuscripta Syriaca*, pp. 49–63.

[10] For example, Scott Johnson's plenary lecture "Linguistic Turns, Disciplinary Boundaries: The Role of Syriac in the Concept of Late Antiquity" at the *XVIII. International Conference on Patristic Studies* (Oxford, 21 August 2019). For a brief survey of translation activities for texts, secular, and religious, from Greek into Syriac, see A. C. McCollum, "Greek Literature in the Christian East: Translations into Syriac, Georgian, and Armenian", *Intellectual History of the Islamicate World*, 3:1–2 (2015), 15–65.

siastical politics or similar international relations. The originals or copies of several of them are now in the Vatican Library, for example. The Peshitta was taken into account already by Humanist biblical scholars. In Europe, Syriac texts were printed early on, arguably for the first time, although at least in India texts have been printed in Syriac for centuries too.[11] Nowadays, early Syriac authors such as Bardaişān and Ephrem, the West-Syrian lives of saints featured in Peter Brown's and Susan Ashbrook Harvey's studies and the so-called "School" of Edessa can be regarded as well established fields of research.[12] Indeed, since the late 1980s, edited Syriac works have received an attention that only few had had when the arrival of new Syriac manuscripts in Europe sparked a flurry of first editions published from *c.* 1885 until the First World War. They changed Patristics significantly. Conciliar studies would be utterly different without the Syriac version of the Acts of the 449 council of Ephesus,[13] homiletics without the Syriac works of Ephrem,[14] Patristic theology without

[11] See J. F Coakley, *The typography of Syriac: a historical catalogue of printing types, 1537–1958* (New Castle, DE, London: Oak Knoll, British Library, 2006), J. F. Coakley, "Edward Breath and the Typography of Syriac", *Harvard Library Bulletin*, 6:4 (1995), 41–64, and Stewart, "Yours, Mine, or Theirs?", p. 614.

[12] See M. L. D. Riedel, "Syriac Sources for Byzantinists: An Introduction and Overview", *Byzantinische Zeitschrift*, 105:2 (2012), 775–801 (pp. 798–99) and P. R. L. Brown, "Wealth, Work and the Holy Poor: Early Christian Monasticism between Syria and Egypt", *Irish Theological Quarterly*, 81:3 (2016), 233–45 (pp. 233–35).

[13] *Akten der Ephesinischen Synode vom Jahre 449: syrisch / mit deutscher Übersetzung und Anmerkungen*, ed. by J. P. G. Flemming, G. Hoffmann & H. Lietzmann, *Abhandlungen der Königlichen Gesellschaft der Wissenschaften zu Göttingen. Philologisch-historische Klasse. Neue Folge* XV, 1 (Berlin: Weidmannsche Buchhandlung, 1917), S. Acerbi, "Polarizzazioni sociali, clientelismi e rivolte popolari a Edessa in epoca tardoantica: un approccio attraverso gli Atti siriaci del II Concilio di Efeso (449)", *Veleia*, 27 (2010), 267–83.

[14] See U. Possekel, *Evidence of Greek Philosophical Concepts in the Writings of Ephrem the Syrian*, Corpus scriptorum Christianorum Orientalium, 580 (Leuven: Peeters, 1999), pp. 1–12, S. P. Brock, *The luminous eye: the spiritual world vision of Saint Ephrem*, Cistercian studies series 124 (Kalamazoo, MI: Cistercian Publications, 1992), pp. 13–21 and pp. 143–57, and C. Shepardson, *Anti-Judaism and Christian Orthodoxy: Ephrem's Hymns in Fourth-century Syria*, Patristic Monograph Series (Washington, DC: Catholic University of America Press, 2011), pp. 31–46. Ephrem's works were seldom copied in complete form after the sixth century because of concerns over his Christological language, as shown in A. M. Butts, "Manuscript Transmission as Reception History: The Case

the *Liber Heraclides*,[15] philosophy of religion without the Syriac *Corpus Dionysiacum*[16] and our understanding of the Cassians and of asceticism, monasticism and Origenism without the Syriac version of Evagrius.[17]

The theme of this section points naturally to the core of the making and reception of these objects that led to the sanitised picture of the later witnesses. Transmission and especially translation were much affected by religious and social contexts, which influenced linguistic-conceptual strategies. Translation can often be related to the relevance of presenting in contemporary polemics textual evidence for the views and rhetoric of earlier authors, interacting with the regard in which the community held them. The Syriac traditions received quite similarly the writings of the early Syriac authors, which were then mostly transmitted within their own literary cultures for centuries. However, some readings show that not only later works but also manuscripts from other denominations could be taken into account.[18] Because

---

of Ephrem the Syrian (d. 373)", *Journal of Early Christian Studies*, 25:2 (2017), 281–306.

[15] See G. A. Bevan, *The New Judas: The Case of Nestorius in Ecclesiastical Politics, 428–51 CE*, Late Antique History and Religion 13 (Leuven: Peeters, 2016), and the still influential L. I. Scipioni, *Nestorio e il concilio de Efeso: Storia, dogma, critica*, Pubblicazioni della Università Cattolica del Sacro Cuore. Studia Patristica Mediolanensia, 1 (Milano: Vita e pensiero, 1974).

[16] For an overview of the contribution of the Kerala manuscripts to current views on Pseudo-Dionysius Areopagite's identity, theology, philosophy, and historical context, taking into account publications such as A. P. & I. Perczel, "A New Testimony from India to the Syriac Version of Pseudo-Dionysius (Pampakuda, Konat Collection, MS 239)", *Iran & the Caucasus*, 6:1/2 (2002), 11–26, see C. M. Stang, *Apophasis and Pseudonymity in Dionysius the Areopagite: 'No Longer I'*, Oxford early Christian texts (Oxford: Oxford University Press, 2012), pp. 24–26.

[17] On Cassian, see P. Tzamalikos, *The Real Cassian Revisited: Monastic Life, Greek Paideia, and Origenism in the Sixth Century*, Supplements to Vigiliae Christianae, 112 (Leiden: Brill, 2012), p. 82; on the relevance of the Syriac texts of works by Evagrius and about him, see, for example, C. Stewart, "Evagrius beyond Byzantium: The Latin and Syriac Receptions", in *Evagrius and His Legacy*, ed. by J. Kalvesmaki & R. D. Young (Notre Dame: University of Notre Dame Press, 2016), pp. 206–35.

[18] See, for example, C. Noce, "Eusebius' *Historia Ecclesiastica* in Syriac and Latin: A First Comparison", *Aramaic Studies*, 14:2 (2016), 98–117 (p. 116) on the Syriac translator's censorship of passages of Eusebius *H.E.* that suggest subordination, and B. Ter Haar Romeny, "Athanasius in Syriac", *Church History and*

of the diversity of denominations[19] and their rise and development under "foreign" rule of Rome, Persia, New Rome, and Arab courts, these manuscripts are ideal in helping to understand why Patristic works were written, copied, edited or compiled.

## 2. Late Antique Syriac Intellectual Cultures

Most modern Westerners who hunted for manuscripts claimed it was out of scholarly interest, using arguments which echo the reasons overtly mentioned for acquiring items for late antique Syriac monastic libraries. Moses of Nisibis wrote of the spiritual and intellectual benefit for the monks of his Deir al-Surian monastery of the more than 250 manuscripts he acquired during the five years (927–32 CE) he was in Baghdad, where he successfully appealed to the Caliph al-Muqtadir for the return of the exemption from poll-taxation of the monasteries of the Egyptian desert:

> To the honour and glory and magnificence of this Syrian Orthodox monastery of the Mother of God in the Desert of Sketis, Mushē known as "of Nisibis", an insignificant sinner and abbot, strove to acquire this book; together with 250 others (many of which he himself bought, while others were given to him as a present), when he went to Baghdad

---

*Religious Culture*, 90:2/3 (2010), 225–56 (p. 230), on the East Syrian reception of Athanasius.

[19] The doctrinal positions of Syriac denominations reflect their stance towards a number of late antique synods, which can be more or less arranged in three groups:
- Non-chalcedonian, which reject Chalcedon (451) and accept Ephesus I (431) & II (449) (e.g. Syrian Orthodox)
- Chalcedonian, which reject Ephesus II (e.g. Maronite; Melkite; Syrian Catholic; Syro-Malankara; Chaldean; Syro-Malabar)
- "Non-chalcedonian", which reject Ephesus I & II and are ambivalent over Chalcedon (e.g. Church of the East)

(*apud* http://syri.ac/brock/chalcedon). The terminology for the religious, literary, and historical traditions is extremely ambiguous and contentious. Several of the names used in Western scholarship until the middle of the twentieth century were repudiated by the communities themselves or reflect mistaken historical assumptions. A set of terms for the doctrinal positions of the Syriac Churches now widely accepted in Anglophone academia and interfaith dialogue was discussed in Brock, "The 'Nestorian' Church", p. 27.

on behalf of this holy Desert and the monks dwelling in it. May God, for whose glory, and for the benefit of those who read these books, grant forgiveness to him and to his departed ones, and to everyone who has shared with them. By the living word of God no one is permitted to cause harm to any of them in any way; nor to appropriate them to himself. Nor should anyone delete this commemorative note, or make any erasure or cut anything out – or order anyone else to do so; nor may they be given away from the monastery. If anyone dares to do so, let him realise that he is under an anathema.

These books arrived with the above-mentioned abbot Mushē in the year 1243 of the Greeks (= AD 932).[20]

He could acquire a considerable number of very early manuscripts because their relevance in the Syriac cultural centres had waned. Those who could afford them preferred sanitised witnesses, such as florilegia, catenæ, and newer, more idiomatic, works.[21] As in the case of the libraries available to Origen, Eusebius of Caesarea, Theodoret of Cyrrhus, and the Babylonian Jewish communities, Syriac collections included texts now split between theology, classical philosophy, and science. They then reflected enterprises which were not in opposition, but rather were seen as aspects

---

[20] Note in British Library, MS Add. 14445, transl. Brock, "Without Mushē", p. 16.

[21] See M. J. Martin, "Athanasiana Syriaca and the Library of Dayr al-Suryan", *Ancient Near Eastern Studies*, 40 (2003), 225–34 and Butts, "Manuscript Transmission". See also M. Kahlos, "Ditches of Destruction – Cyril of Alexandria and the Rhetoric of Public Security", *Byzantinische Zeitschrift*, 107:2 (2015), 11–33. On books in Syriac monastic settings, see M. Debié, "Livres et monastères en Syrie-Mésopotamie d'après les sources syriaques", in *Le Monachisme syriaque*, ed. by F. Jullien, *Études syriaques*, 7 (Paris: Geuthner, 2010), pp. 123–68. For eulogising accounts of Moses' acquisition, see the article by the librarian of Deir al-Surian, B. el Suriany, 'The Manuscript Collection of Deir al-Surian in Wadi al-Natrun', *Journal of the Canadian Society for Coptic Studies*, 2 (2011), 53–64, *From Dust to Digital: Ten Years of the Endangered Archives Programme*, ed. by M. Kominko (Cambridge, MA: Open Book Publishers, 2015), URL http://dx.doi.org/ 10.11647/OBP.0052 (p. lii), Brock, "Without Mushē", and M. J. Blanchard, "Moses of Nisibis (fl. 906–43) and the Library of Deir Suriani", in *Studies in the Christian East in Memory of Mirrit Boutros Ghali*, ed. by L. S. B. MacCoull, *Publications of the Society for Coptic Archaeology, North America*, 1 (Washington, DC: Society for Coptic Archaeology, 1995), pp. 13–24; D. King, "Logic in the Service of Ancient Eastern Christianity: An Exploration of Motives", *Archiv für Geschichte der Philosophie*, 97:1 (2015), 1–33.

of the same intellectual endeavour.[22] The abundant details clearly point to small purpose-driven collections in private hands and show that nothing hints at the existence of a patriarchal or public "library" in Antioch or most cities of the late-antique Eastern Roman Empire.

What then of the myth about philosophy's narrow escape from the clutches of the clergy by way of Antioch, Harran, and Baghdad, where this endeavour could finally be pursued anew? A passage of Ibn Abī Uṣaibiʿa's, in which he quoted al-Fārābī,[23] gained undue visibility when Max Meyerhoff included a translation in an influential essay:

> Nachdem Fārābī zuerst phantastische Nachrichten über die alte Akademie und Bibliothek von Alexandrien und über die angebliche Einrichtung einer Zweigakademie in Rom durch Augustus gegeben hat, fährt er fort: "Somit befand sich die (philosophische) Lehre an zwei Orten, und so blieb es, bis das Christentum kam. Da hörte die Lehre in Rom auf und verblieb in Alexandrien, bis der Christenkaiser sich damit befaßte und sich die Bischöfe versammelten und darüber berieten, was von der Lehre belassen und was abgeschafft werden sollte; da entschieden sie, daß von den Büchern der Logik nur bis zum Ende der Figuren des Wirklichen (*al-aškāl al-wuǧūdijja*) unterrichtet werden sollte, und nicht über das,

---

[22] D. Gutas, *Greek Thought, Arabic Culture: The Graeco-Arabic Translation Movement in Baghdad and Early ʿAbbasaid Society (2nd-4th/5th-10th c.)* (London: Routledge, 1998), pp. 83–94, D. Gutas, "The 'Alexandria to Baghdad' Complex of Narratives: a Contribution to the Study of Philosophical and Medical Historiography Among the Arabs", *Documenti e studi sulla tradizione filosofica medievale*, 10 (1999), 155–93. On Origen and Eusebius see A. Grafton & M. H. Williams, *Christianity and the Transformation of the Book: Origen, Eusebius, and the Library of Caesarea* (Cambridge, MA: Harvard University Press, 2006), pp. 18, 56–58, and on the Babylonian Jewish communities, S. M. Gross, "Irano-Talmudica and Beyond", *Jewish Quarterly Review*, 106:2 (2016), 248–55 (p. 253). Theodoret's access to compilations and florilegia and his familiarity with a wider range of texts are discussed by Théodoret de Cyr. *Histoire ecclésiastique*, ed. by J. Bouffartigue, A. Martin & P. Canivet, *Sources chrétiennes* 501, 530 (Paris: Éditions du Cerf, 2006–2009) II (2009), pp. 38–45 and C. Scholten, *Theodoret – De Graecarum Affectionum Curatione = Heilung der Griechischen Krankheiten*, Supplements to Vigiliae Christianae, 126 (Leiden; Boston: Brill, 2015), pp. 106–22, especially pp. 112–13.

[23] (*Ibn Abī Uṣaybiʿah*) *History of the Physicians (Kitāb ʿUyūn ʾal-ʾanbāʾ fī ṭabaqāt ʾal-ʾaṭibbāʾ)*, ed. by A. Müller (Cairo: Königsberg i. Pr.), 1882–1884, II (1884), pp. 134–35.

was danach kommt, weil sie der Meinung waren, daß darin ein Schaden für das Christentum läge, und daß in dem, was sie zum Unterricht zuließen, eine Hilfe für den Sieg ihres Glaubens enthalten sei. Das Öffentliche (Exoterische) der Lehre blieb also auf dieses Maß beschränkt, während das Studium des Übrigen insgeheim (*mastūr*, esoterisch) betrieben wurde, bis lange Zeit danach der Islam erschien." [...] "Dann (nach Erscheinen des Islams) wurde die Lehre von Alexandrien nach Antiochien verlegt und verblieb dort lange Zeit; schließlich blieb nur noch ein einziger Lehrer übrig, und von ihm lernten zwei Männer und zogen (dann) fort, und mit ihnen die Bücher. Der eine von ihnen war ein Bewohner von Ḥarrān, der andere ein solcher von Merw. Von dem Manne aus Merw lernten zwei Männer: der eine war Ibrāhīm al-Marwazī, der andere Jūḥannā b. Ḥailān; und von dem Harranier lernten der Bischof Isrā"īl und Quwairī. Diese beiden reisten nach Baghdad, und Isrā'īl wurde durch die Religion in Anspruch genommen; während Quwairī zu lehren begann. Was Jūḥannā b. Ḥailān betrifft, so wurde er ebenfalls durch seinen Glauben in Anspruch genommen; Ibrāhīm al-Marwazī aber ging nach Baghdad hinunter und machte sich dort ansässig. [...]'[24]

Syriac manuscripts are key evidence to prove beyond doubt that Al-Fārābī tried rather ingenuously to suggest that only then and there the whole logic of Aristotle could be read and taught freely again, that for many centuries the Byzantine clerical hierarchy had outlawed the irreligious subtleties of the foremost philosopher, and that the bishops were terrified of what an extensive knowl-

---

[24] M. Meyerhof, "Von Alexandrien nach Bagdad. Ein Beitrag zur Geschichte des philosophischen und medizinischen Unterrichts bei den Arabern", *Sitzungsberichte der Berliner Akademie der Wissenschaften: Philosophisch-Historische Klasse* (1930), pp. 389–429 (393–94, 405). For an English translation, see F. Rosenthal, *The Classical Heritage in Islam*, Islamic world series (London: Routledge, 1975), pp. 50–51. See also J. W. Watt, "The Syriac Aristotle Between Alexandria and Baghdad", *Journal for Late Antique Religion and Culture* 7 (2013), 26–50 (p. 27), D. King, "Logic in the Service of Ancient Eastern Christianity: An Exploration of Motives", *Archiv für Geschichte der Philosophie*, 97:1 (2015), 1–33 (pp. 1–2), S. P. Brock, "Two Letters of the Patriarch Timothy from the Late Eighth Century on Translations from Greek", *Arabic Sciences and Philosophy*, 9:2 (1999), 233–46, and especially H. Biesterfeldt, "Secular Graeco-Arabica – Fifty Years After Franz Rosenthal's *Fortleben der Antike im Islam*", *Intellectual History of the Islamicate World*, 3:1–2 (2015), 125–57 (p. 130).

edge of peripatetic straight-thinking might do to their precious doctrines of Trinity and Incarnation. None of this applies to late-antique Syriac cultures. In most disciplines, such as astronomy, medicine, and grammar, the adoption of different teaching methods followed a pattern in which, after some time without any Arabic sources on the topic, first can be found poems, possibly for memorisation of the content, then instructional texts, especially on handling teaching materials and dealing with the specificities of local nature and, at last, commentaries on earlier works, which point to scholastic settings and lectures. The default interpretation for the earlier periods is that the lack of Arabic writings reflects an absence of the later intellectual endeavours.[25] Instead, their existence as oral discourses resorting to written material in Greek, Latin, Persian, and especially in Syriac should be taken for granted, seeing in the presence of the last a continuation of the pre-Islamic teaching environment in the Roman and Persian Empires which remained relevant and current.[26] The aggressive rhetoric of Arabic programmatic statements can then be seen as a diatribe to carve a niche among respected oral or written teachings in Arabic or other languages, with which it competed directly.[27] To exalt

[25] See, for example, J. Thomann, "From Lyrics by Al-Fazārī to Lectures by Al-Fārābī: Teaching Astronomy in Baghdād (750–1000 CE)", in *The Place to Go: Contexts of Learning in Baghdād, 750–1000 C.E.*, ed. by J. Scheiner & D. Janos, Studies in late antiquity and early Islam, 26 (Princeton, NJ: Darwin Press, 2014), pp. 503–25 (pp. 503–06).

[26] See M. Debié, "Christians in the Service of the Caliph: Through the Looking-Glass of Communal Identities", in *Christians and Others in the Umayyad State*, ed. by A. Borrut & F. M. Donner, Late antique and medieval Islamic Near East, 1 (Chicago, IL: Oriental Institute of the University of Chicago, 2016), pp. 53–71 (pp. 55–56) (on Athanasius bar Gūmōyē's teaching positions under ʿAbd al-Malik), and also M. Mavroudi, "Translations from Greek into Latin and Arabic during the Middle Ages: Searching for the Classical Tradition", *Speculum* 90:1 (2015), 28–59.

[27] On further concealed intellectual indebtedness and overt repudiation of earlier authors in Arabic culture see S. Vasalou, *Moral Agents and their Deserts: the Character of Muʿtazilite Ethics* (Princeton, NJ: Princeton University Press, 2008), pp. 2–8. On the gradual supersession of Greek and Syriac expertise by texts in Arabic see J. W. Watt, "Why did Ḥunayn, the Master Translator Into Arabic, Make Translations Into Syriac? On the Purpose of the Syriac Translations of Ḥunayn and his Circle", in Scheiner & Janos, pp. 363–88 (pp. 366–69). On the contribution of Christians, especially of the Assyrian Church of the East, to the Abbasid translation project and further references, see S. H. Griffith, "From Patriarch Timothy I to Ḥunayn Ibn Isḥāq: Philosophy and Christian Apology

the caliph's court, Ibn Abī Uṣaibi'a elaborated the traditional theme of rival intellectual centres, opposing freedom of thought to repressive courts and quasi-tyrannical legislation.[28] As effective as Roman legislation could sometimes be in capitals, in most provinces it was never enacted. Justinian's ruling on the teaching of *paideia* signalled that Greek logic, and especially Aristotelian thought, would do little good in arguments directed to the imperial administration or in their supporting documentation, such as rounded up in synodical collections and other compilations.[29] On the contrary, writings containing such arguments could be used as material evidence against an author and his followers. The decrease of Greek and Latin texts which might be called "philosophical" is therefore hardly surprising. The unfounded rhetoric of Fārābī's narrative is exposed by Syriac works, which point to ongoing philosophical traditions, and the limited enforcement of institutional ecclesiastical or imperial control. They testify amply to the interest in and interaction with Greek (specifically Aristotelian) logic by Syriac speakers between the sixth and the ninth/tenth centuries.

Why was Fārābī's tirade believed? It was transmitted by Ibn Abī Uṣaybiʿa, and made it into the Arab philosophical tradition which was translated into Latin, at a time when any argument which could minimise the intellectual and religious authority of Byzantium came in handy, not least because of religious controversies, such as that over the *filioque*. They involved, for theological and ecclesiastic reasons, also the main Latin authors, such as Anselm of Canterbury. Their concerns and those of their students and readers are reflected in the discourses "against the

---

in Abbasid Times; Reason, Ethics and Public Policy", in *Christians and Muslims in dialogue in the Islamic Orient of the Middle Ages = Christlich-muslimische Gespräche im Mittelalter*, ed. by M. Tamcke, *Beiruter Texte und Studien*, 117 (Beirut, Würzburg: Orient-Institut, Ergon, 2007), pp. 75–98 (pp. 77–79).

[28] Several similar anecdotes about the hiding of classical Greek texts by both Arab and Greek authors are discussed by Gutas, *Greek Thought*, pp. 156–57 and Y. Hunt, "Bang For His Buck: Dioscorides as a Gift of the Tenth-Century Byzantine Court", in *Byzantine Culture in Translation*, ed. by A. Brown & B. Neil, *Byzantina Australiensia*, 21 (Leiden, Boston: Brill, 2017), pp. 73–94 (pp. 77–83).

[29] See E. J. Watts, *City and School in Late Antique Athens and Alexandria* (Berkeley, CA; London: University of California Press, 2006), pp. 111–41.

Greeks" which inform their written output.[30] Also for the modern historian, the general purport of Fārābī's version of events seems sufficient evidence of an independence of philosophy from religion that is regularly sought for by scholars but rarely found in the ancient sources. A case in point of the context in the intellectual competition of scientific and philosophical works expressed with the discourse of ethnic and religious polemics and opposition is Elias of Nisibis's work on Syriac and Arabic languages.[31]

East-Syriac texts have been the main evidence to nuance the earlier literal acceptance of the medieval Arabic account about Patristic Syriac and Greek cultures. The East-Syriac literature, from regions with less contact with European churches, remains underrepresented in the printed editions.[32] Still, its importance for Patristics has been increasingly explored, yielding, for example, further proof that Constantine's "crusade" against Persia is just another of Eusebius's constructions, and that the ensuing Persian persecution of Christians for the sake of their faith is only a much later rendition or invention of facts with the *topoi* of Eusebian and Lactantian hagiography.[33] These recent results draw attention to the drawbacks of linguistic, cultural and political frontiers typical of compartmentalised scholarship. Spliting the labor between Hellenists and Syriacists, they prevent adequate analysis of Patristics.

[30] See A. E. Siecienski, *The* Filioque: *History of a Doctrinal Controversy*, Oxford studies in historical theology (New York, NY, Oxford: Oxford University Press, 2010), pp. 118–19 and P. Gemeinhardt, *Die Filioque-Kontroverse zwischen Ost- und Westkirche im Frühmittelalter*, Arbeiten zur Kirchengeschichte, 82 (Berlin: Walter de Gruyter, 2002), p. 463.

[31] See D. Bertaina, "Science, Syntax, and Superiority in Eleventh-Century Christian–Muslim Discussion: Elias of Nisibis on the Arabic and Syriac Languages", *Islam and Christian – Muslim Relations*, 22:2 (2011), 197–207. See also A. H. Becker, "The Comparative Study of 'Scholasticism' in Late Antique Mesopotamia: Rabbis and East Syrians", *AJS Review*, 34:1 (2010), 91–113.

[32] J. T. Walker, *The Legend of Mar Qardagh: Narrative and Christian Heroism in Late Antique Iraq*, The transformation of the classical heritage, 40 (Berkeley; London: University of California Press, 2006), pp. 6–7.

[33] K. Smith, *Constantine and the Captive Christians of Persia: Martyrdom and Religious Identity in Late Antiquity*, The transformation of the classical heritage 57 (Berkeley; London: University of California Press, 2016), p. 63; R. Payne, "Review of *Constantine and the Captive Christians of Persia: Martyrdom and Religious Identity in Late Antiquity*. By Kyle Smith", *BMCR* 2016.10.41, 2016. URL http://bmcr.brynmawr.edu/2016/2016-10-41.html.

## 3. Syriac Manuscripts in Time and Space

Syriac manuscripts are particularly difficult to date unless they contain dated scribal annotation such as colophons.[34] Eastern manuscripts yield several examples of scribes' inconsistency or conscious attempts to preserve earlier writing types. For example, in Vatican Library, Syriac MSS, Vat. Syr. MS 192, Estrangela and more characteristically Eastern letter forms were used side-by-side.[35]

Plenty of Syriac manuscripts have colophons or other meta-textual remarks, sometimes about translation. Usually they are ego-narratives which cannot be taken at face value because of the characteristics of late-antique egodocuments. For example, Philoxenus cast blame on his predecessors to validate and promote his project in several programatic passages. When criticising a poetic description of the Incarnation by Ephrem, he compared his choice of words, infelicitous from Philoxenus's monophysite perspective, with:[36]

> Those who have translated the Scriptures from Greek to Syriac were not concerned to preserve the precise terms used

---

[34] See F. Briquel-Chatonnet, "Le temps du copiste. Notations chronologiques dans les colophons de manuscrits syriaques", in *Proche-Orient ancien: temps vécu, temps pensé. Actes de la table-ronde du 15 novembre 1997 organisée par l'URA 1062 'Études Sémitiques'*, ed. by F. Briquel-Chatonnet & H. Lozachmeur, *Antiquités sémitiques*, 3 (Paris: J. Maisonneuve, 1998), pp. 197–210, F. Briquel-Chatonnet, "Cahiers et signatures dans les manuscrits syriaques. Remarques sur les manuscrits de la Bibliothèque Nationale de France", in *Recherches de codicologie comparée: la composition du codex au Moyen Âge, en Orient et en Occident*, ed. by P. Hoffmann, *Collection bibliologie*, (Paris: Presses de l'École normale supérieure, 1998), pp. 153–69, Brock, "Two Letters".

[35] Vat. Syr. MS 192 is a case in point of conservative use of letter forms and codicological features. Thus, on f. 73r, the *alaf* in ܪܕܝܬܐ ("fever") is written in Estrangela on l. 3 and in Eastern script on l. 10. See E. J. Wilson & S. Dinkha, *Hunain Ibn Ishaq's 'Questions on Medicine for Students': Transcription and Translation of the Oldest Extant Syriac Version (Vat. Syr. 192)*, Studi e testi, 459 (Città del Vaticano: Biblioteca apostolica vaticana, 2010), pp. xv; 471 (facsimile/edition). See now also K. Bush, M. Penn, R. J. Crouser, N. Howe & S. Wu, "Challenging the Estrangela / Serto Divide: Why the Standard Model of Syriac Scripts Just Doesn't Work", *Hugoye: Journal of Syriac Studies* 21:1 (2018), 43–80.

[36] See L. Van Rompay, "*Mallpânâ dilan Suryâyâ*: Ephrem in the Works of Philoxenus of Mabbog: Respect and Distance", *Hugoye: Journal of Syriac Studies*, 7:1 (2007), 83–105 (pp. 96–97) and Brock, "Charting the Hellenization", pp. 102–03.

among the Greeks, nor the true sense; instead they thought up and put whatever pleased them, or [used] wording that they considered more in harmony with the usage of the Syriac language.[37]

As reason for his revision of the Syriac New Testament, Philoxenus claimed:

> When those of old undertook to translate [certain] passages of the Scriptures they made mistakes in many things, whether intentionally or through ignorance. These mistakes concerned not only what is taught about the Economy in the flesh, but various other things concerning different matters.[38]

Such programmatic statements and colophons show the awareness of textual and codicological alterations and that deliberate intervention in the contents was admissible. They suggest that more or less literal translation techniques could be consciously adopted for the reception of Greek texts in Syriac. However, they are not accurate about the processes and agents of changes in Syriac translation and transmission. The scope of influence of the translators and copyists is quite evident in Syriac manuscripts, because of the language gap. Also Greek and Latin patristic texts have only reached the present in edited, sometimes compiled versions. They went through similar engagement with the quality of earlier manuscripts. Nothing guarantees that they replicate their "originals" "authentically", regardless of how close they are in time, space and idiom.

Patristic interpretation of a passage could be informed by another text. The most explicit case of biased reception is probably the reading of an annotated text. The relevance of the marginalia in Syriac culture is attested by the manuscripts in which the annotations of the source were (selectively) reproduced, as in the marginal notes to Severus's *Cathedral Homilies* in BL Add.

---

[37] *Philoxène de Mabbog. Commentaire du prologue johannique*, ed. by A. de Halleux, *Corpus scriptorum Christianorum Orientalium* 380 (*versio*) and 381 (*textus*), Scriptores Syri 165, 166 (Louvain: Secrétariat du Corpus SCO, 1977), I, p. 53.

[38] *Philoxène de Mabbog. Lettre aux moines de Senoun*, ed. by A. de Halleux, *Corpus scriptorum Christianorum Orientalium* 231 (*versio*) and 232 (*textus*), Scriptores Syri 98, 99 (Louvain: Secrétariat du Corpus SCO, 1963), I, p. 54.

12,159. It attests several words found in the Syriac *Masoras*, which point to the influence of this layer of information.[39]

The relevance of codicological information for understanding a work and the intellectual cultures in which it was made or used can be illustrated by Tûr ʾAbdîn homiliaries such as British Library, MS Add. 12,165 and Vatican Library, Syriac MSS, Vat. Syr. MS 253. They show that by the end of the eleventh century, between every two sermons credited to Greek Fathers a *memra* by Jacob of Serugh started to be included. These metrical homilies by an author particular to that Syriac tradition were visually, linguistically, stylistically and ideologically closer to most literary and contemporary discourses of the users of these manuscripts. Did the "Greek sermons" still have intrinsic value for the communities? Did the *memre* affect their interpretation?[40]

### 3.1 Editions of Syriac Patristic Manuscripts

Hidden behind critical apparatuses or especially behind translations are objects which are unique and the testimony of particular stories of translation, composition or copying. Despite their status, critical (printed or digital) editions have severe limitations. For one, the editor's choices reflect the tradition and context of what is essentially a subjective engagement with the material available directly or indirectly, or going beyond it, as in the systematisation or addition of diacritical points and vocalisation. More seriously, critical editions derive from concepts closely associated with notions retrospectively rooted in Enlightment and colonial endeavours to save texts from uncivilised neglect or misuse for

---

[39] See J. Loopstra, "Jacob of Edessa and Patristic Collections in the 'Syriac Masora': Some Soundings", in *Syrien im 1.-7. Jahrhundert nach Christus: Akten der 1. Tübinger Tagung zum Christlichen Orient (15.-16. Juni 2007)*, ed. by D. Bumazhnov, H. R. Seeliger, and C. B. Horn, Studien und Texte zu Antike und Christentum, 62 (Tübingen: Mohr Siebeck, 2011), pp. 157–68 (pp. 164–65).

[40] See J.-M. Sauget, "Pour une interprétation de la structure de l'homéliaire syriaque: MS *British Library Add. 12,165*", *Ecclesia Oriens*, 3 (1986) 121–46, and on the related Arabic *Sammlungen* of Jacob and their relevance for the reception of his homilies among Coptic Christians, see A. M. Butts, "The Christian Arabic Transmission of Jacob of Serugh (d. 521): The *Sammlungen*", *Journal of the Canadian Society for Syriac Studies*, 16 (2016), 39–59 (p. 55).

the clear, clean, and lean use in scientific projects.[41] Manuscripts testify to the availability of a work, and indicate the likely use or the interest in some parts.[42] They reflect settings which shaped the transmitted versions of early Patristic works and in which the later texts were written. They clarify the engagement of the authors, translators and copyists familiar with earlier Syriac works, including a number of versions of canonical and apocryphal biblical texts. Thus, writers such as Ephrem and Ps-Dionysus can be seen to engage primarily with the vocabulary and meaning a text had in a native or colloquial language when citing or quoting a passage from the Septuagint, for example.[43] Until the seventh century, the manuscripts of the Syriac biblical versions exhibit a remarkable textual individuality, dominated by singular readings. After three centuries in which Eastern and Western traditions of the text of the Peshitta remained quite separate, their distinctive profiles

---

[41] The critical edition regarded as only one more stage of engagement with the texts that renders it with a specific audience in mind can be seen in B. Stefaniw, "The School of Didymus the Blind in the Light of the Tura Find", in *Monastic Education in Late Antiquity*, ed. by L. Larsen & S. Rubenson (Cambridge: Cambridge University Press, forth.) and B. Stefaniw, *The Grammarian and his History: Imagining Christian Knowledge in the Tura Papyri* (Berkeley: University of California Press, 2018). The relevance of the genealogical method of textual criticism for Syriac manuscripts is presented in C. Macé, A. Bausi, J. den Heijer, J. Gippert, P. La Spisa, A. Mengozzi, S. Moureau & L. Sels, "Textual Criticism and Text Editing. Introduction", in *Comparative Oriental Manuscript Studies: An Introduction*, ed. by A. Bausi *et al.* (Hamburg: COMSt; Tredition, 2015), pp. 321–27 (pp. 321–23).

[42] Michael the Syrian's treatise on ecclesiastical administration exemplifies what could be achieved when the necessary manuscript sources were available, as discussed by A. Vööbus, "Discovery of a Treatise About the Ecclesiastical Administration Ascribed to Michael the Syrian: A Unique Document in the Literary Genre of Canon Law", *Church History: Studies in Christianity and Culture*, 47:1 (1978), 23–26 (p. 24).

[43] See respectively Y. Monnickendam, "How Greek Is Ephrem's Syriac? Ephrem's Commentary on Genesis as a Case Study", *Journal of Early Christian Studies* 23:2 (2015), 213–44 and I. Perczel, "The Pseudo-Didymian *De trinitate* and Pseudo-Dionysius the Areopagite: A Preliminary Study", in *Studia Patristica Vol. LVIII: Papers presented at the Sixteenth International Conference on Patristic Studies held in Oxford 2011: Volume 6: Neoplatonism and Patristics*, ed. by M. Vinzent, *Studia Patristica* (Leuven: Peeters, 2013), pp. 83–108 (pp. 97–98) and on Ps-Dionysius's Syriac milieu, in which he was as likely to find Syriac speakers, texts, and translations as Greek ones, see R. A. Arthur, *Pseudo-Dionysius as Polemicist: the Development and Purpose of the Angelic Hierarchy in Sixth-Century Syria*. Ashgate new critical thinking in religion, theology, and biblical studies (Aldershot: Ashgate, 2008) – to be used with caution.

were weakened by mutual assimilation and Eastern manuscripts began to dominate. The ongoing relevance of dealing with the various versions of biblical texts and their availability are attested by "collections of šmāhē" in the so-called Syriac *Masoras*' (known in Syriac simply as "tradition", ܡܫܠܡܢܘܬܐ), which are eighth- to tenth-century collections of difficult words from the Peshitta, the Harklean version, Patristic writings and various philological and grammatical materials. Their development coincides with the increasing independence of Byzantine influence and the parallel consolidation of regularised texts in the rising Islamic traditions.[44]

Among the widely known and available printed editions, Paul Bedjan's still influential publications of vast swathes of Syriac literature at first glance resemble Syriac manuscripts. He selectively incorporated features of Western critical editions and Syriac manuscripts, such as the use of red and of ornaments. Bedjan used mannerist frames, which, albeit found in some Syriac printing traditions, are largely unrelated to the transmission of the text in the volumes. Closer to the codicology of Syriac manuscripts are, for example, the seventeenth-century volumes of the Propaganda Press in Rome, which rather ingeniously replicate typographic, floral or simple geometric patterns found in late-antique Syriac manuscripts.[45]

---

[44] See A. Juckel, "'Syriac Masora' and the New Testament Peshiṭta", in *The Peshiṭta: its Use in Literature and Liturgy: Papers Read at the Third Peshiṭta Symposium*, ed. by B. ter Haar Romeny, *Monographs of the Peshiṭta Institute, Leiden* 15 (Leiden: Brill, 2006), pp. 107–22 (pp. 113–14) and Loopstra, pp. 164–65.

[45] On the layout of Syriac manuscripts, see A. Desreumaux, "Des couleurs et des encres dans les manuscrits syriaques", in *Manuscripta Syriaca*, pp. 161–94 (p. 169) (with further information on the inks) and Borbone, "Codicology", p. 258). See F. Briquel-Chatonnet, "Les manuscrits syriaques", in *Sources syriaques*, ed. by R. Jabre-Mouawad, *Nos sources: arts et littérature syriaques*, 1 (Antélias-Beyrouth: Centre d'Études et de Recherches Orientales CERO, 2005), pp. 43–73 (p. 58) on the traditional layout of printed Syriac books. On the ornaments, see, with an album of colour plates, E. Balicka-Witakowska, "Syriac Decorated and Illuminated Manuscripts: a Codicological Approach", in *Manuscripta Syriaca*, pp. 328–30. On Paul Bedjan's editorial activity, and the extension of editorial accretions in the modern editions, see Coakley, "Edward Breath", pp. 41–43; J.-M. Vosté, "Paul Bedjan, le lazariste persan (27 nov. 1838–9 juin 1920). Notes bio-bibliographiques", *Orientalia Christiana Periodica*, 11 (1945), 45–102; H. L. M. van den Berg, "Paul Bedjan, Missionary for Life (1838–1920)", in *Paul Bedjan: Homilies of Mar Jacob of Sarug*, ed. by P. Bedjan & S. P. Brock, *Homiliae Selectae Mar-Jacobi Saurgensis*, 6 (Piscataway: Gorgias, 2006), pp. 339–69.

The Syriac manuscript cultural expression offers a wealth of sources to understand multicultural identity from the nearest to the farthest East, as long as naïve generalisations or comparative studies are avoided.[46] They are related to the dynamics of the Syriac Christian identities, and the relation of Syriac to various cultures within the Roman Empire and, beyond its frontier, in the Persian Empire, China, Indian and under Arab rule. Likewise in the research of Latin Patristics, the analysis of manuscripts has to consider cultural factors such as the endogenous North-African populations, barbaric immigrants, and the Greek culture of the Demotic, Copt, and Arab Alexandria and Egypt. The contribution of Syriac manuscripts for Patristic studies is represented in the next session by four brief case-studies of destruction of manuscripts.[47] They stand for different patterns, defined by the involvement of the holders of the volumes as agents of their destruction and by their intention, distinguishing largely accidental damage of the objects from deliberate and content-aware targeting. The wide temporal and geographic scope of the case-studies reflects that the manuscripts are key evidence that Syriac "was perhaps the strongest common religious marker for all the Syriac-speaking Churches and remained so even in Central Asia where Syriac was used as a script for other local languages as a sign that they belonged to

---

[46] The abundance of Syriac and archaeological sources allows close analysis of Syriac speaking regions, such as Anatolia, and also shows that a generic "East" cannot be extrapolated from one cultural sphere to others. These areas differed significantly from other areas such as Armenia and the very hellenised and then romanised Egyptian province(s), as discussed by G. Greatrex, "Review of *Rome in the East. The transformation of an empire*. By Warwick Ball", *BMCR*, 2001.08.32, 2001. URL http://bmcr.brynmawr.edu/2001/2001-08-32.html and L. E. Patterson, "Review of *Rome in the East. The Transformation of an Empire. Second edition (first published 2000)*. By Warwick Ball", *BMCR* 2017.01.57, 2017. URL http://bmcr.brynmawr.edu/2017/2017-01-57.html.

[47] A survey of momentous losses of Syriac manuscripts is provided by Stewart, "Yours, Mine, or Theirs?". On the survival of ninth-century manuscripts from Edessa see S. P. Brock, "Syriac Manuscripts of the 9th-10th Centuries from a Codicological Perspective", *Semitica et Classica*, 8 (2015), 157–64. This article contextualises the main changes in Syriac palaeography and manuscript culture.

this Christian communion", that is, receivers, conveyors and producers of Patristic writings.[48]

## 4. Patristic Syriac Manuscripts and Cultural Identities

### 4.1 Kerala and Orality

At the beginning of the three pages long encomiastic colophon of Vatican Library, Syriac MSS, Vat. Syr. MS 22, the scribe refers to his and the manuscript's provenance, mentioning the city of ܫܝܢܓܠܐ (Shingly or Chingala, modern day Kodungallur/Cranganore), in ܡܠܒܪ (Malabar). He also mentions the date in 1301, so that it is possibly the only surviving Indian manuscript with Christian content predating modern contacts with Europe.[49] This manuscript stands out because of the historical context of its survival, which shows that Patristic legacy was not necessarily expressed or preserved in writing. In the sixteenth-century, the Portuguese presence in India led to the synodical decision of the Council of Diamper in 1599. It stipulated the destruction of writings with heretical content, listing preventively, but inconsequently, all literary genres associated with the Church of the East in which works with Nestorian con-

---

[48] This is shown by M. Debié, "Syriac Historiography and Identity Formation", *Church History and Religious Culture*, 89:1-3 (2009), 93-114 (quotation on p. 112).

[49] A Latin translation of the colophon can be found in the catalogue, Assemani (I. 2, *Complectens Codices Chaldaicos sive Syriacos*), pp. 187-88, and for the reliability of the detailed descriptions it provides, see *Comparative Oriental Manuscript Studies: An Introduction*, ed. by A. Bausi et al., (Hamburg: COMSt; Tredition, 2015), pp. 493, 502. Although an unicum, the manuscript is represented in William Henry Paine Hatch, *An Album of Dated Syriac Manuscripts. Monumenta palaeographica vetera*. 2nd ser. (Boston: American Academy of Arts and Sciences, 1946), p. 226/Plate CLXXV. A few other manuscripts which may predate the Portuguese arrival in India are discussed by I. Perczel, "Malayalam Garshuni: A Witness to an Early Stage of Indian Christian Literature", *Hugoye: Journal of Syriac Studies*, 17:2 (2014), 263-323 (pp. 264-69), F. Briquel-Chatonnet, "Syriac Manuscripts in India, Syriac Manuscripts from India", *Hugoye: Journal of Syriac Studies*, 15:2 (2012), 289-99 (pp. 292-93), I. Perczel, "Classical Syriac as a Modern Lingua Franca in South India Between 1600 and 2006", *Aram*, 21 (2009), 289-321 (pp. 292-94), and T. Koonammakkal, "An Introduction to Malayalam Karshon", *The Harp*, 15 (2002), 99-106.

tent were known in the West.⁵⁰ Despite vivid narratives of its enforcement, it seems few Patristic manuscripts were destroyed. In a literate society, the Christian tradition in Kerala apparently did not have at all or in any significant numbers manuscripts except the liturgical and biblical copies owned by religious men, as reflected by the few extant early manuscripts. Patristics was for them predominantly an oral legacy. Also most of the intellectual culture of Early Christianity and Late Antiquity was oral,⁵¹ and texts were produced not as handbooks of uncontested authority but as constructions of the literary persona of the Christian leader who defended his piety and religious commitment, not least in his exposition of theological and religious views. Transmission reflects similar textual constructions of literary personæ who refer to earlier works for the sake of positive or negative values associated to them, or attempts to actively propagate and implement the views and rituals found in the texts. The manuscripts contributed material proof of the pedigree of a "tradition" that is more an endoxography than a genuine doxography. After Christians in Kerala were confronted with these processes of religious disputation anchored in textual evidence, a complex cultural dynamic led to the rise of a rich Patristic literary output in which the destruction of the few manuscripts was only an early episode. The contact with European literary culture in the form of the Portuguese presence spread the making and use of printed and manuscript Syriac texts in India. The versions extant in Eastern and Western Syriac communities indicate that they had access to Patristic works by virtue of waves of importation of manuscripts, sometimes of "unorthodox" provenance.⁵²

---

[50] See Briquel-Chatonnet, "Syriac Manuscripts in India", pp. 292–93, Perczel, "Classical Syriac", p. 294 and "Some Early Documents about the Interactions of the Saint Thomas Christians and the European Missionaries", in *Malabar in the Indian Ocean: Cosmopolitanism in a Maritime Historical Region*, ed. by M. Kooria & M. N. Pearson (New Delhi: Oxford University Press, 2018), pp. 76–120.

[51] D. MacRae, *Legible Religion: Books, Gods, and Rituals in Roman Culture* (Cambridge, MA: Harvard University Press, 2016), pp. 79–85, W. Kelber, "The History of the Closure of Biblical Texts", in *The Interface of Orality and Writing: Speaking, Seeing, Writing in the Shaping of New Genres*, ed. by A. Weissenrieder & R. B. Coote, *Wissenschaftliche Untersuchungen zum Neuen Testament*, 260 (Tübingen: Mohr Siebeck, 2010), pp. 71–99 (pp. 81–82).

[52] See Perczel, "Malayalam Garshuni", p. 278. The manuscripts can be placed in branches associated with traditions at odds with the doctrinal alignment sig-

Syriac manuscripts in India are an active area of research and conservation efforts. Unknown texts and recensions are still being found in local archives of Christian communities in Malabar and Kerala. István Perczel has drawn attention to MS Ernakulam MAP 4 of Mar Abraham's (Metropolitan of Malabar between *c.* 1555 and 1597) personal copy of the East Syriac canon law collection, copied in 1563, in Gazarta; MS Piramadam Syr 14 with anonymous Nestorian and Isho'dad of Merv's commentaries on the Gospels, Piramadam MS Syr. 25, f. 41v with the colophon of the translation of the Revelations of St Gregory the Theologian, from the Arabic to Syriac, by Mor Yovannis Hidayat' Allah; the bilingual (*v.* Garshuni / *r.* Syriac) Ernakulam MAP Syr 7, ff. 516v–517r with a Letter of Mor Dionysius I (1759–1809) to Pope Pius VI, and the palm leaf in Kolezhuttu script with the 1768 (= 1770) date of a Malayalam chronicle from Kuruppampady, which tells, for example, of the separation of the Catholic and Jacobite communities.[53] These manuscripts also challenge the definition of manuscript, since many are made of rectangularly cut and cured palm leaf sheets on which the text is engraved, and which are usually bound together. They differ from painted or incised wooden beams, for example, only in their portability.[54]

---

nalled by the more or less independent connections established by most dioceses in India, from the sixteenth century on, with dioceses and patriarchates in Europe and Asia. See W. Baum & D. W. Winkler, *The Church of the East: a Concise History* (London: Routledge, 2003), pp. 115–16. The expansion of print culture in response to foreign presence as sign of the resilience of a literary and religious culture can also be seen in the late nineteenth- and early twentieth-century vibrant market for Punjabi books in both the Gurmukhi and the Indo-Persian scripts, as discussed in F. Mir, *The Social Space of Language: Vernacular Culture in British Colonial Punjab* (Berkeley; Los Angeles; New York: University of California Press, 2010), pp. 63–64.

[53] I. Perczel, "History of Kerala Christianity on the Basis of Newly Found Documents: Methodological Challenges and Possible Answers", *IIS Centre for Contemporary Studies*, 24 July, 2008 – unpublished. Images of these manuscripts were shown at the conference and were available as of November 2017 on pp. 38, 45, 49, 59 and 65 of http://ces.iisc.ernet.in/hpg/ragh/ccs/photoGallery/2008-07-24-Istvan/2008-07-24-Istvan.pdf.

[54] See F. Briquel-Chatonnet, "De l'usage du parchemin à celui du papier dans les manuscrits syriaques", in *Manuscripta Syriaca*, pp. 141–59 (p. 151).

## 4.2 Maronite Manuscripts and Written Evidence

The second case-study points to the value of manuscripts as material witnesses which could be used in dispute resolution processes for or against individuals or communities. The seventh-century Monothelete controversy left traces in the Maronite manuscript culture which contributed to the Maronite communities themselves deliberately destroying their Syriac manuscripts when, in the twelfth century, they came again into closer contact with Roman Catholic views. Thus only a handful of liturgical manuscripts survive. It seems that unlike the filleting of the archives carried out in Armenia,[55] the Maronites destroyed manuscripts in general, regardless of the content of the main matter, simply because they were likely to harbour, for example in prayers of colophons, wording then suspected of heresy in view of being at variance with the translations from Greek and Latin of the time. Actually, the differences reflected local changes in translation practices over the intervening centuries and the largely independent development of the languages involved, including Greek and Latin. Thereby the Maronites destroyed what seems, from extant Arabic translations and earlier references, to have been the material remains of a rich but by then largely inaccessible literary culture. It is likely that in the twelfth century most Maronites could not read or find out the content of their manuscripts. Under Arab rule, bilingualism receded and daily use of Syriac decreased, as well as fluency in reading and writing, in part reflecting increased availability of newer writings and teaching material on non-religious topics in Arabic.[56] Surviving texts (in later copies), such as the *Kitab*

---

[55] See T. Greenwood, "'New Light from the East': Chronography and Ecclesiastical History through a Late Seventh-Century Armenian Source", *Journal of Early Christian Studies*, 16:2 (2008), 197–254 (p. 252).

[56] See n. 25 and J. Moukarzel, "Le portrait des maronites et du Mont-Liban au début du XVIIe siècle", in *Le latin des maronites*, ed. by M. Issa (Paris: Geuthner, 2017), pp. 157–88 (p. 169) on the information provided in G. Dandini, *Missione apostolica al patriarca, e maroniti del Monte Libano del p. Girolamo Dandini della Compagnea die Giesú, e sua pellegrinazione a Gerusalemme* (Cesena: il Neri, 1656) (revised and augmented edition by Kram Rizk, Kaslik, 2005). See also Jack Tannous, "You Are what you Read: Qenneshre and the Miaphysite Church in the Seventh Century", in *History and Identity in the Late Antique Near East, 500–1000*, ed. by P. Wood, Oxford studies in late antiquity (Oxford: Oxford University Press, 2013), pp. 83–102 (pp. 92–97), T. S. Richter, "Greek, Coptic and

*al-Huda*, Thomas of Kafartab's *Ten chapters* and works by Theophilos of Edessa, and al-Mas'ūdī's reference to Qays al-Maruni, suggest that Maronite Syriac literature included works in a wide range of genres, including non-religious poetry and prose. They also refer to the existence of significant libraries or archives.[57] The destruction eliminated the evidence of anathematised views, but Maronite religious vocabulary and practices were largely unaffected, as in the veneration of Barṣawmo. Although "protection" by Catholic Rome was desirable to Maronites beleaguered by Mamluk and Ottoman rule, closer contact, for example during the Frankish presence in Syria during Crusades and in the early twelfth century led to conflicts, especially in rural areas, where it seems that ritual practices were less affected by episcopal theological and disciplinary rulings.[58] Some information about the continuity of Maronite religious vocabulary and practices, such as the veneration of Barṣawmo as saint can be found, for example, in the very partial accounts by the Maronite Joseph Simon Assemani, who worked in Rome and addressed Latin Europeans. Assemani's printed output has largely obscured earlier European scholarship about Syriac Patristic manuscripts, such as Eusèbe Renaudot's considerations about Nestorians in the East (in Bibliothèque nationale de France, Département des manuscrits, MS NAF 7474

the 'Language of the Hijra': the Rise and Decline of the Coptic Language in Late Antique and Medieval Egypt", in *From Hellenism to Islam: cultural and linguistic change in the Roman Near East*, ed. by H. M. Cotton, R. G. Hoyland, J. J. Price & D. J. Wasserstein (Cambridge: Cambridge University Press, 2009), pp. 402–46 (pp. 431–34).

[57] The works are discussed by R. G. Hoyland, *Seeing Islam as others saw it: a survey and evaluation of Christian, Jewish, and Zoroastrian writings on early Islam*, Studies in late antiquity and early Islam, 13 (Princeton, NJ: Darwin Press, 1997), pp. 136–37. See J. Tannous, "In Search of Monotheletism", *Dumbarton Oaks Papers*, 68 (2014), 29–67, and K. S. Salibi, "The Traditional Historiography of the Maronites", in *Historians of the Middle East*, ed. by B. Lewis & P. M. Holt (London: Oxford University Press, 1962), pp. 212–25 (pp. 213–14), as well as S. P. Brock, "A Syriac Fragment on the Sixth Council", *Oriens christianus*, 57 (1973) 63–71, republished in *Syriac perspectives on late antiquity*, Variorum reprint, CS199 (London: Ashgate, 1984), XIII (p. 71). M. P. Penn, "A Temporarily Resurrected Dog and Other Wonders: Thomas of Margā and Early Christian/Muslim Encounters", *Medieval Encounters*, 16:2–4 (2010), 209–42.

[58] See K. S. Salibi, "Maronite Church in the Middle Ages and its Union with Rome", *Oriens christianus*, 42 (1958), 113–58 (p. 93).

and 7475).[59] This case-study further demonstrates that extant manuscripts draw an incomplete picture of past literary cultures. The Patristic bias of the manuscripts of most Syriac traditions is unrepresentative of the literary and documentary cultures in which they were made and transmitted.

### 4.2.1 The Use of Patristic Writings: Magical Manuscripts, Ostraca and Incantation Bowls

The Kerala Syriac manuscripts mentioned above reflect the fact that Patristic works were in many cases part of lived religions in which tradition was created and preserved orally, so that the deliberate choice to express something in writing was linked to the meaning manuscripts had in the culture, regardless of its literacy. Syriac manuscripts which may be considered magical reveal the power associated with writing in the cultures from which Patristic texts stem. They are small, often tiny objects with prayers and excerpts from Scriptures and Patristic texts, sometimes adorned with illustrations.[60] This material is widely spread and was often

---

[59] See A. Palmer, "The West-Syrian Monastic Founder Barṣawmo: A Historical Review of the Scholarly Literature", in *Orientalia Christiana: Festschrift für Hubert Kaufhold zum 70. Geburtstag*, ed. by P. Bruns and H. Luthe (Wiesbaden: Harrassowitz, 2013), pp. 399–414 (pp. 401–04), J.-M. Sauget, "Le 'codex liturgicus' de J.-L. Assémani et ses sources manuscrites pour les 'ordines' de l'initiation chrétienne selon la tradition syro-occidentale", *Gregorianum*, 54:2 (1973), 339–52, B. Heyberger, *Les chrétiens du Proche-Orient au temps de la Réforme catholique: Syrie, Liban, Palestine, XVII<sup>e</sup>-XVIII<sup>e</sup> siècles*. Bibliothèque des Écoles françaises d'Athènes et de Rome, 284 (Rome: École française de Rome, 1994), pp. 247, 429 and 535, and B. Heyberger, "'Pro nunc, nihil respondendum'– Recherche d'informations et prise de décision à la propagande: l'exemple du Levant (XVIII<sup>e</sup> siècle)", *Mélanges de l'Ecole française de Rome. Italie et Méditerranée*, 109:2 (1997), 539–54 (pp. 545–46). On E. Renaudot, see J. Leroy, "La renaissance de l'Église syriaque aux XII<sup>e</sup>-XIII<sup>e</sup> siècles", *Cahiers de Civilisation Médiévale*, 14 (1971), 131–48 (p. 139). I thank Walter Beers and Cornel Zwierlein for respectively drawing my attention to Palmer's article and to the wider early eighteenth-century European interest in Syriac Patristic manuscripts.

[60] See the images in H. Gollancz, *The Book of Protection: Being a Collection of Charms, Now Ed. for the First Time from Syriac Mss.* (London: H. Frowde, 1912), Cod A p. 6 and the small but poignant repertory in P. Gignoux, *Incantations Magiques Syriaques*, Collection de la Revue des Études Juives, 4 (Leuven: Peeters, 1987), and Pl.- XXXII.3 in Balicka-Witakowska, pp. 321–42. On the problematic use of "magical" and possible characterisations of this category, see R. Gordon, "Astrology, and Magic: Discourse, Schemes, Power, and Literacy", in *Panthée: Religious Transformations in the Graeco-Roman Empire*, ed. by L. Bricault & C. Bonnet, *Religions in the Graeco-Roman world*, 177 (Leiden: Brill,

neglected or dismissively catalogued. Now the corpus is growing, with new evidence being found even in European libraries. Recently, the group of three sixth- or seventh-century amulets in the Bibliothèque Nationale de France edited by P. Gignoux in 1987 was enlarged when the Cambridge University Library acquired a further member of the group, now MS Or. 2,480.

This contains a healing and protection incantation written for a client in minute letters on a leaf of vellum which was folded vertically into 3 "columns", then presumably rolled up. The verso was left blank.[61]

Ostraca were common writing materials in Syriac cultural contexts too, and also texts on ceramic objects and vessels provide relevant evidence about Patristics.[62] A case in point are two of the so-called incantation bowls. Bowl 49 has atypical formulæ closer to formal Christian prayers, possibly related to Maronite liturgical practices, and Bowl 48 bears a text that echoes Christian formulæ but is not specifically Christian. On the inner-side of the bowl, at the bottom of which a bearded facial design can be seen, most writing is Estrangela, with some letter forms similar to Manichaean, Serto, and Eastern Syriac scripts.[63] Syriac incantation bowls and epigraphic evidence show that the vocabulary of the disputes and controversies were not rarefied conflicts of intellectuals, but could be present among groups to the point of characterising their social identity. These objects point to Patristic texts in less erudite registers and show clearly the

---

2013), pp. 85–111, J. N. Bremmer, "From Books with Magic to Magical Books in Ancient Greece and Rome", in *The Materiality of Magic*, ed. by D. Boschung & J. N. Bremmer, *Morphomata*, 20 (Paderborn: Wilhelm Fink, 2015), pp. 241–69 and B.-C. Otto, "Historicising 'Western Learned Magic': Preliminary Remarks", *Aries*, 16:2 (2016), 161–240.

[61] I thank Dr J. F. Coakley for the preliminary version of the catalogue entry of this magic scroll, now published in his *A Catalogue of the Syriac Manuscripts in Cambridge University Library and College Libraries Acquired since 1910* (Ely: Jericho Press, 2018).

[62] See Gross, "Irano-Talmudica", p. 252, Tannous, "In Search", p. 68, Becker, "The Comparative Study", p. 111, J. N. Ford, "A New Parallel to the Jewish Babylonian Aramaic Magic Bowl IM 76,106 (Nippur 11 N78)", *Aramaic Studies*, 9:2 (2011), 249–77 (p. 257).

[63] See the detailed analysis and excellent images in M. Moriggi, *A Corpus of Syriac Incantation Bowls: Syriac Magical Texts from Late-Antique Mesopotamia*, Magical and Religious Literature of Late Antiquity, 3 (Leiden; Boston: Brill, 2014), pp. 206–11.

fluidity of the boundaries between Christian groups defined by the creeds they, or at least their bishops, confessed. Syriac "magical" manuscripts, moreover, make explicit the fuzziness of linguistic and narrative borders between Christians, Jews, Zoroastrians, and Muslims, since contemporary Sassanid, Arabic, and Rabbinic sources contain similar material.[64] The liminal position between formal Maronite liturgy attested in manuscript evidence made by and for institutionalised Christianities and the literary register of "magical" rites shows the multifarious reception of Patristic literature in lived Christian religion not isolated from other local practices of lived ancient religions.

### 4.3 Turfan Manuscripts and Modern Written Cultures

The gradual spread and the changes in the use and status of printed materials in European societies long ago contributed for manuscripts to be regarded no longer as objects of cultural and religious significance, but rather as artefacts, to be protected and studied.[65] The positivistic approach to texts, the Enlightenment's concepts of authorship and modern relation to manuscript and printed materials are embodied in books such as Robert Curzon, *Visits to the Monasteries of the Levant* (London: Murray, 1849). It is easy to identify in its illustrations the sanitising and denigrating distortion of reality characteristic of this travel literature, which was informed by and made within a conceptualization of a bourgeois individualist subjectivity of which the scholars, such as Alphonse Mingana, searching for or working on Syriac manuscripts in the nineteenth and early twentieth century were affirmatively or antagonistically part.[66] They are important documents for the

---

[64] See further examples of linguistic and theological evidence in Gross, "Irano-Talmudica", Penn, "A Temporarily Resurrected Dog", A. Gasimova, "Models, Portraits, and Signs of Fate in Ancient Arabian Tradition", *Journal of Near Eastern Studies*, 73:2 (2014), 319–40, and E. C. D. Hunter, "Syriac Inscriptions from a Melkite Monastery on the Middle Euphrates", *Bulletin of the School of Oriental and African Studies*, 52:1 (1989), 1–17. See also Shepardson, pp. 112–53.

[65] *From Dust to Digital*, p. liv.

[66] On the socio-cultural place of this travel-literature see, for example, A. Olsaretti, "Urban Culture, Curiosity and the Aesthetics of Distance: The Representation of Picturesque Carnivals in Early Victorian Travelogues to the Levant", *Social History*, 32:3 (2007), 247–70 (pp. 249–50), as well as K. S. Heal, "Notes

History of Ideas and can provide some entertainment (or consternation). Also part of this genre of literature are Albert von Le Coq's stories about the search for "Hellenic culture" in Turfan (Xinjiang, China). The *Berichte und Abhandlungen der II. und III. Deutschen Turfan-Expedition* (published in 1926) had as main title *Auf Hellas Spuren in Ostturkistan*. This was replaced by the entrepreneurial search for discoveries in the publication of *Buried Treasures of Chinese Turkestan* in 1928, which the author characterised as

> a personal narrative – free from scientific ballast – of our experiences in those distant sunny lands, which, remote, and dusty as they undoubtedly are, will ever be endeared to by the memory of many efforts crowned with success and of the many valuable friends that we made during our stay there. This narrative is interspersed with all kinds of remarks referring to the life and character of our native friends – Eastern Turkestan and Chinese alike – and to interesting developments of the history of art, etc. But the main object of the book is to give to the public at large a general idea of our expeditions and their results. I would refer any reader desiring more detailed information to the great number of publications of quite a popular character and mostly published by Dietrich Reimer, which are given in the bibliography which appears as an appendix to my narrative.[67]

His story about the destruction of manuscripts regarded by their holders as "old volumes" shows that they no longer had a textual culture which would assign value to the volumes for the sake of their content, even if it was unreadable because of the language or writing.

---

on the Acquisition History of the Mingana Syriac Manuscripts", in *Manuscripta Syriaca*, pp. 11–38.

[67] On the spread of Christianities and other religions of the Roman empire in Asia, see M. Dickens, "Patriarch Timothy I and the Metropolitan of the Turks", *Journal of the Royal Asiatic Society of Great Britain*, 20:2 (2010), 117–39 (pp. 122–24) and M. Dickens, "Scribal Practices in the Turfan Christian Community", *Journal of the Canadian Society for Syriac Studies*, 13 (2013), 3–28; on the libraries, see E. C. D Hunter, "The Church of the East in Central Asia", *Bulletin of the John Rylands University Library*, 78:3 (1996), 129–42 (p. 138).

Our expeditions arrived too late at Karakhoja. Had they come earlier, more of these remarkable Sassanian-Hellenistic paintings would certainly have been secured. We would have saved, too, very much more of the literature of the religious community, important as it is to the history of religions and languages alike; one of the peasants told me that five years before the arrival of the first expedition he had, in the ruins of one of the temples, which were pulled down to turn their site into fields, found great cartloads (araba) of those manuscripts "with the little writing" (i.e. Manichæan) for which we were making such diligent search. Many had been ornamented with pictures in gold and colours. But he was afraid, to begin with, of the unholy nature of the writings and, secondly, that the Chinese might use the discovery as a pretext for fresh extortions, so he straightway threw the whole library into the river![68]

The story is quite typical of late nineteenth- and twentieth-century representation of manuscripts waiting to be rediscovered, whether by foreigners or by the communities themselves.[69] Alien interest and prestige self-reflected in monetary value of the volumes. What was initially driven by economic or political factors in reaction to European attention contributed to their internal reassessment.[70] Now, their physical presence informs the identity of many communities, several of which rely on literal interpretations of Patristic narratives, spurning the results of History and Patristic Studies. Cultural values, such as mentioned in the Turfan reports and the notion derived from Classical culture, that the violent destruction of written objects is a highly charged symbolic aggression against their owners or those who value them,[71]

---

[68] A. von Le Coq & A. Barwell, *Buried Treasures of Chinese Turkestan*. (London: George Allen & Unwin Ltd., 1928), pp. 58–59.

[69] See also J. F. Coakley, "The Teaching of Syriac at Cambridge", in *A Man of Many Parts: Essays in Honor of John Westerdale Bowker on the Occasion of His Eightieth Birthday*, ed. by E. E. Lemcio & R. Williams (Eugene, Oregon: Pickwick, 2015), pp. 15–29, and for a sober appraisal of the contents of modern monastic libraries in the East, see Leroy, "La renaissance", p. 139.

[70] See Stewart, "Yours, Mine, or Theirs?", pp. 607, 612–15, 626–27.

[71] See J. N. Bremmer, "Religious Violence between Greeks, Romans, Christians and Jews", in *Violence in Ancient Christianity: Victims and Perpetrators*, ed. by A. C. Geljon & R. Roukema, Supplements to Vigiliae Christianae, 125 (Leiden; Boston: Brill, 2014), pp. 8–32 (pp. 23–26), D. Rohmann, *Christianity*,

has contributed to the targeting of Syriac manuscripts during the twentieth century. In this regard, their destruction during the recent violent political developments in the Near East differs from the loss of the collection of manuscripts from the ʿAmādīyā and ʿAqrā regions which was rather a side-effect of the military operations of the Iraqi army against Kurdish guerillas in 1961, which led to the destruction of the episcopal residence at ʿAmādīyā, where the manuscripts had been.[72]

### 4.4 Syriac Manuscripts and Linguistic Registers

A comparison of the importance of Syriac manuscripts in these four case-studies reveals that Syriac manuscripts were written in settings in which other languages were possible options to express Patristic content and their writers's choice of Syriac was directly related to the identity of their Christian tradition.[73] Greek and

---

*Book-Burning and Censorship in Late Antiquity: Studies in Text Transmission*, Arbeiten zur Kirchengeschichte, 135 (Berlin: Walter De Gruyter, 2016), pp. 38–39, D. Rohmann, "Book Burning as Conflict Management in the Roman Empire (213 BCE – 200 CE)", *Ancient Society*, 43 (2013), 115–49, D. C. Sarefield, "The Symbolics of Book-Burning: the Establishment of a Christian Ritual of Persecution", in *The Early Christian Book*, ed. by W. E. Klingshirn & L. Safran, Catholic University of America Studies in Early Christianity (Washington, DC: The Catholic University of America Press, 2007), pp. 159–73, F. H. Cramer, "Bookburning and Censorship in Ancient Rome: A Chapter from the History of Freedom of Speech", *Journal of the History of Ideas*, 6:2 (1945), 157–96, W. Speyer, *Büchervernichtung und Zensur des Geistes bei Heiden, Juden und Christen*, Bibliothek des Buchwesens, 7 (Stuttgart: Hiersemann, 1981), M. P. Penn, "Moving Beyond the Palimpsest: Erasure in Syriac Manuscripts", *Journal of Early Christian Studies*, 18:2 (2010), 261–303 (pp. 297–98), and, on the legislation M. V. E. Paño, "Impios libros ...publice conburi decernimus. el control de la palabra en la legislación de los ss. IV y V", in *Atti dell'Accademia Romanistica Costantiniana XIX 2013: Convegno internazionale. Organizzare, sorvegliare, punire. Il controllo dei corpi e delle menti nel diritto della tarda antichità*, ed. by S. Giglio Atti dell'Accademia Romanistica Costantiniana, 16 = OAW Phil.-hist. Kl., Denkschriften 379 (Roma: Aracne Editrice, 2009), pp. 541–66.

[72] See D. Wilmshurst, *The Ecclesiastical Organisation of the Church of the East, 1318–1913*, Corpus scriptorum Christianorum Orientalium, 582. Subsidia 104 (Leuven: Peeters, 2000), p. 12.

[73] Other aspects of the formal or erudite discourse, such as elaborate illuminations and other costly decorations of the pages or of the binding are also seldom attested in Syriac manuscripts, pointing to similar conceptual and practical options, as discussed by Briquel-Chatonnet, "Cahiers et signatures", p. 169. The absence of "luxury Syriac manuscripts", especially of costly bindings, may reflect the vicissitudes of their transmission and of nineteenth-century conser-

Latin Patristic literature likewise reflects deliberate choices to copy a version of a text which someone decided to make to express a discourse very formally. It was made in multilingual contexts.[74] In the capitals of the Latin West and of Byzantium at least a diglossia of formal and vernacular linguistic registers existed and Patristic authors were competent in both. However, discourses on the Christian faith were seldom registered in the vernacular, since its literacy, especially for "literary" works, was frowned on. The familiarity of Patristic authors with the various linguistic strata is revealed by less formal types of text such as papyri letters, and the excellent vernacular works from periods when the literary use of this register was more widely accepted, including Manganeios's *politikos stichos*.[75] Very little evidence of varieties of Syriac that depart from the classical language remain, and most is found on the incantation bowls.[76] They point to long oral traditions of expressing Patristic topics without resorting to writing, so that the textual material preserves only a fraction of the full range

---

vation practices rather than utilitarian raisons d'être suggested, for example, by J. Leroy, *Les manuscrits syriaques à peintures conservés dans les bibliothèques d'Europe et d'Orient: contribution à l'étude de l'iconographie des Églises de langue syriaque*, Bibliothèque archéologique et historique, 77 (Paris: Geuthner, 1964) and Y. Dergham & F. Vinourd, "Les reliures syriaques: essai de caractérisation par comparaison avec les reliures byzantines et arméniennes", in *Manuscripta Syriaca*, pp. 271–306 (pp. 271, 292–96). See Borbone, "Codicology", pp. 265–66.

[74] On the intellectual and educational background of Christian translators working on classical works for Arab thinkers, see, for example, A. Treiger, "Palestinian Origenism and the Early History of the Maronites: In Search of the Origins of the Arabic *Theology of Aristotle*", in D. Janos (ed.), *Ideas in Motion in Baghdad and Beyond: Philosophical and Theological Exchanges Between Christians and Muslims in the Third/Ninth and Fourth/Tenth Centuries*, Islamic History and Civilization, 124 (Leiden; Boston: Brill, 2015), pp. 44–80 (p. 48).

[75] See E. Jeffreys, "Medieval Greek Epic Poetry", in *Medieval Oral Literature*, ed. by K. Reichl, De Gruyter Lexikon (Berlin, Boston: De Gruyter, 2011), pp. 459–84 (pp. 460–62), E. Jeffreys & M. Jeffreys, "The Traditional Style of Thirteenth-Century Greek 'Politikos Stichos' Poetry and the Search for its Origins", *Byzantine and Modern Greek Studies*, 40:1 (2016), 69–81, and C. Cupane, "Wie volkstümlich ist die byzantinische Volksliteratur?", *Byzantinische Zeitschrift*, 96:2 (2004), 577–600.

[76] See L. Van Rompay, "Some Remarks on the Language of Syriac Incantation Texts", in *V Symposium Syriacum 1988*, ed. by R. Lavenant, Orientalia Christiana Analecta, 236 (Roma: Pontificium Institutum Studiorum Orientalium), pp. 369–81, and A. M. Butts, "Review of *A Corpus of Syriac Incantation Bowls. Syriac Magical Texts from Late-Antique Mesopotamia*. By Marco Moriggi", *Journal of Near Eastern Studies*, 74:2 (2015), 361–62 (p. 361).

of religious discourses of the contexts in which it was written and used. It furthermore shows that the choosing of a linguistic register and the written medium were more related to the wider sociopolitical interests of the author, editor or translator than to his pastoral and ecclesiastic concerns. Thus, no hypothetical "Library of the Church Fathers" or a rather extensive *BKG* with an ideal *CPG* as table of contents can convey the unadultered thought of the Fathers.

## 5. *Contemporary Syriac Manuscript Studies*

A vast literature of editions and studies about Syriac Patristic manuscripts exists already, but much more needs to be done. Scores of Syriac manuscripts have not yet been edited. This applies especially to later specimens and new finds, not least from regions such as Turfan and Malabar, which can provide important early Patristic sources, such as Isaiah of Scetis in manuscript C2 of Turfan, and still new readings or even recovered works, such as Babai of Nisibis's *Homily* and the *Counsels* of Šem'ōn d-Ṭaibūtēh, both seventh-century East Syriac ascetics. Turfan manuscripts have offered passages not known to be extant elsewhere, or known to have been destroyed, as is the case of the *Counsels*, which were in the collection of the Chaldean Archbishopric Library in Seert, destroyed during the First World War, with only thirteen manuscripts previously taken to Paris now surviving.[77]

Flourishing in only a few universities and research centres, research into Syriac manuscripts is nevertheless a very active field of research, with a large community of scholars and a significant digital presence. However, most of the projects announced in the first decade of this century to digitise and create searchable databases did not achieve their optimistic goals on schedule, or became an authoritative reference until now.[78] Several projects

---

[77] See G. M. Kessel & N. Sims-Williams, "The Profitable Counsels of Šem'ōn d-Ṭaibūtēh: The Syriac Original and its Sogdian Version", *Le Muséon*, 124:3–4 (2007), 279–302, and N. Sims-Williams, *The Christian Sogdian Manuscript C2*, Schriften zur Geschichte und Kultur des alten Orients. Berliner Turfantexte, 12 (Berlin: Akademie-Verlag, 1985), pp. 165–67 (= no. 12), 87–100.

[78] For example, E. Ringger, K. Heal, C. Griffin, K. Seppi, D. Lonsdale & D. Taylor, "Compiling and Annotating a Syriac Corpus", *All Faculty Publica-*

were largely abandoned or postponed, not only for financial reasons. Digital and technological developments are meaningless resources without "the slow work of reading and pondering the contents of these manuscripts to draw out their significance for understanding the peoples and cultures that produced them", the wearisome pleasure which cannot be spared by some chimeric algorithm to automate the paleographical, codicological, and editorial work.[79] Full disclosure of the information in Syriac manuscripts by the Digital Humanities in the near future is unlikely, but already now the tools in this area are helping Patristics by making vast and increasing numbers of manuscripts accessible to every scholar. The efforts will only lead somewhere if the importance of the Patristic manuscripts is recognised.

## 6. Concluding Remarks

The information conveyed by Syriac should not lay dormant. It helps to understand better what the Greek, Latin, and vernacular texts now regarded as Patristic "sources" actually were and are. This is clearly set out in the abundant literature protesting the importance of Syriac manuscripts on which this paper builds. It points out ways in which they can be further explored and especially how they can contribute much more to Patristics than they already have. As important as unpublished works and new variants is the significant evidence they provide for the dynamics which led to the writing of the works, which affected their transmission, and which made them a part of the lived religion of many.

---

*tions* (2008), 1297 URL http://scholarsarchive.byu.edu/facpub/1297. Recently, a number of websites were (re-)launched. Usually acknowledging the existence of other digital resources, including digitised manuscripts, they contain thorough reviews of the literature on many subjects. It remains to be seen if they will share the fate of earlier initiatives.

[79] Paraphrase of C. Stewart, "HMML and Syriac Manuscripts", in *Manuscripta Syriaca*, pp. 49–63 (p. 60). See also the claims in Ringger *et al.*, "Compiling and Annotating", K. S. Heal, "Corpora, eLibraries, and Databases: Locating Syriac Studies in the 21st Century", *Hugoye: Journal of Syriac Studies*, 15:1 (2013), 65–78, P. Felt, E. K. Ringger, K. Seppi, K. S. Heal, R. A. Haertel & D. Lonsdale, "Evaluating Machine-Assisted Annotation in Under-Resourced Settings", *Language Resources and Evaluation*, 48:4 (2014), 561–99.

This section has thus shown that the corpus of Syriac manuscripts has a clear Patristic bias, which is unrepresentative of the full range of the cultural traditions in which they were made and used over a wide timeframe. Focusing on narratives of the destruction of manuscripts and cultural scenarios in which they or their content was or was not meaningful, this paper has shown that active engagement with the riches of the collections and electronic depositories of Syriac manuscripts is essential for a proper understanding of the New Testament, Early Church, Latin or Greek fathers, papal primacy, asceticism, monasticism, the philosophical legacy of the Cappadocians, Ps.-Dionysius the Areopagite, and Maximus the Confessor, among other topics of Patristic Studies. The Syriac manuscripts have and will continue to yield new texts and important information on their philosophical and political implications. Their preservation and interdisciplinary research is essential for Patristics Studies.

## *Abstract*

The chapter shows that since its beginnings Patristic Studies has occasionally taken into account the additional or unique readings of a fraction of Syriac manuscripts. It argues that this misrepresents the full range of the cultural traditions in African, Near-Eastern and Asian regions, where they were made and used over a wide timeframe. Taking these into account is important, for example, to counter the negative view of late antique Syriac cultures found in most Arabic and European accounts, and to challenge the reliability of critical editions, especially for Patristic Studies. The chapter analyses four brief case-studies of the use and destruction of manuscripts, which differ in the agency of the holders and the intention behind the destruction. These blur traditional assumptions about religious identity, materiality of writing and the relevance of texts among Christians.

# CHAPTER 5
# THE DISCOVERY OF COLLECTIONS OF LETTERS FROM THE PATRISTIC ERA: ITS IMPACT ON WESTERN HISTORY

PATRICIA CINER
*Universidad Católica de Cuyo, Argentina*

# BRIEF INTRODUCTION TO THE TOPIC

This section is dedicated to another of the new lines of research in Patristic Studies, the study of collections of letters as sources of information on theological, political and judicial positions, among others. These sources exceed the autobiographical perspective of their writers and allow for a clearer and deeper understanding of the Patristic era. The articles included in this chapter belong to the prestigious academics Dr Oscar Velásquez and Dr Bronwen Neil. Though they study different authors and different issues, both have sought to design new theoretical and methodological approaches that take advantage of the rich content found in the epistles of the Patristic period.

Dr Velásquez's article is entitled "The Vision of God and Augustine's De uidendo deo liber unus (= ep. 147)". The first thing that becomes apparent upon reading this text is its author's great intellectual capacity. However, this should come as no surprise as Dr Velásquez is one of the leading specialists on Augustine. His analyses stand out due to the fact that his reading of the philosopher is always connected to Platonic and Neoplatonic tradition, traditions to which Dr Velásquez has also contributed with his excellent translations. This research methodology is evident in his analysis carried out regarding the mind's ability to contemplate the divinity without intermediaries. He calls this path of ascent the "dialectic of interiority", in which the soul becomes progressively illuminated by the truth. Dr Velásquez concludes that:

> To find this object, it is necessary beforehand, methodologically, to clear the way and to undertake research that, as it seems, has discernible Platonic features. This supposes an

effort to make the vision of mind transparent to the object, in other words, to liberate the spirit by means of a stripping of all that hinders and obscures that mentis obtutus. Thus liberated, and resembling as much as possible an object always present but normally invisible to human vision, Christian souls could finally be counted, in futuro saeculo, among those clean-hearted capable of seeing God.

For its part, Dr Neil's article reflects great theoretical and methodological soundness, both the result of her extensive research experience. For this reason, Dr Neil is considered one of the most consolidated scholars in the academic world. In addition to the many awards she has won, she has coauthored with Dr Pauline Allen volumes that mark a turning point in her lines of research, including *Crisis Management in Late Antiquity (410–590 CE): The Evidence of Episcopal Letters* (2009) and *Collecting Early Christian Letters. From the Apostle Paul to Late Antiquity* (2015). This experience undoubtedly contributes to the excellence of her work presented here, entitled "Pope Leo I's Letters on 'the Manichean Perversity'". The analysis that Dr Neil makes of a letter that Leo the Great (440–61) sent to the Senate in Rome demonstrates the consequences that a brief and not well-studied text can have in the academic realm (we must remember that Leo's homilies have received much more academic attention than his 143 surviving letters). In effect, Leo's announcement to the Senate that the "Manichean Perversity" and its instigator Mani should be condemned by orthodox Christians and its followers expelled from Italian churches had a direct impact on the edict (*Constitutio*) published by Emperor Valentinian III. In this document, one year after Leo the Great sent his letter, the emperor proclaims that the "incestuous perversity" of the Manicheans should be declared a public crime with the corresponding punishment.

Dr Neil also analyzes the consequences of the letter Pope Leo sent to Turibius of Astorga in July 447 in which he again attacks Manicheanism and, through this heresy, Priscillianism, a doctrine which according to him led back to Mani, among other "philosophers". His declarations had important consequences, as the followers of Priscillian, who had been condemned to death for heresy in 385, were forced to live in absolute secrecy in order not to be persecuted. Effectively, Pope Leo's final objective was to completely exile them from their country, where they would live outside the kingdom of God and outside the limits of imperial civilization. Dr Neil concludes her article by convincingly illustrating how letters can have just as much power as long theological treatises, stating that "the rhetoric of vilification in Leo's letters and homilies was, it seems, quite persuasive, when combined with religious, social and legal proscriptions. Both letters laid the ground for the inquisitions of the Middle Ages".

OSCAR VELÁSQUEZ
*Former Vice-President of AIEP, Chile*

# THE VISION OF GOD AND AUGUSTINE'S *DE VIDENDO DEO LIBER UNUS* (= EP. 147)

*De uidendo deo liber unus* was originally conceived as a letter (= *ep*.147), but it gained such consistency that Saint Augustine himself finally decided to include it among his books ("de uidendo deo librum scripsi": *retr.* 2, 41). This was probably because the issue of the vision of God had already acquired a great complexity in his thought. The present study intends to focus especially on certain aspects that have to do with the search method of the central issue in question, that is to say, the vision of God especially at the present time. Augustine proposes here what I would call a dialectical methodology of interiority. The central issue raised here is to establish the vision of God, but to achieve this a search method is necessary, and this is none other than a kind of Platonic dialectics.

Two variants of the dialectical method are proposed here, both originating in Plato himself, continued in substance by his Neoplatonic successors. One is paradigmatically revealed and analyzed in The *Republic*, another is representatively examined in the *Phaedo*. I consider them as variants, because supposedly there is a single dialectic method that is precisely the platonic, regulated search for an intelligible truth. Within these two central research species ("research", "investigation" is usually called ζήτησις or σκέψις in Plato) there are also sub-species, but the central issue of a truth (not always clearly "intelligible") that is sought through a dialectical method is always maintained, so to say from the *Apology of Socrates* to *The Laws*. Accordingly, both Plotinus and Porphyry followed this path. What takes a central stage in this case is the inner road to truth. St Augustine's proposal to Pauline is to follow, as I suggest, the method exemplified in the *Phaedo*, which I would identify in substance as a dialectic method of interiority.

## *A Letter Converted into a Book*

An account of the importance of *De uidendo deo* in the context of the Augustinian work, should take into consideration its double condition of letter and *opusculum*. Throughout its 57 pages, a constant spiritual closeness is maintained with the addressee, and through it, with other possible readers of its circle. For this very reason, it seems reasonable to characterize this type of epistolary exchange as direction of conscience,[1] as it shows clearly a concern for the spiritual life of those who access its pages. In this work we will also insist on the other aspect that most distinguishes this writing – shared with a small number of other writings – that of being a true treatise on the important subject of the vision of God. That is possibly the reason for its inclusion by St Augustine himself among his books, and the fact that he categorized it as an epistle, although that was not in its original formulation.

Now, the letter has been a long-lasting means of connection and transmission of information among people, and an irreplaceable instrument of communication. Among Christian authors, St Augustine proves to have been the most prolific, gathering a total of 254 letters for a period of 43 years, according to relatively recent computations. These include the discovery of new correspondence, unknown until over thirty years ago.[2] The epistolary corpus of St Augustine, like that of various other Fathers, often includes extensive letters. The *ep.* 147 happen to be a missive in response to a question, although the motive and the contents

---

[1] P. Descotes (2017) 422, 436–437. "Les lettres 147 *De uidendo Deo* et 187 *De praesentia Dei* d'Augustin d'Hippone: entre exposé doctrinal et direction de conscience", in *Conseiller, diriger par lettre*, É. Gavoille & F. Guillaumont (2017). Tours: Presses universitaires François-Rabelais.

[2] There are other 44 letters addressed to him. Cf. Claire Sotinel, "Agustine's Information Circuits", in *A Companion to Augustine*, ed. by M. Vessey, Oxford: Wiley Blacwell (2015) 125–37. Sotinel adds: "Augustine's correspondence involves 197 persons"; that Ambrose wrote 91 letters, Jerome 144 and John Chrysostome, 246.

of these different letters are in fact very varied. The pre-Christian Greek epistolary, on the other hand, had already established certain canons for letters in general, both private and official.

An intended purpose for them was probably the dissemination of ideas, so it is not rare to see letters written among philosophers, such as Epicurus or Seneca, or numerous religious authors, such as the epistles of St Paul and other NT apostles. In these circumstances, and considering that Cicero had already established a model in the Latin world – without forgetting the later Seneca – it is natural that from the origins of Christianity the letter had a relatively recognizable format.[3] Its importance for communication and diffusion of ideas within the vast Roman Empire – and consequently among Christian communities – was soon apparent for that very reason.[4]

It is, therefore, only natural to note the existence of letters that, although having a clear addressee, are often intended to be read also by those who belong to a certain private circle. In this opuscule-letter 147, to Paulina, St Augustine refers significantly to the fact that, along with the addressee, there could be other readers as well.[5] Hence, it is not surprising that some letters by St Augustine acquired the dimension of a book, or that of a more extensive document, a treatise. Letters of this kind are transformed, thus, into real *opuscula* on a certain matter raised by the addressee. The importance acquired by the letters by Saint Augustine for an evaluation of his life and thought is, for this reason, considerable. Many of them became also documents rich in historical information. The same may be said of other authors of Antiquity, not only of the Fathers of the Church.

---

[3] Cf. *letters, Latin*, in *The Oxford Classical Dictionary*. Oxford, OUP, S. Hornblower/A. Spawforth (2012) p. 823, General Editors.

[4] In Africa the presence of the bishop St Cyprian was fundamental both to Catholics and to Donatis. It was a precedent that Augustine could not ignore. On Cyprian's letters, cf. J. A. Gil – Tamayo, *Obras completas de san Cipriano de Cartago*, Madrid: BAC (2013) LXXVIII s: "Este conjunto consta de 81 cartas, no todas escritas o recibidas por Cipriano, y constituyen el primer epistolario cristiano en lengua latina".

[5] *Vid. deo.* 5 = *ep.* 147, 5, CSEL vol. xxxxiiii, Al. Goldbacher (1904) Vindobonae - Lipsiae: F. Tempsky & G. Freytag: "... sed te atque alios qui ista lecturi sunt ...".

Letter 147 to Paulina is just an exemplary case, to the extent that it deserves a chapter among the "books" in his *Revisions* (*Retr.* 2, 41, now with the name *de uidendo deo liber unus*). Only eight other letters he includes here explicitly among books. It was in *Revisions* precisely when the *ep.* 147 – written by the end of 412 or the beginning of 413 – received the name of: *De uidendo deo liber unus*.[6] Together with letter 187 (year 417), called *De praesentia dei*, to Dardanus (also mentioned in *Revisions* with this name), put together, as has been said that: "they offer a set of interesting common points".[7]

*Ep.* 147 is a "...work with the character of a letter",[8] addressed to a "religious servant of God" (*religiosa famula dei*) called Paulina (*uid.* deo, I 1). There is another previous letter, *ep.* 127,[9] written by the end of 410, addressed to her in conjunction with her husband Armentarius. They are both treated as "exemplary sirs" and "sons".[10] The marriage has passed through difficulties for having made a private vow of *continentia*,[11] and it has turned out that on the part of the husband things have taken a turn for the worse ("reddite igitur, quod uouisti [...] reddite obsecro".). That letter 127 reveals the problem, and while it is addressed to both, most of it has Armentarius as the main recipient. For it is clear that, in this case, Paulina has always been willing to assume her part in that vow of continence between spouses.[12]

---

[6] It was written between the summer of 412 and the first days of 413. Cf. J. Anoz, "Cronología de la producción agustiniana", in *Augustinus* XLVII 186–87 (2002), 250. See *retr.* 2, 41: "de uidendo deo librum scripsi".

[7] P. Descotes (2017) 421.

[8] "...durch dieses Werk mit Briefcharacter", J. Divjak, "Epistulae", in *Augustinus Lexicon*, ed. by Cornelius Mayer, Basel - Stuttgart : Schwabe & Co. AG: (1996–2002) vol. 2, 978.

[9] J. Anoz (2002) 250. *Epistula* 127, in *Corpus Christianorum, Epistulae* CI–CXXXIX, Series Latina XXXI B Pars III, 3. Aurelii Augustini Opera, cura et studio Kl. D. Daur (2009) Turnhout: Brepols Publishers.

[10] Women consecrated could be addressed as *famulae dei*, but if, as it seems, this Paulina of the epistles 147 and 127 are both the same person, it may be a woman consecrated who lives in a private and familiar milieu. See *ep.* 212: *honorabiles dei famulas*.

[11] *Ep.* 127, Kl. D. Daur (2009): "Vir egregius, filius meus Ruferius, affinis uester, rettulit mihi, quid domino uoueritis", *ep.* 127, 1.

[12] *Ep.* 127, 6: "Si continentia uirtus est, sicuti est, ... Noli ergo uir abhorrere a uirtute, quam mulier est parata suscipere".

*Peculiarities of* De uidendo deo:
*A Protreptic for Spiritual Life*

Now, letter 147 is instead directed only to Paulina; about the husband and the rest of the intricate matter of the vow there is total silence. Apparently, the contacts between Augustine and Paulina have been maintained, and even more, they have seemingly intensified during the last two years. It is remarkable the delicate tact of the bishop, who also shows a certain affectionate familiarity with the addressee.[13] We can deduce it in the first place from its initial words, but it is also revealed in the development extension and depth of the response.

An attentive reading, likewise, reveals that, more than "a work with the character of a letter" (J. Divjak) it is rather a letter that assumes the character of a book. Accordingly, it maintains its epistolary format until the end, although as it progresses, a consistent modification is produced that finally transforms the script into a true book. In addition to the direct references to his addressee, there is a constant awareness in Augustine of who will read the letter. The verbal use of the second person of the singular is frequent,[14] as well as that of the imperatives, strategically present at the right moment.[15] This is a way to keep alive the intention to communicate with the recipient, not simply to produce a written piece of work. A feature which I would like to stress, especially being that letter 147 happened to turn out extremely long. Likewise, the use of the subjunctive mood is another courteous way to call attention, or to exhort. St Augustine, nearly concluding his letter, gives it the literary name that it now deserves:

---

[13] *Vid. deo*, I 2: "... quia nec ibi marcuisti, cum sis annis grauis". It may be something personal: "circumspicere autem potes finis anuli tui", *uid. deo* IX 21. It could be not accurate what is said in P. Descotes (2017) 430: "autant dire qu'il s'agit de lettres bien impersonnels".

[14] *Vid. deo* I 3: praestruaris, uides; III 9 distinguis; IV 11 recognouisti; XV 37 "quod mihi proposueras", "si enim quaeris", *et passim*.

[15] *Vid. deo*, 2 : "percipe"; 4, "tene", "attende recolendo" XV 37, XVII 43; "uigilanter attende: intuere caelum et terram", *et passim*. On the use of the imperative in Latin, see B. L. Gildersleeve, Gonzalez Lodge (1992) 174 (1ª ed. 1895), *Gildersleeve's Latin Grammar*: "The imperative is the mood of the will. It wills that the predicate be made reality. The tone of the Imperative varies from stern command to piteous entreaty. It may appear as a demand, an order, an exhortation, a permission, a concession, a prayer".

that of an *opusculum* (*uid. deo* XXIII 54: "quae ab initio huius opusculi").[16] So, his response to the topic that has been proposed begins just thus:

> "Since you had asked me to write to you in a rather detailed and eloquent manner about the invisible God, if it could be seen through corporeal eyes, I could not deny doing it so as not to offend your devotion to study" (*uid. deo* 1).[17]

The question set out the central theme, that is, the invisibility of God, and how it could be seen. A rather particular case is also added: that of whether it can likewise be seen with bodily eyes. From the beginning St Augustine is ready to answer the matter in its entirety, without remaining in the attached question only, rather tangential to the main issue. His procrastination (*dilationi*) is understandable, since there was much to consider before writing (*diutius cogitari*). In addition, for a matter of such magnitude (*cum tanta res esset*), it was necessary to undertake the more difficult consequent task that is to persuade. Hence, it goes far beyond her initial question, she being apparently a habitual correspondent, and his response would soon exceed the limits of a formal letter.

Nevertheless, it is evident that Paulina succeeds in raising an issue that undoubtedly had worried its correspondent, Augustine.[18] It is also natural to think that she perhaps did not fully imagine the vast scope of her question. Because beyond the invisibility of God, there is an even more relevant issue that of the "question of the divine substance". It is undeniable that this divine substance opens up many questions in the human mind, particularly when the ability of man to see and comprehend it is at stake. The very qualification of *inuisibilis* for the divine reality, points out an impossibility of vision on the part of humankind *in praesenti saeculo*. St Augustine mentions not only the human

---

[16] *Vid. deo*, 54: "Sed haec iam satis dicta sint, quae ab initio huius opusculi ...".

[17] *Vid. deo*, 1: "cum enim petiuisses, ut de inuisibili deo, utrum per oculos corporeos possit uideri, prolixe aliquid copioseque ad te scriberem, negare non potui, ne sanctum studium tuum offenderem ...".

[18] It may be seen in *ep.* 99 to Italica (a. 408), and also in the *Commonitorium Fortunatiano* (= *ep.* 148, written the 411 or at the beginning of the 412). After *uid. deo*, see *ep.* 159 y *ep.* 162, to Evodius (a. 414/15). Cf. Anoz (2002) 245-54.

senses but also the mind and its various ways of perceiving.[19] For this incapacity is owed fundamentally to the inabilities of cognitive powers, be they sensitive or spiritual, to perceive an object that is always present but inaccessible in its transcendence.

There are accordingly several previous questions that become manifest and Paulina herself must keep in mind. There are things that are perceived with the mind but not with the eyes. And it is not negligible that look that comes from the inner man: "that you ought not to despise this very vision that is seeing that you do not know".[20] It is necessary, then, to rectify in depth the attitude of the gaze that recognizes its ignorance. We may say that she is concerned about the difficulties that arise from the question of an invisible God who, nevertheless, has manifested himself – judging by testimonies of the Scriptures – visibly to many.

The mind, points out Augustine, sees through an intense action more interior (*interius*) that is, the one that is realized with the power of the gaze of the mind. In other words: it sees with a *mentis obtutu* (*uid. deo* 3), that is, with an "intense gaze of the mind"; or, with a *mentis intuitu*, i.e. in a look of the mind; or even (*uid. deo* I 6), with a *mentis aspectu*, i.e. a glance of the mind (*uid. deo* 3). For the act of believing is realized by the capacity of the mind (*mens*), not merely by means of the visual faculties of the senses.

## *A Methodology of Intimacy: The Dialectical Access to Truth*

In *uid. deo* 3, there is an invitation to Paulina to change her search method, "while she has been reading this letter".[21] If it is possible to see God, I surmise, the actual manner here is not *per uisibilia*, a kind of roundabout way through Creation toward God. It is rather through an intellectual path like the one Socrates invites to perform in the *Phaedo*. For it is in fact an exhortation to Pauline, so I understand, to see the *inuisibilia dei* in the light of her own inner experience. This means that he does not invite her to a simple intellectual examination: "So", he writes, "what

---

[19] *Vid. deo* 3: "cum igitur nec corporis oculis [...] nec mentis aspectu [...] nunc uideamus deum [...]".
[20] *Vid. deo* 3: "quia nec ipsa est contemnenda uisio uidere quod nescias".
[21] *Vid. deo*, 3: "tu itaque ipsa lectis his litteris...".

matters most in this search is more the way of living than the way of speaking" (*uid. deo* 1).[22]

The path consists, therefore, in a kind of methodological "shortcut" (cf. ἀτραπός τις, *Fd.* 64b 4), in other words, an inner experience of mind that leads to truth. It is the Platonic shortcut, that is, an alternative dialectical way to ideas and truth, which passes through and takes place inside the mind. This is a sort of *express* Platonic dialectic, a methodological procedure that comes especially from Plato's *Phaedo* and widely used by platonic philosophers of late Antiquity. It passes over the long road of The *Republic* through the cavern, and proceeds in the manner of the dialectical path of the *Phaedo*. The purpose is to return inside of our own and find there with what, in the allegory of the cave, is at the end of a long road. The former is necessary, no doubt, for the *paideia* of the *Republic*, in which an extensive period of learning of the pre-dialectic disciplines is shown.

For these stages of study in the *Republic* are in obvious connection with certain propaedeutic disciplines, which predispose the young future ruler to think according to the dialectical method. Thus, finally, the student will be transformed into a man who is capable of dialectically thinking intelligible objects, in other words, truth in itself. Dialectic creates a disposition to comprehend intelligible truth, and souls have paved their way for contemplating intelligible good by means of those disciplines. In the case of *Republic*, contemplation of the good itself is a necessary condition for rulers of the ideal city to govern. Here, on the other side, Paulina is invited to understand the difficult issue she has proposed in the light of the interior truth: "sed aut scripturis canonicis credas, si quid nondum quam sit uerum uides, aut interius demonstranti ueritati, ut hoc plane uideas" (*uid.deo* 2): "But if you do not see yet, or give you credence to the canonical scriptures, or to the truth that more inwardly reveals".

On the other hand, with respect to the previous methodology, it is convenient to remember that both previous rational methods obviously are mutually supportive, as we see in Plato, because in

---

[22] "in hac inquisitione": see θήραν (hunting, search), Plato, *Fd.* 66c2; θηρεύειν, 66a3. Man ought to dispose himself of all the corporeal and sensorial in the search of real beings and truth. See *inquisitio* as "the action of hunting out, search", see OLD 919.

fact the dialectical method is only one. The character of *express* that I assign to this dialectical path emphasizes the fact that the Socrates of the *Phaedo* seems to skip the long road of *paideia*, and encourage his friends to investigate the truth inwardly. Hence the hortatory character we find in many pages of the *Phaedo* and of Plotinus' *Enneads*. Because the "shortcut", as Plato puts it, supposes in any case a long-term internal preparation. This makes it necessary, methodologically, that the inquirer of intelligible ideas and truth remain ἐν φιλοσοφίᾳ, as in a habitual attitude of intellectual asceticism. Because Socrates is "a man who has spent his life in philosophy",[23] so that this "shortcut" means rather the following: that the search for intelligible truth and ideas is made in this case more expressly and directly in reference to the soul, and its inner capacity to recognize truth.

It is therefore to a path of intimacy that Paulina is invited to proceed. St Augustine manifestly points it out when he says: *sed credas [...] interius demonstranti ueritati*. That is to say, to perform a similar task to search truth. In this case, is the truth at issue: God's invisibility. It is something appealing no longer to the vision of senses but to a "simpler and more interior" look (cf. *uid. deo* 3: "simplicius interiusque"). It is about a simpler and inner search, performed by an "intense gaze of the mind" (*mentis obtutu*). Because the consistency of that "god" that one seeks to contemplate, is "the first, the good, the one", *more platonico*. Something that it is itself, among other characteristics, "simple and pure" (ἁπλοῦν, καθαρόν, *Enn*. I 6, 7, 9–10). This keeps us between Plato (*Fd*. 65e–66a, cf. *Bq*. 211e) and Plotinus, who used to interpret these texts written by the master. St Augustine understands perfectly that the gaze must be adapted to the object, so that the most appropriate means of accessing the understanding of the invisible reality of God is through a simplicity of mind (*mens*).

It is not difficult to understand the propriety of the simplicity of this interior gaze put at the service of the faithful Christian, us Augustine does here. This means, it seems to me, a true spiritual conquest open to man and women alike of any social condition. If it is permitted to say, it points to a democratization of the inner life, open to all. Paulina is exhorted here to experience for her-

---

[23] *Fd*. 63e: ἀνὴρ τῷ ὄντι ἐν φιλοσοφίᾳ διατρίψας τὸν βίον: cf. *Fd*. 68c.

self in this path of spiritual inquiry. It is mainly from these pages of Plato that the Neoplatonists obtained what many have thought that only they devised. But, as it seems, it is derived directly from Plato's *Phaedo* and other platonic texts, especially since the dialectical ascent of the *Symposium*, as by scales,[24] is more in tune with the *Republic*. We can thus verify in *De uidendo deo* one of the most expressive texts of what I would call an Augustinian dialectic of interiority. This dialectic leads to a certain emancipation of the individual, be it man or woman, slave or free, in the words of Saint Paul. It is something that allows you to see, he says to Paulina, "so that you see it in you".[25] He affirms, thus, summarizing these lines full of meaning: "tanto clarius et certius quanto simplicius interiusque conspicias". That is to say, "in order that with the more greater clarity and certainty you can see, the more it is in the simplest and most interior way" (*uid. deo*, 3).[26]

This connects St Augustine with his old readings of Plotinus, with an *Ennead* that he certainly read. It is the vision of beauty as the divine reality itself, which takes place in a "rise" of the soul (ἐν τῇ ἀναβάσει, *Enn.* I 6, 7, 9).[27] But this peculiar ascent is not, so to speak, upwards to the opening of the cavern, but towards the interior of soul that rises naked, as when advances ritually towards the *sancta sanctorum* of the temples: οἷον ἐπὶ τὰ ἅγια τῶν ἱερῶν [...] τὸ γυμνοῖς ἀνιέναι (*Enn.* I 6, 6, 8).

> ἕως ἄν τις παρελθὼν ἐν τῇ ἀναβάσει πᾶν ὅσον ἀλλότριον τοῦ θεοῦ αὐτῷ μόνῳ αὐτὸ μόνον ἴδῃ εἰλικρινές ἁπλοῦν, καθαρόν.[28]
>
> Until, passing through its ascent everything that is alien to the God, someone sees, while being alone, to that alone without mixture, simple, pure.

---

[24] *Bq.* 211c: ὥσπερ ἐπαναβασμοῖς χρώμενον. *Bq.* 210e: θεόμενος ἐφεξῆς τε καὶ ὀρθῶς τὰ καλά.

[25] *Vid. deo*, 3: "ut in te uideas".

[26] "simplicius" could correspond to the platonic ἁπλοῦς. See *Rep.* 2, 382e: κομιδῇ ἄρα ὁ θεὸς ἁπλοῦν καὶ ἀληθὲς ἔν τε ἔργῳ καὶ ἐν λόγῳ: "God is absolutely simple and true as in his action as in his word"; cf. *Cra.* 405c. But here, more probably, is the plotinian ἁπλοῦς. Cf. *Enn.* I 6, 7, 9.

[27] *Vid. deo*, 2: "erige itaque spiritum mentis tuae, qui renouatur in agnitione secundum imaginem eius, qui creauit eum".

[28] Plotinus, *Enn.* I 6, 7, 8–10, cf. Plato, *Bq.* 211e1, *Fd.* 66a, *et passim*.

I would rather like to understand παρελθὼν as "bypassing <the long road>" that leads to the God. There is something similar to the "shortcut", that is to say the alternative path of the *Phaedo*, which recalls the short path, instead of the long letters of the *Republic*. The dialectical journey from the cave to the light and the intelligible world is now transformed into a direct ascent into the interior of himself. For the intelligible inhabits also in the inner self of the individual being. In other words, Paulina is exhorted to an inner predisposition, so that with transparent eyes she would be able to see the intelligible. Thus, St Augustine is inviting her to prepare herself to understand the profound meaning of God's invisibility. The eyes must be predisposed to look at what, otherwise, could not be seen. Because the "clean of heart will see God".

The starting point here, therefore, seems to be how to elucidate what one sees when one sees the God who lets himself be seen. Because that invisible God has arguable sometimes been seen, according to the Scriptures. Hence the tension that is established between the present and the absent. For a distinction appears between seeing and believing. Believing does not consist in seeing, but in understanding. In spite of being expressed in the form of a question, it is also worth to remember what Augustine says: "Because the present things are seen, the absent ones are believed".[29]

The effort of Augustine is now directed mainly to create in Pauline, by means of this inner purification, a new disposition towards the words that come from his letter: "Tu itaque lectis ipsa his litteris" (*uid.deo* 3). She is exhorted to see both all that surrounds her both physically and intellectually. Augustine exhorts her to simplify and interiorize the sight of her mental perception.[30] This means a sort of purification of sight. Plotinus, on the other hand, had pointed out the stripping of the garments (καὶ ἱματίων ἀποθέσεις: a sort of an *edifying striptease*). For this renunciation indicates not only a profound change in personal attitude, but also a methodological abandonment of the sensible as a way of accessing the truth. "You will increase yourself, therefore, when

---

[29] *Vid. deo* II 7: "quia praesentia uidentur, creduntur absentia".
[30] *Vid. deo* 3: "tanto clarius et certius quanto simplicius interiusque conspicias".

you have detached yourself from the rest, and the whole becomes present in detachment" (*Enn.* VI 5, 24). St Augustine on the other hand urges Paulina to return to her inner soul:

> Therefore, perceive the words of the intellect according to the inner man [...] raise accordingly the spirit of your mind [...] Christ dwells in you [...] there is no Jew or Greek [...] man or woman [...] raised with this your interior self pay attention and see what I mean [...] (*uid. deo* 2).[31]

With almost prophetic words Augustine intimates her: "erige itaque spiritus mentis tuae". But now, the time has come for St Augustine to respond more properly to the question posed, and he finds in St Ambrose the answer he need. The paragraphs of the *Expositio Euangelii secundum Lucam*, collection of sermons to the people of Milan between 377–78 years, were subsequently published in a comment form the year 389.[32] St Ambrose inspires the fundamental lines of some of the central answers of the *De uidendo deo*. It soon becomes apparent though the extensive and deeply personal contribution of St Augustine to the clarification of the issue. This transforms his epistle into an *opusculum*, which I think should be considered among the most relevant works of his speculative theology.

For that very reason, his capacity to transform a letter into a treatise is very impressive. He knows how to preserve the personal atmosphere that matters, with serious tone of a real treatise on a central theme in Revelation. St Augustine also manifests in this way, apart from his condition as a theologian, the character of "directeur spirituel" strongly present in this writing.[33] An attitude that is not unique to this letter, in a period he manifests an

---

[31] *Vid. deo*, 2. "secundum interiorem igitur hominem percipe verba intellectūs [...] erige itaque spiritum mentis tuae, qui renouatur in agnitione secundum imaginem eius [...] in te habitat Christus, ubi non est Judaeus et Graecus, seruus liber, masculus femina, ubi non morieris cum solui corpore coeperis [...] hoc interiore tuo erecta intende et uide quae loquor [...]".

[32] "Hi sermones, retractati ad formam commentarii, iam ° 389 euulgato erant", Sancti Ambrosii Mediolanensis Opera, *Expositio Euangelii secundum Lucam*, ed. by. M. Adriaen (1958), VII\* Turnholti: Brepols.

[33] P. Descotes (2017) 430: "... et c'est en cela qu'Augustin fait œuvre non seulement de théologien, mais également de directeur spirituel"; cf. *ibid.* (2017) 436-37.

intense concern about the subject of God's vision. It is revealed by the appearance of other more or less contemporary writings of the Bishop, such as epistle 148, (autumn of 411), sermon 23 (January 20 of 413), sermon 53 (January 21 of 413), sermon 277 (January 22 of 413), and the book XII of *De Genesi ad litteram* (413–14).[34]

There is a difficult and continuous balance in the Scriptures between a God to whom nobody has ever seen, and the evangelical promise that the pure in heart will eventually see him. Augustine, commenting on the words of Ambrose, points out:

> Nobody ever saw God, and how the ancient just could see him, if the reason why that was said is because God is by nature invisible, still why those who saw him whoever saw God, <is> because to whom he wished, just as he happened to wish, appears in that figure as he could have wished, to whom his will has chosen, although his nature remains hidden.[35]

And of the Trinitarian Persons who are supposed sometimes to be present, quoting Ambrose textually, he adds: "they are seen in that figure that the <divine> will decided to choose, not what nature could form".[36] So then, Augustine finally interprets this central aspect in the following way: "thus, he appears to those he happened to wish, in the figure he wished". For this is the way of preserving the immutable and invisible nature of God integrally (*uid. deo* VIII 20). Moses, Abraham, and others saw a God who remained invisible, because they saw a *species* of him, not his *natura*. It is a vision of God "in praesenti saeculo", which is realized only when he wants (Ambrose, *in Luc.* 1, 27); but "*in futuro saeculo* <shall see him> those who are about to receive the kingdom", that is, the clean ones of heart (*uid. deo* X 23).

---

[34] Confer dates in J. Anoz (2002). On *Gen. litt.* 12, see P. Agaesse & A. Solignac, Œuvres de Saint Augustin 48 *La Genèse au sens littéral en douze livres.* Brugge : Desclée de Brouwer (1972) 20: "On s'étonne qu'Augustin ait annexé ce traité à son commentaire en guise de conclusión, mais la chose paraît moins étrange si l'ont remarque qu'aux environs de l'année 413, il intéresse tout spécialement au problème de la vision de Dieu, se préoccupe d'en préciser la nature et les modalités pour la distinguer des visions inférieures ou suspectes, comme en témoignent les lettres qu'il adresse à certains de ses correspondants". Cf. P. Descotes (2017) 423.

[35] *Vid. deo* VII 19.

[36] *Vid. deo* VII 19: "ea specie uideri, quam uoluntas elegerit, non natura formauerit"; Ambrosius, *Expositio Euangeli secundum Lucam* I 25.

It arises from this an issue of great theological depth, which St Ambrose points out with admirable precision (*uid. deo* XII 29): "Et cum absens putatur, uidetur et, cum praesens est, non uidetur" (*Expositio Euangelii secundum Lucam* I 27, 421–22). That is: "He is seen while he is thought to be absent, he is not seen while he is present". The "cum" can be interpreted as: "though", "even though" (OLD[7a] 469), in which case the perspective becomes perhaps more interesting. This makes more sense in the context that Ambrose himself understands it, i.e. that those who are clean of heart will see God (Mt 5, 8). The main relationship is here between the absence and the presence of God, between eyes unable to see and eyes transparent to the divine presence. It is possible that Ambrose uses "uidetur" in the usual classical sense of "it appears", "it manifests".[37]

This does not change the fundamental meaning of the expression, but it brings perhaps it closer to what the bishop meant. Because I presume that there is a contrast between πάρεστι and φαίνεται, which in Plotinus arises from the philosopher's analysis along *Enn.* VI 5, 12. This apparent paradox of a God (here more likely the intelligible reality "as boiling over with life": οἷον ὑπερζέουσαν ζωῇ, *Enn* VI 5, 9), who manifests itself, even though it is considered absent, and the God that does not manifests when in fact it is present. This idea and similar expressions seem to have, then, in Ambrose, a Plotinian origin, although we could not rule out that, apart or in conjunction with Plotinus, he read it in Porphyry (*Sent.* 40). A little more than ten years after the publication of *Confessions*, and by means of his renewed readings of St Ambrose, St Augustine now uses these doctrines, already established in his understanding, as an effective instrument for the direction of conscience.

There is here, I think, a clear indication of what I would call the presence of a spiritual dynamic of proximity and distance, something we can see, for example, in important steps of *Confessions*. It could be said that the most strictly biographical section of his conversion is sustained on this metaphor: the "quia fecisti nos ad ad te", reveals the presence of an object that at first, and for a long time, remains distant, and therefore absent, that is to say,

---

[37] See OLD 2060, uideor [20] (pass.): "Appear, seem, be thought".

God. The "donec requiescat in te", indicates the consummation of a drama that culminates in a definite nearness to a God, before whose presence soul finally rests. It could be suggestive to think of a closeness with Porphyry (*Sententiae* 40, 50, 3): αὐτὸς γάρ σοι παρὼν οὐκ ἀπῇς αὐτοῦ: "Because he is present to you, you are not far from him".

Now, Plotinus and Porphyry were authors intensely studied among the cultivated circles of Milan, both pagan and Christian; and we know of St Augustine's lectures of Plotinus, and his appreciation of Porphyry, with reservations. St Ambrose, on the other hand, dominated the Greek language, unlike the hesitant knowledge of St Augustine, who however improved opportunely the practical use of this language. I refer not only to the paragraph quoted above about detachment (*Enn* VI 5, 12, 24), but also to the deep meaning on what was said in the *Expositio Ev. sec. Luc.* I 27, 421–22. This important chapter of *Eneads* VI 5, 12, reappears in the *Sententiae* 40 of Porphyry.[38] There is a similar emphasis between the present and the absent, and both the presence the Being and the God are mutually emphasized (τὸ ὄν, *Sent.* 40, pp. 49, 10, 15, *et passim*).

It turns out however that St Augustine, when commenting this place, points out to the fact that Ambrose said "cum absens putatur", not "cum absens est". And Augustine explains:

> Nusquam enim est absens, qui caelum et terram implet nec spatiis includitur paruis magnisue diffunditur, sed ubique totus est et nullo continetur loco (*uid. deo* XII 29).

This complements our proposal about the presence, in both authors, not only of *Enn.* VI 5, 12 but also of *Sententiae* 40. First of all, it is the exclusion of all that prevents us from raising our minds to the search for the truth. Then, the reaffirmation that it is possible to approach and see "the whole" (*Enn.* VI, 12, 16–17 ... ἢ ὅτι προσῆλθες ...). In other words, to contemplate Being, which is the Intelligence.

Because Plotinus have said: εἰ δ'ἀπῆλθες, οὐκ ἀπ'αὐτοῦ – αὐτὸ γὰρ πάρεστιν – οὐδὲ τότε ἀπῆλθες ἀλλὰ παρὼν ἐπὶ τὰ ἐναντία

---

[38] Porphyrius *Sententiae ad intelligibilia ducentes*, edidit E. Lamberz. Leipzig: Teubner (1975) 47–52.

ἐστράφης (*Enn.* VI 5, 12, 27 ss). That is: "But if you separated yourself it was not from him – in fact he is still present – neither in that case you absented yourself, but, although you were present, you turned to the opposite way". Only some are able to look at the gods when they appear. And, recalling again Plotinus in the final paragraph of VI 5, 12, 32–34, close to concluding this *Ennead*, there exists also that <God>: "the one towards whom [...] the cities and the whole earth and the whole sky turn towards": Εἰς ἐκεῖνον αἱ πόλεις ἐπιστρέφονται, καὶ πᾶσα γῆ καὶ πᾶς οὐρανός. So, accordingly, we can see in *uid. deo* XII 29: "nusquam enim est absens qui caelum et terram implet [...] sed ubique totus est et nullo continetur loco". This may be considered a concise formula of: πανταχοῦ ἐπ' αὐτοῦ καὶ ἐν αὐτῷ μένοντα (VI 5, 12, 34).

So then, we could see how certain fundamental traits of the theme of divine vision are harmonized. Without having properly entered into the core of the matter, I have sought to clarify certain aspects that, although preliminary, I consider of decisive importance. These aspects are related with the attitude of the spirit that undertakes the search of a truth, in this case the vision of God. To find this object, it is necessary beforehand, methodologically to clear the way, and to undertake a research that, as it seems, has discernible platonic features. This supposes an effort to make the vision of mind transparent to the object, in other words, to liberate the spirit by means of a stripping of all that hinders and obscures that *mentis obtutus*. Thus liberated, and resembling as much as possible to an object always present but normally invisible to human vision, Christian souls could be finally counted, *in futuro saeculo*, among those clean-hearted capable of seeing God.

## Abstract

*De uidendo deo liber unus* was originally conceived as a letter (= *ep.*147), but St Augustine decided to include it among his books. That was probably because the issue of the vision of God finally acquired a great complexity in his thought. The present study intends to focus especially on certain aspects that have to do with the method of inquiry of the central issue in question, *i. e.* the vision of God especially at the present time. Augustine proposes here what I would call a dialectical methodology of interiority. The central issue raised here is to establish the vision of God but to achieve this, an inner research is necessary, and this is Platonic dialectics. I call it a methodology of intimacy in St Augustine, that is, a dialectical access to truth. To find the object, God, it is necessary beforehand, methodologically to clear the way and to undertake a research that, as it seems, has discernible platonic features. This supposes an effort to make the vision of mind transparent to the object, in other words, to liberate the spirit by means of a stripping of all that hinders and obscures that *mentis obtutus*.

BRONWEN NEIL
*Macquarie University, Australia*

# POPE LEO I'S LETTERS ON "THE MANICHEAN PERVERSITY"

Leo the Great (440–61) presided over the see of Rome during one of the most turbulent periods in that turbulent city's history. Leo's homilies have received much greater scholarly attention than his one hundred and forty-three surviving letters, probably due to the absence of a critical edition of the full collection. These letters corroborate the evidence of Leo's sermons for the bishop of Rome's close attention to pastoral care, especially regarding heresy among his Roman flock. In his letters to bishops throughout Italy and, more broadly, through the divided western and eastern churches, Leo sought to establish the status of the bishop of Rome as the highest authority on questions of doctrine.[1]

In January 444 Pope Leo informed the bishops of Italy of the outcome of his investigations into the activities and beliefs of the Manicheans in Rome. His sole surviving letter on the subject gives

---

[1] In the absence of a critical edition we are reliant on the Migne edition of PL 54. Selected letters are translated by E. Hunt, *St Leo the Great. Letters*, Fathers of the Church, 34 (Washington, DC: The Catholic University of America Press, 1957). Selected letters and sermons pertaining to Manicheism are edited and translated by H. G. Schipper & J. Van Oort (eds), *St Leo the Great: Sermons and Letters Against the Manicheans. Selected Fragments*, Corpus Fontium Manichaeorum Series Latina 1 (Turnhout: Brepols, 2000). Other selected letters on theological controversies appear in Acta Conciliorum Oecumenicorum 2.2.1 and 2.4, ed. by E. Schwartz (Berlin: W. de Gruyter, 1932); and in Textus et documenta, series theologica, 9, 15, 20 and 23, ed. by C. Silva-Tarouca (Rome: Pontificia Universitas Gregoriana 1923, 1934, 1935, 1937). The sermons have been edited by A. Chavasse, *Sancti Leonis Magni Romani pontificis tractatus septem et nonaginta*, CCSL 138 and 138a (Turnhout: Brepols, 1973) and by R. Dolle, *Sermons de Léon le Grand*. SC 22bis, 49bis, 74bis, 200 (Paris: Cerf, 1961–2000).

a detailed account of the senate tribunal over which Leo presided.[2] Leo announced the tribunal's judgement that "the Manichean perversity", and its instigator Mani, the self-styled "Paraclete", ought to be condemned by orthodox Christians, and its believers expelled from Italian churches. Leo's strong statement against the Manicheans bears a distinct resemblance to the edict (*Constitutio*) published by Emperor Valentinian III in the following year, in which the "incestuous perversity" of the Manicheans is declared a public crime with appropriate penalties. In July 447 Leo again attacked Manichaeism in his lengthy letter to Turibius of Astorga against Priscillianism,[3] a heresy that he traced back to Mani among other "philosophers".

Placing the two letters side by side with an imperial rescript of 445, I consider how the letter form could be used to exercise both ecclesiastical and judicial authority in the Manichean persecution, and the grounds on which the two authorities – Leo I on the one hand, and Valentinian III and Theodosius II on the other – defended their judgements to their addressees. This textual comparison will reveal how bishops and emperors sought to define and contain acts of sacrilege in mid-fifth-century Rome. Leo's accusations of sexual immorality find confirmation in contemporary North African sources and in two later Sogdian letters from Turfan, Central Asia.

## Manichean Immorality in Rome

Leo I's investigation into Manicheism in Rome is a good example of a bishop's use of the rhetoric of social exclusion – backed by a successful appeal to imperial authority – to deal with a religious dispute, which was exacerbated by the influx of Manicheans to the city of Rome.[4] Manicheans were first discovered in Rome in the time of Pope Anastasius (399–401/2).[5] An imperial edict

---

[2] *ep.* 7, Schipper & van Oort, *St Leo*, pp. 46–49.

[3] *ep.* 15, Schipper & van Oort, *St Leo*, pp. 50–76.

[4] The following section is a modified version of B. Neil, *Leo the Great* (London – New York: Routledge, 2009), pp. 31–33 and 73–74.

[5] *Liber Pontificalis*, ed. by L. Duchesne and C. Vogel, 3 vols, 2nd edn (Paris: de Boccard, 1955–1957), I, p. 218.

of 425 expelled "Manichean heretics or schismatics or astrologers and every sect opposed to the Catholics" from the city of Rome.[6] The followers of Mani posed a particular threat to the Christian community in Rome because they challenged it from within, by claiming to be Christians and participating in mainstream worship. Their ascetic regime differed from mainstream Roman Christian practices, with fasting on Sundays and abstinence from the Eucharistic sacrament of the cup enjoined upon its followers.[7] Due to their radical dualism of heavenly spirit and earthly matter, they abstained from meat and wine at all times, and most significantly, perhaps, they proscribed procreation.[8]

Leo cut his teeth as a scourge of heretics on the controversy caused by the return of Pelagian clergy to Italy in the 430s.[9] The language and images that he deployed to vilify them, to ostracize them from other Christians, and to isolate their leaders, were to prove equally applicable in the next decade to Manicheans and Priscillianists. In his response to the Manicheans, as in his response to Pelagian theology, Leo was strongly influenced by Augustine.[10] Indeed, many Manicheans from North Africa sought refuge in Rome in the years following the Vandal occupation of their homeland. In 443, Leo launched a campaign against the Manicheans in Rome which lasted for eighteen months. In a climate of social instability the violent suppression of dissenters or heretics served the important social functions of group delineation and reinforcement of the leader's authority, helping "to reaffirm and reinforce the commitment of group members to the ideals

---

[6] *Codex Theodosianus* 16. 5. 62; ed. by T. Mommsen, trans. by J. Rougé, *Le code Théodosien. Livre XVI*. SC 497 (Paris: Cerf, 2005), p. 328.

[7] Leo, *serm.* 42. 5; Chavasse, *Sancti Leonis*, p. 247.

[8] On the Manichean anthropology that gave rise to this dualism, see Schipper & van Oort, *St Leo*, pp. 8–9 and 98–99.

[9] On Pelagianism in Italy, see further S. Pietrini, *Religio e ius romanum nell'epistolario di Leone Magno*, Materiali per una palingenesi delle costituzioni tardo-imperiali 6 (Milan: Guiffre, 2002), pp. 85–88; Neil, *Leo the Great*, 33–37; in North Africa, Italy and Gaul: P. Allen & B. Neil, *Crisis Management in Late Antiquity (410–590 CE): A Survey of the Evidence from Episcopal Letters*, Supplements to Vigiliae Christianae 121 (Leiden: Brill 2013), pp. 115–18.

[10] Pietrini, *Religio*, p. 283. Leo knew of the effects of vacillation on the question of Pelagianism, when the future pope Sixtus III, as deacon under Zosimus (417–18), found first for Pelagius and then against him. See Augustine, *ep.* 191, PL 33, cols 867–68 and *ep.* 194, PL 33, cols 874–91.

of the community",[11] as Maier notes in his social-anthropological study of the Manichean investigation at Rome. Rome in the 440s was certainly in a state of social flux, with external threats to urban stability pressing on all sides.[12] The North African settlement of the Vandals was uncomfortably close, allowing Gaiseric to continue his attacks on Sicily, and Attila and his forces were drawing near to Rome from the north.

Thus in late 443 Leo convoked a commission over which he presided, in the presence of bishops, members of the Senate and other aristocracy, using state laws that had been instituted to deal with the threat in 425 during the pontificate of Celestine.[13] He sought to bring to trial several members of the highest echelon in the sect, the "Elect" or "Chosen Ones" (*serm.* 16.4). On the basis of the findings of these trials, he presents a horrifying picture of the Manicheans as insidious perverts preying on the young and unwary, with his allusion to the confession of several of the Elect concerning a religious ritual of sexual intercourse with a ten-year-old girl who had been raised for this sole purpose (*serm.* 16.4).

## *Manichean Immorality in North Africa and Central Asia*

Given that such "confessions" may well have been extracted under torture, as they were later in the episcopacy of Pope Hormisdas (514–23),[14] it is impossible to assess the truth of this allegation. Such an act would certainly have been at odds with the Manicheans' alleged distaste for the body and the act of procreation. Allegations of sexual immorality were also made against Manicheans in North Africa where a similar trial was staged under the

---

[11] H. Maier, "Manichee!: Leo the Great and the Orthodox Panopticon", *JECS* 4/4 (1996), 441–60 (pp. 447–48).

[12] On the various ways that Leo responded to these threats by expanding the civic role of the bishop of Rome, see S. Wessel, *Leo the Great and the Spiritual Rebuilding of a Universal Rome*, Supplements to Vigiliae Christianae 93 (Leiden: Brill, 2008), esp. pp. 179–83 on care for the poor; cf. B. Neil, "Leo I on Poverty", in P. Allen, B. Neil, & W. Mayer, *Preaching Poverty in Late Antiquity* (Leipzig: EVA, 2009), pp. 171–203.

[13] S. N. C. Lieu, *Manichaeism in the Later Roman Empire and Medieval China*, Wissenschaftliche Untersuchungen zum Neuen Testament 63, 2nd edn (Tübingen: J. C. B. Mohr, 1992), pp. 204–06.

[14] *LP* I, p. 270, *Hormisdas* ch. 9.

tribune Ursus between 421 and 428. In the course of this trial Augustine claimed that he witnessed no such thing as a Hearer of the sect,[15] while not denying that it was possible. The bishop's silence is perhaps understandable in view of his former standing in the Manichean community.[16] While it may seem at first glance that such acts of the flesh would be incompatible with the Manichean denial of the body, it could also be argued that their radical dualism lent itself to abuses of the flesh, even of others' bodies, since the flesh was accorded little spiritual value.[17]

Manicheans persisted in North Africa until at least the eighth century, as we know from the Arabic catalogue of books, *Al-Fihrist*, which was composed in Baghdad by the Shia (and probably Persian) literary scholar Muhammad ibn Ishāq al-Nadīm in 987/88. Al-Nadīm records that an African Manichean leader came to Babylonia, that is, southern Mesopotamia, in the time of al-Mansūr (754–75).[18] In the ninth Discourse of the longer edition, al-Nadīm gives an extensive account of eastern Manicheism, which includes details about Mani's life and his death under the Persian king Shapur I (d. *c.* 271), and about his teachings, especially on creation, the Fall and the afterlife.[19] He also described the persecution of the Manicheans in various Islamic countries, including Iraq where he lived. Al-Nadīm wrote that he had known about 300 Manicheans in Baghdad, but at the time of writing (987/88) there were only about five left.[20]

---

[15] *nihil turpe fieri vidi*: Augustine, *Contra Fortunatum* 3, ed. by J. Zycha, CSEL 25/I (Vienna: Verlag der Österreichischen Akademie der Wissenschaften, 1892), p. 85. Lieu, *Manichaeism*, p. 199.

[16] See J. van Oort, "Manichean Christians in Augustine's Life and Work", *Church History and Religious Culture* 90/4 (2010), 505–46.

[17] This case may be strengthened by Jan van Oort's recent work on the Manichean ritual of "semen eucharist": J. van Oort, "'Human semen eucharist' among the Manicheans? The Testimony of Augustine Reconsidered in Context", *Vigiliae Christianae* 70/2 (2016), 193–216.

[18] *Kitāb al-Fihrist*, chapter 9 (ed. R. Tadjaddod, *An Edition of Kitāb al-Fihrist by Ibn al-Nadīm*, rev. edn [Tehran, 1973], p. 398; Engl. transl. B. Dodge, *Fihrist of an-Nadim*, 2 vols [New York: Columbia University Press, 1970], p. 793): "...until Abū Hilāl ad-Dayḥūrī came from Africa and the leadership of the Manicheans fell to him. That was in the time of Abu Ja'far al-Manṣūr". I thank Dr Diego Santos for alerting me to this source.

[19] *Kitāb al-Fihrist* 9, Tadjaddod, *An Edition*, pp. 391–402.

[20] *Kitāb al-Fihrist* 9, trans. Dodge, *Fihrist*, p. 803.

The reason for their dwindling numbers in the East may be found in the conflict between different sects of Manichees over the keeping of the five commandments by the Elect, and especially over chastity (the third mandate of Mani to the Elect).[21] This appears to be confirmed in the allegations against a Syrian bishop made in two Sogdian letters from Turfan, a city of Central Asia,[22] and written in the late eighth or late ninth century.[23] This bishop, who had a malady in the lower part of his body, on two occasions received a servant girl in his house to minister to him behind closed doors, which set tongues wagging. According to the girl, she had only been required to take blood from him "behind the door".[24] The Manichean author of the first Sogdian letter described the behaviour of "western" Manicheans as "loose and shameless" in matters of religious law (chastity).[25] In his sec-

---

[21] Hearers, the second grade of Manichean followers, lived secular lives and could engage in sexual activity. Their role was to minister to the Elect, who lived like monks. Hearers maintained their inferior status in the afterlife, while the Elect went straight to heaven.

[22] *Turfan Letters* 1 (in several fragments) and 2, ed. by W. Sundermann, "Eine Re-edition zweier manichäisch-soghdischer Briefe", in *Iranian Languages and Texts from Iran and Turan: Ronald E. Emmerick Memorial Volume*, ed. by M. Macuch, M. Maggi, & W. Sundermann (Wiesbaden: Harrassowitz Verlag, 2007), pp. 403–22 (pp. 405–11 and 411–16) with German translations; Eng. trans. H.-J. Klimkeit, *Gnosis on the Silk Road: Gnostic Parables, Hymns and Prayers from Central Asia* (London: HarperCollins, 1993) pp. 261–62. See S. Lieu, "From Iran to South China: The Eastward Passage of Manichaeism", in *Worlds of the Silk Roads: Ancient and Modern*, ed. by D. Christian and C. Benjamin, Silk Road Studies 2 (Sydney – Turnhout: Brepols, 1998), pp. 1–22 (p. 12). I am very grateful to Dr Diego M. Santos for alerting me to these Sogdian letters and their modern editions and commentaries. On other Sogdian Manichean texts of this period, see Santos's chapter in this volume.

[23] A later dating, after 880, is preferred by W. Sundermann, "Iranian Manichean Turfan Texts concerning the Turfan Region", in *Turfan and Tun-Huang. The Texts: Encounter of Civilizations on the Silk Route*, ed. by A. Cadonna (Firenze: Leo S. Olschki, 1992), pp. 63–84 (pp. 74–76). Klimkeit, *Gnosis*, p. 261, follows Henning's dating of between 763, when Manicheism first came to Central Asia, and 840, when the schism between the two Syrian Manichean groups, Miqlasiya and Mihriya, was settled: W. Henning, "Neue Materialien zur Geschichte des Manichäismus", *Zeitschrift der Deutschen Morgenländischen Gesellschaft* 90/1 (n.F. 15) (1936), 1–18 (pp. 17–18).

[24] *Turfan Letter* 1, Sundermann "Eine Re-edition", p. 408.25–31; trans. Klimkeit, *Gnosis*, p. 262.

[25] *Turfan Letter* 1, Sundermann "Eine Re-edition", p. 408.24–25; trans. Klimkeit, *Gnosis*, p. 262. The gloss (chastity) is Klimkeit's, but is warranted by the context, a discussion of the bishop with the malady in his nether regions. Sunder-

ond letter, he again refers to the foreign customs and practices of the "vile Syrians".[26] Henning and Sundermann agree that we can identify them with the two main Manichean groups who conflicted in Mesopotamia, loyal to the leaders Mihr and Miqlāṣ, in the account of al-Nadīm.[27] Their libertine practices were disapproved of in Central Asia.

## Against the Manicheans: Ep. 7 to the Bishops of Italy

In spite of devoting eighteen months to the persecution of Manicheism in Rome, Leo wrote only one surviving letter on the subject, *Letter 7* to the bishops of Italy, sent on 30 January 444. In this letter he proudly announced that the sect had been extinguished in Rome and restrained by his authority and judgement, and warned the bishops to be vigilant lest its take root among them.[28] Leo too encouraged the laity and clergy in Rome and all of Italy to search out and denounce suspected Manicheans.[29] Lay people were encouraged to do so by relaxation of the normal penalties for false denunciations,[30] meaning that no contrary law suit could be brought against the accusers, with stiff penalties if their accusa-

---

mann, "Eine Re-edition", p. 408 n. 38, notes that his suspected liaison with the servant was a transgression against the third commandment of chastity for the Elect. See further Klimkeit, *Gnosis*, pp. 262–63 on the five commandments for the Manichean elect, which were described as follows by Al-Nadīm in *Kitāb al-Fihrist* 9, trans. Dodge, *Fihrist*, p. 288: subdue lust and covetousness; refrain from eating meat, drinking wine, and marriage; and avoid injury to water, fire, trees, or any living thing.

[26] *Turfan Letter* 2; Sundermann, "Eine Re-edition", p. 412.15; trans. Klimkeit, *Gnosis*, p. 262. On their provenance, see Sundermann, "Iranian Manichean Turfan Texts", p. 75.

[27] Henning, pp. 17–18; Sundermann, "Iranian Manichean Turfan Texts", p. 75.

[28] Leo, *ep.* 7. 1; Schipper & van Oort, *St Leo*, p. 46. On the Christological basis for Leo's preaching against the Manichean doctrine, see B. Green, *The Soteriology of Leo the Great*, Oxford theological monographs (Oxford: Oxford University Press, 2008), pp. 168–80, L. Casula, *La Cristologia di San Leone Magno, Il fondamento dottrinale e soteriologico*, Dissertatio series Romana 27 (Milan: Giuffre, 2000), pp. 132–38 and pp. 140–45 calls Manicheism and Priscillianism respectively "heresies against the humanity" of Christ.

[29] Leo, *ep.* 7. 1, Schipper & van Oort, *St Leo*, p. 48; cf. *serm.* 16. 5, Chavasse, *Sancti Leonis*,, pp. 65–66.

[30] e.g. Leo, *serm.* 9. 4, Chavasse, *Sancti Leonis*, p. 37; *serm.* 16. 5, Chavasse, *Sancti Leonis*, p. 66; *serm.* 34. 5, Chavasse, *Sancti Leonis*, pp. 186–87; *serm.* 42.5;

tion was found to be false.[31] Christians were instructed to inform the authorities of places where Manicheans held private meetings, and to avoid all contact with them. They were especially advised to avoid allowing them into their houses, where unsuspecting Christian women had fallen prey to their fanciful stories.[32] Some opportunities were given for penance and repentance,[33] but Leo's emphasis was on punishment rather than reconciliation. Prosper of Aquitaine claimed that Leo's investigation in Rome had salutary effects for the whole world since the Manicheans made confessions naming the members of other urban networks of teachers, bishops and priests. Leo's zeal was said to have inspired many eastern clerics,[34] among them probably Theodoret of Cyrrhus who wrote to Leo to congratulate him on his success in Rome.[35]

Leo was on secure ground with his persecution of the sect. An imperial edict of 425 expelled from Rome "Manichean heretics or schismatics or astrologers and every sect opposed to the Catholics".[36] Leo's efforts were backed by the emperors Valentinian III and Theodosius, who issued a constitution on 19 June 445, declaring Manicheism a public crime with severe penalties. Its adherents were to be exiled and their books burnt. Those identified as Manicheans were forbidden to enrol for military service, to live in cities, to receive or leave inheritances. These were the same penalties applied to others found guilty of sacrilege: "For nothing seems to be too severe to be decreed against those persons whose incestuous perversity in the name of religion commits deeds that are unknown and shameful even in brothels."[37]

---

Chavasse, *Sancti Leonis*, pp. 246–48. See Maier, "Manichee!", 448–50, and 455–57; Lieu, *Manichaeism*, pp. 204–06.

[31] *Val. Nov.* 18, Schipper & van Oort, *St Leo*, p. 50.

[32] Leo, *serm.* 16. 5, Schipper & van Oort, *St Leo*, pp. 26–28.

[33] Leo, *ep.* 7. 1, Schipper & van Oort, *St Leo*, pp. 46–48; *serm.* 16.6, Chavasse, *Sancti Leonis*, p. 66.

[34] Prosper, *Epitoma Chronicon* 1350, ed. by T. Mommsen, *Chronicorum minorum saec. IV–VII*, vol. 1, MGH auctorum antiquissimorum, tomus IX (Berlin: Weidmann, 1892), p. 479.

[35] Theodoret, *ep.* 113, ed. by Y. Azéma, *Théodoret de Cyr, Correspondance III*, SC 111 (Paris: Cerf, 1965), p. 58. See discussion of Lieu, *Manichaeism*, pp. 205–06.

[36] *Codex Theodosianus* [= *CTh*] 16. 5. 62, Mommsen & Rougé, *Le code*, p. 328.

[37] "Neque enim aliquid nimium in eos videtur posse decerni quorum incesta perversitas religionis nomine lupanaribus quoque ignotavel pudenda committit." *Valentiniani III Novella* 18, Schipper & van Oort, *St Leo*, pp. 50–51.

Leo's view of the bishop's responsibility has been widely recognized as greater than his predecessor bishops of Rome in the fourth and fifth centuries, but on the same trajectory as Popes Damasus and Innocent, who issued letters of instruction on matters of clerical discipline which were later taken up as having universal application.[38] Innocent, like Leo, sought also to regulate lay behaviour in some areas which had previously been matters of civil law, such as the right to remarry when one's spouse was taken in captivity by barbarians. Leo issued letters of similar ilk, recommending pastoral flexibility to other bishops in times of increasing uncertainty, caused by the invasions of Vandals and other Gothic leaders into previously Roman territory.[39] An example is his letter to Bishop Rusticus of Narbonne, which advised giving people the benefit of the doubt on questions of baptism due to the displacement caused by war.[40] When it was impossible to know whether a candidate for baptism had been previously baptized, whether into the Homoian faith or the Catholic faith or neither, Leo recommended that Catholic baptism be accorded to those who sought it. The implementation of Leo's expansive concept of the law would not have been possible without the wide circulation of his written replies to bishops who sought his advice. In this sense the letter form enabled the development of canon law beyond the canons of local synods, Roman synods or ecumenical councils. While Leo's letter on the Manicheans did not obtain the status of decretal, his letter to Turibius of Astorga on the related problem of the Priscillianists did.

---

[38] The remarriage of citizens whose spouses had been taken captive in wars was a pastoral problem for Innocent I and Leo I, since Roman law deemed such marriages void. The quasi-judicial authority of the bishop of Rome was tested by such cases as that presented to Innocent by Probus (*ep.* 36). Leo upheld Innocent's opposition to remarriage in such instances. See Neil, *Leo the Great*, pp. 139–40.

[39] *Ep.* 167 to Rusticus of Narbonne, PL 54, cols 1199–1209, trans. with intro. Neil, *Leo the Great*, pp. 138–46. On Leo's use of letters to manage various social crises, see Allen & Neil, Appendix, pp. 216–17; and in theological crises, Green, passim.

[40] Leo, *ep.* 167, questions 16–19; PL 54, cols 1208–09; trans. Neil, *Leo the Great*, pp. 145–46.

## Ep. *15 to Turibius of Astorga against the Priscillianists*

Leo's campaign against Manichaeism was not the only occasion when he sought to influence household religious practices,[41] as we see in relation to Leo's condemnation of Priscillianists in Spain. Named after its founder, Priscillian, bishop of Avila in 380–81 CE, the sect originated in Spain. The new emperor and zealous defender of the faith, Magnus Maximus, had Priscillian executed *c.* 385, together with several of his followers, on charges of sorcery.[42] Even orthodox bishops censured the emperor's radical action at the time. Priscillianism refused to be put down, however, and the cult of its "martyrs" added to its growing appeal in Spain. Followers of Priscillian continued to flourish, especially in Galicia in the 390s, until the condemnation of their practices at the Synod of Toledo in 400.[43] They survived underground for several decades, having been allowed to flourish, free from imperial persecution, due to the Suevi and Vandal domination of the region. The remote and mountainous province of Galicia had fallen under the control of the Suevi after the Vandals and Alans had passed through Spain on their way to settlement in North Africa.[44] In the 440s Priscillianism resurfaced in the Iberian peninsula, causing the bishop of Astorga to consult Leo for advice.

In 447 Turibius wrote to Leo, describing and condemning Priscillianism. Turibius's dossier included an account of the heresy's major deviations in sixteen points, a tract and a personal letter. The documents were delivered to Leo by Turibius's deacon for endorsement. Leo's response, dated 21 July 447, is a commentary upon the sixteen points of Priscillianist error raised in Turibius's

---

[41] H. O. Maier, "Religious Dissent, Heresy and Households in Late Antiquity", *Vigiliae Christianae*, 49/1 (1995), 49–63 (53 and 58).

[42] H. Chadwick, *Priscillian of Avila: The Occult and the Charismatic in the Early Church* (Oxford: Clarendon Press, 1976), pp. 128–38.

[43] Chadwick, *Priscillian*, p. 157.

[44] J. Moorhead, *The Roman Empire Divided, 400–700* (Harlow: Longman, 2001), p. 61. In the early fifth century, Orosius of Braga addressed the North African bishop Augustine of Hippo on the matter in his *Commonitorium*. Our main primary source for this period in Spain is Hydatius, *Chronicle*, trans. by R. W. Burgess (ed.), *The Chronicle of Hydatius and the Consularia Constantinopolitana: Two Contemporary Accounts of the Final Years of the Roman Empire*, Oxford Classical Monographs (Oxford: Clarendon, 1993).

tract.[45] Leo rejected their Trinitarian beliefs, their Christology, their fasting regime, their beliefs about the relationship between the human soul and the material order and God, and their belief in the devil having substance, that is, an independent existence.[46] Leo again levelled accusations of sexual deviance against them, claiming that they aimed to dissolve the marriage bond by rejecting procreation.[47] In the context of the recent criminal persecution of the Manicheans, the severity of Leo's response is not surprising. Priscillianism had already been proscribed by Emperor Honorius in 407, just as Valentinian later outlawed Manicheism in 445. Indeed, Leo likened the Priscillianists to Manicheans on several occasions in this letter. They shared with the Manicheans their belief in the consubstantiality of the human and divine – namely, that the human soul is made of divine substance – and in the independent existence of evil, and their negative disposition toward human physicality and sexuality. His portrait of their theological and sacramental commonalities stretches the facts: however, Leo's *Letter* 15 was not aimed at giving an accurate précis of their beliefs, but at terminating their existence as a group.

That group, like the Manicheans, challenged the Christian religion from within by using its name while manifesting some extreme and occasionally bizarre ascetic behaviours. Leo uses the language of disease and contagion – familiar to us from *Homily* 16 – to describe the heresy and how it spreads to others in the Christian community. Priscillianism is likened to a "plague", a "deadly disease", "filthy dregs"[48] and a "poison".[49] Leo's figures of speech seem quite mild compared with those of Turibius, who comments that those infected by "the pestilence of depraved doctrines" are expelled by the church "as if they were either the fruit of a miscarriage or illegitimate bastards".[50] Its belief system – like that of Manicheism – was said to be derived from all the heresies that had preceded it, including those of Arius, Paul of Samosata, Pho-

---

[45] Leo, *ep.* 15, Schipper & van Oort, *St Leo*, pp. 50–74; trans. Neil, *Leo the Great*, pp. 83–94. See also Wessel, *Leo the Great*, pp. 106–13.
[46] Schipper & van Oort, *St Leo*, Preface, p. 4.
[47] Leo, *ep.* 15. 7; cf. *serm.* 16. 5.
[48] Leo, *ep.* 15. prol., Schipper & van Oort, *St Leo*, pp. 52–54.
[49] Leo, *ep.* 15. 15, Schipper &d van Oort, *St Leo*, p. 70.
[50] Turibius, *ep.* 1, Schipper & van Oort, *St Leo*, pp. 78–79.

tinus, Cerdo, and Marcion, but it is also influenced by the pagan art of astrology. Like Manicheism, it "corrupts" catholic priests. Like Mani, Priscillian is described as "a servant of the devil".[51]

Followers of Priscillian operated in secret, Leo claimed, just like the Manicheans, seducing the gullible through "the enticements of fables" and "miraculous tales" (*ep.* 15.15). Leo did not single out women for special mention here, as he had done in *Homily* 16. In *Letter* 15, he recommended the same remedy of vigilance by the priesthood as he did for the laity in *Homily* 16. Leo hoped that the delineation of clear boundaries by denunciation and excommunication would serve to reinforce papal authority over the church of Spain and North Africa, and he requested Turibius to see to it in his final exhortation.[52] Leo's proscription of Priscillianism and other heresies also gave people a sense of comfort in "an ambiguous social situation", as Maier points out in relation to the Manichean investigation in Rome.[53] Clergy under barbarian rule in a region as remote from Rome as Galicia could feel safe in the knowledge that the shepherd was keeping the wolf of heresy from their door. It was not novel for a Spanish bishop to turn to Roman authority – Innocent I had been called upon to uphold the decision of the Council of Toledo to readmit bishops who had renounced Priscillianism.[54] In contrast, Spanish bishops Vitalis and Constantius turned to Capreolus, bishop of Carthage, for advice on Nestorianism, at the time of the Council of Ephesus.[55]

Leo appealed to the authority of secular princes to reinforce his own attacks on Manicheans and Priscillianists as pretend-

---

[51] Leo, *ep.* 15.prol., Schipper & van Oort, *St Leo*, p. 54.

[52] Leo, *ep.* 15. 17, Schipper & van Oort, *St Leo*, p. 76: Ad tuae dilectionis sollicitudinem pertinebit ut nostrae ordinationis auctoritas ad praedictarum provinciarum episcopos deferatur. ("It will be a matter for your beloved's concern that the authority of our rank should be recommended..."). Schipper & van Oort, *St Leo*, p. 77, translate: "It will be the task of your good self to ensure that the official instrument which contains our decision is delivered to the bishops of the aforesaid provinces", noting (n. 124) that *auctoritas* here "denotes an authoritative writing".

[53] Maier, "Manichee!", p. 460.

[54] Innocent I, *ep.* 3; PL 20, cols 485–93.

[55] PL 53, cols 847–49. This request is discussed by Moorhead, *Roman Empire*, p. 60.

ing to confess Christ with sacrilegious intent (*sacrilege sensu*). In *Letters* 7 and 15, he recalled the laws of princes which had indicted these sects as heretical. Priscillian offered a clear example to Emperors Valentinian and Theodosius of the appropriate measures against heresy. This may in fact explain why he exaggerated the similarities between the blasphemous Priscillianists and the Manicheans, even though their differences were apparent, both in their liturgical practices – Manicheans refused the Eucharistic cup and rejected the Old Testament – and in their beliefs.[56] Although ordained bishop of Avila in 381, Priscillian had the distinction of being the first to be executed by imperial command as a Christian heretic. In 385 or 386, he was found guilty of practising magic, together with several of his disciples.[57] The usurper Magnus Maximus may have hoped to gain legitimacy for his rule by championing the faith in this way. After he was accused by Ithacius (possibly the bishop of Ossonuba)[58] of Manicheism, Priscillian fled to Rome, seeking protection from its bishop, Damasus. The pope refused to hear his case, but Priscillian's party did gain a rescript from the *magister officiorum* Macedonius, which allowed them to return to Avila where he recovered his see.[59] The imperial officer's rescript could not save him, however, when Ithacius travelled to Trier and gained the ear of Magnus Maximus. After the Council of Bordeaux condemned Priscillian in 384 or 385, his fate was sealed. Priscillian's devout followers did not cease to follow their late leader's teachings, however; the sect merely went underground.

Its continued survival is indicated by an edict issued by Honorius, Arcadius and Theodosius II in Rome in 407, against "Manicheans and Phrygians or Priscillianists" who are to be con-

---

[56] Priscillianists and Manicheans were deeply suspicious of the material realm, rejecting demands of the flesh such as marriage and procreation. On their similarities and differences, see Schipper & van Oort, *St Leo*, pp. 4–5.

[57] On the evidence for the date of Priscillian's execution, see Chadwick, *Priscillian*, pp. 132–38; M. Conti, *Priscillian of Avila. The Complete Works*, Oxford Early Christian Studies (Oxford: Oxford University Press, 2010), p. 5, agrees, writing that the trial "probably occurred in 385".

[58] Schipper & van Oort, *St Leo*, p. 3.

[59] Chadwick, *Priscillian*, pp. 38–41.

sidered as committing a "public crime".[60] Their property was to be confiscated,[61] and any property where a Manichean or Priscillianist meeting was held with the landowner's knowledge was forfeit to the state.[62] A stronger edict of 408 permitted Catholics to seize Donatist, Manichean and Priscillianist churches and property.[63] This handing over of powers previously confined to the state illustrates the extent of the new cooperation of the bishop of Rome and the emperors in the time of Innocent I. It is noteworthy that it occurred in the midst of Alaric's three sieges of Rome, between 408 and 410. The invasion of Spain in 409 by the Visigoth, Vandal, Suevi and Alan peoples caused widespread chaos and destruction there, but it also allowed heretics to flourish unopposed. Ongoing warfare in Roman territory hindered both the execution of laws against heretics and the gathering of local episcopal councils, as Leo noted in the prologue of *Letter* 15, quoted below. In this context, the power and perceived responsibility of the bishop of Rome to maintain social and civic order increased to unprecedented levels.

Sometime before 447, the "most fetid sewage" of Priscillianism, as Leo put it,[64] erupted again on Spanish soil, this time in Galicia. Leo's letter to Turibius indicates that times of war necessitated stronger measures by bishops against heretics. Leo advises Turibius to convene a council to make "a very minute investigation" of the beliefs of all bishops, so as to weed out the contagion of heresy.[65] If such a synod of the bishops of Tarragon, New Carthage, Lusitania, and Galicia could not be arranged, then

---

[60] *CTh*. 16. 5. 40. 1–2, Mommsen & Rougé, *Le code,* pp. 284–86, addressed to Senator, the urban prefect or praetorian prefect of Rome. There is some doubt as to whether followers of Priscilla, the Montanist prophetess, are meant here. The grouping with Manicheans suggests that western Priscillianists, that is, followers of Priscillian, are meant. See *CTh*. 16. 5. 40, p. 285 n. 4; cf. *CTh*. 16. 5. 40. 5, p. 286: *qui aut manichaeus aut fryga aut priscillianista fuisse conuincitur*. The same ambiguity applies to Priscillianists proscribed with Donatists and Manicheans in *CTh*. 16. 5. 43, Mommsen & Rougé, *Le code,* p. 292.

[61] *CTh*. 16. 5. 40. 2, Mommsen & Rougé, *Le code,* pp. 284–86.

[62] *CTh*. 16. 5. 40. 7, Mommsen & Rougé, *Le code,* pp. 286–88.

[63] *CTh*. 16. 5. 43, Mommsen & Rougé, *Le code,* pp. 292–94; addressed to Curtius, the praetorian prefect in Rome.

[64] Leo, *ep.* 15, prol., Schipper & van Oort, *St Leo,* p. 52: *Priscillianistarum apud vos foetidissimam recaluisse sentinam.*

[65] Leo, *ep.* 15. 17, Schipper & van Oort, *St Leo,* pp. 74–76.

at least the bishops of Galicia should convene, so that "a remedy can be applied all the more quickly to such gaping wounds".[66]

> Merito patres nostri sub quorum temporibus heresis haec nefanda prorupit, per totum mundum instanter egerunt ut impius furor ab universa ecclesia pelleretur; quando etiam mundi principes ita hanc sacrilegam amentiam detestati sunt ut auctorem eius cum plerisque discipulis legum publicarum ense prosternerunt.

> Our fathers, in whose times this abominable heresy erupted, were right to take firm action throughout the whole world in order that this impious fury might be expelled from the universal church; at which time, the leaders of the world likewise began to detest this sacrilegious madness: to such an extent that they struck down its originator with the sword of the public laws together with a great number of his disciples.[67]

This last sentence probably refers to Mani's death sentence passed by the Sasanian King Bahram I in 276 or 277,[68] but the remainder of the passage, which refers to the "severe constitutions of Christian rulers", calls to mind both to Roman laws against Manicheism and the execution of Priscillian by the western Roman emperor Magnus Maximinus *c.* 386:

> Profuit diu ista districtio ecclesiasticae lenitati; quae etsi sacerdotali contenta iudicio cruentas refugit ultiones, severis tamen Christianorum principum constitutionibus adiuvatur, dum ad spiritale nonnumquam recurrunt remedium qui timent corporale supplicium.

> This severity was for long conducive to ecclesiastical lenience, which, though it avoids bloody revenges, content as it is with priestly judgement, is aided by the *severe constitutions of Christian rulers*: not rarely do those who fear corporal punishment take recourse to spiritual remedy.[69]

---

[66] Leo, *ep.* 15. 17, Schipper & van Oort, *St Leo*, pp. 76–77: *quo citius vel provinciali convenit remedium tantis vulneribus afferatur.*
[67] Schipper & van Oort, *St Leo*, pp. 53–55.
[68] e.g. Schipper & van Oort, *St Leo*, p. 53 n. 70 and p. 55, n. 71.
[69] Leo, *ep.* 15, prol., Schipper & van Oort, p. 52, trans. p. 55. My emphasis.

No one had been executed on the grounds of heresy since Priscillian's death. It is not clear that Leo wished to reinstate the death penalty for Manicheans or Priscillianists, but he was adamant that they deserved the worst punishments that the state could offer the living: a life of exile in poverty after their goods had been confiscated by the imperial fisc, with no opportunity to inherit or pass anything on to their heirs. They could not make a living in business or the military. They could not even defend themselves against slander (*iniuria*) in the courts. They became stateless persons, living outside the kingdom of God and outside the civilizing boundaries of empire. This was a big step for a bishop to take, and Leo was the first after Augustine to take it. After him, Popes Gelasius, Symmachus and Hormisdas took decisive steps against Manicheans. The success of Leo's and Augustine's ventures against Manicheans is reflected in a forgery composed in the early sixth century, a memorandum issued in the name of Augustine of Hippo (*Commonitorium Sancti Augustini*), which outlined the conditions under which a Manichean who had repented could return to the church. While, as Schipper and van Oort note, the prosecution of Manicheans was a joint effort by both ecclesiastical and secular authorities, the *Commonitorium Sancti Augustini* credits the former with leading the charge.[70]

## *Conclusions*

While Leo certainly exaggerated the similarities between Priscillianism and Manicheism, the Priscillianists did share with Manicheans certain doctrines and rituals that were unorthodox, such as the Sunday fast, and a rejection of marriage and procreation (or as Leo put it, they wanted to "untie the conjugal bond").[71] In

---

[70] Schipper & van Oort, *St Leo*, p. 2, give the *terminus ante quem* for this memorandum as 536. Ps-Augustine, *Commonitorium sancti Augustini*, ed. by J. Zycha, CSEL 25/II (Vienna: Verlag der Österreichischen Akademie der Wissenschaften, 1892), pp. 979–82.

[71] Leo, *ep.* 15, prol., Schipper & van Oort, *St Leo*, p. 52: [Patres nostril] videbant enim omnem curam honestatis auferri omnemque coniugiorum copulam solvi simulque divinum ius humanumque subverti, si huiusmodi hominibus usquam vivere cum talii professione licuisset. ("For [our fathers] saw that all care for reputation would be taken away and every conjugal bond would be loosed, and

spite of these similarities, Schipper and van Oort rightly conclude that Priscillianism was not a true heresy, but rather "a dissident movement within the Catholic Church, marked by a strong preference for asceticism and esotericism".[72] Priscillian disavowed the "pseudo-bishops and the Manicheans".[73] In the same tract he repudiated the Manicheans thus:[74]

> Inter quae tamen omnia Manichaeos, iam non hereticos, sed idololatras et maleficos servos Soli et Lunae, invictiacos daemones cum omnibus auctoribus sectis moribus institutis libris doctoribus discipulisque damnamus, quia de his scribtum (*sic*) est: *cum tali nec quidem cibus sument.*
>
> Among them all we condemn the Manicheans not simply as heretics, but as idolaters and evil servants of the sun and the moon, as demons worshipping the Unconquered Sun together with all their authors, sects, customs, institutions, books, teachers, and disciples, because it is written about them: *Do not even eat with such a one* (I Corinthians 5, 11).

This made no impression on Leo the Great, however. The slightest trace of Manicheism was enough for him to label a marginal group like the Priscillianists as heterodox and therefore illegal.[75] According to Leo, Manicheans and Priscillianists differed in name alone, and were guilty of the same sacrileges. Disguised as Catholics they attended mass in order to convert churchgoers. They both practised rituals that were at best unorthodox, at worst depraved.[76] Citizens were encouraged to report them, and Catholic bishops to expose their clerics.

Leo's policies of exclusion of Manicheans were not irreversible: they could redeem themselves if they informed on their leaders and co-religionists. Leo managed to have his strictures enforced by

---

divine and human law would be subverted at the same time, if people of this kind were allowed to live anywhere with a profession [of faith] of this kind").

[72] Schipper & van Oort, *St Leo*, p. 19.

[73] Priscillian, *tract.* 2. 50; ed. by G. Schepps, *Priscilliani quae supersunt, accedit Orosii Commonitorium de errore Priscillianistarum et Origenistarum*, CSEL 18 (Vienna: Verlag der Österreichischen Akademie der Wissenschaften, 1889), pp. 40–41. See Maier, "Manichee!", p. 441 n. 1.

[74] Conti, *Priscillian*, pp. 74–75, lines 103–06; following Schepps's edition.

[75] *ep.* 15. 4 and *ep.* 15. 7.

[76] *ep.* 15. 16; Schipper & van Oort, *St Leo*, p. 72.

imperial law. A combination of religious, social and legal proscriptions proved fairly effective, if we are to believe Prosper's *Chronicon*.[77] The rhetoric of vilification in Leo's letters and homilies was, it seems, quite persuasive, when combined with religious, social and legal proscriptions. Both letters laid the ground for the inquisitions of the Middle Ages.

## *Abstract*

In January 444, Leo the Great informed the bishops of Italy of the outcome of his investigations into the activities and beliefs of the Manicheans in Rome. His sole surviving letter on the subject gives a detailed account of the senate tribunal over which Leo presided. Three years later, Leo again attacked Manicheism in his lengthy letter to Turibius of Astorga against Priscillianism. Leo's accusations of sexual immorality against certain members of the Manichean Elect find confirmation in contemporary North African sources and in two later Manichean letters from Turfan, Central Asia. The connection between the Turfan letters and the immoral practices of North African Manicheans is demonstrated. These disparate sources, when considered in combination, force us to reassess and take seriously Leo's claims that ritual sexual intercourse, perhaps involving children, was practised by the Manichean Elect in Rome as part of their liturgy.

---

[77] See note 34 above.

## CHAPTER 6
# MANUSCRIPTS FROM LATE ANTIQUITY AND FROM THE PATRISTIC PERIOD: THEIR DISCOVERY, CONSERVATION AND DIGITAL PUBLICATION

PATRICIA CINER
*Universidad Católica de Cuyo, Argentina*

# BRIEF INTRODUCTION TO THE TOPIC

The sixth chapter is devoted to the issue of discovery, conservation and digital publication of manuscripts, both from Late Antiquity and from the Patristic period. These three aspects constitute a kind of "trinity" of essential technical skills for the scientific study of manuscripts. Included here are articles written by three prestigious scholars: Dr Ira Rabin, Monsignor Cesare Pasini and Father Angelo di Berardino.

This chapter is divided into two sections. The first deals with the Dead Sea Scrolls, undoubtedly one of the most important discoveries of Late Antiquity, which has had a decisive impact on Patristic Studies. The prestigious specialist Ira Rabin, who is dedicated to the care of the Dead Sea Scrolls, presents an analysis of the conditions that have allowed these scrolls to survive for so many centuries and describes the conservation methods which ensure their preservation. On the one hand, these issues are essential for ensuring the survival of this invaluable historical material, but on the other they are essential for our understanding of the circumstances in which these scrolls were written (geographical origin, community in charge of writing, spiritual content, etc.) and the material or other vicissitudes that accompanied their storage in the caves of Qumran.

It is important to mention some of the most important milestones in Dr Ira Rabin's academic formation in order to understand the experience needed by a scholar dedicated to this type of task. She first studied chemistry at the Hebrew University of Jerusalem. From 1979 to 1983, she worked as a student and later as a staff member of the Conservation Department of the

Jewish National and University Library (JNUL), with specialization in paper and parchment conservation. In 1983, she returned to the Hebrew University of Jerusalem to continue her studies in physical chemistry. In 1987, she moved to Berlin where she obtained a PhD in physical chemistry at the Free University of Berlin in collaboration with the Max-Planck Society. Until 2003, she worked in basic research in cluster physics at the Fritz-Haber Institute of the Max-Planck Society and continued her research on parchment as a hobby. Since 2003, her main research interest is the Dead Sea Scrolls. From 2005 to 2006, she worked in Israel as a scientific advisor for the Israel Antiquities Authority and the Jewish National Library. From 2007 to 2010, she coordinated the international Dead Sea Scrolls project. Currently, she is senior scientist at the Federal Institute of Material Research and Testing (BAM) in Berlin and the Centre for the Studies of Manuscript Cultures (CSMC) in Hamburg, Germany. Her breadth of experience makes her invaluable to our discussion of manuscript preservation.

The second section of the chapter will be devoted to the issue of digital discovery, conservation and publication in the specific field of Patristic Studies. Here the reader will find impressive articles by Monsignor Cesare Pasini and Father Angelo di Berardino. Though their academic merits have been recognized internationally, I would like to take a moment to mention and link their respective contributions to this volume on the topic of the discovery of manuscripts.

In Monsignor Pasini's article "Patristic Vocation at the Vatican Library", readers will immediately note that this specialist has both the rigor of an academic and the delicacy of an erudite, a specialist who does not separate his spiritual life from his intellectual life. Monsignor Cesare was born in Milan in 1950 and was ordained into the priesthood in 1974. In 1979, he received his doctorate in Oriental Ecclesiastical Studies from the Pontifical Oriental Institute in Rome. He worked as a Professor of Patrology at the Seminary of the Diocese of Milan from 1978 to 1989 and entered the Ambrosian Library in Milan as a PhD in 1986, becoming its Vice-Prefect in 1991. Since June 2007, he has been the Prefect of the Vatican Apostolic Library. This last position is undoubtedly of utmost importance in terms of the preservation of Patristic manuscripts. In particular, we must mention the monumental task currently being undertaken, that of digitizing all of the Vatican Library's manuscripts. As Monsignor Pasini explains at the end of his article, this is a huge job as it encompasses the entire collection of eighty thousand manuscripts held by the Library, that is, 40 million pages or 45 petabytes of data (equivalent to 45 billion million bytes!). He also points out that this challenging project of digitization does not take away from the humanist spirit upon which the Library was built, but rather renews it by adding to the passion and scientific rigor behind current research and by making it possible for scholars to access source documents, especially those concerning the Church Fathers. This humanist spirit also refers to the idea of sharing, which is exactly what the Library is doing by making the cultural treasures that the Library possesses available to all scholars at no cost. In this sense, the mission and "Patristic vocation" of the Vatican Library continues unchanged, as in the words of Monsignor Pasini, the Library collaborates with the path set forth by the Church Fathers, a path "in search of truth, the truth of man loved by God, found and redeemed by Him."

Father Angelo di Berardino has contributed to this volume with his magnificent article entitled "The Impact of Recent Archaeological, Historical and Literary Discoveries on the Study of Patristics". Father Angelo was born in Furci, Italy in the year 1936 and was ordained in 1962. He obtained his Doctorate in Theology in 1967 and his Doctorate in History and Philosophy in 1990. The characteristics that define Father Angelo are, without a doubt, his enthusiasm and his creativity for new initiatives. This enthusiasm is especially reflected in his participation in the International Association of Patristic Studies (IAPS/AIEP), of which he served as Secretary from 1983 to 2000 and then as President from 2000 to 2004. Since 1970, he has been Professor of Patrology at the Institutum Patristicum Augustinianum in Rome and he has been invited to be a visiting professor at numerous universities around the world. His lengthy bibliography includes Patristic dictionaries and encyclopedias on the Old Church, among many other works.

Father Angelo's article is organized around three central themes: a) the history of the International Association of Patristic Studies and its current situation, b) the reach of the term Patristics and c) the principal discoveries of manuscripts in the field of Patristics and their subsequent publication. This article has two strengths which make it accessible to both specialized and non-specialized readers: its clarity and its precision with respect to the information provided. In some cases, this information is an autobiographical account of the effort and dedication that it took to strengthen AIEP. As regards the discovery of manuscripts from the Patristic era, this article is a true academic gem as it very precisely synthesizes diverse information that is at times difficult to put together.

In summary, this chapter shows that the conservation of past sources has no "raison d'être" if those sources are not available for analysis and consultation by any researcher who wishes to study them. The current techniques of digitization, storage and retrieval allow access to sources that for economic or geographical reasons were previously inaccessible to many. As an example of one of the initiatives that all Patristic specialists are grateful for, we must mention the great contribution of Brepols Publishers, which provides dictionary tools and online databases on its website for access by scholars around the world.

Finally, we would also like to point out that this interesting chapter teaches us that investment in preserving the great wonders of the past allows us to better understand our present and to envisage a more hopeful future.

IRA RABIN

*Bundesanstalt für Materialfrschung und-prüfung (BAM), Berlin, Germany*

# WRITING MATERIALS OF THE DEAD SEA SCROLLS

The paramount importance of the Dead Sea Scrolls (DSS) for the historical evaluation of the time of Jesus doesn't require specific analysis. The very many publications largely devoted to text analysis and reconstruction, however, have largely neglected the material components of the DSS. Yet, the discovery and the post-discovery history of the scrolls play an important role in addressing the questions of the origin, archaeological provenance, and attribution of the fragments. To address these questions, the BAM Federal Institute for Materials Research and Testing conducted the international Qumran project aimed at establishing an optimal methodology for recovery of the original and acquired properties of the scrolls' material.[1] The scrolls excavated by Bedouins and archeologists in the eleven caves around Khirbet Qumran in the middle of the last century underwent complicated post-discovery treatments that gave the skin-based material of the scrolls a stratified structure that varies from fragment to fragment and from spot to spot.[2] Our approach was based on identifying the traces accumulated on a fragment in the course of time. In this view, production of a writing support and its inscription, use, storage

---

[1] I. Rabin, "Archaeometry of the Dead Sea Scrolls", *Dead Sea Discoveries* 20 (2013), 124–42; I. Rabin & O. Hahn, "Characterization of the Dead Sea Scrolls by advanced analytical techniques", *Analytical Methods*, 5 (2013), 4648–54.

[2] E. Boyd-Alkalay & E. Libman, "Conservation of the Dead Sea Scrolls", *Restaurator*, 18 (1997), 92–101; O. Hahn *et al.*, "Non-Destructive Investigation of the Dead Sea Scrolls", Proceedings of the ART2008 international conference, Jerusalem May 25–30, 2008. Internet edition. https://www.ndt.net/article/art2008/papers/209Hahn.pdf (accessed am 08.01.2021)

in caves, and post-discovery treatments are distinct events in the history of a scroll, each of which leaves a recognizable trace or so-called fingerprints. Spatially resolved distributions of the elements present in the scrolls coupled with chemical analysis of the regions of interest made it possible to determine these fingerprints, i.e., to reveal characteristic patterns that we, in turn, can correlate with the specific layer or event. The sketch of the cross section in Figure 1 presents schematically the main periods of different trace accumulation as spatially separated layers. Though in reality the layers are not clearly separated, their intermixing presents a problem only in the rare cases of complete gelatinization of skin-based writing surface accompanied by full dispersion of the ink in the material. In general, we were able to recognize the traces of the post-discovery events, such as humidification/freezing cycles and treatment with oils, adhesives, and various consolidating agents. Equally clearly, a characteristic set of salts could point to storage in caves rich in specific minerals, whereas the water used during the processing of the hides suggested a fingerprint of the source in a number of cases. During our Qumran project, we proposed to correlate the origin of writing surfaces and materials based on the impurities introduced with the water during the production or the inscription stage, since both skin and ink preparation involve handling with water. After the drying and finishing stages, a skin-based writing surface has a homogeneous distribution of the elements that were present as impurities in the water.[3] Carbon ink produced from soot is handled with water twice: to produce a dry ink pellet, soot is mixed with a binder dissolved in a small amount of water, whereas liquid ink for inscription is prepared directly before writing by adding water to the dry ink. Therefore, the text on the scroll would have the impurities representative of the water used at the location of writing. Since the spring water of the coastal region of the Dead Sea has a salt composition similar to that of the Dead Sea and different from the water sources in the rest of the country, we suggested using the ratio of the elements chlorine and bromine as the markers of the area.

---

[3] I. Rabin *et al.*, "Characterization of the writing media of the Dead Sea Scrolls", in *A holistic view on Qumran and the Dead Sea Scrolls*, ed. by J. Gunneweg, A. Adriaens & J. Dik (Leiden: Brill, 2010) 123–34.

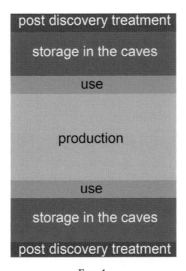

Fig. 1.
Schematic depiction of the accumulation of traces on a fragment.
The traces from production are distinguishable from those left by use and storage in the caves, as well as from those left by conservation attempts.
(Reprinted from ref. 3)

To check and validate our hypothesis, we first used samples that we prepared ourselves. Then we applied the same analysis to the un-inscribed samples from Qumran cave 4, Nahal Hever, Ein Feshkha, and Murabba'at, which belonged to the Ronald Reed archive and were made available to us by the John Rylands library of the Manchester University. Ronald Reed Archive contains a collection of small un-inscribed fragments allegedly originating from the find sites along the western shore of the Dead Sea.[4] The samples were given to Ronald Reed of Leeds University for material analysis shortly after the initial discovery and were never treated chemically, therefore presenting an excellent initial testing material. Simulating some of the most aggressive interventions, we tested the effects of the possible post-discovery treatments. Finally, we investigated inscribed fragments of the scrolls from Qumran Cave 1 and Cave 11, which were provided by the Shrine of the Book in Jerusalem.

---

[4] I. Rabin *et al.*, "The Ronald Reed archive at the John Rylands University Library", *e-Preservation* 4 (2007), pp. 9–12.

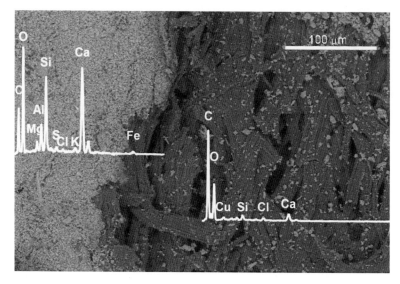

Fig. 2.
Electron scanning micrograph with the corresponding EDX spectra (white curves) of the surface of a fragment from Cave 4 (Reprinted from ref 5).

The testing was first conducted with an electron scanning microscope equipped with an energy-dispersed X-ray detector (EDX) and micro-X-ray fluorescence (XRF) applied in two- and three-dimensional manner to obtain distributions of the elements present in the object under investigation. We found the elements chlorine (Cl) and bromine (Br) to be distributed evenly inside the fragments, confirming that chlorine and bromine could be associated with the water used for the production of the parchment and inks. In contrast, we registered the elements silicon (Si), calcium (Ca), and iron (Fe) mostly as islands on the surface of the fragments, which fact allowed us to connect these elements with the sediments from the caves.[5] Figure 2 shows two regions on the surface of a fragment from Qumran Cave 4, each of which can be used for a separate study of the production and storage in the caves.

[5] T. Wolff et al., "Provenance studies on Dead Sea scrolls parchment by means of quantitative micro-XRF", *Analytical and Bioanalytical Chemistry*, 402 (2012), 1493–1503; I. Mantouvalou et al., "3D Micro-XRF for cultural heritage objects – new analysis strategies for the investigation of the Dead Sea Scrolls", *Journal of Analytical Chemistry*, 83 (2011), 6308–15.

In the field view of the micrograph in Figure 2, we see two clearly independent regions, each of which corresponds to a certain event in the life history of our fragment. To study these events separately, one needs to identify different regions using high-resolution spatial element maps. In the second step of the testing, one can identify the minerals constituting the sediments in different caves. So, a certain ratio between two polymorphs of calcium carbonate, aragonite, and calcite can help distinguish between natural and manmade caves, assisting the establishment of archaeological provenance – one of the important questions of the Qumran research. On the other hand, testing the collagen fibers for the presence of tannin answers an even more important question about the technology of the parchment production.[6]

Since Ronald Reed's first publication on the production technology of the Qumran parchment, it has been generally tacitly assumed that the surfaces of skins depilated without the aid of lime solutions and stretched to dry were invariably subjected to treatments with tannins before sacred texts could be inscribed on them.[7] Such a rule, together with the rule requiring biblical scrolls to be inscribed on the hair side, can indeed be found among the Talmudic prescriptions for ritual writing. Later, Reed himself acknowledged that some of the samples in his possession were never tanned.[8] The famous, almost 8-meter Temple Scroll was never treated with tannins, either. Moreover, it was inscribed on the flesh side.[9] This finding alone would be sufficient to raise doubts about the belief that the Talmudic prescriptions for writing sacred texts were already universally respected in the late Second Temple period. Reed's and our finding of a number of such a parchments in Qumran allowed us to conclude that different parchment-making traditions coexisted in Ancient Israel of the Hellenistic period.

---

[6] M. Bicchieri et al., "New results in Dead Sea Scrolls non-destructive characterisation. Evidence of different parchment manufacture in the fragments from Reed collection", *Journal of Cultural Heritage* 32 (2018), 22–29.

[7] J. B. Poole & R. Reed, "The Preparation of Leather and Parchment by the Dead Sea Scrolls Community", *Technology & Culture*, 3 (1962), 1–36.

[8] R. Ronald, *Ancient Skins, Parchments and Leathers* (New York: Seminar Press, 1972), pp. 261–64.

[9] R. Schütz et al., "The Temple Scroll: Reconstructing an ancient manufacturing practice", *Science Advances* 2019; 5: eaaw7494.

Tanned parchments that closely resemble Aramaic documents from the fifth century BC are most probably associated with the "Eastern" or Babylonian tradition, whereas un-tanned pale parchments that look quite similar to the early Christian Greek ones would correspond to the "Western" one.[10] It is noteworthy that our study of the scrolls in the Genizah collection confirmed our classification into the East and West traditions.[11]

In addition to the presence of tannin, we discovered that elemental potassium (K) and sulfur (S) could serve as another important marker for the identification of "Eastern" and "Western" technology, respectively. Potassium is always associated with plants and the use of organic liquors for depilating the hides in the first step of parchment production. Tannins extracted from the bark of trees or gallnuts also contain considerable amounts of potassium. In contrast, inorganic salts containing sulfur were most probably used to depilate the pale scrolls that were either not tanned at all or only very lightly tanned. In the collection of the Shrine of the Book, the Great Isaiah scroll and the Community Rule present the best example of scrolls lightly tanned.[12]

In the course of our 10 years of studies of the Dead Sea Scrolls, we have shown that organic (parchment) and inorganic (sediments from the caves) phases of the ancient fragments were not completely intermixed and could be resolved spatially. Since a spatial resolution of $c.$ 50 μm is sufficient, the characterization of the Scrolls can be conducted at the collections using mobile scanning micro XRF and micro Raman techniques. Using microscopy and scanning X-ray techniques, we could also differentiate among materials introduced by conservation, as well as the effects of excessive humidification.

I believe though that our most important discovery is the evidence for the coexistence of at least two different techniques

---

[10] G. R. Driver, *Aramaic Documents of the Fifth Century B.C.* (Oxford: Oxford University Press, 1954).

[11] I. Rabin, "Building a Bridge from the Dead Sea Scrolls to Mediaeval Hebrew Manuscripts", in *Jewish Manuscript Cultures. New Perspectives*, ed. by I. Wandrey (Berlin, Boston: De Gruyter, 2017), pp. 309–22.

[12] I. Rabin, "Material Analysis of the Dead Sea Scrolls Fragments", in *Gleanings From the Caves. Dead Sea Scrolls and Artefacts of The Schoyen Collection*, ed. by T. Elgvin (Bloomsbury: T&T Clark, 2016), pp. 61–77.

of parchment production in Ancient Israel of the Hellenistic period. We hope that the classification of the scrolls in accordance with these production techniques will be carried out as a part of the treatment and documentation protocol.

## *Acknowledgements*

My thanks go to the Shrine of the Book and the John Rylands Library for supplying us with the material to study. I would also like to thank the scholars Michael Stone, George Brooke, Emanuel Tov, and Adolfo Roitman for their great help in identifying the questions of interest in the DSS research.

## *Abstract*

The first manuscripts from the Qumran caves were found in 1947. Within the following 10 years, clandestine and legal excavations revealed some 900 highly fragmented manuscripts from the late Second Temple period. This collection is generally known as Scrolls of the Judea Desert or Dead Sea Scrolls (DSS).

For many years after their discovery, text analysis and fragments attribution were the main concern of the scholars dealing with the scrolls. The uncertain archaeological provenance of the larger part of the collection added an additional difficulty to the formidable task of sorting some 19000 fragments. After 60 years of scholar research the questions of origin, archaeological provenance and correct attribution of the fragments are still hotly debated.

To determine a possible contribution to the debate from the point of view of writing materials, we used optical and electron microscopy, various X-ray based techniques as well as vibrational spectroscopy. We validated our approach with SY- based studies using the advantages of the synchrotron radiation source with respect to the benchtop devices.

Our laboratory studies showed that often production and storage locality could be distinguished thanks to the specific residues ("fingerprint") they left on the material. Moreover, we have discovered that different parchment production processes coexisted in the antiquity, and the resulting writing materials can readily be distinguished.

CESARE PASINI
*Prefect of the Vatican Apostolic Library*

# LA "VOCACIÓN PATRÍSTICA" DE LA BIBLIOTECA VATICANA

Es un honor [1] y les agradezco el poder encontrarme aquí para abrir este Congreso de estudios sobre los descubrimientos de textos patrísticos que se han realizado durante este último siglo. Permítanme que les diga con sinceridad, que es para mí una ocasión para recordar los Padres de la Iglesia. De alguna manera se puede decir que dejé en Milán los estudios patrísticos y en particular las investigaciones sobre San Ambrosio, a los que he dedicado una pequeña parte de mi vida. Ahora me han brindado la oportunidad de reencontrarlos en ocasión de este importante evento. El panorama general que presenta este Congreso es de lo más amplio y pretende tener en cuenta el impacto que han tenido en los estudios patrísticos y en la contemporaneidad los descubrimientos de manuscritos de la Antigüedad Tardía llevados a cabo por la arqueología, paleografía y codicología.

---

[1] Dejo que sea el mismo preludio a dar el importante matiz narrativo de la presentación uniendo a ello notas adecuadas al texto. Agradezco a los organizadores del Congreso y en particular el Gran Canciller de la Universidad Católica el Arzobispo Monseñor Alfonso Delgado Evers, el Arzobispo Coadjutor Monseñor Jorge Lozano y el Rector de la Universidad Doctor Claudio Larrea Arnau y a las Autoridades gubernamentales de la provincia de San Juan que han colaborado en la realización del Congreso. Un agradecimiento en especial a Patricia Ciner, que se ha puesto en contacto conmigo desde el principio y que con su amabilidad ha facilitado mi participación. Además agradezco tanto a Victoria E. Bosch Uuttu como a Ángela Núñez Gaitán la traducción completa del texto. Y agradezco también al doctor Antonio Manfredi (junto al doctor Delio Proverbio y al reverendo Giacomo Cardinali) por la ayuda en la preparación de esta conferencia.

## 1. *El ejemplo de Giovanni Mercati*

Me he preguntado: ¿cómo y por qué la Biblioteca Vaticana puede entrar en este discurso? y me ha venido a la mente un personaje fundamental que ha contribuido de manera exponencial, tanto a nuestros estudios y descubrimientos en edad moderna como sigue siendo una figura importante para la historia de la Vaticana del último siglo: me refiero a Giovanni Mercati, conocido por muchos como el editor de los *Exapla* y como escrupoloso investigador de Ambrosio, Cipriano y otros Padres y escritores bizantinos.[2] Con él querría empezar.

Me ha impresionado mientras ojeaba las publicaciones y cartas escritas por él, una anécdota que narra ciertos descubrimientos y estudios que estaba realizando en la Biblioteca del Archivo del Arzobispado de Rávena a finales del siglo XIX.[3] Mercati pertenecía a la diócesis de Reggio Emilia y en el año 1893 fue nombrado doctor de la Biblioteca Ambrosiana en Milán. Cinco años más tarde lo encontramos en la Biblioteca Vaticana como *scriptor* convirtiéndose en el año 1918 en pro-prefecto y al año siguiente como prefecto. Fue nombrado Cardenal Bibliotecario en el año 1936 hasta su muerte en el 1957. Se había presentado en Rávena el 19 de febrero del 1894 y en aquella ocasión había descubierto textos de Ambrosio de Milán en algunos pergaminos de los siglos V y VI, conocidos como *Códice de Rávena* de San Ambrosio.[4] Mercati pudo corroborar que aquellos folios contenían fragmentos de obras muy conocidas del Obispo de Milán: el *De Fide*, el *De incarnationis dominicae sacramento* y el *De Spiritu Sancto*.

---

[2] Por lo que se refiere a la abundante bibliografía sobre Giovanni Mercati (1866–1957) deseo señalar los numerosos contributos que lo conciernen en *I fratelli Mercati nella storia e nella cultura del Novecento*, a cura di F. D'Aiuto, C. Debbi, C. Gazzini & P. Vian (Città del Vaticano: Biblioteca Apostolica Vaticana, 2021), en fase de publicación.

[3] Sobre este tema y su relativa documentación véase C. Pasini, "*Giovanni Mercati e il manoscritto ravennate di s. Ambrogio*", en *Miscellanea Bibliothecae Vaticanae*, XXIV (Città del Vaticano: Biblioteca Apostolica Vaticana, 2018), pp. 497-552.

[4] Cfr. E. A. Lowe, *Codices latini antiquiores. A palaeographical guide to Latin manuscripts prior to the ninth century* (Oxford: The Clarendon Press, 1934-1966), IV, nb. 410a–410b.

Narrando su descubrimiento en un artículo de 1897,[5] Mercati comenta con una frase no demasiado clara que había podido "copiar todo con la comodidad que requería este tipo de trabajo largo y difícil",[6] sin embargo no explicó cuándo y cómo sucedió. En una carta del 10 de agosto de 1895 dirigida al entonces prefecto Antonio Maria Ceriani,[7] le resumía el viaje de estudio que había hecho de nuevo a Rávena y en dicha carta nos da a entender que Mercati debía tener a su disposición el manuscrito en Milán, evidentemente en la Biblioteca Ambrosiana; de hecho le escribe que el 2 de agosto "en Rávena" había "devuelto el manuscrito de San Ambrosio".[8]

El descubrimiento de Mercati concernía textos patrísticos conocidos, pero los había encontrado en un códice antiquísimo, realizado durante la espléndida edad de Rávena entre Justiniano y Teodorico, cuando los enlaces con Oriente eran muy fuertes. Un códice que, junto con el Orosio de Viliaric,[9] representa uno de los monumentos paleográficos de la Rávena exarcal que quizás formara parte de la antigua biblioteca diocesana y que ha llegado hasta nosotros milagrosamente. Por lo tanto era evidente la importancia de aquellas obras para las sucesivas ediciones críticas y también su importancia como testimonio de la difusión más antigua de las obras de Ambrosio.

Vale la pena añadir algún que otro detalle sobre la historia de dicho descubrimiento que marcó, no sólo su vida, sino también los estudios en Italia, e indica como esos descubrimientos "juveniles"

---

[5] G. Mercati, "*Le Titulationes nelle opere dogmatiche di s. Ambrogio, con due appendici*", en *Ambrosiana* (Milano: L.F. Cogliati, 1897), VIII, p. 26; reed. en Id., *Opere minori*, I (Città del Vaticano: Biblioteca Apostolica Vaticana, 1937), pp. 446–81.

[6] "[...] trarre copia di tutto con la comodità, che esigeva la lunghezza e la difficoltà del lavoro" (*Ibid.*, p. 26; p. 464 de la reedición).

[7] Milano, Biblioteca Ambrosiana, W 28 bis inf., nb. 129: editado en *Ceriani-Mercati. 1893–1907*. Introducción, edición y anotaciones por C. Pasini, con la colaboración de M. Rodella (Città del Vaticano: Biblioteca Apostolica Vatiana, 2019), pp. 170–173, nb. 24.

[8] "Il 2° [agosto 1895] faceva a Ravenna la restituzione del manoscritto di S. Ambrogio".

[9] Firenze, Biblioteca Medicea Laurenziana, cod. 65.1 (con las *Historiae adversus paganos* de Paolo Orosio). Para este códice véase Lowe, *Codices latini antiquiores*, III, nb. 298.

acompañaron a Mercati incluso durante su estancia en la Vaticana hasta su vejez.

Según los documentos del archivo de la Vaticana [10] resulta que desde el año 1908 se había organizado, por deseo de Mercati, la restauración de dicho manuscrito que llegó al laboratorio de la Biblioteca Vaticana el 5 de febrero del año 1908 y volvió a Rávena en el año 1957. En ese mismo año fallecía el anciano Cardenal y en una carta del Cardenal Eugène Tisserant al Monseñor Salvatore Baldassari, arzobispo de Rávena, con fecha del 19 de noviembre del año 1957, se explica que Mercati "quería el códice en la Vaticana para controlar mejor el proceso de restauración, lo volvió a estudiar y lo dio a conocer a Lowe para su obra titulada *Codices latini antiquiores*, lo tuvo con él con infinito amor como si de veneradas reliquias se tratara".[11] En una nota adjunta a esta información se revela que el manuscrito se devolvió después de la muerte de Mercati, el cual por su interés había siempre retrasado la devolución.[12]

Es necesario añadir que el 28 de febrero del año 1900 el texto copiado por Mercati fue solicitado por August Engebrecht por encargo de la *Österreichische Akademie der Wissenschaften* de Viena para usarlo en una edición crítica de las obras de Ambrosio en el *Corpus Scriptorum Ecclesiasticorum Latinorum*; el 8 de marzo Mercati respondía a Engelbrecht confirmando el envío de su transcripción y pidiéndole al mismo tiempo que se lo devolviese para dejarlo como herencia a la Biblioteca Ambrosiana.[13] En los *Prolegomena* hasta el *De Fide* publicados en 1962, en el volumen 78 del *Corpus Scriptorum Ecclesiasticorum Latinorum*, el padre jesuita Otto Faller afirma, haciendo referencia a la copia del Mercati, que "ese apógrafo se envió a la Academia de Viena, que posteriormente

---

[10] La documentación se encuentra en la Biblioteca Apostolica Vaticana, *Arch. Bibl.* 242, XV: para mayores detalles cfr. Pasini, *Giovanni Mercati e il manoscritto ravennate*.

[11] "volle il codice nella Vaticana per sorvegliarne il restauro, di nuovo lo riprese e studiò, lo segnalò al Lowe per i suoi *Codices latini antiquiores*, lo tenne presso di sé con l'infinito amore che Gli ispiravano le venerande reliquie del passato": Biblioteca Apostolica Vaticana, *Arch. Bibl.* 242, XV, f. 218 (copia de la carta).

[12] Cfr. *ibid.*, ff. 211-13.

[13] La petición de Engelbrecht se conserva en la Biblioteca Apostolica Vaticana, *Carteggi Mercati*, cont. 7, ff. 1717-18; la respuesta de Mercati en una minuta de la cual posteriormente declara haber abreviado bajo las indicaciones del prefecto Franz Ehrle, en los ff. 1719-21.

me lo devolvió; en el año 1942 lo cotejé en Roma con el códice que había sido restaurado por deseo del ilustre investigador".[14]

He buscado la copia de Mercati tanto en la Ambrosiana como en la Vaticana sin encontrarla, ni siquiera en los archivos jesuitas donde podrían estar los documentos del padre Faller. Podría ser un manuscrito, obviamente no antiguo, pero todavía por encontrar.

## 2. Hacia la biblioteca humanística del papa Parentucelli

Pero es evidente que en la Vaticana, Mercati podía encontrar otros extraordinarios tesoros patrísticos, cuyos descubrimientos hicieron historia en las investigaciones de época humanística y que terminaron en la biblioteca de los Papas a lo largo de los siglos desde su fundación. De hecho, el origen de la Biblioteca Vaticana es humanístico, a mediados del siglo XV, y se debe a la figura de Tommaso Parentucelli, que fue Papa con el nombre de Nicolás V. Permitidme hacer un salto en el tiempo, antes del nacimiento de la Biblioteca Vaticana, cuando en la Teología del Occidente Latino, entre los siglos XII y XIV, ocurre el cambio decisivo con la Escolástica.[15] Con el origen de la Escolástica, la Teología, que era el punto neurálgico de los estudios universitarios, dio frutos decisivos. Tomás de Aquino, Alberto Magno, Buenaventura y un gran número de pensadores cambiaron radicalmente, con un método muy preciso, la teología y la filosofía de ese tiempo. Según una apropiada definición de Marie-Dominique Chenu,[16] la Teología fue vista como una disciplina científica con un propio estatuto metodológico soportado por la filosofía aristotélica.

---

[14] "Quod apographum Academiae Vindobonensi postea liberalissime traditum mihique ab ea commissum anno 1942 Romae cum codice interim ab eodem cl. v. restaurato contuli atque aliquibus locis corrigere potui": Sancti Ambrosii *Opera*, pars VIII: *De fide*. Recensuit O. Faller (Vindobonae: Hoelder-Pichler-Tempsky, 1962), pp. 21*–22*.

[15] Sobre la historia de la Escolástica es útil tomar como referencia el manual E. Gilson, *La philosophie au moyen âge: des origines patristiques à la fin du XIVᵉ siècle* (Paris: Payot, 1947); un cuadro más general y actualizado se haya en *Storia della teologia nel Medioevo*, bajo la dirección de G. D'Onofrio, II: *La grande fioritura* y III: *La teologia delle scuole* (Casale Monferrato: Piemme, 1996).

[16] En el título de esta importante obra se resume la definición de M. D. Chenu, *La théologie comme science au XIIIᵉ siècle* (París: J. Vrin, 1957), un panorama general sobre la historia de la teología de la Escolástica con la figura de San Tomás como centro del discurso.

Ello no excluía a los Padres; al contrario, los englobaba ampliamente, pero desde una perspectiva metodológica diferente al de los Padres. Estos grandes teólogos fueron llamados por parte de sus contemporáneos los "modernos" por excelencia, en oposición, no por fe o fidelidad a la Iglesia sino por su metodología y relación, a los antiguos, es decir, a los Padres. Es por eso que durante la historia de la Iglesia la palabra "Padres" se ha asociado con la palabra descubrimiento, y con ello volvemos a la edad Humanística. De hecho, como consecuencia de la crisis propulsora de la Escolástica, se vieron entonces con otra perspectiva los teólogos y los pastores del primer milenio cristiano, empezando por los latinos para proseguir con los griegos y finalmente con los orientales, leídos en sus lenguas de origen y en sus textos íntegros que poco a poco las bibliotecas más antiguas desvelaban.

Como sabemos, en este proceso de reanudación de los estudios de la Antigüedad, no solamente fueron implicados los autores paganos sino también los cristianos como Orígenes, Hilario, Cipriano, Arnobio, Lactancio, y otros escritos que la Escolástica había apartado.[17] A este punto me vienen a la mente casos excepcionales como la *Carta a Diogneto*, que fue descubierta al final de un texto que llegó a Italia en el siglo XV y fue estudiada con esmero en el siguiente siglo; o el inestimable Minucio Félix, para citar algunos textos de los primeros apologetas e, incluso yendo más atrás con el tiempo a los Padres Apostólicos, el Pastor de Hermas. También se rescataron textos de los Padres de la Iglesia, que se habían quedado en el olvido durante siglos, como por ejemplo Ambrosio, poco conocido y estudiado fuera de su propia diócesis en época medieval y recuperado a partir del siglo XV y XVI.[18] Fue en esa época de grandes descubrimientos sobre los Padres

---

[17] Una serie de ejemplos y actualizaciones sobre el redescubrimiento de los Padres se pueden encontrar en la muestra *Umanesimo e Padri della Chiesa. Manoscritti e incunaboli di testi patristici da Francesco Petrarca al primo Cinquecento*, a cura di S. Gentile (Roma: Rose, 1997); véase también la válida aportación de M. Ferrari, "*Il rilancio dei classici e dei padri*", en *Lo spazio letterario del Medioevo*, 1: *Il Medioevo latino*, directores G. Cavallo, C. Leonardi & E. Menestò, III: *La ricezione del testo* (Roma: Salerno, 1995), pp. 435–36, 439–41.

[18] Sobre el origen de la Vaticana en relación con el Humanismo y el redescubrimiento de los antiguos, véase el volumen *Le origini della Biblioteca Vaticana tra Umanesimo e Rinascimento (1447–1534)*, a cura di A. Manfredi (Città del Vaticano: Biblioteca Apostolica Vaticana, 2010).

de la Iglesia, en edad Humanística, a mediados del siglo XV, cuando nació la que hoy conocemos como Biblioteca Vaticana, la gran biblioteca papal que ha llegado hasta nuestros días conservada perfectamente a nivel institucional. En lo que se refiere a la Antigüedad clásica y cristiana la Vaticana fue uno de los mejores ejemplos de Occidente por la nueva metodología de investigación adoptada. Fue un modelo a seguir por muchas otras bibliotecas coetáneas y sucesivas y como centro de innovación en los estudios de Patrología, mientras el método filológico se hacía de cada vez más minucioso y preciso. Esto fue posible gracias a un gran humanista, Tommaso Parentucelli de Sarzana (Papa Nicolás V desde el 1447 hasta el 1455), considerado uno de los pioneros en la investigación de la Patrología moderna, que fundó y dirigió los primeros años de la Biblioteca.[19]

Mi intención de ahora en adelante es describir tan sólo una lista de hechos, iniciativas, eventos y publicaciones sobre los Padres de la Iglesia en la Vaticana desde los orígenes hasta la actualidad. No es éste el momento para desarrollar esta mole de datos; espero que sólo el mero hecho de citarlos permitan reflejar la riqueza y la vocación patrística de la Vaticana dentro del espíritu humanístico que la caracteriza.

## 3. *Los Padres en los inicios de la Biblioteca Vaticana*

El Papa Parentucelli introdujo en el núcleo de origen de su biblioteca numerosos volúmenes de los Padres, alrededor de unos 200 ejemplares latinos, empezando por San Agustín, estudiado minuciosamente por él mismo, seguido por San Ambrosio, contribuyendo a su revalorización, y continuando con San Jerónimo (con Orígenes), León y Gregorio Magno, Ireneo, Hilario, Tertuliano, Cipriano, y un gran número de manuscritos griegos de los Padres griegos, de entre los que destacan Juan Crisóstomo, seguido por Basilio, Gregorio de Nacianzo y otros.[20]

---

[19] Cfr. A. Manfredi, "*La nascita della Vaticana in età umanistica: libri e inventari da Niccolò V a Sisto IV*", en *Le origini della Biblioteca Vaticana tra Umanesimo e Rinascimento*, pp. 160–82.

[20] Cfr. *ibid.*, pp. 167–74.

Quisiera citar un caso singular que narra el hallazgo y la adquisición de la obra de Ireneo.[21] Para ello es necesario recordar que en sus múltiples viajes, Parentucelli visitó antiguas bibliotecas y recuperó en ellas libros que habían quedado en el olvido. Él había realizado estos descubrimientos en Nonantola, Lodi y Milán y en la *Grande Chartreuse*, donde había ido numerosas veces acompañando al Cardenal Niccolò Albergati. Allí mandó copiar de un apógrafo de ésta biblioteca (posteriormente perdido) un ejemplar en papel de la traducción latina del *Adversus Haereses* de Ireneo[22] que en el 1435 pudo llevarse a Italia. Este códice "de viaje", copiado en una rápida escritura gótica, se prestó temporalmente a Nicoló Niccoli y una vez devuelto a su propietario, Parentucelli lo añadió a la biblioteca que había creado. En la Vaticana, el texto del manuscrito fue corregido por el primer bibliotecario, Giovanni Tortelli, y fue copiado en un ejemplar[23] donde se percibe el cuidado en la composición, la delicadeza en la grafía y en las decoraciones elegantes y al mismo tiempo discretas: en definitiva, un códice pensado para la consulta en una biblioteca filológica tan esmerada como la biblioteca del Papa pretendía ser.

Fue gracias a esta adquisición que el texto de Ireneo entró en el círculo de los humanistas. No olvidemos que en el año 601, el papa Gregorio Magno había confesado a Eterio de Lyón que no encontraba ningún ejemplar en Roma, ni siquiera buscando durante mucho tiempo.[24] El manuscrito Vaticano fue de nuevo copiado y difundido y a partir de ese texto en el 1526, Erasmo de Rotterdam sacó la primera edición impresa de Ireneo.[25]

Una vez Papa, Parentucelli siguió cultivando su interés como patrólogo, no sólo haciendo copiar de nuevo textos que había

---

[21] Cfr. L. Gargan & A. Manfredi, *Le biblioteche dei Certosini tra Medioevo e Umanesimo. Antichi inventari – manoscritti superstiti – ricerche di codici nel sec. XV* (Città del Vaticano: Biblioteca Apostolica Vaticana, 2017), pp. 269–93.

[22] Hoy Biblioteca Apostolica Vaticana, Vat. lat. 187: cfr. *ibid.*, pp. 275–78, 281–82.

[23] Hoy Biblioteca Apostolica Vaticana, Vat. lat. 188: cfr. *ibid.*, pp. 282–85.

[24] Cfr. Gregorius Magnus, *Epistulae*, XI, 40: *Gregorii magni Opera* (Roma: Città Nuova, 1999), V/4, pp. 126–29.

[25] Divi Irenaei, episcopi Lugdunensis, *Opus eruditissimum in quinque libros digestum, in quibus mire retegit et confutat veterum haereseon impias ac portentosas opiniones*, ex vetustissimorum codicum collatione quantum licuit emendatum opera D. Erasmi Roterodami (Basileae: Froben, 1526).

descubierto y corregido, como en el caso de Ireneo, sino también recuperando numerosos textos desconocidos en ámbito Occidental, sobre todo de la vasta sección en lengua griega que él quiso enriquecer con escritos de los Padres, gran parte de los cuales eran accesibles en Occidente sólo a través de textos latinos que no eran particularmente fieles a los originales. Nicolás V no sólo fue baluarte para la recuperación de escritos patrísticos en lengua original, sino que también favoreció la difusión de nuevas y mejores versiones latinas idóneas a una escuela teológica que en aquel momento carecía de conocimientos de lengua griega.

Un caso particular es la versión latina del *Comentario* de Juan Crisóstomo *sobre el Evangelio de Mateo*, conocido parcialmente (es decir menos de la mitad) en Occidente por medio de una antigua traducción.[26] El mismo Tomás de Aquino se lamentaba por no conocer el texto completo.[27] Nicolás V se ocupó de recuperar la versión completa que tuvo como consecuencia no sólo una gran difusión y apertura al conocimiento de la exégesis patrística griega hacia los textos bíblicos sino también un mayor conocimiento de Juan Crisóstomo en Occidente.

Las investigaciones que se están realizando durante estos años sobre el núcleo más antiguo de la sección griega en la Vaticana,[28] nos desvelan la importancia de los estudios efectuados por obra de Nicolás V y su interés por recuperar libros griegos en el momento crítico de la caída del Imperio de Oriente. De hecho ordenó traer a Roma 400 manuscritos griegos, muchos de los cuales procedían de Constantinopla; algunos, como se ha podido constatar, vinieron de monte Athos. Se prevé que los estudios que se están realizando revelen nuevos datos que puedan ayudar a conocer mejor

---

[26] La traducción de las faltantes homilías fue realizada por el humanista Giorgio Trapezunzio entre los años 1448 y 1450; actualmente se conserva en la Biblioteca Apostólica Vaticana, Vat. lat. 388 (en parte autográfico) y fue impreso a principios del siglo XVIII. El códice con la dedica es el Vat. lat. 385. Respecto a éste (y junto algunas indicaciones bibliográficas sobre la traducción) véase A. Manfredi, *I codici latini di Niccolò V. Edizione degli inventari e identificazione dei manoscritti* (Città del Vaticano: Biblioteca Apostolica Vaticana, 1994), p. 42 nb. 68.

[27] La anécdota se encuentra en Vespasiano da Bisticci, *Le vite*, a cura di A. Greco, I (Firenze: Istituto nazionale di studi sul rinascimento, 1970), p. 69.

[28] Sobre la biblioteca griega de Nicolás V cfr. ahora *I codici greci di Niccolò V*, a cura di A. Manfredi & F. Potenza (Città del Vaticano: Biblioteca Apostolica Vaticana, en prensa).

la llegada de los Padres griegos a Occidente en época humanística, además de conocer la historia de importantes testimonios manuscritos.

## 4. La renovación patrística bajo el pontificado del papa Pablo III

Fue así que en la Biblioteca Vaticana se constituyó la primera sección de manuscritos patrísticos latinos y griegos. Sixto IV de la Rovere, elegido papa el año 1471 y quien reorganizó la Biblioteca, fue también un experto teólogo dotado de carácter escolástico con bases franciscanas. Por este motivo, durante su pontificado el interés humanístico por la Patrología parece venir a menos;[29] sin embargo la inmensa mole de volúmenes patrísticos, quizás el más importante de Europa en aquel momento, ya estaba consolidado.

La vocación patrística de la Vaticana sufrió, poco antes de la primera mitad del siglo XVI, un cambio radical con nuevas connotaciones, gracias a la situación inédita de Pablo III Farnese. En el año 1545, el Papa convocó el Concilio de Trento y, pasados tres años, delegó la gestión de la Biblioteca al cardenal Marcello Cervini junto a su joven colaborador Guglielmo Sirleto.[30] La celebración del Concilio impuso a la Curia y a la Vaticana ciertas exigencias de carácter bibliotecario: se necesitaban textos de Padres de la Iglesia, tanto griegos como latinos, no sólo para sostener y dar fundamento a las reflexiones teológicas, sino también para definir cuestiones jurídicas, procesales y litúrgicas. La presencia de un custodio (prefecto) como Sirleto, especializado en griego y latín e infatigable trabajador, hizo posible, motivando al resto del personal, llevar a cabo una revisión global de los fondos

---

[29] Sobre la formación y sobre la biblioteca personal de Sixto IV véase P. Piacentini, "*Ricerche sugli antichi inventari della Biblioteca Vaticana: i codici di lavoro di Sisto IV*", en *Un pontificato ed una città: Sisto IV (1471–1484)*, a cura di M. Miglio, F. Niutta, D. Quaglioni & C. Ranieri (Città del Vaticano: Scuola vaticana di paleografia, diplomatica e archivistica, 1986), pp. 114–78.

[30] Sobre Cervini y Sirleto en la Vaticana veanse, respectivamente, P. Piacentini, "*Marcello Cervini (Marcello II). La Biblioteca Vaticana e la biblioteca personale*", en *La Biblioteca Vaticana tra Riforma cattolica, crescita delle collezioni e nuovo edificio (1535–1590)*, a cura di M. Ceresa (Città del Vaticano: Biblioteca Apostolica Vaticana, 2012), pp. 105–43, y S. Lucà, *Guglielmo Sirleto e la Vaticana, ibid.*, pp. 145–88.

de la biblioteca con el objetivo de individuar los textos solicitados por el Concilio de Trento. Ello condujo a una nueva catalogación del fondo griego; y de consecuencia emergieron textos patrísticos de gran importancia: entre ellos Teodoreto de Ciro, Eustrazio de Constantinopla y los *Actos* del Concilio de Éfeso. Estas solicitudes externas junto al trabajo de búsqueda abrieron un nuevo camino de descubrimientos, todo ello documentado con espontaneidad en la correspondencia entre Cervini y Sirleto de los años 1545 a 1555. Un ejemplo (que en este caso trata un texto hagiográfico) lo encontramos en la carta que escribió Cervini a Sirleto que dice: "Le ruego me avise si encuentra algún texto donde se mencione que el emperador Constantino haya sido bautizado por el papa San Silvestre; porque me haría un gran favor". Sirleto le responde: "He encontrado este libro en el armario de la Biblioteca Vaticana donde se encuentran los libros griegos sin cadenas; ha sido un milagro que abriendo aquel libro, haya encontrado en la parte final del volumen el título de ésta maravillosa obra".[31]

En este mismo periodo, a partir de los descubrimientos del patrimonio de la Vaticana, se empezó por deseo de Cervini el gran proyecto sobre las ediciones impresas de los Padres griegos y latinos, empezando por Teodoreto.[32] Tras la muerte de Cervini, el proyecto se continuó gracias a curiales de rango como los cardenales Sirleto, Carafa y Peretti, con el patrocinio del doctísimo Gregorio XIII. Fue un proyecto que empezó varias décadas después del inicio de la Reforma y que terminó confluyendo en un con-

---

[31] Las dos cartas se encuentran en la Correspondencia entre Cervini y Sirleto que abarcan los años 1545 hasta 1555; la primera de ellas fué enviada por Cervini a Sirleto el 5 de agosto de 1545: "Et avvisatemi se havete per le mani alcun loco, dove si faccia mentione che Constantino Imperatore fusse battizato da San Silvestro Papa, che me ne farete piacere" (Biblioteca Apostolica Vaticana, *Vat. lat.* 6178, f. 62r); la segunda fue enviada por Sirleto a Cervini el 29 de febrero de 1548: "Questo libro l'ho ritrovato drento l'Armario, dove stanno li libri greci senza catena, dico in Libraria Vaticana, e certo è stato un miraculo che, havendo aperto quel libro, circa il fine ritrovai il titulo di questa bella opera" (Biblioteca Apostolica Vaticana, *Vat. lat.* 6177, f. 127r).

[32] Cfr. G. Cardinali, "*Legature 'alla Cervini'?*", Scriptorium 71 (2017), pp. 39–78; Id., "*Il Barbierinianus gr. 532, ovvero le edizioni mancate di Marcello Cervini, la filologia di Guglielmo Sirleto e il* surmenage *di Giovanni Onorio*", Byzantion 88 (2018), pp. 45–89. Mayores detalles de ello se darán en la edición de la correspondencia Cervini-Sirleto y en el volumen dedicado a la editorial promovida por Cervini entre los años 1540 y 1555, de ambos se está ocupando el mismo G. Cardinali.

junto amplio de proyectos culturales post conciliares. A ese lapso de tiempo es donde se remontan las ediciones de Juan Casiano, de Tertuliano y de Minucio Félix (cuyo *Octavius* fue reconocido como obra por sí misma, ya que hasta entonces era considerado el VIII libro del *Contra gentes* de Arnobio).

A este mismo período corresponde la creación de la dificilísima edición del Arnobio, publicado entre los años 1542 y 1543 [33] por mano de Fausto Sabeo, custodio de la Biblioteca Vaticana, basado en el único manuscrito conocido hasta entonces (y además colmo de errores).[34] Vale la pena citar la carta escrita por el tipógrafo Francesco Priscianese a Pier Vettori el 18 de octubre de 1543, donde se percibe la desesperación a propósito de esa edición, y que dice así: "Me dieron el Arnobio para imprimir; un texto, como dicen, único en el mundo, pero tan incorrecto y malaventurado [...], carente de signos de puntuación, de ortografía, de estructura y poca claridad en las palabras [...], que san Pietro o un Pier Vettori no habrían podido sacar algún beneficio" al enmendarlo ni siquiera utilizando todas sus habilidades. "Le corregimos más de tres mil errores con toda la fatiga que suponía un trabajo bien hecho, tanto que el Correggio [es decir Girolamo Ferrari de Correggio, colaborador del tipógrafo] [35] murió, el pobre hombre, y casi yo también. Finalmente lo imprimí y lo controlé otra vez".[36]

---

[33] Arnobii *Disputationum adversus gentes libri octo*, nunc primum in lucem editi (Romae: Francesco Priscianese, 1543).

[34] Dos testimonios resultan haber sobrevivido: Paris, Bibliothèque Nationale, *Paris. lat.* 1661 (que fue usado por Sabeo) y Bruxelles, Bibliothèque Royale Albert I<sup>er</sup>, 10847. Sobre ellos cfr. Arnobe, *Contre les Gentils*, I. Texte établi, traduit et commenté par H. Le Bonniec (Paris : Les Belles Lettres, 1982), pp. 96–100.

[35] Girolamo Ferrari da Correggio murió el año 1542 a la edad de 41 años: cfr. G. Tiraboschi, *Biblioteca modenese, o Notizie della vita e delle opere degli scrittori natii degli stati del serenissimo signor duca di Modena*, II (Modena: Società tipografica, 1782), pp. 273–74; Id., *Storia della letteratura italiana*, IV (Milano: Nicolò Bettoni, 1833), p. 40.

[36] "Questi miei papali mi diedero a stampare Arnobio, cioè un testo solo et unico (come dicono) al mondo, ma tanto scorretto, tanto sciagurato et di scrittura tanto ribalda et spenta et senza punti o altra ortografia o capiversi o distintione di parole o ben niuno, che san Pietro o un Pier Vettori non ne harebbe havuto honore, non che un Priscianese o un Correggio, come che egli, nello emendar libri se l'allacciasse molto in su, come sapete. Noi ne levammo più di tremila errori et vi durammo su tanta fatica et massimamente che la stampa ci incalciava, che 'l Correggio vi crepò l'anima, il poveretto, et io fui per creparvela. Finalmente e' si stampò, al quale io ho dato poi un'altra rivedidura bestiale, di maniera che mi pare ch'egli sia quasi fatto un huom da bene et che possa venire nel cospetto de'

## 5. Los Padres en la biblioteca de Sixto V

El mundo de las investigaciones había cambiado completamente: la Vaticana, fundada como una colección de manuscritos, se abría a las necesidades de los nuevos editores de imprenta, los cuales adoptaban métodos todavía muy rudimentarios basados sobre la interpretación que daban los filólogos a los textos y no por una cotejación entre manuscritos antiguos para dar una mayor fidelidad a la edición. Durante el siglo XVI la Biblioteca de los papas contribuyó de manera decisiva al campo de los descubrimientos, en respuesta a una necesidad cada vez más nítida por parte de los teólogos de comparar no sólo los autores escolásticos sino también las fuentes de tradición antigua, tanto bíblicas como patrísticas, con el objetivo de llegar lo más posible a los orígenes del cristianismo.

A finales del siglo XVI, debido a una serie de necesidades biblioteconómicas y estructurales, fue necesario la creación de un nuevo edificio para la biblioteca que aumentaba cada vez más, y fue papa Sixto V Peretti, implicado anteriormente con su trabajo en las ediciones de los Padres, quien mandó construir rápidamente una nueva sede, en la que todavía hoy se encuentra la Biblioteca Vaticana.[37]

Con la ocasión se aprovechó para reorganizar las colecciones de libros en su nueva ubicación. La colección de manuscritos bíblicos y patrísticos se fusionó con el fondo principal de manuscritos (hoy conocido como Vaticano latino). Se creó un núcleo de alrededor de 670 manuscritos de los cuales 150 eran bíblicos y 450 patrísticos, desde Tertuliano hasta Gregorio Magno, donde confluyeron tanto códices de Nicolás V como adquisiciones posteriores: todos por orden de autor y por orden cronológico y catalogados con criterios modernos para la época. Se creó así la más vasta biblioteca de manuscritos patrísticos latinos de toda Europa, asiduamente

---

galanti huomini": editado en P. Paschini, "*Un cardinale editore: Marcello Cervini*", en *Miscellanea di scritti di bibliografia ed erudizione in memoria di Luigi Ferrari* (Firenze: Olschki, 1952), pp. 383–413: 392–93.

[37] Sobre el origen y la historia de este fondo y en particular sobre la reordenación ranaldiana, véase A. Di Sante & A. Manfredi, "*I Vaticani latini: dinamiche di organizzazione e di accrescimento tra Cinque e Seicento*", en *La Vaticana nel Seicento (1590–1700). Una biblioteca di biblioteche*, a cura di C. Montuschi (Città del Vaticano: Biblioteca Apostolica Vaticana, 2014), pp. 461–502.

frecuentada por filólogos durante las épocas sucesivas y muy reconocida incluso en los últimos tiempos, gracias al amplio catálogo impreso realizado en el año 1902 por dos expertos catalogadores, Marco Vattasso y Pio Franchi de' Cavalieri, ayudados por Giovanni Mercati en lo que se refiere a la sección griega.[38] Esto significa que fue el primer volumen impreso realizado con los nuevos criterios de catalogación y promovido por el entonces prefecto, Franz Ehrle.[39] Ello contribuyó en manera exponencial a los estudios patrísticos en un momento en el que las diferentes escuelas patrísticas promovían sistemáticamente colecciones de ediciones como el *Corpus Scriptorum Ecclesiasticorum Latinorum*, las *Sources Chrétiennes* y el *Corpus Christianorum*.

Ojeando los volúmenes editados desde el siglo XX hasta nuestros días, cada vez que nos enfrentamos a la edición de un Padre de la Iglesia, se percibe con evidencia la presencia constante de éste núcleo de libros de origen humanístico y de su moderna catalogación. De ello nos da la prueba el censo bibliográfico que estamos haciendo en la Vaticana[40] y que quiere demostrar el uso de nuestros manuscritos en las ediciones patrísticas, y al mismo tiempo dar acceso a los investigadores a una bibliografía *on-line* cada vez más actualizada. De hecho estamos haciendo un escrutinio sistemático de nuestros manuscritos en algunas colecciones patrísticas de mayor relevancia: *Texte und Untersuchungen*, *Corpus Scriptorum Ecclesiasticorum Latinorum* y *Corpus Christianorum*. Con ello esperamos contribuir mayormente a los estudios de patrística y filología del período tardo antiguo y dar a conocer cada vez más nuestro patrimonio manuscrito, poniendo al día nuestros catálogos seculares.

---

[38] *Codices Vaticani Latini*. Recensuerunt M. Vattasso et P. Franchi de' Cavalieri, I: *Codices 1–678* (Romae: Bibliotheca Apostolica Vaticana, 1902). Por lo que se refiere a la colaboración de Giovanni Mercati cfr. p. xiv.

[39] Según las *Leges quas curatores bibliothecae Vaticanae in codicibus Latinis recensendis sibi constituerunt*: reproducidas *ibid.*, pp. x–xiv.

[40] Se ha empezado una búsqueda bibliográfica de todos los manuscritos vaticanos citados en las principales colecciones donde están editados los textos patríticos tanto griegos como latinos. Dicha búsqueda se ha centrado en el *Corpus scriptorum ecclesiasticorum latinorum* y parte de los *Texte und Untersuchungen* a los cuales se puede acceder a través del catálogo informático de la Vaticana; el objetivo es continuar con las principales colecciones patrísticas como el *Corpus Christianorum* y las *Sources Chrétiennes*.

## 6. *El siglo XVII*

Vuelvo de nuevo al trascurrir de los siglos y con ello a la relación entre los estudios patrísticos y la Vaticana, con un comentario rápido sobre todo en el siglo XVII: un siglo de gran expansión para la Vaticana gracias a la llegada de tres bibliotecas enteras: la Palatina de Heidelberg, la biblioteca de los duques de Urbino y la biblioteca que perteneció a la reina Cristina de Suecia.[41] Estas bibliotecas incrementaron el ya gran patrimonio de testimonios patrísticos de la Vaticana. En particular, con la llegada de la colección de Cristina, la Vaticana se enriqueció de un imponente número de manuscritos altomedievales de ámbito carolingio, y por otra parte, con la Biblioteca Palatina, de un rico patrimonio de la biblioteca monástica de Lorsch, uno de los centros de investigación más vigorosos de Europa del Norte.

Los doctos custodios de aquellos tiempos, además de catalogar el material, se propusieron valorizar el contenido textual. Aquí me paro para hablar de la figura de Leone Allacci, originario de Grecia, pero totalmente integrado en el ambiente cultural de Roma en su época. Trabajó en la Vaticana durante más de cincuenta años como *scriptor graecus*,[42] y fue mérito suyo que la Biblioteca Palatina llegara a Roma. En el último decenio de su permanencia en la Vaticana se convirtió en segundo custodio, para terminar como primer custodio en los últimos años, cargo correspondiente al actual prefecto. Griego de Quíos, se formó en Roma adquiriendo pleno conocimiento de ambas lenguas, tanto latina como griega. Su gran competencia le permitió dirigir la preparación de un catálogo de manuscritos griegos,[43] publicar estudios sobre teología y llevar a cabo búsquedas sobre las relaciones entre las Iglesias romana y griega. Entre las ediciones de textos antiguos destacan, junto a los clásicos y bizantinos, las *editiones principes* de los Padres griegos con traducción latina. En el año 1629 se editó bajo su

---

[41] Sobre la adquisición de las tres bibliotecas véanse, respectivamente, C. Montuschi, *Le biblioteche di Heidelberg in Vaticana: i fondi Palatini*, en *La Vaticana nel Seicento*, pp. 279–336, M. Peruzzi, *"Lectissima politissimaque volumina": i fondi Urbinati, ibid.*, pp. 337–94, y E. Nilsson Nylander, *"Ingens est codicum numerus": i fondi Reginensi, ibid.*, pp. 395–426.

[42] Sobra Leone Allacci cfr. D. Surace, *Lo sviluppo dei Vaticani greci tra fondo antico e accessioni seicentesche, ibid.*, pp. 503–42: 523.

[43] Cfr. T. Janz, *Vita e opere di Leone Allacci, ibid.*, pp. 199–204.

supervisión la homilía de Orígenes sobre la maga de Endor y el estudio de Eustacio de Antioquía sobre el mismo argumento contra la interpretación de Orígenes, precedido por un comentario del *Hexamerón* atribuido a Eustacio de Antioquía, pero no suyo.[44] En el año 1656 salió el *Symposium* de Metodio de Olimpo[45] y en el año 1668 los cuatro libros del epistolario de Nilo de Ancira, discípulo de Juan Crisóstomo.[46]

Una carta de Allacci a Antonio Caracciolo con fecha del 1 de marzo de 1631 nos permite ver su gran sentido crítico: para la edición de las cartas de Teodoreto de Ciro, que en el 1642 salieron gracias a Jacques Sirmond,[47] se mandó a Francia una copia de un manuscrito vaticano al que habían sido eliminadas dos cartas definidas peligrosas por la fama de Cirilo de Alejandría y del obispo de Roma de aquel tiempo.[48] Allacci narra en su carta su oposición a aquella mutilación, primero porque el contenido de esas cartas ya había sido usado por Baronio y eran ya de dominio público y segundo porque (cito textualmente) "no era cosa buena mandar un libro mutilado, sobre todo viniendo del Vaticano, porque los malintencionados habrían tenido la oportunidad de decir que al igual que este libro, también a los otros se quitaba aquello que no gustaba o no era favorable y se hacía salir solo aquello que podía dar beneficios".[49] Allacci proponía sin embargo que se pusiera alguna anotación marginal en las zonas más críticas, para así poder advertir adecuadamente al lector de supuestos peligros. No tuvieron en

---

[44] Eustathii *In Hexahemeron commentarius* ac *De engastrimytho dissertatio aduersus Originem*. Origenis *De eadem engastrimytho*. Leo Allatius primus in lucem protulit, latine vertit (Lugduni: L. Durand, 1629).

[45] Methodii *Convivium*. Leo Allatius hactenus non editum primus graece vulgavit, latine vertit (Romae: S. Congreg. de Propaganda Fide, 1656).

[46] Nili Ascetae *Epistolarvm libri IV* interprete Leone Allatio (Romae: Typis Barberinis, 1668).

[47] Theodoreti episcopi Cyri *Opera omnia in quatuor tomos distributa*, cura et studio I. Sirmondi (Lutetiae Parisiorum: Sebastiani Cramoisy, 1642).

[48] Cartas 112 (*ibid.*, III, pp. 982–84) y 125 (*ibid.*, IV, pp. 702–04).

[49] "Risposi che non era ben fatto mandare il libro mutilo mentre si diceva che usciva dal Vaticano, perché haveriano preso occasione li maligni di dire, che come in questo così anchora nelli altri libri si cavava quello che non piaceva, ò favoriva, solo si dava fuora quello che faceva per se, et a mè mi pareva meglio farci qualche annotatione marginale all'istesso loco dove s'avvertisse il lettore, e si scoprisse il veleno" (Napoli, Biblioteca Nazionale, XIII.B.39, ff. 141v–142r): testo citato en Th. Cerbu, *Tra servizio e ambizione: Allacci studioso e bibliotecario nella corrispondenza con Antonio Caracciolo*, en *La Vaticana nel Seicento*, pp. 175–98: 186.

cuenta las observaciones de Allacci y se mandó una copia carente de las cartas incriminadas. Sucesivamente, cuando estas dos cartas fueron pedidas de nuevo a la Vaticana, el custodio Lucas Holste las envió, siguiendo las mismas observaciones que había hecho Allacci en su momento,[50] y la edición salió con las dos cartas que faltaban.

En este clima erudito va remarcada la relación entre la Vaticana y los editores Maurinos, es decir los benedictinos de la congregación de Saint-Maure, que en el siglo XVII se dedicaron con gran empeño a realizar una famosa y conocida edición de Agustín, en la cual participaron, utilizando numerosos testimonios manuscritos de gran nivel, investigadores que hoy resultan ser pioneros en la paleografía y en la catalogación de manuscritos.[51]

La edición maurina, reeditada en Migne, ha sido por siglos un instrumento fundamental para leer Agustín y se usa todavía hoy para obras donde falta una edición más fiable. Un examen cuidadoso en ámbito patrístico realizado actualmente nos desvela que los Maurinos no se interesaron por todas las colecciones que poseía la Vaticana, sino casi exclusivamente por los *Vaticani latini*, exceptuando algún que otro códice Urbinate. Este dato podría sorprender si se piensa que la investigación se hizo a mitad del siglo XVII, cuando en la Vaticana habían ya llegado otras colecciones de manuscritos pero con testimonios de gran importancia sobre Agustín. Esto podría explicarse si se estudian las condiciones de los catálogos que estaban a disposición en aquel momento: sólo los *Vaticani latini* tenían un inventario manuscrito, hoy todavía en uso; y por eso nace la necesidad de poner al día los catálogos para poder así ayudar a los editores de textos.

### 7. *Assemani, Mai y Pitra*

En el siglo XVIII la Biblioteca Vaticana se enriqueció de numerosos manuscritos orientales – coptos, etíopes, árabes, persas, turcos y sirios – adquiridos por el Maronita Giuseppe Simonio Assemani

---

[50] Cfr. Cerbu, *Tra servizio e ambizione*, pp. 186–87.
[51] Cfr. la recensión de A. Manfredi a M. M. Gorman, *The Manuscript Traditions of the Works of St Augustine* (Firenze: Sismel-Edizioni del Galluzzo, 2001), en *Studi medievali*, s. III, 44 (2003), pp. 253–59.

en el viaje que hizo por Oriente durante los años 1715 y 1717.[52] Cuando regresó a Roma, Assemani, por aquel entonces *scriptor orientalis* de la Biblioteca (más tarde segundo y después primer custodio), publicó una obra histórico-literaria de gran calidad científica, titulada *Bibliotheca Orientalis Clementino-Vaticana*[53] basada en la investigación directa de las fuentes manuscritas del Oriente Cristiano. De hecho, en ella se ofrecía un desarrollo histórico del mundo patrístico sirio, con sus múltiples articulaciones de carácter dogmático-ritual, dedicando tres diferentes volúmenes: el primero a los autores sirio-ortodoxos, el segundo a los sirio-monofisitas y el último a los sirio-nestorianos, en base a la denominación en uso de aquella época. Investigador versátil y docto, Assemani se había instruido también en las lenguas latina y griega en Roma. Gracias a su competencia en ámbito griego, publicó una gramática griega de más de mil páginas,[54] imprimida en la Tipografía de la Venerable Capilla del Santísimo Sacramento de Urbino. En esa tipografía se había impreso el *Menologio griego de Basilio segundo*, documento de gran relevancia para la hagiografía bizantina, de cuya publicación fue autor el mismo Assemani, como lo afirman los últimos estudios que se han realizado sobre el argumento.[55] En este contexto recordamos el gran trabajo patrístico al que Assemani asoció su propio nombre como editor del conocido Efrén griego – textos legados en griego bajo el nombre de Efrén – que publicó en tres volúmenes; a éstos le siguieron otros tres volúme-

---

[52] Precisamente entre el 30 de junio de 1715 y el 9 de enero de 1717, "iubente Clemente XI": cfr. A. Mazzoccone & D. V. Proverbio, *Giuseppe Simonio Assemani e la Biblioteca Vaticana: una cronaca evenemenziale*, en *La Biblioteca Vaticana e le arti nel secolo dei Lumi (1700–1797)*, a cura di B. Jatta (Città del Vaticano: Biblioteca Apostolica Vaticana, 2016), pp. 313–35: 314.

[53] *Bibliotheca orientalis Clementino-Vaticana* (Roma: S. Congreg. de Propaganda Fide, 1719–1728) I: *De scriptoribus Syris orthodoxis*, 1719; II: *De scriptoribus Syris monophysitis*, 1721; III/1: *De scriptoribus Syris Nestorianis*, 1725; III/2: *De Syris Nestorianis*, 1728.

[54] G. S. Assemani, *Nuova grammatica per apprendere agevolmente la lingua greca* (Urbino: Stamperia della Venerabile Cappella del SS. Sagramento, per lo Stampator Camerale, 1737).

[55] *Menologium Graecorum jussu Basilii imperatoris Graece olim editum*. Nunc primum Graece et Latine prodit, studio et opera A. Albani (Urbini: ex Typographia venerabilis Cappellae SS.mi Sacramenti apud Antonium Fantauzzi, 1727). Por lo que refiere a la atribución de la obra a Assemani cfr. Mazzoccone & Proverbio, *Giuseppe Simonio Assemani*, pp. 318, 330 nt. 50 (en particular, Biblioteca Apostolica Vaticana, *Arch. Cap. S. Pietro*, caps., XII.277, f. 452r).

nes dedicados a los textos de Efrén en lengua siria, publicados por el jesuita Maronita Pietro Benedetti (Butrus Mubarak/Ambarach).[56] Fue una obra extremadamente amplia y costosa, que se hizo notar en las cajas administrativas de la Biblioteca, como se puede leer en la documentación consultada recientemente.[57]

El siglo XIX se caracteriza por dos notos investigadores y editores: el prefecto y más tarde cardenal bibliotecario Angelo Mai, que trabajó principalmente en la primera mitad del siglo, y el cardenal bibliotecario Jean-Baptiste Pitra, en la segunda mitad de siglo. Cuando fue nombrado prefecto de la Vaticana, Angelo Mai ya poseía diez años de experiencia y de estudio sobre los códices palimpsestos en la Biblioteca Ambrosiana de Milán y había investigado sus fondos, como él mismo afirma: "Empecé a examinar por orden los códices de esta prestigiosa Biblioteca Ambrosiana. ¡Oh, qué riqueza en cada lengua y materia! He encontrado varias cosas raras e importantes [...] ¡Cuántos proyectos me venían a la mente!",[58] y empezó enseguida a publicar textos inéditos. Una vez llegado a la Vaticana repitió la misma operación, revisando los manuscritos, en particular los palimpsestos, reconociendo en ellos los textos inéditos. Mai no tenía un interés específico hacia los Padres: anhelaba hallar textos inéditos, fueran paganos o cristianos, clásicos o tardo antiguos.

De todas formas debemos a Mai la genialidad de una organización editorial moderna, con la creación de varias colecciones editoriales: una dedicada a la copia de los códices más célebres, después la *Scriptorum veterum nova collectio*,[59] de mayor formato,

---

[56] *Sancti* Ephraem Syri *Opera omnia quae exstant*, Graece, Syriace, Latine, in sex tomos distributa (Romae: Typographia Pontificia Vaticana apud Joannem Mariam Henricum Salvioni, 1732–1746): Graece et Latine, I: 1732, II: 1743, III:1746; Syriace et Latine, I: 1737, II:1740, III, 1743.

[57] Cfr. Mazzoccone & Proverbio, *Giuseppe Simonio Assemani*, pp. 317, 329 ntt. 33–38 (en particular, véase Biblioteca Apostolica Vaticana, *Arch. Bibl.* 42, f. 329rv).

[58] "Io mi rivolsi ad esaminare per ordine i Codici di questa insigne Ambrosiana. Oh, che ricchezze in ogni lingua e materia! Ho trovate varie cose rare e importanti, e ne ho fatto memoria. Quanti progetti mi si presentavano alla mente!": carta del 30 de marzo de 1813 dirigida a su maestro Giovanni Andrés: A. Mai, *Epistolario*, I: *giugno 1799 – ottobre 1819*, a cura di G. Gervasoni (Firenze: Le Monnier, 1954), pp. 76–79: 77.

[59] *Scriptorum veterum nova collectio e Vaticanis codicibus edita ab A. Maio*, I–X (Romae: apud Burliaeum, 1825–1838).

destinada a las obras más importantes (que inicia con las *Quaestiones evangelicae* de Eusebio de Cesarea); luego los *Classici auctores e Vaticanis codicibus*,[60] casi de bolsillo y más económica, pensados para ciertas obras seleccionadas; y finalmente el *Spicilegium romanum*,[61] con textos también en lengua vulgar con carácter educativo y moralizante (entre ellos, por ejemplo, las *Laudes* y la *Narratio miraculorum sanctorum Cyri et Iohannis* de Sofronio de Jerusalén).

De interés más patrístico fue sin embargo la dirección que tomó Jean-Baptiste Pitra, quien había colaborado con Jacques Paul Migne en la *Patrologia* y que se acercaba más a la tradición de la erudición benedictina (de los Mabillon y de los Montfaucon). Son de él el *Spicilegium Solesmense*[62] (con estudios adjuntos de las cartas de Pablo atribuidos a Hilario de Poitiers, la *Apología* de Melitón de Sardes en sirio y la *Clavis Scripturae* del Pseudo Melitón); los *Analecta Sacra*[63] (donde publica los *Cantica* de Romano el Mélodo, el himno *Akathistos* y otros textos himnográficos, otra recensión de la *Clavis Scripturae*, muchos textos de Padres antenicenos, de entre ellos Hipólito y los *Comentarios in salmos* de Orígenes); y los *Analecta novissima*.[64]

En su edad madura, el mismo Angelo Mai se apoyará a la obra de Pitra, cuando en la *Nova Patrum Bibliotheca*[65] publicará textos inéditos de los Padres. Quien revise los índices encontrará varios *Sermones* de Agustín y su *De Scriptura sacra speculum*, el *Comentario a Lucas* de Cirilo de Alejandría, las *Cartas festales* de Atanasio en siriaco con traducción latina, los *Comentarios a los doce profetas, a los salmos* y *al evangelio de Juan* de Teodoro de Mopsuestia, textos de Hilario de Poiters, Basilio Magno, Gregorio de Nisa, Juan Crisóstomo, Dídimo de Alejandría.

---

[60] *Classicorum auctorum e Vaticanis codicibus editorum tomi I–X* (Romae: Typis Vaticanis, 1828–1838).

[61] *Spicilegium Romanum*, I–X (Romae: Typis Collegii Urbani, 1839–1844).

[62] *Spicilegium Solesmense*, I–IV (Parisiis: Firmin Didot fratres, 1852–1858).

[63] *Analecta sacra Spicilegio Solesmensi parata*, I–VIII (Parisiis: A. Jouby et Roger, 1876–1884).

[64] *Analecta novissima. Spicilegii Solesmensis altera continuatio*, I–II (Parisiis: Roger et Chernowitz, 1885–1888).

[65] *Novae Patrum bibliothecae tomi I–X* (Romae: Typis sacri Consilii Propagando Christiano nomini, 1852–1905). Tras la muerte de Angelo Mai, Giuseppe Cozza-Luzzi continuó con la publicación.

## 8. *Los siglos XIX y XX*

Con esto llegamos a los años de la generación de investigadores que apenas preceden la figura de Giovanni Mercati, del cual empecé a hablar: me refiero en particular al alumno preferido de Mai, Giovanni Battista de' Rossi, que en cierto modo fue maestro de Mercati y es conocido como arqueólogo y epigrafista de la Roma cristiana de los orígenes, colaborador de igual grado de Theodor Mommsen. Aquí también entra en juego la Patrología, con los descubrimientos que iban ampliando el panorama de las investigaciones arqueológicas. De Rossi no sólo fue alumno de Mai, que lo sostuvo en sus investigaciones arqueológicas, sino también por muchísimos años empleado en la Vaticana como escritor y catalogador de manuscritos.

Nos acercamos así a la escuela histórica que, perfeccionando el método de los humanistas con el rigor de las ciencias histórico-filológicas modernas, llega a los primeros años del siglo XX, chocando en relación al modernismo con la exigencia no fácil de mantener alto el nivel de rigor en los estudios y a la vez no decaer de la sana doctrina y del método teológico que en esos momentos estaba influido a menudo por la apologética. También la Vaticana ha sido testigo de estas tensiones: los personajes ya nombrados como Erhle, Mercati y Tisserant supieron hacer síntesis de éstas, produciendo obras de gran valor e iniciando una verdadera escuela de estudios eruditos y filológicos que mantuvo durante todo el siglo XX el rigor de aquellos tiempos y el gusto de los descubrimientos en plena relación con otras escuelas, no necesariamente confesionales, sino incluso abiertas al método riguroso y a la tensión por la búsqueda de la verdad. Salieron así numerosos estudios de nuestras disciplinas, una de ellas ya mencionada al principio con el descubrimiento del *Códice de Rávena* de San Ambrosio.

No es un caso que el primer volumen de los *Codices latini antiquiores* esté dedicado a la Vaticana, primera de la lista y lugar predilecto de los estudios paleográficos y codicológicos cada vez más abierta a aquel aflujo internacional, sobre todo después de la reforma tan anhelada por León XIII de favorecer los estudios históricos y que todavía hoy hace de la biblioteca de los papas un centro internacional de la diplomacia de la investigación y la cultura.

## 9. La *"vocación patrística"* de la Biblioteca Vaticana en nuestros días

Y así llegamos a nuestros días: además de mantener vivo en nuestros investigadores y en las relaciones institucionales el carácter riguroso nacido en aquellos años lejanos del Humanismo, la Vaticana evoluciona tecnológicamente para facilitar y mejorar el acceso a sus manuscritos, fuente de grandes descubrimientos durante tantos siglos. En la vasta campaña de digitalización se ha pensado por lo tanto en dar un espacio privilegiado a aquella colección originaria bíblica y patrística al principio de los *Vaticani latini*, casi totalmente ya disponible *on line* y dentro de poco dotada de un sistemático aparato de metadatos que facilitará las investigaciones y búsquedas del amplio material conservado.

La digitalización de los manuscritos de la Biblioteca Vaticana es una empresa titánica: un proyecto que abarca la colección entera de los ochenta mil manuscritos conservados en la Biblioteca, es decir unos 40 millones de páginas, con una mole de datos informáticos del orden de 45 petabytes (es decir 45 mil millones de millones de bytes!) No es éste el momento ni el lugar para comentarlo, pero cabe decir que es un reto muy importante y delicado bajo muchos puntos de vista, y no sólo por el coste. Implica la elección del método apropiado para fotografiar, para facilitar la consultación *on line*, para ocuparse de la conservación a largo tiempo de los datos y muchas cosas más.[66]

Pero quisiera subrayar que se renueva de esta manera el espíritu humanístico que la Vaticana ha recibido desde sus orígenes en los años del papa Nicolás V: ese espíritu que nos ha enseñado la pasión y el rigor científico en las investigaciones que se realizan, y la necesidad de consultar las fuentes y sopesar los documentos sobre todo en lo que concierne a los Padres, como he intentado describir hasta ahora. El mismo espíritu humanístico nos ha llevado a valorar al hombre y sus inquietudes, que se pueden escrutar sólo gracias a una búsqueda multiforme y compartida. Y quien

---

[66] Cfr. *"La digitalizzazione dei manoscritti presso la Biblioteca Apostolica Vaticana"*, *DigItalia* 9 (2014), n° 2 (*Atti del Convegno "Manuscript digitization and on line accessibility. What's going on?" International workshop, Roma, Biblioteca Vallicelliana, 23 ottobre 2014*, a cura di E. Caldelli, M. Maniaci, S. Zamponi), pp. 10–16.

estudia los Padres participa a esta pasión y siente viva la búsqueda de la verdad como verdad del hombre amado por Dios, encontrado y redimido por Él.

Y por último, y no de menor importancia, el espíritu humanístico nos ha inculcado el empeño a ofrecer todos los medios posibles que permitan compartir la información. De entre ellos ahora forma parte la reproducción digital. Desde sus orígenes la Biblioteca Vaticana ha puesto a disposición de los investigadores y de forma gratuita los bienes culturales que posee; hoy este mismo servicio se integra con otro instrumento que pone a merced del investigador los mismos bienes por vía telemática. Se han estudiado los Padres, se han realizado ediciones, se ha facilitado la consulta por vía telemática. El espíritu humanístico, que anima la Biblioteca Vaticana y que acabo de mencionar, ha ofrecido un nido fecundo para los estudios de los Padres y para la "vocación patrística".

## *Abstract*

The rediscoveries of manuscripts from Late Antiquity are linked to the rediscoveries of the humanistic age, when the Vatican Library was instituted by the will of Pope Nicholas V Parentucelli (1447-1455). This contribution initially focuses on describing the discovery of the *Codice ravennate di Sant'Ambrogio* by Giovanni Mercati in 1894. Then, it delves more directly into the topic, mentioning the renewal that, with the advent of Humanism, leads to the rediscovery of the Fathers. In this context, the *Vaticana* is marked, from its inception, by a "humanistic spirit" and, in it, by a specific "patristic vocation". To corroborate this, a list of facts, in research and publications, is offered, which testifies over the centuries to this "vocation", which begins with the arrival in the library of the writings of Irenaeus, Ambrose, Augustine, John Chrysostom. In the sixteenth century studies and editions of the Fathers stand out (by Cervini and Sirleto). Then the time came for the Greek studies of Allacci, the browsing of the manuscripts by the Maurinis for their editions, the arrival of new important patristic witnesses in the Palatine codices of Heidelberg and in the library of Queen Christina of Sweden, the study of oriental patristic by the Assemani. In the nineteenth century, the researches and editions of unpublished works by Angelo Mai and Jean-Baptiste Pitra stand out. Finally, we come back to Giovanni Mercati and the most recent researches, to reaffirm that "patristic vocation" of the Vatican Apostolic Library, which remains alive even today in an uninterrupted development.

ANGELO DI BERARDINO
*Institutum Patristicum Augustiniamum, Italy*

# THE IMPACT OF RECENT ARCHAEOLOGICAL, HISTORICAL AND LITERARY DISCOVERIES FOR THE STUDY OF PATRISTICS

*The International Patristic Association.* Who would have thought, only a few years ago, that a congress of this magnitude, due to the large number of scholars of so many nationalities, would have taken place in a city little-known in Europe, a city in the Cuyo region of Argentina? This is not just any congress, but a congress rich in papers, ideas and scholars from the five continents. Yet another very significant element is the large number of native participants from Latin America. This is also a sign that the winemakers of the vast vineyard of the Fathers of the Church are now also found on all continents. In the Far East there are numerous conferences among scholars of the Pacific Rim, that is, between Japan, Korea and Australia, with connections to the Pacific coast of the United States.

It is enough to leaf through the *Annuaire of the International Patristic Association*, which is published every two years, to realize the growth of Patristic Studies, not only worldwide, but also in Latin America itself. Dr Patricia Ciner suggested that I mention something about the AIEP / NAPS before proceeding with my intervention. AIEP was born in France, in Paris, in 1965 above all by the work of French scholars, the most qualified during those years. However, the official foundation took place at Oxford in 1967 and the association was refounded at Oxford in 1979. With the work of C. Mondésert, the *Bulletin* resurfaces in 1980, which from then on will be published and distributed freely by Brepols.

Fr. Mondésert, in the introduction to the Bulletin, talks about the postal difficulties of preparing the *Bulletin*. At that time strikes were common in Europe and took place at different times in European countries, delaying or eliminating letters. Sometimes the letters took months to arrive at their destinations. I myself prepared the *Bulletin* for 17 years. Today, thanks to Lorenzo Perrone and Marco Rizzi, it has become a good volume of information and bibliography. I think I can say that each issue contains more information about the individual volumes of the glorious *Bibliographia Patristica*, which disappeared in 1997 (nos 34–35). In my time, communication was still difficult, especially with Eastern Europe. Today we send information anywhere by e-mail, which immediately reaches the recipient and without the additional charge of stamps. I must also mention another difficulty of my time: many professors sent their letters written by hand. It was not easy to decrypt their writing.

In the early years of the association, members came from only a few countries: England, the two Germanies, Austria, Belgium, France, Greece, Italy and Ireland (one person). The nations with richer activities were Germany, France and Belgium. In 1980 there were 244 members, of whom over half (128) were French or foreigners residing in France. Only a few were from Eastern Europe and some were not European (24 countries, or 25 with the two Germanies). In 1983 the paying members rose to 420. In Issue 14 of the Bulletin (1987) the abbreviation AIEP / IAPS is used for the first time. The use of English increases, but the members of North America do not increase because there is a North American Patristic Society (NAPS) which was founded on December 29, 1980. After the fall of the Berlin Wall, members of Eastern Europe increased in number, in fact in 1995 members of AIEP / IAPS numbered 620. In 2006, 650 members came from forty nations. Today there are over 900 members from 53 nations.

In 1982, only four academics from Latin America were members of AIEP / IAPS: two from Chile, Sergio Zañartu and the young Oscar Velásquez; one from Argentina, the malagueño Francisco García Bazán, a very fruitful scholar, and a Mexican, the Dominican Ramos. Today there are 18 Chilean members, and 38 from Argentina, many more than from Spain with just 24. There are also other members of other nations.

*Terminology issues.* In October 1983 I was a guest, along with Adolf Martin Ritter, of Willy Rordorf in his home on the outskirts of Neuchâtel. During the conversation I used the term "patristic". The two Protestant friends were amazed, that I, a Catholic, used a term typical of the Protestant tradition. I too was surprised that they were so surprised. For me that use was normal, coming from the Augustinianum, which in its header uses the adjective *patristicum*: *Institutum Patristicum Augustinianum*, an institution officially founded in 1969. As we know that adjective was coined by Johannes Gerhard (1582–1637).

The work of Jerome – *De viris illustribus* –, who uses Eusebius of Caesarea, constitutes the premise of the kind of treatment and studies that from the seventeenth century onwards, with the impulse of the Lutheran Johannes Gerhard (1582–1637), will be called "patrology". The question of terminology is important because the modern manuals bear different titles: Patrology, (History of) Ancient Christian literature, ancient ecclesiastical literature, sometimes also Patristic literature or even Patristics.

Gerhard is the author of *Patrologia sive de primitivae Ecclesiae christianae doctorum vita ac lucubrationibus opusculum posthumum*,[1] which goes from the second century (Hermas) up to Bellarmine († 1621), his contemporary. With this title, he creates the term "patrology", which for him embraces "the life and thought of the doctors of the primitive Christian church". The concept of "primitive church" is too vast, as it extends until its time. In the dedication he writes that the Fathers are a divine blessing: *Patrum scripta fidei regulam ac credendi vel Scripturam exponendi unicam vel primam normam*, provided that the word of God is found in the Sacred Scriptures *unicum credendi principium esse et articulorum fidei normam* (p. a2). Of each author he cites the sources, describes the content of the work and makes numerous critical observations. He often quotes the opinions of Baronius (*Annales Ecclesiastici*) and Bellarmine.[2] Among the early Christian writers, he also places Dionisius the Areopagite and the Ps.-clementines, which he criticizes for inaccuracies. Bellarmine, with the *De scriptoribus ecclesiasticis*, which includes the

---

[1] Ienae: Sengenwaldus, 1653, reprinted 1668 and 1773.
[2] R. Bellarminus, *De scriptoribus ecclesiasticis liber unus, cum adiunctis indicibus undecim et brevi chronologia ab orbe condito usque ad annum 1612* (Romae: Ex Typographia Bartholomaei Zannetti 1913) (The work was defined by Dupin as a "traité expres").

biblical books and some Jewish authors – Joseph Flavius –, writes a very schematic introductory summary for the reading of the writers up to his time, staggered down the centuries. Bellarmine's work – the first handbook – has been a huge success, because not only has it been reprinted dozens of times in the sixteenth century, but it has also been carried out by several authors (Ph. Labbe, Oudin, A. du Saussay [3]) and many have drawn from him.

Now the adjective "patristic" has changed meaning, especially in the last century. First of all, it became a noun: and we say the *patristic*; the patristics; Patristik, patristique, patrística, patristica, etc. Since it also means the historical and doctrinal study of ancient Christian writers, it has become synonymous with patrology. Moreover, in historiography, it also indicates the historical period in which these authors have lived and worked, the complex of their works, and the doctrine contained in them. Its horizon has expanded or narrowed in many directions of time, space and languages. In the authors of 1600, the treatises reached until their years; then the period reduced slowly: for example, the Migne goes up to 1200. In the studies of the last centuries it went even farther back: to Beda / John Damascene; Gregory the Great († 604); the council of Chalcedon (451).

*Growth of studies.* From the beginning of the 1900s, an expansion began in terms of the geographical space of the authors and of the ancient languages studied.[4] This phenomenon is even more significant for the growth of patristic studies. The manuals normally did not mention the ancient Christian writers who had written in languages which were not Greek or Latin. When the

---

[3] Philippe Labbe (Labbaeus; † 1667), *Dissertatio de scriptoribus ecclesiasticis*, Parisiis: *Sebastian Cramoisy*, 1660 (in two volumes); Casimir Oudin, a catholic who became a protestant († 1717), wrote a work in three volumes, the scope of which was carried to the fifteenth century, and which was published posthumously. In 1668 he had published another work as a supplement to that by Bellarmine and those by other authors, in three volumes (*Supplementum de scriptoribus vel scriptis ecclesiasticis a Bellarmino omissis, Parisiis, Apud Antonium Dezallier 1686*); André Du Saussay, *Insignis libri de scriptoribus ecclesiasticis, eminentissimi cardinalis Bellarimini continuatio: ab anno 1500, in quo desinit, ad annu[m] 1600. quo incipit sequentis sæculi exordium*, Tulli Leucorum: Les Laurents, 1635.

[4] Hanns Christof Brennecke, Volker Henning Drecoll, Christoph Markschies, "Patristik vor Begin des Ersten Weltkrieges zwischen Altertumswissenschaft und Theologie", *Zeitschrift für Antikes Christentum. Journal for Ancient Christianity* 15 (2011), 7–196.

Assemani[5] relatives published translations of Syriac works into Latin, some Syrian authors also began to be considered, but very sporadically. In the manuals in circulation at the beginning of the last century, Christian authors who had not written in Greek or Latin were excluded, as is still the case today in the manuals of the Byzantine tradition, which are interested only in Greek writers, and only sometimes in Latin writers.[6]

As we can see from this congress, the horizon is now much broader, because we also study the authors of Syria, Armenians and Georgians, Copts, Ethiopians, texts in ancient gothic, Celtic, Pahlavi, etc. Still in the nineteenth century, the Catholic clergy did not read the Fathers. They were forced to study the calendar and how to calculate the date of Easter – a special course was mandatory – but they did not go deeper into the ancient Christian tradition. In an American Protestant environment, one passed from the study of the Bible to Luther, neglecting centuries of Christian reflection and theological elaboration.

The growth of bibliographic collections, such as the AIEP / NAPS Bulletin, the Année philologique, and the other bibliographic collections (RHE, *Bibliographia spiritualitatis*, *Archivum Historiae Pontificia*, *Ephemerides Theologicae Lovanienses*) marks a greater interest in the study of Christian antiquity. In this case the term "patristic" may seem reductive, as we also see in this rich congress. In fact, we are not talking only about Christian authors, the interventions in the program deal with the discovery of manuscripts of different fields (Qumran, Gnostics, Origen, Augustine, etc.), of codicology, of archeology, etc. Our horizon has become increasingly interdisciplinary, so we often use the syntagma "Christian antiquity", "Christian antiquities", or Early Christian Studies. Elizabeth C. Clark of Duke University high-

---

[5] Five members of a Maronite Catholic family who lived in Rome in the eighteenth and nineteenth centuries. They were Orientalist scholars and catalogers of oriental manuscripts preserved in Italy and in the Vatican. Translators into Latin of many works written in oriental languages (*Bibliotheca Orientalis Clementino-Vaticana, Romae*: Sacrae Congregationis de Propaganda Fide, 1719-1728), in particular the translation of Ephrem *(Sancti Ephraemi Syri opera omnia,* Typographia Vaticana, J.M.H. Salvioni, 1732).

[6] Indeed, often these manuals of Byzantine tradition also exclude the Latin authors.

lighted this process in the evolution of studies in *From Patristics to Early Christian Studies*.[7]

What are the reasons? Here I list the main ones but I will then only focus on some issues. 1) Recourse to sources, starting with the study of liturgy and theology; 2) Geographical and linguistic extension of the studies; 3) Great interest for late antiquity; 4) the multiplication of journals and study centers; 5) Reforms in churches and recourse to ancient tradition; 6) Ecumenism for rediscovery; 7) The numerous discoveries of the last decades in the archaeological and papyrological fields; 8) New research methodologies; 9) New questions, new trends in studies determined by new sensitivities;[8] 10) New editions of texts; 11) Greater interdisciplinary attention. 12) Finally, new discoveries and publications of unknown texts.

I will cover only some of these issues, because offering a brief overview of patristic research in relation to some specific issues reported is simply an act of unpardonable presumption. It is encouraging that an attempt can be made by each reader with his personal input and knowledge. Mine is only an attempt to synthesize my very limited knowledge, which guides me in the vast patristic production of the last century.

Reading the extensive treatises of the patrologies of the authors of the early centuries in relation to the information offered by Eusebius, Jerome, Fotius and others, seems to mean reading an obituary of a long lists of works lost or preserved only in fragments. The reasons for the lost manuscripts are many, however, sometimes it can also be the lack of interest given to an author. A very significant case is that of Irenaeus of Lyon, an author much read and used in the third century and very much studied today as he is the greatest theologian of the second century and a champion of orthodoxy. At the end of the fourth century a silence begins on his main work – *Adversus haereses* – which is no longer read or is only cited by means of extracts. Only fragments of the original Greek text are preserved. The discovery of the Latin translation

---

[7] In *The Oxford Handbook of Early Christian Studies*, ed. by Susan Ashbrook Harvey and David G. Hunter (Oxford 2008), pp. 1–41.

[8] For example: Gender studies, Cultural studies, Studies on childhood, and so on.

then allows the enhancement of his theology. His other works have completely disappeared or are preserved in Oriental languages (the Apostolic Demonstration). This example introduces a correct observation on the actuality and non-relevance of an author or a text at a precise moment in history. When is a text current? When is a text inactive, and then forgotten, neglected and lost?

Therefore, the progress of studies on any subject, even in the historical field, takes place when previously unknown, unused, or incorrectly interpreted sources of information are discovered, published, or used. But it seems to me that sometimes – at least in a specific sector – there may also be a decline, as we have seen with Irenaeus. That happened for many ancient Christian writers.

1) I begin with the first point because I consider it the most important and fundamental: recourse to sources, starting from the study of liturgy and theology. Although a few decades ago Latin and Greek were studied more, the level of culture of the clergy was very low. The Catholic clergy normally did not read the texts of the Fathers, not even in translations. The clergy or scholars of other Christian confessions were even less interested in the Fathers. In the tradition of the various Protestant confessions, one passed from the Bible to Luther; the entire intermediate period was neglected. The American theologian of the United Methodist Church, Thomas Oden, recently deceased (December 8, 2016) and my dear friend, is an example of what happened in the Catholic Church and what is now taking place in other confessions.

Thomas Oden, after a brilliant university teaching career at Madison's Drew University, said he had a dream discovering the inscription on his grave: *He made no new contribution to theology*. In other words, after a long intellectual and theological journey, he dedicated himself to the study of the Fathers and to the diffusion of their teaching. Among the works promoted are the 29 volumes of the *Ancient Christian Commentary on Scripture* series, translated into many languages – also in Mandarin Chinese – and the five volumes on the Creed. His intention was to introduce the wealth of the Fathers to American Protestants. To his great surprise, the first volumes immediately sold many thousands of copies. The intellectual and theological parable of Tom Oden is narrated in his autobiography, *A Change of Heart*.[9] He tells of the change in his life and career, converting from a liberal theology at the middle of the century to being a child of "paleo-orthodoxy", that is, a return to the Fathers. This return would have brought new life to evangelical churches and would have created bridges between the various Christian confessions. Therefore, he wanted to involve all the churches. His closest collaborator, Joel Elowsky, writes: "It appeared at a time when Evangelicals were ripe to read the Fathers, and Catholics and Orthodox were looking for allies in the Great Tradition against the tide of modernist and postmodernist assumptions undercutting the faith and life of the church".[10]

Linked with the renewal of biblical studies from the late nineteenth century, a renewal of the historical ecclesiastical sciences also develops, within which the liturgical and theological sciences can also be placed.[11] From the sixteenth century onward, an appeal to the Fathers began to take place for polemical reasons between Protestants and Catholics. Even the study of Christian archeology served a theological and apologetic interest. Christian antiquity in a broad sense served to build a confessional identity (Catholics, Lutherans and Calvinists) (Irena Backus). Catholics widely used the writings of the Fathers with the aim of converting the "errant", because they attached great importance to Tradition. Patristic writings enjoyed authority in dogmatic matters along with the conciliar canons. The ascetic writings also served as a renewal of Christian spirituality. The use of the writings of the Fathers also aroused controversy. In this polemical context there was talk of *theologia patristica*, which was a collection of texts of the Fathers in relation to Christian doctrine.

---

[9] Thomas C. Oden, *A Change of Heart: A Personal and Theological Memoir*, Downers Grove (Illinois: InterVarsity Press, 2014) reprinted in 2016.

[10] First Things 12/13/2016.

[11] I point out some work that deal with this phenomenon of Christian antiquity studies at least partially. *Le devenir de la théologie catholique mondiale depuis Vatican II (1965–1999)*, ed. by J. Doré, Beauchesne, Paris 2000; *La teologia del XX secolo, un bilancio*. Vol. 1. *Propsettive storiche*, ed. by G. Canobbio e P. Coda, Città Nuova, Roma 2003; The Oxford Handbook of Early Christian Studies, ed. by S. Ashbrook Harbey and D. G. Hunter, Oxford Press, Oxford 2008.

In the second half of the nineteenth century and in the first half of the twentieth century, the findings of other Christian-inspired texts increased; some of which come from papyrus;[12] also, texts originally written in Greek and lost, were found in translations into the Eastern languages. The philological method allows for better critical editions, for identifying anonymous texts, and for improving the study of language and style. Not only is the theological thought of the Fathers investigated, but also other aspects of their reflection; the too marked apologetic intentions are set aside and frontiers between the scholars break down. Patristics, which was at the exclusive service of theology, becomes a science. Theology always keeps the patristic tradition present, but the study of ancient Christianity also acquires its own autonomy: The Fathers are studied as writers and thinkers, their work and their personality, their sources and their influence are taken into account. The discussions are concentrated in the first centuries; one abandons the medieval period, now a specific area of research. Many scholars arrive at the eighth century, but after the fifth they limit themselves to naming only the great and famous names.

2) *Geographical and linguistic expansion in the study of ancient Christian authors* First, recently scholars have taken into consideration totally or partially neglected geographical areas, in particular the regions outside the Roman or Byzantine Empire in the East. But they also give attention to literary products written in many languages (Syriac, Armenian, Georgian, Coptic, Ethiopian, etc.). Even some Western languages come into play, like Gothic and Celtic.

As I have mentioned, in the old manuals Eastern writers who did not speak Greek were completely neglected and ignored. The most well-known manual, that of Berthold Altaner, in its last edition of 1962 edited by Alfred Stuiber, dedicates just three pages to the Syrian and Armenian authors; among the Coptic, he mentions Shenute of Atripe. This is almost the same number of pages as the Rauschen-Altaner edition of 1931 (pp. 213–19). The best Italian manual, Mannucci – Casamassa, dedicates a bit more space

---

[12] *Christian Oxyrhynchus: Texts, Documents, and Sources*, eds Lincoln H. Blumell, Thomas A. Wayment, Waco, TX: Baylor University Press, 2015; 2018.

(pp. 133-34) and deals with new topics which were previously ignored (Gnosticism and apocrypha). The manual that I edited in the fifth volume gives ample space to oriental literature. Meanwhile, manuals for the most important oriental languages are published.[13]

An almost totally new sector is the interest in Ethiopia, its history, archeology and literature. Surprising discoveries are made in the ge'ez language, i.e. translations of texts from the Coptic or from Arabic. The Coptic Encyclopedia, now edited by Alessandro Bausi, makes rich knowledge of the Christianity of that region available outside the Roman Empire and helped to evangelize as early as the first decades of the fourth century.[14]

Discoveries of some inscriptions and palimpsest manuscripts, some dating back to the fifth and sixth centuries, helps us to know something of the Aramaic-Christian Palestinian language. The texts are generally translations from the Greek. Some are useful for the knowledge of local liturgy.[15]

The lectures in this congress on the Syrian, Armenian, Georgian, and Coptic manuscripts show the change in perspective of the studies in these fields. Not only are manuscripts discovered and editions published, but they are also translated into Western languages. All these languages are important for two reasons; above all because they allow us to understand the richness of their traditions, theology and local liturgy, and because they allow for the discovery of translations of lost works in the original language. Many ancient works are preserved only in translations (e.g. in Ethiopian, Arabic, Armenian, etc.).

3) Scholars of classical literature used to have a kind of prejudice against Christian texts, and they were therefore not taken into consideration. The twentieth century slowly reversed this conception, showing ever greater interest in Christian literary texts. This also arises from the awareness of the fact that there has not been

---

[13] Cf. *Encyclopedia of Ancient Christianity*, ed. A. Di Berardino, Intervarsety Press, Downers Grove 3,693-94 (Sebastian Brock).

[14] *Encyclopaedia Aethiopica*, I-V, ed. S. Uhlig, A. Bausi, Wiesbaden: Harrassowitz Verlag, 2003-2014.

[15] Cf. *Encyclopedia of Ancient Christianity*, ed. A. Di Berardino 3,693-94 (Sebastian Brock).

a real break between the Greek-Roman and the Christian world. The studies of Greek and Latin literature stopped at the second century, the golden age; then there was the decadence of society and culture, following the scheme of the great Edward Gibbon, of a slow and long decline. The shift in interest to the later period, once called the Bas-Empire, a French syntagma, has led to a great flourishing of studies even on Christianity, since the main sources were the Christian Fathers and monuments.

4) When I was a student, it was enough to browse fifteen reviews to be updated. Today it is almost impossible to follow the hundreds of new ones, some very specialized, published in the five Continents. This is a wealth, but also a difficulty in staying well-informed. Bibliographies do not substitute for the direct vision of the texts. How many times have I been disappointed by the bibliographic title in relation to the content of the article?

5) *Some discoveries of the last decades*. What does the term discovery suggest? First, it means bringing to knowledge, to the light, something previously unknown, discovering facts, places, objects and the like; also, it means the acquisition of unknown phenomena, laws and the like by human knowledge. But it is also the acknowledgment of the value of someone or something (= appreciation). Finally, and by extension, it is identification, detection, and recognition. Therefore, its meaning is broad.

I mention some discoveries – not dealt with directly in this congress – that have profoundly influenced the life of western churches and which concern the liturgy. A strong impulse to the revision of the traditional reconstruction of the ancient Christian liturgies also came from the discovery of numerous texts. The most important texts are: the *Didache*, the *Itinerarium Egeriae*, the paschal homily of Melito of Sardis,[16] the homily *In sanctum Pascha*,[17] the *Euchologion* (Sacramentary) of Serapion of Thmuis,[18] the

---

[16] *On Pascha: with the fragments of Melito and other material related to the quartodecimans*, translated, introduced and annotated by Alistair Stewart-Sykes, St Vladimir's Seminary Press, Crestwood 2001.

[17] G. Visonà, *Pseudo Ippolito. In sanctum Pascha*. Studio, edizione, Milano, Vita e Pnesiero, 1988.

[18] M. E. Johnson, *The Prayers of Serapion of Thmuis: a literary, liturgical, and theological analysis*, Roma, Orientalia Christiana Aanalecta, 1995.

papyrus Dêr-Balizeh,[19] the so-called papyrus of Strasbourg[20] and many other papyri, the *Odes of Solomon*,[21] and the hypothetical reconstruction of the *Apostolic Tradition*, first done by H. Connoly and then by Dix and later by Botte.[22]

Recently, the Ethiopic text of the *Apostolic Tradition* was published by Alessandro Bausi from a different manuscript.[23] Previously another translation had been known.[24] This text is unanimously considered of incalculable importance for our knowledge of the evolution of ecclesial organization at the beginning of the third century. It was once known in oriental versions with the name of *Egyptian ecclesiastical order*. After the discovery of the Latin version at the end of 1800 and the publication of the Arabic and Ethiopian versions, it was attributed to Hippolytus of Rome, who lived at the beginning of the third century and was an opponent of local bishop Callistus and well involved with the imperial court. The reason for this attribution is based on the mention carved at the base of the statue, considered as being of Hippolytus. Only a few fragments of the Greek original redaction are preserved, instead we received translations into Oriental languages and into Latin, a palimpsest manuscript of the Biblioteca Capitolare di Verona (Code LV [53]) and into

---

[19] C. H. Roberts, D. B. Capelle, *An early euchologium. The Dêr-Balizeh papyrus enlarged and reedited*, Louvain: Bibliothèque du Muséon 1949; J. Van Haelst, *Une nouvelle reconstitution du Papyrus liturgique due Dêr-Balizeh*: Eph. Theol. Lovaniensis 45 (1969), 444–55 (= Bibloth. Eph. Theol. Lovaniensis 27[1970]201–12.

[20] W. D. Ray, *The Strasbourg papyrus*, in: *Essays on Early Eastern Eucharistic Prayers*, ed. by P. F. Bradshaw, Collegeville: Liturgical Press, 1997, pp. 39–56.

[21] James H. Charlesworth, *The Odes of Solomon*, Missoula, Montana: Scholars Press, 1977.

[22] B. Steimer, *Vertex Traditionis. Die Gattung der altchristlichen Kirchenordnungen*, Berlin – New York, De Gruyter, 1992, pp. 28–48.

[23] A. Bausi, *La Nuova versione etiopica della TRADITIO APOSTOLICA: edizione, e traduzione preliminare*, in *Christianity in Egypt: Literary Production and Intellectual Trends: Studies in Honor of Tito Orlandi*, Edited by Paola Buzi and Alberto Camplani, Roma, Augustinianum, 2011, pp. 19–69.

[24] An Ethiopic translation published by G. Horner was already known, *The Statutes of the Apostles or Canones Ecclesiastici Edited with Translation and Collation from Ethiopic and Arabic MSS.; also a Translation of the Saidic and Collation of the Bohairic Versions; and Saidic fragments*, London 1904, 10–48 [text], 138–86 [translation]; H. Duensing, *Der äthiopische Text der Kirchenordnung des Hippolyt* [Abhandlungen der Akademie der Wissenschaften in Göttingen. Philologisch-historische Klasse 3/32], Göttingen 1946.

re-elaborations of later works.[25] I quote Bausi: "The emersion of a 'new', independent and hitherto unknown version of the Apostolic Tradition in the recently discovered *codex unicus*, attesting an archaic Ethiopian canonical-liturgical collection by me (Bausi) called the aksumita Collection clearly shows that the Ethiopian review handed down in the *Sinodos* it represents the final result of the complex conflation of a more ancient translation – probably directly dependent on a Greek model – and of a more recent translation dependent on an Arabic model".[26]

In Tura, near Cairo, in 1941, several original Greek papyri of the sixth century were discovered. Among other texts, works by Didymus the Blind or of Alexandria and two important texts by Origen were discovered, the *Dialogue with Heraclides* and a work *On Easter*. Only a few texts were known by Didymus and many fragments preserved in the exegetic chains.[27] The ancient sources instead list many of his works, even by personalities who had known him personally, such as Jerome and Rufinus of Aquileia. With Tura's discoveries, we now know much more of this great teacher. Of the eight codes of Tura, six are works of Didymus (about 313–98), codes III–VIII. Comparing these texts with catenary fragments and other quotes by later authors, there are six new works by him: *Commentary on Genesis, Comment on Job, Comment on Zechariah, Comment on Ecclesiastes, Commentaries on the Psalms* (22–44.4) and a booklet against the Apollinarists (*Protocol of a Dialogue between Didymus and a heretic*). These discoveries allow us to understand an important author of the second half of the fourth century from Alexandria.[28]

The first two codices of Tura contain works by Origen. The first one contains two unknown works: The *Dialogue with Heraclides* and two treatises *On Easter*; the second one pieces of Origenian

---

[25] M. Geerard, *Clavis Patrum Graecorum*, Turnhout: Brepols: 1974, I, nos 1730–43.

[26] A. Bausi, *La Nuova versione etiopica della TRADITIO APOSTOLICA*, o.c., p. 22.

[27] Justin M. Rogers, *Didymus the Blind and the Alexandrian Christian Reception of Philo SBL Press*, Atlanta 2017.

[28] CPG 2544–72; R. A Layton, *Didymus the Blind and His Circle in Late-Antique Alexandria: Virtue and Narrative in Biblical Scholarship*, Chicago, Uni. of Illinois, 2004; E. Prinzivalli, *Didimo il Cieco, Lezioni sui Salmi*, Milano, Edizioni Paoline, 2005.

works.²⁹ Between scholars there is controversy regarding whether the Origenian text *On Easter* is a single treatise in two books or two separate treatises. Origen explains the term Easter which becomes very important explanation for the later Easter theology. He begins: "Most of the brothers, perhaps even all of them, believe that the term Easter takes its name from the Savior's passion; on the contrary, according to the Jews, the feast is not called Easter, but Fas, being the name of this festival – which, translated, corresponds to 'passage'". Melito of Sardis derived the term *pascha* from the Greek *paschein*, therefore it refers to passion. Origen expressly criticizes Melito's interpretation.³⁰

An important author of the second century for understanding the passage from the Hebrew to the Christian Easter today is Melito of Sardis.³¹ Now the discovery of the homily of the quartodeciman Melito has aroused great interest because it is the oldest evidence of the liturgical celebration of the origins of Easter (it dates to 160–70) and is therefore capable of illustrating a period of great importance which was previously poorly understood. In 1960, a papyrus was published – Bodmer XIII³² – which contains his homily *On Easter*.³³ Starting in 1940, the work was known in fragments divided into different collections by C. Bonner. This work bears close resemblance to *In sanctum Pascha* attributed to Hippolytus or to John Chrysostom, both expressions of the fourth quartodeciman theology of Asia (the western part of Turkey).³⁴ A first discovery dates to 1936; successive finds of Greek, Coptic, Syriac, Latin, and Georgian fragments and above all the Bodmer

---

[29] O. Guéraud – P. Nautin, Origène, *Sur la Pâque. Traité inédit publié d'après un papyrus de Toura*, Paris, Cerf, 1979; G. Sgherri, *Origene, Sulla Pasqua. Il papiro di Tura*, Introduzione, traduzione e note, Milano, Edizioni Paoline, 1989.

[30] G. Sgherri, Origene, *Sulla Pasqua*, Milano, Vita e Pensiero, 1989, p. 63, n. 2.

[31] Cf. F. Trisoglio, "Dalla pasqua ebraica a quella cristiana in Melitone di Sardi", *Augustinianum* 28 (1988), 152–85, with rich bibliography.

[32] Michel Testuz, *Papyrus Bodmer XIII. Méliton de Sardes. Homélie sur la Pâque, manuscrit du III<sup>e</sup> siècle*. Cologny-Genève, Bibliotheca Bodmeriana, 1960.

[33] Alistair Stewart-Sykes, *On Pascha: with the fragments of Melito and other material related to the quartodecimans*, Crestwood: St Vladimir's Seminary Press, 2016, II edition.

[34] G. Visonà, *Pseudo Ippolito in sanctum Pascha*, Milano, Vita e Pensiero, 1988.

papyrus,[35] which gives us back almost the entire text, allows us today to have a complete version of this important document.

With the study of these three works – Melito, Origen, and *In sanctum Pascha* – the origin and development of Easter theology has been totally renewed by these discoveries. In the Asian tradition – Roman Province of Asia –, and elsewhere in the East, Easter was celebrated on the fourteenth of the month of Nisan according to the Hebrew calendar, therefore on any day of the week, and in other parts, as in Rome and Alexandria, on the following Sunday.

In recent years, another Origenian discovery has also attracted interest. The manuscript of the Staatsbibliothek – *Codex Monacensis Graecus 314* – of Munich was known because of the image of Origen drawn on it, which we had published at the Augustinianum to pay homage to Henri Crouzel. Leafing through this manuscript, Marina Molin Pradel realized its importance, and it was later studied by Lorenzo Perrone.[36] It contains 29 Origenian homilies on the psalms, i.e. texts collected shorthand and therefore the echo of his voice. The new discovery allows us to compare the Origenian interpretation of Ps. 36 with the Latin translation of Rufinus.[37]

Regarding knowledge of the ancient liturgy of Jerusalem and not only of Jerusalem, the oldest manuscripts of the two liturgical collections in use during the celebrations were discovered: the Armenian and Georgian lectionary and the hymnal of the first half

---

[35] The homily of Melito is found in a papyrus from the collection of papyrus of the Chester Beatty Museum, in Dublin, bought in 1930–1931, and in the collection of Bodmer, in Cologny-Geneva, purchased in 1955–1956 are of incalculable importance both for the biblical manuscripts and patristic. See J. van Haelst, *Catalog of the Papyrus littéraires juifs et chrétiens*, Paris: Pubblications de La Sorbonne 1976, p. 6s; p. 115s; the Tura collection, near Cairo, has an exclusively patristic interest, which contains otherwise unknown texts. See J. van Haelst, *Catalog of the Papyrus littéraires juifs et chrétiens*, opus citatum, p. 643 f.

[36] M. Molin Pradel, "Novità origeniane dalla Staatsbibliothek di Monaco di Baviera: Il Codex graec. 314", *Adamantius* 18 (2012), 16–40; L. Perrone, "Riscorpire Origene oggi: prime impressioni sulla raccolta di omelie sui salmi nel Codex Monacensis Graceus 314", *Adamantius* 28 (2012), 41–58; L. Perrone, "The Find of the Munich Codex. A Collection of 29 Homilies of Origen on the Psalms", in *Origeniana Undecima. Origen and Origenism in the History of Western Thought*, ed. by Anders-Christian Jacobsen (Leuven – Paris – Bristol CT: Peeters), 2016, pp. 201–33.

[37] E. Prinzivalli, "Il Cod. Mon. Gr. 314, il traduttore ritrovato e l'imitatore", *Adamantius* 20 (2014), 194–216.

of the fifth century.[38] Before this discovery, only a few references to the liturgy of Jerusalem are found in the baptismal catechesis of Cyril and in the work of Egeria, her travel notes. Already there existed in Jerusalem a Greek lectionary containing the biblical readings taken from the Old and New Testaments. The Armenians and Georgians in the city translated the lectionary into their languages. The translations then spread to Armenia and Georgia.

The discovery of Egeria's *Itinerary* in 1884 – also known as Journal – in a manuscript of Arezzo shone great light on the pilgrimages and the liturgy of Jerusalem in the second half of the fourth century. The text is written in the form of a letter by a noblewoman from an ascetic circle.

Chromatius of Aquileia (AD 406/07), still ignored in Berthold Altaner's 1960 edition, becomes an important author for knowledge of the preaching and Christian life of North-Eastern Italy in the north at the end of the fourth century after the discoveries of J. Lemarié and R. Etaix. These two authors have published homiletic texts and commentary on the *Gospel of Matthew*.[39] He was related to Ambrose, Jerome and Rufinus. St Jerome dedicated to him translations and commentaries, and his personal works were almost unknown.

Here I must mention other discoveries which are also important. The publication by Frede of an unpublished manuscript of the Latin text of a complete commentary on the Pauline letters was preserved in the National Museum of Budapest; it was published in 1983–1984.[40] The codex, written in Salzburg around the year 800, contains all the Pauline letters, as well as the epistle to the Hebrews, according to the usual order in the Latin church. The Pauline text belongs to the lineage of the ancient tradition of the Latin Vetus of the Bible and seems to date back to the environment of Aquileia. The commentary is by an anony-

---

[38] Ch. Renoux, "Lectionnaires et hymnaires arméniens et géorgiens", *Ecclesia Orans* 33 (2016), 279–302.

[39] CCL 9A (1974); 9A suppl. (1977) (cf. J. Doignon, RSPh 63 [1979], 241–50); Sources Chrétiennes, 154 e 164; G. Banterle, *Commento a Matteo,* Roma: Città Nuova: 1990. – J. Lemarié, *Italie. Aquilée*: DSp 7, 2162–65; D. Corgnali, *Il mistero pasquale in Cromazio di Aquileia*, Udine: La Nuova Base, 1979.

[40] H. J. Frede, *Ein neues Paulustext und Kommentar*. Band I: Untersuchungen; Band II: Die Texte, Freiburg: Herder, 1983–1984.

mous author, but already known by Cassiodorus at Vivarium in Calabria. Drafted between 396 and 405, it is strongly influenced by the exegetical school of Antioch, both in its method and in its explanation of the texts. This is notwithstanding that in the West, the Alexandrian exegetical method predominated at that time. The knowledge of Greek allows the anonymous author to open himself to the richest oriental theological and exegetical tradition. Moreover, the comment indicates the great interest in Paul during those years in the West.

Asterius, the Sophist from Cappadocia (d. *c.* 341), perhaps a disciple of Lucianus of Antioch, spread Arianism in his *Syntagmation* (little treatise) and was a companion of Arius from the first hour, as well as an ill-known and poorly studied author. According to Jerome, he wrote many texts: "He wrote during the reign of Constantius commentaries on the Epistle to the Romans, on the Gospels and on the Psalms and also many other works which are diligently read by those of his party".[41] John Chrysostom knew his commentary and psalms; many pieces are quoted in the *catenae*. Thanks to the discoveries of Richard and Skard, one can learn more about his doctrine and especially his exegesis.[42] Is he the same as Asterius the Homilist? According to W. Kinzig, they are two different writers. The Homilist lived later in Syria.[43]

In the first centuries, between Christians and Jews there existed a certain parallel destiny, which lasts over time, sometimes not through the main roads, but through others such as daily contact in life and in society. For example, an anonymous text discovered by Bischoff and published in 1984, *Anna's letter to Seneca of Rome* written at the end of the fourth century, reflects this climate.[44]

---

[41] *Asterius, Arianae philosophus factionis, scripsit, regnante Constantio, in Epistolam ad Romanos et in Evangelia et Psalmos commentarios, et multa alia, quae a suae partis hominibus studiosissime leguntur*: *De viris illustribus* 94; see Ep. 112, 20.

[42] G. Gelsi, Kirche, *Synagoge und Taufe in den Psalmenhomilien des Asterios Sophistes*, Karl-Franzens-Universität Graz 1978; R. P. C. Hanson, *The Search for the Christian Doctrine of God*, Edinburgh 1988, pp. 32–41; Markus Vinzent. *Asterius von Kappadokien, Die Theologischen Fragmente*, Leiden: Brill, 1993.

[43] Wolfram Kinzig, *In Search of Asterius. Studies on the Authorship of the Homilies on the Psalms*, Göttingen: Vandenhoeck und Ruprecht 1990.

[44] B. Bischoff, *Anedocta Novissima*, Stuttgart: A. Hiersemann, 1984, pp. 1–9; A. Momigliano, "The New Letter by 'Anna' to 'Seneca' (MS 17 Erzbischöfliche Bibliothek in Köln)", *Athenaeum* n.s. 63 (1985), 217–20, now in Id., *Ottavo*

The anonymous author – we are at a time when there is a germination of anonymous and apocryphal sources – preaches religious tolerance and unites Christians and Jews in the persecution. Meanwhile, the author intends to win the sympathies of no Jewish readers. Perhaps the author has connections with the redactor of *Collatio Legum mosaicarum et romanarum (Lex Dei) quam præcepit Dominus ad Moysen*).

From the Bodmer collection,[45] only in 1984 did the *Vision of Dorotheus* appear, a poem of 343 hexameters which narrates a vision of a certain Dorotheus who finds himself in heaven, in the palace of God, represented as a Roman court.[46] Gianfranco Agosti has recently studied it.[47] Several unpublished works exist by authors who live in Syria and who write in Greek.[48] Bausi and Camplani have edited *The History of the Episcopate of Alexandria* (HEpA) in its Ethiopian and Latin text, a partially unpublished story (in Adamantius), composed in Greek at the end of the fourth century.

Augustine also benefited from recent discoveries, which were not as important as those of Didymus and the Easter texts. Augustine, as bishop, preached four or five times a week. He has therefore pronounced thousands of speeches. However, most have been lost forever. Already in 1930 Germain Morin had published

---

*Contributo alla storia degli studi classici e del mondo antico*, Roma; Edizioni Storia e Letteratura, 1987, pp. 329–32. Cf. L. Cracco Ruggini, "La Lettera di Anna a Seneca nella Roma pagana e cristiana del IV secolo", *Augustinianum* 28 (1988), 301–25; Leonard Victor Rutgers, *The Jews in Late Ancient Rome: Evidence of Cultural Interaction in the Roman Diaspora*, Leiden, Brill, 2000, pp. 253 ff.

[45] J. M. Robinson, *The Story of the Bodmer Papyri. The First Christian Monastery Library*, Nashville 1987. Now see the monographic section of the review *Adamantius* 21 (2015), 6–172.

[46] *Papyrus Bodmer XXIX : Vision de Dorothéos*, édité avec une introduction, une traduction et des notes par A. Hurst, O. Reverdin et J. Rudhardt, Cologny-Genève: Bibliotheca Bodmeriana 1984; A. H. M. Kessels, P. W. van der Horst, *The Vision of Dorotheus (Pap. Bodmer 29)*, edited with Introduction, Translation and Notes : VC 41 (1987) 313–59.

[47] Gianfranco Agosti, "Papiri Bodmer: biblioteche, comunità di asceti e cultura letteraria in greco, copto e latino nell'Egitto tardoantico", *Adamantius* 21 (2015), 6–172.

[48] See the chapter written by Bettiolo, in *Patrologia*, vol. v, a cura di Angelo di Berardino (in the English Translation, *Patrology: The Eastern Fathers from the Council of Chalcedon 451 to John of Damascus 750*, Cambridge: James Clarke, 2008).

many sermons discovered after Maurini's edition.[49] In recent years, thirty-three other sermons have been published by François Dolbeau and Raymond Étaix beginning in 1988. Twenty-two of them were totally unknown; the other eleven were known in reduced or altered form.[50] A few years ago, in 2007, another six sermons were discovered in Erfurt, Germany, in a twelfth-century manuscript.[51]

Years ago, a block of letters was discovered and published – a total of 29 – by Johannes Divjak in 1981 in a Marseille library. Some were meant to ask him for his theological help. These letters show us an Augustine engaged as a bishop in his pastoral activity in North Africa.

6) This is not the place to talk about the vast so-called apocryphal literature, which today is increasingly studied. In particular, the Gospel of Thomas deserves mention, beginning with this phrase: "Here are the secret words that Jesus Living said and that Didymus, Judas Thomas, has transcribed". It includes 114 sayings of Jesus and is considered very old and dated to before 140. It was found among the texts of the Gnostic library of Nag Hammadi, discovered in 1946. The Gospel of Thomas is not to be confused with the Gospel of childhood of Thomas, also from the second century; it tells of a series of miracles performed by baby Jesus.

7) Mention has been made of the Nag Hammadi discoveries that have led to a vast field of study on the Coptic language, texts, publication of editions and translations, at the same time giving impetus to a great variety of research. The prospect of resolving the question of the origins of Gnosticism still seems distant. For the Fathers it was a heresy, a deformation of the Christian faith. Authors today still discuss its origin. According to recent research, it is a movement of Christian thought which is inscribed in the

---

[49] *Sancti Augustini Sermones post Maurinos reperti: probatae dumtaxat auctoritatis, nunc primum disquisiti in unum collecti et codicum fide instaurati*, Romae: Miscellanea Agostiniana, 1930.

[50] These sermons are published in *Nuovi Discorsi*, volumi XXXV, 1–2, Roma, Città Nuova 2001.

[51] *Sant'Agostino, Sermoni di Erfurt, introduzione, traduzione e note* di Giovanni Catapano, Venezia: Marcianum Press, 2012.

Christian, Judaic, Iranian and Hellenistic traditions, while at the same time linked to the political and social environment of the Roman Empire. In the second century the great Gnostic schools expanded. The debate on the relationship between the New Testament and gnosis remains important.[52] Gnostic texts dating back to the first century are lacking and for this reason we try to identify some currents found in the NT; one goes in search of Gnostic concepts and representations and their meaning in the NT.

Manicheism, which depends on Gnosticism, is defined by Ménard as "the definitive and consequent systematization of the ancient gnosis in the form of a revealed religion with a missionary character".[53] Manichaeism was known only through the controversial writings of the controversists.[54] Numerous discoveries have renewed our knowledge of it. Great discoveries regard Manichaeism, founded by Mani (216–76), originally from Asuristan (northeast Mesopotamia). It spread over a vast geographic area: from the Roman Empire to China. There are many Manichaean manuscripts discovered in many countries: in Egypt (Medînet Mâdi, and Asyut, the ancient Lycopolis), in distant China in Dunhuang (there Nestorian and Manichaean manuscripts), in the Tarim Basin, in Gaochang (Manichaeans and Nestorians).

First, those of the Turfan (northwest of Chinese Turkestan) in 1904; then in 1918 a text in Algeria. In 1930 a Manichean library was found at Medînet Mâdi southwest of the Fayum in Middle Egypt and of Kellis in the Great Oasis. There are seven collections in Coptic, but originally they were in Syriac or Greek and belong to the first Manichean generation. Even more recently, a *Vita Mani* in Greek was discovered (*Codex Manichaicus Coloniensis; Cologne Mani-Codex*), from the tomb of Oxyrhynchus in Egypt, published between 1975 and 1982.[55] It is given the name

---

[52] G. Chiapparini, *Valentino gnostico e platonico: il valentinianesimo della "grande notizia" di Ireneo di Lione: fra genesi gnostica e filosofia medioplatonica*, Milano: Vita e Pensiero, 2012.

[53] J. Ménard J., *De la gnose au manichéisme*, Paris : Cariscript, 1986, p. 69.

[54] J. Ries, "Gnosticisme, manichéisme, encratisme : découvertes récentes et recherches actuelles", *RTL* 16 (1985), 122–26; Id., *Les études manichéens. Des controverses de la Reforme aux découvertes du XXᵉ siècle*, Louvain-La-Neuve : Centre d'histoire des religions, 1988.

[55] *Zeitschrift für Papyrologie und Epigraphik* (1975–1982).

of Codex Manichaicus Coloniensis (it is preserved in Cologne in Germany). The strong spread of Manichaeism, from China to North Africa and to European countries, has given rise to a variety of sources in different languages. These discoveries, which range from Latin, to Coptic, to Chinese and to ancient Turkish, require the collaboration of more scholars.[56] Manichaeism was a missionary religion and therefore of conquest, and for this it attracted persecution. And it was persecuted a bit by everyone: the Roman empire, Christians, Zoroastrians, and Muslims.[57] The last three chapters of Lieu's volume present a panorama of Manichaeism in the kingdom of Uighur and in China, where it continued to exist until at least 1600. In this sense they constitute the first history of Chinese Manichaeism and are therefore of great utility for the Western scholars. A Manichean sanctuary built in 1339 in Fukien still exists, renovated in 1922, and is now a Buddhist center.[58]

8) To understand nascent Christianity, it is important to keep in mind the Judaism of the time of Jesus and the one after the destruction of the Temple of Jerusalem. In the past, almost exclusively, importance was given to classical culture; it had been forgotten that Jesus was a Jew and that the early Christians were Jews. There was almost exclusively talk of the Hellenization of Christianity. For some decades, the study of patristic exegesis has been carried out, especially of Ancient Testament (which the Jews call Tanakh); it has contributed to deepening the relationship with the

---

[56] Claudia Leurini, *The Manichaean church: an essay mainly based on the texts from Central Asia*, Serie orientale Roma, N.S., 1 (Roma: Scienze e lettere – ISMEO, 2013); Zsuzsanna Gulácsi, *Mani's Pictures: The didactic images of the Manichaeans from Sasanian Mesopotamia to Uygur Central Asia and Tang-Ming China*, Nag Hammadi and Manichaean Studies 90 (Leiden & Boston: Brill, 2015).

[57] Samuel N. C. Lieu, *Manichaeism in the Later Roman Empire and Medieval China: a historical Survey*, Manchester University Press, Manchester 1985. For the merits and defects of the volume see the review of H. J. W. Drijvers: VC 41 (1987), 399–402. See The International Association of Manichaean Studies (IAMS): http://www.manichaeism.de/.

[58] G. Gnoli, *Il Manicheismo*, 3 volumi, Milano, Mondadori, 2003–2008 (A great anthology of manichaic texts); Jennifer Marie Dan, *Manichaeism and its Spread into China*. University of Tennessee, 2002; Anna Van Den Kerchove & Luciana Gabriela Soares Santoprete (eds), *Gnose et manichéisme. Entre les oasis d'Égypte et la Route de la Soie. Hommage à Jean-Daniel Dubois*, Bibliothèque de l'École des Hautes Études, Sciences Religieuses 176 (Turnhout, Brepols, 2017).

Judaism of the time. Even the discovery of the Dead Sea Scrolls has revealed a world that has not been studied, including a variety of Jewish life and thought in both Palestine and the Diaspora. The study of the close connection of Christian communities with ancient Judaism has led to new questions. Two are fundamental: a) When does the separation of Christians from Jews occur? And b) When does Catholic Christianity begin?

The answers vary and research is ongoing. Today, unlike a few decades ago, everyone admits that Jesus was truly a Jew, but many would contest the distinctive thesis of Daniel Boyarin,[59] according to which the divine Christ is also Jewish, because the title the "Son of Man" already had the meaning of divine figure. Boyarin bases his research on Dan 7, Isa 53, and the gospel of Mark 7. Christology is itself a Jewish discourse. The Trinity doctrine and the doctrine of the Incarnation – the most typical Christian innovations – were already in some way at play at the time when Jesus was born. Boyarin does not talk about the Holy Spirit. The volume ends with this statement: "The exaltation and resurrection experiences of his followers are a product of the narrative, not a cause of it. This is not to deny any creativity on the part of Jesus or his early or later followers, but only to suggest strongly that such creativity is most richly and compellingly read within the Jewish textual and intertextual world, the echo chamber of a Jewish soundscape of the first century" (p. 160).

9) Today the most important and glaring discoveries are not so much from research in libraries, which is still possible, but from archeology. It seems that the happy time of frequent discoveries of unpublished texts has come to an end, though they were still possible in 1800 and the first decades of the last century. At least in Latin or Greek, no scholar seems to be able to repeat the exhilarating experience of Dom Germain Morin with frequent discoveries of unpublished works.[60] This is more possible for other Eastern languages, such as Coptic, Syriac, Armenian or Georgian, etc. For these languages there are still libraries, especially monastic ones,

---

[59] Daniel Boyarin, *The Jewish Gospels: The Story of the Jewish Christ* (New York: The New Press, 2012).

[60] See G. Ghysens, P.-P. Verbraken, *La carrière scientifique de Dom Germain Morin (1861–1946)*, Steenbrugis : Abbatia S. Petri, 1986.

not yet fully explored. They are often translations from Greek originals, but always useful for our knowledge. Ethiopian manuscripts have made considerable contributions in recent years.

Christian archeology has been and still is a very fertile field of research. From 1950 to today, incredible discoveries have been made in every part of the *Orbis Christianus antiquus*, even outside the Roman Empire. The edition of the *Nuovo Dizionario Patristico e di antichità* (*Encyclopedia of Ancient Christianity*) makes a balance, in the hundreds of lemmas of an archaeological nature, in the activity underway.

Many other archaeological discoveries, starting from the synagogue of Dura Europos, the synagogues of Palestine, the Jewish catacombs of Rome, the Jewish inscriptions within the empire, the Babylonian centers, etc. are offering us a much more complex view of Judaism in general, both the rabbinical, and that of the diaspora. There have been numerous discoveries made in Roman Palestine in recent years because of commitment to excavations (just remember Caesarea ad Mare, Scythopolis). The frescoes of the Dura-Europos synagogue, discovered in 1932, changed the historical approach of art both for synagogue architecture and the representation of images.[61] There are Christian witnesses even in unimaginable places like the Kharg slab in the Persian Gulf.

As an example, I would like to focus briefly on three cases of the importance of archeology. In Rome – the most studied city in Christian archeology – two long Greek Christian inscriptions of the second half of the second century of the Valentinian content were discovered.[62] Both were dedicated to women. A find along the Via Latina, now in the Capitoline Museums,[63] and the other, a funerary epigram, is dedicated to Flavia Sophe.[64] The two inscriptions are the oldest direct testimonies of Valentinian teaching. They attest to the importance of the two women

---

[61] Rachel Hachlili, *Ancient Synagogues – Archaeology and Art: New Discoveries and Current Research*, Leiden: Brill, 2013.

[62] M. Guarducci, *Epigrafia greca*, vol. IV, Roma, Ist. Poligrafico dello Stato, 1978, pp. 528–35.

[63] H. G. Snyder, "A Second-Century Christian Inscription from the Via Latina", *Journal of Early Christian Studies* 19 (2011), 157–95.

[64] H. Gregory Snyder, "The Discovery and Interpretation of the Flavia Sophe Inscription", *Vigiliae christianae* 68 (2014), 1–59.

of high culture among the Valentinians, because their community – or communities – rather were cultural circles. Another cultured woman was Flora, the recipient of a long letter from Ptolemy. Three women, living in Rome in the same years, possessed a high cultural and social level, and all were Valentinians.

The second example is from Roman Britannia and the Balkans. In Britannia there was almost no evidence of Christian archeology; from 1960 onwards, there were discoveries of Christian witnesses even in the most unexpected places. Even richer are the testimonies from the Balkans, the land of origin of numerous Roman emperors from the third century on. In recent years, not only external, but also local archaeologists are rewriting the Roman and Christian history of Pannonia, of Moesia and of Thrace, due to the countless archaeological finds that have come to light. A generation of young scholars is making great contributions.

An immense mine of information is now offered by the Proceedings of the last international congress of Christian archeology, just published.[65] In these two big volumes we now find what we want to know "on the material traces of the Constantinian period, during which Christianity becomes part of public life in the Greco-Roman world" (from a speech by Olof Brandt).

10) Other times there are no real discoveries but rather identifications of texts or authors. For example, a few years ago Schlatter found that the anonymous author of *Opus imperfectum in Matthaeum* refers to previous comments. Now some of these references are found in an anonymous manuscript of Arian inspiration at the Bobbio monastery, which had a rich Scriptorium. Stylistic similarities lead one to think that it could be the same author who writes in Latin.

Another important and delicate task is the identification of works circulated under other names, and they are not few. Sometimes pseudepigraphy is only a question of the manuscript

---

[65] *Acta XVI congressus internationalis archaeologiae christianae (Romae 22, 28-9-2013). Costantino e i Costantinidi: l'innovazione costantiniana, le sue radici e i suoi sviluppi*, a cura di Olof Brandt, Vincenzo Fiocchi Niccolai, Città del Vaticano: Pontificio Istituto di Archeologia Cristiana, 2016; *The Eerdmans Encyclopedia of Early Christian art and archaeology*. Ed. P. Corby Finney, 3 vols, Grand Rapids: Wm. B. Eerdmans Publ. 2017.

tradition or the confusion of names, while other times it is desired and sought.[66] Pseudepigraphy in this case is a literary operation by which a writer circulates his writings under the name of a known and famous person, both to give greater value to certain writings and to defend ideas, perhaps otherwise unacceptable.[67] The psychological reasons for using pseudepigraphy are not always the same and vary from author to author. Often it arises precisely from doctrinal disputes. To impose or circulate an opinion, writers use the aegis of the apostolic age or an appreciated and esteemed name. Two sensational cases include that of Dionysius the Areopagite,[68] a great writer rich in theology and that of Macarius / Simeon, whose many texts were still unpublished until a few years ago and are now being published. Indeed, the most important manuscripts have only recently been discovered. Macarius is a character who has exerted an enormous influence on Christian spirituality. He was active between 380 and 430 in Syria / Mesopotamia.[69] The name of Athanasius,[70] of John Chrysostom, of Ambrose, of Augustine, was a guarantee. Incredible numbers of works are circulated under their names.[71] The case of a true falsification or

---

[66] See A. Hamman, *L'épopée du livre. La transmission des textes anciens, du scribe à l'imprimerie*, II ed., Paris, Perrin, 1985. For the vast public, not for specialists: has as its subject the history of the text, that is how the written documents of antiquity have come down to us. See an important recent work: *Le livre au Moyen Âge*, sous la direction de Jean Glénisson, Turnhout 1988. Besides dealing with the various problems associated with the technique of book making: the parchment (the palimpsest, the paper, the workshops of the monks and the laity; scribe, the use of the book: readers and libraries) also speaks of the transmission of ancient texts: Greeks, Latins, Hebrews and Arabs. Also, of the analysis of the manuscript.

[67] Cf. L. R. Donelson, *Pseudoepigraphy and Ethical Arguments in the Pastoral Epistles*, Tübingen, Mohr Siebeck, 1986; D. Farkasfalvy, "The Ecclesial Setting of Pseudoepigraphy in Second Peter and its Role in the Formation of the Canon", *Second Century* 5 (1985/1986), 3–29; B. M. Metzger, *The Canon of the New Testament. Its Origin, Development, and Significance*, Oxford, Clarendon Press, 1987.

[68] Converted by Paul in Athens.

[69] Cf. Jean Gribomont, "Macarius/Simeon", in *Encyclopedia of Ancient Christianity*, ed. A. Di Berardino, 2,643–44.

[70] *Pseudo-Atanasio: dialoghi IV e V sulla santa Trinità* (testo greco con traduzione italiana, versione latina e armena), Alessandro Capone, Louvain, Peeters, 2011.

[71] Cf. *Pseudepigraphy: Encyclopedia of Ancient Christianity*, ed. by A. Di Berardino 3,346–47; W. Speyer, *Die literarische Fälschung im heidnischen und christlichen Altertum. Ein Versuch iher Deutung*, München, C. H. Beck, 1971; B. Metzger, "Literary Forgeries and Canonical Pseudepigrapha", *JBL* 91 (1972), 3–24; J. H. Charlesworth, "A History of Pseudepigrapha Research: The Re-

manipulation of text is very different. Internal and external criticism has a difficult task to look for possible attributions.

Today we have at our disposal five fundamental *instrumenta* which help us to untangle ourselves from the labyrinth of false attributions and anonymous ones: they are Clavis Patrum Latinorum of Dekkers, Clavis Patrum Graecorum of Geerard, Verzeichnis of Frede[72] especially Clavis Patristica Pseudepigraphorum Medii Aevi (CPPM),[73] and Clavis Scriptorum Latinorum Medii Aevi: Auctores Galliae (CSLMA).[74]

A better critical edition of a text can more profoundly indicates the steps needed to be followed in order to find new answers and new solutions, or perhaps to read the text with different eyes. Some recent examples are very eloquent. The edition of Irenaeus' *Adversus haereses*, recently published,[75] is the result of thirty years of work by various specialists and presents many new features compared to those in circulation. New solutions of a textual redaction sometimes arouse new interpretations. Similarly, the superb new edition of Athanasius' *Historia acephala* allows, with its vast commentary and the Syriac Index of the festive letters, allows a more objective and faithful reconstruction not only of Athanasius' vicissitudes, but of many aspects of the history of the fourth century.[76]

---

emerging Importance of the Pseudepigrapha", *ANRW* II,19:1 (1979), 54–89; N. Brox (ed) *Pseudepigraphie in der heidnischen und Jüdisch-christlichen Antike*, Darmstad: Wissenschaftliche Buchgesellschaft, 1977. See the volumes *ANRW* II,25,5 e 6 del 1988 with another article of J. Charlesworth.

[72] E. Dekkers-A. Gaar, *Clavis Patrum Latinorum*, Steenbrugis: Abbatia S. Petri, 1995; M. Geerard, *Clavis Patrum Graecorum*, Turnhout: Brepols, 1974ss; H. J. Frede, H. J. Hermann, R. Gryson *Kirchenschriftsteller: Verzeichnis und Sigel*, Freiburg: Herder, 1995, Aktualisierungsheft 1999. Compléments 1999, par Roger Gryson, 1999.

[73] Five volumes. This Clavis presents all the Latin pseudepigraphical texts which during the Middle Ages circulated under the name of patristic authors. Besides the incipit and explicit of each text, information on the most important editions has been gathered. The catalogue also tries to identify the real names of the authors and gives references to all studies which involve a particular text.

[74] Four volumes: *Clavis Scriptorum Latinorum Medii Aevi: Auctores Galliae* (CSLMA), Turnhout: Brepols, 1994ss.

[75] A. Rousseau – L. Doutreleau, Sources Chrétiennes, Paris, Cerf, 1969. 1982, six volumes.

[76] Histoire "acéphale" et Index syriaque des Lettres festales d'Athanase d'Alexandrie par Annik Martin, avec la collaboration pour l'édition et la traduction du texte syriaque de Micheline Albert, SCh 317, Paris : Cerf, 1986.

Some examples of the importance of a new edition include *Opus imperfectum in Matthaeum* by J. van Banning, Augustine's *Enarrationes in Psalmos* by Franco Gori, and the new edition of the *Shepherd of Hermas* by Simonetti.

## *Conclusion*

In recent decades, historical research has seen an expansion of its fields of investigation for the period called Late Antiquity, using new tools of investigation, in particular, with the affirmation of Cultural Studies. It has also become invested in the sphere of private life, social and relational changes, the affirmation of new values, different perceptions of time and space, public and private sentiments, family, kinship, etc. – according to a perspective of diachronic anthropology. Today we are more aware that the ancient world is far from us. Though it seems close, it is a different world with different systems of values. In addition, there has been a semantic evolution.

The formative and founding period are the most discussed. For the period after the second century, there is general consensus and research, especially after the Second Vatican Council clarified many aspects. Those who know the ancient sources cannot but think how these have been manipulated, misunderstood, forced, even often distorted for some kind of interest, even by serious historians, who often dream of an ideal church to be traced in them. Those same theologians who fully accept the incarnation imagine a primitive church almost disembodied by the human, often too spiritual. Sometimes there is the conviction that God's plan must be seen as something unorganized and not institutional. The charism for Paul is not opposed to an office, but distinct and connected to it. The numerous sociological studies of primitive Christianity, which have flourished in recent years especially in the Anglo-American environment, are moving towards greater concreteness and a more disenchanted vision. The European scientific tradition is more interested in discovering new texts, in creating new editions, as it has more philological sensitivity. In fact, all the new editions are made by Europeans or by those who have European education.

## Abstract

If we take a look at the bibliographic collections, we see a huge expansion of publications on Christian antiquity in its various aspects. There are numerous factors in the exponential growth of the bibliography. 1) The creation of numerous new study centers in many countries and the dizzying increase of number of scholars. 1) Use of ancient sources, starting from the study of history, ancient languages, liturgy and theology. 2) Geographical and linguistic expansion of studies. 3) The numerous discoveries in the recent decades in the archaeological and papyrological fields. 4) Numerous discoveries and publications of unknown texts in all ancient languages (Augustine, Origen, Didymus, Chromatius, liturgical texts, Manichaeism, Melito of Sardis, Asterius, the Sophist, Bodmer papyri, Nag Hammadi discoveries, Turfan and Tun-huang texts in 22 languages, anonymous texts, and so on). 5) The expansion of the geographical space of the authors and of the ancient languages studied (Coptic, Ethiopian, Syriac, Armenian, Georgian, Arabic, Sogdian, Palestinian Aramaic, Gothic, Nubian, Pahlavi, Paleoslav) began in the early 1900s. The handbooks normally did not name the ancient Christian writers who had written in languages other than Greek or Latin.

# CHAPTER 7
# THE DISCOVERY OF MANUSCRIPTS FROM LATE ANTIQUITY AND ITS IMPACT ON THE CONTEMPORARY WORLD

PATRICIA CINER
*Universidad Católica de Cuyo, Argentina*

# BRIEF INTRODUCTION TO THE TOPIC

The International Conference on Patristic Studies organized in Jerusalem in 2013 to mark the 50th anniversary of the creation of the International Association of Patristic Studies (IAPS/AIEP) makes evident the fact that Patristics is relevant both in and for the contemporary world. In effect, its central theme was "Patristic Studies in the Twenty-First Century".[1] This theme then influenced much of the subsequent academic work in the field. One of these subsequent activities was the organization of the Second International Conference on Patristic Studies in San Juan, Argentina in 2017, with the theme "The Discovery of Manuscripts from Late Antiquity: Their Impact on Patristic Studies and the Contemporary World". Roundtable presentations have become the articles included in this volume.

One of the most well-attended Specialist Roundtables was that referring specifically to "The Discovery of Manuscripts from Late Antiquity: Their Impact on Patristic Studies and the Contemporary World", as this represented the conference's central theme. This roundtable included presentations by two first-rate academics, Dr Marco Rizzi and Dr Theodore de Bruyn, who provided their perspectives on the issue and whose texts now close this volume published by Brepols.

---

[1] B. Bitton-Ashkelony, T. De Bruyn, C. Harrison, *Patristic Studies in the Twenty-First Century. Proceedings of an International Conference to Mark the 50th Anniversary of the International Association of Patristic Studies* (Turnhout-Belgium: Brepols, 2015).

As regards Dr Theodore de Bruyn, I would like to highlight his immense contributions to Patristic Studies as President of the International Association of Patristic Studies from 2011 to 2019. As President, he sought to strengthen the paradigm affirming that Patristic Studies should be studied interdisciplinarily, which implies that although Patristic Theology and Philosophy have an important role, they should not be isolated from the contributions of other disciplines such as History, Art, Archaeology and Sociology, among others. This interdisciplinary view provides an integral understanding of this fascinating period in human history, as it situates its diverse issues within a precise historical and cultural context. This context allows us to discover the everyday nature of existence with which not only the Church Fathers but also the general population of the Patristic Era lived. This perspective is clearly present in Professor de Bruyn's article entitled "Papyri, Parchments, and Ostraca and the Study of Ancient Christianity Today". Precisely, the focus of his research centers on common findings which, until recently, were not considered important in Patristic Studies. In his words:

> By "commonplace finds" – if anything that has survived for several millennia can be called "commonplace" – I mean whatever people wrote or had written for institutional, administrative, or personal purposes: the numerous and often fragmentary remains of literary and technical works; official and personal correspondence; petitions and proceedings; legal documents; registers, accounts, and receipts; school exercises and ad-hoc jottings; amulets and recipes for amulets. Only a fraction of texts gathered in the course of archaeological excavations or purchased through the antiquities trade has in fact been edited or published: publication has itself become a form of discovery. Nevertheless, the amount of published materials is large. I will not attempt to discuss its significance as a whole. Rather, I will offer some comments on the significance of a few types of writing – patristic works, liturgical texts, and letters – for the contemporary study of ancient Christianity.

I would also like to quote Dr de Bruyn's words from his lecture in San Juan because they summarize precisely the change of perspective that Patristic Studies has experienced in the contemporary world:

> Patristics is not a uniform or stable field of study, because we as scholars are the children of different social, political, ecclesiastical, and cultural contexts. What this means for the study of ancient manuscripts, I cannot predict. But I hope that it will result in new interpretative insights into the complex but fragmentary remains of ancient Christianity.

With respect to Dr Marco Rizzi, he is not only the Secretary of the International Association of Patristic Studies (IAPS/AIEP), but also a very prestigious specialist at the Catholic University of Sacred Heart in Milan. His lines of research center mainly upon Origen and Alexandrian tradition, however, he seeks to link this tradition with the contemporary world. His article is unique in this volume as it combines intelligent humor with profound reflection on the consequences that the discovery of manuscripts has for our world today. In this sense, it is a text that is to be re-read several times as it presents the great challenges that we must assume as intellectuals dedicated to these issues, challenges which include, for example, the need to separate the content of these manuscripts from any partisan interest that might use them to support fragmentary visions of a reality that, like that of early Christianity, exceeds any closed categorization.

To conclude both this introduction and this volume, I would like to quote the last fragment of Dr Rizzi's article. His message, in effect, represents a clear direction to follow for Patristic scholars dedicated to manuscripts and their interpretations and puts into words the motivation that prompted us to carry out the 2nd International Conference on Patristic Studies and the subsequent edition of this volume, which Brepols Publishers so generously publishes today:

> Nonetheless, as scholars and intellectuals, we have the responsibility to safeguard as much as we can the message of these texts that are no more a prerogative of the faithful or the Churches, since they have become a common, universal heritage.

THEODORE DE BRUYN
*University of Ottawa, Canada*

# PAPYRI, PARCHMENTS, AND OSTRACA AND THE STUDY OF ANCIENT CHRISTIANITY TODAY

In the panel to which this paper contributed during the conference in San Juan, the topic for discussion was "The Discovery of Manuscripts from Late Antiquity and Its Impact on the Contemporary World". It quickly became apparent that one's approach to the topic depended on what one meant by the words "manuscripts" and "the contemporary world". If we are thinking of a wide public audience, then, yes, certain discoveries have had a broad impact. The manuscripts uncovered at Qumran and Nag Hammadi, themselves the topics of panels at the conference, come immediately to mind. These finds not only have forever altered the terrain for scholars of early Judaism and emerging Christianity, but also have enjoyed public attention in the form of exhibitions, documentaries, and popular publications. One might also include manuscripts held in the collections now known as the Chester Beatty Biblical Papyri and the Bodmer Papyri.[1] These papyri are more widely known because they each consisted of a group of manuscripts that included major early witnesses to portions of the Old and New Testaments (as well as other texts).[2]

---

[1] On the former, see A. Pietersma, "Chester Beatty Papyri", in *The Anchor Yale Bible Dictionary*, ed. by D. N. Freedman, 6 vols (New Haven: Yale University Press, 1992), I, pp. 901–03. On the latter, see J.-L. Fournet, "Anatomie d'une bibliothèque de l'Antiquité tardive: l'inventaire, le faciès et la provenance de la 'Bibliothèque Bodmer'", *Adamantius*, 21 (2015), 8–40; J. M. Robinson, *The Story of the Bodmer Papyri: From the First Monastery's Library in Upper Egypt to Geneva and Dublin* (Eugene, OR: Cascade Books, 2011), should be used with caution.

[2] B. Nongbri, *God's Library: The Archaeology of the Earliest Christian Manuscripts* (New Haven: Yale University Press, 2018), chapters 4 and 5, narrates events following the discovery of these two groups of manuscripts, describes their

But other discoveries, even important ones, are not so well known outside scholarly circles. How many people today are aware of the discovery in 1941 of the Tura codices,[3] which have given us biblical commentaries of Didymus the Blind previously known only from catenae, as well as manuscripts of several works by Origen, most notably the previously unknown *Treatise on Easter* and *Disputation with Heraclides*? Or, reaching further back into the nineteenth century, how many people would recall the significance of the publication for the first time of the so-called ancient "church orders": the *Didache*, the *Didascalia Apostolorum*, the *Apostolic Church Order*, the *Apostolic Tradition* (as a component in other ancient collections), the *Canons of Hippolytus*, and the *Testamentum Domini*?[4] It would be hard to overstate the importance of these publications for our knowledge of the liturgies, organization, offices, and activities of the institutional church in various regions of the ancient world. Moreover, because of their contribution to the liturgical renewal that occurred in Western churches in the second half of the twentieth century, the study of these documents indirectly has had an enormous impact on the way in which many Christians worship today.[5] But while liturgical scholars and Christian clergy might recognize this, most Christians would not. In short, the impact of manuscript discoveries is usually greatest among those most directly interested – typically scholars. Discoveries of some types of manuscripts –

---

codicological features, and discusses problems in determining their find-spot, provenance, and time of writing.

[3] On this discovery, see the paper by Lorenzo Perrone in this volume. See also K. Treu, "Referate: Christliche Papyri 1940–1967", *Archiv für Papyrusforschung*, 19 (1969), 169–206 (pp. 188–99, 191–92); *Repertorium der griechischen christlichen Papyri. II. Kirchenväter Papyri. Teil 1: Beschreibungen*, ed. by K. Aland & H.-U. Rosenbaum, Patristische Texte und Studien, 42 (Berlin: Walter de Gruyter, 1995), pp. lxxv–lxxxiii.

[4] For an overview, see P. F. Bradshaw, *The Search for the Origins of Christian Worship: Sources and Methods for the Study of Early Liturgy*, 2nd edn (Oxford: Oxford University Press, 2002), pp. 73–87. On the reception of the *Didache*, see the paper by Marco Rizzi in this volume.

[5] For an overview of the reform of eucharistic liturgies, see P. F. Bradshaw & M. E. Johnson, *The Eucharistic Liturgies: Their Evolution and Interpretation* (Collegeville, MN: Liturgical Press, 2012), pp. 293–336. See also G. Wainwright, "Recent Eucharistic Revision", in *The Study of Liturgy*, rev. edn, ed. by C. Jones *et al.* (London: SPCK; New York: Oxford University Press, 1992), pp. 328–38 (pp. 333–34).

usually those dealing with religious origins or scriptures – may be felt more widely. But only a few discoveries have become household names.

Even fewer people will be aware of the commonplace finds which in fact constitute the vast majority of ancient manuscripts held today in major collections, many of which come from Egypt, whose dry climate south of the Nile Delta resulted in the preservation of much material. By "commonplace finds" – if anything that has survived for several millennia can be called "commonplace" – I mean whatever people wrote or had written for institutional, administrative, or personal purposes: the numerous and often fragmentary remains of literary and technical works; official and personal correspondence; petitions and proceedings; legal documents; registers, accounts, and receipts; school exercises and ad-hoc jottings; amulets and recipes for amulets.[6] Only a fraction of texts gathered in the course of archaeological excavations or purchased through the antiquities trade has in fact been edited or published: publication has itself become a form of discovery. Nevertheless, the amount of published materials is large. I will not attempt to discuss its significance as a whole.[7] Rather, I will offer some comments on the significance a few types of writing – patristic works, liturgical texts, and letters – for the contemporary study of ancient Christianity. If, then, we expand the purview of "manuscripts" under consideration in this conference to this wider array of written materials and reduce the purview of "the

---

[6] For an overview of the types of documents that have survived from Graeco-Roman Egypt, see B. Palme, "The Range of Documentary Texts: Types and Categories", in *The Oxford Handbook of Papyrology*, ed. by R. S. Bagnall (Oxford: Oxford University Press, 2009), pp. 358–94.

[7] Examples of studies of Egyptian Christianity that draw on a wide range of sources are A. Papaconstantinou, *Le culte des saints en Égypte des Byzantins aux Abbassides: l'apport des inscriptions et des papyrus grecs et coptes* (Paris: CNRS Éditions, 2001); G. Schmelz, *Kirchliche Amtsträger im spätantiken Ägypten nach den Aussagen der griechischen und koptischen Papyri und Ostraka*, Archiv für Papyrusforschung und Verwandte Gebiete, Beiheft 13 (Munich-Leipzig: K. G. Saur, 2002); E. Wipszycka, *Les ressources et les activités économiques des églises en Égypte du IV<sup>e</sup> au VIII<sup>e</sup> siècle*, Papyrologica Bruxellensia, 10 (Brussels: Fondation égyptologique Reine Élisabeth, 1972); E. Wipszycka, *Moines et communautés monastiques en Égypte (IV<sup>e</sup>-VIII<sup>e</sup> siècles)*, The Journal of Juristic Papyrology Supplements, 11 (Warsaw: Journal of Juristic Papyrology, 2009); E. Wipszycka, *The Alexandrian Church: People and Institutions*, The Journal of Juristic Papyrology Supplements, 25 (Warsaw: Journal of Juristic Papyrology, 2015).

contemporary world" to the contemporary study of the ancient Christianity, what do we find?

## Patristic Works

I begin with manuscripts of patristic works, since patristic studies was a focus of the conference in San Juan. They are arguably the "poor cousins" within the family of ancient Christian manuscripts; witnesses to texts that were read as "scripture"—in the broadest sense of that term—are far more numerous. By way of illustration, I consider manuscripts whose assigned date falls between 100 and 399 CE,[8] using, for convenience, the conventional categories of biblical, apocryphal, and patristic literature.[9] Manuscripts of books in the Old and New Testaments, of course, constitute the largest class,[10] followed by manuscripts of the writings of Hermas, also widely read at the time for their spiritual benefit.[11] Apocryphal gospels, acts, and apocalypses or visions

---

[8] I recognize that the selection of this time frame is somewhat arbitrary since most literary manuscripts cannot be dated precisely and a strict limit of 399 CE excludes manuscripts assigned to the fourth or fifth century (or longer windows). However, my purpose here is to be illustrative rather than exhaustive. For a discussion of the problems associated with dating literary manuscripts, particularly by means of comparative paleography, see Nongbri, *God's Library*, 56–72.

[9] An initial search was conducted by means of the Leuven Database of Ancient Books (LDAB; http://www.trismegistos.org/ldab/about.php) in January 2017, setting the date as "AD01 – AD04" and the religion as "Christian." A supplementary search was conducted in December 2020 prior to publication. Unbeknownst to me in 2017, Brent Nongbri conducted a similar inventory of "Christian" books found at Oxyrhynchus, using a larger time frame and different literary categories; see Nongbri, *God's Library*, 228–34, 273–80. Patristic works constitute a minority of the manuscripts in his inventory as well.

[10] P. Orsini & W. Clarysse, "Early New Testament Manuscripts and their Dates: A Critique of Theological Palaeography", *Ephemerides Theologicae Lovanienses*, 88 (2012), 443–74, Table 1, assign eighty New Testament manuscripts to dates between 100 and 399 (II to IV). For an earlier count, see *Repertorium der griechischen christlichen Papyri. I. Biblische Papyri: Altes Testament, Neues Testament, Varia, Apokryphen*, ed. by K. Aland, Patristische Texte und Studien, 18 (Berlin: Walter de Gruyter, 1976), pp. 434–35.

[11] See M. Choat & R. Yuen-Collingridge, "The Egyptian Hermas: The Shepherd in Egypt before Constantine", in *Early Christian Manuscripts: Examples of Applied Method and Approach*, ed. by T. J. Kraus & T. Nicklas, Texts and Editions for New Testament Study, 5 (Leiden: Brill, 2010), pp. 191–212, giving a list of extant papyrus manuscripts at p. 212; T. Wayment, *The Text of the New Testament Apocrypha (100–400 CE)* (London: Bloomsbury, 2013), pp. 81–169

are individually attested by one or two, and sometimes more, manuscripts,[12] some of them remarkably complete, with the *Gospel of Thomas*, the *Acts of Paul (and Thecla)* and the *Protevangelium of James* each enjoying several witnesses.[13] Manuscripts of known patristic works are relatively few: a lacunary Coptic translation of Clement of Rome's *Letter to the Corinthians*;[14] two fragmentary witnesses to Aristides' *Apology*;[15] one fragment of Justin's *First Apology*;[16] two portions, one short, the other long, of Irenaeus' *Against Heresies*;[17] multiple witnesses in Greek and Coptic to Melito's sermon *On the Pasch*;[18] two fragments from Clement of Alexandria's *Stromateis*;[19] an excerpt from Julius Africanus' *Cesti*;[20] fragments from a few works of Origen

---

(transcriptions) and pp. 286–390 (plates); D. Batovici, "The Reception of Early Christian Apocrypha and of the Apostolic Fathers: Reassessing the Late-Antique Manuscript Tradition and the Patristic Witnesses" (unpublished doctoral thesis, KU Leuven, 2015), pp. 92–125 (discussion of scribal habits). My thanks to Dr Batovici for sending me his thesis.

[12] In what follows, to avoid lengthy footnotes, I refer to entries in the LDAB, which gives bibliographical details of editions and emendations, as well as references to older catalogues such as J. Van Haelst, *Catalogue des papyrus littéraires juifs et chrétiens* (Paris: Publications de la Sorbonne, 1976); *Repertorium*, ed. by Aland and Rosenbaum; and the reviews of Christian papyri by K. Treu & C. Römer under the heading "Referate" in *Archiv für Papyrusforschung* from 1969 to 2007. I exclude works from the Nag Hammadi codices (LDAB 107741–107753) unless they are attested by other witnesses; but see the paper by David Brakke in this volume on the impact of the Nag Hammadi codices on our conceptualization of early Christian culture and identity. For further discussion of the LDAB, see the last section of this paper.

[13] *Gospel of Mary*: LDAB 5329, 5406; *Gospel of Judas*: LDAB 108481; *Gospel of Peter*: LDAB 4872 (?), 5111; *Gospel of Thomas*: LDAB 4028, 4029, 4030, 107742; *Protevangelium of James*: LDAB 2560, 2565, 10616; *Sophia of Jesus Christ*: LDAB 5620, 107743; *Acts of Andrew*: LDAB 108861; *Acts of John*: LDAB 5667, 5724; *Acts of Paul (and Thecla)*: 3138, 5234, 5543, 107970, 108121; *Acts of Peter*: 5677, 107746; *Ascension of Isaiah*: 107888, 108464; *Apocalypse of Elias*: LDAB 108728; *6 Ezra*: LDAB 3181; *First Apocalypse of James*: LDAB 107745, 108481. For transcriptions and plates of many of the manuscripts, see Wayment, *Text*.

[14] LDAB 107764.
[15] LDAB 338, 3470.
[16] LDAB 171876.
[17] LDAB 2459, 2460.
[18] LDAB 2565, 2608, 107771, 107910, 108122, 828618.
[19] LDAB 564, 768444.
[20] LDAB 2550.

(*De principiis*,[21] *Selecta in Psalmos*,[22] and *Homilies on Luke*[23]); a fragment of Eusebius of Caesarea's *Ecclesiastical History*;[24] a Greek translation of several letters of Pachomius;[25] and a Coptic translation of Athanasius' *Letter to Dracontius*.[26] Fragments of unidentified patristic works in fact exceed those of identifiable works.[27]

This may seem to be a meagre harvest. But occasionally these remains have been quite important for modern editors. For instance, the Greek fragments of Aristides' *Apology* led its most recent editor to privilege the Syriac version of the work over the Greek text incorporated into the Greek legend of Barlaam and Ioasaph, even if the former took liberties when translating from the Greek.[28] The Greek fragment of Justin's *First Apology* is the only ancient witness to this work to have been published so far;[29] otherwise we have only indirect citations from the *First Apology* in Eusebius and a few later sources, and only three manuscripts of the entire work, two of which are copies of the first, a manuscript completed in 1364 CE.[30] The remains of an ancient Greek copy of Book Five of Irenaeus' *Against Heresies*,[31] whose only other Greek attestations are from excerpts cited by later writers, confirm that the Latin and Armenian versions are more faithful to the original than the Greek citations – this despite errors

[21] LDAB 3504.
[22] LDAB 117888.
[23] LDAB 3499.
[24] LDAB 1060.
[25] LDAB 3513.
[26] LDAB 749338.
[27] R. Yuen-Collingridge, "Hunting for Origen in Unidentified Papyri: The Case of *P.Egerton* 2 (= *inv.* 3)", in *Early Christian Manuscripts*, ed. by Kraus & Nicklas, pp. 39–57 (p. 55, n. 67).
[28] B. Pouderon, "Introduction", in *Aristide: Apologie*, ed. by B. Pouderon *et al.*, Sources Chrétiennes, 470 (Paris: Les Éditions du Cerf, 2003), pp. 21–177 (pp. 144–50).
[29] *The Oxyrhynchus Papyri*, vol. 78, ed. by R.-L. Chang *et al.* (London: Egyptian Exploration Society, 2012), no. 5129.
[30] *Justin, Philosopher and Martyr: Apologies*, ed. by D. Minns & P. Parvis (Oxford: Oxford University Press, 2009), pp. 3–13; see also *Justin: Apologie pour les chrétiens*, ed. by C. Munier, Sources Chrétiennes, 570 (Paris: Les Éditions du Cerf, 2006), pp. 83–89.
[31] F. Uebel, "Der Jenaer Irenäuspapyrus: Ergebnisse einer Rekonstruktion und Neuausgabe des Textes", *Eirene*, 3 (1964), 51–109.

introduced by the scribe in copying the work mechanically without attending to sense.[32] The final two columns of a roll containing Book Eighteen of Julius Africanus' *Cesti*,[33] produced within several decades of its composition,[34] prove that he was the author of the work, since the text is followed by a subscription attributing it to him.[35] The Greek translation of letters of Pachomius, preserved on a roll held in the Chester Beatty Library,[36] with fragments in the Cologne Papyrussammlung,[37] is the earliest extant manuscript of the letters; its witness is a valuable *comparandum* to Coptic fragments of the letters and Jerome's Latin translation of the letters.[38] Lastly, the Coptic translation of Athanasius' *Letter to Dracontius*, found in a roll in the papyrus collection of the Abbey of Montserrat, Barcelona, is the earliest witness to the letter, antedating the earliest surviving Greek manuscript by six centuries; among other things, it preserves a paragraph that appears to have dropped out of the Greek tradition because of a scribal oversight.[39]

---

[32] *Irénée de Lyon: Contres les hérésies, Livre 5*, ed. by A. Rousseau, L. Doutreleau & C. Mercier, Tome I: Introduction, notes justicatives, tables, Sources Chrétiennes, 152 (Paris: Les Éditions du Cerf, 1969), pp. 140–57.

[33] *The Oxyrhynchus Papyri*, vol. 3, ed. by B. P. Grenfell & A. S. Hunt (London: Egyptian Exploration Society, 1903), no. 412; re-edition: J. Hammerstaedt, "Magie und Religion in den Kestoi des Julius Africanus", in *Die Kestoi des Julius Africanus und ihre Überlieferung*, ed. by M. Wallraff & L. Mecella, Texte und Untersuchungen zur Geschichte der altchristlichen Literatur, 165 (Berlin: Walter de Gruyter, 2009), pp. 53–69.

[34] The *Cesti* was completed around 231 CE; see M.Wallraff, "Dating and Structure", in *Iulius Africanus. Cesti: The Extant Fragments*, ed. by M. Wallraff et al., Die griechischen christlichen Schriftsteller der ersten Jahrhunderte, n.F. 18 (Berlin: Walter de Gruyter, 2012), pp. xix–xxii (p. xix). The *verso* of the papyrus has a document dated to the reign of the Emperor Tacitus (275–76 CE); see *Oxyrhynchus Papyri*, vol. 3, ed. by Grenfell and Hunt, p. 36.

[35] Lines 69–71.

[36] H. Quecke, *Die Briefe Pachoms: Griechischer Text der Handschrift W. 145 der Chester Beatty Library*, Textus patristici et liturgici, 11 (Regensburg: F. Pustet, 1975).

[37] *Kölner Papyri*, vol. 4, ed. by B. Kramer, C. Römer & D. Hagedorn, Papyrologica Coloniensia, 7.4 (Opladen: Westdeutscher Verlag, 1982), no. 174.

[38] Quecke, *Die Briefe Pachoms*, pp. 41–72.

[39] S. Torallas Tovar, "Athanasius' *Letter to Dracontius*: A Fourth-Century Coptic Translation in a Papyrus Roll (P.Monts.Roca inv. 14)", *Adamantius*, 24 (2018), 22–38.

## *Liturgical Texts*

A large number of fragmentary liturgical texts have also been found in Egypt. The impact of some of these finds has been greater, arguably, than discoveries of fragments of patristic texts because of their importance for the reconstruction of early liturgies of the Egyptian church, particularly liturgies of the Eucharist. The numerous fragmentary witnesses to early versions of the eucharistic liturgy of Alexandria,[40] traditionally called the Liturgy of St Mark or St Cyril, have stimulated several generations of scholarship on early Christian eucharistic prayers and, more particularly, the evolution of the anaphora of St Mark or St Cyril.[41] Otherwise this liturgical tradition is known from later and more elaborate medieval liturgical manuscripts.[42] Early witnesses to other "named" Egyptian liturgies – the Liturgy of St Basil and the Liturgy of St Gregory – have likewise been instrumental in establishing early forms of portions of those liturgies.[43] Moreover, fragments from eucharistic liturgies that do not correspond exactly to any "named" liturgy have also survived,[44] revealing that other liturgies were used or preserved in different locales.

Some of these finds have garnered considerable attention. One thinks, for instance, of the literature associated with the Strasbourg papyrus inv. 245,[45] a fourth- or fifth-century witness to the anaphora of St Mark whose text dates from the fourth century.[46]

---

[40] G. J. Cuming, *The Liturgy of St Mark*, Orientalia christiana analecta, 234 (Rome: Pontificium Institutum Studiorum Orientalium, 1990), pp. xxiii–xxix, 61–66; J. Hammerstaedt, *Griechische Anaphorenfragmente aus Ägypten und Nubien*, Papyrologica Coloniensia, 28 (Opladen: Westdeutscher Verlag, 1999), nos 1–8.

[41] For bibliography, see H. Brakmann, "Das Alexandrinische Eucharistiegebet auf Wiener Papyrusfragmenten", *Jahrbuch für Antike und Christentum*, 39 (1996), 149–64 (pp. 151–55); J. Henner, *Fragmenta Liturgica Copta*, Studien und Texte zu Antike und Christentum, 5 (Tübingen: Mohr Siebeck, 2000), pp. 21–26.

[42] Cuming, *Liturgy*, pp. xxix–xxxiv; Hammerstaedt, *Griechische Anaphorenfragmente*, pp. 10–12.

[43] For an overview, see Henner, *Fragmenta*, pp. 26–35.

[44] Hammerstaedt, *Griechische Anaphorenfragmente*, p. 9, with nos 9–19; Henner, *Fragmenta*, pp. 4–16.

[45] See now Hammerstaedt, *Griechische Anaphorenfragmente*, no. 1.

[46] Hammerstaedt, *Griechische Anaphorenfragmente*, p. 22.

It and the fourth-century Euchologion attributed to Serapion are our earliest witnesses to anaphoral prayers in Egypt, which scholars have mined for their relationship not only to later forms of the Liturgy of St Mark and St Cyril but also to earlier forms of Christian worship.[47] But the entire body of finds of a liturgical nature is much broader than texts bearing portions of eucharistic prayers. It includes other liturgical prayers, blessings, litanies, practical instructions (typika), and numerous hymns.

This large and diverse body of material has been charted recently in two doctoral dissertations, that of Céline Grassien on Greek hymns,[48] and that of Ágnes Mihálykó on Greek, Latin, and Coptic texts related to principal celebrations of the Egyptian church (the Eucharist, baptism, ordination, the liturgy of the hours, and the celebration of certain festivals such as Easter and Christmas) from the third to the ninth century CE.[49] I will focus on Mihálykó's study. Not least among its contributions is a list of the 323 liturgical texts on which the study is based, with essential descriptive, papyrological, and bibliographical information.[50] Although, as Mihálykó readily acknowledges, the inclusion criteria of her study entail some inevitable constraints,[51] her comprehensive assembly and analysis of this body of material allows for significant advances. I will highlight two.

Mihálykó observes that the preferred format for many liturgical texts was a single sheet. Of the papyri and parchments written with liturgical texts, 54 certainly came from a codex and 10 probably came from a codex, whereas 101 probably were single sheets and 14 may have been single sheets.[52] Mihálykó also

---

[47] For an overview, see W. D. Ray, "The Strasbourg Papyrus", in *Essays on Early Eastern Eucharistic Prayers*, ed. by P. F. Bradshaw (Collegeville, MN: Liturgical Press, 1997), pp. 39–56; G. J. Cuming, "The Anaphora of St Mark: A Study in Development", in *Essays*, ed. by Bradshaw, pp. 57–72.

[48] C. Grassien, "Préliminaires à l'édition du corpus papyrologique des hymnes chrétiennes liturgiques de langue grecque" (unpublished doctoral thesis, Université Paris-Sorbonne, 2011).

[49] Á. T. Mihálykó, *The Christian Liturgical Papyri: An Introduction*, Studien und Texte zu Antike und Christentum, 114 (Tübingen: Mohr Siebeck, 2019); on the delimitation of the materials studied, see pp. 14–38.

[50] Mihálykó, *Christian Liturgical Papyri*, pp. 287–369.

[51] Mihálykó, *Christian Liturgical Papyri*, pp. 37–38.

[52] Mihálykó, *Christian Liturgical Papyri*, pp. 155–58.

observes a correlation between the type of liturgical text and the format of the material: prayers are more likely to be copied into codices, whereas hymns are more likely to be copied on single sheets or leaflets.[53] Sheets of various dimensions were used, but earlier in the period, from the fifth to the seventh century, short broad sheets were typical, whereas later in the period, from the late seventh century onwards, long narrow sheets were preferred.[54] All this is relevant to the question of the uses to which such sheets were put. Mihálykó argues persuasively that most liturgical texts were copied in order to learn, circulate, or perform the liturgy.[55] For selected prayers, hymns, acclamations, or instructions, single sheets could be handier to use than codices,[56] and easier to produce. Regardless of the format, if most liturgical texts were copied as aids to liturgical performance, they preserve for us the language and imagery that constructed and animated the devotional life of Egyptian Christians. They bring us considerably closer to typical and unique characteristics of prayer and worship.

This brings me to my second point – an opportunity for research. The provenance of about two-thirds of the liturgical texts examined by Mihálykó – all of which come from outside the Nile Delta, since nothing survived there – is known or can be inferred with some confidence. In some regions there is a higher concentration of finds than others: Western Thebes (on account of the monasteries and hermitages there), the Fayum, and Hermopolis and its environs. An in-depth study of liturgical texts found or assigned to one of these regions,[57] or a comparative study of a particular liturgical genre across several regions, could yield further insight into the local or supra-local character of Christian identity and devotion. Here Mihálykó's list of texts is especially valuable; it is a portal to further research.

[53] Mihálykó, *Christian Liturgical Papyri*, p. 161.
[54] Mihálykó, *Christian Liturgical Papyri*, pp. 162–63.
[55] Mihálykó, *Christian Liturgical Papyri*, pp. 188–219.
[56] Mihálykó, *Christian Liturgical Papyri*, p. 217.
[57] Mihálykó, *Christian Liturgical Papyri*, pp. 140–52, offers an overview of services in Western Thebes in the seventh and eighth centuries.

## *Letters*

Since letters were used for routine forms of communication among people otherwise lost to history, they offer us access to a broader cultural and social field than literary or liturgical works. For that very reason, ancient letters have been mined repeatedly for what they can tell us about "daily life" and – closer to the interest of this conference – "everyday Christians".[58] The studies by Malcolm Choat, AnneMarie Luijendijk, Lincoln Blumell, and Erica Mathieson are recent contributions to this literature.[59]

Individual letters convey a sense of the particular because they are written by specific people for some personal reason. This makes them captivating as ancient sources. But since most letters were written for non-religious reasons, what they reveal about the religious character of the writer or the recipient is often minimal or oblique. The only indication that the writer is a Christian may be a formal or formulaic one, as in the presence of a staurogram or a cross, the use of *nomina sacra* (abbreviated forms of the Greek words for "God", "Lord", "father", "son", "spirit", "Jesus", "Christ", and certain other names), the phrasing of opening or closing formulae, and the use of familial language.[60] Many customary turns of phrase are not decisive. For instance, Christian writers cannot necessarily be distinguished from non-Christian writers by how they refer to the divine in their opening or clos-

---

[58] In general: J. L. White, *Light from Ancient Letters* (Philadelphia: Fortress Press, 1986); R. S. Bagnall & R. Cribiore, *Women's Letters from Ancient Egypt, 300 BC–AD 800*, electronic edn (Ann Arbor: The University of Michigan Press, 2008). On Christians: G. Ghedini, *Lettere cristiane: dai papiri greci del III e IV secolo* (Milan: Vita e Pensiero, 1923); M. Naldini, *Il cristianesimo in Egitto: lettere private nei papiri dei secoli II–IV*, Studi e testi di papirologia, 3 (Florence: Le Monnier, 1968); G. Tibiletti, *Le lettere private nei papiri greci del III e IV secolo d.C.: Tra paganesimo e cristianesimo* (Milan: Vita e Pensiero, 1979).

[59] M. Choat, *Belief and Cult in Fourth-Century Papyri*, Studia Antiqua Australiensia, 1 (Turnhout: Brepols, 2006); A. Luijendijk, *Greetings in the Lord: Early Christians and the Oxyrhynchus Papyri*, Harvard Theological Studies, 60 (Cambridge, MA: Harvard Theological Studies, 2008); L. H. Blumell, *Lettered Christians: Christians, Letters, and Late Antique Oxyrhynchus*, New Testament Tools, Studies and Documents, 39 (Leiden: Brill, 2012); Erica A. Mathieson, *Christian Women in the Greek Papyri of Egypt to 400 CE*, Studia Antiqua Australiensia, 6 (Turnhout: Brepols, 2014).

[60] Naldini, *Il cristianesimo*, chapter 1; Blumell, *Lettered Christians*, chapter 2.

ing formulae,[61] nor do they often quote, echo, or recall scripture in their letters.[62] Thus, one impression left by their letters is that, with regards to routine communications and mundane affairs, Christians were often indistinguishable from non-Christians.

Nevertheless, personal letters are an important complement to literary works, since they express the attitudes, concerns, and expectations of individuals. Although letters follow customary forms and employ conventional expressions, the individuality of the writer may still emerge, sometimes in intriguing and revealing ways. For instance, among the personal letters from Oxyrhynchus is a letter from an anonymous Christian woman thanking an anonymous man for a letter she had received from him.[63] The recipient, addressed with great respect as "my lord father", was probably a cleric or possibly a monk.[64] The letter reads: "... greetings. I received your letter, my lord father, and I was so elated and rejoiced that such a one as my father remembers me. For when I received it, I venerated your holy face ...".[65] The letter is remarkable for several reasons. It is written in a formal majuscule hand

---

[61] Choat, *Belief and Cult*, chapters 9 and 10.

[62] Choat, *Belief and Cult*, pp. 74–83; M. Choat, "Echo and Quotation of the New Testament in Papyrus Letters to the End of the Fourth Century", in *New Testament Manuscripts: Their Texts and Their World*, ed. by T. J. Kraus & T. Nicklas, Texts and Editions for New Testament Study, 2 (Leiden: Brill, 2006), pp. 267–92; Blumell, *Lettered Christians*, pp. 208–36. When Christian writers do use scriptural language in their letters, they may adapt it to address the situation at hand; see A. Maravela, "Scriptural Literacy Only? Rhetoric in Early Christian Papyrus Letters", in *Proceedings of the 28th International Congress of Papyrology, Barcelona 1–6 August 2016*, ed. by A. Nodar & S. Torallas Tovar (Barcelona: Publicacions del'Abadia de Montserrat – Universitat Pompeu Fabra, 2019), pp. 162–77.

[63] *The Oxyrhynchus Papyri*, vol. 12, ed. by B. P. Grenfell & A. S. Hunt (London: Egyptian Exploration Society, 1916), p. 285 (no. 1592); Ghedini, *Lettere cristiane*, pp. 131–33 (no. 14); Naldini, *Il cristianesimo*, pp. 159–60 (no. 31); Bagnall & Cribiore, *Women's Letters, Letter* 90, A14.3 (the letter is not included in the print edition of 2006); Luijendijk, *Greetings*, pp. 74–78; Blumell, *Lettered Christians*, pp. 181–82; Mathieson, *Christian Women*, pp. 45–46.

[64] Opinion varies on whether the expression "my lord father" should be taken to refer to a cleric (of high status) or a monk; see Naldini, *Il cristianesimo*, pp. 159–60, comment on line 3; Bagnall and Cribiore, *Women's Letters*, Letter 90; Luijendijk, *Greetings*, p. 76, n. 65; Mathieson, *Christian Women*, pp. 160–61. On "father" as a term of respect, see Mathieson, *Christian Women*, pp. 96–97.

[65] Mathieson, *Christian Women*, pp. 45–46 (see also Papyri.info at http://papyri.info/ddbdp/p.oxy;12;1592): χαί]ρειν. αἰδε- | ξά[μ]ην (l. ἐδε|ξά[μ]ην) σου τὰ γράμμα- | τα, κ(ύρι)έ μου π(άτε)ρ, καὶ πάνυ ἐ- | μεγαλύνθην καὶ ἠγαλλεία- | σα

typically used for literary works rather than for letters.[66] It has been suggested that the professional quality of the hand, whether executed by the woman herself or by a scribe,[67] was meant to convey the woman's esteem for her recipient.[68] Her regard for him is also reflected in the use of *nomina sacra* when writing "lord" and "father" (using two different forms for "father"). Although in other literary and non-literary works these abbreviations are at times used of mundane figures,[69] in letters *nomina sacra* mostly appear in formulaic expressions referring to God.[70] Most remarkable of all, in expressing her joy at having received a letter from this man, the woman's letter echoes the opening words of the song of Mary (Luke 1: 46–47).[71] This is one of a handful of biblical echoes in letters found at Oxyrhynchus, and the only instance where

---

(l. ἠγαλλίασα) ὅτει (l. ὅτι) τοιοῦτός μου π(ατ)ὴρ | τὴν μνήμην ποιεῖται. αὐτὰ | γὰρ δεξαμένη τὸ ἱερόν (ἴερον papyrus) σου | [πρόσωπον προσεκ]ύνησα.

[66] The hand has affinities to both Alexandrian majuscule script (the form of α, κ, and υ) and Biblical majuscule script (the contrast between thick vertical strokes, thin horizontal strokes, and descending diagonals of medium thickness); for descriptions of these scripts, see G. Cavallo & Herwig Maehler, *Greek Bookhands of the Early Byzantine Period: A.D. 300–800*, Bulletin of the Institute of Classical Studies Supplement, 47 (London: Institute of Classical Studies, 1987), pp. 23 and 34. An image of the papyrus can be viewed in the American Theological Library Association's Digital Library (https://dl.atla.com/), entering "Oxy. 1592" when searching the database.

[67] Bagnall & Cribiore, *Women's Letters*, Letter 90, think it more likely that the letter was written by a professional scribe for the woman, whereas Luijendijk, *Greetings*, p. 78, argues that it could have been written by the woman herself. Mathiesen, *Christian Women*, p. 71, points out that, even if the letter was written by a professional scribe, the language is probably the woman's own, given the echoes of the song of Mary.

[68] Luijendijk, *Greetings*, p. 77.

[69] A. H. R. E. Paap, *Nomina sacra in the Greek Papyri of the First Five Centuries A.D.: The Sources and Some Deductions* (Leiden: Brill, 1959), pp. 101, 103.

[70] Blumell, *Lettered Christians*, pp. 311–13.

[71] Luke 1: 46–47: Καὶ εἶπεν Μαριάμ, Μεγαλύνει ἡ ψυχή μου τὸν κύριον, καὶ ἠγαλλίασεν τὸ πνεῦμά μου ἐπὶ τῷ θεῷ τῷ σωτῆρί μου; see Naldini, *Il cristianesimo*, p. 160; Bagnall & Cribiore, *Women's Letters*, Letter 90; Luijendijk, *Greetings*, p. 76; Blumell, *Lettered Christians*, p. 222; Mathieson, *Christian Women*, p. 71. Although the two verbs in question (μεγαλύνω and ἀγαλλιάω) appear in similar expressions in the Greek Psalter (e.g., LXX Pss. 19: 6, 91: 5–6), the more likely source of the echo is the song of Mary; see E. J. Epp, "The Oxyrhynchus New Testament Papyri: 'Not Without Honor Except in their Hometown'?", *Journal of Biblical Literature*, 123 (2004), 5–55 (pp. 26–27, n. 69); Choat, *Belief and Cult*, p. 75; Choat, "Echo and Quotation", p. 288.

the song of Mary is echoed in that corpus.[72] Taken together, the quality of the hand, the *nomina sacra*, and the biblical echo give us a glimpse of how a devout woman related to her "spiritual father" (whoever he might have been): not only did she esteem him highly, her letter employed Christian scribal conventions and biblical language to convey that esteem, implicitly evoking a common, elevated culture between her and him.

The echo from the song of Mary has a broader significance, which is why I have singled out the letter here. The song was one of a few New Testament canticles that, along with a selection of Old Testament canticles, entered into the canon of liturgical hymns known as Odes. Evidence for the use of these canticles in Christian worship in the third and fourth centuries – when the above letter is believed to have been written[73] – is mostly indirect, and the evidence is more plentiful for some canticles – such as the Canticle of the Exodus (Exod. 15: 1–19) and the Canticle of the Three Young Men (Dan. 3: 52–88), which were sung during the Easter vigil[74] – than for others. The earliest extant manuscript preserving the canticles as a distinct collection – the book of Odes – is the fifth-century biblical manuscript Codex Alexandrinus. (Codex Vaticanus and Codex Sinaiticus, written a century earlier, do not include such a collection.) Henry Swete and Heinrich Schneider had independently observed that the text of the canticles in Odes (copied by one scribe) varied from their equivalent texts elsewhere in the manuscript (copied, except for the source of Ode 3, by another scribe).[75] Schneider concluded that the book of Odes in Codex Alexandrinus was based on a different and dis-

---

[72] Blumell, *Lettered Christians*, p. 222. A search of documentary papyri by means of Papyri.info (2 December 2020) yielded no other documents containing the verbs μεγαλύνω or ἀγαλλιάω.

[73] The date assigned by Grenfell and Hunt – late third or early fourth century – has been accepted by all subsequent commentators.

[74] H. Schneider, "Die biblischen Oden im christlichen Altertum", *Biblica*, 30 (1949), 28–65 (pp. 37–38, 43–46).

[75] H. B. Swete, *An Introduction to the Old Testament in Greek*, 2nd edn, rev. by R. R. Ottley (Cambridge: Cambridge University Press, 1914), p. 254; Schneider, "Die biblischen Oden", pp. 55–56. On the two-scribe theory, see H. J. M. Milne & T. C. Skeat, *Scribes and Correctors of the Codex Sinaiticus* (London: British Museum, 1938), pp. 91–93; J. A. Miller, "'Let Us Sing to the Lord': The Biblical Odes in the Codex Alexandrinus" (unpublished doctoral thesis, Marquette University, 2006), pp. 83–86.

tinct *Vorlage* than the rest of the manuscript. James Miller has confirmed this supposition with a rigorous analysis of all the variants.[76] It is safe to assume, as Miller suggests, that the compilers of Codex Alexandrinus adopted a version of the canticles already circulating as a distinct collection.[77] The most obvious reason to produce such a collection would have been for use in the liturgy of the church.

Although we know from occasional remarks from Origen, among others, that canticles were sung in the liturgy already in the third century,[78] the earliest evidence that the song of Mary was one of those canticles is from a sermon on the value of singing psalms and hymns during worship services by Nicetas, bishop of Remesiana (in the Roman province Dacia mediterranea) in the last quarter of the fourth century and the first decades of the fifth.[79] The scribal features of Codex Alexandrinus suggest that a collection of canticles including the song of Mary was circulating in Alexandria, if not more widely in Egypt, at about the same time.[80] Our anonymous letter offers further support for thinking that the song of Mary had taken on a life of its own, apart from reading of the Gospel of Luke, by the fourth century. The echo in the letter was almost certainly an effect of repeated recitation

---

[76] Miller, "'Let Us Sing'", pp. 146–76, summarizes the evidence and conclusions.

[77] Miller, "'Let Us Sing'", pp. 176–78.

[78] Schneider, "Die biblischen Oden", p. 51.

[79] Schneider, "Die biblischen Oden", p. 52. See Nicetas of Remesiana, *De utilitate hymnorum* 9, 11, ed. by C. H. Turner, "Nicetas of Remesiana II", *Journal of Theological Studies*, 24 (1923), 225–52 (pp. 238–39); *Nicetas of Remesiana: Writings*, trans. G. G. Walsh, The Fathers of the Church, 7 (New York: The Fathers of the Church, 1949), pp. 65–76 (pp. 72, 74). For full discussion of this work, with prior bibliography, see J. Rist, "Ein spätantikes Plädoyer für den Psalmengesang: Niceta von Remesiana und seine Schrift *De psalmodiae bono* (CPL 649)", *Ostkirchliche Studien*, 50 (2001), 34–57.

[80] The earliest Eastern source to describe the use of all nine odes in a vigil (which is also the context to which Nicetas refers) comes from an account of the visit of Sophronius of Jerusalem and John Moschus to Abba Nilus in the Sinai at the end of the sixth or beginning of the seventh century; see A. A. Longo, "Il testo integrale della 'Narrazione degli abati Giovanni e Sofronio' attraverso le *Ermeneiai* di Nicone", *Rivista di studi bizantini e neoellenici*, n.s. 2–3 (1965–1966), 223–67 (pp. 251–52); R. F. Taft, *The Liturgy of the Hours in East and West: The Origins of the Divine Office and Its Meaning for Today*, 2nd edn (Collegeville, MN: Liturgical Press, 1993), pp. 198–99; G. W. Woolfenden, *Daily Liturgical Prayer: Origins and Theology* (London: Routledge, 2004), pp. 53–54.

in private devotions or public worship. Moreover, it should not go unnoticed that the echo – the only one of its kind among papyrus letters – occurs in a letter written by or for a woman. It suggests that Mary's song held a special meaning for Christian women.

This letter is just one example of what one can learn about Christian devotion, affiliation, and behaviour from individual letters. Obviously, to make more complete use of letters as a source for understanding ancient Christianity, one must investigate a corpus of letters with a particular question in view. Lincoln Blumell's study of letters from Oxyrhynchus is one example of such an investigation. It illustrates how letters by individual Christians can be examined systematically for information that may be unrelated or tangential to their identity as Christians, but nevertheless important for our understanding of ancient Christianity. For instance, from the correspondence of Christians in Oxyrhynchus it emerges that they travelled mostly for reasons related to their occupation or work and mostly within the Oxyrhynchite nome.[81] The letters also attest to occasional travel to neighbouring nomes and to regular communication between Oxyrhynchus and Alexandria,[82] the principal destination, understandably, for trade outside the nome.[83] One may surmise, therefore, that for most Christians in Oxyrhynchus, the sense of association with a community, embodied in its services, churches, and shrines, would have been local. But local forms and venues of devotion could have supra-local significance. As we know from the relatively rich documentation of Christian churches and shrines in Oxyrhynchus, those sites would have connected Christians in Oxyrhynchus with Christians elsewhere: the list of saints venerated in Oxyrhynchus includes, alongside local saints, saints venerated in Middle Egypt, all of Egypt, and more widely in the Eastern

---

[81] Blumell, *Lettered Christians*, pp. 103–25, 155–57. Egypt had long been divided into territorial districts called "nomes". For their extent in the fourth century, see R. S. Bagnall, *Egypt in Late Antiquity* (Princeton: Princeton University Press, 1993), pp. 331–35.

[82] Blumell, *Lettered Christians*, pp. 125–36.

[83] Blumell, *Lettered Christians*, pp. 157–58, citing R. Alston, "Trade and the City in Roman Egypt", in *Trade, Traders and the Ancient City*, ed. by H. Parkins & C. J. Smith (London: Routledge, 1998), pp. 168–202.

empire.[84] In fact, among names suggesting a Christian identity in letters from Oxyrhynchus, attested in increasing frequency in the sixth and seventh centuries, we find not only names of prominent local saints (notably Philoxenus; also Justus and Serenus), but also Egyptian saints (notably Phoibammon and Menas; also Anoup and Collouthus), as well as saints from elsewhere in the empire (George and Cosmas).[85]

## *Digital Tools*

Whether one is undertaking a systematic investigation of a given body of manuscripts, such as the letters from Oxyrhynchus that formed the basis of Blumell's study, or mining manuscripts selectively to answer a particular philological or historical query, one must be able to survey and search the data comprehensively. In this regard, the development of electronic databases and the use of digital technologies have been especially important. They are giving scholars greater access to basic data about a wide range of manuscripts, and they are making it easier for scholars to conduct palaeographical and philological investigations of those manuscripts.

For instance, the database Trismegistos (http://www.trismegistos.org/),[86] a portal to papyrological and epigraphical sources from Egypt and the Nile valley (800 BCE to 800 CE), allows one to identify manuscripts that may be relevant to one's given query or corpus, review a record of their editions and publications, and consider, if only provisionally, the date and find-spot or provenance of the manuscripts. The Leuven Database of Ancient Books (http://www.trismegistos.org/ldab/), incorporated into Trismegistos, allows for extensive searches

---

[84] Papaconstantinou, *Le culte*, pp. 230–33 (for the derivation of saints venerated in Egypt) and pp. 286–88 (for the saints venerated in Oxyrhynchus); Blumell, *Lettered Christians*, pp. 250–60.

[85] Blumell, *Lettered Christians*, pp. 265–67, 275–76, 349–65.

[86] M. Depauw & T. Gheldof, "Trismegistos: An Interdisciplinary Platform for Ancient World Texts and Related Information", in *Theory and Practice of Digital Libraries – TPDL 2013 Selected Workshops*, ed. Ł. Bolikowski *et al.*, Communications in Computer and Information Science, 416 (Cham: Springer 2014), pp. 40–52.

of metadata of manuscripts of literary works. The Brussels Coptic Database does a similar service for Coptic documents, but has not been updated recently.[87] Papyri.info (http://www.papyri.info/), an aggregator of several papyrological databases, allows one, further, to view and search transcriptions of documentary papyri, and the Digital Corpus of Literary Papyri (http://www.litpap.info/), now merged withPapyri.info, aims to do the same for literary papyri. These two databases broaden the scope of searchable texts beyond those captured by the *Thesaurus Linguae Graecae*, the Library of Latin Texts, or the Corpus dei manoscritti copti letterari.[88] Increasingly, moreover, scholars have access to high-resolution digital images of ancient manuscripts and documents, as institutions with major papyrological collections place images of manuscripts on-line.[89] Usually these images are of manuscripts that have already been edited and therefore are included in Trismegistos and Papyri.info. This allows one to compare images of the manuscript with editions of the manuscript, and to assess independently the material and paleographical aspects of the manuscript.

We are also seeing the development of subject-specific databases that combine multiple types of data (literary, documentary, archaeological, and visual). One may cite such examples as the University of Oxford database of early evidence for the cult of saints (http://cultofsaints.history.ox.ac.uk/), which combines data from different media (saints' lives, histories, liturgical texts, calendars of feast-days, inscriptions, images in paint and mosaic, and papyrus documents); or the PAThs project, which aims to combine literary, codicological, and archaeological data to create a searchable database of Coptic literary manuscripts (many now dismembered into separated fragments) in relation to their

---

[87] The last update was 25 August 2014; see http://dev.ulb.ac.be/philo/bad/copte/baseuk.php?page=accueiluk.php.

[88] Thesaurus Linguae Graecae® Digital Library, ed. M. C. Pantelia (University of California, Irvine), http://www.tlg.uci.edu; Library of Latin Texts, Brepolis®, Brepols Publishers Online, https://about.brepolis.net/library-of-latin-texts/; *Corpus dei Manoscritti Copti Letterari*, http://www.cmcl.it/. On the latter, see the paper by Alberto Camplani in this volume.

[89] Links to the websites of many of these institutions are provided in the list of partners of Trismegistos (https://www.trismegistos.org/partners).

sites of production, transmission, discovery, and current location (http://paths.uniroma1.it/).[90]

Databases such as these will afford more scholars the opportunity to conduct complex, fine-grained studies of aspects of ancient Christianity that draw on a wide range of sources while at the same time integrating into their use of those sources an awareness of their specificity or peculiarity. These databases, one might say, are to scholars in the twenty-first century what the monumental *Dictionnaire d'archéologie chrétienne et de liturgie* was to scholars in the twentieth century. They are not without their limitations or hazards, as, indeed, was Henri Leclercq's prodigious compilatory œuvre.[91] Much depends on the accuracy of the data in the database, as well as on the parameters and terms of one's searches. Moreover, databases cannot substitute for consulting editions or discussions of the artefacts and, if necessary, the artefacts themselves. But databases nevertheless open up for scholars worldwide a massive body of manuscripts of all kinds, and thereby the potential for discoveries of an interpretative, if not material, nature. For the myriad written remains that have survived from antiquity, these databases are now indispensable – and, one hopes, enticing – tools.

## *Abstract*

Although a select number of manuscript discoveries (such as those at Qumran and Nag Hammadi) have become known to the broader public, most manuscripts from Late Antiquity do not enjoy such fame. My paper discusses a diverse body of manuscripts that is not well known beyond the purview of specialists: the numerous papyri, parchments, and ostraca that have survived from late antique Egypt. Because these materials often reflect the lived circumstances, actions, and concerns of individuals, they continue to deepen and alter our understanding of many aspects of late antique society. This can be illustrated, with

---

[90] For a description of the project, see J. Bogdani, "Linking Coptic Literary Manuscripts to the Archaeological Context by Means of Digital Humanities: The Case of 'PAThs' Project", *Adamantius*, 24 (2018), 200–10, and the paper by Alberto Camplani in this volume.

[91] See Th. Klauser, *Henri Leclercq, 1869–1945: Vom Autodidakten zum Kompilator grossen Stils*, Jahrbuch für Antike und Christentum, Ergänzungsband, 5 (Münster in Westfalen: Aschendorff, 1977), pp. 122–35.

regard to ancient Christianity, by examples from recent studies of liturgical texts and letters. Current technologies (databases, inventories, digital images) now make it possible to mine large corpora of materials and examine individual artefacts in ways that in the past only few people would have been able to do, making these materials available to scholars around the world.

MARCO RIZZI
*Università Cattolica del Sacro Cuore di Milano, Italy*

# THE IMPACT OF THE REDISCOVERY OF MANUSCRIPTS ON THEOLOGY AND RELIGIOUS CULTURE AFTER THE SECOND WORLD WAR

In 1883 the orthodox Metropolitan bishop Philotheos Bryennios published in Constantinople the *editio princeps* of what is now known as the *Didachè*, found in a manuscript owned by the Greek Patriarchate of Jerusalem, where it is now stored after it had been moved from Constantinople.[1] The strong impression caused by these 204 lines-long writing laid out in less than 5 sheets of manuscript, ushered in a period of new discoveries after the great and unequalled age of Renaissance findings. In fact, quite the year after *editio princeps* was published, Adolf Harnack, not yet "von", wrote a commentary to the text for the just inaugurated series of *Texte und Untersuchungen zur Geschichte der altchristlichen Literatur*.[2] To Harnack, it was such a discovery that he exclaimed: "The *Didachè* has finally shed light for us".[3] According to his vision of the essence of Christianity and its history, he claimed that now it was possible to read a testament of the first, authentic Christian community born from the Gospel, before the ecclesiastical bureaucracy hid it.

---

[1] Διδαχή των δώδεκα Αποστόλων εκ του ιεροσολυμιτικού χειρογράφου, νυν πρώτον εκδιδομένη μετά προλεγομένων και σημειώσεων, εν οις και της Συνόψεως της Π.Δ., της υπό Ιωάννου του Χρυσοστόμου, σύγκρισις και μέρος ανέκδοτον από του αυτού χειρογράφου από Φιλοθέου Βρυεννίου, μητροπολίτου Νικομηδείας (Costantinople: Voutyra, 1873).

[2] *Die Lehre der zwölf Apostel. Nebst Untersuchungen zur ältesten Geschichte der Kirchenverfassung und des Kirchenrechts, von Adolf Harnack. Anhang: Ein übersehenes Fragment der in alter lateinischer Übersetzung, mitgetheilt von Oscar v. Gebhardt* (Leipzig: Hinrichs, 1884 [Texte und Untersuchungen zur Geschichte der altchristlichen Literatur, II 1–2]).

[3] "Die *Didaché* hat uns endlich Licht gebracht": *ibidem*, p. 94.

The initial enthusiasm was quickly replaced by concern, not only from a theological point of view, since in the so called Eucharistic section contained in the ninth and tenth chapter of the *Didaché*, exactly under the title περὶ δὲ τῆς εὐχαριστίας, there was not any reference to the passion and death of Christ, and neither any reference to his body and blood. What should have been the incunabulum of the Christian rite *par excellance*, the Eucharist, seemed instead the description of a simple Jewish ritual meal. In the following decades, scholars gave the most ingenious answers in order to solve the question, trying to distinguish what was described in the *Didaché* from a real Eucharist, or considering it as an introductive ritual to the real celebration, not reported in the text, or even reducing it as a brotherly meal, an ἀγάπη. Still, it remained unsolved the problem of the relationship between this formula and the one that would have been the Eucharistic anaphora in the following Christian tradition.[4] If the Jewish origins of Christianity were confirmed by the discovery, the absence of any significant reference to the death of the Savior in a ritual defined simply as an εὐχαριστία opened to questions not easy to answer to at that time and it seemed to request a profound revision of the historiographical acquisitions about the first phase of life of the Christian communities.

Something more of a decade later, in winter between 1896 and 1897, Bernard Grenfell and Arthur Hunt started archeological digs in Oxyrhinchus, looking for papyrus texts, in particular those of the New Testament. It took only a few days before their efforts were rewarded: in one case the enthusiasm and the debates arisen looked like the one exploded after the discovery of *Didaché* – and also in this case Harnack had something to say… To highlight the importance of their discovery, Grenfell and Hunt put the fragment as the first number in the series of the papyri of Oxyrhinchus published from 1898 onward, after the preview they had given the year before, right after the discovery, in a booklet that had caused an academic debate inversely proportionate to his small dimension.[5]

---

[4] On this highly debated issue, see for instance Giuseppe Visonà, *Didaché. Insegnamento degli apostoli*, introduzione, testo, traduzione e note di Giuseppe Visonà (Milano: Paoline, 2000), pp. 155–92.

[5] ΛΟΓΙΑ ΙΗΣΟΥ. *Sayings of our Lord from an Early Greek Papyrus*, discovered and edited, with translation and commentary by Bernard P. Grenfell and Arthur S. Hunt (London: Henry Frowde for the Egypt Exploration Fund, 1897).

Under the title of Λόγια (*Sayings*) Ἰησοῦ, the two English scholars had published a series of 8 sentences ascribed to Christ that, according to them, came not from a narrative Gospel but belonged to another work, independent from the four canonic Gospels, yet not heretic, which on a paleographic base could be dated before 140 or even back to the first century. Above all, the first point was subject to criticism and discussions. To Harnack, they were extracts of the lost *Gospel of the Egyptians*; to Pierre Battifol, instead, they were abstracts of the lost *Gospel of the Jews*; and finally, to Theodor Zahn they were part of the *Gospel of the Ebionites*.[6]

After the discovery of the papyri of Tura in the middle of the Second World War (1941), which brought to light unknown works of Origen and Didymus the Blind,[7] the fantastic findings of the Qumran and Nag Hammadi libraries gave answers to several questions arisen from the discoveries of the end of the nineteenth century, and shed some new light on many historical perspectives that were pacifically accepted until then. As a matter of fact, a narrow bond has been created among these discoveries, the academic research, the theological thought and the mass culture, even the pop culture. It is on these binds that I would like to dwell here even if with only a few hints.

The enthusiasm of Harnack has damped but the *Didaché* still remains an enigma. Despite the several studies dedicated to it there are no shared opinions and many of the problems have not been solved. Nonetheless, the discovery of the Qumran scrolls let us know much more on the Palestinian Judaism at the time of Jesus and led us to an in-depth analysis of what was called from Ferdinand Christian Baur on "Jewish-Christianity",[8] even though

---

[6] For this debate, see *The Oxyrinchus Papyri*, Part I, edited with translations and notes by Bernard P. Grenfell and Arthur S. Hunt (London: Egypt Exploration Fund, 1898), p. 2.

[7] On the discoveries in Tura and other findings of Origen's text, see the overview by Antonio Cacciari, "From Tura to Munich: Seventy Years of Origenian Discoveries", in *Origeniana undecima: Origen and Origenism in the History of Western Thought*. Papers of the 11th International Origen Congress, Aarhus University, 26–31 August 2013, ed. by Anders-Christian Jacobsen (Leuven: Peeters, 2009 [Bibliotheca ephemeridum theologicarum Lovaniensium 279]), pp. 191–200.

[8] Ferdinand Christian Baur, *Paulus, der Apostel Jesu Christi. Sein Leben und Wirken, seine Briefe und seine Lehre. Ein Beitrag zu einer kritischen Geschichte des Urchristentums* (Stuttgart: Becher & Müller, 1845).

now this definition is under review, too. In Jean Daniélou's *Théologie du Judéo-Christianisme* (1958), the *Didaché* is defined "maybe the document more venerable of the Jewish-Christian literature",[9] because of the numerous points in common with the texts found in the Dead Sea scrolls, in particular with the *Manual of Discipline* of Qumran. Daniélou wrote: "Despite the text has been reshaped [...] its background appears to be definitely Jewish-Christian. It is self-evident for the moral part, the *Two way section*, with a judaizing character noticed a long time ago, confirmed in a clamorous way by the discovery of the *Manual of Discipline* of Qumran since we find here the same doctrine".[10]

As is well known, in the first phase after the discovery of the Dead Sea scrolls the attention of the public opinion was concentrated on some interpretations that saw in these texts an immediate precedent of the Christian movement or even the testimony of the existence of figures that anticipated Jesus' features. In September 1955, the then-director of the Department of Antiquity of the Reign of Jordan published an article in the review "The illustrated London news" under the evocative title *Where Christ himself may have studied. An Essene monastery at Khirbet Qumran*, in which it was supposed there had been a period of study of Jesus by the Essenes community – or what at the time was believed to be so.[11] In January of the year after, John Marco Allegro, who took part in the early group of scholars involved in the reconstruction and publication of the scrolls, participated at three BBC broadcasts retransmitted by the international press. According to Allegro, some of the scrolls contained the description of teachings and events very similar, if not identical, to those reported by the

---

[9] "[...] le document le plus vénérable peut-être de la littérature judéo-chrétienne": Jean Daniélou, *Théologie du judéo-christianisme*, (Tournai: Desclée, 1958), p. 40 (English translation: *The Theology of Jewish Christianity* [London: Darton, Longman & Todd, 1964]).

[10] "Même si le texte que nous avons a subi des remaniements [...] son fond apparaît comme décidément judéo-chrétien. Ceci est évident pour la partie morale, le *Traité des Deux vies*, dont le caractère judaïsant avait été depuis longtemps relevé et que la découverte du *Manuel de discipline* de Qumran a confirmé de façon éclatante, car on y retrouve la même doctrine": *ibidem*, p. 38.

[11] Gerald Lankester Harding, "Where Christ himself may have studied. An Essene monastery at Khirbet Qumran", *The Illustrated London News*, 3 September 1955, pp. 379–81.

Gospels on Jesus; for this reason they would have been hidden by the scholarly group, conditioned by confessional interests.[12] The spread of such claims caused the reply of the group's members and the storm seemed to quite for a while. Obviously, beside the journalistic polemics the research on the historical Jesus took advantage from the discovery of Qumran and on an academic level the relationship between Jesus and the Essenism, direct or mediated by John the Baptist, was at the centre of several studies such as the ones of Herbert Braun, Jean Carmignac and Duncan Howlett.[13] Generally speaking, while the second phase of the research on the historical Jesus had started and quickly consumed, the discoveries of the Dead Sea created the premises for the *Third quest*, enriching and livening up the frame of our knowledge on the Palestinian Judaism at the time of Jesus, overcoming our traditional interpretations based on the fourfold division described in Flavius Josephus's work.

Nonetheless, from that moment on the way of the historical research and the one of the public opinion started to separate. Maybe it was not a coincidence that in 1991 it was published the first volume of the monumental investigation on the historical Jesus of John Paul Meier, *A marginal Jew*, where the relationship between Jesus and Qumran and the Essenism has been drastically scaled down;[14] in the same year, Michael Baigent and Richard Leigh published *The Dead Sea scrolls deception*, relaunching the Allegro's theory on the concealment of some of the Qumran manuscripts contents, which would have denied the originality and the divine character of Christ.[15] Actually, Baigent and Leigh's fame was due above all to a text of 1982, *The holy blood and the*

---

[12] The broadcasts were on air on 16, 23 and 30 January 1956: see Joseph A. Fitzmyer, *Responses to 101 Questions on the Dead Sea Scrolls* (New York: Paulist Press, 1992), pp. 163-69.

[13] Herbert Braun, *Spätjüdisch-häretischer und früchristlicher Radikalismus. Jesus von Nazareth und die essenische Qumransekte* (Tübingen: J. C. B. Mohr, 1957); Jean Carmignac, *Le Docteur de justice et Jésus-Christ* (Paris: Éditions de l'Orante, 1957); Duncan Howlett, *The Essenes and Christianity. An Interpretation of the Dead Sea Scrolls* (New York: Harper, 1957).

[14] John P. Maier, *A marginal Jew. Rethinking the historical Jesus*, vol. 1: *The Roots of the Problem and the Person* (New York: Doubleday, 1991).

[15] Michael Baigent & Richard Leigh, *The Dead Sea scrolls deception* (London: Jonathan Cape, 1991).

*holy Gral*, in which they supposed the birth of a son by Jesus and Mary Magdalene, with a series of other events in which the protagonists are the Templar Knights and the Priory of Sion.[16] The book had a good success but not as much as a two decades later romance that seemed to be inspired by Baigent and Leigh: *The Da Vinci Code* by Dan Brown.[17] Probably, this is the reason why in 2006 the two indicted Brown's publisher, but were defeated and had to pay for legal expenses. Fortunately for them, the anonymous authors of Qumran scrolls were already killed off by the tenth Roman Legion a couple of millenniums before they could advance in turn the charge of plagiarism.

The quotation of *The Da Vinci Code* by Dan Brown evokes the figure of Magdalene, *The Gospel of Philip* and the whole Gnostic library discovered at Nag Hammadi. In this case too, the discovery, a real *coup de théâtre*, paved the way for polemics, namely a complicated theory of conspiracy concerning the "secrets" contained in the manuscripts, which had to be hidden, since they were Christian texts. However, the discovery at Nag Hammadi of the Coptic translation of the *Gospel of Thomas* led to close, a half century later, at least the academic debate between Grenfell and Hunt, on the one side, and Harnack and his supporters on the other side, giving reason to the editors of the Oxyrhinchus papyrus 1 on its belonging to a collection of Jesus's λόγια and not to a narrative Gospel.

After the difficulties concerning the publication of the texts, Nag Hammadi library has inspired a large number of studies, which have profoundly modified our knowledge of the Gnostic phenomenon. The first effect was the removal of the filter represented by the works of the Christian heresiologists Irenaeus, Epiphanius and others, who, until then, were the unique sources allowing us to access the Gnostic authors' thought. Finally, it was possible to read directly their works, without deformations, misunderstandings and the falsifications made by the "orthodox". It did not seem it was a kind of veil having had all these texts, starting from the Gospel of Thomas, in translation, being Coptic

---

[16] Michael Baigent & Richard Leigh, *The holy blood and the holy Gral* (London: Jonathan Cape, 1982).
[17] Dan Brown, *The Da Vinci Code* (New York: Doubleday, 2003).

a language depending largely from the Greek, especially in vocabulary. Lately, scholars became aware that "translating is always like cheating" and also in this case the texts needed philological cures in order to be well understood and put in the right derivation from the original Greek texts, with a comparison with the heresiological sources, trying to contextualize the reasons, the ways and the cultural- historical context in which the library has known its beginning and its end.[18]

In contrast to the Qumran discoveries, which enriched with many details the frame of our knowledge of the Palestinian Judaism, the discoveries of Nag Hammadi have had an opposite result on a historiographical level. Above all in the first phase, there is no doubt, that the analytic study of the Gnostic texts has freed them from the heresiological prejudice pending on them from the Second century. In this way, it was possible to examine in depth the profile of every author and of every school, even if with a preference for the Gnosis of Valentinian origin, determined by the type and belonging of the manuscripts found in Nag Hammadi. However, in the *long durée* this approach has brought to the dissolution of the very historical- religious category of Gnosticism as a coherent system, compact and with characteristic elements in spite of the variations of each tradition and of each text. Before the discovery of Nag Hammadi, the issue at the stage was not the Gnosticism itself, but its derivation: had it a Christian origin or preceded Christianity? Was it a different development of Judaism, or of Orphism, or of other religious forms of syncretism? In any case, it was considered a distinct phenomenon and somehow in contrast with Christianity, with which it had met and fought during the second century.[19] For example, Rudolf Bultmann was quite convinced of it, having he studied the interference between

---

[18] On the Nag Hammadi library see, for instance, the collections of papers *Die Nag-Hammadi-Schriften in der Literatur- und Theologiegeschichte des frühen Christentums*, ed. by Jens Schröter & Konrad Schwarz (Tübingen: Mohr Siebeck, 2017 [Studien und Texte zu Antike und Christentum, 106]); *The Nag Hammadi Codices and Late Antique Egypt*, ed. by Hugo Lundhaug & Lance Jenott (Tübingen: Mohr Siebeck, 2018).

[19] The milestone of such a scholarly view are the proceedings of the conference *Le origini dello gnosticismo. The Origins of Gnosticism. Colloquio di Messina, 13–18 aprile 1966*, testi e discussioni pubblicati a cura di Ugo Bianchi (Leiden: Brill, 1967).

Gnosticism and the Gospel of John;[20] and his disciple Hans Jonas too, who in fact saw in the anticosmism of the Gnostics a reaction to the optimism of the Greek tradition and saw in their presumption of superiority a feeling of alienation, a "mal de vivre" very similar to the one of the twentieth century's Existentialists.[21]

In the last decades instead, Gnosticism has been much more inscribed within Christianity, as a fundamental element which contributed to define the latter. As the historical and philological studies in Nag Hammadi texts went on, the great figures of the Gnostic *pantheon*, Valentinus, Basilides, Theodotus, have been considered the protagonists of a hard competition among schools, traditions, communities and church-organization models, in which sometimes they win and sometimes they lost. They have been defined as "heretics", "enemies", "Gnostic" by their adversaries, but without reflecting their point of view or their real nature. More in general, recent historiography rejects the same category of "heresy", being it considered an *a posteriori* construction by the equally unhistorical "orthodoxy", therefore without any heuristic value. It is self-evident the influence on such a historiographical turn of the deconstructionist theories and philosophy, from Foucault, Derrida until more recently Agamben, and of the anthropological and post-colonial studies.

It must not be forgotten, however, that the specific case of Gnostics differs from the typical ethnographic and anthropological analysis, since we have both points of views, the winners' one, who categorizes and stigmatizes, and the losers' one, who thanks to the Nag Hammadi texts now talk with their own voice to us. Therefore, we can make a carefully comparison between them. The old heresiologists were not necessary wrong: the case of *The Gospel of Jude*, announced as the last discovery able to unveil Jesus' message and unmask Churches' tricks, has only confirmed that Irenaeus was well informed and at the end quite honest in reporting the positions of his opponents, apart from some

---

[20] Well-known is the early paper of Rudolf Bultmann, "Die Bedeutung der neuerschlossenen mandaischen und manichaischen Quellen für das Verstandnis des Johannesevangeliums", *Zeitschrift für die neutestamentliche Wissenschaft* 24 (1925), pp. 100–46.

[21] Hans Jonas, *Gnosis und spätantiker Geist*, 2 vols (Göttingen: Vandenhoeck & Ruprecht, 1954–1966).

verbal excess.[22] It is quite a paradox, but extremely meaningful, to observe that what was considered a discovery of a Gnostic library, and therefore "heretical", has now been transformed by scholars into a monastic library, suddenly hidden because its texts were considered "heretical" only from some moment on.[23]

The idea of a constitutive opposition between Christianity and Gnosticism was not limited to the field of the history of religion or to the study of the Christian origins. Eric Voegelin, who like Jonas emigrated from Germany to the USA to escape from the Nazi dictatorship, saw in Gnosticism the profound evil of modern civilization, as estrangement and antithesis from Christianity, a civilization destined to fall in the great and violent dictatorship of the twentieth century.[24] Therefore, if in the pop imaginary, from *Jesus Christ Superstar* to Scorsese's *The Last Temptation of Christ*, to Saramago's *The Gospel of Jesus Christ*, the institutional Christianity of the Churches had hidden the real nature of Jesus, his relationship with Magdalene, Jude and the Essenes, in the last decades in the ecclesiastical rhetoric, above all the Catholic one, the category and the charge of Gnosticism, inside and outside the Church, has become synonym of self-redeeming intellectualism, of refusal of ecclesiastical mediation and community dimension, of satisfied subjectivism and disembodied elitism. The Gnostic poison would have been spread by the secularized society even inside the Church. In the name of tradition and truth, individualism and relativism of contemporary world should be fought, like Justin, Irenaeus and other heresiologist did in the second century against Gnosticism.[25]

---

[22] See Irenaeus *Adv. haer.* 1.31.1.

[23] This view was firstly propounded by John W. B. Barns, "Greek and Coptic Papyri from the Covers of the Nag Hammadi Codices", in *Essays on the Nag Hammadi Texts. In Honour of Pahor Labib*, edited by Martin Krause (Leiden: Brill, 1975[Nag Hammadi Studies 6]), pp. 9–18; and developed by Frederik Wisse, "Gnosticism and Early Monasticism in Egypt", in *Gnosis. Festschrift für Hans Jonas*, in Verbindung mit Ugo Bianchi, Martin Krause, James M. Robinson und Geo Widengren, herausgegeben von Barbara Aland (Göttingen: Vandenhoeck & Ruprecht, 1978), pp. 431–40.

[24] Eric Voegelin, *The New Science of Politics. An introduction* (Chicago: University of Chicago Press, 1952).

[25] See for instance Massimo Introvigne, *Il ritorno dello gnosticismo*, Introduzione di Giovanni Cantoni (Milano: Sugarco Edizioni, 1993).

However, this fight could reserve unexpected surprises. At the beginning of the theological conflict around the Eucharistic communion to divorced and remarried people, the well-known American scholar John Rist, an expert of Augustine and the Fathers, has made a strong historiographical critic to the introduction of cardinal Walter Kasper to the first synod on family summoned by Pope Francis in 2015.[26] In his argumentation Kasper quoted Origen's Commentary on Matthew, where the Alexandrian Father says that some bishops of some local Churches had given communion to the remarried divorced, adding a positive evaluation – "not without reason" as Origen commented. Kasper's patristic authorities, in addition, were Basil (letters 188 and 199), Gregory of Nazianzus (Oration 37) and Augustine, who were aware of the attitude of these Churches. Rist objected that in the same passage of the Origen's Commentary on Matthew the incompatibility of Scriptures with such a sinful behaviour was claimed 3 times, while in respecy to the three bishops (and saints) Rist recours to an *argumentum e silentio*, by which he reproaches Kasper of omitting to notice that there were no proof that they had really shared an opinion which contradicts their normal teaching. Besides, Rist recognised more exegetic and theological clearness to Origen than to the three Fathers of the fourth century in this sentence: "Hardly endorsement, nor even toleration from so biblical a theologian!". A surprising statement if we recall that the mentioned hypothesis about the Nag Hammadi library hidden by Christian monks because of the condemnation of its texts, is based exactly on the precedent of Origen's and Didymus the Blind's papyri found in Tura.

In fact, the first editor of the *Dialogue of Origen with Heraclides*, Jean Scherer, thanks to the founding of the papyri, had made clear that these texts belonged to the library of the near Greek monastery of Saint Arsenius, former preceptor of Emperor

---

[26] J. Rist, "Remarriage, Divorce and Communion. Patristic Light on a Recent Problem", *The National Catholic Register*, 2 April 2014. Rist has developed his reasoning in a miscellaneous book: *Remaining in the Truth of Christ. Marriage and Communion in the Catholic Church*, ed. by R. Dodaro (San Francisco: Ignatius Press, 2014), pp. 64–92.

Arcadius in Constantinople.[27] After the condemnation of Origen and Didymus at the Constantinople Council of 553, according to Scherer, the monks wanted to expel from the library their heretical works; in Egypt, they did not use to burn heretic books but they threw them into water, as some anecdotes reported in the life of Saint Pacomius show, talking about the removal of some Origen's works. But the Nile was far away from Arsenius monastery and because of the large amount of material they had to destroy there was the risk that not everything went deep in the river and that the dangerous ideas of Origen were saved by someone (as it happened to Moises). For this reason, they decided to put the books in a cavern apparently unreachable. The poor monks could not imagine that precisely the cave would become the ideal place to preserve, 1500 years later, the ammunition and weapons of the English Army during the battle against the Italian-German military forces in North Africa.

There is no doubt that the revival of Origen in contemporary theology is due more to Henri De Lubac and Hans Urs von Balthasar or to the *Sources Chrétiennes* than to the discovery of Tura. Nonetheless, these too have contributed to free Origen and his school from the shadow of heresy and make them both recognize by Catholic orthodoxy. In fact, Rist could count on an authoritative precedent, while applying Origen by his side. Pope Benedict XV had dedicated the audience of April 25th and May 2nd, 2007, to Origen, defining him as "a decisive figure for all the development of the Christian thought", author of a "irreversible turn" in theology, which reaches with him a "perfect symbiosis" with the exegesis and inviting the audience to receive "the reaching of this great master in faith".[28]

The re-discovery of the lost works of the Fathers of the Church has had an impact also on other aspects of the life of the Catholic Church. No doubt that the liturgical reform of the Second Vatican Council was prepared by the renew of spiritual and pastoral

---

[27] See *Entretien d'Origène avec Héraclide*, Introduction, traduction et notes de Jean Scherer (Paris: Éditions du Cerf, 1960 [Sources Chrétiennes 67]), p. 47 note 1.

[28] The audiences have been published in Benedetto XVI, *Testimoni del messaggio cristiano*, a cura di Giuliano Vigini (Milano: Mondadori, 2012); quotations are taken from pp. 22, 23, 26.

sensibility began in the first years of the Twentieth century with the so called "Liturgical movement";[29] even the changed attitude toward the Jews is the result of a long reflection, dramatically accelerated by the Shoah.[30] Nonetheless, it is worth to be read what the Congregation for the Catholic education wrote in 1979 on the teaching of liturgy in seminars: "As far as possible, the Jewish prayer must be presented, as it was in the synagogue, in the private houses and in the Easter celebration at the time of Jesus, in a way that both the similarity and the originality of the Christian prayer could be evident. It must be described, then, the liturgical assembly of the Apostolic age. It is desirable that the students get access to the liturgical sources of the first centuries (for example the *Didaché*, saint Clement of Rome, saint Justin, saint Irenaeus, Tertullian, Hippolytus, the Apostolic Constitutions, the Peregrination of Egeria), to selected texts of the first anaphors and the catechesis of the Fathers".[31] This program could not be imagined without the studies of the Jewish-Christian legacy started from the discovery of the *Didaché*, like Daniélou's *Théologie du Judéo-christianisme*.

The *Orientations about the admission to Eucharist between the Chaldean Church and the East Syrian Church*, stated in October 2001 by the Pontifical Council for the Promotion of the Unity among Christians, recognized as fully valid the anaphora of Addai and Mari.[32] This could not have been possible if the study of the ancient disciplinary and liturgical texts would not have made clear, starting exactly from the *Didaché*, that until the IV century there were no Eucharistic anaphora containing the narration of the last supper with the words to which would have been subsequently associated the idea of the consecration

---

[29] See for instance Franco Brovelli, *Ritorno alla liturgia. Saggi di studio sul movimento liturgico* (Roma CLV-Edizioni liturgiche, 1989); *Liturgia. Temi e autori. Saggi di studio sul movimento liturgico* (Roma CLV-Edizioni liturgiche, Roma 1990).

[30] See for instance Daniele Menozzi, *"Giudaica perfidia". Uno stereotipo antisemita fra liturgia e storia* (Bologna: Il mulino 2014).

[31] Sacra Congregazione per l'Educazione Cattolica, *Istruzione per la formazione liturgica nei seminari*, Roma 1979, n. 26.

[32] Pontificio Consiglio per la promozione dell'unità dei Cristiani, *Orientamenti per l'ammissione all'Eucaristia fra la Chiesa Caldea e la Chiesa Assira dell'Oriente*, Roma 2001, n. 3.

of the species.[33] In my opinion, the discovery of the *Didaché* has helped the re-discovery of the original genetic bond of the Christian prayer with the Jewish one and, therefore, has favoured the re-thinking of the two religious traditions, much more than the recent North-American historiographical debate on the *parting of the ways*, often misleading.

To conclude, if we want to suggest a balance about the circumstances which have led to the contemporary link between academic research, theological thought, mass culture and the influence on it of the discovery of the codices and papyri of ancient Christian texts, we can claim that they gave a contribute to the progressive dissolution of consolidated cultural categories, even if only in a limited part. The diffusion of a variegated and multifaceted historical-religious knowledge has been determined by and has contributed to the process of secularization, since this knowledge was no more put under the control of the traditional religious authorities, or of the traditional academic framework; they were both substituted by the means of mass culture developed from the 50s on, even if they twist and distort them, as we have seen in a few cases. Actually, neither scholars seem to escape this trend. A certain attitude to sensationalize their academic work looking for the scoop and success through the media, urges them to emphasise unilaterally the results of their researches in order to *épater le bourgeois* (if there could be still any *bourgeois* or someone who could be scandalized when we talk about Christianity). An example of this is the recent story of the supposed discovery of a papyrus containing the proof of the existence of the "wife of Jesus".[34]

However, I think there is another and subtler temptation. What Harnack said when the *Didaché* was discovered reveals how much he wanted to have a demonstration of his ideas of Christianity and of the Church, beyond what the texts were actually

---

[33] Enrico Mazza, *La celebrazione eucaristica: genesi del rito e sviluppo dell'interpretazione* (Milano: San Paolo, 1996). English translation: *The Celebration of the Eucharist. The Origin of the Rite and the Development of its Interpretation*, translated by Matthew J. O'Connell [Collegeville, Minn.: The Liturgical Press, 1999]).

[34] See the monographic issue of *New Testament Studies*, 61 (2015), pp. 292–394.

saying. Surely, we are aware today that we cannot read them with the absolute objectivity pretended by Harnack, freeing ourselves from our pre-comprehensions and from our existential interests. Nonetheless, as scholars and intellectuals, we have the responsibility to safeguard as much as we can the message of these texts that are no more a prerogative of the faithful or the Churches, since they have become a common, universal heritage.

## *Abstract*

The paper focuses on some important discoveries of patristic papyri and manuscripts during the twentieth century and shows their impact not only on scholarship, but also on the theological reflection and self-understanding of the different Christian churches (e.g. in their relations with Judaism) on the one hand, and more generally on the ordinary people culture mostly through the mediation of the mass media, on the other hand. In this way, since the second half of the twentieth century, many established historical categories have been redefined and this has contributed to the secularization of the studies on ancient Christianity and more generally of Western culture. Thus, paradoxically, patristic texts are no longer a property only of the Christian churches, but they have become a common, universal heritage.